D1562575

PHILO OF ALEXANDRIA
AN ANNOTATED BIBLIOGRAPHY
1937-1986

SUPPLEMENTS TO

VIGILIAE CHRISTIANAE

Formerly Philosophia Patrum

TEXTS AND STUDIES OF EARLY CHRISTIAN LIFE
AND LANGUAGE

EDITORS

A.F.J. KLIJN – G. QUISPEL
J.H. WASZINK – J.C.M. VAN WINDEN

VOLUME VIII

PHILO OF ALEXANDRIA

AN ANNOTATED BIBLIOGRAPHY
1937-1986

BY

ROBERTO RADICE AND DAVID T. RUNIA

IN COLLABORATION WITH
R.A. BITTER • N.G. COHEN • M. MACH
A.P. RUNIA • D. SATRAN • D.R. SCHWARTZ

E.J. BRILL
LEIDEN • NEW YORK • KØBENHAVN • KÖLN
1988

This work was prepared with the financial support of:
The Netherlands Organization for Scientific Research (N.W.O.).

It was also partially supported by the contributions of:
"C.N.R., Centro di studio del pensiero antico"

and of:
"Centro di ricerche di metafisica dell'Università Cattolica
del Sacro Cuore di Milano".

The text was prepared on an Apple Macintosh Computer System; software
programs Word, File and Excel of MICROSOFT; additional fonts Kadmos
(Allotype Typographics, Ann Arbor), Laser Hebrew, Laser Transliterator
(Linguists Software, Boston). The text was printed on an Apple Laserwriter.

Library of Congress Cataloging-in-Publication Data

Radice, Roberto.
    Philo of Alexandria: an annotated bibliography, 1937-1986 / by
Roberto Radice and David T. Runia; in collaboration with R.A.
Bitter ... [et al.].
        p.   cm.—(Supplements to Vigiliae Christianae, ISSN
0920-623X; v. 8)
    Includes indexes.
    "The core of this book consists of an English translation of
Roberto Radice's Filone di Alessandria"—Jacket.
    ISBN 90-04-08968-1
    1. Philo, of Alexandria—Bibliography. I. Runia, David T.
II. Radice, Roberto. Filone di Alessandria. English. III. Title.
IV. Series.
Z8685.R3   1988
[B689.Z7]
016.181'06—dc19   88-26242
                                                               CIP

ISSN   0920-623x
ISBN   90 04 08986 1

PRINTED IN THE NETHERLANDS BY E.J. BRILL

TO

MARIA LUISA
MARIA ANNA ALLEGONDA

TABLE OF CONTENTS

PREFACE

This bibliography, which the authors hope will become an instrument of great usefulness for all scholars working in the areas of Philonic and related studies, has had a complex history of development, further details of which will be furnished in the Introduction. It goes without saying that the authors and collaborators could not have produced a work of this kind without incurring debts of gratitude to a large number of persons and institutions.

Roberto Radice wishes to thank Prof. G. Reale for having proposed the original project and for offering guidance and stimulation during all the phases of its preparation. He also thanks once again Prof. R. Stefanini of the University of Berkeley (California), who generously helped to collect part of the American contributions. A particular debt of gratitude is owed to Prof. V. Nikiprowetzky for the often extremely rare and valuable material which he provided. Fortunately he was able to see the completed work before his unexpected and untimely death in December 1983. He also wishes to record his gratitude to the staff of the Biblioteca Cantonale in Lugano and to the library and technical staff of the Catholic University of Milan, for their ever prompt and courteous assistance in the preparation of both editions of the work.

Two sources of financial assistance are gratefully acknowledged. The work was partially supported by the "C.N.R., Centro di studio del pensiero antico". Both authors thank its director, Prof. G. Giannantoni, for giving permission for the original bibliography to be reissued in a revised form. A generous grant from the "Centro di Ricerche di Metafysica dell'Università Cattolica del Sacro Cuore di Milano" enabled the original work to be translated from Italian into English. The authors cordially thank the director of the Centre, Prof. G. Reale, for making this subvention possible.

David Runia received financial support during the preparation of the revised edition of the bibliography from the Netherlands Organization for Scientific Research (N.W.O.). Much of the labour was carried out during his stay in 1986-87 at The Institute for Advanced Study, Princeton, U.S.A. He would like to thank the Institute's Director for extending an invitation to him and allowing him to make full use of the splendid library facilities that the Institute provides. Other libraries he wishes to thank are the Speer Theological Library in Princeton, The Library of the Australian National University, Canberra, The Library of the Free University in Amsterdam, The Library of the University of Utrecht.

David Runia also wishes to record his gratitude to Prof. J. C. M. van Winden (Leiden), who encouraged the work from the first, and kindly proposed its inclusion in the series Supplements to Vigiliae Christianae. A vote of thanks is due to Prof. M. Stone (Jerusalem), who warmly supported the venture of adding material written in Hebrew to the work and introduced him to a group of scholars who were willing to lend a hand. The team of four Israeli scholars under the leadership of Dr. David Satran were not looking for this task; it was imposed on them in addition to other onerous and more important duties. Their friendly and conscientious cooperation made a deep and lasting impression. He would also like to thank Dr. R. A. Bitter (Zeist) for giving most valuable assistance in the tracking down of Philonic material written in the Dutch language. His brother Drs. A. P. Runia (Groningen) offered to translate the original bibliography from Italian into English. Not only did he perform this burdensome task with admirable diligence, but he also offered valuable assistance in the task of correcting the proofs. Other scholars that Runia would wish to thank for various kinds of assistance are: Miss E. Birnbaum (Harvard), Prof. L. H Feldman (New York), Drs. P. Goedendorp (Groningen), Prof. E. Hilgert (Chicago), Dr. P. van der Horst (Utrecht), Prof. J. P. Kenney (Portland, Oregon), Prof. J. Mansfeld (Utrecht), Prof. A. Méasson (St. Étienne), Prof. A. Mendelson (Hamilton, Canada), Prof. J. R. Royse (San Francisco), Prof. A. Terian (Berrien Springs, Michigan). He is also thankful to Mr. Julian Deahl of E. J. Brill (Leiden) for the assistance he readily gave in relation to the more technical aspects of the book's production.

The team in Israel consisting of Dr. D. Satran (Jerusalem), Dr. N. G. Cohen (Haifa), Dr. M. Mach (Tel Aviv), Dr. D. R. Schwartz (Jerusalem), wish to express their thanks to Miss Holly Irene Smith and Mr. Oron Joffe, whose expertise and unfailing good humour made the production of a difficult bilingual text possible. Financial support for the work in Israel was generously provided by the Faculty of Humanities of the Hebrew University of Jerusalem.

Last, but most certainly not least, the two authors wish to record their deep feelings of gratitude to their respective wives, Maria Luisa Parietti Radice and Maria Anna Allegonda Runia-Deenick, for years of support and companionship during the preparation of this study.

Luino, Italy   Roberto Radice
Soest, Netherlands   David T. Runia
July 1988

INTRODUCTION

1. Genesis and aim of the bibliography
2. Method of compilation and analysis
3. Division of labour
4. Brief observations on fifty years of Philonic scholarship

1. *Genesis and aim of the bibliography*

In 1983 Roberto Radice published an annotated bibliography of Philonic scholarship under the title *Filone di Alessandria: bibliografia generale 1937-1982*.[1] On its appearance the work was critically acclaimed as a truly valuable instrument for all those who wish to consult and find their way through the extensive scholarly literature on the life, writings and thought of Philo of Alexandria.[2] In some quarters, however, it was felt that the fact that the work was written in Italian might restrict its circulation and usefulness to some degree.[3] The growing cultural imperialism of the English language in the world of scholarship is a force that has to be reckoned with. At the beginning of 1986 David Runia suggested to the author that the work be translated into English and brought up to date so that it would cover exactly half a century of Philonic studies, from 1937 to 1986. The suggestion was welcomed; the present volume is the result of a close cooperation between the two scholars.

As Radice explains in his Introduction to the Italian edition, the year 1937 was deliberately chosen as starting-point. For in 1938 H. G. Goodhart and E. R. Goodenough published their well-known *General Bibliography of Philo Judaeus*, a virtually complete record of studies on Philo up to the year 1937.[4] Since the record for 1937-38 in Goodhart and Goodenough was naturally far from complete, it seemed wise to have a year of overlap. Hence the starting date chosen by Radice. The method that he pursued, however, differed radically from that of his famous predecessors. The American scholars had first devoted a lengthy section to a complete listing of all manuscripts containing Philonic texts, 386 in number. This work did

---

[1] Published by Bibliopolis in the series Elenchos: Collana di testi e studi sul pensiero antico (Naples 1983).

[2] See the reviews listed under **1113** in this volume.

[3] Cf. the remarks of D. T. Runia in *VChr* 39 (1985) 190, *NTT* 40 (1986) 187 (for the abbreviations see the list immediately following the Introduction).

[4] Published by Yale University Press (New Haven 1938) (see our **1001**). Note that this work is often referred to as Goodenough's Bibliography, even though strictly speaking Goodhart is the first author. The fact that it is included as a kind of Appendix to a monograph by Goodenough may have contributed to this development.

not need to be redone. After an extensive section on translations, they divided all their remaining entries into a further 31 sections, which between them covered all aspects of Philo and his relation to other fields of scholarship. Within these sections the bibliographical items were listed in chronological order; their contents could only be surmised from the listing and the information provided in the title. This method has since been continued by E. Hilgert in his splendid 'Bibliographia Philoniana 1935-1981', published in 1984.[5] The method chosen by Radice, in contrast, was to present a 'bibliographie raisonnée' giving a brief account of the contents for each item that the bibliography contains. The precise contours and constraints of this method will be outlined in the following section.

In his monumental critical bibliography *Josephus and modern scholarship (1937-1980)*, L. H. Feldman declares that 'there is hardly an author for whom we have such exhaustive bibliographies as for Philo'.[6] This is true, as a glance at our section on bibliographies will confirm.[7] Nevertheless the authors are convinced that the current work can justify its existence. This for three distinct but interrelated reasons.

Firstly, during the past half-century, but especially during the past two decades, there has been an explosive growth of scholarly production in Philonic studies. We shall document this growth in more detail in the Brief observations on fifty years of Philonic scholarship presented later in this Introduction. But, anticipating that discussion somewhat, we can say that in 50 years there have been 1666 separate studies pertaining in some way to Philo. This is considerably more than the 1120 studies which Goodhart and Goodenough collected for the entire period up to 1937.[8] In the last twenty years alone no less than 1045 studies have dwelt on Philo in some way or other, and have thus gained admission to our bibliography. It is true that such explosive growth has occurred in other areas of scholarship and science.[9] Nevertheless there are also circumstances peculiar to the study of Philo alone. As Radice stressed in the Introduction to the earlier bibliography, there has in recent years been a 'Philo renaissance', particularly in France and the United States of America, but more recently also in Italy, the Spanish-speaking world and Israel, which has led to a remarkable production of translations, instruments of research, and studies of every description. It would appear that Philo, whose corpus of writings is one of

---

[5] In *ANRW* II 21.1 (Berlin 1984) 47-97 (see our **1019**).

[6] Berlin-New York 1984, 412. That this bibliography also commences in 1937 is no coincidence. Feldman had previously compiled an annotated bibliography up till 1962 for both Philo and Josephus, for the former also taking the end of Goodhart-Goodenough as starting-point (see our **1108**).

[7] See below Part I, section A.

[8] Counting sections II to XXX only. It is inaccurate to quote 1603 items, as A.-J. Festugière does (*La révélation d'Hermès Trismégiste,* vol. 2 (Paris 1949) 519), for the total number of entries in Goodhart and Goodenough includes manuscripts, mentions of Philo in incunabala, and Pseudo-Philonica.

[9] Compare the complaints of the bibliographers of Plato and Josephus respectively: L. Brisson, 'Platon 1958-75', *Lustrum* 20 (1977) 6; L. H. Feldman, *op. cit.* (n.8) 2-3.

the largest to survive from the Greco-Roman world, had – relatively speaking – not received as much attention as he deserved, and that once research on him had reached a certain momentum, many scholars jumped on the bandwagon and discovered how interesting he really was.

Moreover, and now we come to our second reason for producing the bibliography, research on Philo has been carried out from a large number of different perspectives. To start with, there are the studies which concentrate on *Philo for his own sake*, e.g. editions and translations, introductory presentations, critical studies of themes and texts and so on. These studies are numerous, but naturally form but a fraction of the whole. Philo can also be seen against the background of the *Greco-Roman culture* – including both classical literature and religion – amid which he, an Alexandrian born and bred, lived his entire life. Two particular facets need to be mentioned separately here. Firstly, Philo's relation to *Greek philosophy* and the later philosophical tradition constructed on the foundations laid by the Greeks. Of particular value is the evidence Philo supplies on the nascent movements of Middle Platonism and Neopythagoreanism. Secondly Philo provides much important material on the *history of the Roman Empire*, in which he himself, as leader of the Alexandrian Jewish embassy to Gaius Caligula, played a minor role. Needless to say he is also an important witness for the contemporary political, social, cultural and religious situation in the *metropolis of Alexandria*. This brings us to the area of Philo's *Judaism*. Neglected for a millenium and a half by the Jewish world, he has now made a spectacular come-back. Numerous studies have been devoted to Philo from the perspective of Jewish thought and history, dwelling not only on the particular nature of Philo's Judaism – whether this be called Hellenistic, Alexandrian, or Diaspora Judaism –, but also comparing him with the mainstream Judaism located in Palestine. During Philo's lifetime a Jew was crucified in Jerusalem. The *Christian movement* that commenced soon afterward was to be of crucial importance for the survival of Philo's writings. Much labour has been expended in determining the relation between Philo's thought and the early Christian documents that constitute the *New Testament*, and also the early Christianity described in those documents. By the late second century A. D. Philo was being extensively studied by Christian intellectuals who laid the basis for what we now call *Patristic thought*. Philo's relation to the Church Fathers has also been an area of extensive research. Finally, since the spectacular find at Nag Hammadi in 1945 there has been a great increase in our knowledge of the *Gnostic movement* which in many ways ran parallel to Christianity until the fourth century. The evidence which Philo supplies on the origin of Gnosticism has also attracted the attention of a number of scholars.

It is surely an impressive list. Philo can be seen as the hub of an axle with spokes leading to at least seven 'encyclical studies', i.e. classical culture, ancient philosophy, Greco-Roman history, Alexandrian and mainstream Judaism,[10] New Testament and Early Christianity, Patristic thought, and Gnostic studies. In each of these areas much research has been carried out, further aspects of which we will discuss later on in this Introduction. The important fact to recognize here is that a good proportion of scholarship on Philo is being carried out by scholars for whom Philo himself is only of secondary interest, namely as a source of evidence for other areas of research. This is the third reason for the compilation of this bibliography. Even for Philonists who spend all their spare time reading and studying Philo, it is virtually impossible to keep abreast of developments in research. For those whose interest in Philo is more peripheral, such an orientation is completely out of the question. For this reason we think it is of the utmost importance that scholars and students who are interested in Philo for whatever reason are given an instrument of research that will enable them quickly and efficiently to gain a sound orientation in the daunting diversity of studies that have been carried out during the past fifty years.

The compilers of this bibliography have asked themselves more than once whether the considerable effort involved in the task was worthwhile. After all compiling such a study does not represent the kind of creative work that will advance the frontiers of research. Much of the labour is tedious, especially when one has to read discussions of subjects that have been dealt with dozens of times before. Nevertheless, we believe that, given the vastly increased productivity of modern scholarship, scholars today will have to pay more attention to the compilation of instruments of research that will enable themselves and their colleagues to surmount the barriers of extreme specialization and to continue to make relevant and effective contributions. The mere listing of works of scholarship will not be enough, for titles can often be insufficiently informative or even positively misleading. Some form of annotation is highly desirable, indeed virtually mandatory.[11]

It is above all the completeness and the inclusion of annotation that distinguishes this bibliography from its various predecessors (except, of course the bibliography of Radice that forms its nucleus). But at the same time we wish to say with a great deal of emphasis that we would not have been able to produce the current work if we had not been able to build on the foundations laid by distinguished predecessors in the field of Philonic studies, most notably by the bibliographers G. Delling, L. H. Feldman, A. V. Nazzaro and E. Hilgert. If this particular area is now better served than almost any other in classical and Judaic studies, this the result of the cumulative efforts of a large number of scholars.

---

[10] We do not want to give the impression here that we take sides in the extensive modern debate on the place of Alexandrian and Hellenistic Judaism in the Judaism of the Second Temple and the early Rabbinic period as a whole!

[11] Compare the splendid service offered by the repertory *New Testament Abstracts*.

2. *Method of compilation and analysis*

The method that has been followed in the presentation of the material is in all essentials the same as that devised by Radice in his *Bibliografia generale*. Much of the explanation that now follows reiterates what was said in the Introduction to that volume. We will present the various features of our methodology under a number of separate headings.

(a) sources

In addition to the previous bibliographies of Philonic scholarship already mentioned above, we have made extensive use of a number of standard repertories in the area of Classical and Biblical studies. Prominent among these are *L'année philologique* (Paris), *Répertoire bibliographique* (Louvain), *Elenchus bibliographicus Biblicus* (Rome), the bibliographical sections of the *Tijdschrift voor Filosofie* and *Gnomon*, *Bulletin Signalétique* (for both Sciences Religieuses and Philosophie), *New Testament Abstracts*, and *Religion Indexes* I and II. Other valuable sources of material have been specialized bibliographies found in various monographs, and the generous assistance of other scholars mentioned in the Preface.

Following the example of Goodhart and Goodenough we have attempted to gain physical access to all works in order to check the relevant bibliographical data. The one exception to this rule is formed by a large group of American Ph.D. dissertations, the treatment of which will be discussed presently. Only four works remained entirely inaccessible.[12]

(b) selection

The criteria of selection established by Radice for his bibliography were both linguistic and quantitative. He restricted the inclusion of material to those publications written in English, French, Italian, German, Spanish and Latin. Moreover he stipulated that contributions of less than three pages in length would not be listed unless they made a significant contribution to Philonic studies. For this work we have retained the quantitative minimum of three pages. The number of languages admitted, however, has been increased by two. All contributions written in the Dutch and Modern Hebrew languages have been added. Especially the last-named items gave rise to a number of practical difficulties, which will be discussed at some length below. It has not been possible to include contributions written in Modern Greek, Slavic, Scandinavian and other languages. These items, however, represent no more than the tiniest fraction of the whole body of Philonic literature.[13]

We have, on the other hand excluded three categories of items that were listed in Radice's original bibliography. (1) All bibliographical

---

[12] Staples (**5115**), Gurov (**6724**), Fabbrini (**8329**), Landmann (**8342**). The annotation accompanying the last-named work is based on the short notice in *APh.*

[13] They are at least partially listed in Hilgert's bibliography cited above in n.5.

material pertaining to Pseudo-Philo *Liber Antiquitatum Biblicarum*, which Radice retained because it had been included in Goodhart and Goodenough's work, has now been omitted. This material, though of great intrinsic interest, really has nothing to do with Philonic studies proper. (2) Unaltered reprints of works published prior to 1937 have not been retained. (3) There is no section corresponding to the extremely useful appendix on work in progress included by Radice.[14] Almost all the items he mentioned in that section have by now been published, and have thus found their way into the new bibliography. We do record studies that have been published in the years since 1986 and propose a continuation of the bibliography in something like its present form. We return to the subject at the end of this section.

(c) arrangement

The organization of the present work is identical to that of its predecessor. It is divided into three parts. Part One lists all those works that give immediate access to Philo's writings or serve as instruments of research. It includes bibliographies (unannotated and annotated), editions (also of fragments), translations (in series, and of single works), anthologies, commentaries, indices and lexica, and the separate journal devoted to Philonic studies. Within each category the items are listed in chronological order. Part Two contains the critical studies that concern Philo and related subjects. Here the principle of organization is strictly chronological. The items are listed in yearly groups, and alphabetically within each year.[15] The third part of the bibliography consists of Indices, the principles of which will be discussed in greater detail below.

Each item in turn consists of two parts. The first consists of an assigned number and the complete bibliographical reference. The second contains a description of the contents of the study in question.

One importance difference in the arrangement of this bibliography compared with that of Radice is that it has adopted an open instead of a closed system of numeration. Whereas the former work numbered its items consecutively from **1** to **1095**, we have now devised a system in which each section starts off with a new round number. Thus unannotated bibliographies start at **1001**, annotated bibliographies at **1101**, and so on. Moreover in Part two there is a direct correspondence between the year of publication and the assigned number. Thus the list of works written in 1937 begins with the number **3701**, that of works written in 1938 with **3801** and so on. For all works listed in Part two it is therefore possible immediately

---

[14] This section could only be compiled at the time with the invaluable assistance of V. Nikiprowetzky (Paris), who, like a spider in the middle of his web, was able to keep track of developments in Philonic research by means of his numerous contacts and the vast correspondence he conducted with other scholars. His death in effect removed the possibility of continuing this section.

[15] Note that if the date of a work covers two years, it is placed in the latter year; this often occurs in Hebrew journals which follow the Jewish year.

to determine the year of publication. This is particularly useful when consulting the indices. A great advantage of the open system of numeration is that it will be extemely straightforward to add missing items to the bibliography in subsequent supplementary publications.[16]

(d) abbreviations
Since a high proportion of the studies contained in this bibliography have appeared either as articles in journals or as monographs in series, it is necessary to make extensive use of abbreviations. The abbreviations that we use in referring to such journals and series have been collected together in a list located directly after the Introduction. The reader will observe that there are two differences between this work and its predecessor in its use of abbreviations. Firstly, scholarly series are much more frequently referred to by means of abbreviations. Secondly, the actual abbreviations used by Radice have in many cases been modified in order to correspond better to Northern European and North American conventions. Basis of the new list are the recommendations of two authoritative publications, one in the area of classical studies, the other in the area of biblical studies:

L'année philologique: bibliographie critique et analytique de l'anti-quité gréco-latine, Paris 1924- (= *APh*).

S. SCHWERTNER, *Internationales Abkürzungsverzeichnis für Theo-logie und Grenzgebiete*, Berlin-New York 1974 (= *IATG*); also published as Abkürzungsverzeichnis of the *Theologische Real-enzyklopädie* (Berlin-New York 1976).

Further details on the journals and series cited in our list can be found by consulting these publications. Where there is a conflict between the two, as is not seldom the case, we have generally chosen to follow *APh*. But we have refused to be dogmatic in any particular case. Thus for the *Reallexikon für Antike und Christentum* we have retained the customary *RAC*, and not the *RLAC* employed by *APh*. Moreover, like *IATG*, we have abbreviated some titles consisting of a single word (e.g. *Gnomon, Mnemo-syne*), which *APh* does not do.

(e) summaries
The summaries given in this bibliography are of diverse origin: (i) for the years 1937-81 most summaries have been taken over from Radice's Italian bibliography and translated into English (indicated by the formula =R and the original number placed in brackets at the end of the summary); (ii) additional items from those years not in Radice and from the years 1982-86 have been prepared by the various members of the present team (indicated by initials placed in brackets at the end of the summary). Given the diverse origin of the summaries, a wholly uniform procedure cannot be expected. In general terms the aim has been to give a summary of the

---

[16] It has been necessary to add a number of items at the last minute, and these have been assigned a number augmented with the letter a. One number (**7629**) has been left vacant on account of a mistake discovered just before publication.

contents of each item that will enable the interested researcher to determine whether the subject matter that it contains will be of relevance for his or her own concerns. The length of the summaries is generally in proportion to the relative importance of the study involved. Here too uniformity is impossible and practicality must be the aim. The longest summary in the book is that of Wolfson's famous work in two volumes and 900 pages, but this summary could hardly be made 90 times the length of the summary of an article of 10 pages. The tone of the annotations has been kept resolutely objective. Some indication is often given of the quantitative (e.g. short, extensive...) and qualitative (e.g. superficial, in-depth, valuable...) aspects of the contributions. But we have been careful not to make evaluations or criticisms of the validity of the results of research surveyed. In this regard the bibliography differs significantly from the survey of Josephan scholarship presented by Feldman for the years 1937-80.[17]

One category of studies has been treated differently from the rest. These are the unpublished Ph.D. dissertations submitted to Universities in North America. In a number of cases summaries have been made with reference to a copy or a microfilm of the dissertation.[18] More frequently, however, summaries have been made through consultation of the abstract placed by the author in the compendium *Dissertation Abstracts*. If this is the case, it is indicated in brackets at the end of the summary. Dissertations that were later published as monographs have of course not been summarized in their original submitted form.[19]

(f) reviews

In this bibliography we have retained its predecessor's practice of listing reviews of those monographs which are specifically devoted to the study of Philo. For the references to these reviews we are greatly indebted to a number of standard repertories, notably *L'année philologique*, *Répertoire bibliographique*, and *Elenchus bibliographicus Biblicus*. Review articles of a length exceeding one or two pages are generally listed twice, both as article under a separate number and as review under the book being reviewed.[20] Here as elsewhere completeness has been the aim, but we are well aware that, in this area more than any other, our bibliography is likely to be very incomplete. But if the lists of reviews are of service to readers of the monographs being reviewed, then they will have sufficiently served their purpose.

---

[17] See above n.6.

[18] This was also case in Radice's bibliography, in which a number of such works were extensively summarized.

[19] An exception is the Ph.D. thesis of A. Mendelson (**7115**), because it differs in a number of ways from the later work (**8235**).

[20] Note also the following convention: a single page number indicates that the review occurs on that page only, a number followed by f. (e.g. 123f.) on that and the subsequent page (i.e. 123-124), a number followed by ff. (e.g. 345ff.) on that and more than one subsequent page (i.e. 345-347).

(g) Hebrew articles

As indicated above, the inclusion of articles written in Hebrew has raised a number of practical difficulties. In consultation with the team members in Jerusalem a number of guidelines were established which have been consistently followed in the presentation of the Hebrew material. Firstly we summarize our procedure for the listing of the article.

(i) Items have been listed under the Romanized version of the author's name, as indicated by the author in publications written in other languages.

(ii) Following the author's Romanized name is his or her name in Hebrew, placed in square brackets.

(iii) The title of the book or article is first given in its Hebrew form.

(iv) Following the Hebrew title an English title is given in square brackets. If there is a title authorized by the author (i.e. given in an English summary or elsewhere in a translation) this is the title that is given; if there is no authorized title, then the Hebrew title is translated into English and cited as such, *preceded by an = sign*. The absence of such a sign generally indicates that the work in question is accompanied by an abstract, the existence of which we have indicated in each case.

Further problems are caused by the fact that a large number of studies published in Hebrew also exist in versions presented in other languages. Sometimes the Hebrew study appears first and a translated version is published later (often with minor modifications); sometimes the study is first presented in a European language and then later published in Hebrew; sometimes Hebrew and English or German versions or summaries are published simultaneously. Our procedure in this complex situation has been as follows:

(i) If similar versions exist in both Hebrew and another language but the Hebrew study was published first, then a cross-reference is given to the version in the other language and the summary is found there.

(ii) If the Hebrew version was made on the basis of a study already published elsewhere in another language, we retain a separate listing, but once again there is no summary, only a cross-reference. Works of non-Israeli authors translated into Hebrew are generally not separately listed, unless there is some specific reason for doing so.[21]

(iii) Cross-references are also given at the end of summaries of articles in European languages if there is a Hebrew version in existence, whether this was published previously or subsequently.

(iv) Summaries of studies written in Hebrew are therefore only presented when they have not appeared in any other language.

A special section of our list of Abbreviations has been devoted to the Journals in which the Hebrew articles have appeared. Special characteristics of these publications, if relevant to our purpose, are briefly indicated.

---

[21] Exceptions are made in the case of the translation of classic works by Wolfson (**7038**) and Ginzberg (**7516**).

(h) indices

Since the organization of the greater part of our bibliography is based on a formal (i.e. primarily chronological) principle, the need for comprehensive indices is a *sine qua non* if the user is going to be able to find what he is looking for. As Radice already pointed out, however, the preparation of indices for an annotated bibliography such as this is fraught with difficulties.[22] We have decided this time on six indices. Five of these – listing authors of studies, authors of reviews, biblical passages and passages of Philonic works referred to in the title of studies or in our summaries, and Greek terms – yield no difficulties. It is the methodology and organization of the subject index that is decidely problematic. Radice divided his index of subjects into some ten different sections covering the diverse aspects of Philonic studies, such as philosophical and religious concepts, ancient authors, exegetical figures and so on. We have decided that this approach was excessively fragmented, and so now include all these subjects in a single index.

But what to include, and how to organize? The subjects dealt with in our studies range from general presentations of vast areas of discourse and theory, such as theology, ethics, mysticism etc., to very precise studies on points of detail. Clearly there is no alternative but to base the subjects of the index on the contents of the summaries that constitute the bulk of our book. The purpose of the index is thus to point the reader to the right bibliographical titles by means of the contents of the summaries. We have aimed to make the process of referral as accurate and efficient as possible by adopting the conventions of subject indices as recommended by the *Chicago Manual of Style*.[23] This method entails extensive use of sub-categories and even sub-sub-categories, so that the occurrence of large subjects (e.g. God, Alexandria etc.) followed by a forest of numbers is avoided as much as possible. Use is also made of frequent cross-references, in order to limit duplication of similar concepts. It is difficult to determine how comprehensive to make an index. We have endeavoured to make it very complete, and so no doubt have erred on the side of excessive detail. If this means that the result is somewhat cluttered and unsystematic,[24] we ask the user's forgiveness in the spirit of *faute de mieux*.

Three more important principles of the index must be explained in some detail.

(i) It must be constantly born in mind by the user that virtually all references in the index pertain in some way or other to Philo, his writings or his

---

[22] *Op. cit.* (n.1) 309.

[23] 13th edition, Chicago 1982; see chapter 18.

[24] Especially in the case of a number of key terms and concepts, such as Logos, Sophia, powers etc., it has been extremely difficult to reach any kind of consistency on account of the differing conventions prevalent in Philonic scholarship. In the case of Logos and Sophia we distinguish between concept and entity, and use a capital when *the* Logos or Sophia is being referred to.

thought. Thus, for example, when one reads 'Ambrose, cosmic theology 6416', this should not be taken to mean that in **6416** a discussion of Ambrosian cosmic theology will be found, but rather that Philo's influence on or relation to Ambrosian cosmic theology is being discussed.

(ii) A considerable problem is presented by the numerous general or synoptic presentations of Philo or broad aspects of his thought. Under the heading 'Philo' in the index we have listed many of these, dividing them into the following nine categories:

> short introduction to (up to 10 pages);
> general account of (10-30 pages);
> detailed introduction to (30-100 pages);
> in-depth presentation of (entire monographs);
> historical situation of, introduction to;
> introduction to from Jewish perspective;
> philosophical thought of, introduction to;
> political thought of, introduction to;
> religious thought of, introduction to.

Some of these categories, if they contained a considerable number of items, have been further sub-divided into the various languages in which the accounts were written. Also in some other areas we have listed synoptic presentations under the sub-heading 'general account', which always appears first under the subject heading concerned. Note also that general references to individual treatises have been collected together under the heading 'Corpus Philonicum'.

(iii) Studies which are of seminal importance for the areas of research with which they are concerned are indicated in bold type, both in the subject index and in the index of authors. Such labelling is used relatively sparingly.

Finally it is to be noted that studies published subsequent to 1986 have not been included in the indices.

(i) continuation

The present bibliography covers the years 1937-86. The final year or two will certainly not be entirely complete, for a number of *repertoria* covering these years have not yet seen the light of day. On the other hand it seemed a pity not to give some indication of items that have been published since 1986 and have come to the authors' notice. We have included these under the headings 1987 and 1988, but have given no summaries (and, as indicated above, not included them in the indices). The provisional nature of the numbers assigned to these items is indicated by an asterisk.

It is the sad fate of all bibliographies not only that they are incomplete, but that they are also going out of date even before they have been published. The authors of this particular bibliography have no illusions about the completeness of their listings, and invite scholars, either in reviews or by means of private communications, to indicate to them items that should have been included but are missing. It is the intention of the authors to continue the bibliography in the future by publishing supplementary lists at regular intervals. The most ideal way to do this would be to publish these yearly in the journal *Studia Philonica*. Unfortunately the future of this publication, which has not appeared since 1980, is by no means certain. If scholarly research on Philo continues at the present high rate of production, then a supplementary volume can be expected in ten years time.

3. *Division of labour*

This bibliography is the result of a collective enterprise involving contributions on the part of no less than eight scholars. The division of labour and responsibility for the various parts of the work will now be outlined.

As indicated above, the nucleus of the present work is formed by the Italian bibliography compiled single-handedly by Roberto Radice in the years 1978-82. Without this foundation the present work would hardly have been possible. The translation from Italian into English was carried out by Anthony Runia.

Leadership of the project to produce an updated version was in the hands of David Runia. He and Radice were responsible for collecting the additional material in all languages except Hebrew and Dutch. The Dutch articles were collected and summarized by Rudolf Bitter; the summaries were then translated from Dutch into English by David Runia. The Hebrew articles were collected by the Jerusalem team.[25]

The task of making summaries of the additional items – except once again the Dutch and Hebrew contributions – was in the hands of the two main authors. Radice summarized all items in the languages other than English. On account of the sheer bulk of material in English he also summarized a number of English articles, the remainder being done by Runia.

The Jerusalem team was led and coordinated by David Satran, who received assistance from Naomi Cohen, Michael Mach and Daniel Schwartz. The task of locating the material was carried out mainly by Satran and Schwartz, while the summaries were made chiefly by Mach, Satran and Cohen. Satran also supervised the difficult task of getting the Hebrew into print.

The Introduction is the work of David Runia, who also drew up the list of Abbreviations (aided by Radice's original list) and compiled the Indices. The general layout of the book and the production of the camera-ready copy were also his responsiblity.

---

[25] Much assisted by Hilgert's bibliography (cf. n.5).

4. Brief observations on fifty years of Philonic scholarship

The material contained in this bibliography allows the reader to gain a remarkable conspectus of the highways and byways of half a century of scholarship on Philo and his direct *Umwelt*. It would be a pity not to take the opportunity to make some brief observations on this collected material. In so doing it is not our intention to present an analytical survey of developments in the scholarly interpretation of Philo's writings and thought. This task, illuminating though it would certainly be, we leave to others, who are welcome to utilize the abundant material we have assembled.[26] In this section we will take a more statistical approach, which will illustrate the growth and development of Philonic scholarship, as witnessed by the languages in which it has been presented and the shifting perspectives from which it has been undertaken. In order to illustrate some of the results of our analyses we will present a number of graphic charts. We are aware that it is not customary to use these in the area of the humanities, but they would seem to be particulary suitable to illustrate the kind of observations we wish to make.

Let us commence with the purely quantitative aspect of the number of studies devoted to Philo during the period 1937-86. In its two parts our bibliography contains 1666 separate items. From the viewpoint of our statistics these have to be treated as discrete units of equal worth. Obviously, in reality this is not the case; it is absurd to regard the two massive tomes of Wolfson's *Philo* as amounting to the same as a short article of three pages. Nevertheless, even allowing for this element of simplification, it is not difficult to tabulate the remarkable growth of production in Philonic scholarship during the half century covered by our work. Figure 1 shows the number of studies dealing with Philo, taken in groups of 5 years at a time.

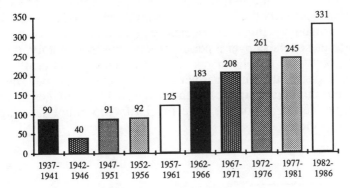

figure 1: number of studies 1937-86

---

[26] See most recently the excellent survey of P. Borgen, **1114** in our bibliography.

The conclusions to be drawn from these numbers will come as no surprise to those who have already had occasion to use our bibliography. Up to about 1960 the amount of scholarship done on Philo was relatively stable, with a predictable lapse in activities during the period of the war and the direct aftermath. Since 1960, however, there has been a truly explosive growth of Philonic studies, which shows no sign of abating. Such growth has certainly also taken place in other scholarly fields. But in the case of Philo one might wonder whether the commencement of the French translation project in 1961 may have been a direct stimulus to greater productivity.

A further area of interest is represented by the eight languages in which scholarship on Philo has been written.[27] Here our material yields the following results. First we take the entire period 1937-1986:[28]

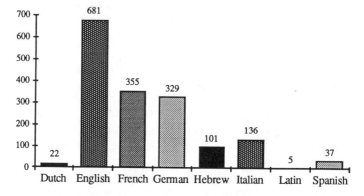

figure 2: languages of research 1937-86

Once again the results are rather predictable. English is by far the dominant language, with as many studies written in it as in French and German combined. Hebrew and Italian, though less well represented than French and German, nevertheless represent a considerable body of scholarship. The three remaining languages are clearly peripheral.

Since these totals cover a period of an entire half-century, the results lack precision. The developments of the period can be better illustrated if we show the use of the languages per decade, as in the next two figures. In figure 3 absolute numbers are given, in figure 4 percentages of the total number per decade. For the sake of clarity the minor languages are grouped together.

---

[27] It would no doubt be equally, if not more, interesting to analyse the different countries in which Philonic scholarship has taken place. But it is impossible to determine the national provenance of all articles, since five of the languages used are not confined to the limits of one country.

[28] Spanish includes Portugese and Castilian contributions.

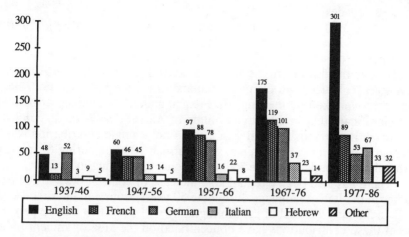

figure 3: languages per decade in absolute numbers

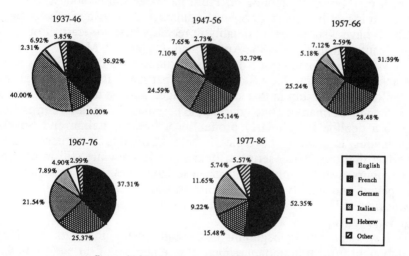

figure 4: languages per decade in percentages

These statistics are of considerable interest, because they document a marked shift in the use of the five major languages of Philonic studies. In absolute figures the use of English has undergone an exponential growth during the half century. In terms of percentages, however, it actually receded in importance during the second and third decades. In the past decade its dominance has become undisputed, and it alone accounted for more than half of all the studies dealing with Philo. The 'linguistic imperialism' which we mentioned at the beginning of our Introduction thus emerges with full force. The increase is primarily due to the massive amount of scholarship being published in North America. A contributory factor is also the fact that Dutch and Scandinavian scholars now publish almost exclusively in English, and no longer in German and French as in previous decades.

The amount of scholarship produced in French grew strongly during the first four decades, but now seems, relatively at any rate, on the decline. The figures for studies in German are much more dramatic. In terms of percentages the drop from the first to the last decades is from 40% to less than 10%.[29] In 1937-46 German scholarship led the field; by 1977-86, it had been overtaken by the English, French, and also Italian contributions. It is significant that in the large volume of *Aufstieg und Niedergang der römischen Welt* published in Berlin in 1984 not a single contribution was in German. Given the total dominance of German scholars during the century before the beginning of our period, this decline is startling indeed.

There has also been a remarkable increase of contributions to Philonic studies in the Italian language during the 50 years, from 3 in the first decade to 67 in the last. Perusal of the bibliography will show that a large percentage of these contributions have concentrated on the area of ancient philosophy, a direct result of the great popularity of that subject in Italy. The growth of articles in Hebrew on Philo has been more modest, but very steady. It is worth noting that Spanish studies (hidden away in the category 'Other') have also increased notably in recent years, not least through the significant contributions of the Argentinian scholar J. P. Martín.

A final conclusion to be drawn is the undoubted correlation between the appearance of translations of Philo in a particular language and growth of Philonic scholarship in that same language. Almost no translation work was done in German or Dutch during the period under review, corresponding to a decline in scholarly production. French, Italian and Spanish translations, in contrast, have clearly been a stimulus to further research. The fact that translation series in Italian and Hebrew are still in progress thus augurs well for scholarship in those languages. The existence of a competent and readily available English translation (also including the *Quaestiones*) in the Loeb Classical Library has certainly aided research on Philo in English.

It was noted at the beginning of this Introduction that Philo's writings and thought furnish important evidence for a number of different scholarly fields of research. A third aspect of Philonic scholarship that the evidence of our bibliography allows us to examine is the relative contributions made by these various fields. For the sake of the exercise we propose a nine-fold division: (1) Philonic studies proper (i.e. concentrating on Philo for his own sake); (2) classical studies; (3) ancient history; (4) history of philosophy; (5) New Testament; (6) Patristic studies; (7) general theology (including also history of religions); (8) Jewish studies; (9) Gnostic studies (including Gnosis). It is important to note that, in contrast to the previous two tables – after all a study can be written in only one language at a time –, there is a subjective element in the assignation of studies to these various fields. A

---

29 Note that 11 of the 53 studies in 1977-86 are in fact translations of articles by Y. Amir originally written in Hebrew or English (**8301-11**).

study can easily combine Jewish studies and philosophy, classical studies and New Testament, and so on. We have tried to assign studies to the field which appears to the focal point of the author's research.

In the following figure the division of studies between these nine fields over the period 1937-86 is presented:

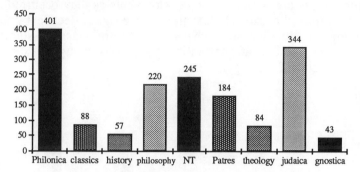

figure 5. subjects of research 1937-86

Less than a quarter of all the studies contained in our bibliography focus directly on Philo, a significant indication of his interest and importance for other fields of learning. The amount of research done on Philo from the viewpoint of classical studies and ancient history is relatively quite meagre. This is no surprise, for most classicists have hardly heard of Philo,[30] while in the field of ancient history Philo's evidence, though of great significance, only relates to a limited number of topics in imperial politics and Alexandrian social and cultural history. The number of studies done from the viewpoint of ancient and Jewish philosophy is certainly quite respectable, especially considering how controversial Philo's status as a philosopher is. More copious, however, is the research done on him from the viewpoint of theology and religion. The material comparing Philo with the New Testament is very rich indeed – especially on his relations to the Gospel of John, the Epistle to the Hebrews, and Pauline thought. Research on Philo's influence on Patristic thought has been less extensively and thoroughly analyzed. It should be noted, however, that the field of theology – consisting of New Testament, Patristic, and general theological studies added together – is responsible for more research on Philo than any other area. From this perspective the tradition of Philo Christianus going right back to Eusebius is still alive and well. The days that Philo was little studied by Judaic scholars are most definitely over. A vast amount of research has been carried out from a Jewish perspective, both on the specific nature of Philo's Judaism and its relation to his involvement in other fields. Mention might be made here of the extensive references to Philo in studies on the Essenes and the Therapeutae in relation to the finds at Qumran (clearly a 'growth area' during the 50's and 60's). Research on Philo's relation to the

---

[30] Cf. our remarks below at **8519**.

Gnostic movement, inspired largely by the discovery of the Nag Hammadi library, has had a slow growth as the material has gradually become more generally accessible to scholars.

So far our comments have been based on a synoptic view of the entire period of fifty years. Once again it would be interesting if we could gain a more precise picture by following developments as they occurred during the fifty years. We can tabulate these once again decade by decade, simplifying the situation somewhat by combining classical studies and ancient history into the category antiquity, and subsuming Gnostic studies under the heading of theology.

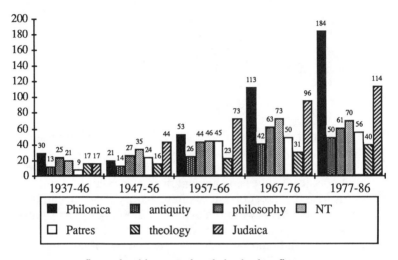

figure 6: subjects per decade in absolute figures

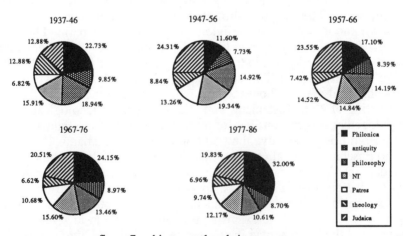

figure 7: subjects per decade in percentages

On the basis of these figures a number of interesting observations can be made. (1) There has been marked tendency to concentrate more on Philo as a thinker and personage in his own right. In the last decade nearly a third of all studies could be placed in this category. Without doubt the increased tendency towards specialization in recent scholarship has contributed here. (2) Interest from the viewpoint of classical and historical studies has been very steady, fluctuating between 8 and 10% of the whole. (3) The interest in Philo from the perspective of philosophy has declined somewhat in recent decades. The stimulus provided by the monumental study of H. A. Wolfson is certainly reflected in the percentages during the decades 1947-56 and 1957-66. (4) New Testament and Patristic studies flourished greatly during the second, third and fourth decades,[31] but are now, it would seem, entering a period of relatively less prominence. (5) The study of Philo from a Jewish perspective during the past fifty has gone from strength to strength. Our figures suggest that at the present time – leaving aside the studies that concentrate on Philo for his own sake – this area of research is gaining a position of dominance in Philonic studies.

---

[31] Note that we should not attribute too much significance to the figures for the first decade, on account of the extraordinary circumstances of the period.

ABBREVIATIONS

1. *Philonic treatises*

Abr.	*De Abrahamo*
Aet.	*De aeternitate mundi*
Agr.	*De agricultura*
Anim.	*De animalibus*
Cher.	*De Cherubim*
Contempl.	*De vita contemplativa*
Conf.	*De confusione linguarum*
Congr.	*De congressu eruditionis gratia*
Decal.	*De Decalogo*
Deo	*De Deo*
Det.	*Quod deterius potiori insidiari soleat*
Deus	*Quod Deus ist immutabilis*
Ebr.	*De ebrietate*
Flacc.	*In Flaccum*
Fug.	*De fuga et inventione*
Gig.	*De gigantibus*
Her.	*Quis reum divinarum heres sit*
Hypoth.	*Hypothetica*
Ios.	*De Iosepho*
Leg. 1-3	*Legum allegoriae* I, II, III
Legat.	*Legatio ad Gaium*
LAB	*Liber Antiquitatum Biblicarum* (Pseudo-Philo)
Migr.	*De migratione Abrahami*
Mos. 1-2	*De vita Moysis* I, II
Mut.	*De mutatione nominum*
Opif.	*De opificio mundi*
Plant.	*De plantatione*
Post.	*De posteritate Caini*
Praem.	*De praemiis et poenis, De exsecrationibus*
Prob.	*Quod omnis probus liber sit*
Prov. 1-2	*De Providentia* I, II
QE 1-2	*Quaestiones et solutiones in Exodum* I, II
QG 1-4	*Quaestiones et solutiones in Genesim* I, II, III, IV
Sacr.	*De sacrificiis Abelis et Caini*
Sobr.	*De sobrietate*
Somn. 1-2	*De somniis* I, II
Spec. 1-4	*De specialibus legibus* I, II, III, IV
Virt.	*De virtutibus*

2. *Philonic editions, translations*

Aucher	*Philonis Judaei sermones tres hactenus inediti* (cf. **1701**), *Philonis Judaei paralipomena* (cf. **1702**)
C-W	*Philonis Alexandrini opera quae supersunt*, ediderunt L. COHN, P.

WENDLAND, S. REITER (cf. **1501-1508**)

G-G   H. L. GOODHART and E. R. GOODENOUGH, 'A general bibliography of Philo Judaeus', in E. R. GOODENOUGH, *The Politics of Philo Judaeus: practice and theory* (New Haven 1938, reprinted Hildesheim 1967²) 125-321 (cf. **1001**)

Loeb   *Philo in ten volumes (and two supplementary volumes)*, English translation by F. H. COLSON, G. H. WHITAKER (and R. MARCUS), Loeb Classical Library (London 1929-62) (cf. **2101-2112**)

OPA   *Les œuvres de Philon d'Alexandrie*, French translation under the general editorship of R. ARNALDEZ, C. MONDÉSERT, J. POUILLOUX (Paris 1961-) (cf. **2201-2234**)

3. *Journals and series*

AAAbo.H	Acta Academiae Aboensis, Ser. A. Humaniora
AAHG	Anzeiger für die Altertumswissenschaft
AB	Analecta Bollandiana
ABG	Archiv für Begriffsgeschichte
AC	L'Antiquité Classique
ActBibl	Actualidad Bibliografica
Aeg	Aegyptus
Aev	Aevum
AFLM	Annali della Facoltà di Lettere e Filosofia della Università di Macerata
AFLN	Annali della Facoltà di Lettere e Filosofia della Università di Napoli
AFLPer	Annali della Facoltà di Lettere e Filosofia della Università di Perugia
AGI	Archivio Glottologico Italiano
AGPh	Archiv für Geschichte der Philosophie
AHAW	Abhandlungen der Heidelberger Akademie der Wissenschaften, philosophisch-historische Klasse
AHR	American Historical Review
AIHS	Archives Internationales d'histoire des Sciences
AIPhO	Annuaire de l'Institut de Philologie et d'Histoire Orientales et Slaves de l'Université Libre de Bruxelles
AISP	Archivio italiano per la storia della pietà
AJPh	American Journal of Philology
AKG	Arbeiten zur Kirchengeschichte
ALGHJ	Arbeiten zur Literatur und Geschichte des hellenistischen Judentums
ALMA	Archivum Latinitatis Medii Aevi
ALW	Archiv für Liturgiewissenschaft
AnBib	Analecta Biblica
Ang	Angelicum
ANRW	Aufstieg und Niedergang der römischen Welt
Ant	Antonianum
AOH	Acta Orientalia Academiae Scientiarum Hungaricae
APh	L'Année Philologique (founded by Marouzeau)
ArAg	Archivo Agustiniano
ArFil	Archivio di Filosofia
ArPh	Archives de Philosophie
ASNP	Annali della Scuola Normale Superiore di Pisa, Classe di Lettere e Filosofia
ASNU	Acta Seminarii Neotestamentici Upsaliensis
ATA	Archivo Teológico Agustiniano

ATG	Archivo Teológico Granadino
Ath	Athenaeum
AThA	L'Année Théologique Augustinienne
AThR	Anglican Theological Review
Aug	Augustinianum
Augustinus	Augustinus
BAGB	Bulletin de l'Association G. Budé
BASP	Bulletin of the American Society of Papyrologists
BBB	Bonner Biblische Beiträge
Bel	Belfagor
BEThL	Bibliotheca Ephemeridum Theologicarum Lovaniensium
BEvTh	Beiträge zur evangelischen Theologie
BFC	Bollettino di Filologia Classica
BFCL	Bulletin des Facultés Catholiques de Lyon
BGBE	Beiträge zur Geschichte der biblischen Exegese
BGBH	Beiträge zur Geschichte der biblischen Hermeneutik
BHTh	Beiträge zur historischen Theologie
BIAO	Bulletin de l'Institut Français d'Archéologie Orientale
Bib	Biblica
BibFe	Biblia y Fe
BibNot	Biblische Notizen. Beiträge zur exegetischen Diskussion
BibOr	Biblica et Orientalia
BICS	Bulletin of the Institute of Classical Studies of the University of London
Bijdr	Bijdragen
BiOr	Bibliotheca Orientalis
BJRL	Bulletin of the John Rylands Library
BJudSt	Brown Judaic Studies
BLE	Bulletin de Littérature Ecclésiastique
BoL	Book list. The Society for Old Testament study
BPW	Berliner philologische Wochenschrift
BR	Biblical Research
BRev	Biblical Review
BSAC	Bulletin de la Société d'Archéologie Copte
BSFA	Bollettino della Società Filosofica Italiana
BThAM	Bulletin de Théologie Ancienne et Médiévale
ByS	Byzantine Studies
ByZ	Byzantinische Zeitschrift
Byz	Byzantion
BZ	Biblische Zeitschrift
BZAW	Beihefte zur Zeitschrift für die alttestamentliche Wissenschaft
BZNW	Beihefte zur Zeitschrift für die neutestamentliche Wissenschaft und die Kunde der älteren Kirche
CB	The Classical Bulletin
CBQ	The Catholic Biblical Quarterly
CBQ.MS	The Catholic Biblical Quarterly Monograph Series
CCARJ	Central Conference of American Rabbis Journal
CCGR	Cahiers du Centre George-Radet, Talence, Université de Bordeaux III
CCist	Collectanea Cisterciensia
CDios	La Ciudad de Dios
CE	Chronique d'Égypte
ChH	Church History
Chir	Chiron
CHR	Catholic Historical Review

CHSHMC	The Center for Hermeneutical Studies in Hellenistic and Modern Culture
Cith	Cithara
CivCatt	La Civiltà cattolica
CJ	The Classical Journal
ClF	Classical Folia
CPh	Classical Philology
CQ	The Classical Quarterly
CQR	Church Quarterly Review
CR	The Classical Review
CRAI	Comptes Rendus de l'Académie des Inscriptions et Belles-Lettres
CRINT	Compendia Rerum Iudaicarum ad Novum Testamentum
Cris	Crisis
Crit	Critique
CrozQ	Crozer Quarterly
CuBi	Cultura Biblica
CuS	Cuadernos del Sur
CW	The Classical World
DA	Dissertation Abstracts
Dav	Davke
DB	Dictionnaire de la Bible
DLZ	Deutsche Literaturzeitung für Kritik der internationalen Wissenschaft
DoC	Doctor communis
DOP	Dumbarton Oaks Papers
DR	Downside Review
DS	Dictionnaire de Spiritualité, Ascétique et Mystique, Doctrine et Histoire
DT	Divus Thomas
DUJ	Durham University Journal
EAJTh	East Asia Journal of Theology
EBB	Elenchus Bibliographicus Biblicus
EE	Estudios Eclesiásticos
EM	Emerita
EPh	Études Philosophiques
EPRO	Études préliminaires aux religions orientales dans l'Empire romain
Er	Eranos
Eras	Erasmus
ErJb	Eranos-Jahrbuch
EstB	Estudios Bíblicos
EstFil	Estudios Filosóficos
EstFr	Estudios Franciscanos
ET	The Expository Times
EtCl	Les Études Classiques
EThL	Ephemerides Theologicae Lovanienses
ETR	Études Théologiques et Religieuses
Études	Études
Euph	Euphrosyne
EvQ	Evangelical Quarterly
EvTh	Evangelische Theologie
FaT	Faith and Thought
Fil	Filosofia
FKDG	Forschungen zur Kirchen- und Dogmengeschichte
Fl	Le Flambeau
Fr	Franciscana

FreibRund	Freiburger Rundschau
FRLANT	Forschungen zur Religion und Literatur des Alten und Neuen Testaments
FrRu	Freiburg Rundbrief
FuF	Forschungen und Fortschritte
FZPhTh	Freiburger Zeitschrift für Philosophie und Theologie
GGA	Göttingische Gelehrte Anzeigen
GIF	Giornale Italiano di Filologia
Glotta	Glotta
GM	Giornale di Metafisica
Gn	Gnomon
Gr	Gregorianum
GRBS	Greek, Roman and Byzantine Studies
GrJ	Grace Journal
Gymn	Gymnasium
HDSB	Harvard Divinity School Bulletin
HebAR	Hebrew Annual Review
Hel	Helikon
Helm	Helmantica
Herm	Hermes
Herma	Hermathena
HeyJ	Heythrop Journal
HibJ	The Hibbert Journal
HistJud	Historia Judaica
HR	History of Religions
HThR	Harvard Theological Review
HThS	Harvard Theological Studies
HUCA	Hebrew Union College Annual
Hum (B)	Humanitas
HZ	Historische Zeitschrift
IATG	Internationales Abkürzungsverzeichnis für Theologie und Grenzgebiete
IEJ	Israel Exploration Journal
InfLitt	L'Information Littéraire
Irén	Irénikon
Isis	Isis
IsrW	Israelitisches Wochenblatt
IThS	Innsbrucher Theologische Studien
JAAR	Journal of the American Academy of Religion
JAOS	Journal of the American Oriental Society
JbAC	Jahrbuch für Antike und Christentum
JbAC.E	Jahrbuch für Antike und Christentum Erganzungsband
JBL	Journal of Biblical Literature
JBL.MS	Journal of Biblical Literature Monograph Series
JBR	The Journal of Bible and Religion
Jdm	Judaism
JEA	The Journal of Egyptian Archaeology
JEvTS	Journal of the Evangelical Theological Society
JFKA	Jahresbericht über die Fortschritte der klassischen Altertumswissenschaft
JHI	Journal of the History of Ideas
JHS	The Journal of Hellenic Studies
JJML	Journal of Jewish Music & Liturgy
JJP	Journal of Juristic Papyrology

JJS	The Journal of Jewish Studies
JNES	Journal of Near Eastern Studies
JŒByz	Jahrbuch der Österreichischen Byzantinistik
JPh	The Journal of Philosophy
JQR	The Jewish Quarterly Review
JR	The Journal of Religion
JRJ	Journal of Reform Judaism
JRS	The Journal of Roman Studies
JS	Journal des Savants
JSAS	Journal for the Society of Armenian Studies
JSJ	Journal for the Study of Judaism (in the Persian, Hellenistic and Roman Period)
JSNT	Journal for the Study of the New Testament
JSNT.S	Journal for the Study of the New Testament. Supplementary Series
JSocS	Jewish Social Studies
JSOT	Journal for the Study of the Old Testament
JSOT.S	Journal for the Study of the Old Testament. Supplementary Series
JSSt	Journal of Semitic Studies
JTC	Journal of Theology and Church
JThS	The Journal of Theological Studies
Jud	Judaica
JWCI	Journal of the Warburg and Courtauld Institutes
Kairos	Kairos
Klio	Klio
L'Histoire	L'Histoire
Labeo	Labeo
Lat	Latomus
LCL	Loeb Classical Library
LCM	Liverpool Classical Monthly
LeDiv	Lectio Divina
LF	Listy Filologické
LM	Lutherische Monatshefte
LThPh	Laval Théologique et Philosophique
LuthQ	The Lutheran Quarterly
Lychnos	Lychnos
LZD	Literarisches Zentralblatt für Deutschland
Maia	Maia. Rivista di letterature classiche
MBTh	Münsterische Beiträge zur Theologie
MCom	Miscelanea Comillas
MD	La Maison Dieu
MEAH	Miscelánea de Estudios Árabes y Hebraicos
Mesures	Mesures
MGWJ	Monatsschrift für Geschichte und Wissenschaft des Judentums
MH	Museum Helveticum
Mind	Mind
Mnem	Mnemosyne
MSR	Mélanges de Science Religieuse
MThS	Münchener Theologische Studien
MThZ	Münchener Theologische Zeitschrift
Muséon	Le Muséon
NatGrac	Naturaleza y Gracia
NAWG	Nachrichten der Akademie der Wissenschaften in Göttingen
NBl	New Blackfriars

NDid	Nuovo Didaskaleion
NHS	Nag Hammadi Studies
NieuwTT	Nieuw Theologisch Tijdschrift
NouvC	Nouveaux Cahiers
NPh	Neophilologus
NPhR	Neue Philologische Rundschau
NRTh	Nouvelle Revue Théologique
NSchol	The New Scholasticism
NT	Novum Testamentum
NT.S	Supplements to Novum Testamentum
NTA	Neutestamentliche Abhandlungen
NTS	New Testament Studies
NTT	Nederlands Theologisch Tijdschrift
Numen	Numen
OLZ	Orientalistische Literaturzeitung
OMRL	Oudheidkundige Mededelingen uit het Rijksmuseum van Oudheden te Leiden
Or	Orientalia
OrChr	Oriens Christianus
OrChrP	Orientalia Christiana Periodica
OrOcc	Oriente-Occidente
PAAJR	Proceedings of the American Academy for Jewish Research
Paid	Paideia
ParPass	La Parola del Passato
ParV	Parole di Vita
Pers	Personalist
Phil	Philologus
PhilAnt	Philosophia Antiqua
PhilRef	Philosophia Reformata
PhPhenR	Philosophy and Phenomenological Research
PhQ	Philological Quarterly
PhR	Philosophical Review
PhW	Philologische Wochenschrift
PI	Le Parole e le Idee
POC	Proche Orient Chrétien
PrOrth	Présence Orthodoxe
PThMS	Pittsburgh Theological Monograph Series
QJS	The Quarterly Journal of Speech
QLB	Quaderni di Lettura Biblica
QVetCh	Quaderni di Vetera Christianorum
QVM	Quaderni di Vita Monastica
RAAN	Rendiconti della Accademia di Archeologia, Lettere e Belle Arti di Napoli
RAC	Reallexikon für Antike und Christentum
RAM	Revue d'Ascétique et de Mystique
RAMIF	Revue de l'Association des Médecins Israélites de France
RB	Revue Biblique
RBen	Revue Bénédictine de Critique, d'Histoire et de Littérature Religieuses
RBP	Répertoire Bibliographique de la Philosophie
RBPh	Revue Belge de Philologie et d'Histoire
RCCM	Rivista di Cultura Classica e Medioevale
RCSF	Rivista Critica di Storia della Filosofia
RE	PAULY-WISSOWA-KROLL, Real-Encyclopaedie der classischen

	Altertumswissenschaft
REA	Revue des Études Anciennes
REArm	Revue des Études Arméniennes
REAug	Revue des Études Augustiniennes
RecSR	Recherches de Science Religieuse
RefR	Reformed Review
REG	Revue des Études Grecques
REJ	Revue des Études Juives
REL	Revue des Études Latines
RelSt	Religious Studies
RelStR	Religious Studies Review
Ren	Rencontre
RenCJ	Rencontre Chrétiens et Juifs
RenOO	Rencontre Orient Occident
RET	Revista Española de Teologia
RevBib	Revista Biblica
RFIC	Rivista di Filosofia e de Istruzione Classica
RFL	Revista de Filosofía Latinoamericana
RFN	Rivista de Filosofia Neoscolastica
RGG	Die Religion in Geschichte und Gegenwart
RH	Revue Historique
RHE	Revue d'Histoire Ecclésiastique
RHEF	Revue d'Histoire de l'Église de France
RhM	Rheinisches Museum für Philologie
RHPhR	Revue d'Histoire et de Philosophie Religieuses
RHR	Revue d'Histoire des Religions
RicRel	Ricerche Religiose
RIFD	Rivista Internazionale di Filosofia del Diritto
RIL	Rendiconti dell'Istituto Lombardo, Classe di Lettere e Scienze Morali e Storiche
RivAC	Rivista di Archeologia Cristiana
RivBib	Rivista Biblica
RivBib.S	Supplementi a Rivista Biblica
RivLas	Rivista Lasalliana dei "Fratelli delle Scuole Cristiane" delle Province d'Italia
RMeta	Review of Metaphysics
RMI	Rassegna Mensile di Israel
RMM	Revue de Métaphysique et de Morale
RPF	Revista Portuguesa de Filosofia
RPh	Revue de Philologie, de Littérature et d'Histoire Anciennes
RPh	Revue de Philologie
RPhilos	Revue Philosophique de la France et de l'Étranger
RPhL	Revue Philosophique de Louvain
RQ	Revue de Qumran
RR	The Review of Religion
RSC	Rivista di Studi Classici
RSHum	Revue des Sciences Humaines
RSLR	Rivista di Storia e Letteratura Religiosa
RSPhTh	Revue des Sciences Philosophiques et Theologiques
RSR	Revue des Sciences Religieuses
RThAM	Recherches de Théologie Ancienne et Médiévale
RThL	Revue Théologique de Louvain
RThom	Revue Thomiste

RThPh	Revue de Théologie et de Philosophie
RVV	Religionsgeschichtliche Versuche und Vorarbeiten
Salm	Salmanticensis
SAO	Studia et Acta Orientalia
Sap	Sapienza
SBF	Studii Biblici Franciscani
SBFA	Studium Biblicum Franciscanum Analecta
SBFLA	Studii Biblici Franciscani Liber Annus
SBLDS	Society of Biblical Literature. Dissertation Series
SBLSPS	Society of Biblical Literature. Seminar Papers Series
SC	Sources Chrétiennes
ScC	La Scuola Cattolica
ScEs	Science et Esprit
Script	Scriptorium
ScrTh	Scripta Theologica
Sef	Sefarad
Sem	Semitica
Semeia	Semeia
SHR	Studies in the History of Religions. Supplements to Numen
SicGymn	Siculorum Gymnasium
Sil	Sileno. Rivista di studi classici e cristiani
Sist	Sistematica
SJLA	Studies in Judaism in Late Antiquity
SMSR	Studi e Materiali di Storia delle Religioni
SNTSMS	Society for New Testament Studies, Monograph Series
SNVAO.HF	Skrifter utgitt av Det Norske Videnskaps-Akademi i Oslo. hist.-filos. Klasse
SO	Symbolae Osloenses
SO.S	Symbolae Osloenses Fasciculi Suppletorii
Sophia	Sophia
SPAW	Sitzungsberichte der preussischen Akademie der Wissenschaften. Philosophisch-historische Klasse
SPB	Studia Post-Biblica
Spec	Speculum
Spud	Spudasmata. Studien zur Klassischen Philologie und ihren Grenzgebieten
SR	Studies in Religion
SSR	Studi Storico-Religiosi
STA	Studia et testimonia antiqua
StAns	Studia Anselmiana
StANT	Studien zum Alten und Neuen Testament
StEAug	Studia Ephemeridis Augustinianum
StGen	Studium Generale
StNT	Studien zum Neuen Testament und seiner Umwelt
StPh	Studia Philonica
StTeol	Studii Teologice
StTh	Studia Theologica
StudCl	Studii Clasice
StudFilGal	Studi Filosofici. Centro Studi Filosofici di Gallarate
StudH	Studia Hellenistica
Studium	Studium
StudMon	Studia Monastica
StudPat	Studia Patavina

StudPatr	Studia Patristica
StUNT	Studien zur Umwelt des Neuen Testaments
SudhAr	Sudhoffs Archiv: Vierteljahrsschrift für Geschichte der Medizin und der Naturwissenschaften der Pharmazie und der Mathematik
Sura	Sura
TAPhA	Transactions and Proceedings of the American Philological Association
TF	Tijdschrift voor Filosofie
ThBl	Theologische Blätter
ThD	Theology Digest
Theok	Theokratia. Jahrbuch des Institutum Judaicum Delitzchianum
Theoph	Theophaneia, Beiträge zur Religions- und Kirchengeschichte des Altertums
ThG	Die Theologie der Gegenwart
ThH	Théologie historique
ThLB	Theologisches Literaturblatt
ThLZ	Theologische Literaturzeitung
Thom	The Thomist
ThPh	Theologie und Philosophie
ThQ	Theologische Quartalschrift
ThR	Theologische Rundschau
ThRv	Theologische Revue
ThS	Theological Studies
ThZ	Theologische Zeitschrift
TPh	Tijdschrift voor Philosophie
TSAJ	Texte und Studien zum antiken Judentum
TU	Texte und Untersuchungen zur Geschichte der altchristlichen Literatur
TWNT	Theologisches Wörterbuch zum Neuen Testament
TyV	Teologia y vida
UaLG	Untersuchungen zur antiken Literatur und Geschichte
UNDCSJCA	University of Notre Dame Center for the Study of Judaism and Christianity in Antiquity
USQR	Union Seminary Quarterly Review
VC	Verbum Caro
VChr	Vigilae Christianae
VChr.S	Supplements to Vigiliae Christianae
VD	Verbum Domini
VetChr	Vetera Christianorum
Vich	Vichiana
Viv	Vivarium
VoxTh	Vox Theologica
VT	Vetus Testamentum
VT.S	Supplements to Vetus Testamentum
WMANT	Wissenschaftlichen Monographien zum Alten und Neuen Testament
WS	Wiener Studien
WThJ	The Westminster Theological Journal
WUNT	Wissenschaftliche Untersuchungen zum Neuen Testament
WZ(H)	Wissenschaftliche Zeitschrift der Martin-Luther-Universität. Halle-Wittenberg
WZKM	Wiener Zeitschrift für die Kunde des Morgenlandes
YClS	Yale Classical Studies
ZAW	Zeitschrift für die alttestamentliche Wissenschaft
Zet	Zetemeta. Monographien zur klassischen Altertumswissenschaft
ZKG	Zeitschrift für Kirchengeschichte

ZKTh	Zeitschrift für Katholische Theologie
ZNW	Zeitschrift für die neutestamentliche Wissenschaft und die Kunde der älteren Kirche
ZRGG	Zeitschrift für Religions- und Geistesgeschichte
ZThK	Zeitschrift für Theologie und Kirche

4. *Hebrew journals and series*

Bar-Ilan	(בר-אילן)	Bar-Ilan University, Ramat Gan.
Cathedra	(קתדרה)	Yad Izhak Ben-Zvi, Jerusalem.
Daat	(דעת)	Department of Philosophy. Bar-Ilan University, Ramat Gan.
Eshel Beer-Sheva	(אשל באר-שבע)	Ben-Gurion University, Beer-Sheva.
Eshkolot	(אשכולות)	Jerusalem.
Horeb	(חורב)	Yeshiva University, New York.
Kiryat Sefer	(קרית ספר)	Jewish National and University Library, Jerusalem.
Knesset	(כנסת)	Tel-Aviv.
Mahanayyim	(מחניים)	Chief Rabbinate, Israel Defense Forces.
Milet	(מלאת)	Everyman's University, Tel-Aviv.
Niv Hamidrashia	(ניב המדרשיה)	Jerusalem.
Shnaton	(שנתון)	Israel Bible Society, Jerusalem.
Sinai	(סיני)	Mossad HaRav Kook, Jerusalem.
Sura	(סורא)	Jerusalem.
Tarbiz	(תרביץ)	Institute of Jewish Studies. Hebrew University, Jerusalem.
Te'uda	(תעודה)	Chaim Rosenberg School of Jewish Studies. Tel Aviv University.
Zion	(ציון)	Historical Society of Israel, Jerusalem.

5. *Scholars responsible for summaries*

RAB	R. A. Bitter
NGC	N. G. Cohen
MM	M. Mach
RR	R. Radice
DTR	D. T. Runia
DS	D. Satran
DRS	D. R. Schwartz

PART ONE

BIBLIOGRAPHIES
EDITIONS FRAGMENTS
TRANSLATIONS ANTHOLOGIES
COMMENTARIES
INDICES LEXICA JOURNAL

A. BIBLIOGRAPHIES

1. Bibliographies without annotation

In this section we cite only bibliographies which are wholly devoted to Philo and his intellectual milieu or have a section specially devoted to him. The numerous bibliographies of no more than introductory value have therefore not been cited. On the use of existing bibliographies and other bibliographical tools in the compilation of our own bibliography, see the Introduction.

1001. H. L. GOODHART and E. R. GOODENOUGH, 'A general bibliography of Philo Judaeus', in E. R. GOODENOUGH, *The Politics of Philo Judaeus: practice and theory* (New Haven 1938, reprinted Hildesheim 1967²) 125-321.

This systematic bibliography, which contains 1603 entries and covers a period of time stretching from the beginnings of Philonic research to 1937, is by far the most extensive and complete one of its kind. The work is divided into 33 sections: some devoted to philological, paleographical, and historical subjects; others – from section XIII onwards – to various philosophical *topoi*; yet others – from section XXV onwards – to the relations between Philo and other thinkers and philosophical movements. Further information on this work has already been given in the Introduction. For reviews cf. **3805** below. (= R1)

1002. J. HAUSSLEITER, 'Nacharistotelische Philosophen: Bericht über das Schrifttum der Jahre 1931-1936', *JFKA* 281 (1943) 1-177, esp. 107-116.

Although containing few entries for Philo, this bibliography does give a brief description of the contents of many of the works cited. On occasion it also records the judgement of eminent reviewers. For the period 1931-1936 it forms a useful supplement to Goodhart and Goodenough's bibliography (**1001**), which is not annotated. (= R2)

1003. R. MARCUS, 'Selected bibliography (1920-1945) of the Jews in the Hellenistic-Roman Period', *PAAJR* 16 (1946-47) 97-181, esp. 175-178.

From the Philonic point of view the bibliography offers a limited selection from G-G (**1001**) and some additions for the years 1938-45. The bibliography is above all useful for its copious references to works on more general historical topics. (DTR)

1004. *Bibliographie zur antiken Bildersprache,* unter Leitung von V. PÖSCHL, bearbeitet von H. GÄRTNER und W. HEYKE, Heidelberger

Akademie der Wissenschaften. Bibliothek der Klassischen Altertums-wissenschaften N.F. 1. Reihe (Heidelberg 1964), esp. 289-294.

Cites primarily works of literary analysis dealing with 'figures, symbols, metaphors, allegories, and similar phenomena' in classical literature and language. As far as Philonic studies are concerned, the work is the only one of its kind and furnishes a number of entries not found elsewhere. (= R3)

1005. W. TOTOK, 'Philon von Alexandrien', in *Handbuch der Geschichte der Philosophie*, vol. 1 *Altertum* (Frankfurt 1964) 328-331.

Following his usual method, the author devotes a few lines to Philo's life and works and provides a respectable bibliography arranged according to subject-matter. (RR)

1006. S. SHUNAMI, *Bibliography of Jewish Bibliographies* (Jerusalem 1936, second enlarged edition 1965), esp. 723.

Contains our **1001-1003, 1108,** and some sporadic pre-1937 collections. (DTR)

1007. G. DELLING, *Bibliographie zur jüdisch-hellenistischen und intertestamentarischen Literatur 1900-1965*, in Verbindung mit G. ZACHHUBER und H. BERTHOLD, TU 106 (Berlin 1969), esp. 34-50.

Cf. **1012.** (= R4)

1008. U. RAPPAPORT, "Bibliography of Works on Jewish History in the Hellenistic and Roman Periods, 1946-1970", in B. ODED *et al.* (edd), מחקרים בתולדות עם-ישראל וארץ-ישראל [*Studies in the History of the Jewish People and the Land of Israel*] vol. 2 (Haifa 1972) 247-321.

A very restricted number of entries on Philo are given in this bibliography on account of the fact that 'most Philonic works are not historical'. This criterion also determines the subsequent contributions of the team of scholars from Haifa University (cf. **1014, 1018, 1020***). (DS)

1009. E. HILGERT, 'A bibliography of Philo studies 1963-1970', *StPh* 1 (1972) 57-71.

This bibliography, which extends to the five entries listed below and also includes works written in Hebrew, links up chronologically with those by G-G and Feldman (**1108**). The entries are alphabetically ordered, without any description of contents or critical judgements. Ample space, however, is devoted to the reviews of several fundamental studies. This work is above all indispensable for its knowledge of literature written in English and, in particular, American literature, in which respect it is more complete than any other bibliography for the corresponding period. See further **1011, 1013, 1015-1017,** and also **1019.** (= R5)

1010. S. P. BROCK, C. T. FRITSCH, S. A. JELLICOE, *Classified bibliography of the Septuagint*, ALGHJ 6 (Leiden 1973), esp. 57-58.

Brief bibliography of works on Philo relevant to the study of the Septuagint, with useful cross-references to other specific areas of study (e.g. proper names, biblical text etc.). (DTR)

1011. E. HILGERT, 'A Bibliography of Philo Studies in 1971, with additions for 1965-1970', *StPh* 2 (1973) 51-54. (=R6)

1012. G. DELLING, *Bibliographie zur jüdisch-hellenistischen und intertestamentarischen Literatur 1900-1970*, in Verbindung mit M. MASER, TU 106² (Berlin 1975), esp. 56-80.

In this second edition, which is distinguished by the range and precision of its citations, Delling has expanded the first by some 700 titles, including some 130 for Philo. The bibliography of Philo, neither annotated nor systematic, is divided into four large sections. It lists in alphabetical order 483 works, as well as about 100 sometimes very brief references (compared with some 60 in the first edition) to texts not specifically concerned with Philo. On the whole it is a very useful compilation, one of the most detailed, solid, and accurate to appear on the subject. (= R7)

1013. E. HILGERT, 'A Bibliography of Philo Studies 1972-1973', *StPh* 3 (1974-75) 117-125. (= R8)

1014. U. RAPPAPORT (with M. MOR), *Bibliography of works on Jewish history in the Hellenistic and Roman periods, 1971-1975* (Jerusalem 1976).

See above **1008**.

1015. E. HILGERT, 'A Bibliography of Philo Studies 1974-1975', *StPh* 4 (1976-77) 79-85. (= R9)

1016. E. HILGERT, 'A Bibliography of Philo Studies 1976-1977', *StPh* 5 (1978) 113-120. (= R10)

1017. E. HILGERT, 'A Bibliography of Philo Studies 1977-1978', *StPh* 6 (1979-80) 197-200. (= R11)

1018. M. MOR and U. RAPPAPORT, *Bibliography of works on Jewish history in the Hellenistic and Roman periods 1976-1980* (Jerusalem 1982).

See above **1008**.

1019. E. HILGERT, 'Bibliographia Philoniana 1935-1981' in W. HAASE (ed.), *Hellenistisches Judentum in römischer Zeit: Philon und Josephus, ANRW* II 21.1 (Berlin-New York 1984) 47-97.

A systematic but unannotated bibliography, valuable above all for its completeness and precision (it includes titles in Slavic and Scandinavian languages, as well as numerous titles in Hebrew). This vast amount of material is organized in 21 sections covering all areas of Philonic research. This work, despite its different approach, has been of great assistance in the preparation of our own bibliography. (RR)

1020*. D. DIMANT, M. MOR and U. RAPPAPORT, *Bibliography of works on Jewish history in the Hellenistic and Roman periods 1981-1985* (Jerusalem 1987).

See above **1008**.

2. *Critical bibliographies and surveys of research*

1101. W. VÖLKER, 'Neue Wege der Philoforschung?', *ThBl* 16 (1937) 297-301.

The article is primarily a review of E. R. GOODENOUGH's book *By light, light* (New Haven 1935). We cite it in this section because Völker closely links the work to the 'Religionsgeschichtliche' school of criticism generally, so that in the end his attention focusses, not only on Goodenough's work, but on the whole exegetical trend which influenced it. (= R12)

1102. H. J. SCHOEPS, 'Rund um Philo', *MGWJ* 82 (1938) 269-280.

This brief contribution analyzes the thought of four theologians (M. Peisker, W. Knuth, G. Kuhlmann, E. Peterson) on theological and moral themes in Philo's work, comparing their positions to that of Heinemann. At the conclusion of the article there is a note by Heinemann which deals in particular with the works by H. WILLMS, Εἰκών: *eine begriffsgeschichtliche Untersuchung zum Platonismus* (Münster 1935) and E. R. GOODENOUGH (**3805**). The survey makes some useful points. (= R13)

1103. W. VÖLKER, *Fortschritt und Vollendung bei Philo von Alexandrien; eine Studie zur Geschichte der Frömmigkeit*, TU 49.1 (Leipzig 1938) 1-47.

The idea which underlies this enquiry and is set out in its initial pages is that, essentially, Philo's philosophical thought lacks a dominant centre and that fragmentation and vacillation are in fact inherent in his mode of thought as well as in the style of his writings. Having thus provided the criteria of his inquiry, the author advises that his concern will be with 'the major points of view' and that he will attempt to avoid 'dispersion on minor points'. Tracking the evolution of Philonic studies, Völker lays emphasis on the following: (a) the efforts to order the Philonic corpus and works of textual criticism; (b) specialist contributions on major themes in Philonic thought and on minor points; (c) monographs attempting an overall reconstruction of the figure of Philo. The author thus takes his point of departure in the work of E. H. Stahl (1793) and goes as far as the major monographs of the thirties. Völker's extensive knowledge and sense of balance make this contribution a highly useful tool. (= R14)

1104. J. LLAMAS, 'Filón de Alejandria', *Sef* 2 (1942) 437-447.

A rather succinct presentation of several fundamental works on Philo written in the twenties and thirties. It is chiefly useful for introductory purposes. (= R15)

1105. G. A. VAN DEN BERGH VAN EYSINGA, 'Was Philo philosoof?', in *idem, Godsdienst-wetenschappelijke studiën*, vol. 8 (Haarlem 1950) 36-53.

The title of the article takes its cue from the publication of Wolfson's study (**4714**), but it is not a review of that work in the narrow sense. Rather it embarks on a broad discussion of Philo in the light of a hundred years of scholarship, including some interesting references to Dutch interpreters. The author strongly attacks the views of Völker and Wolfson, who emphasize the Jewishness of Philo at the cost of giving due credit to the influence of Hellenism, and especially the mystery religions, on his thought. Philo might be considered a philosopher on account of his deep knowledge of Greek philosophy and his influence on later thinkers. But he is a 'believing philosopher' or a 'philosophizing believer', drenched in the idea of the mysteries, a mystic and not an orthodox Jew. In fact the 19th century scholars A. F. Dähne and A. Gfrörer were right in seeing him as a typical representative of Alexandrian theosophy. (DTR)

1106. H. THYEN, 'Die Probleme der neueren Philo-Forschung', *ThR* 23 (1955) 230-246.

The central theme of Philonic studies in the first decades of the century is summarized by Thyen in the following questions: who is Philo really? How should his work be considered? The answers showing the most divergence are those of Wolfson and Wendland; between these extremes are found the positions of Völker, Goodenough, Bréhier, Heinemann, and others. Though brief, this work makes many useful points and shows a sound general orientation. (= R16)

1107. R. ARNALDEZ, 'Introduction générale', in *De opificio mundi* (**2202**) 17-112.

This introduction aims to be 'a map showing only the points necessary for the guidance of readers venturing into Philo's work' (112). In it Arnaldez analyzes the answers which scholars, over a length of time (from the end of the 18th to the middle of the 20th century), have given to two fundamental questions: (a) is there a relation between Philo's treatises on the exegesis of the Mosaic laws and the political and social life of the Jews in Alexandria? (b) is there a relation between Philo's moral, religious, and philosophical ideas and Alexandrian Judaism? In the final section, entitled 'New points of view in the approach to Philo's thought', the author takes stock of the most recent trends in Philonic studies. It is a solid and very useful work, even if it does not enter into the specific themes of Philonism and to some degree fails to take German literature on the subject sufficiently into account. (= R17)

1108. L. H. FELDMAN, *Scholarship on Philo and Josephus (1937-1962)*, Studies in Judaica (New York n. d., = 1963) 1-26.

A systematic and annotated bibliography in which the texts cited are grouped according to type and subject under numerous headings and then given a brief description and critical evaluation. The work also pays ample attention to scholarly literature written in

Hebrew. It is divided into twenty-two sections and as many subsections, ranging from philological, paleographical, historical, and stylistic problems (which mainly occupy the first part of the work) to philosophical issues (to which six sections and numerous subsections are dedicated). The concluding part of the bibliography is concerned with the relations between Philo and other thinkers or movements. Feldman's monograph is valuable for the copiousness of its material, but even more for its structure, which allows a summary of scholarship on each of the subjects dealt with and at the same time makes clear which gaps have yet to be filled in the field of Philonic studies. We note that the *Addenda and Corrigenda* found at the end of the work have been amplified in two successive publications: a first supplementary list is reproduced in the review by Orbe cited below, a second is found in *StPh* 1 (1972) 56. REVIEWS: P. Boyancé, *Lat* 23 (1964) 632; G. Fohrer, *ZAW* 76 (1964) 229; A. Guillaumont, *RHR* 166 (1964) 240; H. Musurillo, *ClF* 18 (1964) 68; V. Nikiprowetzky, *REJ* 223 (1964) 526ff.; P. Nober, *Bib* 45 (1964) 461f.; F. Petit, *RThAM* 31 (1964) 144f.; J. Pouilloux, *REA* 66 (1964) 205ff.; N. Scivoletto, *GIF* 17 (1964) 77f.; A. Solignac, *ArPh* 27 (1964) 314f.; J. Carmignac, *RQ* 5 (1965) 288f.; R. Henry, *RBPh* 43 (1965) 248f.; A. Orbe, *Gr* 46 (1965) 864f.; J. Préaux, *AC* 34 (1965) 595f.; C. Schedl, *FZPhTh* 12 (1965) 365; E. M. Smallwood, *CR* 99 (1965) 227f.; A. Benoît, *RB* 63 (1966) 294f.; H. Bolkestein, *Mnem* 19 (1966) 423; M. Stern, *JHS* 86 (1966) 201f.; J. Kirchmeyer, *RAM* 44 (1968) 247f.; J. H. Waszink, *VChr* 22 (1968) 78f.; A. V. Nazzaro, *Vich* n.s. 1 (1972) 76f. (= R18)

1109. A. V. NAZZARO, 'Recenti studi filoniani (1963-1970)', *Vich* n.s. 1 (1972) 76-125, n.s. 2 (1973) 114-155.

This work is chronologically linked to that of Feldman and also adopts its method, which it improves and amplifies by using more notes and offering more citations of reviews. Divided into eleven sections and twenty-three subsections, the work concentrates on texts with a philosophical content, treating the problem of Philo's relations with other thinkers and trends in a less thorough fashion. In this bibliography – to an even greater degree than we find in Feldman – each section is an autonomous and complete whole and amounts to a concise review of scholarship. Therein lies the work's major value. The two articles into which this contribution is divided were subsequently gathered in a single monograph (Naples 1973). REVIEW: E. Hilgert, *StPh* 4 (1976-77) 110f. (= R19)

1110. G. D. FARANDOS, 'Geschichte der Philon-Forschung', in *Kosmos und Logos nach Philon von Alexandria*, Elementa: Schriften zur Philosophie und ihrer Problemgeschichte 4 (Amsterdam 1976) 7-149.

The value of this bibliography, apart from the large number of references it gives, consists in the clarity and logical organization of its structure and its systematic treatment, often with the aid of diagrams. A large section (18-75) is devoted to explaining the interpretation of Philo put forward by the early 19th century German theologian F. A. Staudenmaier. It is argued that his contribution, though scientifically superseded, is still highly significant from both a historical and a systematic point of view. Farandos accordingly proceeds to employ Staudenmaier's theories as a means of clarifying the transition from the 'ideological' method of interpretation to the 'scientific' interpretation of the 20th century. The limitation of this panorama, highly useful though it is, lies in the excessive concentration on (a) contributions in the German language and (b) on the philosophical side of Philo's thought. See further **7611**. (= R20)

1111. E. HILGERT, 'Central Issues in Contemporary Philo Studies', *BR*

23 (1978) 15-25.

The author puts the accumulated experience which he gained in the course of preparing his numerous bibliographical contributions to the service of the reader by indicating – in addition to the many works in the course of being published or even written – the *desiderata* in Philonic research which still need to be filled. Among these Hilgert laments the absence of a new critical edition which will revise and improve upon C-W, of a commentary on all Philo's works, of a more extensive and complete lexicon than that of Mayer, and of a critical edition of the Armenian version of *Prov.* (= R21)

1112. R. RADICE, 'Bibliografia generale su Filone di Alessandria negli ultimi quarantacinque anni', *Elenchos* 3 (1982) 110-152.

Contains an extract from **1113**.

1113. R. RADICE, *Filone di Alessandria: bibliografia generale 1937-1982*, Elenchos 8 (Naples 1983).

The predecessor of this bibliography; see the Introduction. REVIEWS: B. Amata, *Salesianum* 46 (1984) 543; B. Belletti, *RFN* 76 (1984) 648ff., *Sap* 38 (1985) 89ff. (see **8505**); Colette, *RMM* 90 (1985) 278f.; M. G. Crepaldi, *BSFA* 125 (1985) 61f.; G. Delling, *DLZ* 106 (1985) 618f.; C. Matagne, *EtCl* 53 (1985) 283; P. Nautin *REG* 98 (1985) 207; D. T. Runia, *VChr* 39 (1985) 188ff.; E. Starobinski-Safran, *RThPh* 117 (1985) 246; M. Hadas Lebel, *REJ* 145 (1986) 189f.; P. W. van der Horst, *Mnem* 39 (1986) 496; J. M. Pallarées, *Espiritu* 94 (1986) 177.

1114. P. BORGEN, 'Philo of Alexandria: a critical and synthetical survey of research since World War II', in *ANRW* II 21.1 (cf. **1019**) (Berlin-New York 1984) 98-154.

This full and well-documented *status quaestionis* of Philonic research – the best and most up-to-date account at present available – is divided into the following chapters (which are each in turn divided into various subsections): (a) Philo's situation (from social, political, cultural, and pedagogical points of view); (b) Philo as interpreter of the Pentateuch (Philo's works, Philo's Bible, allegory); (c) 'conqueror or conquered' (Philo's cultural background and his place in the development of philosophy and religion). The more important contributions to Philonic scholarship are critically analyzed in a presentation that emphasizes the need to recognize Philo's fundamental loyalty to Judaism, while also not wishing to neglect the Hellenic side of his achievement. (RR)

1115. L. H. FELDMAN, *Josephus and modern scholarship (1937-80)* (Berlin-New York 1984), esp. 410-418, 936-937.

According to the author of this extraordinarily exhaustive bibliography the subject of the relation between Philo and Josephus remains largely unexplored, although he manages to cite 53 relevant items. Short critical evaluations of these contributions are given. Among major modern scholars I. Heinemann is the only one to deny dependence of Josephus on Philo (see **4008, 5006**; actually Feldman has overlooked the fact that H. Lewy held the same view, cf. **6011**). See also the index of references to Philo at 1007-8. (DTR)

1116. B. L. MACK, 'Philo of Alexandria', in R. A. KRAFT and G. W. E. NICKELSBURG (edd.), *Early Judaism and its modern interpreters* (Philadelphia-Atlanta 1986) 387-410.

A lucid and objective account of trends in Philonic scholarship up to about 1980, accompanied by a selective bibliography. 'The clear tendency in the period under discussion has been the increasing awareness that Philo must be read primarily as an interpreter of scripture. To understand the intention of his language and the composition of his commentaries one must discover the principles that govern his hermeneutic' (393). (DTR)

1117. D. T. RUNIA, 'Recent developments in Philonic studies', in *idem, Philo of Alexandria and the* Timaeus *of Plato,* PhilAnt 44 (Leiden 1986) 7-31.

Although this chapter forms an integral part of the monograph in which it is located, we cite it here because it also furnishes a useful evaluation of recent developments in Philonic scholarship. It examines a 'quintet of recent studies', namely M. Harl (**2219**), scholars associated with the Philo Institute in Chicago – R. Hamerton-Kelly (**7220**), B. L. Mack (**7525**), D. M. Hay (**8020**) –, V. Nikiprowetzky (**7731**), J. Dillon (**7714**), D. Winston (**8133**). Four trends in Philonic research are discerned: (1) a growing awareness of the importance of methodology; (2) the attempt to see Philo against the background of his time; (3) the recognition of the central role of exegesis; (4) agreement on the profound influence of Platonism. The chapter ends with a review of the literature on the monograph's specific subject, the use that Philo makes of Plato's cosmological dialogue, the *Timaeus* (cf. **8656**). (DTR)

B. CRITICAL EDITIONS

1. *Greek texts*

a. Series

1501–1508. *Philonis Alexandrini opera quae supersunt,* vol. I-VII; vol. I-VI ediderunt L. COHN, P. WENDLAND, S. REITER; vol. VII, pars I-II, *Indices ad Philonis Alexandrini opera,* composuit I. LEISEGANG (Berolini 1896-1930, 1962²).

This edition marks a fundamental point of reference in the evolution of Philonic studies, even though later partial editions have brought many and often significant improvements. As Völker observes (**1103**, 14), this work must be considered the crowning achievement of a long series of publications, which, with great acumen and diligence, have corrected the Philonic text to the point of rendering the previous edition by Mangey wholly superseded. It should be noted that the edition also exists in an *Editio Minor* in six vols., without *Prologomena,* critical apparatus, and indices; it reproduces the text of the *Editio Maior,* correcting typographical errors only. This is the edition that was used by Mayer (**3207**) as the basis for his *Index Philoneus*: Vol. VI of the minor edition contains the *Apologia pro Iudaeis*, which is absent in C-W. In the edition by Cohn-Wendland (and also in the English and French translation series), the reader will thus not find a edition of this text with a critical apparatus. He may, however, turn to one of the editions of Eusebius, since those sections of the *Apologia* which have come down to us are taken from the *Praeparatio Evangelica*. We list Cohn and Wendland's edition on account of its seminal importance, even though it falls outside the strict chronological limits of our bibliography. For reviews, the reader is referred to the bibliography by Goodhart-Goodenough (**1001**), 194ff. (= R24)

1501. Volume I, 1896, edited by L. COHN.

Contains: *Prolegomena, Testimonia de Philone eiusque scriptis, Opif., Leg.* I-III, *Cher., Sacr., Det.* In the *Prologomena* Cohn, after a few words on Philo's life, analyzes the Philonic codices. This is followed by a description of previous editions and a brief introduction, largely paleographical, to each of the treatises edited in the volume. The same procedure recurs in all the volumes of the edition.

1502. Volume II, 1897, edited by P. WENDLAND.

Contains: *Prolegomena, Poster., Gig., Deus, Agr., Plant., Ebr., Sobr., Conf., Migr.*

1503. Volume III, 1898, edited by P. WENDLAND.

Contains: *Prolegomena, Her., Congr., Fug., Mut., Somn.* I-II.

1504. Volume IV, 1902, edited by L. COHN.

Contains: *Prolegomena, Abr., Ios., Mos. I-II, Decal.*

1505. Volume V, 1906, edited by L. COHN.

Contains: *Prolegomena, Spec.* I-IV, *Virt., Praem.*

1506. Volume VI, 1915, edited by L. COHN and S. REITER.

Contains: *Prolegomena* by L. COHN (to *Prob., Contempl., Aet.*), *Prolegomena* by S. REITER (to *Flacc., Legat.*), *Prob., Contempl., Aet., Flacc., Legat.* On pp. xviii-xxix there is a critical edition of the ancient Latin translation of *Contempl.*, with a detailed explanation of the manuscript tradition.

1507. Volume VII part I, 1926, *Indices*, compiled by I. LEISEGANG.

Contains: *Index nominum, index locorum Veteris Testamenti (quos Philo in libris suis graeca lingua scriptis aut adfert aut interpretatur), index verborum.* See below **3201**.

1508. Volume VII part II, 1930, *Indices*, compiled by I. LEISEGANG.

Contains the second part of the *Index verborum.*

We note that the original text of Philo's works is also found opposite the translation in the volumes of the English (**2101-2110**) and French (**2201-2231**) translation series. These are not new critical editions, however, for the text is based on the Cohn-Wendland edition, with a few rectifications and improvements added.

b. editions of single works

1551. *Philon d'Alexandrie: La migration d'Abraham*. Introduction, texte critique, traduction et notes par R. CADIOU, SC 47 (Paris 1957).

The reasons which led the author to undertake this edition and translation are set out on 19-21. Cadiou holds that the edition of this work by Cohn-Wendland is not quite as rigorous as their other editions and that the translations by Colson-Whitaker and by Cohn-Heinemann might be improved by employing to some degree 'the vocabulary of moral psychology developed in more recent years'. The Introduction is fairly brief and confines itself to a few remarks on philological and thematic aspects. A work of high quality. REVIEWS: P. Courcelle, *REA* 59 (1957) 424f.; M. T., *VetChr* 11 (1957) 275; F. Petit, *RThAM* 24 (1957) 377f.; E. des Places, *REG* 71 (1958) 483f.; D. Diaz, *RET* 18 (1958) 359; R. M. Grant, *VChr* 12 (1958) 107; C. Martin, *NRTh* 80 (1958) 195; J. Moreau, *AC* 27 (1958) 178; M. Philonenko, *ThZ* 14 (1958) 454; J. Sauter, *RThPh* 8 (1958) 230ff.; J. Sirinelli, *RPh* 32 (1958) 335; J. P. Smith, *Bib* 39 (1958) 250f.; H. Chirat, *RSR* 33 (1959) 83; L. Hermann, *RBPh* 37 (1959) 1137f.; A. Benoît, *RHPhR* 40 (1960) 385. (= R26)

2. *Latin texts*

1601. F. PETIT, *L'ancienne version latine des Questions sur la Genèse de Philon d'Alexandrie*, volume I édition critique, volume II Commentaire, TU 113-114 (Berlin 1973).

Besides a number of Greek fragments, two versions of *QG* have come down to us, one in Armenian and the other, produced in the fourth century and limited to book IV 154-245, in Latin. This work offers a critical edition of the Latin translation, together with a long introduction. The Introduction analyzes the text from a historical and philological point of view and compares it with the other versions (especially with the Greek fragments). The second volume contains a highly detailed commentary on the text, paying not only attention to the philological matters arising out of the highly idiosyncratic Latin translation, but also dealing with many thematic aspects and noting numerous parallels in Philonic works preserved in the original Greek. See also **1819**. REVIEWS: B. Botte, *BThAM* 11 (1973) 470; M. Bogaert, *RBen* 84 (1974) 241; J. C. M. van Winden, *VChr* 29 (1975) 314f.; C. Martin, *NRTh* 98 (1976) 548. (= R27)

3. *Armenian texts*

1701. *Philonis Judaei sermones tres hactenus inediti, I. et II. De Providentia et III. De animalibus, ex Armena versione antiquissima ab ipso* *originali textu Graeco ad verbum stricte exequuta, nunc in Latium (sic!) fideliter translati per* J. B. AUCHER (Venice 1822).

1702. *Philonis Judaei paralipomena Armena, libri videlicet quatuor in Genesin, libri duo in Exodum, sermo unus de Sampsone, alter de Jona, tertius de tribus angelis Abraamo apparentibus: opera hactenus inedita ex Armena versione antiquissima ab ipso originali textu Graeco ad verbum stricte exequuta saeculo V, nunc in Latium fideliter translata per* J. B. AUCHER (Venice 1826); reprinted Hildesheim 1988.

Aucher's edition of the Armenian translations of Philo produced in the sixth century is included in our bibliography, though falling far outside its chronological limits, because it is still the text that scholars have to use, even if it falls far short of modern critical standards. In fact these texts have received little critical scrutiny during the past fifty years; almost all scholars – including those translators referring directly to the Armenian text, cf. **2111-2112, 2233-2234** – have continued to rely on Aucher. The exceptions are the edition by Terian below, and the translation by F. SIEGERT (**2051**).

1703. A. TERIAN, *Philonis Alexandrini de Animalibus: the Armenian text with an introduction, translation and commentary* (diss. Basel 1979).

See the following entry.

1704. A. TERIAN, *Philonis Alexandrini de Animalibus: the Armenian text with an introduction, translation and commentary*, Studies in Hellenistic Judaism: Supplements to Studia Philonica 1 (Chico, California 1981).

This work is to be recommended, not only because it contains the first translation of this treatise in a modern language, but also because it subjects the treatise to a comprehensive examination. The translation is preceded by an extensive introduction dealing with the work's contents and its manuscript tradition (14-25). Taken together with the footnotes to the translation (67-108), these observations form a detailed critical apparatus of the text which improves considerably on Aucher's edition. The second part of the introduction (25-63) deals with questions of authorship, date, dialogic situation, philosophical and exegetical thematics. These themes are pursued in contextual detail in the erudite and accurate commentary (111-207), which in turn is followed by a series of appendices. The first reproduces Aucher's *editio princeps* (indispensable, since the Armenian text is available nowhere else). The second gives an overview of the fragments which have come down to us in the original Greek, with the corresponding Armenian version (263; cf. **1817**). The third relates passages from the *De animalibus* to analogous passages in Plato's *Phaedrus* (265-271). The detailed bibliography is followed by a number of useful indices. REVIEWS: S. P. Brock, *BoL* 1983 124; J. J. S. Weitenberg, *AIHS* 33 (1983) 380f.; R. Thomson, *JSAS* 1 (1984) 185ff.; C. Cox, *JBL* 103 (1984) 463ff.; R. Joly, *AC* 53 (1984) 368; M. Philonenko, *RHPhR* 64 (1984) 73; M. Hadas Lebel, *REJ* 144 (1985) 260f. (= R1094)

4. *Greek fragments*

1800. Up to now a complete critical edition of Philonic fragments has not been produced. Study in this field is still in an exploratory phase and is made particularly complex by the variety of sources in which possible new fragments must be sought and located. F. PETIT is the most productive scholar on this subject at the present time, having made a number of important contributions (**1601, 1810, 1813, 1814, 1819, 1821**). She distinguishes three main types of sources: (a) the Greek *exegetical catenae*, (b) the *Epitome* by Procopius of Gaza, (c) the *Sacra Parallela* ascribed to Johannes Damascus and other *florilegia* derived from it. Another scholar doing important research in this area is J. R. ROYSE (cf. **1816, 1822**). He has announced that he is preparing a new edition of the Greek fragments of Philo, making use of an unpublished collection of fragments prepared by L. FRÜCHTEL from earlier published material, but also utilizing directly the currently available manuscript material (cf. **1801, 1802, 1822**); further details are furnished at *StPh* 5 (1978) 138-139.

The first modern work to collect and order the Philonic fragments was J. R. HARRIS, *Fragments of Philo Judaeus* (Cambridge 1886), which contains, in addition to the material present in previous editions, a large number of unedited fragments, mostly taken from the *catenae* and the *florilegia*. In subsequent years this collection was supplemented by the following studies: P. WENDLAND, *Neu entdeckte Fragmente Philos, nebst einer Untersuchung über die ursprüngliche Gestalt der Schrift 'De Sacrificiis Abelis et Caini'* (Berlin 1891; mainly fragments drawn from Procopius); K. PRAECHTER, 'Unbeachtete Philonfragmente', *AGP* N.F. 9 (1896) 415-426 (fragments from Chronicles by various Byzantine authors); K. STAEHLE, *Die Zahlenmystik bei Philon von Alexandreia* (Leipzig-Berlin 1931) esp. 19-75 (especially fragments from John Lydus dealing with arithmology); H. LEWY, 'Neue Philontexte in der Überarbeitung des Ambrosius: mit einem Anhang; neu gefundene griechische Philonfragmente', *SPAW* 4 (1932) 23-84, to which we owe not only the discovery of some thirty fragments (from *QG, QE, Legat., Somn.*), but also thirteen fragments of uncertain provenance and a classification of the sources of Philonic fragments (72-74). For the fragments taken from the *exegetical catenae,* we refer in particular to the article 'Chaînes exégétiques grecques' in *DB*, Suppl. 1 (Paris 1928) 1084-1233, prepared by R. DEVREESSE, which gives an overview of the Greek *catenae* and lists the authors cited there, among whom the name of Philo is frequently mentioned (cf. 1105, 1119, 1184, 1214, 1225). A similar task has been carried out for the Greek *florilegia* by M. RICHARD in the article 'Florilèges grecs', *DS* 5 (1964) 475-512. During the period covered by our bibliography the following contributions to the study of Philo's Greek fragments have been published:

1801. L. FRÜCHTEL, 'Griechische Fragmente zu Philons Quaestiones in Genesin et in Exodum', *ZAW* N.F. 14 (1937) 108-115.

A number of fragments not classified by Harris are here identified by means of comparison with Aucher's Latin translation. (= R28)

1802. L. FRÜCHTEL, 'Zum Oxyrhynchos-Papyrus des Philon (Ox.-Pap. XI 1356)', *PhW* 58 (1938) 1437-1439.

Früchtel recognizes in this papyrus the beginning of fr. 27 of Lewy's edition (see above) and, on this basis, makes some interesting corrections of the text. We note here that both Goodenough-Goodhart (**1001**) and Früchtel in this article ignore the contribution of this fragment by K. F. W. SCHMIDT in his review of B. P. Grenfell and A. S. Hunt, *The Oxyrhynchi papyri*, vol. 11 (London 1915), in *GGA* 180 (1918) 81-83. On the fragment see also **1816** below. (= R29)

1803. J. MERELL, 'Nouveaux fragments du papyrus 4' *RB* 47 (1938) 5-22, esp. 5ff.

The article discusses P⁴ of the New Testament found inside the cover of the Philo papyrus of *Her.* and *Sacr.* extensively used by C-W in their edition. (RR)

1804. K. STAHLSCHMIDT, 'Eine unbekannte Schrift Philons von Alexandrien (oder eines ihm nahestehenden Verfassers)', *Aeg* 22 (1942) 161-176.

The seven fragments of the Berlin papyrus P.17027 are published here. The author, on the basis of philological arguments and subject-matter, assigns them to a treatise Περὶ θεοῦ written by Philo or by an author close to him, but not identical to the fragment entitled *De Deo* in the Armenian tradition. (= R30)

1805. K. ALAND, 'Eine neue Schrift Philos?', *ThLZ* 68 (1943) 169-170.

The author contests the conclusions drawn by Stahlschmidt (**1804**) with regard to P.17027 and demonstrates that the fragments in question belong to Hermetic literature rather than to Philo or one of his pupils. (= R31)

1806. L. ALFONSI, 'Sul ΠΕΡΙ ΘΕΟΥ del P.17027 di Berlino', *Aeg* 23 (1943) 262-269.

The author agrees with Stahlschmidt's theory (**1804**) and adduces arguments in favour of the hypothesis which assigns the fragments of P.17027 to Philo. We note that this controversy is also alluded to by M. HOMBERT in his 'Bulletin papyrologique XXI (1943 à 1946)', *REG* 61 (1948) 233. (= R32)

1807. R. MARCUS, *Philo in Ten Volumes*, Supplement II (London-Cambridge Mass. 1953, = **2112**): 'Appendix A', 179-263: 'Appendix B', 267-275.

Appendix A reproduces the Greek fragments of *QG* and *QE*, following Harris's edition, supplemented with the passages taken from Procopius and edited by Wendland (cf. above) and with those edited by Praechter (cf. above). On 234-237 we find the unidentified fragments of *QG*, again taken from Harris's edition, but without the fragments which FRÜCHTEL and E. BRÉHIER, *Les idées philosophiques et religieuses de Philon d'Alexandrie*, Études de philosophie médiévale 8 (Paris 1908, 1950³) vii n. 2, had previously identified. On 258-263 the unidentified fragments of *QE* – again drawn from Harris's edition – are published. Appendix B provides a text of the ancient Latin version of *QG* (and also 3 Greek fragments taken from Harris and Wendland), but it is clearly inferior to and also less complete than the edition by Petit (**1601**). The latter scholar (**1601**, I 18 n.1) deplores the frequent inaccuracy of the references and entries, as well as 'the absence of a classification of sources' for these appendices. (= R33)

1808. R. CADIOU, 'Sur un Florilège philonien', *REG* 70 (1957) 93-101; 'Notes complémentaires', *REG* 71 (1958) 55-60.

The author identifies and translates fragments of diverse Philonic writings taken from the Greek *florilegia*. (= R34)

1809. R. DEVREESSE, *Les anciens commentateurs grecs de l'Octateuque et des Rois (Fragments tirés des Chaînes)*, Studi e Testi 201 (Vatican City 1959) 1-21.

After some notes on the Philonic method, the author publishes some fragments of *QG* drawn from the exegetical chains, complementing those published by Marcus (**1807**). (= R35)

1810. F. PETIT, 'Les fragments grecs du livre VI des *Questions sur la Genèse* de Philon d'Alexandrie, édition critique', *Muséon* 84 (1971) 93-150.

This article merges, with considerable additions, into vol. 33 of OPA (**1814**). Compared with the latter study, however, it does offer a more accurate and detailed description of the manuscripts. (= R36)

1811. M. HADAS-LEBEL *De providentia I et II*, OPA 35 [cf. **2229**] (Paris 1973) 355-356.

Ten short fragments of *Prov.*, all from the second book, are reproduced. These are drawn from Theodoret of Cyrrhus, the *Sacra Parallela* attributed to Johannes Damascenus, and other Byzantine authors. (RR)

1812. J. VAN HAELST, *Catalogue des papyrus littéraires juifs et chrétiens*, Université de Paris-Sorbonne, Série Papyrologie 1 (Paris 1976), esp. 251f.

Nos. 695, 696 list papyri containing fragments of *Her.*, *Sacr.*, *Ebr.*, *Post.*, *Leg.*, *Det.*, as well as of other unidentified writings. No. 697 lists 'Stahlschmidt's fragment' (cf. above **1804**). (RR)

1813. F. PETIT, *Catenae graecae in Genesim et in Exodum*, vol. 1, *Catena sinaitica*, Corpus Christianorum. Series Graeca 2 (Turnhout-Louvain 1977) *passim*.

Analysis of the Sinaitic *Catenae in Genesim et in Exodum* leads to the identification of fifteen fragments of *QG* 3 and 4, a fragment from *Mos.* 1.44-47, as well as numerous others either falsely attributed to Philo or of Philonic inspiration. (= R1008/a)

1814. *Quaestiones in Genesim et in Exodum: fragmenta graeca*, Introduction, texte critique et notes par F. PETIT, OPA 33 (Paris 1978).

Collects and examines closely all the Greek fragments of *QG* and *QE* which, from Harris's edition onwards, have gradually been identified, adding new ones drawn from the *catenae*, and giving a better textual basis for many fragments found in the *florilegia*. On 214-228 and 279-306 the (as yet) unidentified fragments of *QG* and *QE* respectively are grouped together. On this occasion Petit, for reasons which are explained, modifies Marcus's numeration. Although part of the French translation series (cf. **2201-34**), only the unassigned fragments are translated. REVIEWS: J. Pouilloux, *CRAI* (1978) 792; E. des Places, *RPh* 53 (1979) 339f.; R. Joly *AC* 48 (1979) 677f.; J. C. M. van Winden, *VChr* 33 (1979) 294f.; N. Zeegers-van der Vorst, *RThAM* 46 (1979) 235f.; M. Bogaert, *RBen* 90 (1980) 152; P. Courcelle, *REA* 82 (1980) 82f.; H. Crouzel, *BLE* 81 (1980) 210f.; E. Junod, *RHPhR* 60 (1980) 256; L. Martin, *NRTh* 102 (1980) 608ff.; P. Nautin, *RHE* 75 (1980) 469; A. Orbe, *Gr* 61 (1980) 185; A. Paul, *RecSR* 68 (1980) 538ff.; E. Cattaneo, *OrChrP* 47 (1981) 274f.; S. Leanza, *ByZ* 74 (1981) 58ff.; A. Solignac, *ArPh* 44 (1981) 335f.; C. Steel, *Script* 35 (1981) 162f.; W. Wiefel, *ThLZ* 106 (1981) 28ff.; H. Chadwick, *JThS* 33 (1982) 536; G. Delling, *OLZ* 77 (1982) 48ff. (= R37)

1815. M. GEERARD, *Clavis Patrum Graecorum*, vol. 4 Concilia Catenae, Corpus Christianorum (Turnhout 1980) 185-259.

Gives detailed lists of the authors cited in the *catenae* of the various books of the Old and New Testament, including Philo. (DTR)

1816. J. R. ROYSE, 'The Oxyrhynchus Papyrus of Philo', *BASP* 17 (1980) 155-165.

A paleographical and philological analysis of the Oxyrhynchus codex containing texts of Philo. The author wishes to contribute to a reconstruction of its contents (the papyrus has come down to us in a mutilated condition) and identify 'the lost works which survive here in part'(155). Three scribes are identified, and the second of these appears to have copied out two works no longer extant in the Philonic corpus. Royse argues that one of these was the first book of Περὶ μέθης (the one in the corpus would thus be the second), the other the section περὶ εὐσεβείας missing from *Virt*. (= R1083)

1817. A. TERIAN, *Philonis Alexandrini de Animalibus* (cf. **1704**), 263.

Reprints from Harris's collection three fragments of *Anim*. (DTR)

1818. E. JUNOD, 'Les fragments grecs transmis et édités sous le nom de Philon, in *Biblia patristica: Supplément, Philon d'Alexandrie* (cf. **3209**) (Paris 1982) 9-14.

Very usefully lists all the fragments in the collections of Harris, Wendland and Lewy which fall outside the scope of Petit's collection (**1814**). A considerable number can be identified with sections of Philo's existing works; others remain unidentified. (DTR)

1819. F. PETIT, 'Le fragment 63 de la Bibliothèque de l'Université de Fribourg-en-Brisgau', *Codices manuscripti* 9 (1983) 164-172.

Identifies the fragment in question as coming from the otherwise lost manuscript previously located at the abbey of Fulda and at Lorsch and used by Jean Sichard in his editions of 1527 and 1538. The fragment preserves a few lines of the ancient Latin version of *QG* hitherto only known from Sichard's (not always accurate) transcription. (RR)

1820. *Philon d'Alexandrie: Questions sur la Genèse II 1-7*: texte grec, versions arménienne, parallèles latins, ed. J. PARAMELLE avec la collaboration de E. LUCCHESI; interpretation arithmologique par J. SEŠIANO, Cahiers d'Orientalisme 3 (Geneva 1984).

Strictly speaking this edition does not contain fragments of the *Quaestiones*. Like the extract *QE* 2.62-68 first edited by Cardinal Mai, the section of interrelated questions and answers *QG* 2.1-7 has come down to us via a direct manuscript tradition. It is located in the ms. *Vatopedinus* 659 discovered at Mount Athos by M. Richard. The Philonic material has been concealed by the scribe among the *Glaphyra* of Cyril of Alexandria, the various extracts amounting to about three-fifths of the original text, such as we find in the Armenian version. Of additional interest is the fact that the same passages have been heavily exploited by Ambrose (and to a lesser extent Augustine). Paramelle in this edition produces a modern *Tetrapla*, with columns of Greek, French translation, Armenian and Latin side by side. The text, providing chiefly an allegorical commentary on the ark of Noah is analyzed and commented on in exhaustive detail, with valuable remarks on aspects of Philo's arithmology. The lavishly produced book ends with an appendix containing other fragments from Philonic works still preserved in Greek located in *Vatopedinus* 659 and eight photographic plates illustrating the eccentric nature of the manuscript in question. REVIEWS: J. Irigoin, *CRAI* (1985) 420f.; A. de Malleux, *RHE* 80 (1985) 664f.; P. Nautin, *REG* 98 (1985) 207f.; M. Philonenko, *RHPhR* 65 (1985) 485ff.; P. H. Poirier *LThPh* 41 (1985) 452f.; M. J. Pierre, *RB* 93 (1986) 467f.; D. T. Runia *VChr* 40 (1986) 204f.; H. Chadwick *JThS* 38 (1987) 190f. (DTR)

1821. F. PETIT, 'En marge de l'édition des fragments de Philon (*Questions sur la Genèse et l'Exode*): les florilèges damascéniens', in E. A. LIVINGSTONE (ed.), *Papers presented to the Seventh International Conference on Patristic Studies held in Oxford 1975*, part 1, StudPatr 15 (= TU 128; Berlin 1984) 20-25.

Some philological and critical notes on the classification of the Damascene *florilegia*. Further contains important general remarks on the difference between the chains and the *florilegia*, as seen in relation to Philo's work. (RR)

1822. J. R. ROYSE, 'Further Greek Fragments of Philo's *Quaestiones*', in F. E. GREENSPAHN, E. HILGERT, B. L. MACK (edd.), *Nourished with peace: studies in Hellenistic Judaism in memory of Samuel Sandmel*, Scholars Press Homage Series 9 (Chico, California 1984) 143-153.

Underlines the problems inherent in the identification of the Greek fragments of the *Quaestiones*. In addition to these structural difficulties, problems are caused by the lack of coordination between scholars, who often discover and proceed to identify fragments already discovered and identified by other researchers. Royse produces many examples of this, taking as his starting-point Früchtel's article from 1937 (cf. **1801**). The article closes with the publication of nine fragments: two were identified in Früchtel's article but were left out of the collections of Marcus (**1807**) and Petit (**1814**); four were identified by Früchtel but left unpublished; the remaining three have been located by Royse himself (*QG* 1.98, *QE* 2.19, 2.115). (RR)

5. *Armenian fragment*

1901. A. TERIAN, 'A Philonic Fragment on the Decad', in *Nourished with peace* (cf. **1822**) 173-182.

Publishes, translates, and attempts to identify an arithmological fragment from the Armenian translation of Philo explaining the significance and value of the decad. An important parallel with the arithmological treatise of Anatolius allows observations to be made on the original Greek text on which the Armenian translation was based. After arguing that the fragment must be Philonic and cannot belong to the *Quaestiones*, Terian attributes it to the lost treatise *De numeris*. (RR)

C. TRANSLATIONS IN MODERN LANGUAGES

1. *Translations into German*

a. Comprehensive translation

2001-2007. *Philo von Alexandria, Die Werke in deutscher Über- setzung*, herausgegeben von L. COHN, I. HEINEMANN, M. ADLER und W. THEILER, vols. I-VI, (Breslau 1909-1938, Berlin 1962²); vol. VII 1964.

The German translation of Philo cannot be regarded as a single whole. The main bulk of the work is formed by volumes I-VI, published before the Second World War. Vol. VI was published in 1938, so falls just inside the period covered by our bibliography. These six volumes contain all of Philo's exegetical treatises surviving in Greek. Noteworthy is that the translation does not follow the order of C-W, but translates the Exposition of the Law (including *Opif.*) before the Allegorical Commentary. Each Philonic treatise is preceded by a brief Introduction containing a summary of contents. The translation is, for the most part, amply annotated and of a high standard, particularly in view of the period in which it was produced. It is, however, not without inaccuracies and obscurities, so that today we can, on the whole, say that it retains mainly a historical and retrospective value, having been superseded in clarity and precision by the Loeb English translation. Preparations were well under way for the seventh volume, but these were wiped out by the tragic events of 1933-45 (see the tantalizingly brief foreword to the second edition by W. THEILER). The translation was completed with the publication of volume VII in 1964, containing not only the historical-apologetic and philosophical works still extant in Greek, but also a complete translation of the *De Providentia* by L. FRÜCH-TEL. The notes to this volume are a little more extensive than in the earlier volumes. For the sake of completeness we also include in our list the reviews made of volumes published before the beginning of the period covered in our bibliography. (= R40)

2001. Vol. I, 1909, 1962², edited by L. COHN.

Contains: *Ueber die Weltschöpfung* (= *Opif.*) translated by J. COHN; *Ueber Abraham* (= *Abr.*) translated by J. COHN; *Ueber Joseph* (= *Ios.*) translated by L. COHN; *Ueber das Leben Mosis* (= *Mos.*) translated by B. BADT; *Ueber den Dekalog* (= *Decal.*) translated by L. TREITEL. The General Introduction is an overall presentation of the figure and work of Philo in which a certain emphasis is given to the classification of Philo's writings and to the relations between Philo, the Sapientia Salomonis, and the Septuagint. In conclusion a few words are devoted to Philo's influence, which is regarded as considerable in the doctrinal development of Christianity, but as almost non-existent in Rabbinic Judaism. REVIEWS: P. Heinisch, *ThRv* 8 (1909) 302f.; I. Heinemann, *MGWJ* 54 (1910) 504ff.; G. Heinrici, *ThLZ* 35 (1910) 195ff.; E. Nestle, *BPW* 30 (1910) 1277ff.; E. Weber, *ThLB* 31 (1910) 121ff.

2002. Vol. II, 1910, 1962², edited by L. COHN.

Contains: *Ueber die Einzelgesetze Buch* I-IV (= *Spec.* I-IV) translated by I. HEINEMANN; *Ueber die Tugenden* (= *Virt.*) translated by L. COHN; *Ueber Belohnungen und Strafen* (= *Praem.*) translated by L. COHN. REVIEWS: P. Heinisch, *ThRv* 10 (1911) 382; G. Heinrici, *ThLZ* 36 (1911) 713ff.; E. Nestle, *BPW* 21 (1911) 1333ff.; E. Weber, *ThLB* 32 (1911) 512f.

2003. Vol. III, 1919, 1962², edited by L. COHN.

Contains: *Allegorische Erklärung des heiligen Gesetzbuches*, Buch I-III (= *Leg.* I-III) translated by I. HEINEMANN; *Ueber die Cherubim* (= *Cher.*) translated by L. COHN; *Ueber die Opfer Abels und Kains* (= *Sacr.*) translated by H. LEISEGANG; *Ueber die Nachstellungen, die das Schlechtere dem Besseren bereitet* (= *Det.*) translated by H. LEISEGANG. REVIEWS: P. Heinisch, *ThRv* 19 (1920) 48f.; G. Helbig, *ThLZ* 45 (1920) 30; E. Weber, *ThLB* 41 (1920) 388f.; G. Grützmacher, *ThG* 15 (1921) 117ff.; O. Stählin, *PhW* 41 (1921) 721ff.

2004. Vol. IV, 1923, 1962², edited by I. HEINEMANN.

Contains: *Über die Nachkommen Kains* (= *Post.*) translated by H. LEISEGANG; *Über die Riesen* (= *Gig.*) translated by H. LEISEGANG; *Über die Unveränderlichkeit Gottes* (= *Deus*) translated by H. LEISEGANG; *Über die Landwirtschaft* (= *Agr.*) translated by I. HEINEMANN; *Über die Pflanzung Noahs* (= *Plant.*) translated by I. HEINEMANN. REVIEWS: G. Helbig, *ThLZ* 49 (1924) 54f.; O. Stählin, *PhW* 44 (1924) 1131ff.; E. Weber, *ThLB* 47 (1926) 278f.

2005. Vol. V, 1929, 1962², edited by I. HEINEMANN.

Contains: *Über die Trunkenheit* (= *Ebr.*) translated by M. ADLER; *Über die Nüchternheit* (= *Sobr.*) translated by M. ADLER; *Uber die Verwirrung der Sprachen* (=

Conf.) translated by E. STEIN; *Über Abrahams Wanderung* (= *Migr.*) translated by A. POSNER; *Über die Frage: Wer ist der Erbe der göttlichen Dinge? Und über die Teilung in Gleiches und Gegensätzliches* (= *Her.*) translated by J. COHN. REVIEWS: G. A. van den Bergh van Eysinga, *NieuwTT* 18 (1929) 274f.; I. Heinemann, *MGWJ* 78 (1929) 442; O. Stählin, *PhW* 49 (1929) 1318ff.; H. Leisegang, *ThLB* 51 (1930) 12; O. Michel, *ThLZ* 55 (1930) 225; H. Drexler, *Gn* 8 (1932) 155ff.

2006. Vol. VI, 1938, 1962², edited by M. ADLER and I. HEINEMANN.

Contains: *Über das Zusammenleben um der Allgemeinbildung willen* (= *Congr.*) edited by H. LEWY; *Über die Flucht und das Finden* (= *Fug.*) edited by M. ADLER; *Über die Namensänderung* (= *Mut.*) edited by W. THEILER; *Über die Träume* I-II (= *Somn.* I-II) edited by M. ADLER. In the Foreword Adler and Heinemann somewhat cryptically describe the contributors to this volume as 'editing' rather than 'translating' their respective works in this volume. Presumably after the death of COHN the editors, possessing the manuscripts of his translation, were concerned only to adapt them to the purposes of the edition, respecting the contents 'even when they would have interpreted or translated differently'. ADLER was responsible for revising the translations and completing the notes relating to the field of classical antiquity. HEINEMANN, who also checked the manuscripts, was the chief contributor of notes on Judaic subjects. REVIEWS: G. A. van den Bergh van Eysinga, *NieuwTT* 27 (1938) 266f.; E. Bikerman, *REJ* 4 n.s. (1938) 150; ; P. Heinisch, *ThR* 37 (1938) 223; K. Prümm, *ZKTh* 64 (1940) 52.

2007. Vol. VII, 1964, edited by W. THEILER.

Contains: *Über die Freiheit des Tüchtigen* (= *Prob.*) translated by K. BORMANN; *Über das betrachtende Leben* (= *Contempl.*) translated by K. BORMANN; *Über die Unvergänglichkeit der Welt* (= *Aet.*) translated by K. BORMANN; *Gegen Flaccus* (= *Flacc.*) translated by K. H. GERSCHMANN; *Gesandtschaft an Caligula* (= *Legat.*) translated by F. W. KOHNKE; *Über die Vorsehung* (= *Prov.*) translated by L. FRÜCHTEL; 'Sachweiser zu Philo', prepared by W. THEILER (on which see **3204**). To our surprise we have found no record of any reviews of this volume.

b. Translations of single works

2051. F. SIEGERT, *Drei hellenistisch-jüdische Predigten: Ps.-Philon, 'Über Jona', 'Über Simson' und 'Über die Gottesbezeichnung, wohltätig verzehrendes Feuer'. I. Übersetzungen aus dem Armenischen und sprachliche Erläuterungen*, WUNT 20 (Tübingen 1980).

This is an important work, because to our knowledge it offers for the first time a complete translation of the treatises *De Jona, De Sampsone, De Deo* which occur in the Armenian Philonic corpus in an up-to-date and well-edited version based on the Armenian text. The notes to the translation are mainly concerned with philological and linguistic matters. The only pages devoted to the genesis and content of the treatises are found in the Preface (1-8, esp. 6-8), where Siegert argues that all three treatises are pseudonymous works (the content of *De Deo* is too Stoic be be from Philo's hand, though it is no doubt the work of someone who has read Philo). The translation is a notable improvement on Aucher's earlier version (1826), which contains many obscurities and inaccuracies. In fact the author himself confesses that in many cases he was able to understand Aucher's text 'only after retranslating it from the Armenian' (1) and that he was forced to turn to the manuscripts on a number of occasions. In the case of *De Jona* he was able to make extensive use of the edition by H. LEWY, *The pseudo-Philonic De Jona*: Part I, Studies and Documents 7 (London 1936), of which the second volume, which was to contain an English translation and commentary, never appeared. The work concludes with an index of biblical references, an index of names, a glossary, and an index of Greek terms. REVIEW: J. Murphy-O'Connor, *RB* 89 (1982) 144. (= R1085)

2. *Translations into English*

a. Comprehensive translation

210t–2112. *Philo in ten volumes (and two supplementary volumes)*, with an English translation by F. H. COLSON, G. H. WHITAKER (and R. MARCUS), Loeb Classical Library (London-Cambridge Mass. 1929-1962).

This is not the first English translation of Philo. Previously there was the translation in four volumes by C. D. YONGE, 1854-55, republished in 1890 (cf. G-G **1001**, 203), and now wholly superseded. The translation by Colson-Whitaker is based on C-W with a few modifications. The notes to the translation are not very extensive, but are almost always of relevance. On the whole the translation is an appreciable improvement on Cohn-Heinemann. (It is worth recording here the division of labour. The following treatises were translated by Whitaker: *Opif.*, *Leg.*, *Det.*, *Post.*, *Agr.*, *Plant.*, *Migr.*, *Fug.*, *Somn.* I (the last four revised by Colson); the remainder were the work of Colson. As a rule the translations of Colson, of whom the editor of the Loeb Classical Library, W. H. D. Rouse, said 'a translator more careful and more competent I never worked with' (preface to vol. 10), are of considerably higher quality.) All the Philonic treatises translated in this work are preceded by a brief analytical introduction and nearly always have appendices supplementing the notes. According to the judgment of scholarly specialists, this translation marks a decisive turning-point in the interpretation of the Philonic text and is still invaluable, even if advance has been made at various points, for instance in some of the volumes of the French translation series. REVIEWS. For the sake of completeness we also include in our list the reviews made of volumes published before the beginning of the period covered in our bibliography. (= R41)

2101. Vol. I, 1929, 1971[5], edited and translated by F. H. COLSON and G. H. WHITAKER.

Contains: *General Introduction*; *On the account of the world's creation given by Moses* (= *Opif.*); *Allegorical interpretation of Genesis* II, III, Book I-III (= *Leg.* I-III). The General Introduction, written by COLSON, covers primarily the first five volumes, which contain the twenty-two treatises published in the first three volumes of C-W. REVIEWS: C. Knapp, *CW* 24 (1930) 3; O. Stählin, *PhW* 50 (1930) 225ff.; I. Heinemann, *MGWJ* 76 (1932) 263ff.; A. D. Nock, *CR* 46 (1932) 173.

2102. Vol. II, 1929, 1968[4], edited and translated by F. H. COLSON and G. H. WHITAKER.

Contains: *On the Cherubim, and the flaming sword, and Cain the first man created out of man* (= *Cher.*); *On the birth of Abel and the sacrifices offered by him and by his brother Cain* (= *Sacr.*); *That the worse is wont to attack the better* (= *Det.*); *On the posterity of Cain and his exile* (= *Post.*); *On the giants* (= *Gig.*). REVIEWS: O. Stählin, *PhW* 50 (1930) 225ff.; I. Heinemann, *MGWJ* 76 (1932) 263ff.; A. D. Nock, *CR* 46 (1932) 173.

2103. Vol. III, 1930, 1968⁴, edited and translated by F. H. COLSON and G. H. WHITAKER.

Contains: *On the unchangeableness of God* (= *Deus*); *On husbandry* (= *Agr.*); *Concerning Noah's work as a planter* (= *Plant.*); *On drunkenness* (= *Ebr.*) transl. F. H. COLSON; *On the prayers and curses uttered by Noah when he became sober* (= *Sobr.*). Following the death of Whitaker the footnotes were compiled exclusively by Colson. REVIEWS: C. Knapp, *CW* 24 (1930) 3; O. Stählin, *PhW* 51 (1931) 1473ff.; I. Heinemann, *MGWJ* 76 (1932) 263ff.; A. D. Nock, *CR* 46 (1932) 173.

2104. Vol. IV, 1932, 1968⁵, edited and translated by F. H. COLSON and G. H. WHITAKER.

Contains: *On the confusion of tongues* (= *Conf.*); *On the migration of Abraham* (= *Migr.*); *Who is the heir of divine things* (= *Her.*); *On mating with the preliminary studies* (= *Congr.*). REVIEWS: C. Knapp, *CW* 26 (1933) 109; O. Stählin, *PhW* 53 (1933) 177ff.; A. D. Nock, *CR* 48 (1934) 153.

2105. Vol. V, 1934, 1968⁴, edited and translated by F. H. COLSON and G. H. WHITAKER.

Contains: *On flight and finding* (= *Fug.*); *On the change of names* (= *Mut.*); *On dreams, that they are God-sent* (= *Somn.* I-II). REVIEWS: A. D. Nock, *CR* 49 (1935) 154; O. Stählin, *PhW* 55 (1935) 1139ff.; L. Vaganay, *RSR* 15 (1935) 603f.; A. D. Winspear, *CPh* 30 (1935) 372; M. Radin, *CJ* 32 (1937) 238ff.

2106. Vol. VI, 1935, 1966⁴, edited and translated by F. H. COLSON.

Contains: *On Abraham* (= *Abr.*); *On Joseph* (= *Ios.*); *Moses I and* II (= *Mos.* I-II). REVIEWS: A. D. Nock, *CR* 50 (1936) 148; L. Vaganay, *RSR* 17 (1937) 212; O. Stählin, *PhW* 58 (1938) 113ff.

2107. Vol. VII, 1937, 1968⁴, edited and translated by F. H. COLSON.

Contains: *On the Decalogue* (= *Decal.*); *On the special laws, Books* I-III (= *Spec.* I-III). REVIEWS: R. Marcus, *CW* 31 (1938) 213; A. D. Nock, *CR* 52 (1938) 146; O. Stählin, *PhW* 59 (1939) 118ff.

2108. Vol. VIII, 1939, 1968⁴, edited and translated by F. H. COLSON.

Contains: *On the special laws, Book* IV (= *Spec.* IV); *On the virtues* (= *Virt.*); *On rewards and punishments* (= *Praem.*). In contrast to Cohn-Wendland, Colson uses in this volume a progressive numeration of the chapters (i.e. sections in Roman numerals) in each treatise, in order to demonstrate the unity of its contents. This method, which thus neglects the internal partitions, was also employed in the preceding volume with regard to *Spec.* I-III. REVIEWS: E. R. Goodenough, *JBL* 59 (1940) 57ff.; A. D. Nock, *CR* 54 (1940) 170; L. Vaganay, *RSR* 20 (1940) 429; O. Stählin, *PhW* 61 (1941) 146ff.; R. Marcus, *AJPh* 64 (1943) 252f.; G. Phillips, *CW* 36 (1943) 197.

2109. Vol. IX, 1941, 1967⁴, edited and translated by F. H. COLSON.

Contains: *Every good man is free* (= *Prob.*); *On the contemplative life or Suppliants* (= *Contempl.*); *On the eternity of the world* (= *Aet.*); *Flaccus* (= *Flacc.*); *Hypothetica* (= *Hypoth.*); *On Providence* (= *Prov.*). Two writings not included in C-W are published here: *Hypoth.* and *Prov.*; of the latter only the Greek fragments preserved in Eusebius are translated. REVIEWS: E. R. Goodenough, *JBL* 61 (1942) 305f.; A. D. Nock, *CR* 57 (1943) 77ff. (= **4304**); R. Marcus, *AJPh* 65 (1944) 85ff.; H. A. Rigg, *CJ* 40 (1945) 301f.

2110. Vol. X, *The embassy to Gaius*, edited and translated by F. H. COLSON; *Indices to Volumes* I-X by J. W. EARP, 1962, 1971².

Contains: *On the Embassy to Gaius (the First Part of the Treatise on Virtues)* (= *Legat.*). For the indices, cf. **3203**. REVIEWS: A. D. Nock, *CR* 13 (1963) 344; K. Vretska, *AAHG* 16 (1963) 88f.; F. W. Kohnke, *Gn* 36 (1964) 352ff.; V. Nikiprowetzky, *RPh* 38 (1964) 311.

2111. Supplement I, *Questions and answers on Genesis translated from the ancient Armenian version of the original Greek*, by R. MARCUS, Books I-IV, 1953, 1979⁴.

A translation of great importance, it being a considerable improvement on the earlier Latin version by Aucher (**1702**). This volume only provides the translation, however, not an Armenian or Latin text. At present a modern critical edition of the Armenian version of *QE* and *QG* is still lacking. The translation is accompanied by relatively few notes, but at the bottom of each page are numerous attempted retranslations of Greek terms back from the Armenian. Although, needless to say, these must be used with great caution, they are nevertheless of great value to the reader in that they give some indication of what the original text might have said (cf. the comment of D. T. Runia, *VChr* 40 (1986) 205 in his review of **1820**). REVIEWS (for both volumes): McKemie, *CB* 30 (1953) 23; J. van Ooteghem, *LEC* 21 (1953) 463; F. Petit, *RThAM* 20 (1953) 340f.; A. Benoît, *RB* 61 (1954) 467ff.; E. R. Goodenough, *JBL* 73 (1954) 169f.; F. C. Grant, *JR* 34 (1954) 217; M. Hadas, *CW* 47 (1954) 91; P. Katz, *Gn* 26 (1954) 224ff.; H. J. Leon, *Jdm* 3 (1954) 1ff.; A. Rostagni, *RFIC* 32 (1954) 104; L. H. Gray, *JNES* 14 (1955) 203; A. D. Nock, *CR* 5 (1955) 108; G. Delling, *ThLZ* 82 (1957) 578f.; G. Rocca Serra, *RHPhR* 39 (1959) 302f.

2112. Supplement II, *Questions and answers on Exodus translated from the ancient Armenian version of the original Greek*, by R. MARCUS, Books I-II, 1953, 1970³.

For the appendices to this volume, cf. **1807**. It should be noted also that this volume contains a subject index to the *Quaestiones*, to our knowledge the only one available.

b. Translations of single works

2151. *Philonis Alexandrini in Flaccum*, edited with an introduction, translation and commentary by H. BOX, Greek Texts and Commentaries (London-New York-Toronto 1939, New York 1979²).

The Introduction is concerned both with the political context in which Philo's activity took place and with the structure of the treatise as seen from a philological, literary, and historical point of view. Three supplementary notes on lvi-lxii develop some of the points made in the Introduction. The translation is based on C-W's text (**1506**); an extensive commentary is found on 68-124. (= R42)

2152. *Philonis Alexandrini Legatio ad Gaium*, edited with an introduction, translation and commentary by E. M. SMALLWOOD (Leiden 1961, 1970²).

The Introduction follows the structure of Box's work (**2151**), of which it is in a sense a complementary volume. Three additional notes (44-50) elaborate a few points brought up in the Introduction. Of particular importance is the third of these, which establishes the date of Philo's embassy in the winter of 39-40 A.D. The commentary, also mainly oriented towards the historical problems raised by the text, is very extensive, with analysis of and comments on nearly every single paragraph. The translation is based on Reiter's edition (C-W, vol. VI). Reviews: L. H. Feldman, *CW* 55 (1962) 202; W. H. C. Frend, *CR* 13 (1963) 60ff.; V. Nikiprowetzky, *RPLHA* 37 (1963) 308ff.; C. Préaux, *CE* 38 (1963) 185ff.; J. H. Thiel, *Mnem* 16 (1963) 75ff.; R. Joly, *Lat* 23 (1964) 148; F. W. Kohnke, *Gn* 36 (1964) 354ff.; J. G. Préaux, *AC* 33 (1964) 180f.; A. V. Nazzaro, *Vich* n.s. 1 (1972) 90f. (= R43)

2153. A. TERIAN, *Philonis Alexandrini de Animalibus: the Armenian text with an introduction, translation and commentary*, Studies in Hellenistic Judaism: Supplements to Studia Philonica 1 (Chico, California 1981).

On this study, which contains the first translation of *De animalibus* into a modern language, see above **1704**.

2154. *Philo of Alexandria: The contemplative Life, The giants and selections,* translation and introduction by D. WINSTON, preface by J. DILLON, The Classics of Western Spirituality (New York-Toronto 1981).

Contains annotated translations of *Contempl.* and *Gig.*, in addition to an anthology of further Philonic passages and a valuable introduction. See further **3013, 8133**. (DTR)

3. *Translations in French*

a. Comprehensive translation

2201-2234. *Les Œuvres de Philon d'Alexandrie,* publiées sous le patronage de l'Université de Lyon par R. ARNALDEZ, C. MONDÉSERT, J. POUILLOUX avec le concours du Centre National de la Recherche Scientifique et de l'Association des Amis de l'Université de Lyon (Paris 1961-).

This splendid series, now nearing completion, can be credited with giving the decisive impetus to the renaissance of Philonic studies that took place during the sixties and seventies. It was initiated by a group of scholars primarily associated with the University of Lyon. Published by the Parisian publishing house of CERF, it received generous support not only from the University and its association of friends, but also from the Centre National de la Recherche Scientifique, and to a lesser degree from L'Académie des Inscriptions et des Belles Lettres, La Faculté des Lettres de l'Université de Lyon (for vols. 22 and 30), and the Foundation Calouste Gulberkian (for vols. 34A and 35). The format for the majority of the volumes is as follows: (1) an introduction presenting the main themes and concluding with a highly useful schematic summary of the treatise's contents; (2) the text of C-W (rarely modified) and the French translation on facing pages; (3) notes printed at the bottom of the page, with longer 'Notes complementaires' placed at the end of the volume; (4) infrequently some indices. Exceptions to this formula are formed by vol. 33, which contains the critical edition of the fragments without translation, vols. 34A and B (= *QG* I-II, III-VI) and vol. 35 (*Prov.*), which contain Aucher's Latin version, but not the Armenian text. It must be emphasized that there is a great amount of difference, also from the qualitative point of view, between the various volumes in the series. At first, when it was thought that the series would be completed within a few years, the volumes consisted mainly of a translation, with short introductions and no more than a few notes. Some of the first volumes are in fact of a mediocre standard. But within a few years volumes were published containing the fruit of several years of research (e.g. the dissertations of Kahn, Starobinski-Safran), with extensive introductions and so much annotation that they virtually amount to commentaries on the works in question (see below section E on Commentaries).

In general it can be said that the series puts forward a line of interpretation which forms a break with the traditional interpretations based on German and English scholarship. The various translators tend to emphasize the determinative role of the biblical text and the theological and philosophical ideas based thereon in Philo's thought. Thus what the chief editor Arnaldez writes in the Introduction to his own translation of the *De opificio mundi* can be taken as representative for the series as a whole: the underlying idea is that one must search for the unity of Philo's thought 'in the Bible and not in philosophical systems; only there does the unity of the commentary originate. Thus whoever reads Philo with purely philosophical demands will fail to grasp this unity and will find nothing but chatter, word-games, and digressions. It is the Bible which we must try to find in his work, and not this or that kind of philosophy' (**2202,** 117). The same assertion is repeated by Mondésert in the Introduction to *Leg.* (**2205,** 19) and put into practice by many other contributors. Perhaps it finds its most significant demonstration in the volume on *Her.* (**2219**), where Harl shows that the Bible can even be used to explain the celebrated doctrine of the *logos tomeus,* which had remained substantially unexplained, in spite of the many Greek parallels hitherto adduced by scholars. A GENERAL REVIEW of the series was presented by G. DELLING in a sequence of three articles: 'Eine französische Übersetzung der Werke Philons von Alexandrien', *OLZ* 60 (1965) 7-10; 'Die Fortschritte der französischen Bearbeitung der Werke Philons', *OLZ* 64 (1969) 229-233; 'Die französische Bearbeitung der Werke Philons vor dem Abschluss', *OLZ* 72 (1977) 5-11. It is worth noting too that J. C. M. VAN WINDEN has reviewed every single volume of the series in the pages of *Vigiliae Christianae*, and that P. BOYANCÉ made interesting comments on the first volumes of the series in the article listed under **6305**. (= R44)

2201. Vol. 9, *De agricultura*, introduction, traduction et notes par J. POUILLOUX (Paris 1961); French title *L'Agriculture*.

Both the notes and the Introduction to this treatise are very succinct. REVIEWS: P. Courcelle, *REA* 63 (1961) 494f.; J. Daniélou, *RecSR* 49 (1961) 610f.; C. Martin, *NRTh* 83 (1961) 873; J. Ortiz de Urbina, *OrChrP* 27 (1961) 453f.; J. R. Palanque, *RHEF* 47 (1961) 318f.; F. Petit, *RThAM* 28 (1961) 345f.; J. G. Préaux, *AC* 30 (1961) 229; C., *RHE* 57 (1962) 292f.; P. T. Camelot, *RSPhTh* 46 (1962) 754f.; L. Früchtel, *Gn* 34 (1962) 45ff.; S. Giet, *RSR* 36 (1962) 201f.; H. Holstein, *Études* 312 (1962) 285; R. Joly, *RBPh* 40 (1962) 1022f.; J. Moreau, *EPh* 17 (1962) 128f.; A. Orbe, *Gr* 43 (1962) 563f.; J. A. de Aldama, *EE* 38 (1963) 392f.; J. Leipoldt, *ThLZ* 88 (1963) 836f.; M. McNamara, *CBQ* 25 (1963) 204f.; H. Crouzel, *RAM* 40 (1964) 80; V. Nikiprowetzky, *RPh* 38 (1964) 142; M. Simon, *RH* 240 (1968) 433f.; J. C. M. van Winden, *VChr* 24 (1970) 138ff.; A. V. Nazzaro, *Vich* n.s. 1 (1972) 79. (= R45)

2202. Vol. 1, *Introduction générale* par R. ARNALDEZ; *De opificio mundi*, introduction, traduction et notes par R. ARNALDEZ (Paris 1961); French title *La création du monde*.

This work essentially reproduces a doctoral thesis presented by the author in 1955 (**2251**). For the General Introduction to the whole translation series, cf. above **1107**. The Introduction to *Opif.* relates this work to the scientific and philosophical culture of Hellenism. On the basis of this analysis and of the allegorical method employed by Philo, Arnaldez determines the place of *Opif.* in the Philonic corpus and discusses the specific themes which characterize it. The notes to the translation are fairly extensive. REVIEWS: J. Daniélou, *RecSR* 49 (1961) 608ff.; S. Daris, *Aeg* 41 (1961) 260; E. L., *Irén* 34 (1961) 583f.; C. Martin, *NRTh* 83 (1961) 873f.; J. Ortiz de Urbina, *OrChrP* 27 (1961) 453f.; J. R. Palanque, *RHEF* 47 (1961) 318f.; F. Petit, *RThAM* 28 (1961) 345f.; J. G. Préaux, *AC* 30 (1961) 226f.; M. Spanneut, *MSR* 18 (1961) 183f.; C., *RHE* 58 (1962) 292f.; P. T. Camelot, *RSPhTh* 46 (1962) 754f.; Q. Cataudella, *SicGymn* 15 (1962) 287f.; H. Crouzel, *RAM* 38 (1962) 228ff.; N. de El Molar, *EstFr* 63 (1962) 299, E. F., *RBen* 38 (1962) 164f.; L. Früchtel, *Gn* 34 (1962) 45ff.; S. Giet, *RSR* 36 (1962) 200f.; H. Holstein, *Études* 312 (1962) 285; R. Joly, *RBPh* 40 (1962) 1022f.; J. Moreau, *EPh* 17 (1962) 128f.; V. Nikiprowetzky, *RPh* 36 (1962) 314ff.; A. Orbe, *Gr* 43 (1962) 563f.; M. Philonenko, *ThZ* 18 (1962) 437f.; H. Quecke, *Muséon* 75 (1962) 470ff.; J. E. Ramirez, *RET* 22 (1962) 458f.; A. Solignac, *ArPh* 25 (1962) 150f.; E. Bellini, *ScC* 91 (1963) 332*f.; J. A. de Aldama, *EE* 38 (1963) 392ff.; J. de Fraine, *Bijdr* 24 (1963) 216f.; M. E. Lauzière, *RThom* 63 (1963) 130; I. Leipoldt, *ThLZ* 88 (1963) 836f.; M. McNamara, *CBQ* 25 (1963) 204f.; G. P., *ZKTh* 88 (1964) 229f.; P. Aubenque, *RPhilos* 90 (1965) 522; F. Bouwen, *POC* 18 (1968) 391f.; M. Simon, *RH* 240 (1968) 433f.; J. C. M. van Winden, *VChr* 23 (1969) 224ff.; P. Bonnard, *RThPh* 104 (1971) 105ff.; A. V. Nazzaro, *Vich* n.s. 1 (1972) 96f. (= R46)

2203. Vol. 28, *De praemiis et poenis, De exsecrationibus*, introduction, traduction et notes par A. BECKAERT (Paris 1961); French title *Les* *récompenses et les châtiments, Les bénédictions et les malédictions.*

The copiously annotated Introduction deals with the place of the treatise in Philo's corpus and its structure, with special attention paid to its theological and ethical themes. REVIEWS: J. Ortiz de Urbina, *OrChrP* 27 (1961) 453f.; F. Petit, *RThAM* 28 (1961) 345f.; C., *RHE* 57 (1962) 292f.; P. T. Camelot, *RSPhTh* 46 (1962) 754f.; P. Courcelle, *REA* 64 (1962) 499; S. Giet, *RSR* 36 (1962) 200ff.; C. Martin, *NRTh* 84 (1962) 744; J. Moreau, *EPh* 17 (1962) 128f.; A. Orbe, *Gr* 43 (1962) 563f.; J. G. Préaux, *AC* 31 (1962) 349f.; J. A. de Aldama, *EE* 38 (1963) 392ff.; J. Leipoldt, *ThLZ* 88 (1963) 836f.; M. McNamara, *CBQ* 25 (1963) 204f.; H. Crouzel, *RAM* 40 (1964) 79ff.; G., *ZKTh* 86 (1964) 229f.; V. Nikiprowetzky, *RPh* 38 (1964) 143; M. Simon, *RH* 240 (1968) 433; J. C. M. van Winden, *VChr* 24 (1970) 218f.; A. V. Nazzaro, *Vich* n.s. 1 (1972) 98. (= R47)

2204. Vols. 11-12, *De ebrietate, De sobrietate*, traduit par J. GOREZ (Paris 1962); French title *L'ébriété, Prières et malédictions prononcées par Noé revenu à la sobriété.*

The Introductions are inadequate, but more care has been taken in the schematic expositions of content. REVIEWS: L. Früchtel, *Gn* 34 (1962) 770ff.; G. Jouassard, *BFCL* 33(1962) 60f.; F. Petit, *RThAM* 29 (1962) 313f.; P. T. Camelot, *RSPhTh* 47 (1963) 425; P. Courcelle, *REA* 45 (1963) 247f.; S. Daris, *Aeg* 42 (1963) 172f.; J. A. de Aldama, *EE* 38 (1963) 392ff.; J. de Fraine, *Bijdr* 24 (1963) 216f.; S. Giet, *RSR* 37 (1963) 211f.; R. Joly, *RBPh* 41 (1963) 240f.; J. Moreau *EPh* 18 (1963) 111; A. Orbe, *Gr* 44 (1963) 366ff.; J. G. Préaux, *AC* 32 (1963) 644; M. Whittaker, *JThS* 14 (1963) 577; J. P. Audet, *RB* 71 (1964) 474f.; M. Bogaert, *RBen* 74 (1964) 191; H. Crouzel, *RAM* 40 (1964) 79f.; G. P., *ZKTh* 86 (1964) 229f.; C. Martin, *NRTh* 86 (1964) 1123f.; V. Nikiprowetzky, *RPh* 38 (1964) 312f.; F. Bouwen, *POC* 18 (1968) 391f.; M. Simon, *RH* 240 (1968) 433f.; J. C. M. van Winden, *VChr* 24 (1970) 142f.; A. V. Nazzaro, *Vich* n.s. 1 (1972) 85f.; P. Bonnard, *RThPh* 108 (1975) 59. (= R48)

2205. Vol. 2, *Legum Allegoriae* I-III, introduction, traduction et notes par C. MONDÉSERT (Paris 1962); French title *Commentaire allégorique des saintes lois après l'œuvre des six jours, livres I-III.*

The Introduction contains a very brief historical-philosophical analysis, together with a quite detailed paraphrase of the contents. We note that there is an earlier French translation of this treatise by E. BRÉHIER, *Philon, Commentaire allégorique des saintes lois après l'œuvre des six jours*, Texte grec, traduction française, introduction et index, Textes et documents pour l'étude historique du Christianisme 9 (Paris 1909). At an early stage the editors planned to include this translation in the series. Later, however, the project was abandoned, because on closer analysis it proved to be superseded on many points by more recent developments in Philonic scholarship. REVIEWS: P. T. Camelot, *RSPhTh* 46 (1962) 754f.; P. Courcelle, *REA* 64 (1962) 497f.; N. de El Molar, *EstFr* 63 (1962) 302f.; L. Früchtel, *Gn* 34(1962) 660ff.; H. Holstein, *Études* 312 (1962) 285; C. Martin, *NRTh* 84 (1962) 744; M. B., *RBen* 72 (1962) 368; J. Moreau, *EPh* 17 (1962) 562; A. Orbe, *Gr* 43 (1962) 563f.; F. Petit, *RThAM* 29 (1962) 313ff.; M. Philonenko, *ThZ* 18 (1962) 438; Q. Cataudella, *SicGymn* 16 (1963) 243ff.; S. Daris, *Aeg* 42 (1963) 172f.; J. A. de Aldama, *EE* 38 (1963) 392ff.; J. de Fraine, *Bijdr* 24 (1963) 216f.; S. Giet, *RSR* 37(1963) 211; R. Joly, *RBPh* 41 (1963) 240f.; J. Leipoldt, *ThLZ* 88 (1963) 836; M. McNamara, *CBQ* 25 (1963) 204f.; R. McL. Wilson, *JThS* 14 (1963) 121f.; J. G. Préaux, *AC* 32(1963) 643f.; J. P. Audet, *RB* 71 (1964) 474f.; H. Crouzel, *RAM* 40,

(1964) 80; G., *ZKTh* 86 (1964) 229f.; V. Nikiprowetzky, *RPh* 38 (1964) 310f.; E. Bellini, *ScC* 93 (1965) 228*; F. Bouwen, *POC* 18 (1968) 391f.; M. Simon, *RH* 240 (1968) 433f.; J. C. M. van Winden, *VChr* 23 (1969) 226f.; P. Bonnard, *RThPh* 104 (1971) 105ff.; A. V. Nazzaro, *Vich* n.s. 1 (1972) 90. (= R49)

2206. Vol. 19, *De Somniis* I-II, introduction, traduction et notes par P. SAVINEL (Paris 1962); French title: *Que les rêves sont envoyés par Dieu.*

The Introduction and the notes are inadequate. The Introduction in particular is limited to very general observations on Philo's exegetical method, with hardly any references to the treatise. REVIEWS: P. Courcelle, *REA* 64(1962) 498; S. Daris, *Aeg* 42 (1962) 172ff.; L. Früchtel, *Gn* 34 (1962) 770ff.; C. Martin, *NRTh* 84 (1962) 984f.; M. B., *RBen* 72 (1962) 368; J. Moreau, *EPh* 17 (1962) 563f.; F. Petit, *RThAM* 29(1962) 313f.; M. Philonenko, *ThZ* 18 (1962) 437ff.; J. A. de Aldama, *EE* 38 (1963) 392ff.; J. de Fraine, *Bijdr* 24 (1963) 216f.; N. de El Molar, *EstFr* 64 (1963) 119; R. Joly, *RBPh* 41 (1963) 240f.; A. Orbe, *Gr* 44 (1963) 336f.; J. G. Préaux, *AC* 32 (1963) 645; G. J. Toomer, *JThS* 14 (1963) 122f.; J. P. Audet, *RB* 71 (1964) 474ff.; H. Crouzel, *RAM* 40 (1964) 81; G., *ZKTh* 86 (1964) 229f.; V. Nikiprowetzky, *RPh* 38 (1964) 312f.; M. B., *RBen* 75 (1965) 170f.; A. Morâo, *RPF* 21 (1965) 216; P. van Doornik, *Bijdr* 26 (1965) 229; J. A. de Aldama, *EE* 42 (1967) 139f.; F. Bouwen, *POC* 18 (1968) 391f.; M. Simon, *RH* 240 (1968) 433f.; J. C. M. van Winden, *VChr* 24 (1970) 300ff.; A. V. Nazzaro, *Vich* n.s. 1 (1972) 100. (= R50)

2207. Vol. 26, *De virtutibus*, introduction et notes de R. ARNALDEZ, traduction de P. DELOBRE, M. R. SERVEL, A. M. VERILHAC (Paris 1962); French title *Des vertus décrites par Moïse et entre autres du courage, de la piété, de la vertu d'humanité et du repentir, Le courage* (= *De fortitudine*) translated by A. M. VERILHAC, *La vertu d'humanité* (= *De humanitate*) translated by P. DELOBRE, *Le repentir* (= *De paenitentia*), translated by M. R. SERVEL, *La noblesse* (= *De nobilitate*), translated by M. R. SERVEL.

The Introduction presents the theme of virtue in Philo in broad outline, without much depth and with scarcely any references to the text. A few remarks are devoted to the place of the treatise in the Philonic corpus. REVIEWS: P. T. Camelot, *RSPhTh* 46 (1962) 754f.; P. Courcelle, *REA* 64 (1962) 498; S. Daris, *Aeg* 42 (1962) 172f.; L. Früchtel, *Gn* 34 (1962) 770ff.; R. Joly, *RBPh* 40 (1962) 1409f.; C. Martin, *NRTh* 84 (1962) 984f.; M. B., *RBen* 72 (1962) 368; J. Moreau, *EPh* 17 (1962) 563; F. Petit, *RThAM* 29 (1962) 313ff.; M. Spanneut, *MSR* 19 (1962) 122f.; J. A. de Aldama, *EE* 38 (1963) 392ff.; N. de El Molar, *EstFr* 64 (1963) 119f.; J. de Fraine, *Bijdr* 24 (1963) 216f.; S. Giet, *RSR* 38 (1963) 211f.; J. Leipoldt, *ThLZ* 88 (1963) 836f.; A. Orbe, *Gr* 44 (1963) 366ff.; J. G. Préaux, *AC* 32 (1963) 645f.; G. J. Toomer, *JThS* 14 (1963) 122f.; J. P. Audet, *RB* 71 (1964) 474f.; H. Crouzel, *RAM* 40 (1964) 79ff.; G., *ZKTh* 86 (1964) 229f.; V. Nikiprowetzky, *RPh* 38 (1964) 144; F. Bouwen, *POC* 18 (1968) 391f.; M. Simon, *RH* 240 (1968) 433f.; J. C. M. van Winden, *VChr* 24 (1970) 218ff.; A. V. Nazzaro, *Vich* n.s. 1 (1972) 101. (= R51)

2208. Vol. 3, *De Cherubim*, introduction, traduction et notes par J. GOREZ (Paris 1963); French title *Les Chérubins. L'épée de feu. La première créature née d'un homme: Caïn.*

Both the notes and the Introduction to this treatise must be considered inadequate.

REVIEWS: G. Jouassard, *BFCL* 35 (1963) 27f.; J. Moreau, *EPh* 18 (1963) 472; F. Petit, *RThAM* 30 (1963) 341ff.; A. Benoît, *RHPhR* 44(1964) 424f.; M. Bogaert, *RBen* 74 (1964) 191; P. T. Camelot, *RSPhTh* 48 (1964) 737; C. Martin, *NRTh* 86 (1964) 1123f.; A. Orbe, *Gr* 45 (1964) 355; J. P. Audet, *RB* 72 (1965) 155ff.; E. Bellini, *ScC* 93 (1965) 228*; S. Giet, *RSR* 39 (1965) 374f.; F. W. Kohnke, *Gn* 37 (1965) 666ff.; J. Leipoldt, *ThLZ* 40 (1965) 602; M. Philonenko, *ThZ* 22 (1966) 361; J. A. de Aldama, *EE* 42 (1967) 139ff.; J. Préaux, *AC* 37 (1968) 686f.; J. C. M. van Winden, *VChr* 24 (1970) 303f.; A. V. Nazzaro, *Vich* n.s. 1 (1972) 80. (= R52)

2209. Vol. 13, *De confusione linguarum*, Introduction, traduction et notes par J. G. KAHN (Paris 1963); French title *La confusion des langues*.

This volume represents a doctoral thesis previously defended by the author at the University of Strasbourg. (From this volume onwards the series starts to improve in quality.) The Introduction deals in a synthetic manner with the dominant themes of *Conf.* as well as with the connections between this treatise and the cultural context which influenced it. The translation is amply furnished with footnotes, in which there is a heavy emphasis on Philo's Judaic background. There are also extensive 'Complementary notes' at 157-187. REVIEWS: P. Courcelle, *REA* 65 (1963) 448f.; J. Moreau, *EPh* 18 (1963) 472f.; F. Petit, *RThAM* 30(1963) 343f.; A. Benoît, *RHPhR* 44(1964) 424f.; Q. Cataudella, *SicGymn* 17 (1964) 271f.; N. de El Molar, *EstFr* 65 (1964) 119f.; M. B., *RBen* 74(1964) 191; J. P. Audet, *RB* 72 (1965) 155f.; E. Bellini, *ScC* 93 (1965) 228*f.; J. Leipoldt, *ThLZ* 90 (1965) 602; F. W. Kohnke, *Gn* 38 (1966) 343f.; M. Philonenko, *ThZ* 22 (1966) 361; J. A. de Aldama, *EE* 42 (1967) 139ff.; A. Orbe, *Gr* 49 (1968) 369; M. Simon, *RH* 240 (1968) 433f.; W. Elliger, *ALW* 11 (1969) 319; A. Grilli, *Paid* 24 (1969) 286ff.; J. C. M. van Winden, *VChr* 25 (1971) 62f.; A. V. Nazzaro, *Vich* n.s. 1 (1972) 80f. (= R53)

2210. Vol. 29, *De vita contemplativa*, introduction et notes de F. DAUMAS, traduction de P. MIQUEL (Paris 1963); French title *De la vie contemplative ou des orants* (quatrième partie de l'ouvrage *Des vertus*.

The very extensive Introduction is divided into three sections. The first and third are respectively concerned with historical and philological problems pertaining to the treatise and its contents; the second (26-66) is entirely devoted to the Therapeutae and amounts to a separate essay on the subject. The very generous notes make this volume tantamount to a commentary on *Contempl.* REVIEWS: A. Benoît, *RHPhR* 44 (1964) 424f.; P. T. Camelot, *RSPhTh* 48 (1964) 737; L. Cilleruelo, *ArAg* 58 (1964) 293f.; N. de El Molar, *EstFr* 65(1964) 120; C. Martin, *NRTh* 86 (1964) 1123f.; J. Moreau, *EPh* 19(1964) 316; F. Petit, *RThAM* 31 (1964) 145ff.; J. G. Préaux, *AC* 33 (1964) 447ff.; J. P. Audet, *RBi* 72 (1965) 155f.; E. Bellini, *ScC* 93 (1965) 229*f.; M. Bogaert, *RBen* 85(1965) 170; P. Bonnard, *RThPh* 98 (1965) 47f.; P. Courcelle, *REA* 66 (1965) 452ff.; M. Delcor, *BLE* 66 (1965) 301f.; C. Dumont, *CCist* 27 (1965) 73f.; S. Giet, *RSR* 39 (1965) 374f.; A. Guillaumont, *RHR* 168 (1965) 95f.; R. Joly, *RBPh* 42 (1965), 1096f.; L., *RThom* 65 (1965) 175f.; A. Morâo, *RPF* 21 (1965) 216; A. Orbe, *Gr* 46 (1965) 865f.; J. Oroz Reta *RET* 25 (1965) 468; P. van Doornik, *Bijdr* 26 (1965) 229; F. W. Kohnke, *Gn* 38 (1966) 344f.; A. Pelletier, *RPh* 40 (1966) 137ff.; M. Philonenko, *ThZ* 22 (1966) 361; M. Whittaker, *JThS* 17 (1966) 127f.; J. A. de Aldama, *EE* 42 (1967) 139ff.; J. C. M. van Winden, *VChr* 25 (1971) 63ff.; A. V. Nazzaro, *Vich* n.s. 1 (1972) 82f. (= R54)

2211. Vols. 7-8, *De Gigantibus, Quod Deus sit immutabilis,* introduction, traduction et notes par A. MOSÈS (Paris 1963); French title *Les Géants, L'immutabilité de Dieu.*

The Introduction to the two treatises is inadequate because it fails to get to the heart of the problems discussed; the notes to the translation, however, are fairly numerous, if not very extensive and detailed. REVIEWS: S. Daris, *Aeg* 32 (1962) 322; E. Bellini, *ScC* 91 (1963) 333*f.; A. Benoît, *RHPhR* 43 (1963) 386; P. T. Camelot, *RSPhTh* 47 (1963) 425; P. Courcelle, *REA* 65 (1963) 448; J. de Fraine, *Bijdr* 24 (1963) 437f.; S. Giet, *RSR* 37(1963) 383f.; J. Moreau, *EPh* 18 (1963) 371; F. Petit, *RThAM* 30 (1963) 161f.; Q. Cataudella, *SicGymn* 17 (1964) 270f.; H. Crouzel, *RAM* 40 (1964) 80; G., *ZKTh* 86 (1964) 229f.; C. Martin, *NRTh* 86 (1964) 1123f.; A. Orbe, *Greg* 45 (1964) 354; J. G. Préaux, *AC* 33 (1964) 479f.; J. P. Audet, *RB* 72 (1965) 155f.; F. W. Kohnke, *Gn* 37 (1965) 666ff.; J. Leipoldt, *ThLZ* 90 (1965) 602; M. Philonenko, *ThZ* 22 (1966) 361; J. A. de Aldama, *EE* 42 (1967) 139ff.; F. Bouwen, *POC* 18 (1968) 391f.; J. Garcìa, *EstFil* 17 (1968) 184; M. Simon, *RH* 240 (1968) 433f.; J. C. M. van Winden, *VChr* 24 (1970) 302f.; P. Bonnard, *RThPh* 104 (1971) 105ff.; A. V. Nazzaro, *Vich* n.s. 1 (1972) 85. (= R55)

2212. Vol. 10, *De plantatione*, introduction, traduction et notes par J. POUILLOUX (Paris 1963); French title *Noé et l'art de la culture; livre second.*

The Introduction is inadequate; the notes to the translation, however, are quite extensive. REVIEWS: E. Bellini, *ScC* 91 (1963) 333*f.; A. Benoît, *RHPhR* 43 (1963) 386; P. Courcelle, *REA* 65 (1963) 448; S. Giet, *RSR* 37 (1963) 384; F. Petit, *RThAM* 30 (1963) 162; M. Bogaert, *RBen* 74 (1964) 191; C. Martin, *NRTh* 86 (1964) 1123f.; J. Moreau, *EPh* 19 (1964) 315f.; A. Orbe, *Gr* 45 (1964) 355; J. P. Audet, *RB* 72 (1965) 155f.; F. W. Kohnke, *Gn* 37 (1965) 666ff.; J. Leipoldt, *ThLZ* 90 (1965) 602; P. J. M. Ozaeta, *RET* 25 (1965) 326; J. A. de Aldama, *EE* 42 (1967) 139ff.; J. G. Préaux, *AC* 37 (1968) 687; J. C. M. van Winden, *VChr* 24 (1970) 140ff.; A. V. Nazzaro, *Vich* n.s. 1 (1972) 98. (= R56)

2213. Vol. 21, *De Iosepho*, traduit par J. LAPORTE (Paris 1964); French title *Une vie d'homme politique: Joseph.*

The Introduction, which deals above all with the political themes implicit in the treatise, is quite extensive and useful, but the notes are infrequent and brief. REVIEWS: J. Moreau, *EPh* 20 (1965) 551f.; M. E. Lauzière, *RThom* 66 (1966) 315f.; F. Petit, *RThAM* 33 (1966) 159f.; A. Orbe, *Gr* 49 (1968) 369; J. C. M. van Winden, *VChr* 25 (1971) 65f.; A. V. Nazzaro, *Vich* n.s. 1 (1972) 89. (= R57)

2214. Vol. 18, *De mutatione nominum*, introduction, traduction et notes par R. ARNALDEZ (Paris 1964); French title *Du changement des noms et pourquoi on le fait.*

The Introduction is limited to a rapid and rather superficial analysis of the treatise's contents. REVIEWS: A. Benoît, *RHPhR* 44 (1964) 424f.; P. T. Camelot, *RSPhTh* 48 (1964) 737; P. Courcelle, *REA* 66 (1964) 453f.; N. de El Molar, *EstFr* 65 (1964) 437f.; J. Moreau, *EPh* 19 (1964) 621f.; M. Pellegrino, *Studium* 60 (1964) 883f.; F. Petit, *RThAM* 31 (1964) 334f.; J. P. Audet, *RB* 72 (1965) 155f.; E. Bellini, *ScC* 93 (1965) 230*; M. Bogaert, *RBen* 75 (1965) 170; E. Boularand, *BLE* 66 (1965) 222f.; S. Giet, *RSR* 39 (1965) 374f.; A. Guillaumont, *RHR* 168 (1965) 96; R. Joly, *RBPh* 43 (1965)

247f.; M. Lauzière, *RThom* 65 (1965) 175; J. Leipoldt, *ThLZ* 89 (1965) 602f.; A.
Morâo, *RPF* 21 (1965) 216; A. Orbe, *Gr* 46 (1965) 866; P. van Doornik, *Bijdr* 26
(1965) 229; M. Whittaker, *JThS* 16 (1965) 482; J. Oroz Reta, *RET* 26 (1966) 106f.; A.
Pelletier, *RPh* 40 (1966) 135ff.; M. Philonenko, *ThZ* 22 (1966) 361; J. A. de Aldama,
EE 42 (1967) 139ff.; C. Martin, *NRTh* 89 (1967) 78f.; W. Wiefel, *ThLZ* 92 (1967)
372ff.; J. G. Préaux, *AC* 37 (1968) 690; J. C. M. van Winden, *VChr* 25 (1971) 65; A.
V. Nazzaro, *Vich* n.s. 1 (1972) 95. (= R58)

2215. Vol. 23, *De Decalogo*, introduction, traduction et notes par V.
NIKIPROWETZKY (Paris 1965); French title *Des dix paroles qui constituent
les principes généraux des lois*.

This work corresponds to the major part of a doctoral thesis defended by the author at
the École pratique des Hautes Études. The Introduction is largely devoted to an analysis
of contents and pays particular attention to the method of interpreting the Law used by
Philo in this work, a method which is directly linked to the essential theme of his
mysticism. The notes are very extensive and are supplemented with 'Appendices' at 133-
166. The volume thus virtually has the status of a commentary. REVIEWS: J. Moreau,
EPh 20 (1965) 551f.; F. Petit, *RThAM* 33 (1966) 159ff.; P. Hadot, *REJ* 129 (1970)
257f.; A. Orbe, *Gr* 51 (1970) 209; J. C. M. van Winden, *VChr* 25 (1971) 140ff.; A. V.
Nazzaro, *Vich* n.s.1 (1972) 83f. (= R59)

2216. Vol. 5, *Quod deterius potiori insidiari soleat*, introduction,
traduction et notes par I. FEUER (Paris 1965); French title *Que le plus
mauvais ordinairement attaque celui qui est meilleur*.

The Introduction is inadequate, in contrast to the analysis of the treatise and the notes,
which are quite detailed and extensive. REVIEWS: P. Courcelle, *REA* 67 (1965) 565f.; J.
Moreau, *EPh* 20 (1965) 371; F. Petit, *RThAM* 32 (1965) 142f.; J. P. Audet, *RB*
73(1966) 627; N. de El Molar, *EstFr* 67 (1966) 106; P. Fransen, *Bijdr* 27 (1966) 433; R.
Joly, *RBPh* 44 (1966) 187; J. Oroz Reta, *RET* 26 (1966) 245f.; M. Bogaert, *RBen* 77
(1967) 203; J. A. de Aldama, *EE* 42 (1967) 139ff.; B. Mondin, *RFN* 59 (1967) 140f.;
A. Orbe, *Gr* 48 (1967) 374; W. Wiefel, *ThLZ* 92 (1967) 372f.; M. Hadas Lebel, *REG* 81
(1968) 301f.; J. C. M. van Winden, *VChr* 25 (1971) 141; A. V. Nazzaro, *Vich* n.s. 1
(1972) 84f. (= R60)

2217. Vol. 14, *De migratione Abrahami*, introduction, traduction et
notes par J. CAZEAUX (Paris 1965); French title *L'émigration*.

This volume reproduces a doctoral thesis defended by the author at the University of
Lyons. Given the scope of the Introduction, the particularly complete and precise
analysis of contents, and the abundance and amplitude of the notes, the work as a whole
may be considered tantamount to a commentary on *Migr.*, especially since the Introduction gives an in-depth examination, chapter for chapter, of the text of the treatise. The
views presented here on the structural method used by Philo in organizing his treatise
anticipate the main theses of Cazeaux's monograph, *La trame et la chaîne* (see **8320**).
REVIEWS: F. Petit, *RThAM* 32 (1965) 337f.; J. P. Audet, *RB* 73 (1966) 626f.; N. de El
Molar, *EstFr* 67 (1966) 105; P. Fransen, *Bijdr* 27 (1966) 433; M. E. Lauzière, *RThom*
67 (1966) 316f.; M. Whittaker, *JThS* 17 (1966) 431 f.; M. Bogaert, *RBen* 77 (1967)
203f.; P. Courcelle, *REA* 69 (1967) 175ff.; S. Giet, *RSR* 41 (1967) 169ff.; C. Martin,
NRTh 89 (1967) 78f.; B. Mondini, *RFN* 61 (1967) 142; A. Orbe, *Gr* 48 (1967) 133; G.
Torti, *Paid* 22 (1967) 366f.; W. Wiefel, *ThLZ* 92 (1967) 373; J. A. de Aldama, *EE* 43

(1968) 603f.; M. Hadas Lebel, *REG* 81 (1968) 302ff.; J. G. Préaux, *AC* 37 (1968) 687ff.; F. W. Kohnke, *Gn* 42 (1970) 29ff.; J. C. M. van Winden, *VChr* 25 (1971) 142f.; A. V. Nazzaro, *Vich* n.s. 1 (1972) 94. (= R61)

2218. Vol. 20, *De Abrahamo*, introduction, traduction et notes par J. GOREZ (Paris 1966); French title *Vie du sage que l'étude a mené à la perfection ou (premier livre) sur les lois non écrites: Abraham.*

Both the notes and the Introduction are inadequate. The analysis of the treatise, however, is accurate and useful. REVIEWS: J. Moreau, *EPh* 21 (1966) 430f.; F. Petit, *RThAM* 33 (1966) 159f.; M. Bogaert, *RBen* 77 (1967) 203; P. Courcelle, *REA* 69 (1967) 175ff.; H. Crouzel, *BLE* 68 (1967) 221f.; S. Giet, *RSR* 41 (1967) 169ff.; M. E. Lauzière, *RThom* 67 (1967) 336f.; C. Martin, *NRTh* 89 (1967) 79; B. Mondin, *RFN* 59 (1967) 140ff.; P. F., *Bijdr* 28 (1967) 214f.; M. Whittaker, *JThS* 18 (1967) 555; J. P. Audet, *RB* 75 (1968) 146; H. Crouzel, *RAM* 44 (1968) 463f.; J. A. de Aldama, *EE* 43 (1968) 603f.; M. Hadas Lebel, *REG* 81 (1968) 304ff.; A. Orbe, *Gr* 49 (1968) 370; J. G. Préaux, *AC* 37 (1968) 689; J. V. Vernhes, *RPh* 42 (1968) 155f.; W. Wiefel, *ThLZ* 93 (1968) 516; N. de El Molar, *EstFr* 70 (1969) 275f.; S. Sandmel, *Eras* 22 (1970) 679ff.; J. C. M. van Winden, *VChr* 25 (1971) 61; A. V. Nazzaro, *Vich* n.s. 1 (1972) 78f. (= R62)

2219. Vol. 15, *Quis rerum divinarum heres sit*, introduction, traduction et notes par M. HARL (Paris 1966); French title *Quel est l'héritier des biens divins; sur la division en partes égales et contraires.*

In this work the series reaches its highest standard. The Introduction amounts to an entire monograph, not only on account of its length (13-162), but also because of the completeness and the originality of the views which it sets out. *Her.* is reread in terms of the theme of levitical spirituality and a wholly original interpretation of the *logos tomeus* is given. The copious and detailed footnotes are supplemented with the Appendices (329-333). Together with the closely packed references to the Introduction, they give this work the importance of a major commentary. REVIEWS: F. Petit, *RThAM* 33 (1966) 159ff.; P. T. Camelot, *RSPhTh* 51 (1967) 674; P. Courcelle, *REA* 69 (1967) 175f.; H. Crouzel, *BLE* 68 (1967) 221f.; A. Jacob, *EPh* 22 (1967) 108f.; M. E. Lauzière, *RThom* 67 (1967) 336; B. Mondin, *RFN* 59 (1967) 140ff.; P. F., *Bijdr* 28 (1967) 214f.; M. Whittaker, *JThS* 18 (1967) 455f.; J. P. Audet, *RB* 75 (1968) 146ff.; M. Bogaert, *RBen* 78 (1968) 169; G. L. Coulon, *CBQ* 30 (1968) 123f.; H. Crouzel, *RAM* 44 (1968) 462f.; J. Daniélou, *RecSR* 56 (1968) 130ff.; J. A. de Aldama, *EE* 43 (1968) 603f.; C. Martin, *NRTh* 90 (1968) 622ff.; A. Orbe, *Gr* 49 (1968) 783f.; A. Pelletier, *REG* 81 (1968) 306ff.; W. Wiefel, *ThLZ* 93 (1968) 516f.; N. de El Molar, *EstFr* 70 (1969) 276f.; G. Lomiento, *VetChr* 6 (1969) 222; S. Sandmel, *Eras* 22 (1970) 679ff.; J. C. M. van Winden, *VChr* 25 (1971) 60f.; A. V. Nazzaro, *Vich* n.s. 1 (1972) 88f. (= R63)

2220. Vol. 4, *De sacrificiis Abelis et Caini*, introduction, traduction et notes par A. MÉASSON, (Paris 1966); French title *Naissance d'Abel et sacrifices offerts par lui et par son frère Caïn.*

This work is the edition of a doctoral thesis defended by the author at the University of Lyons. The Introduction explains the main themes of the treatise, the method used by Philo, and the influence which this writing exercised on the literature and thought of the early Christians and the Church Fathers. The generous annotation of the translation is given further depth by the addition of 'Complementary notes' (189-210). The volume in its entirety can be regarded as equivalent to an extended commentary on *Sacr.* REVIEWS: G. Jouassard, *BFCL* 40 (1966) 49f.; F. Petit, *RThAM* 33 (1966) 161; M. Bogaert, *RBen* 77 (1967) 203; G. Coulon, *CBQ* 29 (1967) 174f.; P. Courcelle, *REA* 69 (1967) 175ff.; H. Crouzel, *BLE* 67 (1967) 221f., *RAM* 44 (1968) 461f.; S. Giet, *RSR* 41 (1967) 169ff.; R. Joly, *RBPh* 45 (1967) 590f.; M. E. Lauzière, *RThom* 67 (1967) 335f.; C. Martin, *NRTh* 89 (1967) 78f.; B. Mondin, *RFN* 59 (1967) 142; M. Whittaker, *JThS* 18 (1967) 313; J. P. Audet, *RB* 75 (1968) 147; J. A. de Aldama, *EE* 43 (1968) 603f.; P. Fransen, *Bijdr* 29 (1968) 209f.; M. Hadas Lebel, *REG* 81 (1968) 645ff.; A. Orbe, *Gr* 49 (1968) 370f.; J. V. Vernhes, *RPh* 42 (1968) 298ff.; N. de El Molar, *EstFr* 70 (1969) 274f.; F. W. Kohnke, *Gn* 42 (1970) 26ff.; S. Sandmel, *Eras* 22 (1970) 679ff.; J. C. M. van Winden, *VChr* 25 (1971) 143f.; A. V. Nazzaro, *Vich* n.s. 1 (1972) 98f. (= R64)

2221. Vol. 16, *De congressu eruditionis gratia*, introduction, traduction et notes par M. ALEXANDRE (Paris 1967); French title *Du commerce de l'âme avec les connaissances préparatoires*.

This work corresponds to a doctoral thesis defended by the author at the Sorbonne. The long Introduction and the extensive and numerous notes – with 'Complementary notes' added at 233-257 – make the work as a whole the equivalent of a commentary. The Introduction analyzes the themes of the treatise and also devotes a chapter to its influence on the Church Fathers; its central section deals extensively with the theme of the ἐγκύκλιος παιδεία, which is held to be the dominant theme of *Congr.* REVIEWS: F. Petit, *RThAM* 34 (1967) 272f.; P. Courcelle, *REA* 70 (1968) 470f.; P. Fransen, *Bijdr* 29 (1968) 209f.; R. Joly, *RBPh* 46 (1968) 950f.; J. E. Menard, *RSR* 42 (1968) 347ff.; J. Moreau, *EPh* 23 (1968) 240f.; J. Ortall, *Cris* 15 (1968) 340; H. Chadwick, *CR* 19 (1969) 238; J. Daniélou, *RecSR* 57 (1969) 115ff.; N. de El Molar, *EstFr* 70 (1969) 279f.; M. E. Lauzière, *RThom* 69 (1969) 157; I. Opelt, *Gn* 41 (1969) 503f.; J. Oroz Reta, *RET* 29 (1969) 86f.; J. Ortall, *Augustinus* 14 (1969) 198; M. Whittaker, *JThS* 20 (1969) 273f.; W. Wiefel, *ThLZ* 94 (1969) 357f.; A. Orbe, *Gr* 51 (1970) 774f.; J. C. M. van Winden, *VChr* 25 (1971) 63f.; A. V. Nazzaro, *Vich* n.s. 1 (1972) 81. (= R65)

2222. Vol. 31, *In Flaccum*, introduction, traduction et notes par A. PELLETIER (Paris 1967); French title *[De Philon] Contre Flaccus*.

The Introduction gives a close analysis of the text with the purpose of placing the various characters who appear in it against their historical background. The final section deals with the political and cultural situation of the Jews in Alexandria. Although the Introduction is fairly brief, the volume does approach the status of a commentary by virtue of the generous notes, to which sixteen 'Complementary notes' are added (157-165), as well as four Excursus (167-184) which explore important themes of the work in greater depth. REVIEWS: P. Courcelle, *REA* 69 (1967) 452ff.; H. Crouzel, *BLE* 68 (1967) 221f.; J. Moreau, *EPh* 22 (1967) 494; F. Petit, *RThAM* 34 (1967) 274; J. A. de Aldama, *EE* 43 (1968) 603f.; P. Fransen, *Bijdr* 29 (1968) 209f.; C. Martin, *NRTh* 90 (1968) 662ff.; D. M. Pippidi, *StudCl* 10 (1968) 312f.; E. M. Smallwood, *JThS* 19 (1968) 258f.; W. Wiefel, *ThLZ* 93 (1968) 438; N. de El Molar, *EstFr* 70 (1969) 277f.; A. Orbe, *Gr* 51 (1970) 208; S. Sandmel, *Eras* 22 (1970) 679ff.; J. C. M. van Winden, *VChr* 25 (1971) 62; A. V. Nazzaro, *Vich* n.s. 1 (1972) 86. (= R66)

2223. Vol. 22, *De vita Mosis I-II*, introduction, traduction et notes par R. ARNALDEZ, C. MONDÉSERT, P. SAVINEL (Paris 1967); French title *La vie de Moïse, Livre I et II*.

Both the Introduction and the notes are extremely brief and do not provide the reader with adequate assistance. REVIEWS: P. Courcelle, *REA* 69 (1967) 452f.; G. Jouassard, *BFCL* 43 (1967) 50; J. Moreau, *EPh* 22 (1967) 493; F. Petit, *RThAM* 34 (1967) 273f.; B. M., *RFN* 60 (1968) 149f.; H. Crouzel, *RAM* 44 (1968) 464; J. A. de Aldama, *EE* 43 (1968) 603f.; P. Fransen, *Bijdr* 29(1968) 209f.; R. Joly, *RBPh* 46 (1968) 950; C. Martin, *NRTh* 90 (1968) 662ff.; N. de El Molar, *EstFr* 70 (1969) 278; M. Hadas Lebel, *REG* 82 (1969) 668ff.; M. E. Lauzière, *RThom* 69 (1969) 156f.; G. Torti, *Paid* 24 (1969) 373f.; W. Wiefel, *ThLZ* 94 (1969) 357f.; A. Orbe, *Gr* 51(1970) 209; S. Sandmel, *Eras* 22 (1970) 679ff.; Z. P., *RMI* 36 (1970) 333f.; A. V. Nazzaro, *Vich* n.s.1 (1972) 94f.; E. Valgiglio, *Maia* 24 (1972) 283ff.; J. C. M. van Winden, *VChr* 26 (1972) 60ff. (= R67)

2224. Vol. 30, *De aeternitate mundi*, introduction et notes par R. ARNALDEZ, traduction par J. POUILLOUX (Paris 1969); French title *De l'incorruptibilité du monde.*

The very extensive Introduction is divided into two parts: the first is concerned with the authenticity of the work, the second contains an analysis of the treatise in which the author, adhering closely to the text, enlarges on its main themes. The notes are relatively ample and numerous, so that the volume as a whole can be regarded as equivalent to a commentary on *Aet.* For extensive comments on this volume, cf. also **7927.** REVIEWS: F. Petit, *RThAM* 36 (1969) 233; P. Courcelle, *REA* 72 (1970) 236f.; J. Daniélou, *RecSR* 58 (1970) 117ff.; J. A. de Aldama, *EE* 45 (1970) 583f.; J. Moreau, *EPh* 25 (1970) 245f.; A. Orbe, *Gr* 51 (1970) 775; A. Solignac, *ArPh* 33 (1970) 994f.; W. Wiefel, *ThLZ* 95 (1970) 750f.; P. de Fidio, *RSLR* 7 (1971) 339ff.; M. Hadas Lebel, *REG* 84 (1971) 243f.; R. Joly, *RBPh* 49 (1971) 672; M. Whittaker, *JThS* 22 (1971) 216f.; C. Martin, *NRTh* 94 (1972) 823f.; A. V. Nazzaro, *Vich* n.s. 1 (1972) 79; J. C. M. van Winden, *VChr* 26 (1972) 64f.; A. Guillaumont, *RHR* 184 (1973) 80ff. (= R68)

2225. Vol. 17, *De fuga et inventione*, introduction, texte, traduction et commentaire par E. STAROBINSKI-SAFRAN (Paris 1970); French title *La fuite et la découverte.*

Given the amplitude of the annotation, this volume may also be considered virtually a commentary. The Introduction, after analyzing the place of the treatise within the Philonic corpus, expands on its basic themes, in particular on the allegorical meaning of some of the characters and figures in the text. The translation, amply furnished with footnotes and with thirty-five 'Complementary notes' (267-294), is based on the text of C-W, with a few modifications listed at 100f. This work corresponds to a doctoral thesis defended at the University of Geneva and published in 1970 by the same publishing house (Cerf), but outside the series. REVIEWS: P. Courcelle, *REA* 72 (1970) 484ff.; J. A. de Aldama, *EE* 45 (1970) 583f.; J. Moreau, *EPh* 25 (1970) 408f.; A. Orbe, *Gr* 51 (1970) 774; F. Petit, *RThAM* 37 (1970) 152; M. Bogaert, *RBen* 81 (1971) 349; A. Solignac, *ArPh* 34 (1971) 162ff.; M. Whittaker, *JThS* 22 (1971) 215f.; W. Wiefel, *ThLZ* 96 (1971) 433ff.; C. Martin, *NRTh* 94 (1972) 823; R. Joly, *RBPh* 50 (1972) 192; G. de Carrea, *RET* 32 (1972) 481; E. des Places, *RPh* 45 (1972) 309; M. Aubineau, *Script* 26 (1972) 217; A. V. Nazzaro, *Vich* n.s. 1 (1972) 87f.; A. Guillaumont, *RHR* 184 (1973) 80f.; J. C. M. van Winden, *VChr* 28 (1974) 62; P. Bonnard, *RThPh* 108 (1975) 59f.; M. Hadas Lebel, *REG* 88 (1975) 360f.; R. Hissette, *RPhL* 73 (1975) 208f. (= R69)

2226. Vol. 25, *De specialibus legibus III et IV*, introduction, traduction et notes par A. MOSÈS (Paris 1970); French title *Des lois spéciales*...

The Introduction pays particular attention to the main legal themes of the treatise and their relations to political and ethical questions. The amply annotated translation is supplemented with seven excursus (351-361), which help to make the volume equivalent to a commentary. At 44f. there is a list of modifications to the text of C-W adopted in the translation. REVIEWS: M. Bogaert, *RBen* 81(1971) 349; P. Courcelle, *REA* 73 (1971) 469ff.; J. Moreau, *EPh* 26 (1971) 391f.; E. des Places, *RPh* 46 (1972) 309; R. Joly, *RBPh* 50 (1972) 193; C. Martin, *NRTh* 94 (1972) 742; A. V. Nazzaro, *Vich* n.s.1 (1972) 100f.; A. Orbe, *Gr* 53 (1972) 789; F. Petit, *RThAM* 32 (1972) 257; M. Whittaker, *JThS* 23 (1972) 187; M. Aubineau, *Script* 27 (1973) 198; A. Guillaumont, *RHR* 184 (1973) 80f.; P. Sousa, *RET* 33(1973) 81; J. C. M. van Winden, *VChr* 28 (1974) 63; R. Winling, *RSR* 48 (1974) 81f.; P. Courcelle, *REA* 77 (1975) 398f.; M. Hadas Lebel, *REG* 88 (1975) 361f.; R. Hissette, *RPhL* 73 (1975) 208; T. Kobusch, *Gn* 48 (1976) 340ff. (= R70)

2227. Vol. 32, *Legatio ad Caium*, introduction, traduction et notes par A. PELLETIER (Paris 1972); French title *Philon, Des vertus I ou de son ambassade auprès de Caius*.

The Introduction offers a stylistic and historical analysis of the treatise, with special attention being paid to the chronology of the events and to the social status of the Jews in the Empire of Philo's day. The notes are exceptionally full and are augmented with a series of nineteen 'Complementary notes' (323-347) and nine Excursus (349-378), which give the work as a whole the character of an extended commentary. REVIEWS: M. Bogaert, *RBen* 82 (1972) 361; C. Martin, *NRTh* 94 (1972) 823ff.; A. Orbe, *Gr* 53 (1972) 789; P. Bonnard, *RThPh* 106 (1973) 262; P. Courcelle, *REA* 75 (1973) 431ff.; H. Crouzel, *BLE* 74 (1973) 77; A. Guillaumont, *RHR* 184 (1973) 80ff.; D. M. Pippidi, *StudCl* 15 (1973) 248ff.; W. Wiefel, *ThLZ* 98 (1973) 297f.; C. W. Macleod, *CR* 24 (1974) 293f.; A. Paul, *RecSR* 62 (1974) 415f.; F. Petit, *RThAM* 41(1974) 211; J. C. M. van Winden, *VChr* 28 (1974) 146; J. A. de Aldama, *EE* 50 (1975) 558f.; J. Moreau, *EPh* 32 (1975) 221; R. Winling, *RSR* 49 (1975) 359. (= R71)

2228. Vol. 6, *De posteritate Caini,* introduction, traduction et notes par R. ARNALDEZ (Paris 1972); French title *La posterité de Caïn, le Sophiste et son exil*.

The Introduction faithfully follows the structure of the treatise and deals at some length with a few of its themes, in particular with the etymologies and names with a double meaning. At the end of the Introduction there is a list of the passages – a dozen in all – where the text differs from C-W. The notes to the translation are quite extensive. REVIEWS: P. Courcelle, *REA* 75 (1973) 433f.; A. Guillaumont, *RHR* 184 (1973) 80ff.; J. Moreau, *EPh* 30 (1973) 99f.; F. Petit, *RThAM* 40 (1973) 218; M. Whittaker, *JThS* 24 (1973) 643f.; M. Bogaert, *RBen* 84 (1974) 241; C. Martin, *NRTh* 96 (1974) 203; A. Paul, *RecSR* 62 (1974) 416f.; J. C. M. van Winden, *VChr* 28 (1974) 147; J. A. de Aldama, *EE* 50 (1975) 558f.; M. Hadas Lebel, *REG* 88 (1975) 362ff.; W. Wiefel, *ThLZ* 100 (1975) 44ff. (= R72)

2229. Vol. 35, *De providentia I et II*, introduction, traduction et notes par M. HADAS-LEBEL (Paris 1973); French title *La providence*.

The Introduction is concerned with the composition and transmission of the text and also with the work's philosophical content, paying special attention to its cosmological and theological themes. The translation is based on Aucher's Latin version, except for the Greek fragments preserved in Eusebius' *Praeparatio Evangelica*, for which the author has relied on the critical edition by K. Mras (Berlin 1954-56). The notes are reasonably extensive, but cannot address all the problems of this work, which on account of its indirect transmission is exceptionally difficult. The volume concludes with ten fragments of *Prov.* transmitted through Patristic literature (cf. **1811**) and a series of indices. REVIEWS: F. Petit, *RThAM* 40 (1973) 218; M. Bogaert, *RBen* 84 (1974) 241; E. des Places, *Or* 43 (1974) 256f.; C. Martin, *NRTh* 96 (1974) 203; A. Paul, *RecSR* 62 (1974) 418f.; W. Wiefel, *ThLZ* 99 (1974) 261ff.; A. Davids, *OrChr* 59(1975) 192ff.; J. A. de Aldama, *EE* 50 (1975) 558f.; N. J. Séd, *REJ* 134 (1975) 153ff.; A. Solignac, *ArPh* 38 (1975) 131f.; J. van Banning, *ThPh* 50 (1975) 98ff.; J. C. M. van Winden, *VChr* 29 (1975) 147; C. Steel, *TF* 38 (1976) 474f.; J. Moreau, *EPh* 32 (1977) 243;.V. Nikiprowetzky, *RHR* 193 (1978) 71ff. (= R73)

2230. Vol. 28, *Quod omnis probus liber sit*, introduction, texte, traduction et notes par M. PETIT (Paris 1974); French title *Tout homme vertueux est libre*.

This volume has the amplitude and the features of a proper commentary. After giving a historical and philological analysis of the treatise, the Introduction is chiefly concerned with its philosophical content, which it relates to the main trends of Greek (classical and Hellenistic) thought and to Jewish culture. Besides the very ample notes to the translation, there are 'Complementary notes' at 249-254. REVIEWS: M. Bogaert, *RBen* 84 (1974) 425; P. Courcelle, *REA* 76 (1974) 449f.; A. Paul, *RecSR* 62 (1974) 419ff.; F. Petit, *RThAM* 41 (1974) 210; J. A. de Aldama, *EE* 50 (1975) 558f.; C. Martin, *NRTh* 97 (1975) 65; A. Solignac, *ArPh* 38 (1975) 485f.; J. C. M. van Winden, *VChr* 29 (1975) 148; M. Whittaker, *JThS* 26 (1975) 182f.; W. Wiefel, *ThLZ* 100 (1975) 134ff.; M. Aubineau, *Script* 30 (1976) 168; G. Filoramo, *RSLR* 12 (1976) 466f.; J. van Banning, *ThPh* 51 (1976) 157; J. Moreau, *EPh* 34 (1977) 243; M. Hadas Lebel, *REG* 91 (1978) 253; V. Nikiprowetzky, *RHR* 193 (1978) 114ff. (= R74)

2231. Vol. 24, *De specialibus legibus I et II*, introduction, traduction et notes par S. DANIEL (Paris 1975); French title *Des lois spéciales...*

The Introduction is divided into two chapters: one devoted to the composition and the structure of *Spec.*, in which it faithfully follows the development of the treatise; the other devoted to the writing's philosophical contents, with particular attention paid to its ethical and pedagogical thought. The footnotes are augmented with 'Complementary notes' at 221-224. REVIEWS: M. Bogaert, *RBen* 85 (1975) 422; P. Courcelle, *REA* 77 (1975) 398f.; J. A. de Aldama, *EE* 50 (1975) 558f.; H. Crouzel, *BLE* 77 (1976) 215; F. Petit, *RThAM* 43 (1976) 256; J. C. M. van Winden, *VChr* 30 (1976) 159f.; Bouttier, *ETR* 52 (1977) 564; J. van Banning, *ThPh* 53 (1978) 574f. (= R75)

2232. Vol. 33, *Quaestiones in Genesim et in Exodum: fragmenta graeca*, introduction, texte critique et notes par F. PETIT (Paris 1978).

See **1814**. (= R76)

2233. Vol. 34A, *Quaestiones et solutiones in Genesim I et II e versione armeniaca*, introduction, traduction et notes par C. MERCIER (Paris 1979);

French title *Questions et réponses de Philon sur la Genèse.*

This volume offers Aucher's Latin translation facing the French translation, but the latter itself is based directly on the Armenian text. In matters of philological detail it shows many improvements on the version of Marcus (**2111–12**), but lacks the latter's attempts at retranslating important terms back into the original Greek. The Introduction is primarily devoted to the manuscript tradition. The notes to the translation are numerous but brief, and focus mainly on philological matters. No attempt is made to further the more general interpretation of these neglected works. REVIEWS: F. Petit, *Muséon* 92 (1979) 403f.; J. Bernard, *MSR* 37 (1980) 40; H. Crouzel, *BLE* 81 (1980) 210f.; R. Joly, *AC* 49 (1980) 347; J. P. Mahé, *REArm* 14 (1980) 473ff; L. Martin, *NRTh* 102 (1980) 608ff.; A. Paul, *RecSR* 68 (1980) 540; F. Petit, *RThAM* 47 (1980) 283; M. Philonenko, *RHPhR* 60 (1980) 257; E. des Places, *RPh* 54 (1980) 170; J. C. M. van Winden, *VChr* 34 (1980) 89ff.; E. Cattaneo, *OrChrP* 47 (1981) 275f.; E. Junod, *RThPh* 113 (1981) 293; W. Wiefel *ThLZ* 106 (1981) 180ff.; M. Bogaert, *Script* 36 (1982) 50; H. Chadwick, *JThS* 33 (1982) 536; G. Delling, *OLZ* 77 (1982) 567f.; A. Orbe, *Gr* 63 (1982) 368; A. Solignac, *ArPh* 45 (1982) 155; M. J. Pierre, *RB* 89 (1982) 305; M. Devriendt, *Byz* 53 (1983) 763f.; A. Terian, *JSAS* 2 (1985-86) 187ff. (= R77)

2234. Vol. 34B, *Quaestiones et Solutiones in Genesim III-IV-V-VI e versione armeniaca*, introduction, traduction et notes par C. MERCIER, Complément de l'ancienne version latine, texte et apparat critique, traduction et notes par F. PETIT (Paris 1984); French title *Questions et réponses de Philon sur la Genèse.*

Contains the French translation opposite Aucher's Latin translation of the Armenian version of *QG*. Mercier has adopted the division into six books, but has maintained the universally adopted continuous numeration of the *Quaestiones* and *Solutiones* in the final three books. Once again the notes are confined to philological matters. The last part of the book (515-549), edited by F. Petit, contains the text and translation of the 11 *Quaestiones* which have come down to us in Latin translation only and are situated between *QG* 4.195 and 196 of Aucher's translation. REVIEWS: J. Pouilloux, *CRAI* (1984) 718; M. Bogaert, *RBen* 95 (1985) 347; C. Granado Bellido, *EE* 60 (1985) 361; L. Leloir, *Muséon* 98 (1985) 376ff.; J. Liébaert, *MSR* 42 (1985) 97; G. Pelland, *OrChrP* 51 (1985) 231f.; M. Philonenko, *RHPhR* 65 (1985) 485; J. C. M. van Winden, *VChr* 39 (1985) 406ff.; A. le Boulluec, *REG* 99 (1986) 214f.; A. Paul, *RecSR* 74 (1986) 156f.; M. J. Pierre, *RB* 93 (1986) 467; A. Terian, *JSAS* 2 (1985-86) 187ff.; W. Wiefel *ThLZ* 111 (1986) 268f. (RR)

b. Translations of single works

2251. R. ARNALDEZ, *Philon d'Alexandrie, De opificio mundi*, traduction avec introduction et commentaire analytique. Thèse complémentaire à la 'Faculté des Lettres' (Paris 1955).

After a general presentation of Philo which focusses on the mediating role he plays between Judaism and Hellenism, the author examines the position of *Opif.* in the context of the Philonic corpus and the method used by Philo in this work. The commentary contains an annotated synthesis, followed by an analysis of each paragraph of the work (xlviii-xcvi). The translation, with brief, primarily philological notes, is found at the end of the dissertation. See also **2202**. (= R78)

2252. R. CADIOU, *Philon d'Alexandrie, La migration d'Abraham* (Paris 1957).

See **1551**. (= R79)

2253. *Le traité de la vie contemplative de Philon d'Alexandrie*, introduction, traduction et notes par P. GEOLTRAIN, Sem 10 (Paris 1960).

After some bibliographical notes, the fairly brief but significant Introduction deals specifically with the sect of the Therapeutae and discusses its connections with the Pythagoreans and the Essenes. With regard to the latter problem, which took on an entirely new dimension in the light of the Qumran manuscripts, the author holds that the Essenes and the Therapeutae were representatives of a single spiritual movement. The translation is based on the text of C-W. REVIEWS: J. Daniélou, *RecSR* 49 (1961) 611; M. E. B., *RB* 69 (1962) 311f.; H. Quecke, *Muséon* 75 (1962) 470f.; W. Rölling, *WZKM* 58 (1962) 226f.; J. P. Asmussen, *AOH* 27 (1963) 55f.; A. Guillaumont, *RHR* 164 (1963) 105f.; A. Neaga, *StTeol* 15 (1963) 631; J. P. Smith, *Bib* 44 (1963) 119; V. Nikiprowetzky, *RPh* 38 (1964) 144ff. (= R80)

4. *Spanish translations*

a. Comprehensive translation

2301-2305. *Obras completas de Filón de Alejandría* (Colección Valores en el tiempo), traducción directa del griego, introducción y notas de J. M. TRIVIÑO, vols. I-V (Buenos Aires 1975-76).

This is the first complete Spanish translation of Philo's works. The Preface, which is essentially popular in aim and style, without penetrating analyses of a scientific kind, emphasizes the philosophical aspects of Philo's thought at the expense of its historical background. The translation follows the same criteria, while the infrequent and brief notes serve mainly to justify and explain choices made in the translation. There are virtually no bibliographical references. For a detailed REVIEW: see especially J. P. MARTIN, 'Las *Obras completas de Filón de Alejandría* editadas recientemente en Buenos Aires y su significación cultural', *Stromata* 37 (1981) 89-98, where the single volumes are analytically reviewed and assessed. (= R81)

2301. Vol. I, 1975.

Contains: Introducción; Sobre la creación del mundo según Moisés (= *Opif.*); Interpretación alegórica de las sagradas leyes contenidas en el Génesis II y III (= *Leg.* I-III); Sobre los querubines, la espada flamígera y Caín primer hombre nacido de hombre (= *Cher.*); Sobre el nacimiento de Abel y los sacrificios ofrecidos por él y su hermano Caín (= *Sacr.*); Sobre las habituales intrigas de lo peor contra lo mejor (= *Det.*).

2302. Vol. II, 1975.

Contains: Sobre la posteridad de Caín y su exilio (= *Post.*); Sobre los gigantes (= *Gig.*); Sobre la inmutabilidad de Dios (= *Deus*); Sobre la agricultura (= *Agr.*); Sobre la obra de Noé como plantador (= *Plant.*); Sobre la ebriedad (= *Ebr.*); Sobre las súplicas e imprecaciones de Noé una vez sobrio (= *Sobr.*); Sobre la confusión de las lenguas (= *Conf.*); Sobre la migración de Abraham (= *Migr.*).

2303. Vol. III, 1976.

Contains: Sobre quién es el heredero de las cosas divinas (= *Her.*); Sobre la unión con los estudios preliminares (= *Congr.*); Sobre la huida y el hallazgo (= *Fug.*); Sobre aquellos cuyos nombres son cambiados y sobre los motivos del so cambios (= *Mut.*); Sobre los sueños enviados por Dios (= *Somn.* I-II); Sobre Abraham (= *Abr.*); Sobre José (= *Ios.*).

2304. Vol. IV, 1976.

Contains: Sobre la vida de Moisés (= *Mos.* I-II); Sobre los diez mandamientos o Decálogo que son compendios de las leyes (= *Decal.*); Sobre las leyes particulares (= *Spec.* I-IV).

2305. Vol. V, 1976.

Contains: Sobre las virtudes (= *Virt.*); Sobre los premios y los castigos (= *Praem.*); Todo hombre bueno es libre (= *Prob.*); Sobre la vida contemplativa (= *Contempl.*); Sobre la indestructibilidad del mundo (= *Aet.*); Flaco (= *Flacc.*); Hipotéticas (Apología de los judíos) (= *Hypoth.*); Sobre la providencia (= *Prov.*); Sobre la embajada ante Cayo (= *Legat.*); Indice de nombres. Of *Prov.* only the Greek fragments preserved in Eusebius are translated. For the index of names, cf. **3205.**

b. Translations of single works.

2351. *Filón, Todo hombre bueno es libre*, traducción del griego, prólogo y notas de F. DE P. SAMARANCH, Biblioteca de Iniciación filosófica (Buenos Aires 1962, 1977⁴). (= R82)

2352. *Filón de Alejandria, El tratado de la vida contemplativa*, versión castellana de R. LEON (Málaga 1964). (= R83)

2353. *Filó d'Alexandria, La llibertat de l'home virtuós, La creació del món, L'emigració d'Abraham*, traducció i edició a cura de J. MONTSERRAT I TORRENTS (Barcelona 1983).

A brief synoptic presentation of Philo and an analytical exposition of the writings presented in this volume (1-26) is followed by the translations of the following treatises: *Prob.* (29-67); *Opif.* (71-127); *Migr.* (129-185). The translations are very briefly annotated. (RR)

5. *Translations in Italian*

a. Comprehensive translation

There is no complete translation of Philo's writings in Italian. From 1978 onwards, however, five volumes have appeared in the series I classici del pensiero, section I Filosofia classica e tardo-antica, published by Rusconi in Milan. When the sixth appears in 1988 the entire Allegorical Commentary, including *Opif.*, will have been translated. Moreover the fifth volume (**2405**) serves as an introduction to the series of translations. In our bibliography we separate these works from other, more incidental publications.

2401. *Filone di Alessandria, La creazione del mondo*, prefazione, traduzione e note di G. CALVETTI. *Le allegorie delle leggi*, prefazione, traduzione e note di R. BIGATTI, a cura di G. REALE, (Milan 1978).

The lengthy Introduction gives a general presentation of Philo, with emphasis on the mediating role he played between Jewish and Hellenistic culture, and, in particular, on the nature of his theological thought. The translations of single works are preceded by a preface and by a schematic analysis of contents. The notes are fairly copious. The translation of *Opif.* is the third to appear in Italian: the previous ones date back to 1570, by M. A. Ferentilli, and to 1922-23, by N. Festa (cf. G-G **1001**, 208 and 196 respectively). *Leg.*, on the other hand, is here translated into Italian for the first time. The volume as a whole has the merit of re-introducing Philo the philosopher to Italy and is the first such work to be based on the principles of modern research. REVIEW: S. Amato, *RIFD* 56 (1979) 133ff. (= R85)

2402. *Filone di Alessandria, L'erede delle cose divine*, prefazione, traduzione e note di R. RADICE, Introduzione di G. REALE, (Milan 1981).

The very extensive Introduction, though focussing on the treatise's own themes, locates in its underlying pattern several themes which are essential to Philo's philosophical thought from theological and anthropological as well as ethical and cosmological points of view. The final part (89-124) also offers an annotated synthesis of the work. At the end of the volume there is, among other things, an index of the biblical characters cited in *Her.* with their allegorical meaning and references to parallels in the rest of Philo's works. To our knowledge this is the first Italian translation of *Her.* REVIEWS: A. Ghisalberti, *RFN* 73 (1981) 741ff.; G. Leonardi, *StudPat* 28 (1981) 410ff. (= R87)

2403. *Filone di Alessandria: Le origini del male. I Cherubini, I sacrifici di Abele e di Caino, Il malvagio tende a sopraffare il buono, La posterità di Caino, I Giganti, L'immutabilità di Dio*, traduzione di C. MAZZARELLI, introduzione, prefazioni, note e apparati di R. RADICE, (Milan 1984).

The Introduction analyzes the basic themes of the treatises in question, with particular emphasis on Philo's allegorical method (10ff.) and aretology (30ff.). The translation –

covering *Cher., Sacr., Det., Post., Gig., Deus* – is furnished with extensive notes and with prefaces and summaries of contents introducing each treatise. The work concludes with a series of indices (of persons and biblical quotations) and appendices which explain the references in the treatises to the biblical text and, in the case of *Gig.* and *Deus*, also give the references to the corresponding *Quaestiones* (*QG* 1.89-99). REVIEW: B. Belletti, *Sap* 38 (1985) 486f. (RR)

2404. *Filone di Alessandria: L'uomo e Dio. Il connubio con gli studi preliminari, La fuga e il ritrovamento, Il mutamento dei nomi, I sogni sono mandati da Dio*, introduzione, traduzione, prefazioni, note e apparati di C. KRAUS REGGIANI, presentazione di G. REALE, (Milan 1986).

The introduction, entitled 'The encounter with God in the Philonic search', presents an overview of the treatises translated in the volume (*Congr., Fug., Mut., Somn.*), and also deals with the theme of progress (19-29) and its anthropological foundations, which can be traced back to the concept of man as μεθόριος between the sensible and the supra-sensible worlds. Each treatise is introduced by extensive prefaces and reading lists, and is furnished with ample notes. The work concludes with a 'systematic thematic index of biblical texts in the four treatises with references to the places in which they are quoted and interpreted' and with indices of persons and biblical quotations. (RR)

2405*. *Filone di Alessandria: la filosofia Mosaica. La creazione del mondo secondo Mosè*, traduzione di C. KRAUS REGGIANI, *Le allegorie delle Leggi*, traduzione di R. RADICE, prefazioni, apparati e commentari di R. RADICE, monografia introduttiva di G. REALE and R. RADICE, (Milan 1987).

2406*. *Filone di Alessandria: la migrazione verso l'eterno. L'agricoltura, La piantagione di Noè, L'ebrietà, La sobrietà, La confusione delle lingue, La migrazione*, presentazione di G. REALE, saggio introduttivo, traduzione, prefazioni, note e apparati di R. RADICE, (Milan 1988).

b. Translations of single works

2451. C. KRAUS, *Filone Alessandrino e un'ora tragica della storia ebraica*, prefazione di A. FERRABINO (Naples 1967).

The initial part of the book should not just be regarded as an introduction, for it is virtually a complete monograph. It starts by discussing the connections between *Flacc.* and *Legat.* and goes on to analyze the contents of *Flacc.*, the guiding motif of which it locates in the concept of Providence. The two chapters entitled 'Composition and structure' and 'Interpretations' are mainly concerned with historical and literary problems pertaining to the two works, while the legal position of the Jews in Alexandria is discussed at length at 143-158. The translations of *Flacc.* and *Legat.* are found at 165-195 and 197-254. Kraus deserves credit for having taken up the task of translating Philo into Italian after a long period of neglect, even if these two works are without philosophical interest. The translation of *Flacc.* is the first to appear in Italian, but there is a complete translation of *Legat.* by G. Belloni dating from 1828 (cf. G-G **1001**, 209, who also make note of a partial translation by G. Bertoli dating from 1885; neither work has a sound scholarly basis). REVIEWS: A. V. Nazzaro, *ParPass* 122 (1968) 396f.; Y. C., *RMI* 35 (1969) 233f.; A. Ferrua, *CivCatt* 121 (1970) 406f.; A. V. Nazzaro, *Vich* n.s. 1 (1972) 86, 93. (= R84)

2452. C. KRAUS REGGIANI, *Filone Alessandrino, De opificio mundi, De Abrahamo, De Josepho*. Analisi critiche, testi tradotti e commentati, Biblioteca Athena 23 (Rome 1979).

Each of the works translated is introduced by a lengthy analysis explaining the main themes and is briefly annotated. The Introduction to *Opif.* is of interest in that it offers reasons – though these are debatable – for giving the treatise a different place in the Philonic corpus from the one in general use since Cohn (but cf. also the German translation, **2001**). The translation of *Opif.* is in fact the fourth to be published in Italian (cf. **2401**); the translation of *Ios.* is the second in Italian – the previous one, by P. F. Zino, dates from 1574 – but the first to be based on sound scholarship. *Abr.*, however, is presented here in Italian for the first time. A revised version of the translation of *Opif.* appears in **2405***. (= R86)

6. *Dutch translation*

2500. In the period 1937-86 no Dutch translations of the writings of Philo were produced, with the exception of some short extracts by D. T. RUNIA; see below **8536**.

7. *Hebrew translations*

a. Comprehensive translation

2601. S. DANIEL-NATAF [ס. דניאל-נתף] (ed.), פילון האלכסנדרוני. כתבים [ס. דניאל-נתף] [Philo of Alexandria: *Writings*]: vol. 1, Historical writings, Apologetical writings (Jerusalem 1986).

This long-awaited volume marks the beginning of the first complete Hebrew translation of the Philonic corpus. The general editor of the series explains that the writings have been organized strictly according to genre, and will be presented in the order suggested by E. R. Goodenough (cf. **4007**). The present volume therefore contains Philo's historical works (*Flacc.*, *Legat.*, translated by A. KASHER) and apologetic works (*Hypoth.*, translated by D. ROKEAH; *Contempl.*, translated by S. DANIEL-NATAF; *Mos.*, translated by S. DANIEL-NATAF, H. WOHLMAN). Succeeding volumes will offer the general (II-III) and allegorical (IV-V) expositions of the Law. The translations are accompanied by substantial introductions and detailed annotation. (DS)

b. Translations of single works

2651. M. STEIN [שטיין .מ] (tr.), כתבי הסטוריה: נגד כתבי הסטוריה. פילון האלכסנדרוני.
פלאקוס. המלאכות אל קאיוס [= Philo of Alexandria: *Historical writings: In Flaccum, Legatio ad Gaium*] (Tel Aviv 1937).

Contains a translation, introduction and notes on the two treatises. Introduction reprinted in **7034**. (DS)

2652. J.-G. KAHN [כהן-ישר .י] (tr.), על החלומות. פילון האלכסנדרוני
(ספר א׳) [= Philo of Alexandria: *De Somniis* I] (Ramat Gan 1968).

Translation only, published in a stencilled form. The author will furnish a complete translation of the treatise (*Somn*. I-II) in the projected Hebrew complete works (cf. **2601**). (DS)

2653. N. G. COHEN [כהן-ישר .י] (tr.), חיי איש המדינה. פילון האלכסנדרוני
הוא על יוסף [Philo Judaeus: *The life of the statesman... On Joseph*] (Jerusalem 1965).

Contains a translation, introduction and notes. (DS)

2654. D. ROKEAH [רוקח .ד] (tr.), על עשרת על ההשגחה. פרקי פילון: על
הדברות. היפותטיקה [Philonis Alexandrini: *De Providentia, De Decalogo, Hypothetica*] (Jerusalem 1976).

Contains a translation and notes on the treatises concerned, preceded by a lengthy general introduction on Philonic research. (DS)

2655. C. SCHUR [שור .ח] (tr.), על אברהם מאת פילון האלכסנדרוני [*De Abrahamo* by Philo of Alexandria] (M.A. Thesis, Tel Aviv University 1981).

Contains a translation, introduction and notes. (DS)

D. ANTHOLOGIES

Most of these works, and particularly those which provide translations by others or which are limited to collections of fragmentary passages, have a primarily introductory or propaedeutic value. We list here the more extensive or important, and make no claim to completeness.

3001. G. BLIN and R. M. GUASTALLA, 'Traité de la Monarchie divine par Philon-le-Juif', *Mesures* 5 (1939) 155-176.

This volume offers a translation and amply annotated commentary of *Spec*. 1.13-65, a section which in the Philonic mss. has the subtitle 'The laws concerning monarchy'. The translation is based on C-W. (= R92)

3002. *Philo, philosophical writings: selections*, edited by H. LEWY, Philosophia Judaica: selections from the writings of the most eminent Hebrew thinkers in English translations (Oxford 1946).

Cf. **3009** (and for a Hebrew translation, **3012**). (= R93)

3003. *Hellenistic Greek Texts*, edited by A. WIKGREN with the collaboration of E. C. COLWELL and R. MARCUS (Chicago 1947, 1969⁶), 81-86.

Reproduces Cohn-Wendland's edition of passages from *Leg*. I and *Mos*. II. The texts are preceded by a brief introduction to the life and works of Philo. (= R94)

3004. *Judaism, postbiblical and Talmudic period*, edited with an introduction and notes by S. W. BARON and J. L. BLAU (New York 1954), 31-53.

Reproduces Colson's translation of passages from *Spec.*, *Opif.*, *Hypoth.*, *Mos.*, *Flacc.*, on theological, religious, ethical, and political themes. (= R95)

3005. M. C. WATHELET, *L'héritier des biens divins de Philon d'Alexandrie et l'héritier de Dieu de Saint Paul* (diss. Louvain 1954) 62-107.

Contains the translation – the first to appear in French – of a large part of *Her.*, preceded by a brief introduction to and description of the treatise. Only the main passages are translated; the rest is given in summary. See further **5413**. (= R96)

3006. C. J. DE VOGEL, *Greek Philosophy: a collection of texts, with notes and explanations*. Vol. III The Hellenistic-Roman Period (Leiden 1959, 1964²) 353-376.

This is not just a selection of numerous Philonic texts printed in the Greek of C-W's edition. The author attempts to place Philo in his philosophical context: he is regarded as belonging to what she calls 'Prae-Neoplatonism', but with the difference that Philo accepts revelation. Moreover the passages are ordered in a systematic fashion and furnished with brief introductions and annotations. The chief emphasis lies on the doctrines of God and the Logos. (= R97)

3007. C. K. BARRETT, *The New Testament background: selected documents* (London-New York 1961), esp. 173-189.

Contains selections from Philo's writings, presented in translation with brief commentary, illustrating his faithfulness to the Law, philosophical eclecticism, the allegorical method, etymological arguments, doctrine of the Logos, and his religious and ethical views. (DTR)

3008. J. L. SAUNDERS, *Greek and Roman philosophy after Aristotle* (New York-London 1966), esp. 10-11, 199-227.

As part of the anthology of texts illustrating the development of Greek philosophy in the Hellenistic and Imperial periods, this text-book contains a complete but wholly unannotated translation (by Whitaker) of the *De opificio mundi*. (DTR)

3009. *Three Jewish philosophers, Philo: selections*, edited by H. LEWY; *Saadya Gaon: book of doctrines and beliefs*, edited by A. ALTMANN; *Jehuda Halevi: Kuzari*, edited by I. HEINEMANN (New York 1969, 1974⁴), esp. 5-110.

An unchanged reproduction of the 1946 edition. The Introduction offers a general presentation of the figure of Philo and clarifies his mediating role between Judaism and Hellenism, between Greek theism and Jewish monotheism, between Stoic morality and Mosaic law. Lacking among the texts translated by Lewy are those with a historical character (*Flacc., Legat.*) and the primarily philosophical works (*Aet., Prob., Prov., Anim.*). (= R98)

3010. *Philo Judaeus: the essential Philo*, edited by N. N. GLATZER (New York 1971).

Photomechanically reproduces C. D. Yonge's – by now totally out-dated – translation (London 1854) of 7 complete Philonic treatises and parts of four others. A brief preface and twenty pages of notes are added. Modern chapter numbers are not furnished. The incipient student of Philo is advised not to make use of this collection. (= R99/DTR)

3011. *Philo of Alexandria: about the life of Moses*, translated by D. L. DUNGAN, in D. L. DUNGAN, D. R. CARTLIDGE (edd.), *Sourcebook of texts for the comparative study of the Gospels*, Sources for Biblical Study 1 (Missoula 1973), esp. 297-345.

Translates passages from *Mos.* I and II. (= R100)

3012. H. LEWY [לוי .י] (ed.), כתביו הפילוסופיים של פילון [Philo: *Philo-sophical writings.*] translated into Hebrew by Y. AMIR [עמיר .י] (Jerusalem 1964, 1975²).

Reproduces Lewy's anthology (cf. **3002**) in a thoughtful Hebrew translation. (DS)

3013. *Philo of Alexandria: The contemplative Life, The giants and selections*, translation and introduction by D. WINSTON, preface by J. DILLON, The Classics of Western Spirituality (New York-Toronto 1981).

On this, by far the best anthology of Philo's writings at present available, see below **8133**.

E. COMMENTARIES

3100. Few commentaries have been written on Philonic writings during the past fifty years. Of the works expressly presented as such, three have already been cited in the sections dealing with critical texts and translations: the commentary on the Old Latin version of *QG* 4.154-245 by F. PETIT (**1601**), on the De animalibus by A. TERIAN (**1704**), on *Flacc.* by H. BOX (**2151**), and on *Legat.* by E. M. SMALLWOOD (**2152**). Moreover the following list of works in the French OPA series can considered tantamount to commentaries on account of the amplitude of their annotation. We list them in order of appearance in C-W: vol. 1 *Opif.* by R. ARNALDEZ (**2202**, cf. also **2251**); vol. 4 *Sacr.* by A. MÉASSON (**2220**); vol. 13 *Conf.* by J. G. KAHN (**2209**); vol. 14 *Migr.* by J. CAZEAUX (**2217**); vol. 15 *Her.* by M. HARL (**2219**); vol. 18 *Congr.* by M. ALEXANDRE (**2221**); vol. 17 *Fug.* by E. STAROBINSKI-SAFRAN (**2225**); vol. 23 *Decal.* by V. NIKIPROWETZKY (**2215**); vol. 24 *Spec.* 1-2 by S. DANIEL (**2231**); vol. 25 *Spec.* 3-4 by A. MOSÈS (**2226**); vol. 28 *Prob.* by M. PETIT (**2230**); vol. 29 *Contempl.* by F. DAUMAS (**2210**); vol. 30 *Aet.* by R. ARNALDEZ (**2224**); vol. 31 *Flacc.* by A. PELLETIER (**2222**); vol. 32 *Legat.* by A. PELLETIER (**2227**); vol. 35 *Prov.* by M. HADAS LEBEL (**2229**). See also **3001** (commentary on *Spec.* 1.13-65). The only other works that can be considered commentaries in the true sense are:

3101. D. WINSTON and J. DILLON, *Two treatises of Philo of Alexandria: a commentary on De Gigantibus and Quod Deus Sit Immutabilis*, BJudSt 25 (Chico 1983).

The book is divided into two sections: an introduction, consisting of a series of contributions by various authors which we shall deal with separately (cf. **8324** etc.) and a commentary (231-358) by Winston and Dillon. The latter is in turn divided into two parts: '(a) general comments on the segment as a whole; and (b) detailed line-by-line commentary' (vii). The commentary is the first to be specifically devoted to an exegetical treatise of Philo. Its observations on detailed points of philology and diverse aspects of the intellectual background (Greek and Jewish) of the treatises are of great value. The authors acknowledge the particularly substantial contribution made by V. NIKIPROWETZKY toward the drafting of this commentary. See also **7815**. REVIEWS: J. A. Hickling, *BoL* (1984) 141; P. W. van der Horst, *JSJ* 15 (1984) 214ff.; J. Morris, *JJS* 35 (1984) 91ff.; D. T. Runia, *VChr* 38 (1984) 226ff. (cf. **8447**); R. Williamson, *Herma* 138 (1985) 75f.; D. M. Hay, *JQR* 76 (1986) 379ff.; J. Mansfeld, *Mnem* 39 (1986) 491ff. (RR)

3102*. R. RADICE, 'Commentario a *La creazione del mondo secondo Mosè* e a *Le allegorie delle Leggi*', in *La filosofia mosaica...* (cf. **2405***) (Milan 1987) 234-533.

F. INDICES AND LEXICOGRAPHICAL WORKS

3201. I. LEISEGANG, 'Indices ad Philonis Alexandrini opera', pars I, II (Berlin 1926, 1930) (= **1507-1508**).

We include this work, even though it falls outside the time span of our bibliography, because of the important place it still occupies among the lexicographical instruments available to the Philonist. As Petit observes in her review of Mayer (cf. **3207**), this index, though highly selective and therefore incomplete (it concentrates almost exclusively on philosophical terms), may still render valuable services. For in contrast to Mayer's *Index philoneus* it orders the terms in accordance with the various meanings which they assume in different contexts. The two lexica may therefore be considered complementary. Unfortunately, the practical value of this index is seriously compromised by the fact that it refers to the page and line numbers of C-W, so that it can only be used in combination with this edition. (= R104)

3202. F. KUHR, *Die Gottesprädikationen bei Philo von Alexandrien* (inaug. diss. Marburg 1944).

The lexical analysis presented in this dissertation supplements Leisegang's index with regard to the predicates used of God. The predicates are divided according to a grammatical criterion: substantive predicates, either direct (referring directly to God) or indirect (used instead of God) (1-31); adjectival predicates (31-50); predicates in the form of a participle (50-57). Unfortunately this work is often very difficult to read, because it exists only in manuscript form. A useful if brief complement found in the dissertation of A. BENGIO, *La dialectique de Dieu et de l'homme chez Platon et chez Philon d'Alexandrie: une approche du concept d' ἀρετή chez Philon* (Paris 1971) 101-104. Bengio examines Platonic influences on Philo's terminology, mainly with regard to the concept of God and the relationship God-man (cf. also **7102**). (= R105)

3203. J. W. EARP, 'Indices to Philo', in **2110**,189-520.

The lexicographical section of volume X of the Loeb edition comprises an index of scriptural references (189-268) and an index of names, plus two other indices which do not refer to the texts, but to the notes of the English translation, and which are therefore of less interest. The Index of names is particularly important, being the most extensive and complete of its kind. Its greatest value lies in the fact that it offers a complete survey of the various allegorical meanings which each name has in Philo's writings (Armenian corpus excluded). (= R106)

3204. W. THEILER, 'Sachweiser zu Philo', in **2007**, 386-411.

Offers a highly useful guide to Philo's thought. A large series of references to his works are organized in relation to a number of mainly philosophical *topoi* (also included are some valuable references to philosophical authors). On 388-389 there is a list of Greek poets to whom Philo alludes in his works. (= R107)

3205. J. M. TRIVIÑO, 'Indice de nombres', in **2305**, 393-462.

Reproduces and sometimes literally translates, without acknowledgement, the Index of names in Earp (**3203**). (= R108)

3206. P. BORGEN and R. SKARSTEN, *A complete KWIC-Concordance of Philo's writings* (Trondheim 1974).

The authors have developed a machine readable text of Philo's works, including the Greek fragments. On the basis of this text a key-word-in-context (KWIC) concordance has been produced, listing every occurrence of a word in Philo in its immediate context (compare the Josephus concordance edited by K. H. Rengstorf). It is greatly to be regretted that this valuable lexical resource has not been published in a form that makes it readily accessible to Philo scholars in general. See further *StPh* 2 (1973) 75, 4 (1976-77) 112. (DTR)

3207. G. MAYER, *Index Philoneus* (Berlin-New York 1974).

In this index all words found in Philo's writings (except some very frequent words such as the articles, prepositions etc.) are exhaustively listed, but without any reference to the context in which they occur. It thus differs from the Index of Leisegang, which is not complete, but does indicate the context. The work is based on C-W's *Editio minor*, which also contains the fragments of *Hypoth.* handed down to us through Eusebius and not included in the *Editio maior*. Lacking, however, are references to the Greek fragments of *Prov.*, to those of *QG* and *QE*, and to all the writings transmitted in Armenian. The writings of Philo are indicated by numbers in the text, and are not ordered alphabetically as usual, but according to the position they occupy in C-W. Another drawback of this lexicon is that no attempt has been made to subdivide the usage of frequently found words on semantic or thematic grounds; in this respect Leisegang's Index still remains indispensable. (In this context it is worth noting that the only modern lexicographical work concerned with Philonic writings transmitted in Armenian is the article by R. MARCUS, *An Armenian-Greek index to Philo's 'Quaestiones' and 'De Vita Contemplativa'*, *JAOS* 53 (1933) 251-282. This index is highly selective, however, and therefore incomplete. In fact, it collects only those terms – some seven hundred – on which the Greek and the Armenian text are certainly in agreement. The Armenian terms and the corresponding Greek terms are placed side by side.) REVIEWS: F. Petit, *RThAM* 41 (1974) 209f.; M. Gilbert, *EtCl* 43 (1975) 212f.; J. Irigoin, *BAGB* 13 (1975) 430; W. Reister, *ZRGG* 27 (1975) 166ff. (= **3208**); L. H. Feldman, *CW* 69 (1976) 398f.; F. Petit, *RPhL* 74 (1976) 458f.; R. Weil, *RPh* 50 (1976) 138; C. W. Macleod, *CR* 27 (1977) 108; V. Nikiprowetzky, *REJ* 135 (1977) 434ff.; J. van Ganning, *ThPh* 53 (1978) 575. (= R109)

3208. W. REISTER, 'Zur Problematik eines Philo-Index', *ZRGG* 27 (1975) 166-168.

A penetrating critique of Mayer's *Index Philoneus* (**3207**), on which many of the observations we have made in our notice are based. Abstract in *StPh* 5 (1978) 133. (DTR)

3209. *Biblia Patristica: Supplément, Philon d'Alexandrie*, Centre d'analyse et de documentation patristiques: équipe de recherche associée au Centre National de la Recherche Scientifique: J. ALLENBACH, A. BENOÎT, D. A. BERTRAND, A. HANRIOT-COUSTET, E. JUNOD, P. MARAVAL, A.

PAUTLER, P. PRIGENT (Paris 1982).

Carried out with admirable technical and scientific rigour and a healthy regard for essentials, this work is extremely valuable because it gives an exhaustive list of all Philo's references to the Bible, ranging from direct quotes to casual allusions. The entire Philonic corpus has been covered, including the Armenian works, which have never previously been analyzed from this perspective. Only the references in *Alex.* are lacking, and these can be found in TERIAN **1704**, 323. For those wishing to study Philo's exegetical method and thematics, this slender volume is an indispensable tool. Indeed it should find a place on the desk of every Philonist. The text referred to is the OPA edition, with references to specific editions for those parts not published in that collection (some fragments, some texts in Armenian, *Hypoth.*). On E. Junod's list of fragments (9-14) see above **1818**. REVIEWS: M. Perraymond, *RivAC* 59 (1983) 241f.; V. Roisel, *NRTh* 105 (1983) 434. (= R1095/a)

3210. L. BERKOWITZ and K. A. SQUITIER, *Thesaurus Linguae Graecae: canon of Greek authors and works* (New York-Oxford 1986) 252-253.

The aim of the *Thesaurus Linguae Graecae* project has been to provide a computer data bank of all literary texts written in Greek from Homer to 600 A.D. The *Canon* lists the texts used for all authors already included in the data bank, as well as for those about to be added in the near future. The Philonic corpus has been available since about 1980 (cf. *StPh* 6 (1979-80) 224). It is primarily based on C-W, but also includes Greek fragments (*Quaestiones*, *Hypoth.*, *Prov.*, and selections from the collections of Wendland, Staehle, Lewy, Harris, Stahlschmidt (cf. **1804**), but not from those of Früchtel, Royse and Paramelle). The text is available on magnetic tape and now on compact disk (the latter accessible on the Ibycus Personal Computer produced by David Packard). (DTR)

G. JOURNAL

3301-3306. *Studia Philonica*, vols. 1-6 (Chicago 1972-80).

Six issues of this journal, devoted to the study of Philo and the Hellenistic synagogue, appeared in the years 1972 to 1980. The articles that it contained have either been mentioned in section A devoted to bibliographies (cf. **1009**, **1011**, **1013**, **1015-17**), or will be referred to in Part II devoted to the critical literature. Every issue contains abstracts of the most important contributions on Philo published throughout the world; references to these we have placed, where applicable, at the end of our summaries. *Studia Philonica* is the official organ of the Philo Institute (Chicago) and has been edited by B. L. MACK, E. HILGERT, and a committee made up of all members of the Institute. Unfortunately new issues have not appeared since 1980. At the present time efforts are being made to revive the journal, so that it can continue to be a unique forum for Philonic scholarship. (= R111)

PART TWO

CRITICAL STUDIES

1937-1986

1937

3701. S. BELKIN, 'The Alexandrian source for Contra Apionem II', *JQR* 27 (1936-37) 1-32.

'The evidence discussed indicates clearly that in *Contra Apionem*, II, Josephus is either directly dependent on the *Hypothetica* of Philo or on one of its sources, more probably the former' (31). (DTR)

3702. H. BOGNER, 'Philon von Alexandrien als Historiker', in *Forschungen zur Judenfrage*, Sitzungsberichte der zweiten Arbeitstagung der Forschungsabteilung Judenfrage des Reichsinstituts für Geschichte des neuen Deutschlands vom 12. bis 14. Mai 1937 (Hamburg 1937) 2.63-74.

A structural analysis of Philo's two historical treatises, *Legat.* and *Flacc.*, with special attention paid to the latter. The author's point of view is that in these writings, as elsewhere, propagandistic and apologetic intentions are predominant and expressive of Philo's personality. His assimilation to Hellenism is regarded as no more than superficial; essentially, he remains faithful to Judaism and its laws, which he attempts to credit with all the discoveries of Greek learning. (= R111/a)

3703. J. DEY, *ΠΑΛΙΓΓΕΝΕΣΙΑ: ein Beitrag zur Klärung der religionsgeschichtlichen Bedeutung von Tit. 3,5*, NTA 17.5 (Münster 1937), esp. 8-11, 109-117.

The expression *secunda nativitas* in *QE* 2.46 is translated in Aucher by the term 'regeneration'. The author discusses this interpretation and, analyzing in particular the views of Pascher and Reitzenstein, notes how in Philo this concept is often spiritualized and introduced in the context of man's mystic ascent towards God. (= R111/b)

3704. C. H. DODD, 'Hellenism and Christianity', in *Independence, convergence, and borrowing in institutions, thought, and art*, Harvard Tercentenary publications (Cambridge Mass. 1937) 109-131; reprinted in *HDSB*, 1937, 24-44.

Although Philo is not specifically dealt with in this profound analysis of Christianity's relation to its Judaic and Hellenistic roots, he is frequently referred to as a point of comparison, especially in relation to Paul, the author of Hebrews and John. His thought is regarded as standing closer to Hellenistic religious or mystical philosophy than that of the New Testament writers. (DTR)

3705. E. R. GOODENOUGH, 'Literal Mystery in Hellenistic Judaism', in P. CASEY, S. LAKE, A. K. LAKE (edd.), *Quantulacumque: studies presented to K. Lake by pupils, colleagues and friends* (London 1937) 227-241; reprinted in *Goodenough on the history of Religion and on Judaism* (cf. **8614**) 49-61.

Philo regarded the Old Testament as a guide to the true philosophy, a road to salvation and a means of gaining access to the supernatural. He thus brings about – as Plutarch did in the case of the rites of Isis and Osiris – an allegorical transfiguration of Jewish rites, which come to be regarded as sacraments leading man to mystic salvation (cf. 236). These views are exemplified with many specific references to Philo's writings. (= R111/c)

3706. E. R. GOODENOUGH, 'New Light on Hellenistic Judaism', *JBR* 5 (1937) 18-28.

The author briefly explains his interpretation of Philo's work as the complete and mature expression of a Jewish mystery, recapitulating the views set out at length in his controversial monograph *By light, light* (New Haven-London 1935, Amsterdam 1969²). (= R112)

3707. E. R. GOODENOUGH, *Religious tradition and myth* (New Haven 1937), esp. 68-72.

A brief account of Philo's 'strange Judaism' in the larger context of the development from Greek religion through Hellenistic Judaism to Christianity. (DTR)

3708. I. HEINEMANN, 'Um Philons geschichtliche Stellung', *MGWJ* 81 (1937) 355-368.

A penetrating critical analysis of the views of Goodenough and other Philonic scholars. (= R113)

3709. N. J. HOMMES, 'Philo en Paulus', *PhilRef* 2 (1937) 156-187, 193-223.

A comparison is made of the thought of Philo and Paul with reference to the following topics: (1) creation and God's image; (2) Logos and God's image; (3) the heavenly and the earthly man. In spite of terminological similarities, a fundamental difference emerges between the two writers. Philo interprets Gen. 1-2 from a Platonic dualistic viewpoint, and so posits a basic division in man's make-up. According to Philo's interpretation of Gen. 1:27, man is related to the true or ideal man by means of his higher part, the nous, and is thus a spiritual and immortal being, while it is through his lower part, the body, that he belongs to sense-perceptible reality and is thus corporeal and mortal. Sin is conceived as being worsted by corporeality; salvation occurs through triumphing over and freeing oneself from corporeal existence. Paul on the other hand relates Gen. 1:27 (man as image of God) to the real man as unity of body and soul. Sin is revolt against God. Salvation is liberation from guilt and involves a new corporeality. For Philo the heavenly man is an idea that precedes the earthly man of Gen. 2:7. The heavenly man in Paul is an actual man, namely Christ, and he appears after the earthly man of Gen. 2:7. Philo thinks in philosophical terms: there is an unbridgeable chasm between spirit and matter. Paul thinks in eschatological terms: the whole man is saved through a new creation in Jesus Christ. (RAB/DTR)

3710. W. L. KNOX, 'Pharisaism and Hellenism', in H. LOEWE (ed.),

Judaism and Christianity II: The contact of Pharisaism with other cultures (London 1937) 61-111.

This learned contribution presents a synoptic view of Philo in the context of the relations between Hellenism and Pharisaism. Knox maintains that Philo was neither an eccentric nor an eclectic philosopher, but rather a compiler (cf. 62) who collected in his writings most of the doctrines taught in the schools and synagogues of Alexandria and, by means of the allegorical method, made a serious attempt to present the culture and faith of the Jews as a 'revelation made by God on the stage of history' (109). (= R114)

3711. H. LEISEGANG, 'Philons Schrift über die Ewigkeit der Welt', *Phil* 92 (1937) 156-176.

What Philo says in *Aet.* about the eternity of the world does not correspond to his own convictions, but to those of an opponent. The sequel of the treatise, which is no longer extant, must have contained a refutation in which Philo himself, by way of reply, defended the concept of Providence and the strictly related concept of creation. According to Leisegang, therefore, *Aet.* should not be considered a scholastic work, as Bousset did, nor a juvenile exercise, 'but it belongs to that group of works in which Philo takes issue with the opponents of both the Stoic *Weltanschauung* and his religious conviction – based on Stoic philosophy – of the existence and value of divine Providence' (176). (= R115)

3712. R. MEYER, *Hellenistisches in der rabbinischen Anthropologie*, Beiträge zur Wissenschaft vom Alten und Neuen Testament IV 22 (Stuttgart 1937) *passim.*

The author wishes to show the numerous points of contact between Rabbinic anthropology and Hellenistic philosophy. Philo plays an important role from this point of view and, although Meyer does not devote a separate section to him, his works are constantly cited in relation to the doctrine of the soul and the doctrine of creation, themes which frequently find exact counterparts in the Rabbinic literature after Philo. (= R116)

3713. H. NEUMARK, *Die Verwendung griechischer und jüdischer Motive in den Gedanken Philons über die Stellung Gottes zu seinen Freunden* (inaug. diss. Würzburg 1937).

The central theme of this dissertation is the relationship God-man in Philo, taken in the double sense of descent (God-man) and ascent (man-God). Philo, Neumark observes, is almost exclusively interested in the bond that exists between God and our soul, a bond based on the natural affinity (συγγένεια) between creator and created. The essence of this relationship is love, ἔρως, the meaning of which goes far beyond Greek limits and is determined in the context of Jewish culture and faith. Philo, in fact, ultimately identifies love with the object of love (= God). Catalyst of the synthesis between the two poles of thought, Jewish and Greek, is the religion of the mysteries and the mystic inspiration which characterizes it, but which Philo does not take to its furthest extent. Thus he is one of those figures who mark the transition from one period to another 'and who cannot be considered pioneers, but, already captured by the new spirituality, do all they can to reconcile their own way of feeling to the cultural heritage of a bygone era' (65). Neumark arrives at this conclusion after a careful analysis of the expressions which describe God's gifts to the man who loves him and those which convey God's relationship towards the pious man. We note, finally, that Neumark's subsequent contributions to Philonic scholarship have been published under the name Y. AMIR. (= R117)

3714. A. D. NOCK, 'The question of Jewish mysteries', *Gn* 13 (1937) 156-165; reprinted in Z. STEWART (ed.), *Arthur Darby Nock: essays on religion and the ancient world*, 2 vols. (Oxford 1972) 1.459-468.

A penetrating critique of E. R. Goodenough's *By light, light* (cf. above **3706**). The metaphor of initiation into the mysteries is highly important for an understanding of Philo, but is not to be taken as referring to actual communal celebrations, as Goodenough suggests. Both for Greek philosophers and for Philo the metaphor was highly appropriate, for it sets them apart from the impure mass of humanity. (DTR)

3715. H. OPPEL, *KANΩN: zur Bedeutungsgeschichte des Wortes und seiner lateinischen Entsprechungen (Regula-norma)*, Phil Supplbd 30.4 (Leipzig 1937), esp. 57-60.

The concept of law in Philo is expressed in terms of a Stoic terminology, but denotes significant notions from Jewish culture. The term κανών is almost always used by Philo to indicate the Decalogue. (= R118)

3716. H. PRIEBATSCH, *Die Josephsgeschichte in der Weltliteratur: eine legendengeschichtliche Studie* (Breslau 1937), esp. 14-37.

An analysis of the connections between Philo and the few remaining fragments of the *Proseuché of Joseph* (mostly going back to Origen). The author establishes that Philo not only knew this work, but regarded it as a canonical writing (cf. 15). In order to reach these conclusions, the author discusses the principal allegorical meanings of the figure of Joseph in Philo's œuvre. (= R119)

3717. M. STEIN [שטיין .מ], ומשנתו וספריו הסופר .האלכסנדרוני פילון הפילוסופית [= *Philo the Alexandrian: the author, his works, and his philosophical doctrine*] (Warsaw 1937).

A systematic introduction to Philo by a leading scholar of Jewish Hellenism. The first section of the work includes a biographical essay (49-101), a survey of the Philonic corpus (102-161), and a discussion of the allegorical method (162-185). The second section examines Philo's philosophical – metaphysics (191-242) and ethics (243-273) – and religious (274-289) doctrines. Philo is characterized as the first in a long tradition of Jewish philosophers who sought to mediate between "religion and knowledge" (290). Remarkably Stein's study remains the only full-length Hebrew monograph on Philo. REVIEW: I. Heinemann, *MGWJ* 81 (1937) 355ff. (DS)

1938

3801. L. DÜRR, *Die Wertung des göttlichen Wortes im Alten Testament und im antiken Orient: zugleich ein Beitrag zur Vorgeschichte des neutestamentlichen Logosbegriffes*, Mitteilungen der Vorderasiatisch-aegyptischen Gesellschaft 42.1 (Leipzig 1938) *passim*.

The author frequently turns to Philo in order to explain the theological conceptions of Hellenistic Judaism. Particular emphasis is given to the theory of the Philonic Logos – regarded as a synthesis of Stoic-Platonic conceptions and biblical theories (162) – in its thematic relation to the Prologue of the Gospel of John. (= R120)

3802. H. FRÄNKEL, 'Heraclitus on the notion of a generation (*Vorsokr.* 22 A 19)', *AJPh* 59 (1938) 89-91.

Some doctrines of Heraclitus are discussed and interpreted on the basis of a Philonic fragment (*QG* 2.5). (= R121)

3803. L. FRÜCHTEL, 'Neue Quellennachweise zu Isidoros von Pelusion', *PhW* 58 (1938) 764-768.

Attention is drawn to some lexical and thematic parallels between Isidore of Pelusium and Philo. (= R122)

3804. L. GINZBERG, *The legends of the Jews*, 7 vols. (Philadelphia 1909-38, 1968²).

Although most of this classic study was written well before the period of our bibliography (1909-13), we include it for two reasons. (1) It was completed through the publication of an excellent index in 1938. (2) It contains the most complete collection ever compiled of Jewish legends or Haggadah, in the collection of which copious use was also made of the material that Philo offers. There are also discussions of Philonic evidence in the notes (esp. 5.1-112). See references in the index prepared by B. COHEN, 7.371, 541-6. For the Hebrew translation see **7516**. (DTR)

3805. E. R. GOODENOUGH, *The politics of Philo Judaeus, practice and theory: with a general bibliography of Philo* by H. L. GOODHART and E. R. GOODENOUGH (New Haven 1938, Hildesheim 1967²).

The importance of this controversial work lies in the particular perspective from which Philo's political themes are approached. Although the author takes his starting-point in the familiar account of the embassy to Gaius, he does not opt for a purely historical reconstruction of the events connected with it, but turns directly to what may be considered Philo's political philosophy. Chapter 2 presents an original interpretation of the figure of Joseph (in an anti-Roman key), while chapters 3 and 4 explore its allegorical meaning. Joseph, in fact, represents the man of politics *par excellence*, not only from a historical point of view, in virtue of the manifest wisdom which guided his exercise of power, but also, and above all, from an ethical and religious point of view; for in the Philonic allegory he is the symbol of God's lordship over man, of which the function of kingship should be an image. This formula, which is seen as the lynch-pin of Philo's political philosophy, is not far removed – at least theoretically – from the Hellenistic ideal of the divine origin of the sovereign, but it is not identical with it either. Philo, in fact, draws a sharp distinction between the divine origin of kingship, which he accepts, and the divinity of the person of the king, which he obviously must reject. For the bibliographical section, cf. **1001**. REVIEWS: I. Heinemann, *MGWJ* 82 (1938) 278ff.; A. Calderini, *Aeg* 19 (1939) 115f.; J. de Gellinck, *NRTh* 66 (1939) 888f.; A. H. M. Jones, *JThS* 40 (1939) 182ff.; M. R. P. M., *CHR* 24 (1939) 509; M. Radin, *CPh* 34 (1939) 269ff.; C. Schneider, *ZKG* 58 (1939) 579ff.; R. de Vaux, *RB* 48 (1939) 318; R.

58 PHILO BIBLIOGRAPHY

Willoughby, *JR* 19 (1939) 183f.; S. Zeitlin, *JBL* 58 (1939) 62ff.; Q. Cataudella, *BFC* 47 (1940) 3f.; P. Collart, *RPh* 14 (1940) 174ff.; D. R. Dudley, *JRS* 30 (1940) 125ff.; M. Ginsburg, *AHR* 45 (1940) 372f.; W. L. Knox, *JEA* 26 (1940) 164; S. Lösch, *ThQ* 121 (1940) 37; A. D. Nock, *CR* 54 (1940) 147f.; E. Stein, *Museum* 47 (1940) cols. 5ff.; W. Theiler, *Gn* 16 (1940) 331ff.; H. C. Puech, *RHR* 123 (1941) 79ff.; K. H. Rengstorf, *OLZ* 44 (1941) cols. 229ff.; F. Petit, *RThAM* 30 (1963) 344f. (= R123)

3806. R. B. HOYLE, 'Spirit in the writings and experience of Philo', *BRev* 13 (1938) 351-369.

A brief presentation of Philonic pneumatology without much scientific depth. The concept of *pneuma* is discussed in its fundamental aspects (physical, physiological, and theological-spiritual), with explanatory references to the most relevant texts in Philo and frequent parallels with the corresponding themes in Paul. (= R124)

3807. G. KITTEL (ed.), *Theologisches Wörterbuch zum Neuen Testament,* vol. 3 (Stuttgart 1938; English translation, Grand Rapids 1966).

Because of his importance in the history of theology, Philo is cited many times in this celebrated work in connection with practically all fundamental words and concepts found in the New Testament. We have thought it worthwhile to draw attention to the enormous fund of evidence readily available to scholars in this dictionary. For this reason we shall give a fairly thorough list of those lemmata containing discussions in which specific attention is paid to Philo. These will be presented under the heading of the name of the general editor (first G. KITTEL, from 1948 onwards G. FRIEDRICH), in the years that successive volumes were published. The reader who wishes to have a more complete overview of the references to Philo may consult the index volume 10.1 (1978) 310-1. For the sake of completeness we include here also lemmata from the first two volumes published in 1933 and 1935. But it should be noted that the articles in the first volumes are on the whole less expansive in scope than in those published later. We do not give references to the English translation *Theological Dictionary of the New Testament,* completed between 1964 and 1976 under the editorship of G. W. BROMILEY, but these can easily be obtained on account of the alphabetical ordering of the entire work and the fact that the German and English volume numbers correspond precisely. Vol. 1 1933: H. M. S. BÜCHSEL, art. ἀλληγορέω (allegorize), 261-2; R. BULTMANN, art. γινώσκω (know), 702 (cf. 694); O. PROCKSCH, art. ἅγιος (holy), 96-7; K. H. RENGSTORF, art. γογγύζω (grumble), 732-3; H. WINDISCH, art. βάρβαρος (barbarian), 547-8. Vol. 2 1935: J. BEHM, art. ἑρμηνεύω (interpret), 661; R. BULTMANN, art. ζωή (life), 862-3; W. FOERSTER, art. δαίμων (demon), 9-10; art. εἰρήνη (peace), 409; G. FRIEDRICH, art. εὐαγγελίζομαι (bring good news), 711; H. GREEVEN, art. εὔχομαι (pray, vow), 781; G. KITTEL, art. εἰκών (image), 392-3; A. OEPKE, art. ἔκστασις (ecstasy), 447ff.; K. H. RENGSTORF, art. δοῦλος (slave), 272; art. ἑπτά (seven), 625-6; K. L. SCHMIDT, art. διασπορά (diaspora), 101-2; J. SCHNEIDER, art. ἡδονή (pleasure), 918-9; G. SCHRENK, art. δίκαιος, δικαιοσύνη (just, justice), 185, 196; art. ἐντολή (injunction), 543. Vol. 3 1938: J. BEHM, art. καρδία (heart), 613-4; G. BERTRAM, art. θαῦμα (wonder), 35-6; R. BULTMANN, art. θάνατος (death), 13; W. FOERSTER, art. κλῆρος (heir), 761-2; W. GRUNDMANN, art. κακός (evil), 474-5; art. καλός (beautiful), 544; W. GUTBROD, art. Ἰουδαῖος, Ἰσραήλ, Ἑβραῖος (Jew, Israel, Hebrew), 370-6; A. MICHAELIS, art. κράτος (might), 906; A. OEPKE, art. ἀποκαλύπτω (reveal), 581-2; H. SASSE, art. κόσμος (cosmos), 867-8; K. L. SCHMIDT, art. ἐκκλησία (assembly), 532; G. SCHRENK, art. ἱερός (sacred), 226-8, ἱερόν (temple), 233-4, 240, ἱερεύς (priest) 259, ἀρχιερεύς (high priest) 272-4. (DTR)

3808. W. L. KNOX, 'Parallels to the N.T. use of σῶμα', *JThS* 39 (1938) 243-246.

Contains some observations on the use of σῶμα as an image to indicate the close relation that exists between the individual and society. Philo provides significant examples of the word in this sense. (= R125)

3809. W. L. KNOX, 'Origen's conception of the resurrection body', *JThS* 39 (1938) 247-248.

Some anthropological passages in Philo contribute to a brief discussion on the view imputed to Origen that the resurrected 'spiritual body' has a spherical shape. (= R126)

3810. H. LEISEGANG, 'Philons Schrift über die Gesandtschaft der alexandrinischen Juden an den Kaiser Gaius Caligula', *JBL* 57 (1938) 377-405.

The greatest obstacle to an understanding of *Legat*. is the fact that it has been incompletely transmitted. The author analyzes the four parts of which the work is composed, following its structure carefully. Special attention is paid to the introduction, which has a philosophical content, and to the 'Palinodia' (cf. 402ff.), which must have constituted the final section, but which has been lost. Leisegang holds that in this part Philo presented a eulogy of Gaius, who is regarded as an unconscious instrument of God's provident will to move his people to a more coherent testimony of faith (cf. 404). (= R127)

3811. R. MARCUS [מרקוס .ר] , ראשי פרקים בשיטת החינוך של פילון האלכסנדרוני [= 'Major themes in Philo of Alexandria's educational system'] in ספר טורוב [= *N. Touroff Jubilee Volume*] (Boston 1938) 223-231.

Philo's writings are surveyed for his viewpoints on the education of children. Subjects discussed include: (a) physical and mental training; (b) the role of parents and teachers; (c) the curriculum of study; (d) ethical and religious instruction. In each instance the author attempts to demonstrate Philo's basic dependence on classical models, a dependence, however, that is significantly tempered by his Jewish values. The ideal is therefore spiritual advancement in service of God based upon the recognition of 'Holy Scripture as the supreme text-book' (231). (DS)

3812. J. QUASTEN, 'Der Gute Hirte in hellenistischer und frühchrist-licher Logostheologie', in *Heilige Überlieferung: Ausschnitte aus der Geschichte des Mönchtums und des heiligen Kultes, I. Herwegen zum silbernen Abtsjubiläum dargeboten von Freunden, Verehrern, Schülern und in deren Auftrag gesammelt von* O. CASEL (Münster 1938) 51-58.

In *Sacr*. 104 reason (= λόγος) is clearly identified with the image of the shepherd, in opposition to the senses, which are identified with wild animals. This allegory refers to an existing doctrine of Stoic and Cynic origins. (= R128)

3813. A. SCHMEKEL, *Forschungen zur Philosophie des Hellenismus* (edited by J. SCHMEKEL), Die positive Philosophie in ihrer geschichtlichen

Entwicklung 1 (Berlin 1938), esp. 527-531.

Philo is cited numerous times in the course of this work, but he is given separate treatment only in the chapter dedicated to logic and the theory of knowledge in the Hellenistic period, where some aspects of his logical thought are examined. Particular attention is given to the interpretation of the hypothetical syllogism, which Philo approaches according to a combinatorial method along the lines of Chrysippean Stoicism. (= R130)

3814. W. STAERK, *Die Erlösererwartung in den östlichen Religionen: Untersuchungen zu den Ausdrucksformen der biblischen Christologie (Soter II)* (Stuttgart-Berlin 1938), esp. 71-85.

The author systematically analyzes some Philonic expressions and themes, linking them to Jewish theology and the Gospel of John. Staerk dwells in particular on the figure of the heavenly man (ἄνθρωπος οὐράνιος, = Adam, of whom all the predicates are listed) and Σοφία-Λόγος. (= R132)

3815. M. STEIN [שטיין .מ], דח ודעת [= *Religion and Knowledge*] (Warsaw 1938), *passim*.

This collection of minor pieces by Stein touches frequently on Philonic themes. The only piece devoted entirely to him, however, is a brief discussion (146ff.) of 'Race and nationality in Philo's thought'. Philo, 'more Jewish in his heart than in his mind', opposed any biological notion of race which might undermine the ethical principles which are the very fundament of Judaism. (DS)

3816. J. H. STELMA, *Christus' offer bij Paulus vergeleken met de offeropvatting van Philo* (diss. Groningen, Wageningen 1938).

In this biblical-theological dissertation Paul's views on the significance of Christ's sacrifice, the communion with his suffering and the notion of personal sacrifice as the fruit of communion in faith with him are compared with the Philonic conception of sacrifice. The author concludes that there are both similarities and differences. Similarities occur because both recognize the meaning of the sacrificial cult at Jerusalem, both are Jews, and both are influenced by Rabbinic thought. The differences between them can be attributed to their different reaction to Hellenistic influences. For Philo sacrifice is basically a human act. Emphasis is placed on the personal purity of the celebrant, i.e. ethics precedes communion with God. For Paul sacrifice is an act of God. Through God's sacrifice in Christ man is freed from sin, i.e. communion with God precedes ethics. In eschatology the two thinkers diverge. For Philo the purpose of life is communion of the soul with God, whereas for Paul it is the peace that results from the atonement of man's enmity towards God. Philo relates salvation to the individual, whereas for Paul it has cosmic significance. (RAB/DTR)

3817. W. VÖLKER, *Fortschritt und Vollendung bei Philo von Alexandrien: eine Studie zur Geschichte der Frömmigkeit*,TU 49.1 (Leipzig 1938).

This work must be considered a fundamental point of reference for Philonic research (cf. also **1101**). The author studies the various concepts relating to the spiritual life (sin, passion, *mathesis, askesis*, faith, virtue, progression, perfection, vision of God), in an attempt to weigh up the relative importance of the Greek and Jewish components. Though certainly not undervaluing the former, Völker demonstrates the decisive weight of the latter: the ideal of the spiritual man in Philo is located on the road which leads from Socrates to the Christian martyrs, and precisely 'at a decisive point on this road' (349). Philo is 'a great mediator between antiquity and Christianity' (*ibid.*), he is a thinker of great importance, in spite of all his uncertainties and inconsistencies, because he stands at the intersection of both cultures. A feature of the book which enhances its value is the numerous analyses of texts related to the above-mentioned themes. REVIEWS: G. A. Van den Bergh van Eysinga, *NieuwTT* 27 (1938) 390ff.; G. Bertram, *ThLB* 64 (1939) 193ff.; D. B. B., *Irén* 16 (1939) 503; H. Delehaye, *AB* 57 (1939) 404; R. de Vaux, *RB* 49 (1939) 317; E. R. Goodenough, *JBL* 58 (1939) 51ff.; J. Lebon, *RHE* 35 (1939) 84f.; J. Lebreton, *RecSR* 39 (1939) 630ff.; J. Pascher, *ThRv* 38 (1939) 94f.; Schilling, *ThQ* 120 (1939) 117f.; H. Strathmann, *ThBl* 18 (1939) 166f.; H. Urs von Balthasar, *Zeitschrift für Askese und Mystik* 14 (1939) 233f.; B. Botte, *RThAM* 12 (1940) 172; Gemmel, *Scholastik* 15 (1940) 631; E. R. Goodenough, *CPh* 35 (1940) 225f.; H. Kleinknecht, *OLZ* 35 (1940) 295ff.; C. Martin, *NRTh* 67 (1940) 111f.; C. Schneider, *ZKG* 59 (1940) 480ff.; W. Theiler, *Gn* 16 (1940) 331; J. Martin, *DLZ* 62 (1941) 145f. Cf. also **3901, 3904, 4007, 4205, 5002.** (= R134)

1939

3901. G. BERTRAM, 'Philo als politisch-theologischer Propagandist des spätantiken Judentums', *ThLZ* 64 (1939) 193-199.

A brief but trenchant analysis of the works by Goodenough (cf. **3706**) and Völker (**3817**). (= R136)

3902. H. BOLKESTEIN, *Wohltätigkeit und Armenpflege im vorchristlichen Altertum: ein Beitrag zum Problem 'Moral und Gesellschaft'* (Utrecht 1939), esp. 426-428, 435-437.

The term φιλανθρωπία in Philo essentially means care for the poor and is strictly connected to religious themes, so that the love of mankind is ultimately identified with the love of God. Yet, in the view of the author, many aspects of Philo's ethical and social thought have a Greek rather than Jewish origin. (= R137)

3903. F. J. FOAKES JACKSON, *A history of Church history: studies of some historians of the Christian Church* (Cambridge 1939), esp. 39-55.

The author presents Philo almost exclusively from a historical point of view, mostly on the basis of evidence supplied by *Legat.* (= R138)

3904. E. R. GOODENOUGH, 'Problems of method in studying Philo Judaeus', *JBL* 58 (1939) 51-58.

An extensive analysis of Völker's work (**3817**), with special regard to its methodological premisses. The author acutely observes that Völker is the first to disregard his own warning not to systematize Philo (cf. 57). (= R139)

3905. L. GOPPELT, *Typos: die typologische Deutung des Alten Testaments im Neuen. Anhang Apokalyptik und Typologie bei Paulus* (Darmstadt 1939, 1969²), esp. 48-62.

The author deals rather summarily with the subject of Philonic allegory and typology, illustrating it with many examples derived from the Allegorical Commentary and giving but superficial indication of the philosophical meaning which it implies and presupposes. (= R140)

3906. E. I. GRUMACH, 'Zur Quellenfrage von Philos *De Opificio Mundi* § 1-3', *MGWJ* 83 (1939) 126-131.

The Philonic passage in question and the parallels in *Mos.* 2.48-51 refer back to Plato. The views presented probably reached Philo in an already Stoicized form by means of an intermediate Stoic source which remains hard to identify. (= R141)

3907. H. HANSE, *'Gott haben' in der Antike und im frühen Christentum: eine religions- und begriffsgeschichtliche Untersuchung*, RGV (Berlin 1939), esp. 98-102.

The theme indicated by the title (the possession of God) is dealt with mainly from a philological point of view. The terms which Philo uses to express this concept are analyzed and commented upon one by one. (= R143)

3908. W. JOST, *ΠΟΙΜΗΝ: das Bild vom Hirten in der biblischen Überlieferung und seine christologische Bedeutung* (inaug. diss. Giessen 1939), esp. 21-22.

According to the author, the Philonic image of the shepherd-king comes from Homer and finds its roots in oriental culture. (= R144)

3909. E. KÄSEMANN, *Das wandernde Gottesvolk: eine Untersuchung zum Hebräerbrief*, FRLANT 55 (Göttingen 1939, 1959³, 1961⁴), esp. 45-52.

Although there are many points of contact between Hebrews and Philo, the overall vision which inspires them is substantially different. This applies particularly to the motif of the 'royal road' and the related motif of the people of God travelling along this road. Both present a doctrine of liberation, but, though there are remarkable similarities between the two and they probably share a common tradition (cf. 52), a direct relation cannot be postulated. (= R145)

3910. H. LEISEGANG, 'Das Mysterium der Schlange', *ErJb* (1939) 151-250, esp. 211ff., 223ff.

In *Spec.* 3.2ff. and *Opif.* 70ff. the metaphors which describe the moment of ecstasy imply a cultic model inasmuch as they are expressed in the form of the theology of mysteries (cf. 211). Other cultic models are suggested by the author in his interpretation of *Contempl.* 30 and *Somn.* 2.126. (= R146)

3911. W. LEONARD, *Authorship of the Epistle to the Hebrews: critical problem and use of the Old Testament* (Vatican City 1939), esp. 184-218.

The author analyzes at length the parallels between the vocabulary and contents of Hebrews and the works of Philo. After briefly indicating the various scholarly views on the subject, Leonard sums up in eight points the common themes, which are for the most part concerned with the identification of Christ with the Logos. The conclusion which the author reaches is that none of the affinities usually recognized is enough to demonstrate that Hebrews depends directly on Philo, whether on a lexical level or on the level of its contents. At most one might think of an Alexandrian influence on Hebrews which does not necessarily go back to Philo (cf. 214ff.). (= R147)

3912. J. P. MAGUIRE, 'The Sources of Pseudo-Aristotle *De Mundo*', *YClS* 6 (1939) 111-167.

Philo's writings are regularly cited in this work, particularly in support of the theory that the *De Mundo* is derived from the Neopythagorean tradition. The treatise is thought to depend on sources very similar to those used by Philo. (= R148)

3913. M. MAHMUD AHMAD, *Die Verwirklichung des Summum Bonum in der religiösen Erfahrung: mit einem Vorwort von* F. HEILER, Christentum und Fremdreligionen: religionsgeschichtliche und religions-philosophische Einzeluntersuchungen 7 (Munich 1939), esp. 55-68.

According to the author Philo regards the mystic state as an inspiration, as a being possessed by God, a being ravished; as an ecstasy, an opening of the eyes of the soul, and a contact of man's spirit with that of God. In this sense, such a state differs both from sensory experience and from thought and abstract reflection. Philonic mysticism – like every mysticism – is at the same time an immanent and a transcendent experience: it is immanent in that it is the experience of a Being who embraces all things; it is transcendent in that it reveals a sublimity which is inexpressible. (= R135)

3914. A. MEYER, *Vorsehungsglaube und Schicksalsidee in ihrem Verhältnis bei Philo von Alexandria* (inaug. diss. Würzburg 1939).

While the Greeks believed in an irresistible force which holds man in its power, Philo's belief in Providence is based on a different concept of God (the Creator) which, in the author's view, sees in Providence a prime example of the physical and theological proof of God's existence. On an ethical level, the concept of Providence is translated into the simple maxim that the good man experiences God's help in life, while the wicked man receives punishment. From a cosmological point of view, on the other hand, divine Providence is limited by matter, regarded as a negative principle dualistically opposed to the action of God. In any case Philo is convinced that there cannot be a better world than the one which God, in his infinite wisdom, has created. As far as the doctrine of fate is concerned, Philo, though influenced by Stoic philosophy, did not accept the principle of absolute determinism. For this purpose he interpreted the Logos – the expression of God's power over the world – as a law in the natural world from which man is exempted. The moral structure too is reduced to this God-Logos principle, and is identified with Mosaic law. Monotheism, therefore, is staunchly defended against the concept of fate, and through this defense human freedom is preserved as well. Summing up, the difference between belief in Providence and the idea of fate is for Philo the difference between faith and lack of faith, for faith, conceived as the acceptance of an 'ethics based on monotheism', excludes the idea of fate (cf. 81). At the end of the work Meyer devotes an appendix to the relation between Philo and the Gnostic concept of fate. (= R149)

3915. R. D. MIDDLETON, 'Logos and Shekinah in the Fourth Gospel', *JQR* 29 (1938-39) 101-133, esp. 101-104.

In spite of its numerous uncertainties, the theory of the Logos in Philo is the most important antecedent of the analogous doctrine in the Gospel of John. Philo's vacillations on this subject have especially to do with the transcendence or immanence of God and are determined by the plurality and heterogeneity of the philosophical elements – Stoic and biblical in particular – which constitute the concept of logos. (= R150)

3916. P. VIELHAUER, *Oikodome: das Bild vom Bau in der christlichen Literatur vom Neuen Testament bis Clemens Alexandrinus* (inaug. diss. Heidelberg 1939), esp. 28-33.

The image of building has three fundamental meanings in Philo: theological, intellectual, and ethical. The author presents a careful analysis of this topic, with frequent references to the texts. (= R151)

1940

4001. A. H. ARMSTRONG, *The architecture of the intelligible universe in the philosophy of Plotinus: an analytical and historical study*, Cambridge Classical Studies (Cambridge 1940, Amsterdam 1967²), esp. 70-74, 107-108.

Although also stressing crucial differences, the author feels constrained to point to fundamental similarities between Philo and Plotinus in the doctrines of the multiplicity of the mind's grasp of the unity of the supreme principle, the passivity of the soul, the importance of ecstasy in the state of mystic contemplation, and the conception of the Logos. See also **6749**. (DTR)

4002. S. BELKIN, *Philo and the oral Law: the Philonic interpretation of biblical law in relation to the Palestinian Halakah* (Cambridge Mass. 1940, reprinted New York 1968, 1970).

The aim of this book is to trace back the essential content of Philo's work (and not only its main lines and spiritual background) to the themes of Jewish culture. Belkin does not, therefore, confine himself to pointing out affinities with the Rabbinic tradition, but arrives at the supposition of a stable oral tradition in Palestine – broadly reconstructed here – from which the Alexandrian Jew is thought to have drawn most of his views. In the light of these considerations, Philo's devotion to the Mosaic law is regarded as fully in agreement with the aforementioned tradition and in perfect harmony with Palestinian Judaism, as is also shown by his harsh attitude to the heretical tendencies of the extreme allegorists. The same loyalty to the Law explains his missionary aims and, consequently, his open-mindedness towards Greek culture. Thus Philo can be characterized as a *halachic Pharisee* on account of his application of the principles of the oral law to the interpretation of the Bible, a *Palestinian allegorist* on account of his particular interpretation of

Holy Scripture, and an *Alexandrian mystic* on account of his aspirations toward the Infinite. It should be noted that Belkin, although he is one of the most forthright proponents of the view that Philo knew the Hebrew language (35 n. 29), does not discuss the pros and cons of this very difficult question here, since he does not consider it fundamental to his views. He maintains in fact that, even if Philo had had no knowledge of the Hebrew tongue, he would have nonetheless been able to draw on the oral tradition through the mediation of people in Alexandria who were acquainted with the Hebrew language. See also **4601**. REVIEWS: E. R. Goodenough, *JBL* 59 (1940) 413ff.; M. Ginsburg, *AHR* 47 (1942) 315f.; G. D. Kilpatrick, *JHS* 62 (1942) 95; E. Bevan, *JThS* 44 (1943) 201ff.; H. Caplan, *PhR* 52 (1943) 214; D. Daube, *BiOr* 5 (1948) 64f. (= R152)

4003. G. BERTRAM, 'Philo und die jüdische Propaganda in der antiken Welt', in W. GRUNDMANN (ed.), *Christentum und Judentum: Studien zur Erforschung ihres gegenseitigen Verhältnisses*, Sitzungsberichte der ersten Arbeitstagung des Institutes zur Erforschung des jüdischen Einflusses auf das deutsche kirchliche Leben vom 1. bis 3. März 1940 in Wittenberg (Leipzig 1940) 79-105.

For Bertram Philo is an eclectic who cannot lay any claim to originality and who nevertheless did manage to exercise a notable influence on early Christian philosophy (cf. 88). His debt to Judaism is rather formal and not always clear: the very attempt to mediate with Hellenism would appear to be foreign to the Jewish mind. On the other hand, several notable differences separate Philo from Hellenism too, e.g. the refusal to deify the emperor (cf. 92). As for the concept of the immortality of the soul – which the author analyzes from various points of view –, this appears to have been adopted from Hellenism in a wholly provisional and superficial way. Yet it is right to emphasize that for Philo, properly speaking, immortality does not extend to man (cf. 101ff.); instead he tends to spiritualize this concept by identifying it with wisdom. Only in this quite specific sense can one say that the wise man already attains immortality in this world. (= R154)

4004. F. H. COLSON, 'Philo's quotations from the Old Testament', *JThS* 41 (1940) 237-251.

Philo's quotations from the Pentateuch easily outnumber those from other Bible books. The author sets out to determine the exact proportion between the two groups, and so can correct the estimations of previous scholars. (= R155)

4005. W. DEN BOER, *De allegorese in het werk van Clemens Alexandrinus* (diss. Leiden 1940).

Frequent comparisons and contrasts are made between the allegorical method as practised by Philo and Clement, e.g. at 58f., 129f. (DTR)

4006. P. FRACCARO, 'C. Herennius Capito di Teate procurator di Livia, di Tiberio e di Gaio', *Ath* 28 (1940) 134-144.

The author cites Philonic evidence (*Legat.* 162-337) in order to reconstruct the figure of Herennius Capito. (= R157)

4007. E. R. GOODENOUGH, *An introduction to Philo Judaeus* (New

Haven 1940); second edition revised and amplified (Oxford 1962, New York 1963).

In itself this work cannot be considered a scientific contribution to Philonic studies, since it is written in an intentionally didactic and popularizing style. Aside from this, however, it is of considerable interest because it contains an abbreviated and much simplified account of all the basic views of the author, who in his day was one of the leading authorities on Philo in the English-speaking world. The second edition is of additional interest, for in it Goodenough discusses the positions of other major Philonic interpreters (Wolfson, Völker, Heinemann, Daniélou) and relates them to his own. The resultant 'summit meeting', though too concise and somewhat superficial, is still well worth reading. REVIEWS: S. Belkin, *JBL* 60 (1941) 61ff.; M. J. Gruenthaner, *CBQ* 3 (1941) 187f.; R. Willoughby, *JR* 21 (1941) 103; F. H. Colson, *CR* 56 (1942) 78ff.; M. Ginsburg, *AHR* 47 (1942) 315f.; W. J. Phythian-Adams, *CQR* 133 (1941-43) 226ff.; A. C. Purdy, *AJPh* 64 (1943) 383; A. Momigliano, *JRS* 34 (1944) 163ff.; M. Radin, *CPh* 39 (1944) 123ff. Of the second edition: F. Petit, *RThAM* 30 (1963) 344ff.; Berkovits, *JR* 44 (1964) 182f. (= R158)

4008. I. HEINEMANN [היינמן .י ,[היהודים קדמוניות בתיאור יוספוס של דרכו ['Josephus' method in the presentation of Jewish Antiquities'], *Zion* 5 (1940) 180-203.

This penetrating investigation of Josephus' historiographical outlook and principles finds several occasions to compare and contrast that author with Philo. Heinemann takes pains to delineate the differences between the two (esp. 188f.) both with regard to exegetical technique and ideological orientation. (DS)

4009. A. HEITMANN, *Imitatio Dei: die ethische Nachahmung Gottes nach der Väterlehre der zwei ersten Jahrhunderte*, StAns 10 (Rome 1940), esp. 47-64.

The impossibility of dealing with Philo's ethics as distinct from his theology basically depends on the fact that the archetypal function of God stands at the centre of Philo's entire thought, including his ethics. Conscious of this dependence, Heitmann first analyzes the ethical attributes of God and then the most important passages in which the imitation of God plays a predominant role. In this concept one recognizes, in the view of the author, a clear syncretism of Jewish and Hellenistic elements (cf. 64). (= R159)

4010. F. R. M. HITCHCOCK, 'Philo and the Pastorals', *Herma* 56 (1940) 113-135.

Hitchcock criticizes here the views of P. N. HARRISON (*Problem of the Pastoral Epistles*, Oxford 1921) directed against the Pauline authorship of the *Pastoral Epistles*. For this purpose he compares the language and style of the latter with that of Philo. The similarities which emerge from this analysis are such that, according to the author, one must allow for a reciprocal influence, albeit indirect (cf. 135). (= R160)

4011. N. JOHANNSON, *Parakletoi: Vorstellungen von Fürsprechern für die Menschen vor Gott in der alttestamentlichen Religion, im Spätjudentum und Urchristentum* (inaug. diss. Lund 1940), esp. 268-292.

Analyzes the various meanings of the term παράκλητος in Philo and shows how it carries, besides its usual meaning, various theological and allegorical connotations. (= R161)

4012. W. L. KNOX, 'A note on Philo's use of the Old Testament', *JThS* 41 (1940) 30-34.

The scarceness of biblical quotations in Philo from books other than the Pentateuch suggests a stratification of influences in the exegetical traditions of Alexandria which is strictly related to the chronology of the Septuagint. (= R162)

4013. J. B. MCDIARMID, 'Theophrastus on the eternity of the world', *TAPhA* 71 (1940) 239-247.

Aet. 117ff. is generally considered to be a fragment from Theophrastus. After a brief but penetrating analysis, McDiarmid confirms this view and puts forward the theory that the fragment is derived from his meteorological works and that it records and interprets Aristotelian views (cf. 246ff.). (= R156)

4014. W. RICHARDSON, 'Philo and his significance for Christian theology', *Modern Churchman* 30 (1940) 15-25.

A synoptic portrait of Philo and his Alexandrian background, presented at a high level of generality and with emphasis on his eclecticism and mysticism. A final note is added on interesting anticipations in Philo of the notion of the 'paraclete'. (DTR)

4015. J. SCHNEIDER, *Lässt sich in der paulinischen Christologie philonisches Gedankengut nachweisen?* (diss. Vienna 1940), esp. 52-133.

Philo's eclecticism is clearly seen in the doctrine of the Logos, which in its complexity reveals Stoic, Platonic, and – with regard to the personal nature of the Logos – also Jewish influences. On the basis of this presupposition the author compares various passages of Paul with corresponding passages in Philo (though a great deal more attention is paid to the former than the latter). On the subject of allegorical exegesis Schneider, basing himself mainly on the way both thinkers interpret the figure of Melchizedek, reaches the conclusion that, while Philo maintains that allegorical meaning is destined for the select few, the author of Hebrews holds that Christ revealed completely, and for everybody, the most profound contents of the Old Testament. If in this sense Philonic exegesis is allegory, that of Hebrews is typology. The work of Paul as a whole should be understood as a bridge erected towards 'Greek dogma', a bridge in the construction of which Philo played a decisive role (cf. 133). (= R163)

4016. W. WIERSMA, 'Der angebliche Streit des Zenon und Theophrast über die Ewigkeit der Welt', *Mnem* III 8 (1940) 235-243.

Aet. 117ff., which presents four scientific arguments in favour of the eternity of the cosmos, is regarded by Zeller and many other scholars as a fragment from Theophrastus in response to the young Zeno, but there have been heated controversies about its meaning and derivation. The author proposes a novel solution, namely that the passage is for the most part a Philonic reconstruction based on a rather slender clue in Theophrastus. (= R165)

1941

4101. B. ALTANER, 'Augustinus und Philo von Alexandrien: eine quellenkritische Untersuchung', *ZKTh* 65 (1941) 81-90; reprinted in *Kleine patristische Schriften*, TU 83 (Berlin 1967) 181-193.

By means of a textual analysis, the author sets out to demonstrate the view that Augustine was influenced by Philo not only indirectly through Origen and Ambrose, but also directly through a Latin version of *QG*. (= R166)

4102. J. BARBEL, *Christos Angelos: die Anschauung von Christus als Bote und Engel in der gelehrten und volkstümlichen Literatur des christlichen Altertums; zugleich ein Beitrag zur Geschichte des Ursprungs und der Fortdauer des Arianismus*, Theoph 3 (Bonn 1941), esp. 18-33.

Philo's angelology has only an indirect relevance to the question dealt with in these pages, namely whether there is a representation of the Messiah as an angel in Jewish religion. Philo consistently distinguishes between the concept of the Messiah and that of the Logos, since for him an 'incarnation of the *logos*' (cf. 19) is inconceivable. Thus the attribute of *angelos* comes to be reserved for the Logos; in fact, on account of its pre-eminent role with respect to the other Powers (also defined as 'angels'), the Logos is often described as archangel. (= R167)

4103. P. BARTH and A. GOEDECKEMEYER, *Die Stoa,* Fünfte Auflage völlig neubearbeitet, Frommanns Klassiker der Philosophie 16 (Stuttgart 1941), esp. 232-242.

Philo's thought is presented in its essential outlines as dependent on Stoic thought, though not without some vacillations. But the mystic-aesthetic dimension in Philo's thought, which represents a climactic development of themes in Hellenistic philosophy, is said to derive from oriental culture. (= R168)

4104. W. BIEDER, *Ekklesia und Polis im Neuen Testament und in der alten Kirche zugleich eine Auseinandersetzung mit Erik Petersons Kirchenbegriff* (inaug. diss. Zürich 1941), esp. 70-78.

Philo's conception of politics is reconstructed by means of his use of the term πόλις and its derivatives. The author emphasizes that Philo's political views cannot be separated from his religious concerns and are embedded in an eclectic context in which Hellenism acts as a 'magnet' for all other philosophical components (cf. 78). (= R169)

4105. C. BONNER, 'Desired haven', *HThR* 34 (1941) 49-67, esp. 57-59.

The author collects numerous Philonic texts containing the spiritualized image of the haven and the storm-tossed ship. (= R170)

4106. F. V. COURNEEN, 'Philo Judaeus had the concept of creation',

NSchol 15 (1941) 46-58.

Courneen's method, in dealing with this very delicate subject, is to limit himself to a rapid enumeration of the most relevant texts, and then consult the views of the best known Philonic scholars in order to demonstrate that Philo did possess the concept of creation. (= R171)

4107. N. A. DAHL, *Das Volk Gottes: eine Untersuchung zum Kirchenbewusstsein des Urchristentums*, SNVAO.HF 1941.2 (Oslo 1941), esp. 105-118.

The author analyzes the concept of Israel and its related themes. He particularly emphasizes the difference between the term Ἰουδαῖοι – used by Philo mainly in political writings (cf. 107ff.) – and the term Ἰσραήλ, used mostly in the allegorical commentaries. (= R172)

4108. J. H. KÜHN, *ΥΨΟΣ: eine Untersuchung zur Entwicklungsgeschichte des Aufschwungsgedankens von Platon bis Poseidonios* (inaug. diss. Stuttgart 1941), esp. 53-71.

The term ὕψος in Philo designates man's supreme aspiration, i.e. possession of the knowledge of God which embraces all other knowledge; this is a gift from God and constitutes the height of virtue. Philo, however, also recognizes a false 'greatness', which is the fruit of human presumption and pride and which, according to Kühn, is to be identified with the doctrine of Posidonius. (= R173)

4109. H. LEISEGANG, art. 'Philo (41)', in *RE* 20.1 (1941) 1-50.

A densely written general overview based on a detailed knowledge of Philo's writings. On the subject of his 'philosophical-theological system' the author affirms: 'The foundation of the whole system and of the general framework in which all the particulars are arranged is from the start the view of reality held by the Stoa, together with the ethics derived from it' (39). This theory, once highly influential, is now most definitely on the decline. (= R174)

4110. A. S. PEASE, 'Caeli enarrant', *HThR* 34 (1941) 163-200, esp. 189ff.

In a long and exhaustive account of ancient authors who discuss the teleological argument from design as evidence for a creating deity, Pease devotes a short passage to 'that interesting eclectic Philo' (189-191). Aristotle's *De philosophia*, but also Stoic and Platonic doctrines exert their influence. The *De opificio mundi* is an important landmark because it 'joins the Mosaic tradition of creation with Greek cosmological theories' (190). Philo's teleological view of nature is also anticipated in Hebrew thought, e.g. Ps. 19 (hence the article's title) and Sap. Sal. 13:1-5. (= R175)

4111. J. H. WASZINK, 'Die sogenannte Fünfteilung der Träume bei Chalcidius und ihre Quellen', *Mnem* III 9 (1941) 65-85.

For his theory of dreams Calcidius relies on Philonic views. The author regards Porphyry and Numenius as intermediaries between the two (cf. 84). (= R164)

1942

4201. L. DELATTE, *Les traités de la royauté d'Ecphante, Diotogène et Sthénidas*, Bibliothèque de la Faculté de Philosophie et Lettres de l'Université de Liège 97 (Liège-Paris 1942), esp. 184-288 *passim*.

Philo's writings are cited very frequently in this commentary on Ecphantus' treatise *On royalty*. Though not specifically concerned with Philo, the work as a whole gives valuable information on the fate and development of many of his views. (= R177)

4202. G. KITTEL (ed.), *Theologisches Wörterbuch zum Neuen Testament,* vol. 4 (Stuttgart 1942; English translation, Grand Rapids 1967).

Cf. above **3807**. Contains: O. BAUERNFEIND, art. νήφω (be sober), 937-8; J. BEHM, art. νοῦς (mind), 954-5, μετανοέω (repent) 988-90; G. BERTRAM, art. μακάριος (blessed), 369; R. BULTMANN, art. λύπη (pain), 320-1; W. GUTBROD, art. νόμος (law), 1044-6; J. HORST, art. μέλος (limb), 562-3; H. KLEINKNECHT, art. λόγος (word), 86-8; W. MICHAELIS, art. μιμέομαι κτλ (imitate), 666-8; O. MICHEL, art. μισέω (hate), 693; A. OEPKE, art. λούω (bathe), 304; art. μεσίτης (mediator), 621; K. H. RENGSTORF, art. μανθάνω (learn), 407; H. STRATHMANN, art. λαός (people), 38-9. (DTR)

4203. M. MÜHL, 'Zu Poseidonios und Philon', *WS* 60 (1942) 28-36.

Collects a large number of theological passages from *Prov.* supposedly related to Posidonian thought. (= R179)

4204. M. POHLENZ, 'Philon von Alexandreia', *NAWG* 5 (1942) 409-487; reprinted in H. DÖRRIE (ed.), *Kleine Schriften* (Hildesheim 1965) 1.305-383.

Taking up and developing Heinemann's views, the author endeavours to show that the substance of Philo's thought is Greek, but that its underlying spirituality is primarily Jewish. For this purpose Pohlenz analyzes the basic elements of Philo's theology – which he holds to be demiurgic, not creationistic (cf. 418) – and his anthropology and ethics. He thus attempts to reconstruct the cultural environment on which the Alexandrian drew and to show that his eclecticism is in reality a faithful expression of the philosophical *koine* of his time, and is largely free from the influence of Rabbinic Judaism. At the root of Philo's philosophy, according to the author, lies a kind of Stoicizing Platonism, but other elements of the philosophical atmosphere of Philo's time, e.g. the influence of Posidonius, the Peripatetic revival and Neopythagorean arithmology, also make their presence felt. Yet these elements are subsumed only insofar as they are compatible with the deepest meaning of the Mosaic law. Philo's value and originality consists precisely in the effort to mediate between the two cultural domains. At the end of the essay (480-487) Pohlenz adds an appendix on the *De Mundo,* in which he shows some sympathy for Bernays' suggestion that the addressee of the work is not Alexander the Great, but his namesake, Philo's nephew. (= R180)

4205. E. VANDERLINDEN, *Vers la contemplation de Dieu avec Philon* *d'Alexandrie* (diss. Louvain 1942).

This study's starting-point is opposition to the work of Völker (**3817**). The German scholar is criticized for his inadequate analysis of Philo's sources, which are almost exclusively limited to Plato and ancient Stoicism. Vanderlinden thinks it is possible to broaden this horizon by paying more attention to what he calls 'the philosophers of the preceding generation': first of all Posidonius, to whom Philo owes his theory of the natural knowledge of God; next Antiochus of Ascalon and the New Academy, who partly influenced his conception of nous, of the ideas as thoughts of God, of the Logos as intelligible cosmos, and who also suggested various Sceptic arguments; and finally, though its influence was less important, the Epicurean philosophy. Philo's original contribution, on the other hand, is thought to be his monotheism. This was not a product of reason, however, but of faith in the biblical revelation inspired by an interior illumination. The dissertation ends with an appendix which attempts to reconstruct, on the basis of Aucher's Latin version, the original Greek text of *Prov.* 1.2-4. (= R181)

4206. H. A. WOLFSON, 'Philo on free will and the historical influence of his view', *HThR* 35 (1942) 131-169.

The author examines with great lucidity the problem of free will in Philo, which he sets in the context of Philo's cosmology, theology, and anthropology. For Philo, according to Wolfson, man asserts his freedom in the struggle between the irrational and the rational, between good and evil – a struggle in which he is involved as part of the cosmos. Yet in man's case the action of divine grace is decisive, whether conceded by God from time to time according to the circumstances, or granted as a permanent gift to some people before birth (cf. 163). In Wolfson's view this notion of free will anticipates many positions in Christian, Jewish, and Islamic theology (cf. 164). (= R182)

4207. H. A. WOLFSON, 'Hallevi and Maimonides on prophecy', *JQR* 32 (1942) 345-370; 33 (1942) 49-82; reprinted in *Studies in the History of Philosophy and Religion*, vol. 2 (Cambridge Mass.-London 1977) 60-119, esp. 99ff., 104-107.

Wolfson points out some similarities between Hallevi and Philo which give rise to the possibility of a direct literary connection between the two. (= R183)

1943

4301. A. BECKAERT, *Dieu et la connaissance de Dieu dans la philosophie de Philon d'Alexandrie: essai sur le mysticisme judéo-alexandrin* (diss. Paris 1943).

The central theme of this long and interesting dissertation is that the figure of Philo should not, historically speaking, be understood as a meeting-point of Judaism and Hellenism, but rather as a convergence of two Hellenisms, Jewish and Christian. Far from being purely eclectic, Philonic philosophy finds its centre of gravity in the religious and psychological perspective which it takes on metaphysical problems; these problems hinge on the concepts of God (cause and end of all things), soul (creature privileged with the vocation of returning to God), cosmos (starting-point of theological knowledge, it too being oriented towards God), and logos (the principle of universal causality). From the interrelation of these elements the internal structure of Philonic thought is derived: the transcendence of God, as transcendence of cause with respect to effect; the created thought, which, in virtue of its similarity to the creating thought, returns, with the mystic vision, to the cause, and thus justifies both the cosmos and God; and finally, Philo's 'historicism', which traces the whole of present reality back to the originating action of God. That which distinguishes Philo from other thinkers, concludes the author, is precisely the concept of a personal God: it differentiates him from Hellenism, which did not yet possess such a concept, and sets him apart from Christianity, which was developing this concept much further. (= R184)

4302. A. BECKAERT, *Les théories psychologiques de Philon d'Alexandrie* (diss. Paris 1943).

In Beckaert's view, Philonic psychology is marked by a lack of method, but also by considerable coherence. Its essence is formed by the biblical revelation of the creation of the soul by God's breath. Having spiritualized the term *pneuma*, Philo deduces from it the substantial affinity between man and God, and, consequently, the possibility of a return to God through the practice of asceticism. According to our author the doctrine of the irrational realm, i.e. of the sense-perceptible, is precisely that which 'inspires asceticism', in that it induces man to overcome his material condition. In the same way the doctrine of the rational realm subsequently inspires the concept of progress, the goal of which is the state of mystic ecstasy (this is at the same time the condition of perfect knowledge and perfect virtue), but which starts from sensation, where sense and intellect meet. (= R185)

4303. M. W. BLOOMFIELD, 'A Source of Prudentius' *Psychomachia*', *Spec* 18 (1943) 87-90.

Philo (especially in *Abr.* 225ff.) is said to have inspired Prudentius' allegorical interpretation of Gen. 14. (= R186)

4304. A.D. NOCK, 'Philo and Hellenistic philosophy', *CR* 57 (1943) 77-81; reprinted in Z. STEWART (ed.), *Arthur Darby Nock: essays on religion and the ancient world* (Oxford 1972) 2.559-565.

Although this article is actually a review of vol. 9 of F. H. Colson's English translation of Philo in the LCL (cf. **2109**), it deserves inclusion here on account of the important observations it makes on various philosophical and historical-apologetic treatises (*Prob., Contempl., Aet., Hypoth., Prov., Anim., Flacc.*). It is attractive to regard the philosophical treatises as youthful works, but the dialogues are certainly later, perhaps about 30 A.D. (DTR)

1944

4401. J. DANIÉLOU, *Platonisme et théologie mystique: essai sur la doctrine spirituelle de Saint Grégoire de Nysse*, Théologie 2 (Paris 1944, 1953²), esp. 73-77, 262-266, 274-276.

In tracing an outline of Gregory's allegorical practice, the author frequently draws on

Philonic exegesis as a point of reference, and especially some of its typical interpretations, such as the double creation of man, the asexuality of the man created 'in the image' (on which Gregory based his doctrine of virginity), the wild beasts, and the theme of 'sober drunkenness'. (= R187)

4402. W. L. KNOX, *Some Hellenistic elements in primitive Christianity*, The Schweich Lectures of the British Academy 1942 (London 1944), esp. 47-54.

Philo's use of various sources (Posidonius, the Old Testament, Jewish literature, the classical philosophers) is illustrated here by means of examples. The work is mainly analytical and does not discuss the complex structure and formation of Philonic thought. (= R188)

4403. R. MARCUS, 'A note on Philo's *Quaestiones in Gen.* II, 31', *CPh* 39 (1944) 257-258.

A brief philological annotation of the passage in question, of which the author gives three different interpretations. (= R189)

4404. C. MONDÉSERT, *Clément d'Alexandrie: introduction à l'étude de sa pensée religieuse à partir de l'Écriture*, Théologie 4 (Paris 1944), esp. 163-183.

The author considers the connections between Philo and Clement from the viewpoint of their use of Scripture. An analysis of Clement's allegorical method (particularly in *Strom.* 5.6), compared with that of Philo, leads Mondésert to reconsider, within the specific context of his study, how great Philo's influence on Clement actually was. This influence is said to be considerable with regard to psychology and morality, but negligible with regard to the method of biblical exegesis (cf. 183). (= R190)

4405. K. J. POPMA, 'Philoonsche en stoïsche allegoristiek', *VoxTh* 15 (1943-44) 61-67.

Philo's use of allegory is to be explained as the result of the type of Judaism which he represents, namely a subjectivist fideism. This is totally non-Greek, the result of a process of reorientalization, but at the same time is heavily determined by the previous movement of Hellenization. The chief emphasis of Philo's thought is on the piety of the individual soul, which is taken as norm and thus leaves little room for respect for Scripture. Hence the quest to locate meaning that is actually not there. The author denies that the influence of Stoic allegory was strong; the movement of reorientalization, self-confidently promoting the cause of Jewish culture, attempts to defeat its opponents with their own weapons. (DTR)

4406. A. SCHALIT [שׁליט .א] (tr.), קדמוניות (פלביוס יוספוס). יוסף בן מתתיהו היהודים [= *Joseph ben Matitiahu (Flavius Josephus), Jewish Antiquities*], vol. 1 (Jerusalem 1944, 1955²) xli-xliii.

The extensive introduction to this translation includes a discussion of the author's sources. Schalit argues forcefully for Josephus' direct dependence on Philo, adducing passages from *Opif.* 1-2 and *Mos.* 2.98ff. which in his view lie behind the first book of the *Antiquities*. (DS)

4407. H. A. WOLFSON, 'Philo on Jewish citizenship in Alexandria', *JBL* 63 (1944) 165-168.

Draws attention to *Mos.* 1.35, where Philo defines the political position of the Jews in Alexandria. (= R191)

1945

4501. D. AMAND, *Fatalisme et liberté dans l'antiquité grecque: recherches sur la survivance de l'argumentation morale antifataliste de Carnéade chez les philosophes grecs et les théologiens chrétiens des quatre premiers siècles*, Université de Louvain, Receuil de travaux d'Histoire et de Philologie III 19 (Louvain 1945), esp. 81-95.

In his argumentation against fatalism, particularly in *Prov.* 1.77-88, Philo 'used the weapons afforded him by the dialectical arsenal of Carneades', but proceeded from assumptions quite foreign to the New Academy, i.e. from the concept of human freedom and from the rejection of the worship of the heavenly bodies in the name of monotheism. (= R192)

4502. P. T. CAMELOT, *Foi et gnose: introduction à l'étude de la connaissance mystique chez Clément d'Alexandria*, Études de Théologie et d'Histoire de la Spiritualité 3 (Paris 1945).

Superficial *obiter dicta* on the relation between Philo and Clement at 24-27, 72-76, 108-110. (DTR)

4503. G. DELCUVE, *L'exégèse de Philon étudiée dans le commentaire allégorique* (diss. Paris 1945).

The author's basic thesis is that not only does Philo's allegorical method follow fixed rules (a thesis already defended by Siegfried), but that the very plan of the works, their division into chapters and their internal structure, also follow a fixed symbolical scheme. This scheme is here reconstructed from diverse elements, such as the many verbal and formal parallels and similarities of content; these allow the association of different sections from the same treatise, or even of parts from different treatises. Next Delcuve asserts his conviction that this type of analysis, if properly applied, might lead to a new overall interpretation of Philo's thought, in that it would provide a new key to the reading of all his writings. In this connection he anticipates a few conclusions: in the first place he demonstrates the completeness of the Allegorical Commentary, basing himself on the completeness of its symbolic structure; in the second place he emphasizes the esoteric nature of Philo's writings. It must be pointed out, however, that, though the author's conclusions are highly stimulating, the analyses on which they are based relate to a very small section of the Philonic corpus; in practice they are limited to three books of *Leg.* and, much less convincingly, to *Legat.* and *Flacc.* (= R193)

4504. M. PULVER, 'Das Erlebnis des Pneuma bei Philon', *ErJb* 13 [*Der Geist*] (1945) 111-132.

Pulver sees in the concept of *pneuma* the fundamental connection between early Christian philosophy and Philo. Although πνεῦμα, from a terminological point of view, belongs to the vocabulary of Hellenism (medical and astrological as well as philosophical, cf. 114ff.), the use which Philo makes of it is considerably wider. The author emphasizes both its cosmological and its anthropological and theological aspects; he particularly focusses on the role which it plays in psychology and concludes that in this context the Philonic *pneuma* has nothing in common with its Old Testament counterpart, but rather shows notable points of contact with Platonic-Aristotelian doctrines (cf. 123). Finally, a few pages (126ff.) are devoted to Philo's angelology and to his theory of ecstasy in relation to the parallel Platonic conception of divine *mania*. (= R194)

4505. A. ROSTAGNI, *Introduzione a Anonimo del sublime* (Milan no date, = 1945?) i-xxxiv, esp. xxv-xxxii.

Philo is probably the philosopher referred to in the final part of the anonymous treatise *On the sublime*. The author bases this conclusion on three kinds of considerations: (1) formal, on account of analogies between the *De sublimitate* and *Ebr.* 198ff.; (2) historical, through Philo's presence in Rome in 40 A.D. as a member of the embassy to Gaius; (3) political, on account of the marked aversion to imperial Roman authoritarianism shared by both treatises. The date we give of this book is based on the reference in **6420**. (RR)

4506. V. TCHERIKOVER [א. צ׳ריקובר], היהודים במצרים בתקופה ההלניסטית הרומית לאור הפאפירולוגיה [*The Jews in Egypt in the Hellenistic Roman age in the light of the papyri*] (Jerusalem 1945, 1963²), esp. 139-155.

The author uses Philo in discussing Claudius' relations to Alexandrian Jewry. The account is mainly based on nos. 153 and 156 of the *Corpus Papyrorum Judaicarum* (**5723**): the former document being Claudius' letter to the Jews of Alexandria, the latter the *Acta Isidori et Lamponis*. English Summary, xviii-xx. (DRS)

4507. V. TCHERIKOVER [א. צ׳ריקובר], שקיעתה של הגולה היהודית במצרים בתקופה הרומית [= 'The decline of the Jewish Diaspora in Egypt in the Roman period'] *Knesset* 9 (1945) 143-162.

Subsequently published in English; see **6323**. Later republished in **6117**.

4508. G. VERBEKE, *L'évolution de la doctrine du pneuma du Stoïcisme à S. Augustin: étude philosophique*, Bibliothèque de l'Institut Supérieur de Philosophie, Université de Louvain (Paris-Louvain 1945), esp. 236-260.

The two main aspects of Philonic pneumatology are the concept of prophetic *pneuma* and the spiritual dimension in which this concept is located. In both cases the influence of Posidonius must be regarded as considerable. The author emphasizes, however, the differences between Posidonian pan-pneumatism and Philo's doctrine of prophecy, and the fact that the *effective* spiritualization of the *pneuma* achieved by the Alexandrian occurs under the decisive influence of Jewish religion (cf. 259). (= R195)

1946

4601. S. BELKIN [בלקין .ש], המקורות של פרשנות פילון האלכסנדרוני [= 'On the question of the sources of the exegesis of Philo of Alexandria'], *Horeb* 9 (1946) 1-20.

Belkin addresses himself exclusively to examples of legal exegesis, arguing that Philo's legal frame of reference is Rabbinic, whereas the Roman and Greek parallels adduced by him and also his Hellenistic terminology served the purpose of explaining and/or justifying these laws to his Hellenized audience. The emphasis on the Rabbinic parallels is primarily motivated by the article's attempt to rebut E. R. Goodenough's critical review of Belkin's *Philo and the Oral Law* (**4002**) in *JBL* 59 (1940) 413-419. (NGC)

4602. P. BOYANCÉ, 'Les muses et l'harmonie des sphères', in *Mélanges dédiés à la mémoire de F. Grat* (Paris 1946) 1.3-16.

The myth of Pythagorean origin which relates the Muses to the harmony of the spheres is here interpreted in the light of Philonic evidence. (= R196)

4603. F. COPLESTON, *A history of Philosophy*, vol. I, *Greece and Rome*, The Bellarmine Series 9 (London 1946, 1947², 1956⁴) 457-462.

The Philonic method of allegorical interpretation stands above, but does not disqualify, the literal meaning of the Old Testament. From it Copleston deduces the aim of Philo's work, which is 'not to destroy Jewish orthodoxy ..., but rather to reconcile it with philosophy'. Copleston's discussion of Philo's thought, presented as a form of Platonic dualism, focusses almost exclusively on his theology. (= R197)

4604. E. R. GOODENOUGH, 'Philo on immortality', *HThR* 39 (1946) 85-108.

This article undertakes to clarify Philo's views on immortality, but also to present copious evidence of the wide-spread eschatological convictions that existed among Hellenistic Jews. Goodenough makes a few prefatory remarks on Philo's expository method, which appears not to be troubled by contradictions, and then illustrates these contradictions in the analyses that follow. In particular he considers Philo's views on the soul and shows how they continually oscillate between Stoicism and Platonism (cf. 108). (= R198)

4605. P. KATZ, 'Notes on the Septuagint', *JThS* 47 (1946) 31-33.

Contains a few paleographical observations on the new Aquila fragment recovered from the text of Philo, *Gig.* 63 (i.e. added by a later scribe). (= R199)

4606. C. W. LARSON, 'Prayer of petition in Philo', *JBL* 65 (1946) 185-203.

The author assigns two meanings to the term εὐχή which Philo uses to express the concept of prayer: petition and thanks. He also speaks briefly about Philo's use of divine epithets, with frequent references to the texts (cf. 192ff.). (= R200)

4607. H. A. WOLFSON, 'Synedrion in Greek Jewish literature and Philo', *JQR* 36 (1946) 303-306; reprinted in *Studies...* (cf. **4207**) 566-569.

In three or four Philonic passages the term συνέδριον means 'court of justice'. (= R201)

1947

4701. S. CARAMELLA, 'I Neoplatonici nelle *Confessioni* di S. Agostino', *NDid* 1 (1947) 49-54.

Philo's influence on Augustine was not direct, but probably mediated through Numenius of Apamea. (= R202)

4702. J. DANIÉLOU, 'La typologie d'Isaac dans le Christianisme primitif', *Bib* 28 (1947) 363-393, esp. 376-380.

The figure of Isaac in Philo represents perfect virtue, understood as a natural gift, in contrast to ascetic virtue (represented by Jacob) and virtue achieved by intellectual effort (represented by Abraham). Philo's interpretation of Isaac is here compared with the interpretations given by Clement of Alexandria, Origen, Gregory of Nyssa and Ambrose. (= R203)

4703. R. M. GUASTALLA, 'Judaïsme et Hellénisme: la leçon de Philon d'Alexandrie', *REJ* 107 (1946-1947) 3-38.

Offers an overall presentation of the figure of Philo (his thought, sources, method, and critical fortunes) introduced by a preface on the historical, political, and cultural characteristics of Diaspora Judaism, which takes up about half of the article. (= R204)

4704. M. HERMANIUK, *La parabole évangélique: enquête exégétique et critique* (diss. Bruges-Paris-Louvain 1947), esp. 411-420.

Philonic allegory is one of the sources of Clement's 'parable'. The author explains this debt by outlining the essence of Philo's allegorical method, which is the transposition of the figurative sense onto the metaphysical level, as practised in Platonic philosophy. (= R205)

4705. H. DE LUBAC, "'Typologie' et 'allégorisme'", *RecSR* 34 (1947) 180-226, *passim*.

An explanation of the difference between allegory and typology. Historically speaking, the former is exclusively Philonic, in the sense that it entered Christian culture (e.g. Origen) through Philo; the latter, on the other hand, is typically Christian. (= R206)

4706. S. PÉTREMENT, *Le dualisme chez Platon, les Gnostiques et les Manichéens*, Bibliothèque de Philosophie Contemporaine (Paris 1947), esp. 216-220.

The author claims that if we were to search in the Gnostic movement for elements 'which are anterior to Christianity, we would find only Philo' (216). For Pétrement, therefore, Philo is the only known representative of pre-Christian Gnosticism. The latter manifests itself particularly in his conception of God, his theories of the Powers and the Logos, and his dualistic opposition of the flesh and the spirit. (RR)

4707. F. PETTIRSCH, 'Das Verbot der opera servilia in der Heiligen Schrift und in der altkirchlichen Exegese', *ZKTh* 69 (1947) 257-327, 417-444, esp. 306-312.

The command of rest on the Sabbath is a basic concept for Philo, the foundation of his religiosity and of many of his philosophical positions. Yet the Alexandrian tends to spiritualize the concept of the feast by identifying it with the joy which is consequent upon fullness of virtue. (= R207)

4708. H. RIESENFELD, 'La voie de charité: note sur I Cor. XII, 31', *StTh* 1 (1947) 146-157, esp. 149ff.

Briefly analyzes the notion of ὁδός in Philo's writings in relation to the meaning which the metaphor of the road assumed in contemporary Judaism. (= R208)

4709. F. M. M. SAGNARD, *La Gnose valentinienne et le témoignage de Saint Irénée*, Études de philosophie médiévale 36 (Paris 1947), esp. 598-602.

The existence of a supreme being which manifests itself through intermediaries and in particular through the Logos is the basic feature shared by Philo and the Valentinian Gnosis. (= R209)

4710. F. TAILLIEZ, 'ΒΑΣΙΛΙΚΗ ΟΔΟΣ: les valeurs d'un terme mystique et le prix de son histoire littérale', *OrChrP* 13 (1947) 299-354, esp. 309-318.

The author confines himself to collecting and briefly annotating the Philonic passages in which the expression in question occurs. (= R210)

4711. E. VANDERLINDEN, 'Les divers modes de connaissance de Dieu selon Philon d'Alexandrie', *MSR* 4 (1947) 285-304.

The article analyzes the philosophical components of Philo's psychology and sees the latter as a coherent structure, capable of giving unity and philosophical justification to much of Philo's so-called eclectic philosophy. In particular man's knowledge of God, which in the highest sense is not rational, but mystical-intuitive, reaffirms God's transcendence, also in respect of our capacity for knowledge. (= R211)

4712. W. VÖLKER, 'Die Vollkommenheitslehre des Clemens Alexandrinus in ihren geschichtlichen Zusammenhängen', *ThZ* 3 (1947) 15-40.

Though not specifically concerned with Philo, this article frequently refers to him as the thinker who provided Clement with the 'schema' of his mystic itinerary. (= R212)

4713. H. WESTHOFF, *Die Lichtvorstellung in der Philosophie der Vorsokratiker* (inaug. diss. Erlangen 1947), esp. 68-70.

The image of light in Philo is of Platonic and Posidonian origin and is important in the areas of both theology and psychology. (= R213)

4714. H. A. WOLFSON, *Philo, foundations of religious philosophy in Judaism, Christianity and Islam*, 2 vols. (Cambridge Mass. 1947, 1948[2], 1962[3], 1968[4]).

This huge study is certainly a landmark *sans pareil* in the history of the interpretation of Philo. Its outstanding merit consists in the attempt to fix an image of the author and to define his place in the history of Western ideas. The novelty of the results has had a disconcerting effect on scholars, especially those at work in the actual field of Philonic studies and in the history of philosophy, and their response has often been to engage in lively polemics against what they see as an unjustified inversion of traditional perspectives. But the book has stood up to criticism and has established itself as a highly important point of reference. Needless to say Wolfson's work raises many problems and requires verification and further study on various points; but it provides a point of departure which earlier general monographs were not able to offer. (Previously only the study of E. BRÉHIER (Paris 1908) had had comparable, if more limited, success in opening up vitally important perspectives.) Wolfson's central position can be summarized as follows. Philo saw himself confronted on the one hand by the philosophy of the Greeks, product of human reason, and on the other hand by divine revelation. Consequently, he tried to mediate between the two by marking out what would later be called the ancillary role of philosophy. In doing so, he determined the path which was subsequently to be taken by medieval philosophy and which hence came to represent a decisive step in the intellectual history of the West. Here are his well-known closing words (2.457):

> This fundamental departure from pagan Greek philosophy, if the facts of the history of philosophy are to be represented as they are actually *known by nature* and not as they merely happen to be *known by us,* appears first in Hellenistic Judaism, where it attains its systematic formulation in Philo. Philo is the founder of this new school of philosophy, and from him it directly passes on to the Gospel of St. John and the Church Fathers, from whom it passes on to Moslem and hence also to mediaeval Jewish philosophy. Philo is the direct or indirect source of this type of philosophy which continues uninterruptedly in its main assertions for well-nigh seventeen centuries, when at last it is openly challenged by Spinoza.

The distinction between facts 'known by nature' and 'known to us' can only be understood in the light of Wolfson's radical 'hypothetico-deductive' method, which forms the indispensable methodological basis of the study, and has received severe scholarly criticism. Few reviewers, however, took note of Wolfson's specifically philosophical interpretation that 'the point of departure of Philo's philosophy is the theory of Ideas' (1.200) and that for Philo this was both a biblical and a Platonic doctrine, forming a hinge, as it were, between biblical thought and philosophy. This assertion, however, together with the evidence supporting it, reincorporates Philo into the history of Platonism and might even furnish reasons for regarding him as the founder of Alexandrian Middle Platonism. Certainly, these conclusions delivered a fatal blow to the theories about

Philo's eclecticism or basically Stoic-Posidonian position. Among the many new elements which Wolfson brings to the interpretation of God, creation (regarded as *ex nihilo*), the Logos, and the Powers, we draw particular attention to his discussion of immortality, which in Philo's view is exclusively reserved – by the grace of God – for the souls of the good and not for those of the evil. Finally we should add that Wolfson's Philo, though thoroughly conversant with all the doctrines of Greek philosophy, nevertheless imports many crucial Jewish themes into his philosophical system: among these we might mention scriptural revelation, faith, God's unconditional omnipotence and the occurrence of miracles. A detailed summary of Wolfson's book (setting out the contents of the work in some fifty points) is found in the article by Marcus cited below (**4912**). REVIEWS: M. V. Anastos, *AHR* 53 (1948) 525f.; H. J. Cadbury, *Spec* 23 (1948) 523ff.; J. Daniélou, *RecSR* 35 (1948) 614ff., *Irén* 22 (1949) 239, *RHR* 138 (1951) 230ff.; E. Garin, *Bel* 3 (1948) 617ff.; G. A. Churgin, *Horeb* 10 (1948) 349ff.; W. R. Inge, *HibJ* 46 (1948) 371f.; F. C. Grant, *AThR* 30 (1948) 185f.; W. L. Knox, *JThS* 49 (1948) 210ff.; G. Berger, *EPh* 4 (1949) 102f.; H. Chadwick, *CR* 63 (1949) 24f.; F. V. Filson, *JQR* 39 (1948-1949) 97ff.; H. Francès, *RPhilos* 74 (1949) 495ff.; W. Gerber, *Eras* 2 (1949) cols. 269f.; M. R. Konvitz, *PhR* 58 (1949) 272ff.; P. O. Kristeller, *JPh* 46 (1949) 359ff.; M. S. Orlinsky, *CQ* 26 (1949) 148ff.; R. T. F., *Pers* 30 (1949) 418ff.; S. Sandmel, *CPh* 44 (1949) 49ff.; G. Vajda, *REJ* 9 (1949) 117ff.; E. Zolli, *Miscellanea Franciscana* 49 (1949) 423ff.; B. Botte, *RThAM* 17 (1950) 342f.; A. Brunner, *Scholastik* 25 (1950) 259f.; B. Celada, *Revista de Filosofia* 9 (1950) 123ff., *Sef* 10 (1950) 437f.; J. Dupont, *RHE* 45 (1950) 217ff.; G. E. Müller, *Sophia* 18 (1950) 383f.; A. Pincherle, *SMSR* 22 (1949-1950) 193ff.; W. Völker, *DLZ* 71 (1950) 290ff.; J. Gilbert, *NRTh* 73 (1951) 1108; H. J. Schoeps, *ThLZ* 76 (1951) cols. 680ff.; P. W. Skehan, *CHR* 36 (1951) 448ff.; J. A. Beckaert, *AThA* 12 (1952) 95f.; H. Jonas, *PhPhenR* 12 (1952) 442ff. Of the third edition: R. Grant, *Spec* 38 (1963) 164f.; T. Burkile, *PhR* 72 (1963) 257ff.; C. Richardson, *USQR* 18 (1963) 179f. Cf. also the following discussions: **4801, 4804, 4808, 4901, 4917, 5002, 5410, 5503, 7420, 7510, 7845, 8220, 8446, 8455**. For the Hebrew translation see **7038**. (= R214)

1948

4801. G. BOAS, 'Professor Wolfson's Philo', *JHI* 9 (1948) 385-392.

An extensive and accurate review of Wolfson's book (**4714**). (= R215)

4802. J. COPPENS, 'Philon et l'exégèse targumique', *EThL* 24 (1948) 430ff.

The comparison of *Opif.* with a rather obscure text in the Targum reveals notable affinities, especially of a theological kind. (= R216)

4803. P. COURCELLE, *Les lettres grecques en occident: de Macrobe à Cassiodore* (Paris 1943, 1948²; English translation, Cambridge Mass. 1969), esp. 70ff., 184.

On the knowledge of Philo's writings possessed by Jerome and Augustine. (DTR)

4804. J. DANIÉLOU, 'The philosophy of Philo: the significance of

Professor Harry A. Wolfson's new study', *ThS* 9 (1948) 578-589.

Wolfson's work (**4714**) 'is not an exhaustive portrait of Philo', for it obscures the religious dimension of his thought. As regards his philosophy, however, the work 'is definitive'. With it, according to Daniélou, 'the study of Philonic philosophy enters the domain of science' (589). (= R217)

4805. J. DANIÉLOU, *Origène*, Le génie du Christianisme (Paris 1948, English translation New York 1955), esp. 179-190.

Philo's influence on Origen is above all detectable in the latter's method of biblical exegesis, which is very artificial in form and owes much to Philo's 'perverse idea' that every detail in Scripture has a spiritual meaning. (= R218)

4806. J. DUPONT, 'Syneidèsis: aux origines de la notion chrétienne de conscience morale', *StudH* 5 (1948) 119-153, esp. 124-126, 146.

Paul and Philo give a similar meaning to the term συνείδησις. According to the author, both derived the term as well as its meaning from the popular philosophy and moralistic preaching of the Hellenistic period. (= R219)

4807. J. GIBLET, 'L'homme image de Dieu dans les commentaires littéraux de Philon d'Alexandrie', *StudH* 5 (1948) 93-118.

Philo revolutionized the concept of εἰκών. If in Rabbinic thought 'the image of God' merely designates material life, and if in Greek thought it refers to the sensible world, in Philo it is the expression of the invisible and spiritual world and of intelligence. That is possible because in Philo the fundamental opposition is no longer between sensible and intelligible, but between creator (God) and created being. In this opposition the body too retains its value – though not in an absolute way – as the material instrument of a transcendent reality. (= R220)

4808. E. R. GOODENOUGH, 'Wolfson's Philo', *JBL* 67 (1948) 87-109; reprinted in *Goodenough on the history of Religion and on Judaism* (cf. **8614**) 77-93.

An extensive and penetrating review of Wolfson's book (**4714**). Goodenough takes a decidedly critical view, especially with regard to Wolfson's method, which in his opinion forces Philo into a general philosophical framework that is largely preconceived. (= R221)

4809. I. HEINEMANN, Art. 'Philo', *The Universal Jewish Encyclopedia*, vol. 8 (New York 1948) 495-496.

A synoptic presentation of Philo's life and thought from a Jewish perspective by one of the greatest Philonic scholars of his time. (DTR)

4810. I. HEINEMANN [היינמן .י'], review of H. A. WOLFSON, *Philo* (cf. **4714**), in *Kirjath Sepher* 24 (1948) 208-212.

Subsequently expanded and published in German; see **5005**.

4811. R. MARCUS, 'A 16th century Hebrew critique of Philo (Azariah dei Rossi's *Meor Eynayim*, Pt. I, cc. 3-6)', *HUCA* 21 (1948) 29-71.

The author draws attention to the 16th century Hebrew commentary on Philo written by Azariah dei Rossi. Though usually neglected by scholars, this scholar is an important figure, for it was he who broke the silence surrounding Philo in the Talmudic and medieval period. Azariah's judgement of Philo is only partly favourable, since he does not agree with Philo's allegorical method and does not understand his vacillations with regard to the concept of creation. In general, however, the 16th century scholar considers Philo's position reconcilable with Jewish orthodoxy. After carefully analyzing Azariah's work, Marcus concludes with two appendices: one gathers some references to Philo in the work of the 16th century Italian scholar Eugubinus; the other reports on Azariah's translation of Gelenius' Latin version of Philo. (= R222)

4812. R. MARCUS, 'Notes on the Armenian text of Philo's *Quaestiones in Genesin*, Books I-III', *JNES* 7 (1948) 111-115.

Adds a few corrections to Aucher's translation of *QG* 1-3. (= R223)

4813. P. MORAUX, 'Une nouvelle trace de l'Aristote perdu', *EtCl* 16 (1948) 89-91.

Philo's allusions to the existence of a fifth substance, according to the author, must derive from Aristotle's lost treatise *De philosophia*. (= R224)

4814. H. RAHNER, 'Der Spielende Mensch', *ErJb* 16 [*Der Mensch*] (1948) 11-87, *passim*.

No chronological limits are set to this study, which is thus not confined to classical antiquity. In his discussion Rahner mentions Philo's work frequently, if only in passing, citing passages in which the idea of play is suggested. A certain prominence is given to the allegory of Isaac, 'the laughter of the soul' (cf. 45-48). (= R225)

4815. W. J. ROBBINS, *A study in Jewish and Hellenistic legend with special reference to Philo's* Life of Moses (diss. Brown University 1948).

This dissertation aims at a non-controversial, constructive study of the Hellenistic treatment of Moses. After a brief analysis of the story of Moses in the Pentateuch, Jewish Apocalyptic and Judaeo-Hellenistic literature, the bulk of the work is devoted to Philo's *Life of Moses* (the task for Philonic scholarship, according to the author, now being to undertake exhaustive studies of each of his works, cf. 46). Robbins proceeds to summarize the various sections of the *De vita Moysis*, adding remarks on points of special interest, but these do not amount to research of any depth. The concluding chapter places Philo's biography in the broader context of the development of biblical and Jewish thought. Philo avoids the excesses of early Judaeo-Hellenistic literature, also leaving out the 'folklorish' elements later included by Josephus. Philo obtrudes his own aims and judgments on the biographical material, in this following Hellenistic practice and departing from the methods of biblical narrative. From the literary point of view, and especially in his striving to see Moses as an ideal figure, Philo perhaps anticipates later hagiography. But it must be immediately added that the Christian writers had a deeper sense of history. (DTR)

4816. M. SIMON, *Verus Israel: étude sur les relations entre Chrétiens et Juifs dans l'empire romain*, Bibliothèque des Écoles Françaises d'Athènes et de Rome 166 (Paris 1948, 1964²; English translation Oxford 1986), esp. 78-82.

Briefly discusses the connections between Philo and Jewish-Alexandrian culture, the reconstruction of the latter being strongly dependent on Philo's evidence. (= R226)

1949

4901. B. J. BAMBERGER, 'The dating of Aggadic materials', *JBL* 68 (1949) 115-123.

The author intervenes in the debate between Goodenough (cf. **4808**) and Wolfson (cf. **4714**) and demonstrates the soundness of the latter's method of using Talmudic parallels. (= R227)

4902. G. BONAFEDE, *Storia della filosofia greco-romana* (Florence 1949), esp. 343-350.

This short outline of Philo's work and thought shows the religious-contemplative dimension which transcends and gives unity to the basic eclecticism of his philosophical thought. (= R228)

4903. R. BULTMANN, *Das Urchristentum im Rahmen der antiken Religionen* (Stuttgart 1949, 1954², French translation Paris 1950), esp. 81ff. of the French edition.

The doctrines of Platonic philosophy, and more precisely of the Platonism which tends towards Neoplatonism (cf. 84ff.), are more important in Philo than Stoic doctrine, because they are more suitable for translating the content of the Bible into philosophical terms. (= R229)

4904. J. DUPONT, *Gnosis: la connaissance religieuse dans les Épîtres de Saint Paul* (diss. Louvain-Paris 1949), esp. 158-180.

Of the many points of contact between Philo and Paul, those related to psychological theory are certainly the most important. In his analysis of these points the author underlines the following aspects. (1) the opposition truth-falsehood, which Philo used to describe the relation between Jews and pagans, is also used by Paul in reference to the relation Christians-Jews. (2) The Pauline antithesis between 'psychic' and 'pneumatic' (ψυχικός-πνευματικός) is readily explained from the Philonic interpretation of the creation of man. (3) The use of the verb καταλαμβάνω in Philo shows that, before Paul, the term had already assumed in philosophy the religious connotation which it has in Eph. 3:18. (= R230)

4905. A. J. FESTUGIÈRE, *La révélation d'Hermès Trismégiste*, vol. 2, *Le Dieu cosmique*, Études Bibliques (Paris 1949), esp. 519-585.

The author recognizes two components in the personality of Philo. The first consists of the complex of motifs or *topoi* which Philo takes from the tradition without adding anything personal or original (it includes literary, scientific-philosophical, and also mystical elements); the second, which constitutes his original contribution, is love for the Bible and philosophy, faith in divine grace, and the supremacy accorded to the activity of contemplation. With regard to the latter, Festugière emphasizes the ambiguity of Philo's attitude towards the cosmos: on the one hand, it is in man's power to arrive at God through knowledge of the world; but on the other hand, the same goal can only be reached through renunciation of the world and withdrawal into oneself. Both attitudes are of Platonic origin: the first derives from the *Timaeus*, the second from the *Phaedo*, the *Symposium*, and the *Republic*. Philo takes up both attitudes (he in fact incorporates them into the very scheme which expresses the soul's ascent to God), but does not hesitate to set the second above the first. Herein lies the importance of Philo for the history of thought. He, in fact, was the first who sought a synthesis between the two attitudes (in this he was later followed by Hermetic thought). Hence it became possible, Festugière concludes, that 'a Jew could keep pure the monotheism of his faith, even while using the language of astral polytheism' (585). (= R231)

4906. A. FUKS [פוקס .א], מרקוס יוליוס אלכסנדר – לתולדות משפחת פילון אלכסנדרוני ['Marcus Julius Alexander – the family history of Philo of Alexandria'], *Zion* 13-14 (1948-49) 10-17.

Subsequently published in English; see **5108**.

4907. I. HEINEMANN [היינמן .י], -היחס שבין עם לארצו בספרות היהודית הלניסטית ['The relationship between the Jewish people and their land in Hellenistic-Jewish literature'], *Zion* 13-14 (1948-49) 1-9.

Mainly a discussion of Philo's relation to the land of Israel. The midrashic praise of the land is not to be found in Hellenistic-Jewish literature, although the love of the 'fatherland' is as important for Philo as for the Stoics. The real relation to the land of Israel comes to the fore when Philo differentiates between μητρόπολις and ἱερόπολις, i.e. there is a religious tie that binds Hellenistic Jewry to Israel more than Greek colonies to the mother-polis. English Summary. (MM)

4908. I. HEINEMANN [היינמן .י], האלגוריסטיקה של היהודים ההלניסטיים פרט לפילון [= 'The allegorical method of Hellenistic Jews aside from Philo'], in M. SCHWABE and I. GUTMAN (edd.), ספר יוחנן לוי [*Commentationes Judaico-Hellenisticae in memoriam Ioannis Lewy*] (Jerusalem 1949) 46-58.

Subsequently published in German; see **5206**.

4909. H. JONAS [יונס .ה], בעיית הכרת האל בתורתו של פילון האלכסנדרוני [= 'The problem of knowing God in the thought of Philo of Alexandria'], in *Commentationes Judaico-Hellenisticae...* (cf. **4908**) 65-84.

Subsequently expanded and published in German (**5408**, 2.40-101).

4910. P. KATZ, 'Das Problem des Urtextes der Septuaginta', *ThZ* 5

(1949) 1-24.

This article is exclusively concerned with philological and paleographical questions. Philo's work is often mentioned and in one case (15ff.) its manuscript tradition is briefly analyzed. For the rest the author refers to his monograph on the subject, at that time in the course of publication (cf. **5007**). (= R232)

4911. R. MARCUS, 'Hellenistic Jewish literature', in L. FINKELSTEIN (ed.), *The Jews, their history, culture and religion*, vol. 2 (Philadelphia 1949, 1955², 1960³) 1077-1115, esp. 1107-1115.

A brief outline of the figure of Philo from a historical-cultural and philosophical point of view. (= R233)

4912. R. MARCUS, 'Wolfson's revaluation of Philo: a review article', *RR* 13 (1949) 368-381.

A lucid and accurate analysis of Wolfson's work (cf. **4714**), which at the same time can serve as a useful reading guide. Marcus briefly summarizes each chapter and thus brings out the structure of the entire work. (= R234)

4913. C. MAZZANTINI, *La filosofia nel filosofare umano: storia del pensiero antico* (Turin-Rome 1949), esp. 356-364.

A sober presentation of the main lines of Philo's thought, showing the centrality of the concept of God and its determinative influence on Philo's ethics and anthropology. (= R235)

4914. R. H. PFEIFFER, *History of New Testament times: with an introduction to the Apocrypha* (New York-Evanston 1949), esp. 212-224.

Insufficient attention is paid to Philo (222-224) in the section which Pfeiffer dedicates to Jewish-Alexandrian philosophy. But the general presentation of this philosophy, in which Philo is continually referred to, is of greater interest. It characterizes Philo's work on three levels: (a) as an attempt to deduce Greek philosophy from the Pentateuch; (b) as a philosophical interpretation of the Bible; (c) as a de-anthropomorphization of Scripture. (= R236)

4915. M. POHLENZ, *Die Stoa: Geschichte einer geistigen Bewegung* (Göttingen 1948-49, 1959², 1964³), esp. 1.369-378, vol. 2.180-184 of the first edition.

Pohlenz first acknowledges the subordinate role which philosophy plays in Philo with respect to wisdom, which in the final analysis is identified with Mosaic philosophy and the faith in a creator God – elements which transcend Stoic thought. Subsequently, he underlines the many points of contact between Philo and the Stoa, in particular with regard to cosmology, anthropology, and ethics. (= R237)

4916. G. QUISPEL, 'Philo und die altchristliche Häresie', *ThZ* 5 (1949) 429-436.

The author sets out to demonstrate, on the basis of philological arguments and an analysis of contents, that the first clear traces of Philo's influence on Christian thought are not to be found in the Prologue to the Gospel of John, but in the Valentinian Gnosis. (= R238)

4917. L. ROBERTS, 'Wolfson's monument to Philo', *Isis* 40 (1949) 199-213.

An extensive and accurate review which brings out the strong points and innovatory aspects of Wolfson's work (**4714**). The Wolfsonian interpretation of Philo is on the whole accepted, though some assertions are said to require further study and analysis. (= R239)

4918. V. TCHERIKOVER [ריקובר צ׳ .א], -היהודית הספרות לחקר פרקים ראשי האלכסנדרונית [='Major Themes in the Study of Jewish-Alexandrian literature'], in *Commentationes Judaico-Hellenisticae...* (cf. **4908**) 139-160.

Subsequently published in English; see **5617**. Later republished in **6117**.

4919. G. VAJDA, 'De Philon aux scolastiques: origine et croissance de la philosophie religieuse', *Crit* 39 (1949) 697-712.

A lucid presentation of Philo, though without much scientific depth. Fundamental importance is attributed to Philo's role in Western thought, regarded as a synthesis of Greek and Jewish culture, of faith and reason. (= R240)

1950

5001. J. DANIÉLOU, 'L'incompréhensibilité de Dieu d'après Saint Jean Chrysostome', *RSR* 37 (1950) 176-194.

The doctrine of the unknowability of God is without doubt of Philonic origin. In Philo it serves to translate the transcendence of God into metaphysical and religious terms. (= R243)

5002. J. DANIÉLOU, *Sacramentum futuri: études sur les origines de la typologie biblique*, Études de Théologie Historique (Paris 1950), esp. 45-52, 112-128, 177-190.

The three allegorical figures examined here by the author (Adamite typology, the marriage of Isaac, the life of Moses) help to throw light on Philo's personality, which is that of a Jewish believer and a mystic (190). This interpretation of Philo intermediates between Völker (cf. **3817**), who sees Philo virtually exclusively as a mystic in the biblical and Christian sense of the word, and Wolfson (cf. **4714**), for whom he is almost solely the founder of biblical philosophy; but it is far removed from Goodenough's views, who regards Philo as a representative of a Hellenistic mystery. (= R 244)

5003. G. DELLING, 'Zur paulinischen Teleologie', *ThLZ* 75 (1950)

705-710, esp. 707-709; reprinted in F. HAHN, T. HOLTZ, N. WALTER (edd.), *Studien zum Neuen Testament und zum hellenistischen Judentum: Gesammelte Aufsatze 1950-1968* (Göttingen 1970) 311-317.

Philo's anthropology, like that of Paul, is clearly influenced by his theology; the goal of man is not man himself, but God. Yet Paul goes beyond Philo in giving a positive value to history (cf. 709). (= R245)

5004. L. FRÜCHTEL, 'Zur Aesopfabel des Kallimachos', *Gymn* 57 (1950) 123-124.

A brief comment on the text in question, here brought in relation to *Conf.* 6-8. (= R246)

5005. I. HEINEMANN, 'Philo als Vater der mittelalterlichen Philosophie?', *ThZ* 6 (1950) 99-116.

An analysis of Wolfson's work (cf. **4714**). Its main value, according to Heinemann, lies in the fact that it has attempted to incorporate Philo not only into the usual context of Greek and Jewish culture, but also into the much larger context of medieval philosophy, though it does so from a point of view with which Heinemann strongly disagrees. Earlier version published in Hebrew; cf. **4810**. (= R247)

5006. I. HEINEMANN [היינמן .י], דרכי האגדה [= *Methodology of the Aggadah*] (Jerusalem 1950) *passim*.

This classic study of Rabbinic thought and literary technique, sadly as yet untranslated, contains much of interest for the student of Philo. Heinemann's basic categories of 'creative historiography' and 'creative philology' are richly illustrated through the comparison and contrast of examples drawn from Rabbinic and Philonic writings. The detailed index listing for Philo (271) helps make these discussions accessible. Of particular note are the sections on the rationalization of commandments (143ff.), on allegory (157ff.), and on the general relationship between Philo's 'logos-directed' thought and the Sages' 'organic' thinking (180ff.). (DS)

5007. P. KATZ, *Philo's Bible: the aberrant text of Bible quotations in some Philonic writings and its place in the textual history of the Greek Bible* (Cambridge 1950).

This work sets out to reconstruct, from a strictly philological point of view and on the basis of a rigorously technical terminology, the entire biblical text to which Philo makes reference, starting from those quotations which do not agree with the text of the LXX. In these quotations – which the author selects and analyzes with great care in the first part of the work – at least three tendencies may be distinguished: '(a) the introduction of a different type of Bible quotations, the text of which follows lines irreconcilable with those of the LXX quoted and expounded by Philo himself; (b) the manipulation of seemingly meaningless Bible quotations – (a) and (b) mostly in the lemmata–; and finally (c) the freely introduced interchanges between quotations from the Bible and Philo's exposition' (96). These aberrant passages, according to Katz, cannot be regarded as sporadic or incidental modifications of the LXX, but on the contrary suggest a special recension of Philo's text which depends, for the biblical references, on a lost recension of the

Pentateuch. Katz also succeeds in specifying the identity of Philo's interpolator, who is said to be a representative of the school of Antioch, probably active in Syria or Palestine, but he finds insufficient evidence for a precise dating. The book concludes with a review of scholarship on the subject (125-138) and with a series of six appendices complementing the analyses contained in the first part of the work. REVIEWS: B. Botte, *RThAM* 18 (1951) 160f.; M. Johannessohn, *ThLZ* 76 (1951) 679f.; G. D. Kilpatrick, *JThS* 2 (1951) 87ff.; C. Larcher, *RB* 58 (1951) 274ff.; C. Matagne, *NRTh* 73 (1951) 424f.; E. L. Rapp, *Gn* 23 (1951) 398f.; J. Ziegler, *ThRv* 47 (1951) 201ff.; D. Amand, *RBen* 62 (1952) 314f.; Hospers-Jansen, *BiOr* 9 (1952) 146; B. J. Roberts, *JJS* 2 (1952) 205ff.; A. Debrunner, *MH* 10 (1953) 251f.; W. C. van Unnik, *VChr* 7 (1953) 187f. (= R248)

5008. F. LANG, *Das Feuer im Sprachgebrauch der Bibel dargestellt auf dem Hintergrund der Feuervorstellungen in der Umwelt* (diss. Tübingen 1950), esp. 109-122.

Within its analytic framework this work carefully follows the various meanings of the notion of fire in Philo. Basic to the author's findings is the dichotomous structure of these meanings, occurring on the cosmological level (in fire as a cosmic element), on the anthropological level (in the relation between fire and spirit), and finally, on the ethical-theological level, in reference to the biblical motif of fire as theophany and the ethical interpretation which Philo imposes on it. (= R249)

5009. E. K. LEE, *The religious thought of St. John* (London 1950), esp. 16f., 87-89, 132-135.

The author indicates the main points of contact between the theological thought of John and Philo. In particular he discusses the doctrine of the Logos and the theme of seeing God. (= R250)

5010. H. LEISEGANG, 'Der Gottmensch als Archetypus', *ErJb* 18 [*Aus der Welt der Urbilder: Sonderband für C. G. Jung zum fünfundsiebzigsten Geburtstag, 26. Juli 1950*] (1950) 9-45, esp. 32-38.

For Philo the superiority of Moses over the other prophets and his own nature as a divine man are due to the fact that he saw God face to face. Philo, however, does not regard that as the fruit of a particular virtue, but as the result of divine grace. (= R251)

5011. D. LERCH, *Isaaks Opferung christlich gedeutet: eine auslegungsgeschichtliche Untersuchung*, BHTh 12 (Tübingen 1950), esp. 20-25.

Philo's interpretation of the sacrifice of Isaac (especially in *Abr.*) moves considerably away from the biblical text. It seems rather to be based on Greek and especially Stoic models, to the extent that the biblical names appear to replace those of classical heroes. (= R252)

5012. A. LEVI, 'Il problema dell'errore in Filone di Alessandria', *RCSF* 5 (1950) 281-294.

In the view of the author the strict relation which Philo establishes between human knowledge and divine grace poses two kinds of problems. On the one hand, in view of the omniscience and omnipotence of God, there is no justification for the existence of error; on the other hand, if knowledge of truth depends solely on divine grace, who could be sure of having obtained this grace? (= R253)

5013. S. V. MCCASLAND, '"The image of God" according to Paul', *JBL* 69 (1950) 85-100.

The concept of the image of God, which in Philo is linked to the concept of logos, is compared with the analogous concept in Paul and with some aspects of the anthropology of Epictetus. (= R242)

5014. R. MARCUS, 'A textual-exegetical note on Philo's Bible', *JBL* 69 (1950) 363-365.

A brief methodological and philological contribution to the study of Philo's biblical exegesis, with specific reference to Philo's exegesis of Gen. 27:41 in *Det.* 46, *QG* 4.238. (= R254)

5015. R. MONDOLFO, *Il pensiero antico: storia della filosofia greco-romana esposta con testi scelti dalle fonti* (Florence 1950) 473-488.

In the Preface the author himself explains the nature of this work, which, far from being a mere collection of texts, rightly claims to be a 'history of ancient philosophy'. Its method is later adopted by Faggin (**6611**), who also places the same heavy emphasis on theological themes. The method seems to be used to greater effect in this work, since it also attempts, if only in outline, to account for the vacillations and ambiguities of many Philonic concepts. Compared to the first edition of 1927, this edition is considerably revised and enlarged. (= R255)

5016. *Reallexikon für Antike und Christentum*, edited by T. KLAUSER *et al.* (Stuttgart 1950-).

The first fascicle of this magnificent lexicon was published in 1941, the first completed volume in 1950. By 1986 13 volumes had been completed, reaching the subject lemma 'Heilgötter'. The lexicon was conceived as an instrument for the study of the relations between the ancient world and early Christianity. Both from the Judaic and the Hellenistic point of view Philo is a major participant in this area of study, and so it is scarcely surprising that his evidence is discussed in a large number of articles. In our bibliography we list all the contributions in which Philo is dealt with under a separate sub-heading, but no resumés will be given (only an English translation of the subject lemma). These lists will be found under the title of the lexicon in the years that complete volumes were published. It should be noted that contributions have tended to become longer as the lexicon progresses. Until vol. 4 Philo rarely gets a section or sub-section all for himself (for example, in the article 'Allegorese' he is dealt with under the heading 'Juden' in less than a column; see 1.287). On the Supplementary articles see **8535**. (DTR)

5017. K. L. SCHMIDT, 'Jerusalem als Urbild und Abbild', *ErJB* 18 [cf. **5010**] (1950) 207-248, esp. 244-247.

The term which Philo uses to designate the holy city Jerusalem is a Hellenistic one. He in fact employs the expression ἱερὰ πόλις, used by the Greeks to indicate holy cities, and not ἁγία πόλις, which is the term used by the LXX and by the New Testament. At the same time the concept of Jerusalem in Philo undergoes a process of psychologization and spiritualization; this brings him close to Platonic political thought, which posits a strict analogy between the structure of the state and that of the soul. (= R256)

5018. H. J. SCHOEPS, 'Religionsphänomenologische Untersuchungen zur Glaubensgestalt des Judentums', *ZRGG* 2 (1949-50) 293-310, esp. 297f.

Man's existential attitude towards God, which is essentially one of reverential fear, depends on the generally creationistic conception of Philonic theology. (= R257)

5019. C. SPICQ, 'Le philonisme de l'Épître aux Hébreux', *RB* 56 (1949) 542-572; 57 (1950) 212-242; reprinted with slight modifications in *L'Épître aux Hébreux*, vol. 1 (Paris 1952, 1961³), esp. 39-91.

Although Philo's influence on Hebrews is widespread and constant, it is particularly noticeable in the apologetic and hortatory parts. Spicq grounds this assertion in a comparative analysis of vocabulary, argumentation, exegetical method, and philosophical themes and schemata. He concludes that the author of Hebrews did not passively reproduce Philo's themes and style, but certainly must have had the opportunity to study his works (cf. 240); it is even likely that he knew Philo personally – perhaps he heard him preach in a synagogue – and that this contributed to the strong influence that Philo exercised on him. (= R258)

5020. D. J. THERON, *Paul's concept of ἀλήθεια (truth): a comparative study with special reference to the Septuagint, Philo, the Hermetic literature, and Pistis Sophiae* (diss. Princeton 1950).

Contains a superficial compilation of passages in Philo that refer to the notion of truth, without references to secondary literature. (= R259)

5021. H. A. WOLFSON, 'The veracity of scripture in Philo, Halevi, Maimonides, and Spinoza', in S. LIEBERMAN (ed.), *Alexander Marx jubilee volume, on the occasion of his seventieth birthday: English section* (New York 1950) 603-630; reprinted as 'The veracity of scripture from Philo to Spinoza', in *Religious philosophy: a group of essays* (Cambridge Mass. 1961) 217-245.

In his attempt to harmonize the Holy Scriptures with philosophical thought, Philo uses four types of arguments to demonstrate the divine origin of the Law: (1) the miraculous interventions of the prophets; (2) their ability to predict events; (3) the revelation on Mount Sinai; (4) the excellence of the Law. In the course of the article Wolfson compares Philo's arguments with those of Halevi, Maimonides, and Spinoza (cf. 622ff.). For the subsequent Hebrew translation, cf. **7853**. (= R260)

1951

5101. S. AALEN, *Die Begriffe 'Licht' und 'Finsternis' im Alten Testament, im Spätjudentum und im Rabbinismus*, SNVAO.HF 1951.1 (Oslo 1951), esp. 211-218.

The author's main thesis is that Philo's authentically Jewish views were modified by Hellenistic universalism. Philo believes that the good cannot be suppressed, just as light cannot be obscured. He is also convinced of man's innate predisposition to the good; from it he infers the ineluctable victory of his faith. On the other hand, where he identifies light with reason, universalism in Philo merges with rationalism. The light to which he refers, however, is not a light which 'spreads', but one which 'attracts' (213). For this reason the triumph of Mosaic law, which according to Philo is achieved in the context of history and not in an eschatological dimension, involves no coercion or violence. This law has an exclusively religious meaning, and not a political-legal one. (= R261)

5102. A. W. ARGYLE, 'Philo and the fourth Gospel', *ET* 63 (1951) 385-386.

The supposed connections between the Gospel of John and Philo are essentially based on the concept of logos. Argyle points out the main similarities between the two authors in their use of this concept. (= R262)

5103. S. BELKIN [בלקין .ש], – יאיר בן פנחס ׳דר מדרש או תרשא מדרש קדום הלניסטי מדרש [= 'Midrash Tadshe or the Midrash of R. Pinchas ben Yair – an early Hellenistic Midrash'], *Horeb* 11 (1951) 1-52.

Belkin takes issue with A. EPSTEIN's hypothesis – in his introduction and commentary to *Midrash Tadshe* (Vienna 1887) –, according to which R. Moses haDarshan, the medieval compiler of this Midrash, was largely dependent upon a hypothetical, more complete Hebrew version of the *Book of Jubilees*, and that Philo was also influenced by the *Book of Jubilees*, thus explaining the parallels between *Midrash Tadshe* and Philo. Belkin notes that while most of the material in *Midrash Tadshe* which is not found in the traditional Midrashic sources is found word for word in Philo, the latter never mentions any of the Apocryphal and Pseudepigraphic works. Comparing the parallels at length, Belkin argues that although the compiler of *Midrash Tadshe* could not have been familiar with the Philonic corpus, the common source of the parallel material is the use on the part of both Philo and *Midrash Tadshe* of the often no longer extant Hellenistically influenced parts of the ancient 'oral' Midrashic tradition which Belkin assumes developed parallel to the 'oral' Halachic tradition. This, in turn, indicates an early date for *Midrash Tadshe*. (NGC)

5104. H. BIETENHARD, *Die himmlische Welt im Urchristentum und Spätjudentum*, WUNT 2 (Tübingen 1951), esp. 178-181.

The concept of the heavenly native land is used by Philo to distinguish between sinners and the virtuous. But above the men of heaven stand the men of God, the prophets and the priests. (= R263)

5105. M. BLACK, 'The origin of the name Metatron', *VT* 1 (1951) 217-219.

The term μετρητής (measurer) is of Philonic origin and is used by Philo as an epithet of the Logos in *QG*. (= R264)

5106. A. CERESA-GASTALDO, 'ΑΓΑΠΗ nei documenti anteriori al Nuovo Testamento', *Aeg* 31 (1951) 269-306, esp. 287.

The term ἀγαπή in Philo expresses the concept of 'intellectual love of God' and recalls Sap. Sal. 6:17-18. (RR)

5107. J. D. EISENSTEIN [אייזענשטיין .ד.י], פילון [= 'Philo'], in אוצר ישראל [*Ozar Yisrael*] (New York 1924, 1951²) 8.230-234.

A somewhat quaint survey of Philonic writings and doctrines, very much in the spirit of an earlier age of scholarship. Philo's position vis-a-vis Rabbinic literature serves here as a recurrent theme. (DS)

5108. A. FUKS, 'Notes on the Archive of Nicanor', *JJP* 5 (1951) 207-216; reprinted in *idem, Social conflict in ancient Greece* (Jerusalem-Leiden 1984) 312-321.

Most of the ostraca of the Coptos find concern the business activities of a transport firm belonging to Nicanor and his family. One of their best customers was Marcus Julius Alexander, almost certainly the son of Alexander the Alabarch and brother of Tiberius Julius Alexander, and thus a nephew of Philo. When the evidence of the ostraca is added to what is known from other sources, it appears that Philo's family may have had a special connection with Upper Egypt. Earlier version published in Hebrew; cf. **4906**. (DTR)

5109. E. R. GOODNEOUGH, 'The menorah among Jews of the Roman world', *HUCA* [*Hebrew Union College seventy-fifth anniversary publication*] 32 (1950-51) 449-492, esp. 467-84.

Passages in Philo (and Josephus) help to explain why, of all the cultic machinery in the temple, it was the menorah which took its place in the synagogue and thus survived in Judaism. The menorah, representing the Light of the world or Logos, was God's mercy revealed to the Jew in both a cosmic and Jewish sense. On the whole the Rabbis condemned this approach, but in the Midrash Rabbah on Numbers 15:4 there is evidence of the mystical Judaism known to us mainly through Philo. (DTR)

5110. J. KLAUSNER [קלוזנר .י], הסטוריה של הבית השני [= *The history of the Second Commonwealth*], 5 vols. (Jerusalem 1949-1951) 4.275-85, 5.65-86.

Klausner gives a general introduction to Philo (5.65-86), emphasizing Philo's Jewishness, including his familiarity with Bible and Hebrew, his pilgrimage to Jerusalem, his reverence for Moses and opposition to anti-nominaism. Separate sections are devoted to surveys of Philo's books, his philosophy and ethics, his views on creation and anthropology, and the contrasting reception he received at the hands of Christians and Jews. The latter rejected him, Klausner suggests, because they found the compromise between Moses and Plato threatening in a hostile world. Also in Klausner's account of the reign of Gaius Caligula (vol. 4) Philo figures prominently, both as an actor on the historical stage and as author of *Leg.* and *Flacc.*, which record the 'first anti-semitic pogrom in Jewish history' (275) in Alexandria and Gaius' attempt to erect his statue in the Temple of Jerusalem. (DRS)

5111. W. LAMEERE, 'Sur un passage de Philon d'Alexandrie (*De Plantatione* 1-6)', *Mnem* IV 4 (1951) 73-80.

The system of pagan demonology is compared by Philo to the doctrine of angels in Scripture. The author analyzes in this connection a few passages from *Plant.* which differ in some respects from the parallel texts in *Somn.* and *Gig.* The source of these ideas, it is suggested, goes back via the Peripatos to Plato and Aristotle. (= R266)

5112. A. LAURENTIN, 'Le pneuma dans la doctrine de Philon', *EThL* 27 (1951) 390-437; published separately in Analecta Lovaniensia Biblica et Orientalia, II 25 (Louvain-Paris 1951).

The term πνεῦμα in Philo appears to have four different meanings: air, active bond between the elements, human soul, and prophetic inspiration. The first part of the work tries to find the unity which possibly underlies the various meanings; the second part, goes on to make an attempt to determine the sense of this unity. In both cases no recourse is made to non-Philonic sources. The conclusion is that the term's unity is not one of number, but of relation: on every level *pneuma* denotes a double relation, with life and with God: a relation of origin and of finality which refers to a theory of participation. (= R267)

5113. S. SANDMEL, 'Abraham's knowledge of the existence of God', *HThR* 44 (1951) 137-139.

The author analyzes some differences between the way that Abraham's knowledge of God is presented in Rabbinic literature and Josephus and the presentation of the same theme in Philo. (= R268)

5114. C. SPICQ, 'Alexandrinismes dans l'Épître aux Hébreux', *RB* 58 (1951) 481-502.

The author qualifies his assertions in the preceding article on the same subject (**5019**) by pointing out the possibility that both Philo and the author of Hebrews may have drawn on the same cultural milieu. For this purpose he analyzes some forty terms from Hebrews which are extraneous to the rest of the New Testament and are of Alexandrian derivation. (= R269)

5115. A. F. STAPLES, *The Book of Hebrews in its relationship to the writings of Philo Judaeus* (diss. Louisville Kentucky 1951).

A work that has remained inaccessible to us, and is not summarized in a Dissertation Index. (= R271)

5116. J. STELMA, 'Philo van Alexandrië', in J. H. WASZINK, W. C. VAN UNNIK, C. DE BEUS (edd.), *Het oudste Christendom en de antieke cultuur* (Haarlem 1951) 1.589-602.

A synoptic portrait of Philo with emphasis on his contact with Greek philosophy and his biblical exegesis. 'The Alexandrian theologian-philosopher came close to the gospel. This did not take place ultimately through his direct contact with the Greek spirit, but through his deep knowledge of the Old Testament writings, which for him too were revelation' (601). (DTR)

5117. T. VERHOEVEN, 'Monarchia dans Tertullien, *Adversus Praxean*', *VChr* 5 (1951) 43-48.

The term *monarchia* used by Tertullian in the work under discussion was already a technical term in the Jewish-Alexandrian apologists, as its use in Philo demonstrates. (= R272)

5118. H. A. WOLFSON, 'Clement of Alexandria on the generation of the Logos', *ChH* 20 (1951) 72-81.

Of the many points of contact between the writings of Clement and Philo the most important are those relating to the theory of the Logos. This article concentrates on a few epithets which both authors use in a rather similar way to characterize the relationship of the Logos to God. Other affinities pointed out concern the concept of *nous* and man's ontological constitution. (= R273)

1952

5201. Y. F. BAER [בער .י], היסודות ההסטוריים של ההלכה [.י] ['The historical foundations of the Halachah'], *Zion* 17 (1952) 1-55, 173.

This wide-ranging programmatic essay proposes 'to transfer [the issue of Greek-Hebrew cultural contact] from the periphery to the center of Jewish history, from later periods to the beginnings of the Halakhah and the faith of 'normative' Judaism' (55). Baer examines the development of various aspects of the Jewish law and polity in the early Hasmonean period – the Sanhedrin, the Temple service, and so on – in an attempt to recover the original ideals and social context underlying this legislation. Philo is invoked regularly (16f., 21f., 37f.) as a witness to this basic ideology of the period of the Second Temple. Extensive English summary. See further **5304, 5502**. (DS)

5202. S. W. BARON, *A social and religious history of the Jews*, 3 vols. (New York 1937), 18 vols. (New York 1952-76²), esp. 1.199-207, 386-390 of the second edition.

An account of Philo's thought written at a rather high level of generality, reaching the following conclusion (206): 'Philo thus stood at the crossroads between Judaism and Hellenism. He tried to reconcile the historical and static. That he did not quite succeed and seemed to be in an almost inevitable discord with the world and himself is due to the ultimate impossibility of such an attempt.' Elsewhere in this massive work Philonic evidence is much utilized; cf. the comprehensive index to volumes 1-8 (New York 1960) 115-116. (DTR)

5203. R. GOOSSENS, 'La secte de la nouvelle alliance et les Esséniens', *Fl* 35 (1952) 145-154.

The evidence in Philo on the Essenes of Alexandria (i.e. the Therapeutae) pleads both against the hypercritical theory which denies their existence and against the opposite view which posits a perfect identity of opinion between the Therapeutae and the Essenes of Palestine. (= R274)

5204. R. M. GRANT, *Miracle and natural law in Graeco-Roman and early Christian thought* (Amsterdam 1952), esp. 89-91, 185-187.

Philo's attitude to the sciences is rather ambiguous: on the one hand, he seems severely critical, on the other hand, profoundly admiring. The first attitude reaches him through Carneades and the New Academy, the second through Antiochus and Posidonius. Philo's belief in miracles remains strong because it is not based on philosophical arguments, but on religious conviction. (= R275)

5205. I. HAUSHERR, *Philautie: de la tendresse pour soi à la charité, selon Saint Maxime le Confesseur*, Orientalia Christiana Analecta 137 (Rome 1952), esp. 21-25.

In Philo φιλαυτία is equivalent to impiety, in the first place because it leads man to attribute to himself absolute ownership of his faculties, which in fact belong to God, and in the second place because it makes him seek material pleasures. (= R276)

5206. I. HEINEMANN, 'Die Allegoristik der hellenistischen Juden ausser Philon', *Mnem* IV 5 (1952) 130-138.

Although Philo is deliberately excluded from the scope of this study, he is nevertheless used as a point of reference in order to clarify the relations existing between allegorical method and apologetic intent. The author concludes that there are no other cases in the Jewish-Hellenistic world in which faith was defended by means of the allegorical method. This pleads for greater caution in characterizing Philonic allegory purely in terms of its apologetic intent. Earlier version published in Hebrew; cf. **4908**. (= R277)

5207. P. KATZ, 'Οὐ μή σε ἀνῶ, οὐδ' οὐ μή σε ἐγκαταλίπω, *Hebr*. XIII 5, the Biblical source of the quotation', *Bib* 33 (1952) 523-525.

A philological and thematic analysis of the relevant expression in Hebrews, Philo, and the LXX. (= R278)

5208. A. LEVI, 'Il concetto del tempo nelle filosofie dell'età romana', *RCSF* 7 (1952) 173-200, esp. 176ff.

Philo's concept of time, which he regards in the Stoic manner as 'an extension of the movement of the cosmos', anticipates in many ways the same concept in Neoplatonism. (= R279)

5209. G. LINDESKOG, *Studien zum neutestamentlichen Schöpfungs-gedanken*, vol. 1, Uppsala Universitets Arsskrift 1952: part 2 Acta Universitatis Upsaliensis (Uppsala-Wiesbaden 1952), esp. 135-161.

In a brief introduction discussing the main interpretations of Philo, the author tends to steer a middle course between the opposing views which see him as entirely dependent either on Greek philosophy or on Judaism (135-140). He goes on to explain at some length the fundamental themes of Philo's doctrine of creation: the idea of God, the Logos, the concept of εἰκών, and anthropology. In terms of the creationistic thought of the New Testament, which is the author's viewpoint, Philo is seen as playing a specific and fundamental role: his work is the first example of a philosophical exegesis, serving missionary purposes, which aims to translate the biblical story of creation into the terms of Greek cosmogony (cf. 161). (= R280)

5210. R. MARCUS, 'Philo, Josephus and the Dead Sea Yahad', *JBL* 71 (1952) 207-209.

A detailed philological analysis of the term ὅμιλος in Philo, which probably translates the Hebrew yahad. (= R281)

5211. H. MERKI, *'ΟΜΟΙΩΣΙΣ ΘΕΩΙ von der platonischen Angleich-ung an Gott zur Gottähnlichkeit bei Gregor von Nyssa*, Paradosis: Beiträge zur Geschichte der altchristlichen Literatur und Theologie 7 (Freiburg in der Schweiz 1952), esp. 35-44, 72-83.

The author refers to Philo on two occasions in particular. At 35-44, where he discusses the concept of ὁμοίωσις θεῷ, Merki asserts that this motif in Philo is of Middle Platonic rather than of biblical origin and that in any case the admission of a direct assimilation of man to God contrasts with Philo's profound conviction of the absolute transcendence of God. The Logos itself, which is the intermediate reality *par excellence*, tends not to play a significant role at all in this connection, which shows that the theme is not well integrated into Philo's thought. In the second part of the work (75-83) the author deals with the concept of εἰκὼν θεοῦ and shows how in Philo this is understood in a wholly spiritualized meaning. A limitation of the study is that it does not consider the evidence in *QG* and *QE*. (= R282)

5212. F. MUSZNER, *ΖΩΗ: die Anschauung vom 'Leben' im vierten Evangelium unter Berücksichtigung der Johannesbriefe; ein Beitrag zur biblischen Theologie*, MThS I 5 (Munich 1952), esp. 32-35.

Philo's concept of life is a direct expression of his philosophical thought. According to Muszner, Philo made Moses into a Stoic-Platonic philosopher by adopting Plato's soul-body dualism and the Stoa's aretology (cf. 32). On these assumptions it becomes apparent that, for Philo, 'life' means the immortal life of the rational soul. It is a gift of God, but man can nevertheless prepare himself for it by the practice of an ascetic and virtuous way of life. (= R282/a)

5213. R. PFEIFFER, 'The image of the Delian Apollo and Apolline ethics', *JWCI* 15 (1952) 20-32.

The evidence in Philo, which agrees with the evidence in Macrobius, is used to determine the exact image of the Delian Apollo. (= R283)

5214. K. F. PROOST, *Tussen twee werelden: Philo Judaeus* (Arnhem 1952).

A general account of Philo, in which he is presented as a thinker who attempts to achieve a synthesis of Judaism and Hellenism. Having made a brief sketch of Hellenistic culture and thought, especially as it was developed in Alexandria, and the position of the Jews in relation to it, the author proceeds to give an account of Philo's views and scriptural interpretation. Special emphasis is given to the psychological aspect of his thought. The synthesis Philo strove for was not achieved; his thought is significant above all in relation to the development of Christianity. (RAB/DTR)

5215. W. VÖLKER, *Der wahre Gnostiker nach Clemens Alexandrinus*, TU 57 (Berlin 1952) 617-623 and *passim*.

In the final chapter of this imposing monograph the author summarizes the relation between Philo and Clement in the area of ethical thought (i.e. following on from the earlier study on Philo, cf. above **3817**). There are remarkable affinities between the thought of the two thinkers, indicating large-scale dependence on the part of Clement. These emerge in the doctrine of God and of man as image, in the treatment of the themes of sin, passion, virtues, gnosis. But close examination of the texts show numerous modifications, as Clement deepens his thought in relation to the central figure of Christ as Logos. Differences emerge particularly clearly in the way faith and the specific virtues are presented. Völker concludes (623): 'In spite of all the dependence Clement read his predecessor with a critical eye and evaluated him from a fixed position.' (= R284)

5216. H. A. WOLFSON, 'Albinus and Plotinus on divine attributes', *HThR* 45 (1952) 115-130, esp. 115-117, 126-129; reprinted in I. TWERSKY and G. H. WILLIAMS (edd.), *Studies in the history of philosophy and religion* (Cambridge Mass. 1973) 115-130.

Plotinus attributes his conception of the hierarchy of three hypostases to Parmenides, or, more precisely, to the image of Parmenides transmitted by Plato. The concepts and the language referred to, however, cannot be directly attributed to Plato; rather they belong to one of his interpreters, possibly Philo (cf. 115). Philonic influence is also traceable in the use of the *via negationis* to describe God's essence, which is common to both Albinus and Plotinus. (= R285)

1953

5301. L. ALFONSI, 'Un nuovo frammento del Περὶ φιλοσοφίας aristotelico', *Herm* 81 (1953) 45-49.

Advances new evidence in support of Moraux's hypothesis (**4813**) concerning the Aristotelian origin of the views expressed in *Her.* 283. (= R286)

5302. G. A. VAN DEN BERGH VAN EYSINGA, 'Christus en de Keizers', in *idem*, *Godsdienst-wetenschappelijke studiën*, vol. 13 (Haarlem 1953) 3-38, esp. 3ff.

Some interesting remarks on B. Bauer's book with the remarkable title *Philo, Strauss und Renan und das Ur-christentum* (Berlin 1874). (DTR)

5303. Y. F. BAER [בער .י], החסידים הראשונים בכתבי פילון ובמסורת העברית ['The ancient Hassidim in Philo's writings and in Hebrew tradition'], *Zion* 18 (1953) 91-108.

A continuation of the author's earlier study (**5201**) on the origins of Jewish religious thought. Philo's doctrine of the 'sage' is explored as primary evidence for the existence of 'ancient Hassidim' (righteous men) who fused the 'heritage of the prophets of Israel and the doctrines of the wise men of Greece' into a new 'social-religious' entity (107f.). The following passages from Philo's works are discussed in some detail: *Spec.* 2.42-55; *3.1-6*; *Migr.* 120-126; *Her.* 1-39; *Sacr.* 121-125; *Prob.* 1-31, 41-73. English summary. See also **5502**. (DS)

5304. J. M. BAUMGARTEN, 'Sacrifice and worship among the Jewish sectarians of the Dead Sea (Qumrân) Scrolls', *HThR* 46 (1953) 141-159, esp. 154-157.

Philonic evidence is used to determine the special religious customs of the Essenes and, specifically, their purificatory rites. (= R287)

5305. J. DANIÉLOU, 'Terre et Paradis chez les Pères de l'Église', *ErJb* [*Mensch und Erde*] 22 (1953) 433-472, esp. 467-472.

The concept of Paradise as an interior dimension of man, a theme very dear to the Church Fathers, is of Philonic origin. (= R288)

5306. G. DI NAPOLI, *La concezione dell'essere nella filosofia greca* (Milan 1953), esp. 217-220.

Philo's thought is explained here without much depth and exclusively in relation to his conception of God and creation. The author emphasizes its innovatory importance for Jewish culture, which is not of itself given to theological speculation on account of the pride in being the depository of divine revelation. (= R289)

5307. W. DITTMAN, *Die Auslegung der Urgeschichte (Genesis 1-3) im Neuen Testament* (diss. Göttingen 1953), esp. 1-37.

In order to demonstrate that the Jewish religion is the *true* philosophy, Philo tries to present a unified interpretation of the various parts of the Torah. Gen. 1-3 is regarded by Philo as a mystical allegory, the real meaning of which underlies the literal meaning. The problem raised by Dittman is whether Philo is interested in coming to a true understanding of the 'proto-history' of Genesis, or is content to use the latter for the purposes of his Jewish-Hellenistic philosophy. It is the ambivalence of the Philonic discourse itself which fuels this doubt. Moses, in fact, is presented both as the subject of the Law and – to the extent that he is inspired by God – as its author. Besides fulfilling the office of a prophet, therefore, Moses is also honoured as a sage and philosopher, and hence as a precursor and anticipator of Greek philosophy. (= R290)

5308. C. H. DODD, *The interpretation of the Fourth gospel* (Cambridge 1953, 1965²; French translation, Paris 1975), esp. 54-73.

As part of the attempt to reconstruct the intellectual background presupposed by the evangelist in his readers, a chapter is devoted to Philo. There are remarkable similarities in the use of symbolism, in the notion that man's quest is the knowledge of God, and in the doctrine of the Logos. 'The gospel certainly presupposes a range of ideas having a remarkable resemblance to those of Hellenistic Judaism as represented by Philo (73).' The decisive difference is that the Logos in John becomes fully personal. The Jewish elements of personal piety, faith and love, which are not satisfactorily integrated in Philo's thought and stand in an uneasy relation to a more philosophical and mystical conception of the divine, come into their own in the Gospel. (DTR)

5309. E. R. GOODENOUGH, *Jewish symbols in the Greco-Roman period*, 13 vols., Bollingen Series 37 (New York 1953-68) *passim*.

In order to discover and elucidate the religious attitudes of Jews in the Greco-Roman world, Goodenough compiled this remarkable collection of symbols and further evidence from excavated synagogues, tombs, lamps, glass ware, coins and amulets. In his explanations and analyses he also calls on copious evidence from literary sources, so that the name, writings and thought of Philo appear constantly throughout the entire work, often with reference to the interpretation which since the publication of *By light, light* has been associated with Goodenough's name (cf. esp. 10.86-97). The reader can consult the comprehensive index in vol. 13 (citations 13-15, subjects 159-160). We confine our notice to giving the following list, in alphabetical order, of the most important Philonic themes dealt with in the 12 volumes: Aaron 10.21-25, Ares 10.112-117, astral symbolism 8.208-218, cosmic Judaism 10.21-40, drunkenness 6.201-207, first fruits 5.87-90, the graces 9.219-222, Hellenized Judaism 1.25-48, the Logos 4.85ff., 6.198-217, Moses 9.117ff. and *passim*, mystic Judaism 6.206-216, 8.209-18, numbers 9.192-195, 10.64-69, Philo as Platonist 12.10-14, the Powers 4.130-132, 9.85-88, Samuel 9.191-194, Sophia 6.198ff., spiritual food 12.128-131, tree symbolism 9.107-110, wine 6.201-16, 12.128-131. Given the controversial nature of many of the views put forward, the reader is well advised to consult the authoritative reviews of the first eight volumes by A. D. NOCK (cf. **5712**) and also the evaluative review article by M. SMITH, 'Goodenough's Jewish Symbols in retrospect', *JBL* 86 (1967) 53-68 (cf. **6755**). See also below **5613, 8614**. (DTR)

5310. A. GRILLI, *Il problema della vita contemplativa nel mondo greco-romano* (Milan 1953), esp. 187-192, 318-321, 328.

Emphasizes the connections between Nilus' *De monastica exercitatione* and a few passages from *Praem.*, with a synopsis of the two texts. Elsewhere (187-192) Philo's evidence on the Essenes is cited in relation to the theme of solitude. (= R291)

5311. K. LAKE, 'Introduction', in *Eusebius: the ecclesiastical history*, LCL (Cambridge Mass. 1953), esp. vol. 1, xl-xliv.

Notes serving as background to the information on Philo given by Eusebius in his *Ecclesiastical History*. (DTR)

5312. J. PÉPIN, 'Recherches sur les sens et les origines de l'expression 'Caelum caeli' dans le livre XII des *Confessions* de S. Augustin', *ALMA* 23 (1953) 185-274, esp. 248-251, 259-274; reprinted in *"Ex Platonicorum persona"*: *études sur les lectures philosophiques de Saint Augustin* (Amsterdam 1977) 39-130.

The biblical expression *caelum caeli* is of fundamental importance in Augustine's allegorical exegesis. The remote origin of this image is Platonic, but before reaching Augustine it was progressively spiritualized by Philo and Origen. This development is also charted in synoptic tables (260-265) in relation to the three thinkers discussed. (= R292)

5313. F. RAVAISSON, *Essai sur la Métaphysique d'Aristote: fragments du Tome III (Hellénisme-Judaïsme-Christianisme)*, edited by C. DEVIVAISE, Bibliothèque des textes philosophiques (Paris 1953), esp. 33-36, 62-70.

The editor has reconstructed the thought of the distinguished mid-nineteenth century French scholar on the basis of unpublished papers. It emerges that he was especially concerned with Philo's theological thought, discussing its importance in the evolution of Jewish theology (Philo marks the transition from emanationism to creationism, cf. 33), as well as its general structure, which in his view is expressed in the trinitarian formula God-Logos-Cosmos. In this hierarchy Aristotle's influence is held to be dominant (62-64). (RR)

5314. K. SCHUBERT, 'Einige Beobachtungen zum Verständnis des Logosbegriffes im Frührabbinischen Schrifttum', *Jud* 9 (1953) 65-80, esp. 65-77.

In Schubert's view it is possible to relate the Rabbinic theory of creation and of the intermediate entities in the Torah to analogous theories in Neoplatonism. In this line of development he also places Philo's cosmogony, to which the dialectic of unity-multiplicity is extraneous. (= R293)

5315. R. McL. WILSON, 'Philo and the fourth Gospel', *ET* 65 (1953) 47-49.

Wilson takes up Argyle's analysis of this subject (**5102**), but instead of positing a direct connection between Philo and the fourth Gospel, he suggests that both thinkers were influenced by a common, though not easily identifiable, Greek-Jewish source. (= R295)

1954

5401. B. BOTTE, 'La vie de Moïse par Philon', *Cahiers Sioniens* 8 (1954) 173-180; reprinted in *Moïse, l'homme de l'alliance* (Paris 1955) 55-62; German translation (Düsseldorf 1963) 173-181.

An analysis of the content and structure of and critical response to *Mos.* 1-2. The author underlines the specific nature of this treatise: it is not exegetical, like most of Philo's works, but largely biographical. (= R297)

5402. P. DALBERT, *Die Theologie der hellenistisch-jüdischen Missionsliteratur unter Ausschluß von Philo und Josephus*, Theologische Forschung 4 (Hamburg-Volksdorf 1954) *passim.*

Although Philo is explicitly excluded from the programme of this work, he is frequently cited in the notes as a source of doctrine and as a point of comparison for the authors dealt with (Demetrius, Philo the Elder, Eupolemus, Artapanus, Ezechiel the Tragedian, Aristeas, Wisdom of Solomon, Aristobulus, *Sibylline Oracles*). This study is a valuable tool for reconstructing the Jewish-Hellenistic tradition to which Philo belongs. (RR)

5403. E. EYDOUX, 'À Philon d'Alexandrie', in *Philon d'Alexandrie: De la charité et amour de son prochain*, Faculté libre de théologie juive: chaire de civilisation judéo-hellénistique (Marseille 1954) 7-86.

A lengthy didactic poem devoted to Philo, who is celebrated as the first thinker to develop a synthesis of 'the soul of Israel' ('messenger of the word of God') and 'the light of Greece'. In an appendix (89-121) the French translation of *Virt.* 57-186 (= *De humanitate, De paenitate*) published by P. BELLIER (Paris 1575) is reproduced with the title *De la charité et amour de son prochain*, from which the title of the entire book is drawn. The same poem is reprinted, together with other works, in E. EYDOUX, *Massilia mater: I le message* (Paris 1980) 15-126. (RR)

5404. A. J. FESTUGIÈRE, *La révélation d'Hermès Trismégiste*, vol. 4, *Le Dieu inconnu et la gnose*, Études Bibliques (Paris 1954), esp. 7-8, 19-22.

The author deals briefly with Philo's arithmology and his use of negative theology, both of which he interprets as being valuable evidence of the Neopythagorean speculation in that period. (= R299)

5405. G. FRIEDRICH (ed.), *Theologisches Wörterbuch zum Neuen Testament,* vol. 5 (Stuttgart 1954; English translation, Grand Rapids 1967).

Cf. above **3807.** Contains: O. BAUERNFEIND, art. πανουργία (technical skill), 722-3; J. BEHM, art. παράκλητος (advocate), 800-1; G. BERTRAM, art. παιδεία (instruction), 611-4; H. BIETENHARD, art. ὄνομα (name), 263-5; G. DELLING, art. παρθένος (maiden), 831-2; J. HORST, art. οὖς (ear), 549; W. MICHAELIS, art. ὁδός (road), 60-64; art. ὁράω (see), 335-6; πάσχω (undergo), 908; O. MICHEL, art. οἶκος (house), 126-7; art. ὁμολογέω (confess), 205-6; A. OEPKE, art. ὄναρ (dream), 231-2; H. SCHLIER, art. παρρησία (boldness of speech), 875; K. L. and M. A. SCHMIDT, art. πάροικος (sojourner) 847-8; G. SCHRENK, art. πατήρ (father), 956-7; E. SJÖBERG and G. STÄHLIN, art. ὀργή (divine anger), 418; H. TRAUB, art. οὐρανός (heaven), 500-1. (DTR)

5406. D. GALLI, *Il pensiero greco*, Collana di Storia della Filosofia I 2 (Padua 1954), esp. 306-309.

A succinct synoptic introduction to Philo, whose thought is traced back to its chief antecedents in Greek philosophy. (RR)

5407. Q. HUONDER, *'Gott und Seele' im Lichte der griechischen Philosophie* (Munich 1954), esp. 189-200.

Philo is confronted by the problem of the relationship between faith and reason from the moment that he grounds his thought both in revelation and in Greek philosophy (cf. 189). He is convinced that the Bible contains the same truth as Greek philosophy. The difference is only that the former expresses itself in images, the latter in abstract thoughts. In order to bring this identical true content to light, Philo resorts to the allegorical reading of the Bible. As signficant examples of this procedure, Huonder cites the Philonic doctrine of God, of the Logos, and of the soul. (= R300)

5408. H. JONAS, *Gnosis und spätantiker Geist*, part 1, *Die mythologische Gnosis: mit einer Einleitung zur Geschichte und Methodologie der Forschung*, FRLANT 51 (Göttingen1934[1], 1954[2], 1964[3]); part 2, *Von der Mythologie zur mystischen Philosophie*, FRLANT 63 (Göttingen 1954), esp. 38-43, 70-121.

Philo's theology contains a structural contradiction in that it simultaneously allows for the knowability and unknowability of God (70). For this reason the expression γνῶσις θεοῦ acquires in Philo a complex meaning, which can be summed up in the following points. (1) Knowledge of God takes on an existential meaning – related to the suppression of egotism – expressing an attitude of the will. (2) It carries an intellectual meaning implying a vision of God, which cannot, however, be fully realized, given the unknowability of his nature (83ff.). Since man is limited to this extent, he can at most demonstrate the existence of God and the fact that God is creator. (3) Yet it is possible to go beyond this initial understanding of God through knowledge of the noetic cosmos (92ff.), which is an irradiation of the divine essence. Moreover the elect may go on to transcend this intermediate ideal form and receive God directly throught his light. But even in this case – as Jonas observes (119) – knowledge of God's nature remains unattainable. (4) Finally, quite apart from these possibilities, man 'is given the real possibility of an ecstatic relationship with God, a relationship which presupposes, however, the "transcendence" and annulment of human individuality' (120, cf. 99ff.). In addition to these topics Jonas also briefly deals with the theme of virtue in Philo (38-43). An earlier version of the chapter on Philo's theology was published in Hebrew; cf. **4909**. (= R301)

5409. A. N. M. RICH, 'The Platonic ideas as the thoughts of God', *Mnem* IV 7 (1954) 123-133.

More than any other Middle-Platonist, Philo helped to transform the Platonic ideas into the thoughts of God. The author discusses this subject at length and shows how the Aristotelian concept of εἶδος ἐν τῇ ψυχῇ favoured this transformation (cf. 131ff.). (= R303)

5410. S. SANDMEL, 'Philo's environment and Philo's exegesis', *JBR* 22 (1954) 248-253.

Summarizes in a schematic way the author's views on Philo. Although he shows a great admiration for the Wolfsonian interpretation of Philo, Sandmel disagrees with it on some points, for instance on the role of philosophy, which in Sandmel's view is not the exclusive key to Philo's thought. (= R304)

5411. C. SCHNEIDER, *Geistesgeschichte des antiken Christentums*, vol. 1 (Munich 1954), esp. 335ff.

As far as their allegorical method is concerned, neither Clement nor Origen should be read in the light of Philo. For the Christian authors allegory is the most privileged method of reading the Bible. For Philo, however, – as the author, in this following the views of Goodenough, observes – it was essentially a means of spreading the Jewish faith. (= R305)

5412. E. G. TURNER, 'Tiberius Julius Alexander', *JRS* 44 (1954) 54-64, esp. 54-57.

Philonic evidence is extensively used by the author to reconstruct the historical and cultural context in which the controversial figure of Philo's nephew lived. (= R306)

5413. M. C. WATHELET, *L'héritier des biens divins de Philon d'Alexandrie et l'héritier de Dieu de Saint Paul* (diss. Louvain 1954).

The dissertation is divided into three parts: the first, which is by far the longest (52-123) and includes large part of the translation of the relevant work (cf. **3005**), is concerned with the concept of 'heir' in Philo; the second (125-163) analyzes the same concept in Paul; the third (165-183) compares the two concepts. The first part is introduced by means of a very extended preliminary section dedicated to the etymology of the term κληρονόμος, with reference to its usage in secular and legal language and to the connections between its secular and religious meanings in Greek, Etruscan, Roman, Egyptian, and Jewish culture. This is certainly the most interesting and original part of the thesis, since for the rest Wathelet does little else than underline the points of contact between the two thinkers, concluding that there was probably a direct dependence of Paul on Philo. (= R308)

1955

5501. A. W. ARGYLE, 'The logos of Philo: personal or impersonal?', *ET* 66 (1954-55) 13-14.

The problem in question is introduced by a brief review of scholarship, followed by a succinct discussion of the relevant Philonic texts. Argyle follows Goodenough in holding that the Logos is for Philo a 'supra-personal' reality, such that it includes and at the same time transcends the concept of person. (= R309)

5502. Y. F. BAER [בער .י], ישראל בעמים [*Israel among the Nations*] (Jerusalem 1955, 1969²).

This small volume is aptly summarized by its subtitle: 'an essay on the history of the period of the Second Temple and the Mishnah and on the foundations of the Halakhah and the Jewish faith'. Baer draws freely upon and elaborates his earlier studies (**5201**,

5304) on this theme. Philo is widely cited, especially in the discussion of the 'religious-contemplative' ideal of the ancient sages (81-98, 130-140). (DS)

5503. K. BORMANN, *Die Ideen- und Logoslehre Philons von Alex-andrien: eine Auseinandersetzung mit H. A. Wolfson* (inaug. diss. Köln 1955).

In this dissertation the author undertakes a systematic refutation of the views of Wolfson (**4714**). The work as a whole, therefore, has a polemical, though not aggressive, tone. According to Bormann, Wolfson sought to transform Philo's philosophical thought into a system, particularly with regard to the doctrine of the intermediaries between God and the world. That is to say, by identifying the Powers with the ideas, he imposed a fictitious interpretation on Philo's thought which transformed all the differences between the two realities into various *status existendi*, thus eliminating all evident contradictions. As a result, Wolfson converted an eclectic philosopher into a systematic one and, in a serious misrepresentation of his thought, made Philo into the originator of religious philosophy. In Bormann's view, Philo neither regarded the ideas as prototypes of possible worlds (cf. 13ff.), nor did he possess the concept of creation (cf. 44); his thought on these problems does not transcend the limits of Greek philosophy. (= R310)

5504. V. BURR, *Tiberius Iulius Alexander*, Antiquitas 1. Reihe: Abhandlungen zur alten Geschichte 1 (Bonn 1955), esp. 16-20.

The author is only indirectly concerned with Philo as the discussion partner of his nephew Tiberius Julius Alexander. Burr explains the basic aspects of the Philonic *paideia* that is directed at Alexander and in so doing briefly discusses *Anim.* and *Prov.*, which are shown to have a predominantly erudite character. The aims of *Prov.* and *Anim.* appear to be pursued in *Aet.* as well (20); the latter treatise, however, expresses a Peripatetic rather than a Stoic point of view. From these works Philo emerges as a profoundly Hellenized thinker. (RR)

5505. E. BRÉHIER, 'La cosmologie stoïcienne à la fin du paganisme', in *Études de philosophie antique*, Publications de la Faculté des Lettres de Paris (Paris 1955) 144-160, esp. 145-150; originally appeared in *RHR* 64 (1911) 1-20.

Philo's presentation of the Chaldeans (i.e. of those who put their faith in astrology) in *Migr.* 178 is significant because it shows the fusion of the Stoic concept of fate with the absolute power of the stars. (= R311)

5506. E. BRÉHIER, 'Philo Judaeus', in *Études de philosophie antique* (cf. **5505**) (Paris 1955) 207-214.

A brief introduction to Philo. The essence of Philo's thought consists of a new moral consciousness which embraces theology and cosmology as well as anthropology. (= R312)

5507. J. CARCOPINO, *Le mystère d'un symbole chrétien, 'l'ascia'* (Paris 1955), esp. 53-59.

An analysis of the allegorical meaning of the knife in Philo's writings, especially in relation to the concept of the Logos. (= R313)

5508. S. S. COHON, 'The unity of God: a study in Hellenistic and Rabbinic theology', *HUCA* 26 (1955) 425-479, esp. 433-436.

A rather limited discussion of the doctrine of God's unity in Philo, concentrating on apologetic rather than theological-philosophical aspects. (DTR)

5509. J. COSTE, 'Notion grecque et notion biblique de la 'souffrance éducatrice' (à propos d'Hébreux V, 8)', *RecSR* 43 (1955) 481-523, esp. 508-522.

The article deals with the word-play ἔμαθον-ἔπαθον that occurs in Hebr. 5:8. Its origin does not lie in classical Greek philosophy, but in Philo, who assigns at least three meanings to the theme of paedeutic suffering: one pertaining to personal experience; another to an existential situation, typical of the person who has left the sphere of the sense-perceptible and is oriented towards God; the third to corrective punishment of the wicked. Paul's debt to Philo here, however, is said to be a purely literary one (cf. 520). (= R314)

5510. H. DÖRRIE, ''Υπόστασις: Wort- und Bedeutungsgeschichte', *NAWG* phil.-hist. Kl. 3 (1955) 35-92; reprinted in *Platonica Minora*, STA 8 (Munich 1976) 12-61, esp. 31, 39, 43, 46.

The characteristic of stability implied in the concept of hypostasis is primarily used by Philo to define the realm of the divine and the spiritual, usually in contrast with the temporary and evolving nature of the sensible world. (RR)

5511. B. GÄRTNER, *The Areopagus speech and natural revelation*, ASNU 21 (Uppsala 1955), esp. 116-125.

Philo's writings are of great assistance in understanding the 'Diaspora missionary' Paul (117). To this end the author briefly outlines Philo's doctrines – extensively influenced by Stoic, Platonic and Neopythagorean ideas – on how man gains knowledge of God. Philonic evidence is also much used in the detailed ᵔnalysis of themes in the Areopagus speech in Acts 17:22-31 (144-228). Gärtner concludes (251f.) that the speech belongs to a tradition going back to Paul, but also carrying the traces of Jewish Diaspora propaganda similar to ideas found in Philo. (DTR)

5512. E. LANNE, 'Chérubim et Séraphim: essai d'interprétation du chapitre X de la *Démonstration* de Saint Irénée', *RecSR* 43 (1955) 524-535, esp. 527-530.

In the text under discussion, Irenaeus relates the Word of God, Wisdom, the Son, and the Holy Spirit to the Seraphim and Cherubim. Lanne observes that this procedure is typical of Philo, who more than once associates the divine Powers with the Cherubim. (= R316)

5513. E. NORDEN, *Das Genesiszitat in der Schrift vom Erhabenen*,

Abhandlungen der deutschen Akademie der Wissenschaften zu Berlin, Klasse für Sprachen Literatur und Kunst, 1954.1 (Berlin 1955), esp. 11-23; reprinted in *Kleine Schriften zum klassischen Altertum* (Berlin 1966) 286-313.

The lecture printed here 14 years after its author's death was orginally delivered before the Berlin Academy in 1923, but could not be published after 1933 for political reasons. The treatise *On the sublime* alludes to a philosopher whose identity cannot be easily established. By means of a careful analysis, the author shows that the philosopher in question is Philo. This identification is supported by a number of lexical and conceptual parallels. One notes especially the use of the term σπάνιος (= rare) in reference to the number of wise men, and also the social question of freedom and slavery which is present in the anonymous author of *On the sublime* and which, though it is elsewhere very uncommon (at least in the ancient world), is also discussed at length in Philo's works, if in a moral rather than political sense. Other significant parallels are noticeable in the pedagogical themes, in the importance assigned to ecstasy and enthusiasm, and in the role of rhetoric. Having demonstrated that the philosopher in question is in all likelihood Philo, Norden tries to establish the place and date of the meeting between the two writers. The place is certainly Rome; the date is to be set in the last months of 41 A.D. (cf. 22). (= R317)

5514. E. PAX, *ΕΠΙΦΑΝΕΙΑ: ein religionsgeschichtlicher Beitrag zur biblischen Theologie*, MThS 10 (Munich 1955), esp. 152-159.

The concept of ἐπιφάνεια, also analyzed here in connection with arithmological themes, plays a fundamental role in Philo's thought. It defines the relationship between man and God, which should not be seen as a benevolent intervention of God in the human realm, but as a true and proper union with God (cf. 153). (= R318)

5515. A. C. PURDY, 'The Epistle to the Hebrews: introduction', in *The Interpreter's Bible: the Holy Scriptures in the King James and Revised Standard Versions with general articles and introduction, exegesis, exposition for each book of the Bible in twelve volumes*, vol. 11 (New York-Nashville 1955) 577-595.

Philo is twice discussed here: once on the subject of sources (Purdy does not believe in a direct connection between Hebrews and Philo) and once with regard to the christological theme of Hebrews, which does appear to have a direct relation to Philo's theory of the Logos. (= R319)

5516. M. REITERER, *Die Herkulesentscheidung von Prodikos und ihre frühhumanistische Rezeption in der 'Voluptatis cum virtute disceptatio' des Benedictus Chelidonius* (diss. Vienna 1955), esp. 196-206.

The author notes how Philo's retelling in *Sacr.* 20-45 of the myth of Hercules at the crossroads – which represents for him the conflict between the ethical ideals of Epicureanism and Stoicism – is extraordinarily rich and full compared with other accounts, for instance in Xenophon. (= R320)

5517. H. RUSCHE, 'Die Gestalt des Melchisedek', *MThZ* 6 (1955) 230-

252, esp. 238-240.

The figure of Melchizedek in Philo constitutes a total departure from the historical characterizations in the biblical narrative and is draped with moral and philosophical meanings quite foreign to Scripture. (= R321)

5518. S. SANDMEL, 'Philo and his pupils: an imaginary dialogue', *Jud* 4 (1955) 47-57.

This popularly written article deals primarily with the problem of Philonic hermeneutics. (= R322)

5519. S. SANDMEL, 'Philo's place in Judaism: a study of conceptions of Abraham in Jewish literature', *HUCA* 25 (1954) 209-237; 26 (1955) 151-332; revised and enlarged edition (Cincinnati 1956, New York 1971²).

The problem which this work attempts to solve is the following: was Philo a Jewish philosopher with a Greek education, or a Greek philosopher with a Jewish background? To solve this problem, the author analyzes the figure of Abraham, which he extracts from Philonic and Rabbinical thought and uses as a measuring standard for both thought-worlds. In Philo's case the choice is a particularly felicitous one, since Abraham, as the symbol of human progress towards perfect virtue, constitutes the structuring and unifying element of his anthropology and ethics. Sandmel recognizes two levels of meaning in Philo's Abraham (literal and allegorical); at the same time he demonstrates their complementarity and congruence. Thus, if the Rabbinical Abraham might be called a Rabbi-Abraham (cf. 66), Philo's Abraham is a mystic philosopher (cf. 161). The following conclusions emerge from these considerations. (1) Philo either knew little about or refuted the content of Rabbinical exegesis. (2) His attitude towards Judaism differs from that of the Rabbis, as his mystic philosophy based on the Bible differs from Halachah legalism. (3) Philonic Judaism is the result of a profound Hellenization. (4) Philo represents a marginal and aberrant, but not contradictory, version of Judaism, testifying to the plurality of forms which was characteristic of the Diaspora. REVIEWS: G. Delling, *ThLZ* 82 (1957) 32f.; L. H. Feldman, *CW* 51 (1957-58) 175f. Of the second edition: S. Légasse, *BLE* 73 (1972) 288f.; M. Hadas-Lebel, *REJ* 132 (1973) 622ff.; H. Dörrie, *AAHG* 29 (1976) 184f.; H. F. Weiss, *OLZ* 71 (1976) 265ff. (= R323)

5520. F. J. SCHIERSE, *Verheissung und Heilsvollendung zur theologischen Grundfrage des Hebräerbriefes*, MThS 9 (Munich 1955), esp. 19-21.

By analyzing some ten terms, the author shows the differences in form and content between Philo and Hebrews. What they have in common, at least as regards the allegory of the sanctuary, is a dualistic structure. (= R324)

5521. J. SCHWARTZ, 'Note sur la famille de Philon d'Alexandrie', *AIPhO* 13 (1953), [*Mélanges Isidore Lévy* (Brussels 1955)] 591-602.

Although these few notes do not add substantially to the biography of Philo, they do show the important position of his family in the Jewish community of Alexandria. (= R325)

5522. C. SPICQ, 'Agapè: prolégomènes à une étude de théologie néo-testamentaire', *StudH* 10 (1955), esp. 171-183.

Although the term ἀγάπη is little used by Philo, the concept which it expresses is extremely important. According to the author, 'the Alexandrian philosopher is the only profane [i.e. non-Christian] writer to have insisted on the role of charity as a motive for moral and religious action' (183). (= R326)

5523. W. THEILER, 'Gott und Seele im kaiserzeitlichen Denken', *Recherches sur la tradition platonicienne*, Entretiens sur l'antiquité classique 3 (Vandœuvres-Geneva 1955) 65-90; reprinted in *Forschungen zum Neuplatonismus*, Quellen und Studien zur Geschichte der Philosophie 10 (Berlin 1966) 104-123, esp. 106-109.

In touching on Philo, who shows traces of the transcendentalism typical of the imperial era, Theiler briefly delineates the theological-cosmological structure of Philo's thought, which emphasizes the vast gap between man's οὐδένεια and the greatness of God. (= R327)

5524. H. THYEN, *Der Stil der jüdisch-hellenistischen Homilie*, FRLANT 65 (Göttingen 1955) *passim*.

A purely literary study which sets out to specify, on the basis of selected Jewish-Alexandrian texts, the characteristics of the homiletic genre. From this point of view Philo's evidence offers a fundamental contribution towards the definition of the genre. (= R328)

5525. J. H. WASZINK, 'Der Platonismus und die altchristliche Gedankenwelt', in *Recherches sur la tradition platonicienne* (cf. **5523**) 137-179, esp. 165-167, 176f.

The figures of the intermediaries and in particular of the Logos are used by Philo to lend philosophical plausibility to his doctrine of ὁμοίωσις which, given the absolute transcendence of God, would otherwise be untenable. (RR)

1956

5601. S. BELKIN, 'The Jewish community in a non-Jewish world: problems of integration and separation', in *Essays in traditional Jewish thought* (New York 1956) 121-143, esp. 124ff.

The Alexandrian Jewish community, as represented by Philo, was a successful example of a community which integrated itself into the broader life of the society in which it lived, not least because it resisted the idea of over-emphasizing Jewish theology or philosophy at the expense of observance of the Halachah. But why did Hellenistic Judaism not become part of historic Judaism, as did the Golden age of Spain? Belkin suggests the answer is that 'the Judaism of the Hellenistic Jews was not rooted in its origins, while their non-Jewish knowledge did come from primary sources' (130). (DTR)

5602. S. BELKIN [בלקין .ש], מדרש השמות בפילון [= 'The onomastic Midrash in Philo'], *Horeb* 12 (1956) 3-61.

The methods of etymologizing practised by the Rabbis and Philo in onomastic Midrash are copiously compared with a view to illustrating their common origin in a traditional Palestinian archtype, which both Philo and the Sages used, and which was part of Philo's Jewish educational baggage. Belkin notes that looking for Philonic influence on Palestininian Midrash is putting the cart before the horse: even when the Greek rather that the Hebrew form of a name is interpreted, this has Rabbinic parallels, and in any event the form of the Greek names in Philo's Midrash often differs from that of the Septuagint (which he otherwise follows) and hence reflects a midrashic tradition. Belkin points out that the onomastic exegeses are homiletic rather than philological in both Philo and Rabbinic Midrash, though quite often they were developed differently. It is not considered likely that Philo developed onomastic Midrash independently from the Hebrew text. (NGC)

5603. G. A. VAN DEN BERGH VAN EYSINGA, 'Philo en het Nieuwe Testament', in *idem, Godsdienst-wetenschappelijke studiën*, vol. 20 (Haarlem 1956) 3-34.

After an introductory section in which the author puts forward his view that, though Philo wanted to be an orthodox Jew, he was thoroughly Alexandrian, i.e. profoundly influenced by a mystically orientated Hellenism, the article presents a long and unsystematic list of parallels between New Testament themes, including both the Gospels and the Pauline corpus, and Philo's writings. The most interesting part of the article is left to the end (30ff.), where the author argues that Philo's influence on the early Church only becomes profound when Catholic Christianity gains the upper hand, e.g. in the case of Ambrose. Earlier, when the radical views of Marcion and the Alexandrian Gnostic Christians were more dominant, Philo would have been regarded as too conservative a thinker. Proof of this is gained from the fact that few of the parallels between Philo and the New Testament can be located in the more limited Marcionitic canon. (DTR)

5604. F. BUFFIÈRE, *Les mythes d'Homère et la pensée grecque*, Collection d'études anciennes (Paris 1956) *passim*.

Refers to some Philonic allegorical interpretations which are grafted onto myths of the Homeric tradition, e.g. the Dioscuri (572ff.), the demons (cf. 524) and various arithmological figures (cf. 663ff.). (= R329)

5605. H. CROUZEL, *Théologie de l'image de Dieu chez Origène*, Théologie 34 (Paris 1956) *passim*, esp. 52-57.

The most important parallels between Philo and Origen are found in their interpretations of the two biblical accounts of man's creation in Gen. 1:26 and 2:7; these interpretations are briefly outlined. (= R330)

5606. J. HERING, 'Eschatologie biblique et idéalisme platonicien', in W. D. DAVIES and D. DAUBE (edd.), *The background of the New Testament and its eschatology in honour of C. H. Dodd* (Cambridge 1956) 444-463, esp. 446-450.

A short introduction to the doctrine of creation in Philo. Hering also discusses Philo's eschatology, in particular the denial of the resurrection of the body, which is to be attributed to the Platonic assumptions that inform this aspect of Philo's thought. (= R331)

5607. P. KATZ, 'The Old Testament Canon in Palestine and Alexandria', *ZNW* 47 (1956) 191-217, esp. 209-212.

The author draws attention to the fact that the Philonic doctrine of prophetic inspiration has often been used to demonstrate the existence of an Alexandrian interpretation of prophecy, which supposedly referred to canonical texts not included in the Jewish Bible. Katz shows that this view is unfounded. (= R332)

5608. P. KATZ, 'Septuagintal studies: their links with the past and their present tendencies', in *The background of the New Testament...* (cf. **5606**) 176-208, esp. 205-208.

Attacks the theory of Kahle (cf. **5917**) that the LXX was formed in the same way as the Aramaic Targums, so that it is not possible to look for the original text in the way initiated by Lagarde and continued by Rahlfs. Philo's aberrant quotations emphatically do not represent pre-LXX remnants of rival translations that were in circulation before the text of the LXX was finally determined. (DTR)

5609. G. KRETSCHMAR, *Studien zur frühchristlichen Trinitäts-theologie*, BHTh 21 (Tübingen 1956), esp. 40-44, 82-94.

The author discusses Philo on two occasions in particular: first, in order to draw attention to the complementarity of the concepts of the Logos and Sophia; secondly, in order to explain the allegory of the two Seraphim (in the fragment *De Deo*) and its connections with the analogous themes in Clement and Origen. (= R333)

5610. R. KRONER, *Speculation in pre-Christian philosophy*, Speculation and revelation in the history of philosophy (Philadelphia 1956), esp. 237-240.

The Stoa prepared the way for the theory which regarded the Platonic ideas as the thoughts of God; yet, as Kroner observes, it 'did not go so far as to pronounce such a doctrine, but they opened the gate through which one of their adherents, who was also inspired by the Bible, could walk: the Alexandrian Jew, Philo' (237). A few remarks, which are quite inadequate to the purpose, link Philo's thought to Kantian criticism, of which Philo is said to be 'potentially' the forerunner (cf. 239ff.). (= R333/a)

5611. H. LEWY, *Chaldaean oracles and theurgy*, Recherches d'archéologie, de philologie et d'histoire 13 (Cairo 1956, Paris 1978³), esp. 311-398 *passim*.

The third edition (1978), edited by M. TARDIEU, is subtitled: *Mysticism, magic and Platonism in the Later Roman Empire*. The author's attempt to reconstruct the doctrine of the Chaldean oracles as a self-contained system takes into account both oriental influences and the metaphysical themes of Middle Platonism. For the latter aspect the evidence supplied by Philo's theological thought is indispensable; we mention in particular the concepts of the Powers, of the Logos, and of the ideas, which also play a fundamental role in the Oracles. Many other affinities are found in the field of psychology and in the use of certain allegorical figures. (= R334)

5612. R. MARCUS, 'The Hellenistic age', in L. W. SCHWARZ (ed.), *Great ages and ideas of the Jewish people* (New York 1956) 95-139, esp. 132-135.

A brief 'portrait of Philo' forms part of a sympathetic overview of the achievements of Hellenistic Judaism by a leading scholar. Philo the religious philosopher is more important than Philo the statesman. The similarities between Philo and contemporary Rabbinic thought is greater than the differences. (DTR)

5613. A. MOMIGLIANO, 'Problemi di metodo nella interpretazione dei simboli giudeo-ellenistici', *Ath* 34 (1956) 237-248.

In this long and thoroughly documented review of Goodenough's *Jewish symbols in the Greco-Roman period* vols. 1-4 (cf. **5309**), Momigliano discusses the interpretation of Philo which underlies this work. (= R335)

5614. R. MONDOLFO, *L'infinito nel pensiero dell'antichità classica*, Il pensiero classico 5 (Florence 1956), esp. 519-539.

The ambiguity of Philonic thought, 'vacillating between the Jewish concept of creation and the Platonic concept of a simple ordering of formless material chaos' (253) would appear to be structural and not accidental. That is shown by the typical notion of a transcendent and infinite God and his essential unknowability, as opposed to the negative infinity of matter. In the views on the relationship between God and man, Mondolfo notes a certain continuity of tradition between classical Greek philosophy, Philo, and Neoplatonic speculation. Consequently, although Philo, Numenius, and Plotinus are given credit for having developed the concept of ecstasy, they should not be accredited with its discovery. Even in its new form, this concept continues to be described 'in colours and features drawn from the design and palette of Dionysian and Orphic mysticism' (536). (= R336)

5615. S. SANDMEL, *A Jewish understanding of the New Testament* (New York 1956), esp. 49-51, 65-67, 99-104.

The affinity between Philo and Paul does not consist in the similarity of their thought on important subjects (Sandmel singles out the concept of law and the doctrine of the Logos), but in the identical goal pursued by both. This goal may be described as the attempt to reconcile, from a missionary perspective, their own faith with the world and with Greek culture (cf. 103). (= R338)

5616. E. M. SMALLWOOD, Some notes on the Jews under Tiberius, *Lat* 15 (1956) 314-329.

In this historical article Philonic evidence (drawn mostly from *Legat.*) is used to articulate some aspects of the politics of Sejanus. (= R339)

5617. V. TCHERIKOVER, 'Jewish apologetic literature reconsidered', *Eos* [*Symbolae Raphaeli Taubenschlag dedicatae*, 3 vols.] 48.3 (1956) 169-193.

This important essay has both a polemical and a programmatic aspect. Firstly it argues forcefully against the common view that Jewish Apologetic literature, including Philo, was directed outwards towards Greeks and other non-Jews. The logistics of ancient book publication make this impossible. Only a few works (among which Philo's historical-apologetic works) may be regarded as memoranda directed at government officials. The main thrust of Jewish apologetic literature, therefore, is inwards, i.e. within the Jewish community itself. Secondly Tcherikover affirms that these works should not be read and interpreted merely as literary or cultural products, but should be approached 'from the historical point of view' (184). The abundant evidence on Egyptian conditions has been insufficiently exploited by scholars. The date and place of origin of a book should be determined, followed by an examination of the conditions prevalent at that period. Careful reading shows that by the time of Philo there is evidence of a deep rupture within the Alexandrian community. Philo, with his wealthy upper-class background, certainly cannot be regarded as a typical representative. Finally any evidence of Palestinian influence has to be taken into careful consideration. Earlier version published in Hebrew; cf. **4918**. (DTR)

5618. H. A. WOLFSON, *The philosophy of the church fathers*, vol. 1, *Faith, trinity, incarnation* (Cambridge Mass. 1956, 1964², 1970³; Italian translation Brescia 1978) *passim*.

The method of Philonic allegory not only provides the Church Fathers with the model for their allegorical practice, but also with a great abundance of material, as is particularly evident in Clement and Origen. Wolfson, who examines both formal and particular aspects of the allegory of the Alexandrians, emphasizes the fact that, historically, it has a double origin: in Philo, who drew on the non-literal method followed by the Greeks in their interpretation of Homer; and in Paul, who drew on the method of the Rabbis in Palestinian Judaism. Given the prominence of Philo in the author's conception of the history of philosophy (see above **4714**), it is no surprise that he is also a central figure in this magisterial, if controversial, account of Patristic philosophy. (= R340)

1957

5701. L. ALFONSI, 'Il Περὶ βίου θεωρητικοῦ di Filone e la tradizione protrettica', *WS* 70 (1957) 5-10.

It is possible to draw a continuous line, though a line filtered through scholastic traditions, between Aristotle's *Protrepticus*, Philo's *Contempl.*, and the *Protrepticus* of Clement of Alexandria. (= R341)

5702. G. ALON [אלון .ג], מחקרים בתולדות ישראל בימי בית שני ובתקופת המשנה והתלמוד [*Studies in Jewish History in the times of the Second Temple, the Mishna and the Talmud*], 2 vols. (Tel Aviv 1957), esp. 1.83-114.

Subsequently published in English (**7702**). The discussion 'On Philo's Halacha' originally appeared in *Tarbiz* 5 (1933-34) 28-36, 241-246; 6 (1934-35) 30-37, 452-459. (DS)

5703. W. BEIERWALTES, *Lux intelligibilis: Untersuchung zur Licht-metaphysik der Griechen* (inaug. diss. Munich 1957) *passim.*

The image of light, which carries fundamental metaphysical meanings in Greek thought, is analyzed here in a wide-ranging, if somewhat superficial, study which attempts to span the whole Greek period. Philo is often cited in this context, but is not separately discussed. (= R342)

5704. H. BRAUN, *Spätjüdisch-häretischer und frühchristlicher Radikalismus. Jesus von Nazareth und die essenische Qumransekte*, vol. 1, *Das Spätjudentum*, BHTh 24 (Tübingen 1957), esp. 67-89.

Philo's evidence on the Essenes is compared with the evidence in Josephus. Analyzing the differences between the two accounts, the author points out that Philo, in contrast to Josephus, is essentially concerned with matters of fact and pays scarce attention to the philosophical ideas and religious convictions which inspired this sect. (= R343)

5705. G. H. CLARK, *Thales to Dewey: a history of philosophy* (Boston 1957), esp. 195-210.

This textbook on the history of philosophy is unusual in that it devotes considerable space to Philo and the development of Patristic thought. In the presentation of a summary of Philo's thought the influence of Wolfson's interpretations are strongly felt. (DTR)

5706. J. DANIÉLOU, 'La symbolique du temple de Jérusalem chez Philon et Josèphe', in *Le symbolisme cosmique des monuments religieux*, Serie Orientale Roma 14 (Rome 1957) 83-90.

The symbol of the temple of Jerusalem in Philo is significant on two levels: from a historical point of view it testifies to a widespread tradition already in existence; from a philosophical-religious point of view it inaugurates a new tradition in which the cosmic symbolism of the temple is placed within the parameters of biblical thought. (= R344)

5707. G. DELLING, 'Wunder-Allegorie-Mythus bei Philon von Alexandreia', *WZ(H)* 6 (1957) 713-739; reprinted in *Gottes ist der Orient: Festschrift für O. Eissfeldt* (Berlin 1959); also in F. HAHN, T. HOLTZ, N. WALTER (edd.), *Studien zum Neuen Testament und zum hellenistischen Judentum: Gesammelte Aufsatze 1950-1968* (Göttingen 1970) 72-129.

According to Dellin, the concept of miracles in Philo finds its supreme illustration not in specific divine interventions, but in the 'miraculous' relationship between God and his people. The analysis of this relationship forces the author to address the subject of allegory in its widest sense, for Philo himself treats the biblical narratives on this theme from a largely allegorical point of view and links them to his own theological-religious ideas. After having thus touched upon many of Philo's fundamental themes, Delling concludes that it is not entirely correct to qualify Philo as a philosopher of religion: in the relationship between faith and religious thought the role of faith would appear to be much more important (cf. 129). (= R345)

5708. H. E. DEL MEDICO, *L'énigme des manuscrits de la mer morte: étude sur la date, la provenance et le contenu des manuscrits découverts dans la grotte I de Qumrân, suivie de la traduction commentée des principaux textes* (Paris 1957), esp. 79-81.

Of the principal sources of evidence on the Essenes (Philo, Pliny, Dio Chrysostom, and Flavius Josephus), Philo is the oldest, but that does not mean he is the most reliable. On the contrary, it was Philo who 'invented' the name and was responsible for creating the 'myth' of the Essenes. (= R346)

5709. R. M. GRANT, *The letter and the spirit* (London 1957) *passim*, esp. 32-38, 120-142.

Even though allegory was not invented by Philo, Grant affirms, the use which he makes of it is strongly innovative; in practical terms it allowed the creation of a Jewish philosophical literature on the basis of biblical exegesis. In Appendix 2 (120-142) the reader finds a discussion of the principal terms used in an allegorical sense by Christian and non-Christian thinkers, in which ample attention is given to Philo. (= R347)

5710. W. GRUBER, *Die pneumatische Exegese bei den Alexandrinern: ein Beitrag zur Noematik der Heiligen Schrift*, Schriften und Vorträge im Rahmen der theologischen Fakultät in Graz, Reihe D, Heft 3/4 (Graz 1957), esp. 15-20.

A succinct presentation of Philo's allegorical method. The author observes that Philonic allegory shows such perfection that one must presuppose a long antecedent tradition. We possess little information about this tradition, however, apart from the evidence, which is in fact provided by Philo himself, on the allegorical method of the Therapeutae. (= R348)

5711. P. KAUFMANN, 'Don, distance et passivité chez Philon d'Alexandrie', *RMM* 62 (1957) 37-56.

The author analyzes the three terms (κάρπωμα, δῶρον, ἀντίδοσις) which express the idea of 'gift' in Philo, each of course having different connotations. The recognition of the irreversibility of divine gifts should lead man to recognize the passivity of his role. Such a recognition is an indispensable condition for overcoming the isolation in which the individual who attributes all activity to himself finds himself, and for arriving at the glorious experience of transcendence. (= R350)

5712. A. D. NOCK, 'Religious symbols and symbolism II', *Gn* 29 (1957) 524-533: reprinted in Z. STEWART (ed.), *Arthur Darby Nock: essays on religion and the ancient world*, 2 vols. (Oxford 1972) 2.895-907, esp. 897ff.

In this critique of vols. 5-6 of E. R. Goodenough's monumental *Jewish symbols in the Greco-Roman period* (cf. **5309**) Nock reiterates some of his criticisms of

Goodenough's interpretation of the Philonic evidence on mystic eating and drinking (esp. of wine). The secrecy often hinted at refers to hidden theological truths, not actual rites. Nock's reviews of vols. 1-4 in *Gnomon* 27 (1955) 558-572 (= STEWART 877-894) and of vols. 7-8 in *Gnomon* 32 (1960) 728-736 (= STEWART 908-918) also contain valuable comments on Philonic material. (DTR)

5713. E. F. OSBORN, *The philosophy of Clement of Alexandria* (Cambridge 1957), esp. 31-37.

The treatment given by Philo, Clement and Plotinus of the problems of God's ineffability and his role as first cause are compared and it is concluded that Clement gives the most consistent account. (DTR)

5714. H. P. OWEN, 'The "stages of ascent" in Hebrews, V.11- VI.3', *NTS* 3 (1956-57) 243-253.

Paul's discussion of the levels of perfection is not very clear in itself, but becomes comprehensible in the light of Philo's ideal of philosophical *paideia*. (= R351)

5715. G. POZZO, 'Logos, uomo e Dio in Filone Alessandrino', *Hum (B)* 12 (1957) 371-374.

A brief, didactic presentation of salient features of Philo's theology and anthropology. (= R352)

5716. *Reallexikon für Antike und Christentum*, edited by T. KLAUSER *et al.*, vol. 3 (Stuttgart 1957).

Cf. above **5016**. Contains: J. HAUSSLEITER, art. 'Deus internus', 794-842, esp. 815-818 (God's presence in the heart or mind).

5717. J. REIDER, *The book of Wisdom: an English translation with introduction and commentary*, Dropsie College Edition: Jewish Apocryphal Literature 4 (New York 1957) *passim*.

Philo is constantly referred to in both the Introduction and the Commentary of this work. An excellent survey is given of the similarities between Philo and the *Book of Wisdom*. (= R353)

5718. W. RICHARDSON, 'The Philonic patriarchs as νόμος ἔμψυχος', in K. ALAND and F. L. CROSS (edd.), *Papers presented to the Second International Conference on Patristic Studies held at Christ Church*, Oxford 1955, part 1, StudPatr 1 (= TU 63, Berlin 1957) 515-525.

An analysis of the archetypal function of the Patriarchs, with particular attention being paid to Abraham, Isaac, Moses, and Joseph. Some pages are also devoted to the relationship God-world and especially to the Philonic doctrine of the Logos. (= R354)

5719. B. J. ROBERTS, 'The Qumrân scrolls and the Essenes', *NTS* 3

(1956-57) 58-65.

The discovery of the Qumran manuscripts has considerably increased our knowledge about the sect of the Essenes, which was previously limited to the evidence supplied by Philo and Josephus. The author uses here the information contained in the manuscripts to weigh the Philonic evidence. (= R355)

5720. E. SCHWEIZER, 'Die hellenistische Komponente im neutestamentlichen σάρξ-Begriff', *ZNW* 48 (1957) 237-253, esp. 246-250.

Schweizer briefly analyzes the Philonic conceptions of flesh and matter, which 'absolutely belong together' (247), particularly in relation to their ethical meaning as the principles contrary to spirituality and virtue. (= R356)

5721. H. SÉROUYA, *La Kabbale, ses origines, sa psychologie mystique, sa métaphysique* (Grasset 1957), esp. 62-70.

Although the points of contact between Cabbalistic literature and Philo are remarkable, the allegorical method and the philosophical principles which characterize Philo's work put him in an entirely different cultural context. (= R357)

5722. E. M. SMALLWOOD, 'The chronology of Gaius' attempt to desecrate the temple', *Lat* 16 (1957) 3-17.

There are some differences in the accounts that Josephus and Philo give of Gaius' attempt to introduce a statue of himself into the temple of Jerusalem. Smallwood considers Philo's account to be the more reliable of the two, because he lived at the time of the events narrated and deals with them in a more objective and historical way. (= R358)

5723. V. A. TCHERIKOVER, *Corpus papyrorum judaicarum*, in collaboration with A. FUKS, vol. 1 (Cambridge Mass. 1957) esp. 55-78.

The *Prologomena* to vol. 1 (written by Tcherikover), the aim of which is 'to present a general survey of the historical development of the Jewish people in Egypt during the Hellenistic-Roman-Byzantine age' (1), naturally contain numerous references to Philo (see the annotated list in the *Index to Prolegomena* on 273). A highly valuable attempt is made to place Philo squarely in the context of Jewish and Alexandrian history and politics (cf. 55-78). The profound intention of Philo's apologetic activity is to transform Judaism into a philosophy that transcends race or nation. Though today his political role is regarded as no more than of minor historical interest, 'his literary work remains as a witness of the last effort of Alexandrian Jewry to bridge the gulf between Judaism and Hellenism by creating a philosophic system uniting both' (78). See also **4506.** (= R359)

5724. H. M. TEEPLE, *The Mosaic eschatological prophet*, JBL.MS 10 (Philadelphia 1957), esp. 34-38.

Although Philo never deified the figure of Moses, he came very close to doing so. The author justifies this assertion by analyzing the epithets assigned to Moses (especially that of prophet). He recognizes in this connection two opposite influences on Philo: on the one hand the influence of Jewish and Greek-philosophical thought; on the other hand, the tendency of popular thought to deify its own heroes. (= R360)

5725. C. T. WAGNER, *Die vielen Metaphern und das eine Modell der plotinischen Metaphysik* (inaug. diss. Heidelberg 1957), esp. 25-27.

In surveying the antecedents of the symbolism of light in Plotinus, the author devotes a brief section to Philo, but does not go into much detail. (= R361)

5726. D. H. WALLACE, 'The Essenes and temple sacrifice', *ThZ* 13 (1957) 335-338.

A brief contribution, based on a few Philonic quotations, to the discussion about the passage in Josephus (*Ant.* 18.1.5) on the religious rites of the Essenes. (= R362)

5727. H. A. WOLFSON, 'Negative attributes in the Church Fathers and the Gnostic Basilides', *HThR* 50 (1957) 145-156.

The principles of negative theology used by the Church Fathers to characterize the divine transcendence are already found in Philo, Albinus, and Plotinus. But whereas in Philo the negative attributes of God are devoid of any logical significance and serve only to create an unbridgeable gap between God and other beings, in Albinus and Plotinus they are dealt with according to the logical scheme of Aristotle. (= R363)

1958

5801. G. J. M. BARTELINK, 'Μισόκαλος, épithéte du Diable', *VChr* 12 (1958) 37-44.

The author traces back to Philo the origin of the term μισόκαλος with reference to the Devil. This epithet was widely used by the Church Fathers in almost the same meaning as in Philo. (= R365)

5802. S. BELKIN [בלקין .ש], יסוד ושורש במוסר היהדות ['A fundamental principle in Jewish ethics'], in S. BERNSTEIN and G. A. CHURGIN (edd.), *Samuel K. Mirsky Jubilee Volume* (New York 1958) 5-25.

This theologico-philosophical essay propounds the thesis that the ideological foundation of Jewish morality stems from the belief in the voluntary creation of the world by a single creator. Belkin develops this and kindred themes with the aid of sources culled from the Talmud, Maimonides, the traditions of midrashic compendia and particularly Philo, whom he introduces as one who 'often incorporates ancient Jewish traditions' (8). The weaving in of Philonic quotations which often – though not always (cf. 23) – express the same thought as the traditional Rabbinic sources quoted, clearly creates the impression that Philonic and Rabbinic thought have much in common. (NGC)

5803. S. BELKIN [בלקין .ש], המדרש הנעלם ומקורותיו במדרשים האלכסנדרוניים ['The Midrash Ha Naeelam of the Zohar and its sources in ancient Alexandrian literature'], *Sura* 3 (1957-58) 25-92.

Belkin seeks to determine the sources upon which the *Midrash ha-Ne'elam* of the Zohar drew, and the principles according to which it was compiled (27). He notes that although most of the midrashim and philosophic ruminations found in the *Midrash ha-Ne'elam* are without parallel in extant Palestinian midrash, they are found in the works of Philo, the spokesman of the Hellenistic Midrash. The large number of parallels between the two works is ascribed to a joint Palestinian midrashic tradition used both by Philo and by the *Midrash ha-Ne'elam*, and it is within this frame of reference that the Zohar (and particularly the *Midrash ha-Ne'elam*) must be considered (91-92). The absence of material from the Rabbinic midrashic corpus, with which we are familiar, is explained as being due to the fact that 'the editors of the Palestinian midrash decided against including such material ...because they were not interested in harmonizing Hellenistic and Jewish tradition' (31). See further discussions in **5921, 6207**. (NGC)

5804. S. BELKIN [בלקין .ש], פילון ומסורת מדרשית ארץ ישראלית] [= 'Philo and a Palestinian midrashic tradition'], *Horeb* 13 (1958) 1-60.

Belkin argues that in contrast to the halachhic material, haggadic Midrash did not find it necessary to quote the chain of tradition since no definitive decisions had to be reached. This, he suggests, explains the dearth of the names of Tannaim (sages from mishnaic times) in the Palestinian midrash as we have it, even though it must have stemmed from a tradition antedating the extant works by many centuries. Belkin finds the basic ideological approach as well as the rules of midrashic exegesis of Philo and the Midrash to be very similar. These parallels are then used to support the thesis of the existence of an early Palestinian Midrashic tradition from which the Alexandrian midrashic tradition, of which Philo is the major extant proponent, was derived. (NGC)

5805. G. BERTRAM, "Ἱκανός in den griechischen Übersetzungen des ATs als Wiedergabe von schaddaj', *ZAW* 70 (1958) 20-31.

The absence of need as a characteristic of God is originally found in Philo, but reached him through the Bible rather than through Greek philosophical thought. (= R366)

5806. J. H. BURTNESS, 'Plato, Philo, and the author of Hebrews', *LuthQ* 10 (1958) 54-64.

In the course of this article the author describes the main scholarly views on the connections between Philo and Hebrews. It thus amounts to a brief *status quaestionis*. (= R367)

5807. M. A. CHEVALLIER, *L'Esprit et le Messie dans le bas-Judaïsme et le Nouveau Testament*, Études d'histoire et de philosophie religieuses 49 (Paris 1958), esp. 36-41.

Philo's work testifies to the presence in Alexandrian Judaism of a Messianic tradition associated with Ez. 9 and 11 and Sap. Sal. 2. Philo himself is thought to have inherited it from the Sibylline books. (= R368)

5808. A. DAIN, 'Le codex Hauniensis NKS 182', *REG* 71 (1958) 61-86.

Describes the Hauniensis codex containing, among other things, extracts from the

Mechanica Syntaxis attributed to Philo. *APh*, 29 (1959) 138, cites this article in the entry for *Philo Alexandrinus*, but in our opinion Philo of Byzantium is referred to here. (Cf. the entry for *Philon*, 48, in *RE* 20 1, 53ff.). We cite this text, therefore, only to correct the error of the French bibliographical resource. (= R369)

5809. J. DANIÉLOU, *Théologie du Judéo-Christianisme: histoire des doctrines chrétiennes avant Nicée*, vol. 1 (Tournai 1958) *passim*.

The author deals cursorily with the problem of the anticipation of the doctrine of the Trinity in Philo's writings. He refers specifically to the concept of logos and to the Philonic interpretation of the two Seraphim in Gen. 18:2. A few remarks are devoted to Philo's influence on Origen. (= R370)

5810. J. DANIÉLOU, *Philon d'Alexandrie*, Les temps et les destins (Paris 1958).

The principal aim of this work is to contribute towards a more precise picture of Philo. In fact, as Daniélou observes, a profound division runs through Philonic studies. On the one hand, Philo is interpreted as a syncretist with Jewish colourings; on the other hand, he is seen as the man who is at heart a Jewish believer and on the surface a Hellenistic scholar. In particular the syncretistic interpretation should be rejected, in the first place because it separates Philo the writer from Philo the man, and secondly, because Philo's theology, far from being syncretistic, is strongly synthetic, even if it retains some incoherencies. At the same time Daniélou intervenes in the discussion about the nature of Philo's philosophy; he chooses as terms of comparison both the great philosophical systems of Greek antiquity (Platonism, Aristotelianism, Stoicism) and some minor figures such as Antiochus of Ascalon, Eudoxus (*sic*! doubtless Eudorus is meant), Chaeremon, and Posidonius, all of whom, in one way or another, in their thought give expression to the philosophical *koine* to which Philo also belongs. The same procedure is used in the analysis of Philo's relations to Judaism and mysticism, where the delicate equilibrium between personal experience and theological thought becomes apparent. The last part of the book emphasizes the continuity of Philonic thought in Christian speculation, particularly in Paul, John, and in Hebrews. REVIEWS: P. T. Camelot, *RSPhTh* 42 (1958) 556f.; G. Daoust, *ScEs* 10 (1958) 282; H. Holstein, *Études* 298 (1958) 215; R. Marlé, *RecSR* 46 (1958) 463f.; J. Moreau, *REA* 60 (1958) 446ff.; J. Sint, *ZKTh* 80 (1958) 340f.; P. Smulders, *Bijdr* 19 (1958) 318; E. Boularand, *BLE* 60 (1959) 154ff.; C. Butler, *DR* 77 (1959) 338f.; F. de Fuenterrabia, *EstB* 18 (1959) 211f.; Roger, *Arbor* 43 (1959) 146f.; P. Rouillard, *RHE* 54 (1959) 300; C. Vansteenkiste, *Ang* 36 (1959) 247f.; C. M., *NRTh* 92 (1960) 888f.; E. Gilardi, *ScC* 88 (1960) 685; M. Vanhoutte, *RPhL* 18 (1960) 295f.; A. Vincent, *L'Ami du clergé* 70 (1960) 254; F. Petit, *RThAM* 30 (1963) 344. Cf. further **5902**. (= R371)

5811. H. E. DEL MEDICO, *Le Mythe des Esséniens, des origines à la fin du Moyen Age* (Paris 1958), esp. 17-41.

'The Essenes were born in the enthusiastic imagination of Philo' (300). In order to demonstrate this view, the author examines *Prob.* 75-87 (curiously cited in the version quoted by Eusebius) and provides a translation which adheres as closely as possible to the text (31-35). The evidence in Philo on the Essenes, often referred to in the course of discussion, is later given in a synoptic form together with the evidence in Flavius Josephus, Caius Julius Solinus, Pliny the Elder, and the interpolators of Philo and Josephus. A survey at the end of the book summarizes and specifies the mutual relationships and nature of the sources on the Essenes. (= R372)

5812. F. W. ELTESTER, *Eikon im Neuen Testament*, BZNW 23 (Berlin 1958), esp. 30-59.

The term εἰκών in Philo essentially expresses the function of mediation between God and created reality. Given the centrality of the theological problem of the distance between creator and created in Philo, it is logical that this function and the related concept of 'image' take on a significance which touches upon practically every level of Philonic thought. The author first analyzes the function of the term *eikon* in cosmology. He shows how the the relation model-image serves to explain the relation God-cosmos and to justify the doctrine of the Powers. Secondly, the same term is studied from the point of view of anthropology. Here it serves to explain the relation God-man according to the hierarchy God-Logos-man. It is significant that this relation – which does not involve the whole of man but only his spiritual part (*nous*, soul, *pneuma*) – works in two directions: from God to man, thus determining man's nature, and from man to God, thus characterizing man's ethical-mystical goal. (= R373)

5813. M. HADAS, 'Plato in Hellenistic fusion', *JHI* 19 (1958) 3-13.

The author proceeds from the supposition that the fusion of Greek thought and Jewish culture was a fundamental event in the history of European civilization. From this point of view, Philo, who is regarded as the principal mediator between Platonism and the Christian tradition (cf. 8), assumes a role of considerable importance. (= R374)

5814. H. JONAS, *The Gnostic religion: the message of the alien God and the beginnings of Christianity* (Boston 1958, 1963²), esp. 278-281; Dutch translation (Utrecht 1969) 302-305.

Although the problem of virtue in Philo is stated in the terms peculiar to Greek thought (for in Philo too virtue is derived from man's essential nature), yet it achieves a solution which radically subverts the positions of Greek antiquity; the affirmation, that is, of the insignificance of human nature and its total dependence on God. (= R375)

5815. W. KELBER, *Die Logoslehre von Heraklit bis Origenes* (Stuttgart 1958, 1976²), esp. 92-132.

The starting-point of Philo's doctrine of the Logos is his conception of God's nature. Here lies the fundamental difference between the Stoic and the Philonic Logos, the first having no other reality above itself, the second being subordinate to God. Moreover, since God is for Philo essentially unknowable, the only means of approaching him in a theoretical way is by means of the Logos. This is explained in the following scheme: (a) the Logos in relation to God; (b) the Logos and Sophia; (c) the Logos in relation to the creation of man, (d) in relation to the cosmos, (e) to the Powers, (f) to the history of the cosmos. In his discussion of these themes the author establishes frequent parallels with Greek authors (Heraclitus and Pythagoras) and Christian authors (Paul, John, Origen). (= R376)

5816. S. LAUER, 'Philo's concept of time', *JJS* 19 (1958) 39-46.

For Philo, time is a human creation which presupposes the movement of the sun and in itself has no objective content, being a convention only. (= R377)

5817. R. MONDOLFO, *La comprensione del soggetto umano nell'* *antichità classica*, Il pensiero classico 6 (Florence 1958), esp. 205-214, 514-524.

Philo, suspended between 'activism' and 'passivism', is presented as having found a synthesis between these extremes in the concept of 'voluntary effort' (cf. 210), to which the author gives particular prominence. The limit of the compromise, however, lies in the fact that our philosopher understood this concept in its negative aspect of 'withdrawal and retreat from lower goods' rather than in its positive aspect of elevation towards God. In other aspects of Philonic morality the author recognizes, besides Jewish influences, a large-scale absorption of Greek themes (e.g. Pythagorean). He concludes that, although Philo's ethics cannot be called 'the first morality of conscience' (Bréhier), it was certainly 'in essence a morality of conscience', perhaps the most explicit found in antiquity, but also the most 'anomalous', separated as it was from the humanism of classical ethics (523ff.). We note that the first edition of this work appeared in Spanish under the title: *La comprensión del sujeto humano en la cultura antigua* (Buenos Aires 1955). (= R378)

5818. J. PÉPIN, *Mythe et allégorie: les origines grecques et les contes-tations judéo-chrétiennes*, Philosophie de l'Esprit (Paris 1958, 1976²) *pas-sim*, esp. 231-244 of the second edition.

Philonic allegory is certainly of Greek, and specifically Stoic, origin. That does not alter the fact that many of Philo's interpretations are original and that his fundamental motives are of an apologetic nature, determined by his faith in the Jewish religion. (= R379)

5819. M. PHILONENKO, 'Le "Testament de Job" et les Thérapeutes', *Sem* 8 (1958) 41-53.

The author analyzes some significant similarities between Philo's evidence on the Essenes and certain passages from the *Testament of Job*. (= R380)

5820. W. SEIBEL, *Fleisch und Geist beim heiligen Ambrosius*, MThS II 14 (Munich 1958) *passim*.

Philonic influences, which are for the most part accurately analyzed by the author, can be traced through many aspects of Ambrose's thought and find their culmination in the theory of double creation. This theory forms the basis of Ambrose's anthropology and is at the same time a subject dear to Philo. From this it should not be deduced that there is an identity of interpretation between both thinkers, but rather that an exegetical tradition runs from Philo through Clement and Origen to Ambrose, a tradition which gathers heterogeneous elements in the course of its development, but which remains essentially faithful to a basic methodology. We see the same relationship in the symbolism of paradise; here it is impossible to determine the extent to which Ambrose, in modifying Philo's doctrine, is indebted to Origen. (= R381)

5821. P. SMULDERS, 'A quotation of Philo in Irenaeus', *VChr* 12 (1958) 154-156.

A few similarities, mostly of a lexical nature, suggest that Irenaeus had a direct knowledge of Philo's writings. (= R382)

5822. R. Mc. L. WILSON, *The Gnostic problem: a study of the relations between Hellenistic Judaism and the Gnostic heresy* (London 1958), esp. 30-63.

Philo's ideas on the nature of the intermediate beings in his theology seem to accept both Platonic views (specifically of the *Timaeus*, though Philo probably knew it only through Posidonius; cf. 41) and Stoic views, but cannot be reduced to either. This particular position is basically due to Philo's Jewish background. In order to safeguard the transcendence of God, he is forced to refute the immanentist and emanative conceptions typical of Middle Stoicism. Yet, at the same time, in order to maintain the religious and revealed character of truth, he is led to subordinate philosophy to biblical revelation. If, however, the essentially Jewish character of Philo's personality led him to adopt unresolved and contradictory positions in his philosophical thinking, his love of Greek philosophy – besides historical factors – determined the weakness of his influence on the Jewish tradition. (= R383)

5823. H. A. WOLFSON, 'Philosophical implications of Arianism and Apollinarianism', *DOP* 12 (1958) 3-28; reprinted in *Religious philosophy: a group of essays* (Cambridge Mass. 1961) 126-157, esp. 134-146, 150f.

The author takes a detour to show that the Arian concept of the intermediaries is indebted to the Philonic concepts of the Logos and the ideas. (= R447)

1959

5901. H. ASCHERMANN, art. 'Philo von Alexandrien', in *Evangelisches Kirchenlexicon*, vol. 3 (Göttingen 1959) 192-193.

A joint entry for the many other contributions in which Philo is cited or discussed. A few words are devoted to the state of Philonic studies. A complete list of references made to Philo is given in the *Indices*, vol. 6 (1961). (= R384)

5902. P. BOYANCÉ, 'Philon d'Alexandrie selon le P. Daniélou', *REG* 72 (1959) 377-384.

A detailed critical review of Daniélou's book (**5810**), adding useful supplementary remarks on Philo's supposed relations to Eudorus and the beginnings of Middle Platonism in Alexandria. (= R385)

5903. F. M. BRAUN, *Jean le théologien et son évangile dans l'église ancienne*, vol. 1, Études Bibliques (Paris 1959) *passim*.

Cf. **6403**. (= R386)

5904. H. CORNÉLIS, 'Les fondements cosmologiques de l'eschatologie d'Origène', *RSPhTh* 43 (1959) 32-80, 201-247 *passim*.

The author frequently refers to Philo in his reconstruction of Origen's cosmology. We cannot list all the Philonic citations in this long article here, since they are for the most part brief and focus on specific subjects. In general Cornélis tends to subordinate the philosophical aspect of Philo's work to its mystical-religious aspect (cf. 54ff.). (= R388)

5905. D. M. CROSSAN, *Imago Dei: a study in Philo and St. Paul*, Excerpta ex dissertatione ad Lauream in Facultate Theologica Athenaei Sancti Patricii (Maynooth 1959).

It is not Crossan's intention in this work to show essential connections between Paul and Philo, either in terms of content or vocabulary, since in his opinion there is not enough material to do this. His aim is rather to underline the similarity of structure which links the two thinkers and which is based on the concept of εἰκών. God-Logos-man in Philo and God-Christ-man in Paul are, formally speaking, equivalent series, because they are both functions of a single paradigmatic function. It is along these lines that Crossan's work unfolds, illustrating each element of the two series in both thinkers. The conclusion that emerges from this analysis is that 'the more fundamental divergence' between Philo and Paul 'is that with Philo the theme is on the level of the natural and the static while with Paul it is in the realm of the supernatural and the dynamic' (49). It should be noted that the present work is part of a much longer dissertation on the same subject, in which the Jewish and Greek contexts and the LXX are also dealt with. This perhaps explains why the references to bibliographical and textual material are inadequate (only the first 14 pages are devoted to Philo – hardly enough, given the vastness of the subject). (= R389)

5906. J. K. FEIBLEMAN, *Religious Platonism: the influence of religion on Plato and the influence of Plato on religion* (London 1959), esp. 96-134.

The relevant section of this work is a synthetic presentation of Philonic thought, or at least of its foundations. The comprehensiveness of this presentation, however, is considerably reduced by the particular perspective from which Philo is approached: in practice the author analyzes Philo's thought only from the point of view of its coherence with the Platonic tradition. Feibleman's assumption is that 'historically, Neoplatonism started when the Jews encountered Greek rationalism' (101), i.e. it started with Philo. In this sense Philo himself – and the Neoplatonism which originated with him – is regarded as having been responsible for a radical transformation of thought which the author summarizes in the following points (cf. 97ff.): (1) Neoplatonism places religion above philosophy; (2) in contrast to Plato, Neoplatonism made wide use of allegory; (3) it abandoned the method of dialogue and expressed its own thought dogmatically; (4) it shifted from the finite to the infinite; (5) it lost interest in nature; (6) it also lost interest in politics. In all this the author sees a devolution of Platonism towards forms of thought which attenuate its philosophical rigour in favour of fideistic and irrational elements. Cf. also **8215**. (= R391)

5907. G. FRIEDRICH (ed.), *Theologisches Wörterbuch zum Neuen Testament*, vol. 6 (Stuttgart 1959; English translation, Grand Rapids 1968).

Cf. above **3807**. Contains: W. BIEDER, art. πνεῦμα, πνευματικός (spirit, spiritual), 370-2; H. BRAUN, art. πλανάω κτλ (wander), 238-9; art. πλάσσω, πλάσμα (form, formation), 259-60; art. ποιέω κτλ (make), 459-60; R. BULTMANN, art. πιστεύω κτλ (believe), 202-3; G. DELLING, art. πλεονέκτης κτλ (greedy), 270;

art. πληρόω (fill, discussed in relation to God's cosmos-filling presence), 287-9; H. GREEVEN, art. προσκυνέω (worship), 763; G. HARDER, art. πονηρός (wicked), 563; F. HAUCK and W. KASCH, art. πλοῦτος κτλ (wealth), 324; J. JEREMIAS, art. ποιμήν κτλ (shepherd), 488-9; K. G. KUHN, art. προσήλυτος (stranger, proselyte), 732; E. LOHSE, art. πρόσωπον (face), 774-5; W. MICHAELIS, art. πηγή (spring), 114; R. MEYER, art. προφήτης κτλ (prophet), 822-3; G. STÄHLIN, art. προκοπή (progress), 709-11; H. STRATHMANN, art. πόλις κτλ (city), 527-8. (DTR)

5908. P. GEOLTRAIN, 'Esséniens et Hellénistes', *ThZ* 15 (1959) 241-254.

Philo exercised a considerable influence on the sect of the Essenes, to the extent that he helped instigate the process of Hellenization which took place in this sect in the first century A.D. (= R392)

5909. P. GEOLTRAIN, 'La contemplation à Qoumrân et chez les Thérapeutes', *Sem* 9 (1959) 49-57.

Philo's works are used here as a source for reconstructing the thought of the Therapeutae, particularly in relation to those aspects which in the author's view are pre-Gnostic. (= R393)

5910. E. R. GOODENOUGH, 'Philo of Alexandria', in S. NOVECK (ed.), *Great Jewish personalities in ancient and medieval times* (New York 1959) 98-119; German translation (Zürich 1972) 9-32.

An introduction to Philo which, for all its brevity, deals with historical and political aspects in a fairly comprehensive way. Philo's philosophy and religion, on the other hand, are given a very summary and general treatment. (= R394)

5911. E. R. GOODENOUGH, 'Philo of Alexandria', *Jewish Heritage* I 4 (1959) 19-22.

A succinct introduction to Philo, who is taken to be 'the outstanding leader in one of the most interesting developments of Judaism, one of the truly great Jews of history' (22). (= R395)

5912. R. M. GRANT, *Gnosticism and early Christianity* (New York-London 1959) *passim*.

Philo incidentally enters into the author's discussion of Gnosticism in connection with his concept of logos, his allegorical interpretation of biblical names, and his influence on John's Gospel. (= R396)

5913. V. GUAZZONI FOÀ, 'Il concetto di Provvidenza nel pensiero classico e in quello pagano', *GM* 14 (1959) 69-95, esp. 87ff.

Philo's concept of Providence is much richer than the corresponding Platonic and Stoic concepts. This is due to the following factors: (1) the connection between the themes of Providence and creation; (2) the admission of two types of Providence (general and individual), one related to natural law and the other to miraculous divine intervention; (3) the introduction of the notion of grace into God's providential design. With Philo – the author concludes – we are already in a fully Christian atmosphere (cf. 89). (= R397)

5914. E. E. HALLEWY [הלוי .א.א], מדרש רבה [= *Midrash Rabbah*] 8 vols. (Tel Aviv 1956-1963), vol. 3 (1959), 38-45 [Hebr. pp. לח-מה].

Hallewy's introduction to the Midrash *Exodus Rabbah* includes a discussion of parallel elements in Josephus, Philo, and the Pseudepigrapha. The examples from Philo are drawn almost exclusively from *Mos.* (DS)

5915. R. P. C. HANSON, *Allegory and event: a study of the sources and significance of Origen's interpretation of Scripture* (London 1959), esp. 37-64.

The sources of Philo's allegorical method are examined with particular reference to Aristobulus (cf. 41ff.). Next the author discusses the Jewish antecedents, with whom Philo seems to agree and differ at the same time. For if on the one hand his exegetical technique seems to approach that of the Rabbis, yet the results which he reaches and the ends which he pursues are clearly different; he in fact translates the biblical text into philosophical terms and essentially avoids messianic concerns. Philo's interest in history is actually small (cf. 52), and it is this which, more than anything else, separates him from Palestinian Judaism. (= R398)

5916. W. JAEGER, 'Echo eines unerkannten Tragikerfragments in Clemens' *Brief an die Korinther*', *RhM* 102 (1959) 330-340.

Contains a brief philological note on the Philonic term μαστοί in relation to an analogous term (μαζοί) in Clement. (= R399)

5917. P. KAHLE, *The Cairo Geniza* (London 1947, Oxford 1959²), esp. 247-249.

In the second edition of this study, which in spite of its title, is primarily a history of the biblical text and translations of the Bible up to the Arabic period, the author has occasion to reflect on the research done at his suggestion by Katz on Philo's aberrant textual quotations (cf. **5007**). He disagrees with Katz's conclusion that the aberrations were added by later scribes under the influence of later translators such as Aquila. They reveal the Greek text as Philo had it before him. (DTR)

5918. *Reallexikon für Antike und Christentum*, edited by T. KLAUSER *et al.*, vol. 4 (Stuttgart 1959).

Cf. above **5016**. Contains: E. FACHER, art. 'Dogma II (sachlich)', 1-24, esp. 4-6 (dogma or doctrine); E. VON IVÁNKA, art. 'Dunkelheit, mystische' 350-358, esp. 354-5 (mystical darkness); G. B. LADNER, art. 'Eikon', 771-786, esp. 773-774 (image, εἰκών); F. PFISTER, art. 'Ekstase', 944-87, esp. 979 (ecstasy).

5919. H. J. SCHOEPS, *Paulus: die Theologie des Apostels im Lichte der jüdischen Religionsgeschichte* (Tübingen 1959, Darmstadt 1972²), esp.

21-25.

In his survey of scholarship on Paul, the author devotes a few remarks to the Philonic concept of piety, which finds its perfect embodiment in the figure of Moses. (= R401)

5920. J. P. SMITH, 'Γένος in Philo on the Essenes (*Hypoth.* = Eus. *Pr. Ev.* 8,11) = νόμος?', *Bib* 40 (1959) 1021-1024.

As it has been handed down, the text in question raises problems of interpretation. The substitution of νόμος for γένος would clarify the sense of the passage. (= R403)

5921. R. J. Z. WERBLOWSKY, 'Philo and the *Zohar*: a note on the methods of the 'scienza nuova' in Jewish studies', *JJS* 10 (1959) 25-44, 113-135.

In this long and amply documented article the author proposes to examine Belkin's thesis (cf. **5803**) that the part of the Zohar known as *Midrash ha-Ne'elam* reveals Philonic influences. To this end he carefully analyzes the themes which the two writings have in common and concludes that it is not only impossible to speak of a direct relation, but that one should also not attach too much importance to the common use of allegory, which in specific cases does not go back to Philo (cf. 134ff.). In the author's view the influence of Philo and Hellenistic Judaism on later Judaism is practically nil. (= R405)

5922. S. WIBBING, *Die Tugend- und Lasterkataloge im Neuen Testament und ihre Traditionsgeschichte unter besonderer Berücksichtigung der Qumran-texte*, BZNW 25 (Berlin 1959), esp. 26-30.

The catalogue of virtues and vices, probably derived from popular-philosophical homiletics, is developed in a particular way by Philo. Its foundations are Stoic, however, and although Philo likes to vary and modify the original scheme of the four cardinal virtues and vices to suit his own purposes, his thought on the subject remains within the philosophical tradition of that school. (= R405/a)

5923. U. WILCKENS, *Weisheit und Torheit: eine exegetisch-religions-geschichtliche Untersuchung zu 1. Kor. 1 und 2*, BHTh 26 (Tübingen 1959), esp. 139-159.

What Philo means by 'knowledge of God' goes beyond the limits of traditional Jewish faith, which reduces the relation man-God to one in which man must listen and obey. For Philo that is only the first step on the road towards God; over and above it there is the *visio Dei* which is peculiar to the race of seers (= Israel) and which involves a deification of the person who does the seeing. The author goes on to examine the basic scheme of the 'royal road', specifically as it occurs in *Migr.* Particular attention is paid to the concept of *sophia* (which constitutes the essential theme of this road) and its relation to *pneuma*. In his handling of these themes, Philo appears to have used an Alexandrian mystery, which strongly anticipates the Gnosis. (= R406)

1960

6001. G. J. M. BARTELINK, 'Zur Spiritualisierung eines Opfer-terminus', *Glotta* 39 (1960) 43-48.

The history of the term μῶμος (blemish) and the group of concepts related to it is one of gradual spiritualization. In the LXX it is already introduced into the language of worship; later in Philo it is subsumed in the general process of spiritualization which the subject of worship undergoes. (= R407)

6002. J. B. BAUER, 'Uxor Loth repetiitne Sodomam?', *VD* 38 (1960) 28-33.

The story of Lot and his wife, narrated in Gen. 19:17-26, is analyzed in the light of *Leg.* 3.213. (= R408)

6003. S. BELKIN [בלקין .ש], מדרש שאלות ותשובות של בראשית ושמות לפילון האלכסנדרוני ויחסו למדרש הארץ-ישראלי [= 'Philo of Alexandria's "Quaestiones et Solutiones" on Genesis and Exodus and their relationship to the Palestinian Midrash'], *Horeb* 14-15 (1960) 1-74.

Beginning with the assumption that different works of Philo were addressed to different audiences, Belkin states that the *Quaestiones* were written for loyal Hellenized Jews with a good grounding in the Torah, who were interested in uplifting spiritual literature based upon traditional sources in the Greek vernacular. At the same time they served as a source book for preachers, providing them with the basic material for working up into sermons, arranged according to the sections read in the Synagogue on the different Sabbaths (8). The main body of the article draws parallels between ideas developed by Philo in the *Quaestiones* and the Rabbinic Midrashic tradition. The similarities between ideas, attitudes, questions, etc. in Philo's work and in the early and late Rabbinic material – and also the fact that at times, even though the biblical verses are quoted according to the Septuagint, Philo's exegeses reflects the Hebrew reading (13-14) –, are explained by means of the hypothesis that, while his audience was Greek-speaking and thus knew the Bible according to the Septuagint, Philo's sources were part of an on-going midrashic tradition which began long before his time and continued long after him. Belkin concludes that the *Quaestiones* are to be regarded as the earliest extant Rabbinic Midrash, even though their actual form is unique. (NGC)

6004. O. BETZ, *Offenbarung und Schriftforschung in der Qumran-sekte*, WUNT 6 (Tübingen 1960), esp. 70-72, 150-152.

If we compare the evidence in Philo and Josephus on the doctrine of the Essenes with the evidence found in the Qumran writings, the typical tendency of Philo to schematize and Hellenize becomes apparent. A surprising similarity between the doctrines of the Essenes, the Therapeutae, and the Jews emerges from Philo's accounts. In the author's view, however, we lack the information for deciding whether this similarity has a historical basis, or whether it is due to Philo's uncertain knowledge on the subject. (= R409)

6005. P. BOYANCÉ, 'Sur le discours d'Anchise (*Énéide*, VI, 724-751)', in *Hommages à G. Dumézil*, Collection Latomus (Brussels 1960) 60-76.

There are many points of contact between *Aeneid* 6.724-751 and *Her.* 269 with regard to the eschatological destiny of the soul and the relations between the soul and the passions. The author analyzes these parallels on the basis of the identification of the Philonic nous with the Virgilian *mens* and the *corporae pestes* (passions) in Virgil with the Κῆρες in Philo. (= R410)

6006. J. CARMIGNAC, 'Étude sur les procédés poétiques des Hymnes', *RQ* 2 (1959-60) 515-532, esp. 530-532.

The hymns which Philo attributes to the Essenian sect are said to show significant metrical affinities with the hymns of Qumran. (= R411)

6007. A. CODY, *Heavenly sanctuary and liturgy in the Epistle to the Hebrews: the achievement of salvation in the Epistle's perspectives* (St. Meinrad Ind. 1960), esp. 26-36, 125-127.

The theme of heavenly sanctuary in Philo is compared with the same theme in Hebrews. After a quite detailed analysis of the similarities, the author reaches the following conclusions: the terminology, philosophical thought, and literary expressions in Hebrews can be traced back to a source which, if not in fact Philonic, is certainly Alexandrian; at the same time the content of this theme is closer to Palestinian Rabbinical and apocalyptic Jewish literature than to the Philonic allegory of the temple. A few brief notes (125-127) are devoted to the Philonic concepts of time and eternity. (= R412)

6008. L. H. FELDMAN, 'The orthodoxy of the Jews in Hellenistic Egypt', *JSocS* 22 (1960) 215-237.

The problem of orthodoxy in Jewish-Hellenistic Egypt is discussed with reference to Jewish-Alexandrian literature in general and Philo in particular. It is Philo himself, in fact, who provides us with the most interesting information on the subject, especially because he distinguishes between two forms of heterodoxy, or rather 'non-observance': one leading to an overly literal interpretation of the Law, the other to an overly allegorical interpretation (230). Because Feldman discusses the views of many scholars in the course of the article, his contribution is also useful from a bibliographical point of view. (= R413)

6009. J. JERVELL, *Imago Dei, Gen. 1, 26 f. im Spätjudentum, in der Gnosis und in den paulinischen Briefen*, FRLANT 58 (Göttingen 1960), esp. 52-70.

Gen. 1:26ff. plays a central role in Philo's thought. The allegorical exegesis of this passage, which is strictly connected to the theory of the Logos and so to the field of theology, serves as a basis for Philo's anthropological conceptions. Moreover, the fact that man is created in God's image justifies the possibility of knowing God and the mystical component of ethics. Thirdly, on the basis of a literal interpretation, one may also recognize here the imprint of later Jewish hermeneutics, which makes Adam lord of the world by virtue of his resemblance to God. Lacking in Philo, however, is a 'historical' interpretation of the passage (cf. 70). (= R414)

6010. H. G. LEDER, *Die Auslegung der zentralen theologischen Aussagen der Paradieseserzählung (Gen. 2, 4b-3, 24) in der ältesten Literatur des Judentums und in der Alten Kirche: ein Beitrag zur Geschichte der Schriftauslegung und zur Dogmengeschichte der Alten Kirche*, part 1 *Die Paradieseserzählung im Alten Testament, im Judentum und im Neuen Testament* (inaug. diss. Greifswald 1960), esp. 452-544.

The author concentrates on the philosophical, and in particular theological, dimension of Philo's achievement, though without ignoring its other aspects. Broadly speaking, Philo's position in the history of thought is determined by his effort to synthesize Judaism and Hellenism and his attempt to bend Hellenistic philosophy in the direction of an interpretation of the Bible. This attitude is also recognizable in his exegesis of Gen. 2:4ff. Here, as Leder observes, 'that which in the Old Testament was understood as a historical fact of man's proto-history is resolved by Philo into a psychology of sin' (539). In this interpretation, moreover, the author sees the strong influence of Hellenistic philosophy as the source of its underlying anthropological motifs. Under such circumstances the delicate equilibrium between the two cultures (Hellenistic and Jewish) is broken and the biblical account of *original sin* becomes a philosophical (i.e. Hellenistic) conception of *sin* in general. This is due to the profound and unbridgeable gap between Jewish and Hellenistic anthropology, and does not diminish the value of Philonic thought in its commitment to synthesis. (= R415)

6011. J. H. LEWY [לוי .י.], עולמות נפגשים [*Studies in Jewish Hellenism*] (Jerusalem 1960) *passim*.

A collection of important studies by the distinguished scholar, whose premature death in 1945 was a severe blow for classical scholarship in Israel. None of the studies specifically concern Philo, but various references to his work and thought are made. Note his firm denial, in opposition to Shalit (**4406**), that Josephus employed Philonic themes, preferring the thesis that common elements in the two authors were drawn from no longer extant Jewish-Hellenistic sources (219 n.16). (DS)

6012. S. LYONNET, 'L'hymne christologique de l'Épître aux Colossiens et la fête juive de nouvel an (S. Paul, Col., 1, 20 et Philon, *De spec. leg.*, 2, 192)', *RecSR* 48 (1960) 93-100.

Underlines some significant parallels between Colossians and certain Philonic passages in connection with the theme of God as peacemaker and the related attribute εἰρηνοποιός. (= R416)

6013. M. NAMBARA, 'Die Idee des absoluten Nichts in der deutschen Mystik und ihre Entsprechungen im Buddhismus', *ABG* 6 (1960) 143-277, esp. 154-164.

The negative theology which exercised such a strong influence on German mysticism (in particular on Master Eckhart) is found for the first time in Philo, and not in Plato, as the German mystics themselves thought. The author demonstrates this view by analyzing the doctrine of negative attributes in Philo's theology. (= R417)

6014. J. DE SAVIGNAC, 'Le Messianisme de Philon d'Alexandrie', *NT*

4 (1960) 319-324.

A large number of Philonic passages, carefully listed and analyzed by the author, testify to the presence of 'a Messianism of earthly happiness' in Philo. This Messianism cannot be reduced to mean the 'mere moral development of his people' or 'bliss beyond death'. (= R418)

6015. M. SIMON, *Les sectes juives au temps de Jésus*, Mythes et Religions (Paris 1960) *passim*.

Philo's thought as outlined here is seen as a continuation of the programme initiated by the tradition of the LXX. This programme has a double aim, to rethink the biblical revelation in spiritual terms and to spread the Jewish faith. The author also addresses the problem of orthodoxy in Philo. Without underestimating the differences between Philonism and Rabbinic thought, he draws a distinction between Alexandrian Judaism (of which Philo is the faithful interpreter and inspirer) on the one hand and Palestinian Judaism or, in more general terms, the Diaspora (in respect to which Philo assumes heterodox positions) on the other. A great deal of other Philonic evidence is used to describe the various Jewish sects, particularly the Therapeutae and the Essenes. (= R419)

6016. E. F. SUTCLIFFE, *The monks of Qumran as depicted in the Dead Sea Scrolls, with translations in English* (London 1960), esp. 125-127, 224-228.

Passages from *Prob.* and *Hypoth.* containing evidence on the Essenes are translated and briefly introduced. (= R420)

6017. G. VERMES, 'Essenes-Therapeutai-Qumran', *DUJ* 52 (1960) 97-115.

Making extensive use of the evidence in Philo, the author attempts to show that the Essenes and the Therapeutae represent two tendencies within a single religious movement, one directed towards action, the other mainly contemplative. (= R421)

6018. G. VERMES, 'The etymology of "Essenes"', *RQ* 2 (1959-60) 427-443; reprinted in *Post-biblical Jewish studies*, SJLA 8 (Leiden 1975) 8-29.

An etymological analysis of the term 'Essenes', a name which is not found in the Qumran manuscripts but which occurs frequently in Philo. The interpretation of 'Essenes' as 'healers' gives an excellent Semitic root for the word, and would illuminate some significant correspondences with the Jewish thought of that period. This article is also to be recommended for its copious bibliographical references on the subject it deals with. (= R422)

6019. S. WAGNER, *Die Essener in der wissenschaftlichen Diskussion vom Ausgang des 18. bis zum Beginn des 20. Jahrhunderts: eine wissenschaftsgeschichtliche Studie*, BZAW 79 (Berlin 1960), esp. 194-209.

In the section of the book relevant to our concerns the author gives a documented review of scholarship on the problem of the Essenes (194-202) and the Therapeutae (202-

209). Particular attention is paid to the sources and, consequently, also to Philo. (= R423)

6020. A. WLOSOK, *Laktanz und die philosophische Gnosis: Untersuchungen zu Geschichte und Terminologie der gnostischen Erlösungsvorstellung*, AHAW 2 (Heidelberg 1960), esp. 50-111.

A long excursus is devoted to Philo as representative of the Jewish 'Religionsphilosophie' which is closely connected to parallel forms of speculative religious thought developed in Alexandria. The chief subject of the excursus is the allegorical theme of light and illumination, but in practice Philo's entire theological-anthropological system is set out with considerable attention to detail. Starting-point is the condition of man, which is characterized by his upright position, his possibility of seeing the heavens, of knowing God, and his kinship with God. On this basis is imposed the biblical doctrine of man as God's image, and the related conception of divine transcendence, which is of Platonic coinage. The ethical discourse which attaches itself to this structure and which is symbolized by the soul's retreat from the sensible world to God is justified only by the concept of grace, so that the entire field of man's ethical goals also acquires a precise religious meaning. As the author sums up (69): 'man's ultimate goal is the spiritual vision of God; but man participates in it only through divine grace'. The theme of illumination which occupies the second part of the contribution is simply the elaboration of this last point, analyzed in all the forms – mostly allegorical – in which it appears in Philo's writings. (= R424)

6021. H. A. WOLFSON, 'The Philonic God of revelation and his latter-day deniers', *HThR* 53 (1960) 101-124; reprinted in *Religious philosophy: a group of essays* (Cambridge Mass. 1961) 1-26.

Revelation is for Philo not merely a new road leading to the knowledge of God: it is the only true road. The God of revelation is distinguished from the God of philosophy by the fact that he is characterized as infinite. Philo specifies three ways in which the infinity of God should be understood: infinity as incomprehensibility, infinity as infinite goodness, infinity as omnipotence (cf. 105ff.). Wolfson regards this problem not just as a legacy of the history of philosophy, but as a universal and recurring category of philosophical thought; he consequently analyzes, in the last part of the article, the ideas of three modern philosophers: Spinoza, Hume, and John Stuart Mill. They are joined by the fact that they denied every form of revelation and in this sense are directly opposed to the views of Philo (cf. 110ff.). For the subsequent Hebrew translation, cf. **7853**. (= R425)

1961

6101. A. ADAM, *Antike Berichte über die Essener*, Kleine Texte für Vorlesungen und Übungen 182 (Berlin 1961), esp. 1-22.

Reports the Philonic evidence on the Essenes, taken from *Prob.*, *Contempl.*, and *Hypoth.* (= R426)

6102. M. BLACK, *The scrolls and Christian origins: studies in the Jewish background of the New Testament* (London 1961), esp. chap. 2.

Turns frequently to the evidence in Philo (especially in *Prob.*, *Hypoth.*, *Contempl.*) in order to reconstruct aspects of the life and thought of the Essenes. (= R427)

6103. C. COLPE, Art. 'Philo', *Die Religion in Geschichte und Gegenwart*, vol. 5 (Tübingen 1961³) 341-346.

A brief survey of Philo's life and works. As far as his thought is concerned, the article indicates its principal themes and refers to other entries for more detailed discussions. (= R428)

6104. P. COURCELLE, 'Saint Augustin a-t-il lu Philon d'Alexandrie?', *REA* 63 (1961) 78-85.

In contrast to the view held by Altaner (**4101**), Courcelle claims that Augustine did not know Philo directly, but through the *De Noe* of Ambrose. (= R429)

6105. J. DANIÉLOU, *Message évangélique et culture hellénistique aux IIᵉ et IIIᵉ siècle*, Bibliothèque de Théologie. Histoire des Doctrines Chrétiennes avant Nicée 2 (Tournai 1961), esp. 298ff.; English translation London-Philadelphia 1975, Italian translation Bologna 1975.

Daniélou emphasizes Philo's contribution towards creating the vocabulary of negative theology. He briefly analyzes the negative attributes of God which are found in Philo and have entered into the language of Christian theology. (= R430)

6106. G. P. GOOLD, 'A Greek professorial circle at Rome', *TAPhA* 92 (1961) 168-192.

Goold draws parallels between some passages in Philo and in the treatise *On the sublime*. The analysis of these predominantly lexical parallels and the conclusions which the author reaches generally follow the lines traced out by Norden (**5513**). (= R431)

6107. H. HEGERMANN, *Die Vorstellung vom Schöpfungsmittler im hellenistischen Judentum und Urchristentum*, TU 82 (Berlin 1961), esp. 6-87.

The author turns to Philo's evidence with the aim of reconstructing the ideas which were current in the culture of the synagogue. For this purpose he is forced to clarify the extent to which Philo was indebted to the cult of the mysteries, since his credibility as a source depends on this debt. A great many texts are analyzed in relation to the theme of the intermediaries, i.e. the Logos, the Powers, the figure of Moses and the high priest, and also the theology of Aeons, which the author does not hesitate to identify with the doctrine of the Powers (cf. 65). This analysis tends to limit the mystic influences in Philo and emphasizes the apologetic and missionary aspects of his work. Hegermann's opinion is that Philo sought to meet the aspirations and desires of his age by presenting Judaism as a true 'mystery'. (= R432)

6108. W. JAEGER, *Early Christianity and Greek paideia* (Cambridge Mass. 1961; Italian translation Florence 1974) *passim*.

Jaeger makes scattered but nonetheless interesting remarks on Philo's stature and other subjects. The Alexandrian is seen as 'the prototype of the Jewish philosopher who has absorbed the entire Greek tradition and makes use of its rich conceptual vocabulary and its literary means in order to prove his point, not to the Greeks but to his own fellow Jews' (30). (= R434)

6109. S. JELLICOE, 'Aristeas, Philo, and the Septuagint "Vorlage"', *JThS* 12 (1961) 261-271.

With regard to the question of the extent to which the Jews of Alexandria held their version of the LXX to be canonical, the evidence of Philo, who categorically affirms its divine inspiration, may be considered decisive. (= R435)

6110. J. LEIPOLDT, *Griechische Philosophie und frühchristliche Askese*, Berichte über die Verhandlungen der sächsischen Akademie der Wissenschaften zu Leipzig, philologische-historische Klasse 106.4 (Berlin 1961), esp. 24-27.

Although in the first centuries Christian asceticism flourishes above all in the East, its first beginnings do not take place there (or at least not in the Middle East) or in Greece (cf. 3). On the contrary, it originates in the Egyptian world during the pre-Christian era, i.e. in Chaeremon and Philo, who share the same ideals, though they are approached from opposite religious positions. Philo's enthusiasm for the kind of life led by the Essenes and the Therapeutae is clearly based on his predilection for asceticism, to which he was powerfully attracted, even if he failed to achieve it personally. (= R436)

6111. A. M. MALINGREY, *'Philosophia': étude d'un groupe de mots dans la littérature grecque des Présocratiques au IVe siècle après J.-C.* (Paris 1961), esp. 77-91.

Although it describes itself as being limited to 'a study of vocabulary' (78), this article actually touches on highly relevant aspects of Philonic thought. Malingrey argues that there are various meanings of the term 'philosophy' in Philo and that these have a hierarchical structure. On the first level philosophy is understood as the preparatory science for *sophia*; on the second level as the contemplation of the cosmos; on the third as a moral effort directed towards God; finally it is also regarded as God's revelation to Israel. The last level, which is not only theoretical, but also ethical (since it assumes allegiance to the revealed Law), clearly transcends the ones prior to it, since it involves the actual will of God who bestows on man the free gift of the true 'philosophy'. (= R437)

6112. A. ORBE, *La uncion del verbo: estudios Valentinianos*, vol. 3, Analecta Gregoriana cura Pontificiae Universitatis Gregorianae edita 113; Series Facultatis Theologicae sectio A 19 (Rome 1961), esp. 617-627.

The relevant section of this work examines the theme of priesthood in Philo and Ambrose. Orbe gives a clear account of the evolution of this concept, which in Philo comes to coincide with the concept of logos, in a context which is undoubtedly influenced by Stoicism, but which also shows some Platonic influences (cf. 625). Thus the common mediating function between God and man emphasized by Philo serves to explain, from a historical and philosophical point of view, the concept of 'priesthood of the Word' developed by Augustine. (= R438)

6113. S. REHRL, *Das Problem der Demut in der profan-griechischen Literatur im Vergleich zu Septuaginta und Neuem Testament*, Aevum Christianum 4 (Münster 1961), esp. 54-57, 66-69.

Humility did not play a central role in Greek ethics, and in any case meant something quite different from the Jewish-Christian concept. An exception is made for Philo, 'who was as much indebted to the Greek cultural heritage as to the religious ideas of his people' (69). In order to specify the meaning which the virtue has in our philosopher, Rehrl considers the word-group ταπεινός κτλ and its occurrence in Philonic writings. In this analysis it becomes clear that humility should be understood in both a vertical and a horizontal dimension, i.e. both in the relationship between God and man and between man and man. It is clear, however, that Philo regards the vertical dimension as more important than the horizontal. (= R440)

6114. J. REUMANN, 'Οἰκονομία, as "ethical accomodation" in the Fathers, and its pagan backgrounds', in F. L. CROSS (ed.), *Papers presented to the Third International Conference on Patristic Studies held at Christ Church, Oxford 1959*, StudPatr 3 (= TU 78; Berlin 1961) 370-379.

The term in question is difficult to translate in the context of Patristic biblical exegesis and thus necessitates an etymological analysis. Philo is important here, since he was the first to use this expression in the exegesis of Scripture. (= R441)

6115. J. B. SCHALLER, *Gen. 1.2 im Antiken Judentum (Untersuchungen über Verwendung und Deutung der Schöpfungsaussagen von Gen. 1.2 im antiken Judentum)* (diss. Göttingen 1961), esp. 80-98, 101-107.

Philo's interpretation of Gen. 1-2 is reconstructed mainly on the basis of *Opif.*, *Leg.* 1, and a few passages in *QE*. The dominant tendency in Philo is to fuse the biblical account of creation with themes from Hellenism, i.e. Platonic, Stoic, and Pythagorean philosophy, and also with oriental mysticism. This tendency – which is already found in the Wisdom of Solomon and Aristobulus – makes Philo into the most important representative of Hellenistic Judaism. The guiding motif of Schaller's analyses is the narrative of Gen. 1-2, which from time to time he confronts with the relevant Philonic passages. Special attention is given to the concept of man 'in God's image', which in Philo's view needs to be understood in three senses. That which 'images' God in man is sometimes the human soul, sometimes the idea of man, sometimes man as he actually is. (= R442)

6116. H. G. SCHÖNFELD, 'Zum Begriff "Therapeutai" bei Philo von Alexandrien', *RQ* 3 (1961) 219-240.

The author criticizes in great detail the views advanced by Vermes (**6018**) on the etymology of the terms 'Essenes' and 'Therapeutae'. He rejects the idea that the former could mean 'healers' and that it corresponds to a Semitic original of which the Greek transcription would be 'Essaioi' or 'Esseioi'. (= R443)

6117. V. TCHERIKOVER [ריקובר ˊצ .א], והרומי היווני בעולם היהודים [*The Jews in the Graeco-Roman world*] (Tel Aviv 1961), esp. 294-315, 366-392.

A collection of important studies, including **4507** and **4918**. (DS)

6118. U. TREU, 'Etymologie und Allegorie bei Klemens von Alexandrien', in F. L. CROSS (ed.), *Papers presented to the Third International Conference on Patristic Studies held at Christ Church, Oxford 1959*, StudPatr 4 (= TU 79; Berlin 1961) 191-211, esp. 197ff.

The first part discusses Clement's etymologies, and it is pointed out that many of these in the biblical domain are taken from Philo. The second part focusses on the allegory of Egypt and Canaan as symbolizing the body and the passions, the origins of which also lie in Philo's works. (DTR)

6119. G. VERMES, 'Essenes and Therapeutai', *RQ* 3 (1961) 495-504; reprinted in *Post-biblical Jewish studies*, SJLA 8 (Leiden 1975) 30-36.

A reply to Schönfeld's criticism (**6116**), turning mainly on the meaning of θεραπεία and θεραπευταί. The author also cites and discusses another etymology of 'Essenes' proposed by J. P. AUDET, 'Qumrân et la notice de Plinie sur les Esséniens', *RB* 68 (1961) 346-387. Cf. also **6018**. (= R444)

6120. A. WEISCHE, *Cicero und die Neue Akademie. Untersuchungen zur Entstehung und Geschichte des antiken Skeptizismus*, Orbis Antiquus 18 (Münster 1961, 1975²), esp. 88-101.

Many Philonic passages echo Sceptic tropes, the exact paternity of which is still uncertain. The author not only summarizes the principal scholarly positions, but also examines Philo's specific relation to Scepticism. The sceptical tendencies found in Philo are motivated by his radical distrust of empirical reality, a distrust which clearly goes back to Plato. But while in Plato this position forms the background to an *a priori* conception of knowledge, in Philo it is the starting-point for a mystical knowledge of God (cf. 100). In Philo, as in the later Platonists, the Neo-Academic doctrines are couched in modes of thought and expression which have their origin in Plato's *Theaetetus*. (= R445)

6121. H. A. WOLFSON, 'Extradeical and intradeical interpretations of Platonic ideas', *JHI* 22 (1961) 3-32, esp. 5-13; also printed in *Religious philosophy: a group of essays* (Cambridge Mass. 1961) 27-68.

The location of the Platonic ideas inside or outside the divine mind is a subject of such philosophical importance as to be determinative for the entire history of theology. Philo plays a crucial role in this history, because it was he who altered Plato's metaphysical location of the ideas. Wolfson reconstructs this transition with great clarity, showing how, starting from the analogous descriptions of creation in the *Timaeus* and the Bible, Philo – in spite of his desire to combine the two accounts – moved away from Plato on three issues: in refuting the concept of the cosmic soul; in locating the ideas in the Logos; in regarding the ideas as created substances (cf. 6ff.). For the subsequent Hebrew translation, cf. **7853**. (= R446)

1962

6201. Y. AMIR [עמיר], .י [פילון אצל עבריים שמות פרושי] ['Explanation of Hebrew names in Philo'] *Tarbiz* 31 (1961-62) 297.

Since Philo alters the Attic form of περιττός to περισσός when interpreting the Hebrew name of Jethro (*Sacr.* 50), Amir concludes that this change betrays the influence of a written source since Philo elsewhere prefers the Attic dialect. See also **6316, 6515**. (MM)

6202. E. BRANDENBURGER, *Adam und Christus: exegetisch-religionsgeschichtliche Untersuchung zu Röm. 5 12-21 (1. Kor. 15)*, WMANT 7 (Neukirchen 1962), esp. 117-131.

The analysis of Rom. 5:12-21 in this work is conducted mainly from a religious-historical point of view. Among the principal antecedents of the passage from Paul's epistle the author analyzes the figure of the two Adam-*anthropoi*, for which Philo's writings provide the most significant evidence in pre-Christian times. According to the author the precise starting-point for the interpretation of Rom. 5:12-21 should not be located in Philo's œuvre, which is dominated by Platonic themes, but rather in the circle around Philo. (= R448)

6203. H. A. BRONGERS, *De Jozefgeschiedenis bij Joden, Christenen en Mohammedanen: een theologische, historische en literaire studie* (Wageningen 1962) *passim.*

Philo's *Life of Joseph* is the oldest of the 15 Jewish sources which, together with Christian and Islamic writings, are constantly referred to throughout a detailed analysis of the way that the story of Joseph was interpreted in Judaism, Christianity and Islam. (DTR)

6204. L. CERFAUX, *Le chrétien dans la théologie paulinienne*, LeDiv 33 (Paris 1962), esp. 206-209.

A few remarks are devoted to the concept of divine inheritance in Philo and Paul. The Philonic tendency to Platonize and spiritualize is absent in his Christian counterpart. (= R449)

6205. É. J. COPPENS, 'Les affinités qumrâniennes de l'Épître aux Hébreux', *NRTh* 84 (1962) 128-141, 257-282, esp. 272-279.

According to the author the affinities which Hebrews shares with Qumran are more apparent than real. Even those elements which at first sight join it to Qumran should rather be interpreted in the light of Jewish-Alexandrian, and specifically Philonic, thought and vocabulary. (= R450)

6206. H. M. ERVIN, *Theological aspects of the Septuagint of the book of Psalms* (diss. Princeton 1962).

When one compares the LXX with the Hebrew text, one notices how many variants can only be explained in terms of a precise theological influence, which may be summarized as an attempt at spiritualization. Philo's evidence is fundamental, because the very method of allegory adopted by him is an instrument for spiritualizing biblical terms (30ff.), and more specifically because Philo rejects all anthropomorphic (58ff.) and zoomorphic (81ff.) interpretations of God. Even the angelology common to Philo and Rabbinical thought is understood by the author as an attempt to moderate divine anthropomorphism (cf. 85ff.). (= R451)

6207. J. FINKEL, 'The Alexandrian tradition and the Midrash Ha-Ne'elam', in M. M. KASHER et al. (edd.), *The Leo Jung Jubilee volume: essays in his honor on the occasion of his seventieth birthday* (New York 1962) 77-103.

Attacks the position of Werblowsky (**5921**) for blindly supporting the position of Scholem against Belkin (**5803**) that no influence of Hellenistic Alexandrian tradition has percolated directly or indirectly into the works of the Cabbalists in the Middle Ages. In this article, however, Finkel examines only passages from the Wisdom of Solomon that he thinks found their way into the *Midrash ha-Ne'elam*. The Philonic material was to be discussed in a subsequent article (cf. 79), but to our knowledge this was not published. (DTR)

6208. E. R. GOODENOUGH, Art. 'Philo Judaeus', *The Interpreter's dictionary of the Bible*, 4 vols. (New York-Nashville 1962) 3.796-799.

A synoptic presentation of Philo's life, writings and thought by one of the leading Philonists of his time. (DTR)

6209. E. E. HALLEWY [הלוי .א.א], מדרש האגדה ומדרש הומירוס ['Biblical Midrash and Homeric exegesis'], *Tarbiz* 31 (1961-62) 157-169, 264-280.

Hallewy provides a detailed comparison of the techniques of Rabbinic exegesis with those found in Greek and Hellenistic commentaries on Homer. The varied aspects of Midrash can all be understood as attempts to resolve biblical passages which (a) explicitly deny or contradict one another, or (b) elicit either surpise of disbelief. Examples from the writings of Philo are often introduced in support and illustration of the author's thesis. English summary. (DS)

6210. M. HARL, 'Adam et les deux arbres du Paradis (Gen. II-III) ou l'homme milieu entre deux termes (μέσος-μεθόριος) chez Philon d'Alexandrie: pour une histoire de la doctrine du libre-arbitre', *RecSR* 50 (1962) 321-388.

From Plato and Aristotle to the Church Fathers, the term μεθόριος underwent a development full of philosophical implications, particularly in relation to the concept of free will. Philo's position is especially interesting in this context, since it was he who first made use of the term in biblical exegesis and specifically applied it to the two trees of Paradise in Gen. 2:16-17. The allegorical meaning which Philo attributes to the two trees, i.e. the contrast between φιλαυτία (self-love) and εὐσέβεια (piety), also enters into the thought of the Fathers and, with it, the notion which sees the human will not as an absolute given, but as a synergy, i.e. a cooperation between man and God. (= R452)

6211. I. HEINEMANN, *Philons griechische und jüdische Bildung: kulturvergleichende Untersuchungen zu Philons Darstellung der jüdischen Gesetze* (Breslau 1932, Hildesheim 1962², 1973³).

In the second edition an appendix is added, containing marginalia taken from the author's copy of the first edition. (= R453)

6212. F. N. KLEIN, *Die Lichtterminologie bei Philon von Alexandrien und in den hermetischen Schriften: Untersuchungen zur Struktur der religiösen Sprache der hellenistischen Mystik* (Leiden 1962).

This work sets out to determine as precisely as possible the meaning of light in Philonic thought. An extensive textual analysis in the first chapter focusses on a series of semantic distinctions between which Philo's thought appears to vacillate: light on the one hand as a natural reality, on the other hand as the symbol of a supernatural or of a religious datum (cf. 68). At a further level the image of light also helps to characterize the relation between God and human cognition. On the basis of these elements, the very structure of Philo's theology and cosmology can be formulated in terms of a hierarchy which extends from God (archetypal light), through the divine Logos (model or place of the noetic light which is sometimes identified with wisdom, sometimes with *pneuma*), the light of the sun and the stars, and natural light, ending in darkness as the absence of light. Thus a scheme of emanation emerges (cf. 71) in which two kinds of light, divine and natural, are readily identifiable. The relation between these two types is not analogical but real, and can be traced back to the different levels which each type occupies in the structure of emanation: 'this proves that divine light must be understood concretely, but never naturalistically' (78). REVIEWS: P. Boyancé, *Lat* 22 (1962) 115f.; G. Delling, *ThLZ* 89 (1964) 135f.; J. Mallet, *RHE* 59 (1964) 1139f.; F. Petit, *RThAM* 32 (1965) 339; A. Wlosok, *Gn* 38 (1966) 237ff.; H. Kraft, *ZKG* 78 (1967) 349f.; P. de Fidio, *RSLR* 5 (1969) 634ff. (= R454)

6213. A. F. J. KLIJN, 'The "single one" in the Gospel of Thomas', *JBL* 81 (1962) 271-278.

The theme of the unity-unicity of God and the 'duality' of man is developed at length by Philo; an exact counterpart is found in the Gospel of Thomas. (= R455)

6214. B. KRIVOCHEINE, 'Le thème de l'ivresse spirituelle dans la mystique de Saint Syméon le Nouveau Théologien', in F. L. CROSS (ed.), *Papers presented to the Third International Conference on Patristic Studies held at Christ Church, Oxford 1959*, part 3, StudPatr 5 (= TU 80; Berlin 1962) 368-376.

A brief analysis of the similarities and differences between St. Simeon and Philo on the theme of 'sober drunkenness'. (= R456)

6215. S. LILLA, 'Middle Platonism, Neoplatonism and Jewish-Alexandrine philosophy in the terminology of Clement of Alexandria's ethics', *AISP* 3 (1962) 3-36.

The author establishes a strict parallel between Clement of Alexandria, Middle Platonist thought, and Philo in the following themes: (a) the definition of virtue in general; (b) the analysis of the four cardinal virtues, their relationship with one and other and with the various parts of the soul; (c) the doctrine of the ὀρθὸς λόγος in connection with the passions and with the principle of 'living according to nature'; (d) the two ethical levels of *metriopatheia* and *apatheia*; (e) the doctrine of ὁμοίωσις θεῷ. The close ties between Clement and Philo are emphasized, and an attempt is made to explain Clement's philosophical eclecticism with reference to the method of cultural synthesis typical of both Philo and Middle Platonism. (= R457)

6216. R. LOEWE, 'Philo and Judaism in Alexandria', in R. GOLD-WATER (ed.), *Jewish Philosophy and Philosophers* (London 1962) 20-40.

A general introductory account of Philo's life, writings and thought against the background of the Jewish community at Alexandria. The author distinguishes between a facile and a risky apologetic approach to Greek wisdom, the former merely asserting that philosophy was ultimately derived from the Jews, the latter undertaking to absorb what is valuable in extraneous thought. The latter course, taken by Philo, is described as being unacceptable to the pure philosopher but attractive to the intellectual. In the description of Philo's thought most emphasis is given to the various aspects of the doctrine of the Logos, which is carefully distinguished from Rabbinic conceptions of the Torah. (DTR)

6217. A. LUNEAU, 'Les âges du monde: état de la question à l'aurore de l'ère patristique', in *Papers presented to the Third International Conference...* (cf. **6214**), 509-518.

The doctrine of the ages of the world lies outside Philo's concerns because of his small interest in historical movements and his preponderant emphasis on the journey of the individual soul. (= R458)

6218. M. MÜHL, 'Der λόγος ἐνδιάθετος und προφορικός von der älteren Stoa bis zur Synode von Sirmium 351', *ABG* 7 (1962) 7-56, esp. 17-24.

A brief analysis of the expressions λόγος ἐνδιάθετος and λόγος προφορικός in Philo and the relation between them. The author observes that although in Philo these two concepts do not introduce any kind of differentiation within God's substance, they do anticipate the process which was to lead from Jewish monotheism to Christian 'ditheism' and later 'tritheism'. (= R459)

6219. A. D. NOCK, 'The exegesis of Timaeus 28C', *VChr* 16 (1962) 79-86.

Evidence from Philo – *Abr.* 57 and the themes of Israel and seeing God – do not support the thesis of Wlosok (cf. **6021**) that, when Plato's words at *Tim.* 28c are taken to mean that it is not only difficult but impossible to know God, this modification takes place under the influence of Gnostic Platonism. (DTR)

6220. J. POUILLOUX, 'Philon d'Alexandrie: recherches et points de vue nouveaux', *RHR* 161 (1962) 135-137.

A brief *status quaestionis* of Philonic studies, in which the statements of principle made on the methodology followed by various Philonic scholars. (= R461)

6221. K. PRUEMM, 'Reflexiones theologicae et historicae ad usum Paulinum termini "eikon"', *VD* 40 (1962) 232-257.

The concept of εἰκών in Philo is of Platonic origin. It is possible that Paul's use of this term involves an element of polemic against Philo. (= R462)

6222. *Reallexikon für Antike und Christentum*, edited by T. KLAUSER et al., vol. 5 (Stuttgart 1962).

Cf. above **5016**. Contains: H. CHADWICK, art. 'Enkrateia', 343-365, esp. 348 (asceticism); J. MICHL, art. 'Engel II (jüdisch)', 61-97, esp. 82-83 (angels in the Jewish tradition); I. OPELT, art. 'Erde', 1113-79, esp. 1117-9 (earth in its various literal, symbolic and metaphorical connotations); K. THRAEDE, art. 'Erfinder II (geistesgeschichtlich)', 1191-1278, esp. 1245-6 (the theme of discoverers-inventors in the history of thought).

6223. S. REYERO, 'Los textos de Flavio Josefo y de Filón sobre la residencia de los procuradores romanos en Jerusalén', *Studium* 1-2 (1961-62) 527-555, esp. 547-555.

Analyzes and compares the evidence in *Legat.* 38 and Josephus on the residence of the Roman governors in Jerusalem. (= R463)

6224. S. SANDMEL, 'Parallelomania', *JBL* 81 (1962) 1-13.

A denunciation of the tendency in Jewish-Christian studies to assume parallels and similarities in an exaggerated and often misleading way. This criticism is applied to various studies on Philo which on account of their excessive use of parallels are guided towards solutions that are determined in advance. (= R464)

6225. H. M. SCHENKE, *Der Gott 'Mensch' in der Gnosis: ein religionsgeschichtlicher Beitrag zur Diskussion über die paulinische Anschauung von der Kirche als Leib Christi* (Göttingen 1962), esp. 121-124.

A brief but well-documented analysis of the various Philonic interpretations of Gen. 1:26ff. with regard to the κατ' εἰκόνα relationship between man and God, as seen in connection with the broader subject of the Logos. (= R465)

6226. A. SCHULZ, *Nachfolgen und Nachahmen: Studien über das Verhältnis der neutestamentlichen Jüngerschaft zur urchristlichen Vorbildethik*, StANT 6 (Munich 1962), esp. 215-221.

The imitation of God is a fundamental idea in Philo, which is expressed in many different ways and involves ethics in all its aspects. The author briefly analyzes the most important passages in this connection and emphasizes the way they synthesize Jewish and Greek elements. (= R466)

6227. L. WÄCHTER, 'Der Einfluss platonischen Denkens auf rabbinische Schöpfungsspekulationen', *ZRGG* 14 (1962) 36-56.

Middle Platonism and Philo in particular profoundly changed Plato's theory of ideas, transforming them into the thoughts of God. Through Philo this interpretation passed into Rabbinic Judaism. Instead of a direct mediation through Philo, however, the author posits a long chain of conceptual transmission connecting Rabbinic thought with Hellenistic Judaism, a chain which probably involved Origen and certainly involved the cultural milieu of Alexandria. (= R467)

6228. P. WILPERT, 'Philon bei Nikolaus von Kues', in *idem* (ed.), *Antike und Orient im Mittelalter: Vorträge der Kölner Mediaevisten-tagungen 1956-1959*, Miscellanea mediaevalia 1 (Berlin 1962) 69-79.

Starting from the evidence on Philo in Nicholas Cusanus, the author attempts a broad reconstruction of the sources on which the latter drew. He thus succeeds in sketching the image of Philo in the Middle Ages, a period in which the Alexandrian played an important role, but one that was in many respects far removed from the historical truth. (= R468)

1963

6301. R. ARNALDEZ, 'Les images du sceau et de la lumière dans la pensée de Philon d'Alexandrie', *InfLitt* 15 (1963) 62-72.

The analysis of the two images of the seal and of light gives the author the opportunity to draw attention to the role of rhetoric in Philo. Arnaldez is convinced that beyond the 'conscious' ends of Philo's work – ends which are not remarkable for their richness and variety (cf. 62) – there lies a world of images, the architectural coherence of which makes a vital contribution to the richness of his thought. (= R469)

6302. L. W. BARNARD, 'The background of early Egyptian Christianity', *CQR* 164 (1963) 300-310, 428-441.

A chiefly historical article. Evidence in Philo, taken mostly from *Flacc.*, is used to determine the situation of the Jewish community in Alexandria. (= R470)

6303. O. BETZ, 'Was am Anfang geschah: das jüdische Erbe in den neugefundenen koptisch-gnostischen Schriften', in O. BETZ *et al.* (edd.), *Abraham unser Vater: Festschrift für Otto Michel zum 60. Geburtstag*, Arbeiten zur Geschichte des Spätjudentums und Urchristentums 5 (Leiden-Köln 1963) 24-43, esp. 39 ff.

A few comments are made on the mediating function of Sophia in Philonic thought, with reference to the well-known passages *Leg.* 2.49 and *Cher.* 48-50. (RR)

6304. P. BORGEN, 'Observations on the midrashic character of John 6', *ZNW* 54 (1963) 232-240; reprinted in *Logos was the true light and other essays on the Gospel of John* (Trondheim 1983) 23-31.

Philonic texts, notably *Det.* 47-48, *Mut.* 141-144, *Leg.* 1.28, are invoked to show that John 6 uses exegetical methods and patterns derived from Midrashic exegesis. (DTR)

6305. P. BOYANCÉ, 'Études Philoniennes', *REG* 76 (1963) 64-110; incomplete German translation in C. ZINTZEN (ed.), *Der Mittelplatonismus*, Wege der Forschung 70 (Darmstadt 1981) 33-51.

An important contribution to the question of Philo's philosophical sources, taking its point of departure in the monograph of Daniélou (cf. **5810, 5902**) and the first published volumes of the French translation series (cf. **2201**ff.). The following subjects are discussed. (a) The Hellenistic background of Philo's method of allegorical exegesis. Philo is very well acquainted with allegorical treatment of poets such as Homer and Hesiod. The types of exegesis he uses – physical, moral, mystical – have philosophical antecedents. (b) Philo's knowledge and use of Plato. Philo's works are full of Platonic reminiscences, especially of the *Timaeus* (heavily exploited in the *De opificio mundi*) and the *Phaedrus* myth. These dialogues are the chief sources for the doctrines of the intelligible world and the ascent of the soul. It is likely that Philo drew on material located in Platonist commentaries. (c) Arithmology and Pythagorean influence. Boyancé shows that Philo's arithmological material contains ancient Pythagorean doctrines that go back to Philolaus, but that his direct sources will have been near-contemporary philosophers such as Eudorus of Alexandria. The article is concluded with some remarks on specific passages which refer to interesting philosophical themes (*Opif.* 69, 77, 82, *Leg.* 3.115); cf. also **6307** below to which the author cross-refers. (= R471-6)

6306. P. BOYANCÉ, 'Note sur la φρουρά platonicienne', *RPh* 37 (1963) 7-11.

A brief philological note in which Philonic evidence is used to determine the precise meaning of the term φρουρά in the *Phaedo*. (= R477)

6307. P. BOYANCÉ, 'Sur l'exégèse hellénistique du *Phèdre* (*Phèdre* p. 246 c)' in *Miscellanea di studi alessandrini in memoria di A. Rostagni* (Turin 1963) 45-53.

Philonic passages which echo Plato's *Phaedrus* are collected together and are subjected to a brief but illuminating analysis. (= R478)

6308. J. B. BURKE, *Philo and Alexandrian Judaism* (diss. Syracuse 1963).

The greater part of this thesis (146-265) is devoted to an explanation of Philo's thought and method and discusses almost all his fundamental themes (God, the Powers, the Logos, angels, man, and the doctrine of the mystic vision). This part of the work, which is critical of Wolfson and more in line with the approach of Goodenough, can be considered no more than a general presentation of Philo's thought without much critical depth. The most interesting section of the study, however, offers a historical interpretation of the relations between Philo and Judaism. Agreeing with Goodenough, the author regards Philo's work as an interpretation of Jewish religion, the later fortunes of which were determined by various historical factors. The silence which surrounds Philo in the Jewish tradition is imputed to a kind of censorship which the Rabbis imposed on his works during the 2nd century as part of a policy of 'homogenization' of thought in response to the rise of Christianity and anti-Semitism. (= R479)

6309. G. A. CHURGIN [ג.א. חורגין], שלושה פילוסופים יהודיים [= 'Three

Jewish Philosophers'], in I. L. HACOHEN MAIMON (ed.), ספר... ישראל
אלפנביין [= *I. Elfenbein Jubilee Volume*] (Jerusalem 1963) 102-110 [Hebrew
pp. קב-קי], esp. 104-108

A discussion of three Jewish-American philosophers: M. R. Cohen, H. A. Wolfson,
and H. Kallen. The section on Wolfson includes a brief statement (105f.) of the centrality
of Philo's perception of the ultimate accord between reason and revelation. (DS)

6310. P. COURCELLE, *Les Confessions de Saint Augustin dans la
tradition littéraire: antécédents et postérité*, Études Augustiniennes (Paris
1963) 49-58.

It is argued that Philo inspired the second half of book 7 of the *Confessions*, which
deals with ecstatic experience and the difficulty of achieving it. It was in fact from Philo,
through Ambrose, that Augustine learnt to express the disappointing nature of his first
mystical experiences (cf. 58). (= R480)

6311. J. GUTTMANN [גוטמן .י.י.], הפילוסופיה של היהדות [=*The philosophy of Judaism*] (Jerusalem 1963) 28-33.

A revision of the original German work (1933) and itself the basis of the subsequent
English version; see **6408**.

6312. B. HEMMERDINGER, 'Karabas ou l'origine alexandrine du Chat
Botté', *CE* 38 (1963) 147-148.

A curious item of erudition linking Καραβᾶς, the Philonic character, to Carabas, the
character in Perrault. (= R481)

6313. K. HRUBY, 'Les heures de prière dans le Judaïsme à l'époque de
Jésus', in Mons. CASSIEN, B. BOTTE (edd.), *La prière des heures*, Lex
Orandi 35 (Paris 1963) 59-84, esp. 72-75.

From Philo's description of the sacrificial rites (especially the burnt offering) we may
infer that he conformed strictly to the biblical text and appealed to ancient ritual, 'the
practice of which by his time had undergone significant changes' (73). (= R482)

6314. A. JAUBERT, *La notion d'alliance dans le Judaïsme aux abords
de l'ère chrétienne* (Paris 1963), esp. 375-442.

The theme of the covenant is fundamental in Philo; it is also an important subject for
scholars, because it makes it possible to 'test' Philo's 'reactions' to each of the biblical
components of the theme. By means of this method the author is able to set a limit to the
discussion concerning Philo's true (Jewish or Hellenistic) nature, a discussion which she
finds as barren as it is old. At the conclusion of the work we read (440): 'Philo
abandoned none of the significant elements of the notion of covenant; neither the worship
of the one and personal God, nor the election of Israel, nor the practice of the law. His
notion of διαθήκη is ... the interior covenant inscribed in the heart, based on holiness
and the knowledge of God'. (= R483)

6315. A. M. JAVIERRE, *El tema literario de la sucesión en el Judaismo, Helenismo y Cristianismo primitivo: prolegómenos para el estudio de la sucesión apostolica*, Carta-prefacio by M. L. Cerfaux, Bibliotheca Theologica Salesiana 1.1 (Zurich 1963), esp. 267-279.

The theme of succession in Philo is discussed and elaborated with reference to the Mosaic διαδοχή. It is regarded as 'the curious fruit of a Hellenistic grafting on a Jewish stock' (cf. 279), producing an appropriate synthesis between the theocratic principle of Judaism and the elective norm typical of Hellenism. (= R484)

6316. H. D. MANTEL [מנטל .ח], [פילון אצל שמות פירושי ['Did Philo know Hebrew?'], *Tarbiz* 32 (1962-63) 98-99, 395.

A reaction to Amir (**6201**) stressing, that the differentiation between the Attic and *koine* forms of περιττός–περισσός is doubtful. That particular change may be explained by Philo's use of Rabbinic material, since Philo, as shown by the studies of Belkin and Wolfson, does know the Midrash and the early Halachah. (MM)

6317. R. MONDOLFO, 'Un precorrimento di Vico in Filone Alessandrino', in *Miscellanea Rostagni* (cf. **6307**) 56-67.

The author stresses how the category of 'action', understood as the source and condition of cognition, is a theory common to both Philo and Vico. (= R485)

6318. P. MORAUX, Art. 'Quinta essentia', *RE* II 24.1 (Stuttgart 1963) 1171-1263, esp. 1235-7, 1241-43.

An analysis of those passages in Philo depicting the heavenly bodies or the soul as consisting of the 'fifth element'. Philo is a 'syncretist' who can give the same basic position a Platonic-Aristotelian, Stoic or Jewish guise depending on context and circumstance (1249). (DTR)

6319. A. NAZZARO, 'Il problema cronologico della nascita di Filone Alessandrino, *RAAN* 38 (1963) 129-138.

Starting from the single established chronological fact of Philo's life, i.e. his embassy to Rome, Nazzaro concludes that Philo cannot have been older than 50 or 55 at that time. (= R486)

6320. V. NIKIPROWETZKY, 'Les suppliants chez Philon d'Alexandrie', *REJ* 122 (1963) 241-278.

The complete title of *Contempl.* ('Treatise of the contemplative life or of the suppliants') embarassed Geoltrain (cf. **2253**) because it seemed to identify the theme of the contemplative life with that of supplication. Nikiprowetzky sees the Levites as the binding element which reconciles these two extremes, in accordance with the following series of equivalents: Therapeutae (= suppliants) = Levites (= contemplative philosophers). The author refrains from discussing the thorny question of the identity of the Therapeutae, but observes that 'the suppliant Theraputae do not constitute, properly speaking, a sectarian deviation from Judaism, that all the apparently irregular features which distinguish them can be explained without having to postulate non-Jewish factors, and finally, that there is an almost complete agreement between the doctrine of the Therapeutae and the Levitic ideal generalized as a rule of life'. (= R487)

6321. P. M. SCHUHL, 'Philon, les banquets et le séder pascal', in *Miscellanea Rostagni* (cf. **6307**) 54-55.

Draws attention to some references in *Plant.* and *Contempl.* to the Jewish ritual of the Passover meal. (= R488)

6322. J. W. SEIBEL, *Shepherd and sheep symbolism in Hellenistic Judaism and the New Testament* (diss. Yale 1963), esp. 48-161.

The aim of the study is to examine the use of shepherd and sheep symbolism in the extant Jewish sources of the Hellenistic period, with a view to determining whether this evidence provides insight into the use and value of such symbolism in the New Testament. Philo is a major source on account of the frequent use of shepherd and sheep symbolism in his works. In fact there is so much material that a principle of organization must be determined. Seibel's method is to group the material around the various Old Testament figures who play a major role in Philo's exegesis and in relation to whom the symbolism is used. Such a systematizing method does no harm to the evidence, it is claimed, and in fact 'a certain characteristic approach emerges with remarkable constancy' (48). Philo has adapted the Hellenistic philosophy of kingship, in which the king is regarded as a good shepherd if he embodies the law and wisdom of God as ideal shepherd. This ideal is applied to the Patriarchs, who become more than allegorical types, for they have themselves achieved the ideal and so can lead the whole of mankind to this goal. In giving the shepherd symbolism a salvational force, Philo had penetrated the Greek tradition with values that are quite foreign to it. At the same time he 'does violence to the faith of his fathers' in radically dehistoricizing the Old Testament (158). One cannot speak of Messianism in Philo, for the apocalyptic framework is lacking. In the final section of the work no systematic attempt is made to relate the Philonic material to what is found in the New Testament, but various observations are made on points of detail. (DTR)

6323. V. A. TCHERIKOVER, 'The decline of the Jewish Diaspora in Egypt in the Roman period', *JJS* 14 (1963) 1-32.

Philonic evidence is frequently used here to reconstruct the political status of the Jews in Alexandria. There are also a few notes on Philo's role and the social position of his family. For earlier Hebrew version; cf. **4507**. (= R489)

6324. M. UNTERSTEINER, *Aristotele. Della Filosofia: introduzione, testi, traduzione e commento esegetico*, Temi e testi 10 (Rome 1963), esp. 24-27, 34-41, 46-49, 240-245.

Reproduces, translates, and comments on various Philonic passages which contain evidence pertaining to Aristotle's lost Περὶ φιλοσοφίας. (= R490)

6325. N. WALTER, 'Anfänge alexandrinisch-jüdischer Bibelauslegung bei Aristobulos', *Hel* 3 (1963) 353-372, esp. 367-372; reprinted in *Der Thoraausleger Aristobulos* (Berlin 1964) 141-147.

See below **6426**. (= R491)

6326. J. C. M. VAN WINDEN, 'In the beginning: some observations on the Patristic interpretation of Genesis 1, 1', *VChr* 17 (1963) 105-121.

In an analysis of the relations between Ambrose and Basil, Philo is used to demonstrate the different exegetical methods of the two writers: literal and Neo-Alexandrian in Basil, allegorical and Philonic in Ambrose (cf. 117). (= R492)

1964

6401. S. BELKIN [בלקין .ש], ארץ מדרשי לאור האלכסנדרוני פילון מדרשי ישראל [= 'The Philonic exposition of the Torah in light of the ancient Rabbinic Midrash'], *Sura* 4 (1964) 1-68.

Belkin argues that Philo knew and often used Palestinian Midrashic sources, methods, etc. – the necessary corollary to this being an early dating of the Rabbinic Midrashic tradition. Many parallels are brought forward (some closer than others). A large percentage of them are either popular Hellenistic, or Jewish religious, commonplaces. Nevertheless it can be argued that the large amount of material which is identical in the extant Rabbinic Midrash and in the Philonic corpus, in spite of their so very different literary styles, strongly points to their both being part of a common Midrashic tradition. The parallels between Philo and the medieval Jewish philosophical commentators, who, Belkin stresses, could not have seen Philo's works (and probably had never heard of him), are brought in support of the thesis that similar thought processes working within the same traditional matrices foster similar results (36, 40). (NGC)

6402. S. BELKIN [בלקין .ש], על ת"שו מדרש – ל"חז למדרשי קדום מקור האלכסנדרוני לפילון ושמות בראשית ['An early source of Rabbinic Midrash – Philo of Alexandria's "Quaestiones et Solutiones" on Genesis and Exodus'], in *Abraham Weiss Jubilee Volume* (New York 1964) 579-633.

A continuation of the preceding article (**6003**), dealing in a similar manner, but in a more clearly organized fashion, with the second book of *QG* (exegesis of the story of Noah). (NGC)

6403. F. M. BRAUN, *Jean le théologien: les grandes traditions d'Israël et l'accord des Écritures selon le quatrième Évangile*, vol. 2, Études Bibliques (Paris 1964) *passim*.

Philo and Philonic themes are repeatedly discussed in the first two volumes of this enormous work (cf. **5903**). Though it is clearly an important study, some of the specific observations on Philo are rather cursory (e.g. 2.279). Nevertheless, the conclusions which Braun reaches on the relations between Philo and John are worth reporting: ' ... to varying extents John and Philo underwent the same Jewish-Hellenistic influences in a parallel way, but each in his own line of thought and according to his own manner of conceiving the Bible as the source of truth' (2.298). Even if Philo had not lived, therefore, the fourth Gospel would have been no different from what it is now. (= R493)

6404. C. COLPE, 'Zur Leib-Christi-Vorstellung im Epheserbrief' in W. ELTESTER (ed.), *Judentum, Urchristentum, Kirche: Festschrift für J. Jeremias*, BZNW 26 (Berlin 1964) 172-187, esp. 179-183.

Some of Philo's cosmological and anthropological notions (man as microcosmos, the cosmos as man writ large, the concepts of λόγος, σῶμα, etc.) are briefly compared to the representation of Christ's body in the Epistle to the Ephesians. (= R494)

6405. E. FASCHER, 'Abraham, ΦΥΣΙΟΛΟΓΟΣ und ΦΙΛΟΣ ΘΕΟΥ: eine Studie zur ausserbiblischen Abrahamtradition im Anschluss an Deuteronomium 4, 19', in *Mullus: Festschrift T. Klauser*, JbAC.E 1 (Münster 1964) 111-124.

A brief analysis of the various senses of the name Abraham in Philo in relation to its allegorical meaning. (= R497)

6406. G. FRIEDRICH (ed.), *Theologisches Wörterbuch zum Neuen Testament*, vol. 7 (Stuttgart 1964; English translation, Grand Rapids 1971).

Cf. above **3807**. Contains: O. BAUERNFEIND, art. στρατεύομαι κτλ (fight in or as an army), 706-7; G. BERTRAM, art. σαλεύω κτλ (shake), 67-8; H. G. CONZELMANN, art. σκότος (darkness), 435; G. DELLING, art. στοιχεῖον (element), 675-6; G. FITZER, art. σφραγίς κτλ (seal), 946-7; W. FOERSTER, art. σῴζω κτλ (save), 988-9; W. GRUNDMANN, art. στέφανος (wreath), 627; art. ἵστημι (stand), 643; G. HARDER, art. σπουδάζω κτλ (endeavour), 564; H. KÖSTER, art. σπλάγχνον κτλ (entrail), 552-3; art. συνέχω (hold together), 880; U. LUCK, art. σώφρων κτλ (temperate), 1098; C. MAURER, art. σύνοιδα κτλ (have a conscience), 910-2; W. MICHAELIS, art. σκηνή (tent), 374; art. συγγενής κτλ (related by family) 738-9; K. H. RENGSTORF, art. σημεῖον (sign), 220-1; J. SCHNEIDER, art. σχῆμα (shape), 954-5; S. SCHULZ, art. σκιά (shadow), 398-9; art. σπέρμα (seed), 543; E. SCHWEIZER, art. σάρξ (flesh), 121-2; art. σῶμα (body), 1046-52; U. WILCKENS, art. σοφία (wisdom), 501-2. (DTR)

6407. D. GEORGI, *Die Gegner des Paulus im 2. Korintherbrief: Studien zur religiösen Propaganda in der Spätantike*, WMANT 11 (Neukirchen 1964) *passim*, esp. 63-96; English translation, *The opponents of Paul in Second Corinthians* (Philadelphia-Edinburgh 1986), with epilogue added (333-450).

The author frequently uses Philonic evidence to explain 2 Cor. 11:22ff., where Paul appears to draw a distinction between Jews, Israelites, and descendants of Abraham. In *Legat*. 4, for instance, Philo boasts of the superiority of the Jews, as Israelites, over the pagans. The most important Philonic text as regards the third title, 'descendants from Abraham', is *Virt*. 187-217, which contributes in many ways to an understanding of Paul's letter. The author sums up Philo's thought as follows: (a) true nobility consists in wisdom (= knowledge of God), and is therefore not hereditary (cf. 78ff.). (b) The spiritual and prophetic gifts typical, for instance, of Abraham are connected with the task of mission, which is why Abraham stands as a model for all proselytes. (c) The idea of mission is bound up with the concept of Mosaic Law, which applies to all men. For Philo, there are essentially two ways of propagating this Law: worship in the synagogue and exegetical interpretation. Worship, especially that on the Sabbath, is presented as an exercise in philosophy, and the allegorical interpretation of the Law clearly corresponds to the act of prophecy. In the English translation published in 1986 the author returns to his subject, discussing scholarly developments in the meantime and some modifications to his views. Note esp. 358ff. on missionary aspects of contemporary Judaism, 390ff. on social aspects of the phenomenon of the divine man, 422ff. on contributions of Jewish apologetics, including Philo. (= R498/DTR)

6408. J. GUTTMANN, *Philosophies of Judaism* (New York 1964), esp. 26-32.

Translated from an earlier version in Hebrew (cf. **6311**), which in turn was based on the original German edition (*Die Philosophie des Judentums*, Munich 1933; reprinted Wiesbaden 1985), this work presents a synthetic account of philosophies produced by Jewish thinkers. The plural in the title is very deliberate. 'The Jewish people did not begin to philosophize because of an irresistible urge to do so. They received philosophy from outside sources, and the history of Jewish philosophy is a history of the successive absorptions of foreign ideas which were then transformed and adapted according to specific Jewish points of view' (3). Philo was the first to undertake the task systematically, and deserves the title 'the first theologian'. (DTR)

6409. H. JONAS, 'Heidegger and theology', *RMeta* 18 (1964) 207-233, esp. 207-211.

The philosophical problem of objectification reaches Western theology and Heidegger via the confrontation of the biblical world with the Greek logos. This confrontation takes place for the first time in Philo and, specifically, in the opposition which he sets up between 'seeing' and 'feeling'. These categories are related to the etymology of the name Israel and play an essential part in the doctrine of the knowledge of God. (= R500)

6410. E. KAMLAH, *Die Form der katalogischen Paränese im Neuen Testament*, WUNT 7 (Tübingen 1964), esp. 50ff., 104-115.

The problem raised in these pages (cf. 50ff.) is the following: what Iranian conception of the cosmos' structure corresponds to Philo's statements in *QE* 1.23 and the doctrine of the two angels found there? It would appear that they originate in a conception which in dualistic fashion opposes a guardian spirit, equivalent to light, and a destroyer spirit, equivalent to darkness. Subsequently (104-115) Kamlah analyzes other Philonic passages which may be indebted to Iranian cosmology, for instance the allegory of Jacob and Esau and that of the two women in Deut. 21:15-17, both found in *Sacr.* 17-19. (= R501)

6411. H. J. KRÄMER, *Der Ursprung der Geistmetaphysik: Untersuchungen zur Geschichte des Platonismus zwischen Platon und Plotin* (Amsterdam 1964, 1967²), esp. 266-284.

Krämer gives a novel interpretation of the Philonic Logos by re-examining Philo's position within the philosophical tradition. The fundamental structure of Philo's thought – apart from some Stoic influences in his anthropology and cosmology – is a development of Platonic doctrine (cf. 266). But this Platonism is closely interwoven with Pythagorean elements and is paralleled point for point by a Neopythagorean scheme which deduces from the principles of the monad, dyad, tetrad, and decad the series of numbers which, in their philosophical significance, become the principles and symbols of all reality. This structure is particularly evident in the concept of logos, and constitutes its essence. From a historical-philosophical point of view all this is enough to put Philo at the centre of an authentic Platonic tradition of thought which goes back to doctrines already developed within the Old Academy. Philo thus gives precious evidence of the continuity of tradition linking the Old Academy to Neoplatonism. (= R502)

6412. R. LOEWE, 'The "plain" meaning of Scripture in early Jewish exegesis', in J. G. WEISS (ed.), *Papers of the Institute of Jewish Studies. London*, vol. 1 (Jerusalem 1964) 140-185, esp. 146-152.

A brief outline of Philonic allegory which also discusses its relation to Jewish tradition. In the author's opinion, the main difference between Philo and the Stoics (and also between Philo and the Rabbinic tradition) is that the latter take the fundamental categories of their exegesis from non-philosophical contexts, whereas Philo elaborates his own concepts from a philosophical point of view and then adapts them to – and imposes them on – the contents of faith. (= R503)

6413. O. MAAR, *Philo und der Hebräerbrief* (diss. Vienna 1964).

This dissertation does not specifically discuss the authorship of Hebrews, but sets out to examine its relations with Philo, starting from the observation that the thought contained in this work is not found in Paul's other works and can only be explained with reference to Philo. The first part of the work analyzes the lexical, stylistic, and exegetical parallels between Philo and Hebrews (9-40). The following parts discuss problems of content. Here the author follows the same analytical method as in the preceding section, isolating shared concepts and commenting on them at length. The third chapter (89-108), which also includes a brief digression on the Prologue and the remainder of the Gospel of John, is of greater interest because it deals with the concept of logos, fundamental to both authors. The conclusions reached by Maar go beyond the scope of his study as initially defined: the author of Hebrews is identified as a disciple of Paul who knew Philo's work (if not Philo himself) and who, taking into account the audience at whom the work was aimed, used the cultural heritage of Alexandrian Judaism with the precise intention of making the announcement of Christ the Redeemer more convincing and penetrating. (= R504)

6414. A. D. NOCK, *Early gentile Christianity and its Hellenistic background* (New York 1964; French translation Paris 1973) *passim*.

This work collects a number of contributions dating from 1924 and 1952; for the occasion a new introduction has been added. Philo is above all presented as a mediator between philosophical paganism and Jewish fideistic religiosity. From this synthesis, according to Nock, arises a religious philosophy which emphasizes the doctrine of grace (cf. 159ff. in the French edition). (RR)

6415. R. PATAI, 'The Shekhina', *JR* 44 (1964) 275-288.

The categories of male and female, used by Philo to indicate two aspects of God, are not very far removed from the concept expressed by the Hebrew term *shekhina*, which in Talmudic literature expresses the visible aspect of God. (= R505)

6416. J. PÉPIN, *Théologie cosmique et théologie chrétienne (Ambroise,*

Exam. I 1, 1-4) (Paris 1964) *passim*, esp. 251-274, 527-532.

The statements in the *Hexameron* about the number of worlds and their duration preserve echoes of Aristotle's *De philosophia*. If we rule out the possibility that Ambrose was able to draw directly on this work, then a probable intermediate source would be Philo and especially three passages from *Aet.* 7-13. We should not, however, extend Philo's mediation to Ambrose's entire cosmic theology; for the latter it seems wiser to postulate a plurality of sources. (= R506)

6417. J. POUILLOUX, 'Le calendrier et un passage de Philon d'Alexandrie', *REA* 66 (1964) 211-213.

Decal. 96 contains important information on the controversy about chronologies based on calendars computed κατὰ θεόν and κατὰ σελήνην. (= R507)

6418. R. REID, *The use of the Old Testament in the epistle to the Hebrews* (diss. New York 1964).

This work does not specifically discuss the connections between Hebrews and Philo. The most relevant section with regard to Philo is the Introduction (1-34), where Reid gives a documented review of scholarship on Hebrews, including the different views on its relations with Philo. For the rest Philo occupies a rather marginal position in this work and is mostly cited only to indicate the distance between him and Hebrews. (= R508/a)

6419. J. M. RIST, *Eros and psyche: studies in Plato, Plotinus and Origen*, Phoenix. Supplementary Volumes 6 (Toronto 1964) *passim*, esp. 188ff.

Plotinus' theory of ecstasy does not reveal a debt to Philo, in spite of a few, mainly formal, similarities. In Philo it is God who in the ecstatic moment draws man beyond his human limits, whereas for Plotinus the unification of the soul with the One restores man to the fullness of his humanity. (= R509)

6420. D. A. RUSSELL, *'Longinus' on the sublime* (Oxford 1964) xxix-xxx and *passim*.

The author is sympathetic to the view that the author may have had a Jewish connection, as suggested by various similarities to Philo. These, relating to the central concept of ὕψος and other details, are noted in the commentary. (DTR)

6421. P. J. SIJPESTEIJN, 'The legationes ad Gaium', *JJS* 15 (1964) 87-96.

Discusses the views of Smallwood (**2152**) on the date and the number of members of the embassy to Gaius. Chiefly on the basis of Philonic evidence, the author modifies Smallwood's conclusions and sets the date of the delegation's departure in the winter of 38-39 A.D. instead of 39-40. (= R512)

6422. A. C. SUNDBERG, *The Old Testament of the Early church*, HThS 20 (Cambridge-London 1964, New York 1969²), esp. 68-74.

In the chapter discussing the existence of an Alexandrian canon as a source of the Christian Bible the evidence in Philo is of some importance and is particularly useful for establishing the chronology of the canonization of various biblical texts. (= R513)

6423. B. TAMM, 'Ist der Castortempel das *vestibulum* zu dem Palast des Caligula gewesen?', *Er* 62 (1964) 146-169.

Evidence in Philo (*Legat.* 330ff.) sheds light on the location and architectural structure of Caligula's palace. (= R514)

6424. E. VANDERLINDEN, 'La foi de Virgile', *BAGB* 4.1 (1964) 448-458.

The polyvalence of Virgil's philosophical and religious positions may imply a conception involving different levels of knowledge and truth, as advocated by the Hermetic writers and, in a different way, by Philo. Abstract in *StPh* 4 (1976-77) 105ff. (= R515)

6425. F. DE VISSCHER, 'La politique dynastique sous le règne de Tibère', in *Synteleia: V. Arangio Ruiz*, vol. 1, Biblioteca Labeo 2 (Naples 1964) 54-65.

The figure of Macro, first in his role of mediator between Tiberius and Gaius and later as prefect of the Praetorium, is reconstructed from the Philonic evidence in *Legat.* (= R516)

6426. N. WALTER, *Der Thoraausleger Aristobulos: Untersuchungen zu seinen Fragmenten und zu pseudepigraphischen Resten der jüdisch-hellenistischen Literatur*, TU 86 (Berlin 1964), esp. 58-86, 141-149.

The theory that Aristobulus was probably indebted to Philo has been rejected in recent scholarship. This theory rested mainly on the authority of Wendland, who in an accurate analysis had related each fragment of Aristobulus to passages in Philo and attempted to show the derivation of the former from the latter. A prominent feature of Wendland's argument was the presence of ἕβδομος λόγος in both authors, a concept of Stoic origin which refers to the seven-part structure of the soul. Walter critically analyzes Wendland's arguments and concludes that, although one may allow for an exegetical tradition common to both thinkers, nevertheless the philosophical contexts incorporating the concept in question are wholly different, i.e. very poor in Aristobulus (where, among other things, a theory of the Logos is lacking), whereas in Philo it is very extensive and profound. In fact Wendland's position should be reversed: it was not Aristobulus who was indebted to Philo, but Philo who utilized and perfected the tradition already present in Aristobulus. The earlier thinker did draw on the same cultural heritage as Philo, but at a much more primitive stage of its development. (= R517)

6427. J. H. WASZINK, 'Bemerkungen zu Justins Lehre vom Logos Spermatikos', in *Mullus* (cf. **6405**) 380-390, esp. 389ff.

A brief analysis and comparison of the concept of *logos spermatikos* as sower of truth as it appears in Philo and Justin Martyr. (= R518)

1965

6501. F. ADORNO, 'Filone l'Ebreo e la nuova concezione di Dio', in *Storia della Filosofia* 1, La Filosofia Antica, vol. 2 (Milan 1965) 204-228.

The author shows how a certain level of coherence can be found in Philo's work if it is interpreted in the light of Sceptic presuppositions. Because of man's inability to reach the truth, it is necessary to turn to a truth which reveals itself, i.e. to the wisdom identical with God, who enlightens man and directs man's knowledge towards him. From the concept of wisdom the author passes on to the conception of God and his relationship to the world. He discusses the vast complex of philosophical problems which this conception raises and, as is natural, pays special attention to the concept of logos, which is said to have determined Philo's political views as well. (= R519)

6502. M. ADRIANI, 'Note sull'antisemitismo antico', *SMSR* 36 (1965) 63-98.

In order to demonstrate that anti-Semitism has pre-Christian origins, the author turns extensively to the evidence in Josephus. He also refers to *Flacc.* and *Legat.*, but much more briefly, only giving an outline of their contents. (= R520)

6503. Y. AMIR [עמיר .י], דרשותיו של פילון על היראה והאהבה ויחסן למדרשי ארץ ישראל ['Philo's Homilies on fear and love and their relation to the Palestinian Midrashim'], *Zion* 30 (1965) 47-60.

Subsequently published in German; see **8308**.

6504. Y. AMIR [עמיר .י], ההלניזם היהודי כתופעה דתית [= 'Jewish Hellenism as a religious phenomenon'], *Mahanayyim* 100 (1965) 233-240 [Hebr. pp. רלג-רם].

Characterizes basic changes in Hellenistic-Jewish understanding of Israel's religious tradition as due to the new Greek framework. The main witness is Philo, whose interpretation of creation is viewed according to Septuagint terminology. His understanding of the Law depends on the meaning of Greek νόμος and herein lies the key to Philo's view of Moses as a prophet. Though influenced by Plato's image of the cave, Philo's two levels of exegesis and their relevance to daily life are not really clear (despite *Migr.* 89-93, which must be read in context!). (MM)

6505. R. A. BAER, *Philo's use of the categories male and female* (diss. Harvard University 1965).

See **7005**.

6506. S. BELKIN [בלקין .ש], המדרש הסמלי אצל פילון בהשוואה למדרשי חז"ל [= 'The Symbolic Midrash in Philo compared with Rabbinic Midrash'], in *Harry Austryn Wolfson Jubilee volume on the occasion of his seventy-fifth birthday: Hebrew section*, vol. 2 (Jerusalem 1965) 33-68.

Belkin divides Philo's symbolic Midrash into two types: (a) the allegorical rendering of the biblical narrative in which it is metaphorically metamorphosed into a spiritual-philosophical disquisition; and (b) the symbolic Midrash which provides a moral or other significance to the literal text. This latter type he finds to be true Midrash and to be a natural offshoot of the traditional Palestinian midrashic tradition. Belkin gives examples of different types of parallels and stresses that the similarities are in content, while the literary edifice is often very different. Examples are also brought forward in which the comparison of the same Midrash in Rabbinic sources and in Philo clarifies puzzling points. It is argued that, unlike Homeric allegory, Philo's allegorical exegesis of Scripture did not annul the literal meaning of the text, comparing the latter to the body which is needed to house the symbolic and allegorical elaborations (6-7). Belkin concludes that Philo founded his work either directly upon the Palestinian midrashic tradition or upon the Alexandrian allegorists, who on their part were familiar with Palestinian midrashic tradition (62). (NGC)

6507. P. BORGEN, *Bread from heaven: an exegetical study of the concept of manna in the gospel of John and the writings of Philo*, NT.S 10 (Leiden 1965).

The allegory of manna is certainly not the only point of contact between John and Philo, but for Borgen it is a significant example of the cultural background common to both authors. At the same time it offers us an insight into Jewish thought, which Borgen does not hesitate to posit as a common source. Both Philo and John in their pericopes on manna – *Leg.* 3.162-168, *Mut.* 253-263, John 6:31-58 – paraphrase quotations from the Old Testament, which are supplemented by fragments of the Haggadah and presented by means of figures typical of the homiletic tradition. There are also traces of the Palestinian Midrash in both, though not in equal measure. A comparative analysis of texts leads Borgen to conclude that John did not depend on Philo, but was 'a parallel phenomenon' (3), i.e. the fruit of an identical cultural soil which the author rapidly identifies as the tradition of synagogal homiletics. An analysis of the latter raises problems, however, since Borgen cannot find a single example relating to the theme of manna which is earlier than Philo; all available evidence is of a later date. Borgen is thus forced to hypothesize a long homiletic tradition, older than Philo and John, which both authors supposedly interpreted at different levels and in different contexts: Philo in the synagogue and in terms of a vast philosophical syncretism, John in a school by then independent of the synagogues and in a climate of thought palpably influenced by Gnosis. Borgen replies to criticisms of his work in 'Bread from heaven: aspects of debates on expository method and form', in *Logos was the true light and other essays on the Gospel of John* (Trondheim 1983) 32-46. REVIEWS: G. Fohrer, *ZAW* 78 (1966) 113f.; M. E. Boismard, *RB* 74 (1967) 140f.; G. Delling, *ThLZ* 92 (1967) 425; B. Gärtner, *JSSt* 12 (1967) 143f.; G. D. Kilpatrick, *ThZ* 23 (1967) 439f.; B. Lindars, *JThS* 18 (1967) 192ff.; L. Martin, *JBL* 86 (1967) 244f.; A. Vanhoye, *Bib* 48 (1967) 469f. Cf. also below **6920**. (= R521)

6508. R. CANTALAMESSA, 'Il papiro Chester Beatty III (P[46]) e la tradizione indiretta di Hebr. 10, I', *Aeg* 45 (1965) 194-215.

Philonic evidence (*Leg.* 3.96ff.) contradicts the vulgate reading of Heb. 10:1, which contraposes σκιά and εἰκών as shadow and reality. (= R522)

6509. P. COURCELLE, 'Tradition platonicienne et traditions chrétiennes du corps-prison (*Phédon* 62 b; *Cratyle* 400 c)', *REL* 43 (1965) 406-

443 passim.

Philonic thought plays an important role in developing the image of the body as a prison, because in it this theme is for the first time compared with biblical thought (cf. 442). (= R523)

6510. E. DASSMANN, *Die Frömmigkeit des Kirchenvaters Ambrosius von Mailand: Quellen und Entfaltung* (Münster 1965), esp. 44-74.

The dependence of Ambrose on Philo is such that their biblical interpretations cannot be separated. The author, aware of this problem, does not discuss the matter in detail, but confines himself to considering Philo from the point of view of his connections with Ambrose. He advances two hypotheses: (1) the agreement between both writers is due to their shared aim of mediating faith through philosophy; (2) the points of contact are a consequence of Ambrose's need to find models for his sermons (cf. 45ff.). According to the author the relationship between Philo and Ambrose was not direct, but was mediated through Alexandrian speculation. Dassmann reaches these conclusions on the basis of a comparative analysis of a group of concepts relating to the theme of sin and the ascent of the soul towards God. (= R524)

6511. G. DELLING, 'Josephus und die heidnischen Religionen', *Klio* 43 (1965) 263-269; reprinted in F. HAHN, T. HOLTZ, N. WALTER (edd.), *Studien zum Neuen Testament und zum hellenistischen Judentum: gesammelte Aufsätze 1950-1968* (Göttingen 1970) 45-52.

The Mosaic law against the cursing of heathen gods mentioned by Josephus is not a product of the latter's interpretation, but was already present in Philo (and implicitly in the LXX). Philo actually speaks of two prohibitions, the one applying to the cursing of heathen gods and the other to the cursing of the Jewish God. The transgression of these involve two different punishments. (= R525)

6512. J. FINKEL, 'The guises and vicissitudes of a universal folk-belief in Jewish and Greek tradition', in *H. A. Wolfson Jubilee volume...: English section*, vol. 1 (Jerusalem 1965) 233-254, esp. 239-243.

Finkel demonstrates some similarities between the many Philonic passages interpreting the figure of the high priest in the Holy of Holies and a popular Greek belief, related by Polybius, according to which the priest is said to lose his shadow on entering the temple. The author himself, however, points out that in a number of particulars Philo moved away from the assumed model and spiritualized the meaning of the image. (= R526)

6513. J. HAMBROER, 'Theogonische und kosmogonische Mythen aus Rumänien', *ZRGG* 17 (1965) 289-306.

Certain ancient Rumanian myths can be interpreted as typical examples of allegorical exegesis according to a technique which it is not difficult to trace back to Philo. (= R527)

6514. H. HEGERMANN, 'Das hellenistische Judentum', in J. LEIPOLDT and W. GRUNDMANN (edd.), *Umwelt des Urchristentums*, vol. 1, *Darstellung des neutestamentlichen Zeitalters* (Berlin 1965, 1971³) 292-345, esp.

326-342.

A brief synoptic presentation of Philo, who is regarded as the representative of an orthodox Judaism that is independent of orthodox Palestinian Judaism. Biblical exegesis is said to stand at the centre of Philo's philosophy. Consequently, his thought should be seen as a theological contribution to creationistic views, while his activity as a preacher – to which Hegermann attaches great importance – should be understood not as an original and personal proposal of new ethical ideals, but as a faithful and profound interpretation of the Torah which never exceeds the limits of orthodoxy, even when it seems to bear the stamp of pagan wisdom (cf. 341f.). (= R528)

6515. J. G. KAHN [כהן-ישר .י], (על פי) האם ידע פילון האלכסנדרוני עברית? פירושיו האטימולוגיים) ['Did Philo know Hebrew? the testimony of the "etymologies"'], *Tarbiz* 34 (1965) 337-345.

Mainly a confirmation of Amir's conclusions (**6201**) with new evidence for the phenomenon of Philo's use of a *koine* form in quotations and the Attic dialect in his interpretations. Kahn supposes that Philo had access to a kind of onomasticon. English summary. See further **7110**. (MM)

6516. I. LÉVY, 'Ceux de la grotte', in *Recherches esséniennes et pythagoriciennes* (Geneva-Paris 1965) 7-17.

A passage from the *Book of lights and guard towers* by the 10th-century Karaite writer Jacob Qirqisani mentions a sect of Magarites that venerated certain writings, among which the work of 'an Alexandrian' was pre-eminent. After discussing the views of earlier scholars (some of whom postulated the existence of a Syriac tradition of Philo's works), Lévy identifies this person as a representative of the Jewish school in Alexandria. Cf. Nikiprowetzky's additional comments on this subject (**6624**). (= R529)

6517. I. LÉVY, 'Le très saint nombre 50 et la clé des faveurs éternelles dans le Manuel essénien de discipline', in *Recherches...* (cf. **6516**) 19-29; first published in *Bulletin de l'Académie Royale de Belgique, Classe des Lettres* 4 (1959) 117-128.

In a comparative analysis of the *Manual of discipline* and some Philonic passages, Lévy corrects Dupont-Sommer's error about the arithmological significance of the number fifty. The characteristic of health which Philo (*Spec.* 2.177) attributes to it has no antecedents in Pythagorean literature, but is of Jewish origin. Cf. also **6624**. (= R530)

6518. I. LÉVY, 'Parabole d'Héraclide: Héraclide et Philon', in *Recherches...* (cf. **6516**) 37-50.

The distinction (which goes back to Heraclides Ponticus) drawn in the Pythagorean parable of the *panegyrion* between the athletes (representing the men of action) and the spectators (representing the men devoted to contemplation) is also made by Philo in his representation of the Essenes and Therapeutae respectively. Cf. also **6624**. (= R531)

6519. I. LÉVY, 'Sur quelques points de contact entre le *Contre Apion* et l'œuvre de Philon d'Alexandrie', in *Recherches...* (cf. **6516**) 51-56.

Points out a number of similarities, relating to common precepts, between Josephus' *Contra Apionem* and *Hypoth.* Cf. also **6624**. (= R532)

6520. V. NIKIPROWETZKY, 'Problèmes du 'récit de la création' chez Philon d'Alexandrie', *REJ* 124 (1965) 271-306.

Philo's interpretation of the biblical account of creation in its different formulations is a highly complex work of philosophical mediation. Philo was not capable of rationally demonstrating the theory of creation because Greek philosophy did not provide him with the means. Yet he could not accept the biblical account in its literal sense either, since he was convinced that the act of creation was atemporal. He was thus forced to put forward an allegorical interpretation of the chronology of creation which transformed the temporal scheme into a logical scheme and which transposed the overall meaning of the account from the ontological to the anthropological level, i.e. the interpretation moves from the macrocosmos to the microcosmos. The account of creation, therefore, 'rather than being a description of the intelligible world', seems to be a study 'of the intelligibility of the world' (302), and the arithmological schemes which Philo discerns in it have a similar function to that of Plato's ideal numbers; i.e. they function as vehicles of the world's rationality. The article is also valuable for its analyses of Philo's interpretations of creation in relation to Greek cosmological thought, and especially the *Timaeus* and the *Phaedrus* myth of Plato. See also the appendix in Runia **8656**. (= R534)

6521. A. PELLETIER, 'Les passions à l'assaut de l'âme d'après Philon', *REG* 78 (1965) 52-60.

The metaphors taken from military language which Philo uses to describe the assault of the passions and the defence of the soul underline the active and virile aspect of man's moral commitment. (= R535)

6522. G. PFEIFER, 'Zur Beurteilung Philons in der neueren Literatur', *ZAW* 77 (1965) 212-214.

A brief note on Philonic scholarship from the end of the 19th through to the first decades of the 20th century. (= R536)

6523. L. M. DE RIJK, 'Ἐγκύκλιος παιδεία: a study of its original meaning', *Viv* 3 (1965) 24-93, esp. 73-88.

An analysis of the phrase in question leads the author to conclude that, in addition to an evident Neopythagorean influence which already shows numerous signs of eclecticism, we encounter in Philo a significant component of the ancient choric terminology with expressions referring to a later concept of education as 'nexus of all the sciences'. (= R537)

6524. G. SCARPAT, 'Cultura ebreo-ellenistica e Seneca', *RevBib* 13 (1965) 3-30.

The author allows for the possibility that Seneca read some of Philo's works. He bases his argument on the following observations. (a) It cannot be denied that there is a certain relation between Senecan thought and Alexandrian culture. (b) The chief intermediary in this relation is supposedly Posidonius, but there may well have been others. (c) The fact that the author of the treatise *On the sublime* reveals a direct knowledge of Philo demonstrates that at least some of Philo's works were present in Rome. (d) Philo's participation in the famous embassy to Gaius cannot but have left lasting traces in Roman culture. (= R538)

6525. G. SCARPAT, *La lettera 65 di Seneca*, Antichità Classica e Cristiana 1 (Brescia 1965, 1970²), esp. 117-128, 158-160.

The author stresses certain conceptual affinities between the thought of Philo and Seneca. In particular he compares the following passages: *Opif.* 17-22 with *Ep.* 65.7; *Cher.* 125-127 and *Prov.* 1.23 with *Ep.* 65.8; *Leg.* 1.44, 3.4 with *NQ pref.* 13-14. On the basis of this analysis the author concludes that it is not impossible that Philo, or at least Jewish-Alexandrian philosophy in general, exercised some influence on the thought of Seneca. (RR)

6526. G. SEGALLA, 'Il problema della volontà libera in Filone Alessandrino', *StudPat* 12 (1965) 3-31.

The structure of this article is in part determined by the author's critical attitude towards Wolfson's method, which he considers to 'proceed from a logical scheme of preordained concepts'. The article as a whole constitutes a systematic examination of the technical terminology which Philo uses in discussing the subject of free will, as faculty of movement and decision, in its relation to freedom of choice, and also in its structural connections with anthropology and theology. (= R539)

6527. W. A. SHOTWELL, *The biblical exegesis of Justin Martyr* (London 1965), esp. 41-45, 93-103, 109-117.

Offers a few critical judgements, mostly second-hand, on the connection between the exegetical methods of Philo and Justin Martyr. According to the present state of scholarship, Justin's dependence on Philo cannot be demonstrated, even if one were to hypothesize a common relation with Rabbinic exegesis. (= R540)

6528. M. SMITH, 'A summary of *On the life of Moses* by Philo', in M. HADAS and M. SMITH, *Heroes and gods: spiritual biographies in antiquity*, Religious perspectives 13 (London 1965) 129-160.

The first part of this book introduces the subject of aretalogical literature, i.e. works that present a 'formal account of the remarkable career of an impressive teacher... used as a basis for moral instruction' (3). Philo's biography of Moses is placed in this tradition. Smith presents a lucid summary of the work, highlighting the elements that are of importance for the tradition under discussion. The summary is preceded by a brief introduction. Philo's work is influenced, according to Smith, by both the Hellenizing Jewish Haggadah developed in Alexandria (e.g. Artapanus), but reacts against its extremes. 'What appealed to Philo in the aretalogical tradition was its combination of the traits of philosopher, prophet, and wonder-worker. This enabled him to represent the prophet and wonder-worker of the Bible as a philosopher, someone socially acceptable to the Hellenized Jewish aristocracy of Alexandria' (131). See also **8454**. (DTR)

6529. S. G. SOWERS, *The hermeneutics of Philo and Hebrews: a comparison of the interpretation of the Old Testament in Philo Judaeus and*

the Epistle to the Hebrews, Basel Studies of Theology 1 (Richmond, Va.-
Zurich 1965; earlier submitted as dissertation, Basel 1963).

The examination of the subject of allegory from various points of view forms the
essential part of the work. Philo was not the first Greek writer to use allegory, but joined
a long line of tradition which probably began with the Orphics and culminated in the
Stoics. Nor should we underestimate Plato's influence, which is especially noticeable in
the double level of interpretation and the theory of prophetic inspiration. Philo, however,
– also influenced in this connection by Jewish culture – attributed a more extended sense
to the concept of inspiration, in which he included not only the moment of actual
revelation, but also the interpretation of that revealed truth. The specific characteristics of
Philonic allegory are dealt with in chs. 3 and 4, while ch. 5 discusses the connections
between Hebrews and Philo. Here the author draws attention to the essential originality
of the Epistle to the Hebrews, both with regard to its content, which refers to the
Christian faith, and its form, in which typological exegesis prevails over allegorical
exegesis (cf. the interesting preliminary observations on 99ff.). REVIEWS: L. Cilleruelo,
ATA 52 (1965) 109; F. Hoyos, *Rivista biblica* (Argentina) 27 (1965) 122f.; R. N.
Soulen, *Interpretation* 20 (1966) 109f.; A. B. Mickelson, *JBL* 86 (1967) 114f.; R. Reid,
AThR 49 (1967) 114f. (= R541)

6530. S. W. TAYLOR, *A study of the major factors determinate for a
meaningful life in the writings of Philo and in the Epistle to the Hebrews*
(diss. Emory University, Atlanta 1965).

The work is divided into two sections devoted to the concept of the meaningful or full
life in Philo and Hebrews respectively. In the first section the author is led by the nature
of the subject to discuss the main themes of Philonic anthropology (ch. 3) and the
relationship between man and God (ch. 4). The most interesting aspect of the work is the
importance which Taylor attaches to the social and humanitarian dimension of the concept
in question. This dimension, often obscured by Philonic scholars, is regarded by Taylor
as the distinctive feature of his Philonic interpretation, and is then exploited in order to
demonstrate the originality of his views compared with previous authors, namely
Goodenough, who in Taylor's opinion exaggerates Philo's mystical side; Wolfson, who
absolutizes the philosophical component in Philo's thought; Völker, who reduced it to an
uncompromising homage to Jewish orthodoxy; and finally H. A. Kennedy (*Philo's contribution to religion*, London 1919), who is reproached for a partially inaccurate and
incomplete analysis. (= R544)

6531. W. THEILER, 'Philo von Alexandria und der Beginn des kaiserzeitlichen Platonismus', in K. FLASCH (ed.), *Parusia: Studien zur Philosophie Platons und zur Problemgeschichte des Platonismus; Festgabe für J.
Hirschberger* (Frankfurt 1965) 199-218.

Several Philonic passages mentioning the soul's journey to heaven are collectively
related to the *Phaedrus* of Plato. This relation is not direct, however, but via the Platonic
tradition, and thus suggests the utilization of a commentary rather than the direct reading
of the original. Only in this way is it possible to explain various similarities between
Philo and Maximus of Tyre, since any direct connection between the two writers must be
ruled out. The author finally puts forward Eudorus of Alexandria as the probable
intermediary between Plato and Philo. (= R545)

6532. L. THUNBERG, *Microcosm and mediator: the theological anthropology of Maximus the Confessor*, ASNU 25 (Lund 1965), esp. 155-157, 195-199.

The author discusses two particular points of contact between Philo and the Church Fathers: the theory of double creation, the elaborations of which chiefly concern Origen, Gregory of Nyssa, and Maximus the Confessor; and the conception of the soul, which shows similarities with Clement's psychology (cf. 195-199). (= R546)

6533. U. TREU, 'Ein merkwürdiges Stück byzantinischer Gelehrsamkeit', *ByZ* 58 (1965) 306-312.

The interpretation of the rivers Tigris and Euphrates in Philo is used in order to clarify some verses by a Byzantine scholar. (= R547)

6534. E. F. TRISOGLIO, 'Apostrofi, parenesi e preghiere in Filone d'Alessandria', *RivLas* 31 (1964) 357-410; 32 (1965) 39-79.

An synoptic interpretation of Philo that is primarily based on two critical judgments: firstly the disqualification of his exegesis, in which the biblical narration seems merely 'a pretext in the hands of an author who could use any myth to achieve ... the same pre-established aims' (74); secondly a renewed emphasis on the protreptic elements in Philo which places them at the centre of his work; these elements 'appear to be parentheses but are in fact genetic principles' (73). From this point of view the philosophical component of Philo's thought and the actual method of his allegory serve merely to support his preaching, i.e. they provide the means by which he subordinates all human knowledge to the wisdom of the Bible. (= R548)

6535. S. ZEITLIN, 'Did Agrippa write a letter to Gaius Caligula?', *JQR* 56 (1965) 22-31.

That Agrippa was favourably inclined towards the Jews is an established fact. But there is less certainty about the means which he used to convince the emperor, because on this subject the evidence in Josephus and Philo is not in agreement. Abstract in *StPh* 2 (1973) 73. (= R549)

1966

6601. Art. 'Philon d'Alexandrie ou Philon le Juif', *Dictionaire de la Bible* vol. 7 (Paris 1966) 1288-1351.

Contains the following entries: 1. C. MONDÉSERT, 'Bibliographie œuvres éditions et traductions bibliographies générales, 1288-90; 2. R. CADIOU, 'La Bible de Philon', 1290-99; 3. J. E. MÉNARD, 'Les rapports de Philon avec le Judaïsme palestinien et Josèphe', 1299-1304; 4. R. ARNALDEZ, 'Philon et les "disciples de Moïse"', 1305-06; 5. R. ARNALDEZ, 'Moïse et la loi', 1306-1312; 6. R. ARNALDEZ, 'Figures et historicité', 1312-1320; 7. R. ARNALDEZ, 'La méthode allégorique', 1320-29; 8. R. ARNALDEZ, 'Philosophie, théologie et mystique', 1329-48; 9. A. FEUILLET, 'Rapports de Philon avec S. Jean, S. Paul et l'Épître aux Hébreux', 1348-51. (= R550)

6602. A. ALTMANN, 'The divine attributes: an historical survey of the Jewish discussion', *Jdm* 15 (1966) 40-60.

Briefly presents the essential aspects of Philo's theology. For the most part the author restates the views of Wolfson. (= R551)

6603. J. R. BASKIN, *Words for joy and rejoicing in the writings of the apostle Paul and Philo Judaeus* (diss. Princeton 1966).

In Philo the term χαρά has theological and ethical-anthropological meanings which can be traced back to the following fundamental themes: joy understood as the attribute of God, as the consequence of virtue, as the fruit of wisdom, as the crown of a religious life, and finally, as the product of ecstasy. From a philosophical point of view this cluster of meanings is given unity by its theocentric structure, so that each aspect of the theme of joy can be related to the ontological essence of God. From a historical-philosophical point of view, however, its main feature is the continual oscillation between Greek thought and terminology on the one hand and Jewish faith and religion on the other. To a certain extent the same bipolarity is also present in Paul, but the results which he reaches are entirely different: 'Paul's joy is largely objective, historically grounded, eschatological, social, spontaneous, and thrives on sufferings. Philo's joy is largely subjective, independent of past or future events on the plane of history, individualistic, introspective, mental, and does not thrive on sufferings' (427). (= R552)

6604. H. D. BETZ, 'Zum Problem des religionsgeschichtlichen Verständnisses der Apokalyptik, *ZThK* 63 (1966) 391-409; English translation *JTC* 6 (1969) 124-156.

Ch. 16 of the Revelation to John seems to contain cosmological references (for example to the theory of elements) which become more comprehensible when related to parallel themes in Philo. Abstract in *StPh* 2 (1973) 55. (= R553)

6605. H. CHADWICK, *Early Christian thought and the classical tradition: studies in Justin, Clement and Origen* (Oxford 1966, 1984²).

Though not systematically presented, this study contains numerous important observations on the relation of Philo to the early Christian thinkers Justin, Clement and Origen. Note esp. 7-11, 55-57, 141-2. On the page last cited Chadwick concludes: '... though minor borrowings are frequent, Clement is not simply producing a hellenized Christianity precisely parallel to Philo's hellenized Judaism; his main problems (notably faith and logic, free will and determinism, and the correct evaluation of the natural order) are different from Philo's and are approached from quite another angle'. (DTR)

6606. H. CHADWICK, 'St. Paul and Philo of Alexandria', *BJRL* 48 (1966) 286-307.

Examines the connections between Paul and Philo and between Philo and Gnosticism. A proficient and useful overview, but lacking in analytical depth. (= R555)

6607. G. L. COULON, *The Logos high priest: an historical study of the theme of the divine word as heavenly high priest in Philo of Alexandria, the* *epistle to the Hebrews, gnostic writings, and Clement of Alexandria* (diss. Paris 1966), esp. 10-33.

Philo's concept of the logos is explained here concisely yet accurately. The author's starting-point is *Mos.* 2.127, which contains all the fundamental themes relevant to the logos: (a) the high priest and his garments; (b) the distinction between the logos in the cosmos and in man, and in the latter, (c) the distinction between *logos endiathetos* and *prophorikos* (11). Coulon's aim is to show how these themes are mutually implied. The logos of the universe is a restatement of the Platonic theory of ideas (cf. 11-13), just as the doctrine of the immanent *logos* is of Platonic origin, albeit expressed in Stoic terms (13ff.). Coulon generally follows the well-known views of Wolfson on the connections between logos and God, while the relation between logos and high priest is explained by the mediating function that they share between man and God. In the final analysis, this mediation also involves 'the mind of the sage' which becomes 'Logos High Priest, because it "enters into" the intelligible world of ideas by contemplation' (27). (= R556)

6608. P. COURCELLE, 'Le corps-tombeau (Platon, *Gorgias* 493a, *Cratyle* 400c, *Phèdre* 250c)', *REA* 68 (1966) 101-122.

Between the Platonic image of the body-as-tomb and the Philonic image of man who 'carries his own corpse' (*Leg.* 1.108) there is a direct relationship which is destined to survive the two thinkers into the Christian period. (= R557)

6609. R. W. CRABB, *The κεφαλή concept in the Pauline tradition with special emphasis on Colossians* (diss. San Francisco 1966), esp. 28-32, 120-122.

The concept of κεφαλή in Philo occurs in various allegorical contexts. The semantic unity found there is mainly a result of the fact that it is continually set in opposition to the term σῶμα. In Philo's cosmology, for instance, the σῶμα is the world and the head is that which transcends the world. The relation between the two is one of subordination which Philo expresses by comparing the head to the logos and the body to the limbs, or, in psychological terms, by attributing to the head conscience and responsibility for the body. In this thesis the author is not so much interested in Philo himself as in the Hellenistic context, which he tries to reconstruct on the basis of Philo's evidence. That would at least partly explain the scarcity of the textual references which characterizes this part of the work. (= R558)

6610. M. DELCOR, Art. 'Pentecôte (la fête de la)' §3.6: 'La fête des Semaines chez Philon', *DB* 7 (1966) 872-873.

Brief account of Philo's presentation of the feast of weeks. (= R559)

6611. G. FAGGIN, 'La filosofia greco-giudaica e Filone d'Alessandria', in *Grande antologia filosofica*, directed by U. A. PADOVANI, coordinated by A. M. MOSCHETTI, vol. 1 *Il pensiero classico* (Milan 1966) 659-673.

We cite this work in the secondary bibliography on Philo and not among the anthologies because in it one recognizes a specific exegetical and critical purpose which manifests itself both in the choice of passages – mostly theological – and in the sober connecting passages which attempt to place Philo in the context of Neoplatonic thought, albeit in an entirely original position. (= R561)

6612. G. GERHOLD, *Mystik und Mysterienreligion, bei Philo von Alexandrien* (inaug. diss. Erlangen 1966 (1939?, 1964?)).

The title-page of this dissertation carries the date 1964, corrected in pen to 1939. E. HILGERT, who devotes a note to this bibliographical *curiosum* in *StPh* 4 (1976-77) 109f., cites 1966 as the date, and in this we follow him. We note, however, that the year in which this work was written was certainly 1939, as can be inferred from the bibliographical references, which do not go beyond that date. The work as a whole suffers from incoherence, since it is fragmented into a series of disconnected analyses which are not synthesized at any point. Thus the basic judgement on Philo's personality, from which the work's general perspective should emerge, is merely pronounced without being adequately supported by the analyses which follow. Gerhold holds that in Philo's time there was both a popular religion of mysteries with Greek and oriental origins, and also a learned, mystical-philosophical religion. Although Philo adopts elements from both types, he seems to identify himself with neither of the two, but rather with the Jewish faith of his people. Nevertheless, on examining the exact nature of this identification, the author concludes by regarding Philo as a mere interpreter of this faith rather than an active propagator. Philo, therefore, is not characterized by his belonging to this or that movement of thought, but precisely by 'the absence of a true philosophical problematic' in his work; at most we can grant him 'a problematic of attitude' (62). (= R562)

6613. W. GUNDEL and H. G. GUNDEL, *Astrologumena: die astrologische Literatur in der Antike und ihre Geschichte*, SudhAr 6 (Wiesbaden 1966), esp. 180-183.

A brief and clear exposition of Philo's astronomical and astrological theories. According to the authors Philo shows considerable familiarity with Hellenistic-Egyptian and Jewish astronomy and also believed to a certain extent, at least in his younger days, in astral mysticism. (= R563)

6614. R. G. HAMERTON KELLY, *The idea of pre-existence in early Judaism: a study in the background of New Testament theology* (diss. New York 1966), esp. 178-230.

The section devoted to Philo in this work shows a rigorously deductive approach which places emphasis on the philosophical dimension of his thought. The focal point of Philonic philosophy is said to be the concept of God who transcends time and space. Given the necessary existence of this category, however, the main theme in Philo is the justification of the relationship God-world. The author divides this problem into two parts: the first accepts the relationship between God and the world as a *datum*; the second discusses its nature. The first leads to the concept of Providence. The second, in contrast, raises two fundamental problems: the problem of the relationship God-Logos-Powers-ideas, which the author resolves in favour of an absolute ontological priority of God; and the problem of the pre-existence of matter, which is resolved by reducing the latter not to an objectively existing reality, but to a mythologically conceived entity functioning as symbol of the necessity which resists the ordering power of reason (cf. 230). See also **7314**. (= R564)

6615. L. HERRMANN, 'La lettre d'Aristée à Philocrate et l'empereur Titus', *Lat* 25 (1966) 58-77.

The author lists a large number of connections between the *Letter of Aristeas* and Philonic writings and concludes that the former is indebted to the latter. (= R566)

6616. N. HUGEDÉ, *Saint Paul et la culture grecque* (Geneva 1966), esp. 40-48.

A general outline of Philo, who is seen as the clearest illustration of the extent to which Hellenistic culture penetrated the Jewish world. (= R567)

6617. E. JUNÈS, 'Étude sur Philon', *RAMIF* 143 (1966) 589-611; 144 (1966) 766-823.

A popularly written, but thorough and interesting article. Philo is introduced by way of some considerations on the culture and history of Jewish Alexandria and, in general, the Judaism of the diaspora (cf. 589-599). Next his work, thought, and critical fortunes are analyzed. Also of interest is the final appendix dealing with the origin and nature of the Gnosis (813-823). (= R568)

6618. E. G. KONSTANTINOU, *Die Tugendlehre Gregors von Nyssa im Verhältnis zu der antik-Philosophischen und jüdisch-christlichen Tradition*, Das östliche Christentum 17 (Würzburg 1966) 63-69.

Philo's doctrine of virtue is Stoic only in a superficial sense. Essentially, it is profoundly religious and rests on the belief in a creator God and on the conviction that human nature is weak and sinful. In this sense salvation no longer depends on man, but on God's grace. In his explanation of this view, the author repeatedly stresses Philo's influence on Gregory of Nyssa. (= R569)

6619. H. KRAFT, *Die Kirchenväter bis zum Konzil von Nicäa*, Sammlung Dieterich 312 (Bremen 1966), esp. 94-123.

Contains a synoptic survey of Philonic thought in which both its exegetical and philosophical components are discussed; the latter is in turn situated against the background of Middle Platonism. The author touches on the main themes of Philo's theology and also deals quite extensively with the doctrine of prophetic inspiration, in which Philo himself supposedly located the foundation of his allegorical method and practice. (= R570)

6620. A. G. LEVIN, *The tree of life: Genesis 2,9 and 3, 22-24 in Jewish, Gnostic and early Christian texts* (diss. Harvard 1966), esp. 74-101.

Philo's exegesis of the tree of life represents an important innovation with respect to the parallel Jewish and Gnostic interpretations because it is elaborated in a predominantly ethical context. More precisely, Philo interprets Gen. 2:9 on at least three levels: cosmological, psychological, and moral. On the latter and most interesting level, Philo opposes the tree of life to the tree of knowledge, as symbols of the two different attitudes to life between which man must choose. The first represents the way of virtue and man's mystic ascent towards perfection; it is entirely spiritualized by our philosopher in a perspective which all but excludes any element of eschatology. According to Levin this is the essential difference between Philo and the Jewish tradition, and at the same time the reason for his closeness to Gnostic exegesis, which took from him, among other things, the general method of its allegorical practice. (= R571)

6621. A. MÉASSON, 'Le *De sacrificiis Abelis et Caini* de Philon d'Alexandrie', *BAGB* IV 1 (1966) 309-316.

An analysis of *Sacr.*, considered by the author to be Philo's most interesting exegetical treatise and a work of great spirituality which combines all the motifs of Philonic exegesis. The main value of the treatise is said to consist in its spiritualization of the concept of sacrifice, which closely relates it to the book of Hebrews. Abstract in *StPh* 1 (1972) 88. (= R572)

6622. A. MÉHAT, *Études sur les 'Stromates' de Clement d'Alexandrie* (Paris 1966), esp. 200-205.

Philo's influence on Clement can be summed up under the following headings: (1) allegorical technique; (2) the use of Stoic psychology and its moral doctrine of *apatheia*; (3) the Platonic theme of man's likeness to God; (4) the use of the phrase 'to follow God'. We note too that in the same year Méhat submitted an unpublished complementary thesis entitled *Kephalaia: recherches sur les matériaux des 'Stromates' de Clément d'Alexandrie*, in which an entire chapter (223-250) is devoted to the subject of Clement's use and adaptation of Philo. (= R573)

6623. E. MÜHLENBERG, *Die Unendlichkeit Gottes bei Gregor von Nyssa. Gregors Kritik am Gottesbegriff der klassischen Metaphysik*, FKDG 16 (Göttingen 1966), esp. 58-64; earlier submitted as inaug. diss. Mainz, 1963-64.

Philo, conceiving God as absolute otherness, was the founder of negative theology; but from this we may not deduce, as Guyot did (cf. G-G 1031), that he also espoused the concept of God's infinity. Philo's thought on this subject stays within the limits of the Platonist tradition. (= R574)

6624. V. NIKIPROWETZKY, "Recherches esséniennes et pythagori-ciennes': à propos d'un livre récent', *REJ* 125 (1966) 313-352.

A review article which discusses in detail and in a rather critical spirit the views advanced by Lévy in the contributions cited above (**6516-19**), with particular regard to the Philonic themes dealt with there. (= R575)

6625. H. NORTH, *Sophrosyne, self-knowledge and self-restraint in Greek literature*, Cornell Studies in Classical Philology 35 (New York 1966), esp. 323-328.

According to North Philo's contributions towards developing the concept of σωφροσύνη or self-knowledge are essentially three: (1) the allegorical interpretation of Scripture; (2) the identification of the Decalogue with the principles of Greek ethics; and (3) the substitution of the moral *exempla* of the Old Testament for the models of Greek mythology and history. (= R576)

6626. F. S. PERICOLI RIDOLFINI, *Alle origini del monachesimo: le convergenze esseniche* (Rome 1966) *passim*.

Study, meditation on the Holy Scriptures, manual labour, and isolation from the rest of mankind are characteristics which Christian monasticism adopted from the spirituality of the Essenes and Therapeutae, which today we are fortunately able to reconstruct on the basis of the evidence in Philo. (= R578)

6627. *Reallexikon für Antike und Christentum*, edited by T. KLAUSER *et al.*, vol. 6 (Stuttgart 1966).

Cf. above **5016.** Contains: C. ANDRESEN, art. 'Erlösung', 54-219, esp. 72-6 (salvation, σωτηρία); A. DIHLE, art. 'Ethik', 646-796, esp. 698-701 (ethics); J. HAUSSLEITER, art. 'Erhebung des Herzens', 1-22, esp. 10-11 (the lifting up or ascent of the heart or mind); D. KAUFMANN-BÜHLER, art. 'Eusebeia', 985-1052, esp. 1020-1023 (piety, εὐσέβεια); G. MAYER, art. 'Exegese II (Judentum)', 1194-1211, esp. 1205-7 (exegesis in the Judaic tradition); I. OPELT, art. 'Esel' 564-595, esp. 568 (the ass, especially with regard to its symbolic aspects); I. OPELT, art. 'Etymologie', 797-844, esp. 822-6 (etymology).

6628. G. REDLOW, *Theoria: theoretische und praktische Lebensauffassung im philosophischen Denken der Antike* (Berlin 1966), esp. 135-141.

Briefly examining the role of contemplation in Philo's thought, the author starts with cosmological and theological considerations and then proceeds to analyze the structure of Philo's ethics, the pinnacle of which is formed by his theory of ecstasy. With regard to the latter, the author observes, science and philosophy merely play a preparatory role. (= R579)

6629. M. RONCAGLIA, *Histoire de l'Église Copte*, vol. 1, *Les origines du Christianisme en Égypte: du Judéo-Christianisme au Christianisme hellénistique (Ier et IIe siècles)*, Histoire de l'Église en Orient 2 (Dar Al-kalima 1966), esp. 14-21.

Taking his starting-point from the contradictory information in Philo about the Essenian rule of celibacy, the author launches the hypothesis that Philo confused the Jewish Essenes with the Jewish Christians. (= R580)

6630. H. RONDET, 'Le péché originel dans la tradition: Tertullien, Clément, Origène', *BLE* 67 (1966) 115-148, esp. 126-130.

The theme of original sin in Philo is derived from the allegorical interpretation of the biblical text and in particular of the figures of Eve and Adam. (= R581)

6631. G. RUHBACH, 'Zum Begriff ἀντίθεος in der alten Kirche', in F. L. CROSS (ed.), *Papers presented to the Fourth International Conference on Patristic Studies held at Christ Church*, Oxford 1963, part 1, StudPatr 7 (= TU 92; Berlin 1966) 372-384.

The term ἀντίθεος is mainly used by Philo in an adjectival function. The author analyzes its meanings in diverse Philonic writings. (= R582)

6632. K. SCHNEIDER, *Die schweigenden Götter: eine Studie zur Gottesvorstellung des religiösen Platonismus*, Spud 9 (Hildesheim 1966), esp. 76-84.

For Philo the highest knowledge can only be acquired in a vision. Yet the superiority of seeing above hearing does not involve an opposition between the two concepts, but a difference in degree. Between human word and divine word, in contrast, there is an essential difference: the latter is creative activity, the former must be transcended if the true philosophy is to be attained. Hence the value of silence, which implies a leap into the supernatural. (= R583)

6633. E. SCHWEIZER, 'Zum religionsgeschichtlichen Hintergrund der 'Sendungsformel'. Gal 4 4f. Rm 8 3f. Joh 3 16f. I Joh 4 9', *ZNW* 57 (1966) 199-210, esp. 204ff.

God's sending of his son down from heaven has an important antecedent in Philo's conception of the Logos and his interpretation of the ideas contained in it, which are angels. (= R584)

6634. R. SCROGGS, *The last Adam: a study in Pauline anthropology* (Oxford-Philadelphia 1966), esp. 115-122.

'When Philo writes about Adam as a concrete human figure he does nothing more than to rephrase Jewish tradition into Hellenistic concepts' (115). Philo in fact keeps the notion of Adam separate from the notion of heavenly man: firstly, because of their origin (the former is Rabbinic, the latter Greek); secondly, because of their nature (the former is mythical, the latter philosophical); thirdly, because of their function (the first man is understood as ideal man, while heavenly man has affinities with the ontological structure of created man). (= R585)

6635. C. SPICQ, Art. 'Hébreux (Épître aux)': §3. 'Philonisme', *DB* 7 (1966) 233-239. (= R586)

6636. R. A. STEWART, 'Creation and matter in the Epistle to the Hebrews', *NTS* 12 (1966) 284-293.

The *locus classicus* for deducing Philo's views on the creation of the world is *Opif.* 16 and 7-12, where it emerges that the world is created by God. It would seem, however, that an opposite view emerges from *Aet.*, where Philo supposedly both affirms the indestructibility of the world and denies its createdness. But *Aet.*, as the author observes, is 'an exercise in dialectic' (292) which has probably been handed down to us in an incomplete state. And in the part which we do have Philo is probably expressing views opposite to his own. Thus it must be agreed that Philo followed the lead of Plato in affirming the idea of the world's creation, but did not elaborate all its consequences. (= R588)

6637. H. F. WEISS, *Untersuchungen zur Kosmologie des hellenistischen und palästinischen Judentums*, TU 97 (Berlin 1966), esp. 18-74,

248-282.

An impressive examination of two aspects of Philo's cosmological thought, with careful attention paid to the evidence located in Philo's writings. According to Weiss the essence of Philonic thought consists in the Jewish doctrine of the creator God. On this doctrine Greek influence superimposed the Platonic conception of pre-existent matter, creating a kind of dualism which was progressively accentuated by further Stoic and Aristotelian influences (note the juxtaposition of an active and a passive principle). The author does not dwell on Philo's possible attempts to strike a philosophical compromise between Judaism and Hellenism; he takes the preponderance of the former for granted and justifies the second almost purely on the basis of the apologetic intent of Philo's work. A similar method is followed in the section devoted to the concept of logos. Here too it is claimed that considerable Stoic and Platonic influences were not able to shake the Jewish foundations of the concept of logos (the Logos as firstborn and instrument of the Creator), and here too the emphasis is put on Philo's apologetic intentions, which are taken to be a sufficient compromise – if not on a philosophical level, then certainly on a religious and cultural level – between the two opposite views. (= R589)

6638. H. A. WOLFSON, 'Plato's pre-existent matter in Patristic philosophy', in L. WALLACH (ed.), *The classical tradition: literary and historical studies in honor of H. Caplan* (New York 1966) 409-420; reprinted in I. TWERSKY and G. H. WILLIAMS (edd.), *Studies in the history of philosophy and religion* (Cambridge 1973) 170-181.

A brief analysis of the concept of matter in Plato, Philo, and some Christian thinkers (Tatian, Augustine) leads the author to distinguish between the problem of the world's creation from pre-existent matter and the problem of uncreated matter: the first, observes Wolfson, does not imply the second. (= R590)

1967

6701. M. ALEXANDRE, 'La culture profane chez Philon', in *Philon d'Alexandrie* (cf. **6747**) 105-129.

Philo shows much admiration for Greek learning and incorporates it into the first level of a pedagogical curriculum which, through philosophy, leads to σοφία, i.e. the 'knowledge of divine and human matters'. In this Alexandre sees a particularly significant instance of the general confrontation between Judaism and Greek culture which forms the essence of Philo's personality. The article also contains valuable accounts of Philo's knowledge of the various subjects of the curriculum of the ἐγκύκλιος παιδεία, such as grammar, rhetoric, arithmetic, geometry, astronomy. Abstract in *StPh* 1 (1972) 73. (= R593)

6702. Y. AMIR [עמיר .י.], דיוקנו של משה אצל פילון [= 'The portrait of Moses in Philo'], *Mahanayyim* 115 (1967) 42-49 [Hebrew pp. מב-מם].

Moses is the central figure for the understanding of Hellenistic Jewry both in its self-understanding and in its apologetic activity. Two main tendencies govern Hellenistic Jewish writings: the rational (e.g. Artapanus: Moses as hero, inventor of writing etc.) and the irrational (e.g. Ezekiel the Tragedian: Moses as 'divine man'). Amir then discusses

Moses as author of the 'divine' Law by combining the rational and the irrational portraits of Moses expressed in Philo's theory of prophecy. (MM)

6703. R. ARNALDEZ, 'La dialectique des sentiments chez Philon', in *Philon d'Alexandrie* (cf. **6747**) 299-330.

The dialectic of sensibility in Philo is a lived dialectic, not just an intellectual one such as one finds in Plato. Human feeling continually takes place between a positive and a negative pole, i.e. between hope and fear, joy and sorrow, and it is a constant struggle to come closer to the positive pole. In this situation – which the author explains by means of a comparison with Moslem mysticism – it is possible to distinguish in Philo a horizontal dimension of sensibility (between spirit and flesh, good and evil on the human level) and a vertical one (between man and God). The dominant element here, however, is not the absoluteness of what one feels, but the idea of effort and progress. Abstract in *StPh* 1 (1972) 75. (= R594)

6704. R. ARNALDEZ, Art. 'Philo Judaeus', in *New Catholic Encyclopaedia*, vol. 11 (New York 1967) 287-291. (= R595)

6705. O. ARNDT, 'Zahlenmystik bei Philo – Spielerei oder Schriftauslegung?', *ZRGG* 19 (1967) 167-171.

In Philo's mystical arithmology the sacred numbers play a special part. Here the meaning of the number hundred (as found in *QG* 3.56) is explained with the aid of mathematical terms and geometrical figures. Abstract in *StPh* 1 (1972) 75-76. (= R596)

6706. R. ARNOU, *Le désir de Dieu dans la philosophie de Plotin*, (Paris 1921; 2nd edition revised and corrected Rome 1967), esp. 260-267.

Philo's theory of ecstasy anticipates the Plotinian theory, not so much because of the terminological affinities – these may go back to Plato – but on account of Philo's implicit use of the category of the One, which is relevant to the first Plotinian hypostasis. (= R597)

6707. L. W. BARNARD, *Justin Martyr: his life and thought* (Cambridge 1967), esp. 82-83, 92-97.

Argues forcefully against the view of Goodenough (*The theology of Justin Martyr*, Jena 1923, Amsterdam 1969²) that Philo exerted direct influence on Justin's doctrine of God and the Logos. (DTR)

6708. D. BARTHÉLEMY, 'Est-ce Hoshaya Rabba qui censura le 'Commentaire Allégorique'? A partir des retouches faites aux citations bibliques, étude sur la tradition textuelle du *Commentaire Allégorique* de Philon', in *Philon d'Alexandrie* (cf. **6747**) 45-78.

The analysis of Hebraicized biblical quotations in Philo, which according to the author add up to 122, suggests a Jewish reviser (perhaps Hoshaya Rabba) in the school of Caesarea, who, it is suggested, corrected Philo's quotations of the LXX by referring to the version of Aquila. Abstract in *StPh* 1 (1972) 76-77. (= R598)

6709. R. BATEY, 'The μία σάρξ: union of Christ and the church', *NTS* 13 (1966-67) 270-281.

Philo rejects the Rabbinic interpretation of the μία σάρξ as the union of man and woman; he spiritualizes the image and uses it to express the unity of the mind and the senses. (= R599)

6710. P. BEAUCHAMP, 'La cosmologie religieuse de Philon et la lecture de l'Exode par le *Livre de la Sagesse*: le thème de la manne', in *Philon d'Alexandrie* (cf. **6747**) 207-218.

Manna in Philo refers to the logos and to wisdom. For Philo, as for the author of the Sapientia Salomonis, ἀφθαρσία is an effect of manna, except that the indestructibility of which Philo speaks belongs exclusively to the soul. Abstract in *StPh* 1 (1972) 77. (= R600)

6711. S. BELKIN, 'Some obscure traditions mutually clarified in Philo and Rabbinic literature', 75th Anniversary Volume of *JQR* (1967) 80-103.

Although the author declares that he does not wish to show Philo's debt to the ancient Rabbinic tradition, his attempt to demonstrate how some passages from the latter can only – or chiefly – be interpreted in the light of other passages (taken mostly from the *Quaestiones*) nevertheless does suggest some kind of dependent relationship. Belkin discusses the following subjects in this article: (a) the structure of the altar; (b) the changing of Abraham's name; (c) the offering of first fruits; (d) the nature of angels; (e) manna; (f) eternal death; (g) the interpretation of Gen. 1:27; (h) marital abstinence; (i) predestination. (= R601)

6712. R. BORIG, *Der wahre Weinstock: Untersuchungen zu Jo 15, 1-10*, StANT 16 (Munich 1967), esp. 120-123.

The image of the vine in Philo is often superimposed on that of the vineyard to indicate the idea of fertility. In both cases Philo is in line with the Jewish interpretation of the Old Testament. (= R603)

6713. P. BOYANCÉ, 'Écho des exégèses de la mythologie grecque chez Philon', in *Philon d'Alexandrie* (cf. **6747**) 169-186.

In the author's view it is possible – provided one goes back to the Middle Platonic context which shaped Philo – to trace echoes of Greek mythology in at least four Philonic allegories: in the return of the soul to the heavenly home, which shows similarities with the myth of Odysseus; in the image of justice, of which some epithets echo the Greek image of Dike; in the representation of the virtues, which resembles that of the Graces; and finally, in the allegory of the intellect lacerated by the passions, which reflects the myth of Dionysus and the Titans. Abstract in *StPh* 1 (1972) 78. (= R604)

6714. P. BOYANCÉ, 'Dieu cosmique et dualisme: les archontes et Platon', in U. BIANCHI (ed.), *Le origini dello Gnosticismo: colloquio di Messina 13-18 aprile 1966* (Leiden 1967) 340-356.

The planetary archons in Gnosticism almost certainly go back to Plato (354). Boyancé reaches this conclusion after examining the passages (esp. *Opif.* 72-75 and *Conf.* 168ff.) in which Philo discusses the Powers. These passages have clearly been influenced by the *Timaeus*, and in particular by the motif of the 'young gods'. (RR)

6715. H. CHADWICK, 'Philo and the beginnings of Christian thought', in A. H. ARMSTRONG (ed.), *The Cambridge history of later Greek and early medieval philosophy* (Cambridge 1967) 137-157, 164-165.

'The history of Christian philosophy begins not with a Christian but with a Jew, Philo of Alexandria' (137). This assertion sets the tone of Chadwick's presentation of Philo, in which he discusses the main elements of Philo's thought and concludes with a penetrating revaluation of its philosophical (and in particular its Platonic) dimension. In the following chapter a lucid summary is given of the differences between Philo's thought and that of Justin Martyr. (= R605)

6716. J. COLIN, 'Philon d'Alexandrie et la "lâcheté" du préfet d'Égypte (Philon, *In Flaccum* 38, 41 et 43)', *RhM* 110 (1967) 284-285.

A brief contribution discussing some Philonic evidence on the responsibility of Flaccus in the anti-Semitic persecutions of 38 A.D. Abstract in *StPh* 1 (1972) 79. (= R606)

6717. S. DANIEL, 'La *Halacha* de Philon selon le premier livre des *Lois spéciales*', in *Philon d'Alexandrie* (cf. **6747**) 221-240.

The essentially Jewish nature of Philo's personality appears not only from the religious dimension of his thought, but also from the halachic aspect of his commitment, i.e. his role as a 'doctor of law' specifically committed to carrying out the precepts of Holy Scripture. This conclusion, which is opposed to that of Heinemann in his famous study (cf. **6211**), is reached on the basis of an analysis which examines the relation between the Philonic commentary and the biblical text to which it refers, which sometimes seems to be the LXX, other times the Hebrew original. The contribution is followed by a discussion which owes some of its liveliness to the fact that the author, in contrast to the views of most Philonic scholars, is convinced that Philo knew the Hebrew language. Abstract in *StPh* 1 (1972) 79-80. (= R607)

6718. J. DANIÉLOU, 'Les tuniques de peau chez Grégoire de Nysse', in G. MÜLLER and W. ZELLER (edd.), *Glaube, Geist, Geschichte: Festschrift für E. Benz zum 60. Geburtstage am 17. November 1967* (Leiden 1967) 356-367.

Of the many points of contact between Philo and Gregory of Nyssa, the author briefly examines the theme of σύμπνοια (concord) and touches on the problem of the incarnation of the soul. (= R608)

6719. J. DANIÉLOU, 'Philon et Grégoire de Nysse', in *Philon d'Alexandrie* (cf. **6747**) 333-345.

The author is convinced that Gregory of Nyssa had a direct knowledge of Philo's works. Such use shows that Philo was part of the library of a well-educated Christian of his time. The subjects which he borrowed from them, however, are peripheral to the central concerns of his thought. These conclusions are reached after a comparative analysis of texts, in particular of *Opif.* and *De hominis opificio*, *Contempl.* and *De virginitate*, and *Mos.* and the *De vita Moysis*. Abstract in *StPh* 1 (1972) 80. (= R609)

6720. F. DAUMAS, 'La 'solitude' des Thérapeutes et les antécédents égyptiens du monachisme chrétien', in *Philon d'Alexandrie* (cf. **6747**) 347-358.

The Therapeutae were among the first to achieve an ideal of monastic life based on solitary meditation. In this sense they paved the way for Christian monasticism. But Daumas notes that a similar attitude was already present in Egypt at the end of the second millennium and that soon after Philo in the 1st and 2nd century A.D. similar views, mainly inspired by Stoicism, are found in the heathen world. Abstract in *StPh* 1 (1972) 80. (= R610)

6721. M. GIUSTA, *I dossografi di etica*, 2 vols., Pubblicazioni della Facoltà di Lettere e Filosofia della Università di Torino 15.3-4 (Turin 1964, 1967) *passim.*

The aim of Giusta's monumental work is to demonstrate the existence of an ethical *Vetusta placita* parallel to the *Vetusta placita* on physics postulated by H. Diels in his celebrated *Doxographi Graeci* (Berlin 1879). This must be regarded as a weighty doxographical anthology, on which various 'school' textbooks then supposedly drew. Philo's works are cited on numerous occasions and are almost always compared with parallel passages in many other philosophical sources. Giusta thus in effect accomplishes one of the most comprehensive comparative analyses of Philonic texts ever carried out in the area of philosophical ethics. (RR)

6722. R. M. GRANT, 'Les êtres intermédiaires dans le judaïsme tardif', *SMSR* 38 (1967) 245-259.

Two tendencies can be distinguished in the evolution of the doctrine of the intermediate substances between God and the world: one Philonic, Christian, and predominantly philosophical; the other apocalyptic, Gnostic, and mythological. (= R611)

6723. A. GUILLAUMONT, 'Philon et les origines du monachisme', in *Philon d'Alexandrie* (cf. **6747**) 361-373.

Although Philo and early Christian monasticism have many elements in common (especially the themes of ἀναχώρησις (retirement), ἀποταγή (renunciation), ξενιτεία (solitude)), one cannot speak of a direct relation between the two. Both represent a continuation of certain tendencies in Hellenistic philosophy. Monasticism, however, embodies more Jewish-Christian than Philonic ideals. Abstract in *StPh* 1 (1972) 81. (= R612)

6724. J. GUROV, *Philo's exegesis and theology – a comparison with the Hebrew Bible and the Rabbinic commentaries* (diss. Hebrew Union College – Jewish Institute of Religion, Ohio 1967).

This study, recorded but not summarized in *DA*, cannot be located, not even at the Institution where it was submitted as a dissertation.

6725. A. HANSON, 'Philo's etymologies', *JThS* 18 (1967) 128-139.

After analyzing a large number of etymologies, the author concludes that Philo was in close touch with Rabbinic teaching and that, contrary to Sandmel's view, he also had an adequate knowledge of Hebrew. Abstract in *StPh* 1 (1972) 82. (= R613)

6726. M. ﬁARL, 'Cosmologie grecque et représentations juives dans l'oeuvre de Philon d'Alexandrie', in *Philon d'Alexandrie* (cf. **6747**) 189-203.

A passage from the *De Deo*, which presents various biblical subjects with their Philonic interpretations (the apparition of three men near the oak grove of Mamre, the divine Logos of God between the two Cherubim, and the vision of Isaiah in Is. 6:2), is used by Harl to show the continual interaction in Philo's cosmological representations between biblical and Greek elements. Abstract in *StPh* 1 (1972) 82-83. (= R614)

6727. A. JAUBERT, 'Le thème du 'reste sauveur' chez Philon', in *Philon d'Alexandrie* (cf. **6747**) 243-253.

The theme of the remnant has various elaborations in Philo, ranging from the figures of Noah and Abraham (where it is thus identified with the theme of the 'just redeemer') to that of Israel, the redemptive people. Nevertheless Philo lacks a doctrine of vicarious expiation, and the redemptive function of Israel does not consist in its suffering, but in the contagious force of its virtue. Abstract in *StPh* 1 (1972) 83-84. (= R615)

6728. G. JOSSA, 'Considerazioni sulle origini dello gnosticismo in relazione al giudaismo', in *Le origini dello gnosticismo* (**6714**) 413-426, esp. 416-419.

A comparative analysis of the basic themes of Philonic thought and Jewish thought shows the extent to which Hellenism had penetrated Jewish culture. The decline of interest in eschatology and Messianism was accelerated by Hellenistic philosophy, but can already be traced in Palestinian Judaism. On the other hand, Philo is described as having anticipated, by virtue of his occasionally dualistic cosmology, a good deal of apocalyptic literature. (= R616)

6729. J.-G. KAHN [ר‎שי-ןהכ .י‏, ןוליפ יבתכב ןיאמ שי האירבה תיעב לע ['A strange passage of Philo about the creation "ex nihilo"'], *Bar-Ilan* 4-5 (1967) 60-66.

Since *Opif.* gives no clear answer to the question whether or not Philo believed in a *creatio ex nihilo*, Kahn examines *Somn.* 1.75 where Philo employs all four Greek terms for 'creation' known from the Septuagint and from Greek tradition alike. It is suggested that Philo may have heard of an interpretation of the conception of 'creation' like that in II Macc 7:23-28 or in IQS 3.15. Philo struggled with the interpretation of creation as *ex nihilo*, but as yet did not know how to express it. See also **7720**. English summary. (MM)

6730. C. KANNENGIESSER, 'Philon et les Pères sur la double création de l'homme', in *Philon d'Alexandrie* (cf. **6747**) 277-296.

This highly compact and complex article is concerned with the theory of the double creation of man, its aim being to specify the role and essential nature of God and of the Logos. The theme of hegemony proves dominant in the discussion of the first subject: God's hegemony over creation, man's hegemony over the cosmos, the hegemony of the nous over man's entire being. The role of the Logos, on the other hand, is that of a paradigm and perfect model (cf. 287) based on a symmetrical conception of the ideal world and the sensible world: the Logos, as God's thought in action, stands at the centre of the ideal world, just as man stands at the centre of the sensible world. Abstract in *StPh* 1 (1972) 84. (= R617)

6731. C. KRAUS, *Filone Alessandrino e un'ora tragica della storia ebraica*, with preface by A. FERRABINO (Naples 1967).

'When a philosopher of Philo's temperament ventures into a field which is uncongenial to him such as that of historical events, the result is necessarily contradictory: the tendency towards abstraction is not easily reconciled with the need to coordinate the concrete facts of an event limited in time and space' (111). This statement implies the kind of judgment Kraus makes on Philo the historian, a judgment which nevertheless does not question the value of the information which Philo provides about the events in which he played a leading role. The line traced by this study never strays far from the contents of *Flacc.* and *Legat.*; these two writings are indeed its principal object, since Philo's historical interest, political commitment, and humanity are largely concentrated in them. It is not for nothing that Kraus ends her book with a chapter on Philo's 'humanism', where the religious dimension of the Alexandrian is presented as non-orthodox and open; its characteristics clearly emerge from his philosophical thought, but even more clearly from his activity as a historian. (= R618)

6732. H. M. KUITERT, *Gott in Menschengestalt: eine dogmatisch-hermeneutische Studie über die Anthropomorphismen der Bibel*, BEvTh 45 (Munich 1967) *passim*, esp. 61-64, 93-95.

The most important point of contact between the theologies of Philo and Origen is the polemic against anthropomorphism, which is directed against any tendency to involve God in the sphere of the sensible. In this sense God's human form is all he can have in common with the corporeal world. (= R619)

6733. O. LORETZ, *Die Gottebenbildlichkeit des Menschen*, Schriften des deutschen Instituts für wissenschaftliche Pädagogik (Munich 1967), esp. 16-19.

Philo's commentary on Gen. 1:26f. in *Plant.* 16-17 links the theme of man's upright stature – already present in various Greek thinkers – and his possibility of contemplating the heavens with biblical motifs such as the creation of man in God's image. (= R621)

6734. W. A. MEEKS, *The prophet-king: Moses traditions and the Johannine christology*, NT.S 14 (Leiden 1967), esp. 100-131.

The figure of Moses in Philo is examined here in its diverse aspects. On the basis of his analysis Meeks reaches the following conclusions: Philo's Moses, as prophet and king, differs essentially from the Jesus figure we find in the Prologue to John's Gospel, although both are characterized by the same attributes. Any connections between the two are due to their common dependence on Jewish tradition and not to any direct relationship. The attribute of prophet-king probably derives from Hellenistic tradition, while the attribute of legislator-king has antecedents in both Judaism and Hellenism. The connections between royalty and prophetic powers, however, are derived exclusively from Jewish culture. The enthronement of Moses is understood as the mystical ascent towards heaven. His essential role as prototypal mystic is thus intimately associated with Philo's personal ideals, and it is not possible to determine on the basis of Philo's evidence alone whether it already contains traditional elements. The connection between Moses' kingship and his mystic deification (Ex. 7:1) become clear through an examination of Rabbinic tradition (cf. 176ff.). (= R622)

6735. L. F. MERCADO, *The language of sojourning in the Abraham Midrash in Hebrews 11, 8-19; its Old Testament basis, exegetical traditions and function in the Epistle to the Hebrews* (diss. Harvard 1967).

This dissertation has the nature of an extensive commentary in which the author follows the semantic evolution of a group of terms which denote the theme of sojourning. Philo is continually used as a point of reference, and although Mercado does not believe in a direct connection with Hebrews, he discusses this problem at length. The author writes (170f.): 'The affinities of the author of Hebrews and Philo in their use of the language of sojourning are unmistakable. These are seen not only in the fact that both use similar biblical figures and quote similar biblical texts to show that the patriarchs and the Old Testament figures were sojourners, but especially in the patternlike fashion in which the language of sojourning functions in both authors.' All in all eight common themes are traced: (1) the opposition between the celestial and terrestrial fatherland; (2) man's need to renounce the body; (3) the centrality of God's promise to Abraham; (4) the theme of obedience; (5) 'sojourning' as proper to every life; (6) the heavenly fatherland as goal; (7) the use of a language peculiar to Middle Platonic dualism; (8) the paradeigmatic nature of the condition of 'sojourning' as a universally valid experience. (= R623)

6736. A. MICHEL, 'Quelques aspects de la rhétorique chez Philon', in *Philon d'Alexandrie* (cf. **6747**) 81-101.

Michel's starting-point is the problem of the relation between philosophy and rhetoric in Philo. The solution presented emphasizes the existence of two levels of rhetoric, of which the level of philosophical rhetoric is pre-eminent. In order to determine its nature more exactly, the author compares Philonic rhetoric with Ciceronian rhetoric and discovers considerable parallels between the two. Since the possibility of a direct relationship must naturally be rejected, there is no alternative but to hypothesize a common source, possibly Antiochus of Ascalon. Abstract in *StPh* 1 (1972) 88-89. (= R624)

6737. B. MONDIN, 'Esistenza, natura, inconoscibilità e ineffabilità di Dio nel pensiero di Filone Alessandrino', *ScC* 95 (1967) 423-447.

The author distinguishes the problems of the existence and the nature of God and deals with them separately. After listing and briefly analyzing the attributes of God (unicity, simplicity, incorporeality, perfection and infallibility, self-sufficiency, transcendence, immutability, omnipotence, eternity, goodness, providence), Mondin focusses on the unknowability of God. Certain contradictory elements here can be resolved by distinguishing the act of comprehending God from the act of knowing his various attributes. The author warns, however, that this distinction runs the risk of compromising God's unity. Abstract in *StPh* 1 (1972) 89-90. (= R625)

6738. B. MONDIN, 'Il problema dei rapporti tra fede e ragione in Platone e in Filone Alessandrino', *PI* 9 (1967) 9-16.

The problem of the relation between faith and reason can be solved in three ways: by admitting the absolute autonomy of both spheres; by positing a reciprocal antinomy; by trying to establish some kind of harmony between the two. Philo chose the last solution. From his point of view, the sole task of philosophy was to give to revelation 'a form of expression which could be understood by men of a given culture, civilization, age, milieu' (14). (= R626)

6739. A. NAZZARO, 'Filone Alessandrino e l'ebraico', *RAAN* 42 (1967) 61-79.

The first part of the article offers an interesting *status quaestionis* on the article's subject. Nazzaro himself is convinced that Philo had a 'modest knowledge of Hebrew'. In order to demonstrate this view, he lists a number of accurate etymologies in Philo and records the many biblical quotations which agree with the Hebrew text rather than with the Septuagint. Abstract in *StPh* 1 (1972) 90. (= R627)

6740. V. NIKIPROWETZKY, 'La doctrine de l'élenchos chez Philon, ses résonances philosophiques et sa portée religieuse', in *Philon d'Alexandrie* (cf. **6747**) 255-273.

ἔλεγχος in Philo is identified with the conscience, i.e. with the internal tribunal that judges man's ethical behaviour. Its relation with the human soul is rather ambiguous: sometimes it seems to be identified with the *nous*, other times it seems ontologically distinct. This vacillation can also be found in Platonic demonology, which appears to have inspired Philo, and so also in what the author calls 'Platonic scholasticism'. This relation is valid only from a formal point of view, however, for in terms of content the Philonic *elenchos* is wholly to be located 'in the period between the two Testaments together with its Christian or Rabbinical prolongations' (273). Abstract in *StPh* 1 (1972) 91. (= R628)

6741. V. NIKIPROWETZKY, 'La spiritualisation des sacrifices et le culte sacrificiel au temple de Jérusalem chez Philon d'Alexandrie', *Sem* 17 (1967) 97-116.

The problem under discussion is particularly important for two reasons: (a) it enables us to specify the relations between Hellenism and Judaism in Philo; (b) it forms part of a polemic against ritualism which involves not only the Greek world, but also to some extent Jewish culture (cf. 97). Philonic allegory, in this context, tends not to condemn the cult of sacrifice, but to defend it intelligently by radically and profoundly spiritualizing the concepts of temple and sacrifice and giving them an ethical-religious interpretation. The fact that later Judaism rejected Philo's thought, therefore, should not be imputed to his views on the cult of sacrifice, but rather to the instrument of allegory. Philo's use certainly remained within the limits of orthodoxy, but in itself it could easily be turned in an opposite direction. Abstract in *StPh* 2 (1973) 60f. (= R629)

6742. V. NIKIPROWETZKY, 'Temple et communauté: à propos d'un ouvrage récent', *REJ* 126 (1967) 7-25.

A review and supplementation of B. GÄRTNER's study, *The temple and the community in Qumran and the New Testament: a comparative study in the temple symbolism of the Qumran texts and the New Testament*, SNTSMS 1 (Cambridge 1965), chiefly in relation to the connections between the Essenes and the Therapeutae and to the symbolism of the temple in Philo and parallel sources. (= R630)

6743. A. PELLETIER, 'Deux expressions de la notion de conscience dans le judaïsme hellénistique et le christianisme naissant', *REG* 80 (1967) 363-371.

The term συνείδησις is used by Philo to express man's moral and psychological conscience and is also found in this sense in the Jewish wisdom literature of Alexandria. The term τὸ συνειδός, however, refers to the conscience in an almost personified sense; it is a purely Greek expression taken from legal language. Abstract in *StPh* 2 (1973) 61. (= R631)

6744. J. PÉPIN, 'Remarques sur la théorie de l'exégèse allégorique chez Philon', in *Philon d'Alexandrie* (cf. **6747**) 131-167.

At the origin of Philo's exegetical method probably stands an implicit equation of allegory with mystic initiation, if only because of the distinction between 'the elect' and 'the unworthy' (corresponding to the initiated and the non-initiated) which allegory allows to be drawn between the readers of the Bible. The literal meaning is thus available to everybody, while the allegorical meaning is only for the few. In this way, however, various biblical passages are not accessible for the majority of people because the literal sense is insignificant. In these cases the truth resides solely in the allegorical sense and the apparent senselessness serves precisely to indicate the necessity of jumping to another level of interpretation. The article gives valuable insights into the actual techniques and procedures of allegory, as practised by Philo and his Hellenistic contemporaries and predecessors. (= R632)

6745. G. PFEIFER, *Ursprung und Wesen der Hypostasenvorstellungen im Judentum*, Arbeiten zur Theologie I 31 (Stuttgart 1967), esp. 47-59.

Philo was the first Jew to make use of a hypostatic theology. This is the result of a theological conception which allows no direct contact between God on the one hand and the world and man on the other. Thus it is possible to sketch a hierarchy which is not systematic (since 'Philo is not a systematic thinker, but an exegete', 59), which is not always worked out philosophically (the relation between God and the Intermediaries is sometimes independent, other times nearly identical), but which can nevertheless clearly be divided into Logos, Sophia, *pneuma*, Powers, logoi, and angels. (= R633)

6746. V. C. PFITZNER, *Paul and the agon motif: traditional athletic imagery in the Pauline literature*, NT.S 16 (Leiden 1967), esp. 38-48.

Paul received the traditional elements of his use of the agon motif via two channels, Stoic moral philosophy and Hellenistic Judaism. Philo is used for evidence for the latter channel. An analysis of diverse Philonic texts shows that he too is indebted to the Cynic-Stoic picture of the agon of virtue, but that he also introduces changes. Philo's moral athlete is not self-sufficient, but fights on behalf of God and with God's help. Philo also places more emphasis than the Stoic tradition on the goal or prize of the agon, which is granted by God and is God himself. 'The ultimate goal and prize are the same – God Himself and His blessings' (48). (DTR)

6747. *Philon d'Alexandrie. Lyon 11-15 Septembre 1966: colloques nationaux du Centre National de la Recherche Scientifique* (Paris 1967).

As the climax of the large project to translate all Philo's works into the French language, the Centre National de la Recherche Scientifique in France organized a national conference on Philo, a unique event of its kind. The eighteen papers published in this volume are listed in our bibliography under the names of their authors. REVIEWS: A. Mosès, *RSLR* 3 (1967) 167ff.; F. Petit, *RThAM* 34 (1967) 274f.; E. I. Watkin, *DR* 86 (1967) 287ff. (cf. **6840**); F. Bouwen, *POC* 18 (1968) 393f.; H. Crouzel, *RAM* 44 (1968) 485ff.; J. Daniélou, *RecSR* 56 (1968) 130; M. Delcor, *BLE* 69 (1968) 132ff.; J. E. Ménard, *RSR* 42 (1968) 349f.; J. Moreau, *EPh* 23 (1968) 241f.; C. Perrot, *BFCL* 44 (1968) 89; A. Solignac, *ArPh* 31 (1968) 477ff.; R. Joly, *RBPh* 47 (1969) 1053f.; M. E. Lauzière, *RThom* 69 (1969) 157f.; A. Maddalena, *RSLR* 5 (1969) 183; I. Ortiz de Urbina, *EE* 44 (1969) 549f.; H. Savon, *REA* 71 (1969) 561ff.; M. Simonetti, *RCCM* 11 (1969) 285f.; W. Wiefel, *ThLZ* 94 (1969) 602f.; R. McL. Wilson, *Gn* 41 (1969) 411ff.; A. Orbe, *Greg* 51 (1970) 166ff.; D. M. Pippidi, *StudCl* 12 (1970) 341ff.; C. Martin, *NRTh* 103 (1971) 110f.; J. C. M. van Winden, *VChr* 25 (1971) 302ff.; cf. also the abstracts of many of these contributions in *StPh* 1 (1972) 72-91. (= R591)

6748. P. POKORNÝ, 'Der Ursprung der Gnosis', *Kairos* 9 (1967) 94-105, esp. 99-100.

The origins of Gnosticism can be related to the Philonic doctrines of the Logos and Sophia. In contrast to the Gnosis, however, Philo postulates a positive relationship between God and the world. (RR)

6749. J. M. RIST, *Plotinus: the road to reality* (Cambridge 1967), esp. 99-101.

The author is not impressed by similarities between the Philonic and the Plotinian Logos reported by Armstrong (cf. **4001**); these are 'almost certainly accidental' (101). (DTR)

6750. S. ROSENBERG, 'Filón de Alejandría', in *Bibliotheca popular judía del Congreso judío mundial*, Colección: Grandes figuras del judaismo 6 (Buenos Aires 1967), 4-24.

This synoptic presentation of Philo's thought concentrates on the cultural aspect (his place in Alexandrian Judaism), the methodological aspect (his use of allegory), and the philosophical aspect (especially the relation to Platonism). Philo is regarded as a thinker who preserves 'a profoundly Jewish spirit' (5) and has been wrongly neglected in the history of Jewish philosophy. Two brief appendices are devoted to a classification of Philo's treatises and a short bibliography. (= R636)

6751. C. SCHNEIDER, *Kulturgeschichte des Hellenismus*, vol. 1 (Munich 1967) 881-898.

The author is not specifically concerned with Philo, but in describing the Jewish-Hellenistic sects from a historical-religious point of view, he devotes some lines to Philo and in particular to his allegorical method (894). The work provides a useful frame of reference for those interested in seeing Philo in the context of Alexandrian Judaism. (RR)

6752. J. SCHWARTZ, 'L'Égypte de Philon', in *Philon d'Alexandrie* (cf. **6747**) 35-44.

This historically oriented contribution sets out to reconstruct the legal status of the Jews in Alexandria and to explain the historical events which determined the Jewish community's political order and relations with Rome in the period immediately prior to Philo, i.e. during the reigns of Augustus and Tiberius. (= R637)

6753. M. SIMON, 'Éléments gnostiques chez Philon', in *Le origini dello Gnosticismo* (cf. **6714**) 359-376.

Following H. Jonas, the author distinguishes two types of Gnosticism: an Iranian type which posits a primordial ontological dualism, and a Syro-Egyptian type which, on the basis of a theory of emanation, deduces its dualism from the concept of God and thus remains essentially monistic. With reference to the views of Dodds, Simon introduces more specific differentiations. He concludes that we find in Philo a kind of dualism mitigated by the Jewish belief in monotheism, in which the diverse types of dualism seem to interpenetrate and it is not easy to separate out the various elements. Abstract in *StPh* 2 (1973) 66f. (= R638)

6754. M. SIMON, 'Situation du Judaïsme alexandrin dans la Diaspora', in *Philon d'Alexandrie* (cf. **6747**) 17-31.

Simon draws a general outline of the Jewish Diaspora, paying special attention to the Syrian, Roman, and Alexandrian contexts. The influence of the last named and of Philo in particular was important in primitive Christianity, but not determinative for Jewish thought, and should not be exaggerated. In the Jewish context the dominant influence remained that of Palestinian Judaism. On the other hand the evidence suggests that the Hellenized form of Judaism found in Alexandrian was not an isolated phenomenon in the Diaspora. (= R639)

6755. M. SMITH, 'Goodenough's *Jewish Symbols* in retrospect', *JBL* 86 (1967) 53-68.

Smith reaches the conclusion that Goodenough, to the extent that he wished his monumental work (cf. **5309**) to be not just a collection of material but above all an interpretation of its significance, must be considered to have failed (65): 'His pandemic sacramental paganism was a fantasy; so was the interpretation of pagan symbols based on it, and so was the empire-wide, antirabbinic, mystical Judaism, based on the interpretation of these symbols. All three are enormous exaggerations of elements which existed, but were rare, in early imperial times.' As is pointed out earlier in the article (61), this mystical Judaism is largely based on the example of Philo. But Smith goes on immediately to add (66): 'So be it. Columbus failed too. But his failure revealed a new world, and so did Goodenough's...' (DTR)

6756. S. SOWERS, 'On the reinterpretation of biblical history in Hellenistic Judaism', in F. CHRIST (ed.), *Oikonomia: Heilsgeschichte als Thema der Theologie, O. Cullmann zum 65. Geburtstag gewidmet* (Hamburg 1967) 18-25.

Briefly analyzes the relations between the sacred history described in the Bible and the history of the world as conceived by Philo. Special reference is made to the non-allegorical works. Abstract in *StPh* 2 (1973) 67f. (= R640)

6757. J. WHITTAKER, 'Moses atticizing', *Phoenix* 21 (1967) 196-201.

Argues against E. R. Dodds that the description of the highest god as ὁ μέν γε ὤν in Numenius fr. 13 Des Places is a reminiscence of the LXX designation in Ex. 3:14. Brief discussion of Philo's use of the text and on the possibility that Numenius was acquainted with Philo's writings (cf. esp. n.28). (DTR)

6758. H. A. WOLFSON, 'Philo Judaeus', in *The Encyclopedia of Philosophy*, vol. 6 (New York 1967) 151-155; reprinted in I. TWERSKY and G. H. WILLIAMS (edd.), *Studies in the history of philosophy and religion*, vol. 1 (Cambridge, Mass. 1973) 60-70.

This contribution derives its chief interest from the fact that it summarizes, in a schematic form, the author's interpretation of Philonic theology. Moreover the order in which the material is arranged offers the reader a useful guide to Wolfson's vast scholarly production on the subject, for a synthesis is given of some of his fundamental views on the interpretation of Philo. At the end of the entry Wolfson restates his well-known views on Philo's place in the history of religious philosophy. For the subsequent Hebrew translation, cf. **7853**. (= R641)

6759. G. ZAMPAGLIONE, *L'idea della pace nel mondo antico* (Turin 1967), esp. 248-251.

In the Philonic concept of peace the author recognizes a cosmopolitan emphasis derived from Stoic thought which leads to a mature affirmation of religious tolerance, as well as to the conception of peace as a liberation from vice and an indifference to passion. (= R642)

6760. J. ZANDEE, 'Die Person des Sophia in der vierten Schrift des Codex Jung', in *Le origini dello Gnosticismo* (cf. **6714**) 203-214, esp. 210-212.

The points of contact between Gnostic and Philonic *sophia* can essentially be reduced to the common link with revelation and to the redeeming and mediating function which wisdom has in both contexts. In Philo's case, moreover, one must take into account Platonic and Stoic influences and the many affinities with biblical wisdom literature. Abstract in *StPh* 2 (1973) 72f. (= R643)

1968

6801. E. L. ABEL, 'Were the Jews banished from Rome in 19 A.D.?', *REJ* 127 (1968) 383-386.

Philo's evidence (*Legat.* 159-161), together with the evidence in Josephus, Tacitus, Suetonius, Dion Cassius, and Seneca, is used by the author to shed light on the subject under discussion. (= R645)

6802. A. ALTMANN, '*Homo imago Dei* in Jewish and Christian theology', *JR* 48 (1968) 235-259.

The author concisely analyzes the fusion of Old Testament and Platonic motifs in Philo's conception of the heavenly man, in which a dominant role is played by the concept of logos. Thereafter Philo's work is used as a fixed point of comparison in order to elucidate the views of Judaism, Paul, and Gregory of Nyssa. (= R646)

6803. J. AMSTUTZ, *ΑΠΛΟΤΗΣ: eine begriffsgeschichtliche Studie zum jüdisch-christlichen Griechisch*, Theoph 19 (Bonn 1968), esp. 49-50, 52-60.

From a strictly ethical point of view, the term ἁπλοῦς in Philo indicates spiritual integrity in the face of evil. From an ontological-philosophical point of view, however, it indicates the simplicity of the soul which, having overcome the lures of passion, approaches God, who is absolute simplicity, in an attitude which is the fruit of divine grace and a prelude to contemplation. (= R647)

6804. P. BORGEN, 'God's agent in the fourth Gospel', in J. NEUSNER (ed.), *Religions in antiquity: essays in memory of E. R. Goodenough*, SHR 14 (Leiden 1968) 137-148, esp. 144-148; reprinted in *Logos was the true light and other essays on the Gospel of John* (Trondheim 1983) 121-132.

Points out the close parallel between the theme of *visio Dei* in John's Gospel and the theme of Israel in Philo. Abstract in *StPh* 1 (1972) 77f. (= R648)

6805. E. BRANDENBURGER, *Fleisch und Geist. Paulus und die dualistische Weisheit*, WMANT 29 (Neukirchen 1968), esp. 114-235.

The closest antecedent of the Pauline dualism inherent in the conception of body and spirit is Hellenistic Judaism, reconstructed here chiefly on the basis of Philo's work. In this connection the author discusses the following themes. (1) Philo was acquainted with the opposition between νοῦς-ψυχή and πνεῦμα (cf. 128-140), understood as a development of the opposition between σάρξ and πνεῦμα (cf. 140-154) peculiar to late Judaism. (2) In connection with this notion, both Philo and Paul posited two dualistically opposed classes of men. (3) Both *sophia* and logos in Philo have a pneumatic basis. (4) The corporeal and earthly element in Philo is, just as in the writings of Qumran, connected with the theme of sin. In this sense *sarx* and *sophia* stand in opposition to one another as the principles of damnation and salvation. (5) The phrase εἶναι ἐν σαρκί does not occur in Philo, but the concept which it expresses can be located in a similar context.

(6) In both authors the concept of salvation corresponds to a redemptive power which is its cause: in Philo this power appears to be identified with the Logos and with *sophia*, in Paul with Christ and the *pneuma*. In spite of all these parallels, the author concludes, a direct relationship between Paul and Philo is to be ruled out; in the case of Paul, the parallels rather refer to a dualistic interpretation of wisdom on the basis of concepts and motifs drawn from popular philosophy (cf. 228). (= R649)

6806. A. J. CLAYTON, 'Remarques sur deux personnages Camusiens: Hélicon et Scipion', *RSHum* 129 (1968) 79-90.

Noting the extraordinary similarities between the Helicon of Philo and Camus, the author thinks it likely that Camus was inspired by *Legat*. 166-168, where this personage is discussed. (= R651)

6807. C. COLPE, 'New Testament and gnostic Christology', in *Religions in Antiquity* (**6804**) 227-243, esp. 231ff.

The Christology of the first centuries is here related to the Gnostic doctrine of the *Urmensch*-redeemer. Philo plays a role of some importance in this comparison, because his thought seems to show traces of such a doctrine. Colpe nevertheless tends to play down this influence, recognizing in Philo's thought a fundamentally positive evaluation of the harmony of the universe which is Stoic of origin and quite foreign to the Gnostic mentality. (= R652)

6808. L. M. CONGDON, *The false teachers at Colossae: affinities with Essene and Philonic thought* (diss. Drew University1968).

The subject of this dissertation is the false philosophy mentioned by Paul in his Epistle to the Colossians. The author's main concern is to identify this philosophy historically and to explain the nature of its doctrine in outline. Philo and his thought scarcely enter into this project, but a central role is reserved for his evidence on the sects of the Essenes and Therapeutae. The frame of reference is rather complex, however, since in addition to Philo, the Essenes, and the Therapeutae as inspirers of the false doctrine, it is also possible to include certain forms of Proto-Gnosticism or Pre-Gnosticism (cf. 3f.) and the Qumran community. The author's documented and extensive analysis does not reach definite results; as he acutely observes (268), the problem confronting scholars here resembles a puzzle of which we have certain pieces that allow us to see enough of the overall picture 'to indicate that the section of the puzzle which represents Hellenistic Judaism of the Philonic type (of which the Therapeutae are examples) comes just before the Colossian error'. At the same time there are other pieces which interlock and which show that first-century Essenism should be put next to the section of the puzzle representing Pauline theology; but these do not seem to be directly attached to the pieces representing the error of the Colossians (cf. 268). (= R653)

6809. M. DELCOR, 'Repas cultuels esséniens et thérapeutes, thiases et haburoth', *RQ* 6 (1967-68) 401-425, esp. 408-410.

One of the most significant features linking the Essenes and the Therapeutae is their common interpretation of the banquet or communal meal as a cultic and sacrificial act. The author analyzes in this connection some passages from *Contempl.* containing evidence on the subject. (= R654)

6810. R. S. ECCLES, 'The purpose of the Hellenistic patterns in the Epistle to the Hebrews', in *Religions in Antiquity* (**6804**) 207-226.

Discusses at some length the most representative views on the relations between Philo and Hebrews, with especial attention to the views of of Goodenough, Friedländer and Bousset. The deficiency of most theories on Hellenistic or Philonic influence is that they do not consider the total pattern and purpose of the Epistle. Eccles sees this as lying in the proclamation of *kerygma* and 'Heilsgeschichte', not Christian Gnosticism. Christ is not a mystagogue like the Philonic Moses. But within this framework a rich theological elaboration is given in terms of Hellenistic thought patterns. (= R655)

6811. A. EHRHARDT, *The beginning: a study in the Greek philosophical approach to the concept of creation from Anaximander to St. John*, with a memoir by J. H. THOMAS (Manchester 1968), esp. 196-205.

Philo is described as rejecting an earlier uncritical approach to the problem of the 'beginning' in Gen. 1:1, which he characterizes as 'an ordering principle of natural numbers to which the events of creation were subjected' (cf. 197). Traces of such an interpretation are also found in Paul, but there is a crucial difference: for Philo the 'beginning' is located in number, for Paul in the supreme cause, which is not identified with God. 'As long as the problem of creation was seen as an ontological and not a teleological one no other explanation of the meaning of the 'beginning' could be logically proposed than those of Philo and Paul. Yet the consequences of their respective choices are of profound significance. The principle chosen by Philo, an ordering metaphysical principle, made the empirical world a secondary consideration in the interpretation of the relation between God and man, whereas the active causative principle stated by Paul made it God's world' (205). (= R656)

6812. U. FRÜCHTEL, *Die kosmologischen Vorstellungen bei Philo von Alexandrien: ein Beitrag zur Geschichte der Genesisexegese*, ALGHJ 2 (Leiden 1968).

As Nazzaro rightly observes in the extensive review cited below, the greatest merit of this work consists in its new approach to the relations between Philo and Middle Platonism. A possible criticism, however, as argued by Daniélou in his review, is its relative neglect of the relations between Philo and the Judaism of his day. The book is divided into two sections. The first explores in four chapters four thematic tendencies in Philonic cosmology: the first, third, and fourth chapters are concerned with the cosmos as πόλις θεοῦ (city of God), φυτὸν θεοῦ (plant of God), and ἱερὸν θεοῦ (temple of God) respectively, while the second deals with the doctrine of the *logos tomeus*. The second part deals with the position of cosmology in Philo's thought as a whole; the subjects discussed here are Philo's exegetical method, the problem of knowledge, and the relationship God-man. The book ends with an excursus devoted to the concept of *sophia*. In the Introduction (cf. 1-4) Früchtel declares that her research was guided by three kinds of interests: historical-religious, historical-philosophical (also as related to the doctrine of dogma), and hermeneutic. In her conclusions she relates the following observations to each of these interests. (1) the multiplicity of traditions traceable in Philo does not destroy the unity of his thought, the structure and goal of which are determined by the problem of knowledge. (2) 'Once the meaning and specific nature of Middle Platonism have been recognized, the necessary consequence must be drawn for Philo as well, and his intellectual efforts as a philosopher must be respected' (185). (3) Philo 'must be distinguished from the many Gnostic systems in which the Old Testament, Homer, the mysteries, and the Apocryphal traditions are reduced to a single level' (186). REVIEWS: F. Petit, *RThAM* 35 (1968) 324f.; J. Daniélou, *RecSR* 57 (1969) 112ff.; R. Pesch, *FreibRund* 21 (1969) 88; H. F. Weiss, *BiOr* 26 (1969) 407ff.; G. Bertram, *ThLZ* 95 (1970) 110ff.; A. V. Nazzaro, *VetChr* 7 (1970) 382ff., *Vich* 1 (1972) 119f. (= R657)

6813. B. E. GÄRTNER, 'The Pauline and Johannine idea of 'to know God' against the Hellenistic background: the Greek philosophical principle 'like by like' in Paul and John', *NTS* 14 (1967-68) 209-231.

The proposition 'like knows like' is here taken to be a category of thought which in Philo's case expresses the dynamics of knowledge and of the ascent to God. Gärtner writes: 'God's revelation comes from heaven to a man's soul and nourishes it, and the soul ascends to heaven in order to get to know the divine Reason' (214). (= R658)

6814. E. R. GOODENOUGH with A. T. KRAABEL, 'Paul and the Hellenization of Christianity', in *Religions in Antiquity* (**6804**) 23-68, esp. 40-43, 64-68.

This analysis of the Epistle to the Romans frequently turns to Philo because especially the last part of the letter shows considerable affinities with Philonic thought. The reason for this, according to the authors, is that Paul 'thinks in Hellenistic terms' and attempts to approach ethics in a very similar way to Philo in *Virt.* (= R659)

6815. A. HENRICHS, 'Philosophy, the handmaiden of theology', *GRBS* 9 (1968) 437-450.

The maxim *philosophia theologiae ancilla*, which played such an important role in medieval thought, is of Philonic origin and derives specifically from Philo's interpretation of Gen. 16:1-2 in *Congr.* 12. Philo, in turn, is said to have been inspired by the Stoic philosopher Aristo (cf. 444ff.), if only vaguely. There can be no doubt, however, that it was by means of Philo that the expression and the related idea passed through to Clement, Origen, and Didymus the Blind. (= R661)

6816. H. KOESTER, 'ΝΟΜΟΣ ΦΥΣΕΩΣ: the concept of natural law in Greek thought', in *Religions in Antiquity* (**6804**) 521-541, esp. 530-541.

By 'natural law' Philo means nothing other than Mosaic law. This conception springs from the encounter of Jewish culture with Greek culture and is unique in the history of ancient philosophy. As the author observes: 'Only a philosophical and theological setting in which the Greek concept of nature was fused with the belief in a divine legislator and with the doctrine of the most perfect (written!) law could produce such a theory, and only here could the Greek dichotomy of the two realms of law and nature be overcome. All these conditions are fulfilled in Philo...' (540). (= R662)

6817. F. W. KOHNKE, 'Das Bild der echten Münze bei Philon von Alexandria', *Herm* 96 (1968) 583-590.

The image of the 'genuine coin' is often used by Philo to indicate the 'spiritual hypostasis' (the *nous* and the soul). This image has very ancient roots in Greek culture and is already found, though almost always connected to ethical values (justice, virtue), in Solon, Theognis, the Sophists, Plato, and Eudorus of Alexandria. The last-named probably forms the last link before Philo. (= R663)

6818. R. J. LEDOGAR, *Acknowledgement: praise-verbs in the early Greek anaphora* (Rome 1968) 94-98.

Philo spiritualizes the term εὐχαριστία and, above all, raises and extends its meaning so that it comes to comprehend the sphere of worship and all religious acts. The pre-eminence of Philonic *eucharistia*, observes the author, 'comes from the fact that it is an *acknowledgement* of God as the source of all, and of man's fundamental incapacity to claim anything for himself' (95f.). (= R664)

6819. M. MCCLAIN, 'Western mysticism from Plotinus and Philo to St. John of the Cross', *MEAH* 16-17 (1967-68) 69-96, esp. 69-73.

The author presents a compressed description of the general features of Philonic thought: its mediating function between metaphysical Neoplatonism and Jewish monotheism, its opposition to divine anthropomorphism, the particular kind of mysticism which does not involve the unification of man with God, but the seeing of God in all his splendour. (= R650)

6820. A. MADDALENA, 'L'ENNOIA e l'ΕΠΙΣΤΗΜΗ ΘΕΟΥ in Filone Ebreo', *RFIC* 96 (1968) 5-27.

Starting from an analysis of *Deus* 1-4, the author develops an interesting interpretation of Philo's thought on the essence of the soul. Its conclusions are worth citing. Having affirmed the spiritual nature of the divine *pneuma* and the material nature of the soul, and distinguishing in these conceptions the diverse influences of Greek philosophy (Platonic, Greek, Aristotelian), Maddalena concludes: no Greek 'had conceived a transformation of the corporeal into the incorporeal, or of the passive element into an active force: for the Greeks there was always an irresolvable antithesis, so that becoming remained becoming, matter matter, the passive element the passive element' (27). In Philo, on the other hand, this ontological leap forms the very essence of the knowledge of God attained by the elect. Abstract in *StPh*, 1 (1972) 86. (= R665)

6821. R. MAYER, 'Geschichtserfahrung und Schriftauslegung: zur Hermeneutik des frühen Judentums', in O. LORETZ and W. STROLZ (edd.), *Die hermeneutische Frage in der Theologie*, Schriften zum Weltgespräch 3 (Vienna-Freiburg 1968) 290-355, esp. 315-322.

Although Philo's loyalty to Judaism remained essentially intact, the geographical and political position of Alexandria favoured his open-mindedness to numerous cultural influences. This explains why Philo based Mosaic law on reason and not only on revelation. As far as theology and ethics are concerned, however, Philo is very close to the Therapeutae and the Essenes, while from a philosophical point of view many of his intuitions take him in the direction of Neoplatonism and away from Stoic materialism, and also beyond the Platonism of his time. Abstract in *StPh*, 1 (1972) 87. (= R666)

6822. W. A. MEEKS, 'Moses as God and king', in *Religions in Antiquity* (**6804**) 354-371, esp. 354-361.

Philo transforms the figure of Moses, in his functions of legislator, prophet, and priest, into the ideal Hellenistic king who symbolically represents an intermediate stage between God and humanity. Texts in Philo indicate a tradition, based on exegesis of Ex. 7:1, that Moses was in some sense deified during his ascent at Sinai. (= R667)

6823. J. E. MÉNARD, 'Le mythe de Dionysus Zagreus chez Philon', *RSR* 42 (1968) 339-345.

The myth of Dionysus Zagreus expresses the drama of the soul torn to pieces by the passions. The same myth is often alluded to in Gnostic texts, where it is connected with the giants of the Bible. It was Philo who unified both themes (biblical and mythological) in a single psychological interpretation. Abstract in *StPh* 1 (1972) 88. (= R668)

6824. B. MONDIN, 'L'universo filosofico di Filone Alessandrino', *ScC* 96 (1968) 371-394.

This very clear and coherent synoptic presentation of Philo's thought concentrates on the concept of God and its cosmological implications. In Mondin's view Philo intentionally maintains, for apologetic reasons, a double interpretation of creation, i.e. creation *ex nihilo* for intelligible reality and demiurgic creativity for corporeal reality. Other subjects dealt with are the Logos, the Powers, the ideas, and their archetypal function. Abstract in *StPh* 1 (1972) 90. (= R669)

6825. V. NIKIPROWETZKY, 'ΚΥΡΙΟΥ ΠΡΟΣΘΕΣΙΣ: note critique sur Philon d'Alexandrie, *De Iosepho*, 28', *REJ* 127 (1968) 387-392.

The phrase under discussion, which gives the Greek interpretation of Joseph's Hebrew name, can only be fitted into the context with some difficulty if rendered as in the translations of Laporte and Colson. The author suggests a variant which simultaneously preserves the grammar and the sense of the passage. Abstract in *StPh* 1 (1972) 91. (= R670)

6826. V. NIKIPROWETZKY, 'Schadenfreude chez Philon d'Alexandrie? note sur *In Flaccum*, 121 sq.', *REJ* 127 (1968) 7-19.

Starting from a quite detailed analysis of the passage in question and the relevant translations of Colson and Pelletier, the author makes some general observations on the subject of method. He shows how 'psychological criticism' applied to ancient authors is in fact quite dangerous; in this case the two translators have mistaken a typically haggadic conception of divine justice for a psychological attitude on Philo's part. Abstract in *StPh* 2 (1973) 60. (= R671)

6827. K. OTTE, *Das Sprachverständnis bei Philo von Alexandrien: Sprache als Mittel der Hermeneutik*, BGBE 7 (Tübingen 1968).

The basic problem addressed by this work is the following: what is the relationship between reality, knowledge, thought, and language in Philo (cf. 3)? The author thus finds himself constrained to deal with a complex of themes going far beyond the mere notion of language. Indeed, in this perspective, cosmology and anthropology are merely a part of hermeneutics (cf. ch. 2), just as the theory of knowledge and the theory of the Logos are its foundation (cf. ch. 3). So far the double function of language stands out: on the one hand it synthesizes object and subject, on the other hand it mediates between past and present. But beyond this mediation Otte recognizes another, equally fundamental one: the word preserves within itself above all the true relation between thing and concept, between thing and man, and finally, between thing, man and concept (cf. 153, 49, 53). This obviously opens up a new line of inquiry directed towards the ideal world and the Logos ('that which the Logos divides or unites the word also divides or unites', 154). The final outcome of this is the ecstatic moment when 'man knows, without the mediation of the object, the measure of Being, as it presents itself through the Logos' (128). (The influence of Heideggerian philosophy makes itself felt here.) On the other hand language, which is also man's creation and belongs only indirectly to God (inasmuch as he grants the faculty), is 'a being' like man and like the sensible world: from the former it reproduces the tripartition of body, soul, and nous (cf. 19ff.); on the latter it operates by revealing the essential nature of immanent logos (cf. 121). For a more detailed and comprehensive judgment on this work, see the extensive and perceptive review by Nazzaro cited below. Reviews: F. Petit, *RThAM* 35 (1968) 324; T. Boman, *ThLZ* 94 (1969) 767f.; F. F. Bruce, *Eras* 21 (1969) 464ff.; J. S. Croatto, *RevBib* 31 (1969) 250; P. di Fidio, *RSLR* 5 (1969) 635ff.; A. V. Nazzaro, *PI* 11 (1969) 339ff.; W. R. Schoedel, *JBL* 88 (1969) 241f.; A. Segovia, *ATG* 32 (1969) 309f.; B. Studer, *FZPhTh* 17 (1970) 251f.; G. Delling, *OLZ* 66 (1971) 536ff. (= R672)

6828. M. PHILONENKO, *Joseph et Aséneth: introduction, texte critique, traduction et notes*, SPB 13 (Leiden 1968) *passim*.

The *Romance of Joseph and Aseneth* and Philo are chiefly linked together by the concept of μετάνοια (repentance). In this sense Aseneth, the model for all proselytes, corresponds perfectly to Philo's Abraham. Other points of contact include the theme of virginity (cf. 58), which, in the spiritual sense, characterizes repentance. (= R673)

6829. J. RAASCH, 'The monastic concept of purity of heart and its sources: III Philo, Clement of Alexandria, and Origen', *StudMon* 10 (1968) 7-55, esp. 8-13.

In Raasch's opinion Philo was the first thinker to combine Platonic *katharsis* and the Stoic ideal of *apatheia* (in its function of guarding the mind) with the Jewish conception of the thoughts of the 'heart' determining a fundamental moral orientation in man (cf. 12). Other scattered references to Philo are found in the section of the article devoted to Clement and Origen. (= R674)

6830. F. RICKEN, 'Gab es eine hellenistische Vorlage für Weish 13-15?', *Bib* 49 (1968) 54-86.

The view that Sap. Sal. 13-15 derives from a pre-existing apologetic schema goes back to Wendland (cf. 54). He noted remarkable parallels between this passage, *Contempl.* 3-9, and *Decal.* 52-81, where five forms of worship are described: worship of the elements, stars, demigods, idols, and animals. The author criticizes these views and, after an analysis which pays ample attention to the bibliography on the subject, reaches the following conclusions. (1) Sap. Sal. 13-15 is an expression of biblical and not of Hellenistic thought. (2) No pre-conceived apologetic schema underlies the three passages; their similarities are to be explained by positing a direct dependence of the passage from *Decal.* on Sap. Sal. and by regarding the passage from *Contempl.* as a summary of *Decal.* (3) The author of Sap. Sal. is said to have freely elaborated motifs which he found in the apologetic literature of his time. Abstract in *StPh* 2 (1973) 64. (= R675)

6831. D. ROKEAH, 'A new onomasticon fragment from Oxyrhynchus and Philo's etymologies', *JThS* 19 (1968) 70-82.

Certain corrupt transcriptions of Hebrew names in an onomastic fragment from Oxyrhynchus significantly anticipate Philo's etymologies. The author concludes from this evidence that Philo had no knowledge of Hebrew. Abstract in *StPh* 2 (1973) 64f. (= R676)

6832. S. SANDMEL, 'The confrontation of Greek and Jewish ethics: Philo, *De Decalogo*', *CCARJ* 15 (1968) 54-63, 96.

Philo's ethics certainly originate in the synthesis he achieves between Jewish and Greek morality. In this synthesis, however, the two components do not play equal parts. Nor was this possible, for they are heterogeneous elements: Greek ethics is the product of speculative analysis, Jewish ethics is revealed by God. In the relationship between the two, the latter prevails over the former. Sandmel in fact concludes (63): 'Philo's exposition of Jewish ethics is Grecian. His explanation of how the ethics is defined is Grecian. His bill of particulars is often Grecian. Yet he never abandons the Jewish assumption that the laws are literally the product of revelation.' Abstract in *StPh* 2 (1973) 65. (= R679)

6833. F. SCHRÖGER, *Der Verfasser des Hebräerbriefes als Schriftausleger*, Biblische Untersuchungen 4 (Regensburg 1968) *passim*.

Any assertion that the author of Hebrews drew directly on Philo's work should be treated with reserve. Instead of an immediate literary dependence, it is better to speak of an influence mediated through a common spiritual background and the heritage of Alexandrian culture. The author of Hebrews was certainly acquainted with the better-known traditions of Hellenistic Judaism in a simplified and philosophically ungrounded form, probably through the vehicle of synagogal homiletics. In comparing Hebrews with the works of Philo, it is legitimate to hypothesize two directions in the development of late Judaic scriptural interpretation: one predominantly allegorical and leading to Philo, the other mainly concerned with the history of salvation and leading to the author of Hebrews. (= R680)

6834. A. SKRINJAR, 'Theologia Epistolae IJ comparatur cum philonismo et hermetismo', *VD* 46 (1968) 224-234.

The author of the First Epistle of John had certainly not read the writings of Philo, but probably heard them being discussed. Both authors reveal influence of the same cultural atmosphere. Abstract in *StPh* 2 (1973) 76. (= R681)

6835. J. Z. SMITH, 'The Prayer of Joseph', in *Religions in Antiquity* (**6804**) 253-294, esp. 265-268.

The points of contact between the *Prayer of Joseph* and Philo, besides their analogous interpretation of the concept of Israel, consist in the use of similar epithets attributed, in the one case, to Jacob-Israel, in the other, to the Logos. (= R682)

6836. R. A. STEWART, 'The sinless high-priest', *NTS* 14 (1967-68) 126-135, esp. 131-135.

A brief analysis of the relations between the Logos, the figure of the high priest, and Melchizedek. Between Logos and high priest there is certainly a model-copy relationship, but without contiguity: the high priest is the copy of a copy, while the Logos is the 'ultimate archetype' (133). Abstract in *StPh* 2 (1973) 69. (= R683)

6837. B. H. STRICKER, 'De praehelleense ascese', *OMRL* 49 (1968) 18-39; 'Tijd', *OMRL* 49 (1968) 40-56.

In these articles the views of Egyptians, Greeks, Romans and Jews on the subjects of asceticism and time are discussed with reference to primary sources, among which are the writings of Philo. In the second article, in the context of a discussion of the two birds of the Sun-god at Delphi (Pindar, *Pyth.* IV 4), the author gives a complete overview and translation of all the texts on the Cherubim in Philo. (RAB/DTR)

6838. F. SZABÓ, 'Le Christ et le monde selon S. Ambroise', *Aug* 7 (1967) 258-305; 8 (1968) 5-39, 325-360, esp. 325-360.

'Ambrose's literary debt to Philo is particularly pronounced in his early writings' (332). In order to demonstrate this, the author compares *Sacr.* 64-68 with *De Cain et Abel* 1.8.32 and shows their similarities. He proceeds to affirm, with regard to the concept of logos, that *all* the Stoic themes and terms traceable in Ambrose may have reached him through Philo. In this passage the doctrine of the Stoa would have thus already been largely purged of its pantheistic connotations. (= R684)

6839. W. H. Wagner, *The paideia motif in the theology of Clement of Alexandria* (diss. Drew University 1968), esp. ch. 3.

As part of the background of the paideia motif in Clement the contribution of Philo to this subject is presented, with special attention paid to Philo's views of the soul, ἀρετή, σοφία, as well as παιδεία itself. (DTR; based on *DA* 29-1595A).

6840. E. I. WATKIN, 'New light on Philo', *DR* 86 (1968) 287-297.

A review of *Philon d'Alexandrie* (**6747**), with a short summary of each contribution. The author's 'personal impression after reading these papers is that Philo was spiritually rather than intellectually great, that his insights were not those of an acute intelligence but of a deep religious experience' (288). (DTR)

1969

6901. G. BOLOGNESI, 'Note al testo armeno del *De Providentia* di Filone', in *Armeniaca: mélanges d'études Arméniennes; publiés à l'occasion du 250ᵉ anniversaire de l'entrée des Pères Mekhitaristes dans l'Île de Saint-Lazare (1717-1967)* (Venice 1969) 190-200.

On the basis of the Armenian version, it is possible to reconstruct the different versions and variants of the Greek original used by the translator of the *De Providentia*. The author also shows how wrong inferences are drawn from the Armenian version by Colson in his edition of Philo's Greek text and by Mras in his edition of the Greek text of

Eusebius' *Praeparatio Evangelica.* (= R685)

6902. M. M. BRAYER, 'Psychosomatics, hermetic medicine, and dream interpretation in the Qumran literature: psychological and exegetical considerations', *JQR* 60 (1969) 112-127, 213-230, esp. 119ff.

Philo is used as a source of historical information on the sects of the Essenes and Therapeutae. (= R686)

6903. I. CHRISTIANSEN, *Die Technik der allegorischen Auslegungswissenschaft bei Philon von Alexandrien*, BGBH 7 (Tübingen 1969).

An important and innovative study which attempts for the first time to examine the subject of allegorical exegesis against the background of Greek (esp. Platonic-Aristotelian) philosophy. In the Introduction the author gives a succinct *status quaestionis*, including the research that has been carried out into the historical antecedents of Philo's allegorical interpretation. The first chapter is devoted to the foundations of the allegorical technique. The thesis presented here is that the method of division (*diaeresis*) in the interpretation of texts forms the technical basis of Philo's hermeneutics. The analysis is mostly based on Platonic texts (*Sophist, Phaedrus*). The connection with Philo is made by demonstrating the close relationship of division to dialectic, of which Philo can be considered a master. The second chapter deals with the subject of symbolic explanation. Here the point of departure is always formed by the words of the scriptural text. These, however, may express several and sometimes contradictory concepts, as is shown in the analysis of diverse passages of Philonic exegesis. The author discovers a fixed pattern in Philo's method of symbolic explanation. In determining the identity or similarity between biblical concept and explanatory other (ἕτερον), the ten Aristotelian categories function as a powerful tool. The third chapter discusses the technique of division. Christiansen holds that allegorical interpretation uses the dialectical procedure of division and that division is in fact the way one comes to a proper understanding of the conceptuality underlying Scripture. This is illustrated by a lengthy analysis of *De agricultura*. The fourth chapter attempts to define allegory, which is understood as a form of interpretation by means of which a unit of ideas, contained implicitly in the text, is explained through an equivalent concept. In Philo's view, as the author concludes in the final chapter, the sacred texts are absolutely infallible revelations of incorporeal and divine truth. Allegory is the method required to come to understand such truth. It is by means of allegory that God, who is the source of all certain knowledge, gives man access to the truth. REVIEWS: F. F. Bruce, *Eras* 21 (1969) 589ff.; W. Pöhlmann, *LM* 8 (1969) 429f.; A. Salas, *CDios* 183 (1969) 329; A. Segovia, *ATG* 32 (1969) 296; H. J. Sieben, *ThPh* 44 (1969) 576ff.; M. Bouttier, *ETR* 45 (1970) 215; W. Schultz, *ThLZ* 95 (1970) 109f.; B. Studer, *FZPhTh* 17 (1970) 252f.; W. A. Bienert, *ZKG* 83 (1972) 396f.; P. Nautin *RHR* (1973) 95ff. (= R687)

6904. C. COLPE, 'Der Begriff "Menschensohn" und die Methode der Erforschung messianischer Prototypen (I und II)', *Kairos* 11 (1969) 241-263, esp. 253f.

A brief analysis of the concept of the heavenly man in Philo, together with a series of references to the relevant texts. The author outlines the connections of the subject with the vast complex of related cosmological and theological themes. (= R688)

6905. H. DÖRRIE, 'Präpositionen und Metaphysik: Wechselwirkung zweier Prinzipienreihen', *MH* 26 (1969) 217-228; reprinted in *Platonica minora*, STA 8 (Munich 1976) 124-136.

Dörrie argues that in addition to the Platonist system of prepositional metaphysics discussed by W. THEILER in his study *Die Vorbereitung des Neuplatonismus* (Berlin 1930, 1964²), there is also a Stoic-Gnostic series. Philo, like Plutarch, is acquainted with both, but shows a preference for the latter because of its focus on a single ἀρχή. Philo's theological thought shows greater sophistication than that of Plutarch. (= R689)

6906. G. FRIEDRICH (ed.), *Theologisches Wörterbuch zum Neuen Testament*, vol. 8 (Stuttgart 1969; English translation, Grand Rapids 1972).

Cf. above **3807**. Contains: H. BALZ, art. ὕπνος κτλ (sleep), 551-2; G. BERTRAM, art. ὕβρις κτλ (violence, arrogance), 302-3; G. DELLING, art. τέλειος (complete, perfect), 71-2; art. ὕμνος κτλ (hymn), 499-500; W. GRUNDMANN, art. ταπεινός κτλ (humility), 15; H. KÖSTER, art. τόπος (place), 201-2; art. ὑπόστασις (existence), 582; K. H. RENGSTORF, art. τέρας (miracle), 121-2; art. ὑπηρέτης κτλ (servant), 536-7; W. SCHRAGE, art. τυφλός κτλ (blind), 285-6; E. SCHWEIZER, art. υἱός κτλ (son), 356-7. (DTR)

6907. M. HENGEL, *Judentum und Hellenismus: Studien zu ihrer Begegnung unter besonderer Berücksichtigung Palästinas bis zur Mitte des 2. Jh.s v.Chr.*, WUNT 10 (Tübingen 1969); second edition revised and enlarged (Tübingen 1973); English trans. (London 1974, 1980²) *passim*.

Although the author discusses subjects very close to Philo and cites his writings countless times, he does not devote a specific section to him. The work is nonetheless of interest because it indicates the fundamental themes arising from the confrontation between Jewish tradition and Hellenistic and Sapiential speculation, themes indispensable to the interpretation of Philo (see esp. 275-318). Moreover the study's controversial thesis of the fundamental Hellenization of Palestinian as well as Diaspora Judaism is of direct relevance to an evaluation of Philo's place in Jewish thought. (= R692)

6908. C. LARCHER, *Études sur le livre de la sagesse*, Études bibliques (Paris 1969) esp. 151-178.

An analysis of the relations between Sapientia Salomonis and Philo, with particular reference to *Mos.* and *QG*. Apart from that, the author stresses that the chief connection between the works is their common postulation of a natural knowledge of God, and that from a philosophical point of view, Philo's themes are richer than those of Sap. Sal. On the other hand, many ethical, religious, and anthropological themes, as well as a large number of verbal expressions (listed on p. 178) testify to the fact that both authors belong to the same tradition of Alexandrian Judaism, but that they underwent different developments within it. See further **7947**. (= R693)

6909. S. LAUER, 'Philon von Alexandrien: sein Leben und seine Welt, sein Werk und seine Wirkung', *IsrW* 69 (1969) 88-90.

A brief outline of Philo and his works. (= R694)

6910. B. LOHSE, *Askese und Mönchtum in der Antike und in der alten Kirche*, Religion und Kultur der alten Mittelmeerwelt in Parallel- forschungen 1 (Munich-Vienna 1969), esp. 95-110.

Two accounts are presented on the place of Philo in the history of asceticism, the first on the Therapeutae, the second on Philo himself. In the case of the former, if Philo's reports are reliable, it is possible to discern a mixture of Jewish and Greek motives for the origin of the movement (note the refusal to eat meat, which is not derived from the Old Testament). In the case of Philo, an examination of his views on the subject of ethics and in particular asceticism, shows his importance in that he was the first to introduce philosophical asceticism into Jewish theology, although this was not carried out in a systematic way. Philo thus plays a mediating role between the Greek tradition and the early Church. The two chief features of his achievement were the incorporation of piety towards God in the catalogue of virtues and the identification of natural law with Mosaic law (cf. 110). (= R695)

6911. P. L. MAIER, 'The episode of the golden Roman shields at Jeru- salem', *HThR* 62 (1969) 109-121.

The author uses Philo purely as a historical source for reconstructing the episode in question. He observes that Philo is the only source of information which we have in this case (cf. 109), but that his hostile attitude to Pilate, which cannot be matched against other sources, does not plead for his objectivity. Abstract in *StPh* 1 (1972) 87. (= R696)

6912. W. H. MARE, 'The Greek altar in the New Testament and inter- testamental periods', *GrJ* 10 (1969) 26-35.

The term βωμός, commonly used by the Greeks to indicate the altar, is rarely found in the New Testament. The author reconstructs the specific sense and historical meaning of this word, summarizing its evolution from the LXX to Philo and Josephus. (= R697)

6913. R. MARTIN-ACHARD, *Actualité d'Abraham*, Bibliothèque Théologique (Neuchatel 1969), esp. 132-137.

Briefly illustrates the character and role of Abraham in Philo's works on the basis of a number of basic texts. The author notes certain similarities between Philo's Abraham and the Therapeutae (cf. 136). (= R698)

6914. C. MERCIER, 'La version arménienne du *Legum allegoriae*', in *Armeniaca* (cf. **6901**) 9-15.

Starting from a re-examination of the codices, the author uses the Armenian version to correct Cohn's text of the *Legum allegoriae*. He proposes 89 variants, some of which are quite significant. (= R699)

6915. A. MICHEL, 'La philosophie en Grèce et à Rome de ~ 130 à 250 [*sic!*]', in *Encyclopédie de la Pléiade* 26, *Histoire de la philosophie*, vol.1 Orient, Antiquité, Moyen-âge (Paris 1969) 773-885, esp. 827-832.

A brief synoptic presentation of Philo and his thought, dealing both with historical and with exegetical and philosophical aspects. Philo is said to culminate 'a movement through which Jewish universalism seeks to assimilate classical universalism' (827), by promoting the contact 'between religion and philosophy' (829). (RR)

6916. B. MONDIN, *Filone e Clemente: saggio sulle origini della filosofia religiosa* (Turin 1969, Vatican City 1984²).

This general presentation of Philo is explicitly propaedeutic (cf. viii) and for the most part recapitulates views expressed in previous articles, which we have described at the appropriate places. The most original and interesting part of the study (no doubt giving us a glimpse of the reasons for the author's particular interest in Philo) is the final part, in which the relations between faith and reason are analyzed. The author's conclusions on the subject are as follows: 'Philo does not assign to philosophy the task with which the Scholastics later entrusted it, namely to prove the appropriateness of revelation and to defend it from the attacks of its adversaries. Philosophy is given not a directly apologetic but rather an indirect function. It will cause revelation be valued by making it understood, for if revelation is understood it compels of its own accord' (76). REVIEWS: V. Grossi, *ScC* Suppl. bibl. 3 (1971) 239ff., *PI* 12-14 (1970-72) 106ff.; C. Vansteenkiste, *Ang* 48 (1971) 243f.; S. Cartechini, *DoC* 25 (1972) 72ff.; C. Martin, *NRTh* 94 (1972) 743. (= R700)

6917. A. NEHER, 'La philosophie hébraïque et juive dans l'antiquité', in *Encyclopédie de la Pléiade* 26 (cf. **6915**) 50-81, esp. 69-81.

Philo is part of a vast and complex philosophical and exegetical tradition centred in Alexandria. But in achieving a synthesis of differing and disparate elements he must also be credited with his own contribution, e.g. the addition of a universal and cosmopolitan dimension to Mosaic law (73). The article goes on to highlight some essential elements of Philo's theology, in particular his theory of creation. (RR)

6918. M. PAGLIALUNGA DE TUMA, 'Séneca y Filón de Alejandría en la temática calderoniana', in *El sueño y su representación en el barroco español*, CuS 1969, 90-105.

The motifs of life-as-a-dream and the 'sudden irruption of the transcendent' (105), characteristic of the work of Calderón de la Barca, have significant antecedents in Philo, especially in the *De somniis*. (RR)

6919. *Reallexikon für Antike und Christentum*, edited by T. KLAUSER *et al.*, vol. 7 (Stuttgart 1969).

Cf. above **5016**. Contains: H. O. SCHRÖDER, art. 'Fatum (Heimarmene)', 524-636, esp. 576-7 (fate, εἱμαρμένη).

6920. K. G. RICHTER, 'Zur Formgeschichte und literarischen Einheit von Joh 6, 31-58', *ZNW* 60 (1969) 21-55, esp. 25-28.

A comparative analysis of the text in question with corresponding passages in Philo, Paul, and the Midrash, as seen in relation to the theme of manna. Richter shows that in this passage John 'deviates' from earlier models. Extensive discussion of the monograph of P. Borgen (**6507**). Abstract in *StPh* 2 (1973) 63f. (= R703)

6921. S. SANDMEL, *The first Christian century in Judaism and Christianity: certainties and uncertainties* (New York 1969), esp. 107-142.

An extensive and clear presentation of Philo which touches on all essential aspects of his thought, including its relations to Early Christianity. Sandmel's point of view is general, however, and he refrains from explaining or assessing specific philosophical subjects; instead, he joins into the broad debate on Philo's personality and his role in ancient thought. In this context Sandmel reaffirms the necessity of taking Philo back to his scriptural roots, which are often neglected. As far as his philosophical thought is concerned, Philo can be described as perfectly Greek, but the philosophy which he expresses serves to clarify religious intuitions which are certainly Judaic. (= R704)

6922. H. SÉROUYA, *Les étapes de la philosophie juive: antiquité hébraïque* (Paris 1969), esp. 189-341.

An overall presentation of Philo which takes its point of departure from the Wolfsonian interpretation, though with due reservations (cf. 339ff.). Philo's thought is regarded as the expression of a particular form of mysticism, anchored to a solid philosophical structure which combines Jewish and Hellenistic elements, but in which the Jewish element prevails. That becomes evident through the central role of theology (cf. 239), in which the concept of God, one, transcendent, spiritual, and creator, blots out the Greek horizon and draws together Philo's entire thought, through his cosmology ('Philo is not concerned ... with cosmology; his only interest is God', 274), through his theory of the Logos ('... the Logos cannot have a truly separate existence; it is an imprint of the Divinity', 257), and through his moral theory ('the essential concern of Philo's metaphysics is to provide and explain the moral relations of all beings with God', 335). For Sérouya the nearest points of reference to Philo are Plotinus and Neoplatonism (cf. 341), and not Spinoza, as Wolfson would have it. Philo and Spinoza represent the two extremes of a single spirituality: 'Philo is the father *par excellence* of the great mystics, just as, on another level, Spinoza is the father of metaphysics' (341). (= R705)

6923. G. C. STEAD, 'The Valentinian myth of Sophia', *JThS* 20 (1969) 75-104, esp. 90-104.

Many assumptions of Valentinian thought can be reconstructed from Philo's 'mental equipment' (90). One cannot speak of a direct relationship between the two (the form of Philonic cosmology is Stoic, whereas Gnosticism contains no traces of Stoicism). What one can affirm is that it is possible to account for the genesis of the *sophia* myth by proceeding from the Philonic type of Hellenistic Judaism. (= R706)

6924. G. THEISSEN, *Untersuchungen zum Hebräerbrief*, StNT 2 (Gütersloh 1969), esp. 143-152.

See below **7021**. (= R707)

6925. E.E. URBACH [אורבך .א.א], פרקי אמונות ודעות – ל"חז [*The sages – their concepts and beliefs*] (Jerusalem 1969) *passim*.

Subsequently published in English; see **7551**.

6926. G. VERMES, 'He is the bread – Targum Neofiti Exodus 16:15', in *Neotestamentica et Semitica: studies in honour of Principal Matthew Black* (Edinburgh 1969) 258-263; reprinted in *Post-biblical Jewish studies*, SJLA 8 (Leiden 1975) 139-146, esp. 143ff.

Philo's association of manna with logos and his attribution of its descent to the intercession of Moses (*Migr.* 121f.) are used to elucidate a curious text in Targum Neofiti. (DTR)

6927. H. A. WOLFSON, 'Greek philosophy in Philo and the Church fathers', in *The crucible of Christianity* (New York-London 1969) 309-316, 354; reprinted in I. TWERSKY, G. H. WILLIAMS (edd.), *Studies in the history of philosophy and religion*, vol.1 (Cambridge Mass. 1973) 71-97.

The author's aim is to explain the relations between Greek philosophy and the Church Fathers. Since, historically speaking, the transition from one to the other runs through Philo, the article essentially confines itself to underlining motifs common to some of the Fathers (above all Origen, Clement, and Justin) and Philo. The chief points of contact are presented as the following: (a) the recognition of a structural analogy between human and divine wisdom; (b) the explanation of this analogy on the basis of a referral – whether direct or indirect – to the divine origin of virtue; (c) a particular use of allegorical interpretation which did not reach the Fathers directly from Greek philosophy, but through Philo and via Paul; (d) the subordination of philosophy to faith; (e) the use of various fundamental philosophical doctrines, e.g. the ideas and the Logos. (= R708)

1970

7001. Y. AMIR [עמיר .י], פרוש דתי למושג פילוסופי אצל פילון ['A religious interpretation of a philosophical term in Philo'], in M. ROZELAAR and B. SHIMRON (edd.), ספר זכרון לב"צ כ"ץ [*Commentationes ad antiquitatem classicam pertinentes in memoriam... B. Katz*] (Tel Aviv 1970) 112-117.

Subsequently published in German and English; see **8310**. (= R709)

7002. Y. AMIR [עמיר .י], הרעיון המשיחי ביהדות ההלניסטית [= 'The messianic idea in Hellenistic Judaism'] *Mahanayyim* 124 (1970) 54-67.

Subsequently published in German and in an English abstract; see **7302**.

7003. Y. AMIR [עמיר .י], האלגוריה של פילון ביחסה לאלגוריה ההומרית [= 'Allegory in Philo and its relation to Homeric allegory'] *Eshkolot* 6 (1970) 35-45.

Subsequently published in German and English; see **8306**.

7004. D. BAËR, 'Incompréhensibilité de Dieu et théologie négative chez Philon d'Alexandrie', *PrOrth* 8 (1969) 38-46; 11 (1970) 143-153.

The theme of God's unknowability and ineffability in Philo discloses a philosophical problem: 'what theophany can reveal God's unknowability without violating it?' (40). Philo does not resolve this aporia. But the author points out that Philo's negative theology is resolved into a series of 'supra-affirmations' in which each 'not' contained in the definition of God corresponds to a 'beyond'. This transfer has no justification in philosophy or exegesis; on the contrary, its foundation is existential. At any rate the point is – and this is the specific concern of the second part of the article – that God's unknowability produces, in a strictly logical sequence of thought, the whole theory of the intermediaries, which does no more than repeat in different guises the same aporia of origin from which it arises. Abstract of the first part in *StPh* 1 (1972) 76. (= R711)

7005. R. A. BAER, *Philo's use of the categories male and female*, ALGHJ 3 (Leiden 1970).

As Daniélou rightly observes in the review cited below, this work shows 'the bipolarity of Philo's thought on sexuality, seen both as an aspect of creation and as the origin of sin'. Yet it needs to be said that this second aspect and all the negative connotations which it carries clearly dominate. For the most part Baer's analyses here confirm the general view of Philo in that they give evidence of his efforts to spiritualize the content of the Bible. The decisive move in this process is the substitution of the male-female dualism by the higher dualism between sexual and asexual, so that, for example, man 'in the image' should not be regarded as 'androgynous', but as transcending the very categories of sexuality. The same applies to all things strictly connected with the divine being: *sophia*, the Logos, *arete*, as well as the rational soul. We should not be misled by the fact that Philo often defines the *nous* as masculine: there is in reality a realignment of meaning here by which 'male' comes to carry asexual (i.e. spiritual) connotations and 'female' sexual connotations (cf. ch. 3). This interpretation becomes clear when transposed to the ethical level. Here the progress of the soul is represented by Philo (though not frequently; cf. 66) as becoming 'man', becoming 'one', becoming 'virgin'. The category of male is therefore the first step on the road of asceticism, at the end of which lies the renunciation of sexuality. It is therefore clear that Philo's dialectic has nothing to do with the mythological-sexual speculation of the Gnostics, which, from a formal point of view, uses the same terminology (cf. 66-83). REVIEWS: F. Petit, *RThAM* 37 (1970) 152; J. Daniélou, *RecSR* 59 (1971) 45ff.; N. Walter, *ThLZ* 98 (1973) 278ff.; H. F. Weiss, *OLZ* 68 (1973) 146ff.; D. Winston, *JBL* 92 (1973) 303f.; F. Bovon, *RThPh* 5 (1975) 304. (= R710)

7006. H. BAUMGARTEN, 'Vitam brevem esse, longam artem: das Proömium der Schrift Senecas *De brevitate vitae*', *Gymn* 77 (1970) 299-323, esp. 320-323.

The author finds in Philo *Somn.* 1.9ff. an important antecedent of the theme in question and, even more significantly, of the Senecan expression *vitam brevem esse*. This observation obviously does not entail a direct connection between the two, but it does allow the hypothesis to be advanced that both thinkers drew on a single intellectual context and, from a literary point of view, on a common genre, possibly the Stoic diatribe. (= R712)

7007. S. BELKIN, 'Levirate and agnate marriage in rabbinic and cognate literature', *JQR* 60 (1970) 275-329, esp. 294-303.

The institutions of levirate and agnate marriages are analyzed in this article in various periods of their development and on the basis of different sources, one of which is Philo. Philo, however, does not deal with the levirate marriage as such, but with the much vaster legal problem of inheritance. Belkin discusses this subject at length and with constant reference to the Rabbinic tradition. (= R713)

7008. H. D. BETZ, 'The Delphic maxim γνῶθι σαυτόν in Hermetic interpretation', *HThR* 63 (1970) 465-484, esp. 477-482.

Because Philo lived in Egypt, the probable origin of the Hermetic writers, Philo is a prime source for explaining the exact cultural meaning of Hermetic literature. An analysis of the Delphic maxim in Philo and in the *Poimandres* reveals many similarities, but also basic differences. Betz observes that the Hermetic author would not have been able to agree with Philo's refutation of astrology, nor, of course, with his loyalty to the Mosaic law. (= R714)

7009. G. BOLOGNESI, 'Giacomo Leopardi recensore e critico di testi armeni', in *Leopardi e l'Ottocento: atti del II Convegno Internazionale di studi leopardiani, Recanati 1-4 ottobre 1967* (Florence 1970) 65-79.

Bolognesi draws attention to G. Leopardi's *Annotazione*, which discusses the Armenian translation of Philo's works, with particular regard to *Prov.* and the question of the usefulness of the Armenian version for reconstructing the original Greek text, corrupted in the indirect tradition as found in Eusebius' *Praeparatio Evangelica*. In addition to the instances reported by Leopardi, Bolognesi lists other cases where the Armenian version helps to correct the traditional Greek text. He also notes that Leopardi isolated errors in the Armenian version which are only partly to be attributed to the ancient translator: sometimes they are due to Aucher's inaccurate Latin translation and sometimes to mistakes made by Leopardi himself. Some of the problems dealt with in this work were taken up again in a lecture held at the Linguistic Institute of the Academy of Sciences of the S.S.R. of Armenia, published in Armenian under the title: 'Meaning and value of the ancient Armenian translations of Greek texts' in *Istoriko-Filologičeskij Zurnal*, Akademija Nauk Armjanskoj SSR 85 (1979) 54-61. (= R715)

7010. G. BOLOGNESI, 'Postille sulla traduzione armena delle *Quaestiones et solutiones in Genesin* di Filone', *AGI* 55 (1970) 52-57.

Taking as its point of departure the quotation of Homer *Od.* 17.485-488 in *QG* 4.2, this work sets out to establish the exact Greek text underlying the Armenian version (not always successfully recovered by R. Marcus), in order to determine possible defects due (a) to wrong readings and erroneous interpretations of Greek forms by the translator, or (b) to variants in the manuscript tradition of the Greek text, or (c), more simply, to inaccuracies in the Armenian manuscript tradition. (= R716)

7011. H. BRAUN, 'Das himmlische Vaterland bei Philo und im Hebräerbrief', in O. BÖCHER and K. HAACKER (edd.), *Verborum veritas: Festschrift für G. Stählin zum 70. Geburtstag* (Wuppertal 1970) 319-327.

The concept of the heavenly home as 'city of God' is connected in both Philo and Hebrews with the dualism earth-heaven and with a whole series of corresponding oppositions (wisdom-vice, heavenly man-earthly man, abstinence-passions, etc.) which are derived from the Old Testament, but only by virtue of an allegorical interpretation which changes their sense. In Philo's case, moreover, the 'heavenly home' is strictly related to the celestial nature of the wise man's soul. On the basis of these elements and a careful analysis of the different types of dualism which characterize the two texts, the author concludes that, in relation to this theme, Hebrews is indebted to Philo, but not in the sense of a 'mere passive reception' (326). Abstract in *StPh* 1 (1972) 78f. (= R717)

7012. G. W. BUCHANAN, *The consequences of the covenant*, NT.S 20 (Leiden 1970), esp. 242-251.

Philo's work is used to reconstruct the essential features of the culture of the Essenes and the Therapeutae. Buchanan discusses not only the specific rules of conduct which characterize these sects, but also the economic rules of the Essenes (cf. 242ff.), on which Philo is particularly well-informed. (= R718)

7013. H. CAZELLES, 'L'anaphore et l'Ancien Testament', in *Eucharisties d'Orient et d'Occident: semaine liturgique de l'Institut Saint-Serge*, Lex Orandi 46 (Paris 1970) 11-21, esp. 16ff.

Cazelles advances a hypothesis of great importance ('Philonic *eucharistia* has a sacrificial character and refers back to the Old Testament *tôdah*', 17), later to be shared and elaborated by Laporte (**7223**), but in this article he does no more than skim over the arguments necessary for a documented justification. (= R719)

7014. J. DANIÉLOU, *L'être et le temps chez Grégoire de Nysse* (Leiden 1970), esp. 116-132.

The image of the borderland (μεθόριος) applied to man in order to indicate his intermediate nature between two realities, is derived from Philo and exercized a huge influence on Nemesius and particularly Gregory of Nyssa. Both he and Philo use the image of the borderland to indicate: (a) the nature of man, intermediate between rational and irrational (cf. 119f.); (b) human life, suspended between good and evil (cf. 122ff.); (c) the concept of the Logos standing at the boundary between created and uncreated (cf. 126ff.); (d) once again man who, at the beginning of his spiritual progress, is suspended between matter and spirit and, at the end, marks the border between human and divine (cf. 128ff.). (= R720)

7015. O. DREYER, *Untersuchungen zum Begriff des Gottgeziemenden in der Antike: mit besonderer Berücksichtigung Philons von Alexandrien*, Spud 24 (Hildesheim-New York 1970).

Although this carefully researched study deals with the subject of 'what is fitting to God' (θεοπρέπεια) in various ancient authors up to and including Plutarch, more than half the book concentrates on Philo (68-145). The two components of Philo's thought, Jewish and Greek, become apparent in his use of the divine attributes. The Greek component is responsible for the philosophical aspect; the Jewish component accounts for the faith in a personal God-father-creator, to whom man can turn in prayer and for mercy. In Philo the latter element is clearly predominant: 'the innate faith in the living God of the Old Testament shatters the ontological armour of Philo's philosophical speculation' (148, quoted from S. J. Klein, *RGG*[3] 2.1742). For Plato too, observes Dreyer, the demiurge was personal, but he was not a god to whom one could turn in prayer. In Philo, however, Plato's first theological principle of Goodness-Being becomes Goodness-Being of God. For Plato as well as for Philo, God is perforce concerned with good; but in the first case that is the result of metaphysical necessity, in the second of free will. For the Greeks it was man who went in search of God, for Philo it is God who reveals himself. Similarly, what was inconceivable for the Greeks (i.e. that man was not the active subject of his deeds and his virtue) becomes dogma in Philo: it is in fact God who creates virtue in man. For both the Greeks and Philo what is fitting for God has an exemplary function for man, but Philo looks less to the divine action than to what that means for man's action towards God. The author also has a keen eye for the methods of allegorical exegesis used by Philo, particularly in relation to texts that portray actions that do not befit the divine nature. (= R721)

7016. U. DUCHROW, *Christenheit und Weltverantwortung: Traditionsgeschichte und systematische Struktur der Zweireichelehre*, Forschungen und Berichte der Evangelischen Studiengemeinschaft im Auftrage des Wissenschaftlichen Kuratoriums 25 (Stuttgart 1970), esp. 80-92.

Philo is regarded as a mediator between the Platonic conception of the 'interior man' and the Pauline conception, especially as the result of his representing the new form of Platonic interpretation typical of Hellenistic Judaism. The concept of interior man is presented by Philo in different ways: (a) as the idea of man as pure *nous*, prior to the creation of earthly man; (b) as *nous* or *hegemonikon* and as the conscience of the empirical individual; (c) as the reality represented by the figure of Moses. These diverse positions are examined by the author with regard to their ethical and political implications. He shows how Philonic thought tends to assume the nature of an anthropological dualism in which Hellenistic-Jewish-Sapiential elements interact with the Stoic-popular philosophical tradition (cf. 90). (= R722)

7017. B. EFFE, *Studien zur Kosmologie und Theologie der Aristotelischen Schrift 'Über die Philosophie'*, Zetemata 50 (Munich 1970), esp. 17-23.

Philo's works are used here mainly to reconstruct Aristotle's arguments on the eternity of the cosmos, the author being convinced (cf. 9) that Philo was – whether directly or indirectly – acquainted with the contents of Aristotle's *De philosophia* and that much of the material in *Aet.* was derived – whether directly or indirectly – from this work. From a historical-philosophical point of view, however, the task of distinguishing accurately between what was originally Aristotelian and what Philo or some other intermediate source has added or modified constitutes a highly delicate problem (cf. 17-20). (= R723)

7018. J. ERNST, *Pleroma und Pleroma Christi: Geschichte und Deutung eines Begriffs der paulinischen Antilegomena* (Regensburg 1970), esp. 30-36.

Having analyzed the instances of the term πλήρωμα in Philo's writings, the author distinguishes four different meanings of *pleroma*, all of which can be traced back to the basic dualism that this concept expresses on a theological level. God is for Philo one and, at the same time, everything; and if he is also in the world and fills it, that does not mean that he ceases both to be creator of the world and to transcend it. (= R724)

7019. G. GIRALDI, 'Filone e il "Dio che si fa uomo"', *Sist* 9 (1970) 65-67.

From Philo's affirmation that 'it is easier for a God to become man than for a man to change into God' (*Legat.* 118) and from the complete absence of messianic concerns in his writings, the author infers that Philo was acquainted with Christian beliefs and that he intentionally made no mention of them because they were too far removed from his mystical and moral ideas and from his method of interpreting the biblical revelation. (= R725)

7020. S. GIVERSEN, 'L'expérience mystique chez Philon', in S. S. HARTMAN, C. M. EDSMAN (edd.), *Mysticism: based on papers read at the symposium on mysticism held at Abo on the 7th-9th September, 1968*, Scripta Instituti Donneriani Aboensis 5 (Stockholm 1970) 91-98.

The aim of this article is to determine how far it is possible in Philo's view to have an experience of God. On the one hand, the author observes, there is the infinite otherness and incomprehensibility of God, and on the other hand there is the possibility for man of attaining to the *visio Dei*. It is probably necessary to make a distinction between seeing (ὁρᾶν) and understanding (καταλαμβάνειν) God: the latter would seem to lie beyond man's power. (= R726)

7021. O. HOFIUS, *Katapausis: die Vorstellung vom endzeitlichen Ruheort im Hebräerbrief*, WUNT 11 (Tübingen 1970), esp. 248-259.

This text makes only fleeting references to Philo, but at the end of the work the author devotes an appendix to the meaning of the term κατάπαυσις in Philo's writings. The appendix is occasioned by Theissen's criticism (cf. **6924**) of certain views which Hofius explains in this book. It is therefore necessary to deal with the two texts together, since separately they lack point. On the basis of a common relation to the Gnosis, Theissen traces a clear parallel between the use of *katapausis* in Philo and in Hebrews. At the same time he affirms that Philo's position on this subject is equivocal, since on the one hand he maintains that God's atemporal nature is rest, and on the other hand asserts that God's nature is creative activity, and that for this reason peace is not proper to man, not even to the pious man. Only the second position, according to Theissen, corresponds to Philo's inmost conviction; the first is explained as a concession to tradition. Hofius rejects these views and on the basis of a well-documented analysis draws the following conclusions. (a) For Philo, God's nature is at the same time rest and creative activity, and the two aspects are not antithetical, but complement one another. (b) Similarly the idea that man can take part in God's rest is not a tradition which Philo simply adopts and later refutes, but it too forms one of his profound convictions. (c) God and rest are not identical, interchangeable concepts in Philo, as they are in the Gnosis. (d) If Theissen's view connecting Philo with the Gnosis cannot be confirmed, his other views relating Philo to the author of Hebrews cannot be substantiated either. (= R729)

7022. H. J. HORN, 'Antakoluthie der Tugenden und Einheit Gottes', *JbAC* 13 (1970) 5-28, esp. 22-24.

In dealing with the relations between Philo and Origen, the author adstrues 'the Philonic interpretation of the virtues in their relations with each other and with the Good to the role which the relationship genus-species plays in Philo's doctrine as a whole' (22). The picture which emerges is clearly Platonic, but the identification of Good and pure Being which was essential to Platonic metaphysics is not found in Philo. (= R730)

7023. R. A. KRAFT, 'Jewish Greek scriptures and related topics: reports on recent discussions', *NTS* 16 (1970) 384-396, esp. 388-390.

A brief discussion of the latest publications in Philonic studies, full of suggestions and proposals for research. (= R731)

7024. J. LAPORTE, 'La chute chez Philon et Origène', in P. GRAN-FIELD and J. A. JUNGMANN (edd.), *Kyriakon. Festschrift J. Quasten*, 2 vols. (Münster 1970) 1.320-335.

With regard to the subject of the fall, Philo 'reasons on the basis of four types or models of man. Origen, on the other hand, follows a scheme of sacred history' (322). Philo's typology is summed up in the two figures of the 'moulded man' and 'man in the image', and, from a religious point of view, in the varying degrees of acceptance of the divine spirit by each type. Thus for Philo the experience of the fall 'happens in man and happens during his sojourn on earth' (326). In contrast to Origen, there is no question of salvation or damnation being discussed in relation to an anterior life or nature. (= R732)

7025. A. MADDALENA, *Filone Alessandrino*, Biblioteca di Filosofia: saggi 2 (Milan 1970).

This book is packed full with ideas, but is also written in a very difficult style, so that at times it has been misunderstood by reviewers. It needs more than one reading for full comprehension, partly because Maddalena does not read Philo in an 'aseptic' and detached (or, as it is usual to say, objective and technical) manner, but rather with great involvement and a deep conviction of the vitality and modernity of Philo's thought. In short, Maddalena deeply believes in what he reads and holds the view that there is meaning in everything Philo wrote. Of his comprehensive views, the following are the most important. In the first place, Philo is an original thinker, but unlike the great Greek thinkers he was not able to create an original language *as well*; that is why he availed himself of existing languages, according to what he found useful, but for the purpose of saying different things from what these languages originally expressed. (The interpreter is therefore not allowed to argue as follows: Stoic language is used here, so a Stoic doctrine of inspiration is involved, etc., but each time he must understand what new element Philo is introducing and why he chooses this particular form of language to say it.) Moreover, Philo wished to give expression to a faith, and for this reason did not want to use the concepts of logically enchained thought, because they would make this faith rigid. Among the key elements of this faith, the most important is the notion of the spirit, a conception which profoundly modifies Greek anthropology, epistemology, ethics, and even eschatology: it is the spirit which converts and transfigures the human mind and the life of man. We also draw attention to Maddalena's original interpretation of the Logos, which is said to coincide in a certain sense with God: 'If I am not mistaken, therefore, the Son of God is, in Philo, God, as the Father is God: but the Father is God inasmuch as we somehow may intuit that He is substantially his secret, beyond what He has manifested of himself to us; but the Son is God as He reveals himself to us through his work. The Father and the Son are a single God...' (313ff.). As Nikiprowetzky concludes in his lengthy review (and as the above quote clearly indicates), this work is the most profound modern attempt to present a *Philo Christianus*. Although problematic as a whole, it is a goldmine of interesting and fruitful ideas. REVIEWS: P. Courcelle, *REA* 72 (1970) 486f.; F. Petit, *RThAM* 37 (1970) 153; J. Daniélou, *RecSR* 59 (1971) 45; R. Joly, *AC* 40 (1971) 247f.; C. M. Pifarré, *StudMon* 13 (1971) 514; P. Sacchi, *RSLR* 7 (1971) 333ff.; G. Scarpat, *Paid* 26 (1971) 236ff.; J. Cazeaux, *Gn* 44 (1972) 651ff.; A. Francotte, *RPhL*

70 (1972) 212ff.; J. E. Ménard, *RSR* 46 (1972) 161f.; A. V. Nazzaro, *Vich* 1 (1972) 180f.; F. Piñero, *EM* 40 (1972) 540f.; R. T. Wallis, *CR* 22 (1972) 341f.; S. Lilla, *ASNP* 3 (1973) 1163ff.; C. Sorge, *GM* 28 (1973) 236f.; V. Nikiprowetzky, *RHR* 187 (1975) 204ff. (= R734)

7026. A. V. NAZZARO, 'Nota a Filone *De migratione Abrahami* 8', *RFIC* 98 (1970) 188-193.

After carefully analyzing Philo's characteristic method of quotation, Nazzaro concludes that the expression πρόσεχε σεαυτῷ should not be read as a textual quotation of the Bible, but as a properly Philonic maxim, although one that is inspired by various Old Testament passages. (= R735)

7027. A. V. NAZZARO, 'Il ΓΝΩΘΙ ΣΑΥΤΟΝ nell'epistemologia filoniana', *AFLN* 12 (1969-1970) 49-86.

The Delphic maxim which plays such an important role in Philo's epistemology and ethics is examined here in a three-way comparison of the Platonic (on which Philo bases himself), the Gnostic and the Neoplatonic conception. Philo's point of view is strongly original; in fact, if for Plato 'know thyself' consists in a 'lucid reflection on one's own faculties and spiritual possibilities' (75), and for the Gnostics and Neoplatonists in a direct knowledge of God, for Philo it corresponds to the first step towards intellectual knowledge of God, which is achieved by admitting one's own insignificance and which is preliminary to the 'flight' towards God. (= R736)

7028. V. NIKIPROWETZKY, *La troisième Sibylle*, Études Juives 9 (Paris 1970) *passim*.

This is certainly the most extensive and in-depth work on the subject to be published in our period. Consequently, the analysis of the relations between the *Third Sibyl* and Philo, who constitutes a constant point of reference, also reaches some important results with regard to the reconstruction of Jewish-Alexandrian culture. See also the post-humously published article, 'La Sibylle juive et le 'Troisième Livre' des 'Pseudo-Oracles Sibyllins' depuis Charles Alexandre', *ANRW* 2.20.1 (Berlin 1987) 460-542. (= R737)

7029. A. P. ORBAN, *Les dénominations du monde chez les premiers auteurs chrétiens*, Graecitas Christianorum Primaeva 4 (Nijmegen 1970), esp. 13-15, 110-111, 150-151.

Analyzes the meaning of the terms κόσμος and αἰών-αἰώνιος in Philo. With regard to the first term, which is more extensively dealt with, Orban shows how, by way of the meaning 'heaven', the term *kosmos* in Philo was also used to indicate the Platonically inspired concept of the intelligible world (κόσμος νοητός), a development which the author appears to regard as an original contribution on Philo's part. (= R738)

7030. A. ORBE, 'El dilema entre la vida y la muerte: exegesis prenicena de Deut. 30, 15.19', *Gr* 51 (1970) 305-365, 509-536, esp. 309-315.

Philo reconciles the conflict between God's omnipotence and infinite goodness and man's free will by conceiving freedom as the possibility of voluntarily choosing good. In this sense 'evil derives from the sinner and good from the single divine cause' (315).

This clearly shows the distance that separates the Stoic sage, for whom virtue is an achievement, and the Philonic wise man, for whom virtue is a gift of God. (= R739)

7031. J. H. RANDALL, *Hellenistic ways of deliverance and the making of the Christian synthesis* (New York-London 1970), esp. 112-117.

A brief outline of Philonic philosophical thought, largely based on Wolfson's views. (= R740)

7032. E. SCHWEIZER, 'Die "Elemente der Welt" Gal. 4, 3.9; Kol. 2, 8.20', in *Verborum veritas* (**7011**) 245-259.

The phrase 'elements of the cosmos' which occurs in the texts indicated can be clarified on the basis of Philo's writings, since, chronologically speaking, these constitute the nearest evidence. Yet Philo's own position here is ambiguous, especially as regards the composition of the stars, of the soul, and the total number of elements (cf. 247f.). Another subject touched on by the author is the conception of the cosmos as the 'harmony of the whole' (cf. 249f., 255f.). (= R742)

7033. D. SOLOMON, 'Philo's use of ΓΕΝΑΡΧΗΣ in *In Flaccum*', *JQR* 61 (1970) 119-131.

In *Flacc.* 74 Philo uses the term γενάρχης to indicate the office usually referred to by ἐθνάρχης. The author is not satisfied with the general view held by scholars, who take the two terms to be synonymous. Attempting a more profound discussion, he indicates some subtle political motives which supposedly guided Philo in his choice of this term. (= R744)

7034. M. STEIN [שטיין .מ.], בין תרבות ישראל ותרבות יוון ורומא [*The relationship between Jewish, Greek and Roman cultures*] (Tel Aviv 1970), esp. 36-55, 93-105.

This collection of Stein's most important Hebrew articles is prefaced by an account of the author's life and work (Philonic research, 15-18) and concludes with a nearly complete bibliography of his writings in Hebrew and European languages. Among the essays collected are Stein's introduction to his translation (**2651**) of Philo's historical works (36-55) and a discussion of 'the Hellenistic midrash' (93-105). The latter article in fact amounts to a summary of Stein's German monographs (1929, 1931, = G-G nos. 910-1 under the name E. STEIN) on the topic. (DS)

7035. H. THYEN, *Studien zur Sündenvergebung im Neuen Testament und seinen alttestamentlichen und jüdischen Voraussetzungen*, FRLANT 96 (Göttingen 1970) *passim*.

Involuntary sins are for Philo the cause of all other sins; hence the charge of 'intellectualism' levelled at him by various scholars. In order to get to the bottom of this problem, the author analyzes the views of major Philonic scholars and reaches the following conclusions. (a) Philo was aware of the negativity of sin and the need for redemption. (b) He regarded man's predisposition to sin as a necessary consequence of being in the world and in the body, a captive of the passions. (c) Nevertheless, he did not have a fatalistic and deterministic view of human destiny, since he considered sin to be guilt and redemption a moral duty. (d) For Philo the redemption of sin can only be achieved through divine grace. In contrast to the 'ethical rigorism' of the Stoics, Philo's morality is one of grace and forgiveness. (= R745)

7036. W. C. VAN UNNIK, '"Tiefer Friede" (1. Klemens 2, 2)', *VChr* 24 (1970) 261-279.

In this analysis the author demonstrates the social-political meaning of the phrase 'profound peace' by considering the various cultural contexts from which it may have been drawn. In Alexandrian Judaism, and in particular Philo, peace is clearly identified with concord and contrasted with war and civil strife. Abstract in *StPh* 2 (1973) 70. (= R746)

7037. R. WILLIAMSON, *Philo and the epistle to the Hebrews*, ALGHJ 4 (Leiden 1970).

Definitive results are achieved in the linguistic analyses in this work, but it leaves the problem of the paternity of Hebrews and its thematic relations with Philo quite unresolved. For a more detailed justification of these assertions we refer to the review by Daniélou cited below, which shows how it is possible, on the basis of Williamson's analyses, to reach different and much more balanced conclusions. The author decisively refutes the views of Spicq – according to whom the author of Hebrews is totally indebted to Philo (cf. **5019**) – by pleading for the essential autonomy of both thinkers (cf. 579, and also below **7730**), though without excluding a common reference to a single cultural context. He reaches these conclusions in three different ways: (a) through an extensive analysis of some thirty terms and phrases common to Hebrews and Philo; to Hebrews, Philo, and the LXX; to Hebrews and the LXX; (b) through a detailed examination of many themes and ideas occurring in both authors; (c) through a comparative analysis of the use of the Old Testament and exegetical methods. With regard to the last two points some of the work's concluding statements are illuminating: while Philo 'has the ability to a very large degree of being able to employ the language of Scripture in a system that is totally foreign to the Bible' (i.e a philosophical system), in Hebrews there is no attempt whatsoever to extract philosophical truth from the pages of the Old Testament (576). At the same time Philo's notion of truth was opposite to that of the author of Hebrews: his Greek background made him try 'to grasp the world in its unalterable stability. The events of a particular, narrow period of human history could never have had for him the ultimate spiritual significance they held for the writer of Hebrews' (577). REVIEWS: J. Daniélou, *RecSR* 59 (1971) 47ff.; K. Berger, *JSJ* 2 (1971) 95ff.; R. McL. Wilson, *BiOr* 29 (1972) 228f.; G. Howard, *JBL* 92 (1973) 464f.; Hugues, *WThJ* 35 (1973) 349ff.; F. Bovon, *RThPh* 5 (1975) 305. (= R747)

7038. H. A. WOLFSON [וולפסון .א.צ], פילוסופיה היהודית היסודות .פילון הדתית [*Philo: foundations of Jewish religious philosophy*], 2 vols. (Jerusalem 1970).

The classic work (**4814**) in a slightly abbreviated Hebrew version. One notes the subtitle, which differs significantly from that of the English edition. See also **7420**. (DS)

7039. M. ZICARI, '"Nothus" in Lucr. V 575 e in Cat. 34, 15', in *Studia florentina, A. Ronconi Sexagenario oblata* (Rome 1970) 525-529.

In his lexical study of the term *nothus* in Catullus, the author tracks down a valuable antecedent in two passages from *Somn.* (1.23, 53). This antecedent would account for both the form and the meaning of the word. (= R748)

1971

7101. Y. AMIR, Art. 'Philo Judaeus', *Encyclopaedia Judaica* vol. 13 (Jerusalem 1971) 409-415; reprinted in S. T. KATZ, *Jewish philosophers* (Jerusalem 1975) 11-21.

A synoptic portrait of Philo's life and thought from a Jewish perspective. Most of the article concentrates on Philo's philosophy, with a strong emphasis on the influence of Stoicism. (DTR)

7102. A. BENGIO, *La dialectique de Dieu et de l'homme chez Platon et chez Philon d'Alexandrie: une approche du concept d'ἀρετή chez Philon* (diss. Paris 1971).

This dissertation is important from a theoretical point of view: it discusses the relationship between man and God in Philo and uses Platonic thought – which is closest to Philo because it is the most religious – as a background to make Philo's specific innovations stand out. Bengio's main subject is dialectic and he shows how it has two meanings in Philo: an ethical one symbolizing the dynamic nature of virtue, and a theological-anthropological one in which 'God and man actively collaborate and human nature raises itself towards God by denying and overcoming itself on successive levels' (1). At the base of this dialectic the author posits a further conviction, namely that Philo's emphasis on man's role and his emphasis on the role of God, far from being distinct or, even worse, opposite, are actually a dialectically unified 'single identical exigency' (100). The author's inquiry also brings out certain differences between Plato and Philo which deserve to be mentioned. (1) Plato's God is the One-Good; Philo's is the biblical God. (2) Platonism ignores the problem of free will; Philo takes it into account, if only in an embryonic form. (3) Platonic wisdom is autonomous, Philo's theonomous. (4) Platonic *arete* shows a naturalistic morality, whereas that of Philo is a theological concept. Finally, we draw attention to the two appendices at the end of the work: one is devoted to Plato's influence on Philonic phraseology (cf. **3202**), the other to Gnostic features in Philo. (= R749)

7103. H. BRAUN, *Wie Man über Gott nicht denken soll: dargelegt an Gedankengängen Philos von Alexandria* (Tübingen 1971).

This work should be considered not as a scientific monograph, but rather as a personal exploration of Philonic thought which contains interesting philosophical and theological points. Philo's thought is approached directly with extensive references to the texts, but without the slightest recourse to secondary literature. We indicate the work's scope by translating the author's conclusion. 'The strong tensions that exist in the Philonic concept of God now lie fully exposed to view: God, the one who is without qualities and affections, but who is upset at the evil man and deals with him, albeit indirectly; God, this spiritual entity whose existence may be grasped, but cannot be understood by human thought; God, the only Being in the true sense, but who acts in a personal way. It was not actually my intention to show the theoretical problems which really exist here. Rather

I wished to demonstrate this: the unconditional, transcendent superiority of the divinity in no way obstructs the recognition of man's striving for reward; yet it certainly devalues the worldliness of the world and the humanity of man. This is not the way, I feel, that we should think about and expound God' (119). REVIEWS: F. Petit, *RThAM* 37 (1970) 295; Görz, *BiOr* 28 (1971) 410; L. Malevez, *NRTh* 94 (1972) 109; W. Wiefel, *ThLZ* 97 (1972) 575f. (= R750)

7104. P. COURCELLE, 'Philon d'Alexandrie et le précepte delphique', in R. B. PALMER and R. HAMERTON-KELLY (edd.), *Philomathes: studies and essays in the humanities in memory of P. Merlan* (The Hague 1971) 245-250.

Self-knowledge is for Philo the first step of the ascent to God. In this way the Delphic precept is incorporated in a perspective which is not purely anthropological, but religious and transcendental from the philosophical point of view. Abstract in *StPh* 2 (1973) 57. (= R751)

7105. G. DELLING, 'Von Morija zum Sinai (Pseudo-Philo *Liber Antiquitatum Biblicarum* 32, 1-10)', *JSJ* 2 (1971) 1-18.

The author notes several points of contact between Pseudo-Philo and *Mos.* 2.291 in relation to the episode of Moses' burial and his ascent to heaven, and concludes that the author of *LAB* is a faithful Jew, 'a witness to the religiosity of the period around 100 A.D.' (18). (= R753)

7106. D. A. HAGNER, 'The vision of God in Philo and John: a comparative study', *JEvTS* 14 (1971) 81-93.

We summarize here the abstract of this article published in *StPh* 1 (1972) 81f. One of the main differences between Philo and John concerns the role played by ecstasy in their religious conceptions. For Philo the vision of God is essential to salvation, whereas for John ethical conformance to the will of God is fundamental to this end. (= R753/a)

7107. L. HENAO ZAPATA, 'San Justino y las anteriores dialécticas Platónicas', *Fr* 38 (1971) 91-124, esp. 105-113.

The section dedicated to Philo in this work carries the title 'mysticism as dialectical road'. By means of this phrase the author refers to the process of the soul's purification which forms the essence of Philonic thought and presupposes, as its foundation, the doctrines of Platonic metaphysics. The theory of the Logos, however, shows Stoic influence, especially in its phrasing and terminology. But in view of the religious meaning of this doctrine and the fact that the Logos is the site of the ideas, the conception as a whole goes beyond Stoicism and stands in a context that is definitely Platonic (cf. 111f.). (= R754)

7108. P. HENDRIX, 'Een paasvigilie in Philo's De vita contemplativa', *NTT* 25 (1971) 392-397.

The form and content of the solemn vigil celebrated once every seven weeks by the Therapeutae (*Contempl.* 64ff.) is compared with the Easter vigil held in the Orthodox church on Easter Saturday (Great Sabbath). The author observes a number of similarities:

table with bread, wheat, singing, allegorical exposition of a biblical text, silence, recitation of the Song of Moses after the crossing of the Red Sea (Ex. 15:1ff.). (RAB/DTR)

7109. M. HENGEL, 'Proseuche und Synagoge. Jüdische Gemeinde, Gotteshaus und Gottesdienst in der Diaspora und in Palästina', in G. JEREMIAS, H. W. KUHN, H. STEGEMANN (edd.), *Tradition und Glaube: das frühe Christentum in seiner Umwelt; Festgabe für K. G. Kuhn zum 65. Geburtstag* (Göttingen 1971) 157-184 *passim.*

The role of the synagogue in Jewish society and religious life is reconstructed partly on the basis of Philo's evidence, who sees it as a school of worship and virtue as well as a school of true philosophy. (= R755)

7110. J. G. KAHN [ישׂר-כהן .י], אל רואה – ישׂראל ['Israel – videns Deum'], *Tarbiz* 40 (1970-71) 285-292.

Interpretation of *Somn.* 1.129-132 and *Praem.* 43ff. based on Kahn's earlier study (**6515**). The etymology of Israel (Gen 32:28) is understood as Jacob's turning in God's direction, that he might see the light of God himself, i.e. a theological application of the ancient theory of vision. English summary. (MM)

7111. S. R. C. LILLA, *Clement of Alexandria: a study in Christian Platonism and Gnosticism*, Oxford Theological Monographs (Oxford 1971) *passim* (esp. 80ff., 92ff., 191ff.).

A discussion of Clement's ethics cannot ignore the parallels with Philo. The author sees a continuity of tradition between Philo and Clement which in certain respects also runs parallel to developments in Neoplatonic thought. The main elements in this tradition can be summed up as follows: the distinction between μετριοπάθεια and ἀπάθεια, and the superiority of the former over the latter, is foreign to Middle Platonism, but links together Philo, Neoplatonism, and Clement. Hence the tendency to regard God as ἀπαθής and, consequently, the inclination to identify ὁμοίωσις θεῷ, the highest goal of ethics, with ἀπάθεια. Also in the areas of cosmology (doctrine of creation) and theology (doctrine of God and the Logos) Clement is greatly indebted to his Alexandrian predecessor. (= R756)

7112. E. LOHSE, *Umwelt des Neuen Testaments*, Grundrisse zum Neuen Testament: das Neue Testament Deutsch: Ergänzungsreihe 1 (Göttingen 1971), esp. 97-101.

A concise outline of Philo and his thought, with particular reference to his allegorical method and to his theology and anthropology. (= R757)

7113. J. MANSFELD, *The Pseudo-Hippocratic tract ΠΕΡΙ 'ΕΒΔΟΜΑ-ΔΩΝ ch. 1-11 and Greek philosophy*, Philosophical Texts and Studies (Assen 1971) *passim.*

In his analytical commentary on chs. 1-11 of the *Peri hebdomadon*, a tract in the Hippocratic corpus which is to be dated to the first century A.D., the author constantly refers to parallel literature, especially on arithmological and medical subjects. Many obscure points in Philo's work (esp. in *Opif.*, *Leg.*, and *Aet.*) are in this way illuminated. (RR)

7114. J. MARLOWE, *The golden age of Alexandria: from its foundation by Alexander the Great in 331 B.C. to its capture by the Arabs in 642 A.D.* (London 1971), esp. 241-244.

Some brief remarks on Philo illustrating Alexandria's 'cosmopolitan religious ferment' (241). (DTR)

7115. A. MENDELSON, *Encyclical education in Philo of Alexandria* (diss. Chicago 1971).

The aim of this work to put the concept of ἐγκύκλιος παιδεία in a proper perspective; for this purpose it conducts an analysis consisting of the following points: (a) an examination, in a Philonic context, of each of the disciplines which constitute the encyclical studies; (b) a study of the philosophical and theological contexts in which they occur in order to determine their function within Philo's entire system; (c) a consideration of the historical and pedagogical context which they express; (d) an analysis of the results of the encyclical studies; (e) a series of eight appendices examining specific themes, two of which are aimed at refuting Wolfson's and Goodenough's interpretations of the subject. The author's basic thesis appears to be this: although the inferior position of the encyclical studies with respect to philosophy must be taken for granted, this does not mean that their value is purely instrumental. The latter view – shared by almost all interpreters – misconstrues the objective of this kind of education, i.e. to develop the common man (cf. 5), who belongs to the class of men which Philo himself defines as being intermediate between the perfect man and the 'earthly' man (cf. 77ff.). Under point (c) the author advances the hypothesis that Philo's pedagogical thought reflects actual practice among some of the Jews in Alexandria (129), and on this basis he attempts to reconstruct the didactic practice and organization of the Alexandrian Jews. Of particular interest are the observations on Philo's so-called 'scepticism' (cf. 189f.). Mendelson holds that, with regard to culture, Philo always maintained a negative attitude balanced by a positive one (189); he attributes the first attitude to Philo's sceptical views and the second to his faith in the encyclical studies. Yet this attitude is not contradictory, in the first place because different classes of men are concerned (the encyclical studies are for the 'intermediate', scepticism for the 'perfect' or for those 'intermediate' men who aspire to perfection); secondly because scepticism does not exclude the encyclical studies, but transcends them by inducing man to a higher form of knowledge: the knowledge of God (cf. 202). See further below **8235**. (= R758)

7116. B. MONDIN, *Il problema del linguaggio teologico dalle origini ad oggi*, Biblioteca di teologia contemporanea 8 (Brescia 1971), esp. 40-55.

The problem of theological language is debated at length by Philo, though not in the form of an organized and exhaustive treatment, but rather in isolated and specific discussions, some of which are of great importance for the evolution of theological language. Philo's thought on the subject is summed up by the author in the following axioms: not positive, but only negative terms can refer to God in a proper sense; positive terms can only be applied to God metaphorically (cf. 53). This procedure – Mondin observes – has a biblical origin and, from a philosophical point of view, probably derives directly from Plato (cf. 55). (= R759)

7117. J. NEUSNER, *The Rabbinic traditions about the Pharisees before 70*, part 3, 'Conclusions' (Leiden 1971).

Though hardly enough space is given to Philo, this work forms a useful preliminary study of the relations between Philo and the oral Pharisaic-Rabbinical tradition, a tradition which, according to the author, almost certainly existed. (= R760)

7118. M. PETIT, 'À propos d'une réminiscence probable d'Isaïe dans le *Quod omnis probus liber sit'*, in A. CAQUOT and M. PHILONENKO (edd.), *Hommages à A. Dupont Sommer* (Paris 1971) 491-495.

A scholarly note on *Prob*. 104, where three destructive elements (worms, mould, time) are alluded to instead of the two usually indicated by the Old Testament. The author recognizes the influence of Is. 51:8. Abstract in *StPh* 2 (1973) 62f. (= R762)

7119. P. POKORNÝ, *Der Gottessohn: literarische Übersicht und Fragestellung*, Theologische Studien 109 (Zurich 1971), esp. 18-21.

A concise presentation of various Philonic themes, with particular reference to the concepts of Israel and 'son of God', as seen in the context of Alexandrian literature. (= R763)

7120. H. R. RABINOWITZ [רבינוביץ .ר.ח], פילון – הדרשן היהודי הראשון בגולה [= 'Philo – the first Jewish preacher in the Diaspora'], *Niv Hamidrashia* (1971) 192-199 [Hebrew pp. קצב-קצט].

This popular survey of Philonic themes, largely dependent on the work of Belkin, portrays Philo as a pastoral figure with an predominant interest in questions of ethics and communal welfare. (DS)

7121. J. REILING, 'The use of ΨΕΥΔΟΠΡΟΦΗΤΗΣ in the Septuagint, Philo, and Josephus', *NT* 13 (1971) 147-156.

Whereas in the Old Testament the term nābî is used for both true and false prophets, in the LXX and Philo one encounters the term ψευδοπροφήτης which distinguishes authentic prophecy from pagan divination. In Josephus, however, no association of false prophecy with divination is found. Abstract in *StPh* 2 (1973) 63. (= R764)

7122. B. REVEL, 'The Karaite Halakah and its relation to Sadducean, Samaritan and Philonian Halakah', in P. BIRNBAUM (ed.), *Karaite Studies* (New York 1971) 1-88.

The author analyzes numerous passages – mostly dealing with legal and ritual subjects – in which Philo seems to depart from the traditional Halachah, while at the same time he shows extraordinary similarities with the Karaite Halachah. To account for this fact, Revel formulates two alternative hypotheses: either the Karaites were indebted to Philo, or both made use of a common tradition (cf. 84). The second hypothesis seems more likely, since it is supported by the evidence of Jacob Qirqisani – a 10th century Karaite – who, in citing a sect of the Magarites and 'an Alexandrian' held in great esteem by this sect, is supposedly referring to the Essenes and Philo. If this theory holds good – and the author is convinced it does –, then we must revise the commonly held opinion that Philo was unknown to the medieval Jewish tradition until at least the 16th century. Instead, we must allow for his influence on the early Karaite philosophers, not only from a theological point of view, but also with regard to their interpretation of biblical law and their religious practices (cf. 88). (= R765)

7123. J. SCHWARTZ, 'Philon et l'apologétique chrétienne du second siècle', in *Hommages à A. Dupont Sommer* (**7118**) 497-507.

Decal. 52-80 and *Contempl.* 3-9 seem to arrange the pagan gods according to a kind of scale of value (elements, planets, idols, animals). This scale recurs, though with appreciable variations – carefully reconstructed by the author – in various Christian thinkers of the 2nd century. Abstract in *StPh* 2 (1973) 66. (= R766)

7124. L. G. SEWELL, *Judgment in the writings of Philo Judaeus and the Epistle to the Hebrews: a study of the influence of Philo upon the author of Hebrews* (diss. New Orleans Baptist Theological Seminary 1971).

This study presents a rather uncritical examination of the entire subject of the relation of Philo and the Epistle to the Hebrews, with a particular focus on the subject of judgment. Chronologically, and from the viewpoint of ideas, style and vocabulary, it is possible that the writer of the Epistle was acquainted with a corpus of Philonic material which influenced his thought. Sewell argues that there are significant similarities between the two on the subject of judgment. Thus for both: (1) judgment has retributive and subjective elements; (2) it is the result of man's choice; (3) the recipients of judgment are all men, but the favoured have a greater responsibility (for Philo the Jews, for the writer of the Epistle the Christian believers; (4) it is a present judgment; (5) apostasy is man's holding himself off from God or refusing to align himself with God. Two differences between the two are put forward: (1) for Philo man's response to God is more passive and contemplative, for the author of Hebrews more active; (2) the latter 'has to contend with the Incarnation' (144). The most likely explanation for the similarities between the two writers is that both were influenced by a corpus of ideas on judgment and that 'the author of the Epistle used these ideas, modified by Christian concepts, while Philo remained committed to Jewish, Old Testament concepts, modified by his philosophical thinking' (142). (DTR)

7125. E. W. SMITH, 'The form and religious background of Romans VII 24-25a', *NT* 13 (1971) 127-135, esp. 133-135.

In Rom. 7:24 Paul follows 'formally and materially' a model of lamentation common in Hellenistic religious literature, as references to *Her.* 309 and Epictetus show. (= R767)

7126. A. STEINER, 'Warum lebten die Essener asketisch?', *BZ* 15 (1971) 1-28.

Philo's work is essentially used here as a historical source for reconstructing the life of the Essenes. His work (which attributes three aims to this sect: love of God, love of virtue, and love of one's neighbour) forms the starting-point of the author's inquiry, which ends with the conclusion that Essenian asceticism was specifically halachic in nature. (= R768)

210 PHILO BIBLIOGRAPHY

7127. W. THEILER, 'Philo von Alexandria und der hellenisierte *Timaeus*', in *Philomathes* (**7104**) 25-35; reprinted in C. ZINTZEN (ed.), *Der Mittelplatonismus*, Wege der Forschung 70 (Darmstadt 1981) 52-63.

Following up his earlier article (cf. **6531**), the author advances further evidence that suggests the existence of a Platonist commentator on whom Philo draws. At the end of the contribution he examines the new elements which Philo himself added to the themes of the *Timaeus*: Philo's 'Hellenistic modernization' of the *Timaeus,* Theiler observes, also underwent influences from the Stoic tradition, especially through Posidonius. Abstract in *StPh* 2 (1973) 69f. (= R769)

7128. U. TODINI, 'La cosmologia pitagorica e le muse enniane', *RCCM* 13 (1971) 21-38, esp. 35-37.

According to the author, Philonic evidence offers us 'a clear proof of the continuity of the theory already adumbrated in Plato and referred to by all later Pythagoreanizing sources, according to which the celestial harmony, achieved through the movement of the spheres, is presided over by the Muses' (36). (= R770)

7129. J. VIDAL, *Le thème d'Adam chez Philon d'Alexandrie* (diss. Paris 1971).

The double account of Adam's creation in the Old Testament is an intersection of many exegetical themes involving just as many philosophical meanings. The basic error made by previous studies on the subject is that they divided and isolated these themes, examining them separately and in this way forcing Philo's thought into perspectives which cannot contain it and which are doomed to dissolve in a sea of contradictions. This error can only be corrected by respecting the semantic unity of the Philonic text, a unity made up of scriptural, exegetical, and philosophical contexts. In the account of Adam's creation, observes the author, two conceptions of man's being are represented, one symbolized by man 'in image' and the other by the 'moulded man'. To these is added haggadic man, i.e. the wise man who unites features of both. The exegetical elaboration particularly emphasizes the identification of Adam with the intellect, while the interpretation of man in the Garden of Eden (cf. 43-47) introduces the ethical aspect of the theme. The creation of the animals and of Eve (cf. 68-91) and the temptation by the serpent are not only expressions of psychology and epistemology, but above all express the vast subject of the relationship between God and man. Adam's fall (cf. 68-91) serves to transform this figure 'into a symbol of mankind in general', i.e. into a τρόπος, a disposition of the soul which corresponds to the inverted image of the Patriarchs (cf. 123). In this sense we are far removed from Patristic thought, which sees in Adam the cause of all evil; instead, we find ourselves within the omnipresent theme of the soul's migration, which the author, following Nikiprowetzky, considers the centre of Philonic thought (cf. 4). The dissertation ends with an appendix on the relations between the figures of Adam and Noah (125-128). (= R771)

7130. W. H. WAGNER, 'Philo and paideia', *Cith* 10 (1971) 53-64.

In spite of the title the analysis of Philonic *paideia* actually only occupies the central part of this article (55-61), which is not so much an examination of this concept as a vigorous plea for Philo's central position in the evolution of religious thought. The theme of *paideia* is regarded as playing a significant role in Philo: it constitutes a study of man, his origins, his experiences, his social life and his destiny (cf. 62). Abstract in *StPh* 2

(1973) 70f. (= R772)

7131. J. WHITTAKER, 'God and time in Philo of Alexandria', in *God Time Being: two studies in the transcendental tradition in Greek philosophy*, SO.S 23 (Oslo 1971) 33-57.

The concept of eternity as 'eternal present', typical of Augustine, is often assumed to be of Philonic origin. The author does not refute this view, but indicates certain difficulties which arise not only from the necessity of accommodating four Philonic texts which are fundamental to the subject and which show many differences, but also from two terms which Philo uses to indicate this concept, αἰών and ἄχρονος. Whittaker concludes that the development of the doctrine of non-durational eternity derived from exegesis of *Timaeus* 37c-38c, possibly by Eudorus of Alexandria. It is unlikely that Philo's formulations are drawn from the same source, because they are too clumsy. Abstract in *StPh* 2 (1973) 71f. (= R773)

1972

7201. D. L. BALCH, 'Backgrounds of I Cor. VII: sayings of the Lord in *Q*; Moses as an ascetic ΘΕΙΟΣ ΑΝΗΡ in II Cor. III', *NTS* 18 (1971-72) 351-364.

The themes of continence and virginity and the strictly related theme of asceticism are characteristic of Christianity from the outset, but are specifically taken up by Paul in 1 Cor. 7 and 2 Cor. 3. They have clear antecedents in Philo (*QG* 2.49, *Mos.* 2.66-70), who represents the Jewish-Alexandrian religious sensibility. (= R774)

7202. M. BALTES, *Timaios Lokros Über die Natur des Kosmos und der Seele* , PhilAnt 21 (Leiden, 1972) *passim.*

In a highly detailed commentary on the text of Ps. Timaeus Locrus, Περὶ φύσεως, the author frequently uses Philo's works for purposes of comparison (though the parallels are not easily located for want of an index). It is concluded that the two authors relate to the same milieu of early Neopythagoreanism and Middle Platonism, possibly through mutual dependence on Eudorus. (RR)

7203. E. M. BARTH, *Evaluaties* (inaugural lecture Utrecht, Assen 1972), esp. 22-32.

Philo's use of the categories 'male' and 'female' is an example of the application of a dyad as an intellectual instrument for the understanding and description of the hierarchical relation 'spiritually superior to' as well as 'more valuable than'. 'Man' is a formal sign of 'the divine' without actually being divine himself, because 'he', in the view of Philo and many other thinkers, is in analogical relation to God, i.e. in contrast to 'woman' he is image-carrier of God. (RAB/DTR)

7204. S. BELKIN, [בלקין .ש], מדרשים בכתבי פילון ומקבילותיהם למאמרים במדרש הגדול ש"מקורם נעלם" ['Midrashim in Philo and their parallels of unknown source in Midrash Hagadol'], in M. ZOHORI, A. TARTAKOVER, H. ORMIAN (edd.), הגות עברית באמריקה [= *Hebrew thought in America*], 3 vols. (Tel Aviv 1972) 1.261-287.

Many midrashim in David b. Amram Adani's 13th century Yemenite anthology, *Midrash Hagadol*, which are not found in the traditional midrashic corpus, are juxtaposed with parallels from Philo and mediaeval commentators. Belkin states (267) that 'the purpose of the comparison is not necessarily to prove that Philo's writings were one of the sources of the *Midrash Hagadol*,... (but) to show that apparently both Philo...and the Midrash Hagadol drew from common sources, or from hidden channels of ancient books and traditions which have been lost ... and to point to the fact that the source of some of the material in *Midrash Hagadol* for which no parallels have been found [in the traditional Rabbinic sources] goes back to very ancient traditions, which antedate the compilations of the Tannaitic Midrash...' Twenty four examples are brought forward to illustrate this thesis. See also further **7402**. (NGC)

7205. H. D. BETZ, *Der Apostel Paulus und die sokratische Tradition: eine exegetische Untersuchung zu seiner 'Apologie' 2 Korinther 10-13'* , BHTh 45 (Tübingen 1972) *passim.*

The author frequently turns to Philonic writings in order to explain various philosophical principles in Pauline thought. In particular he refers at 30f. to the opposition between sophistic and rhetoric typical of Philo (but also common to Flavius Josephus), and at 128ff. to the Philonic (and Socratic) 'know thyself' motif and the related theme of οὐδένεια. (RR)

7206. W. A. BIENERT, *'Allegoria' und 'Anagoge' bei Didymos dem Blinden von Alexandria*, Patristische Texte und Studien 13 (Berlin-New York 1972), esp. 36-40, 44-45, 52-53.

The author turns to Philo on three occasions in particular: to illustrate the allegorical method (36-40); to indicate his connections with Origen (44ff.); and to discuss the concept of allegory (52ff.). Bienert points to the great importance of allegory in Philo as the instrument *par excellence* for interpreting the divine law. (= R775)

7207. P. BORGEN, 'Logos was the true light: contributions to the interpretation of the prologue of John', *NT* 14 (1972) 115-130; originally appeared as 'Logos var det sanne lys', *Svensk Exegetisk Årsbok* 35 (1970) 79-95; German translation 'Der Logos war das wahre Licht: Beiträge zur Deutung des johanneischen Prologs.', in A. FUCHS (ed.), *Theologie aus dem Norden*, StNT A2 (Linz 1977) 99-117; also reprinted in *Logos was the true light and other essays on the Gospel of John* (Trondheim 1983) 95-110.

The term logos, as related to the concept of light, in the Prologue of John is based on Philo's exegesis of Gen. 1:3 in *Somn.* 1.75. (= R777)

7208. J. CAZEAUX, 'Interpréter Philon d'Alexandrie: sur un commentaire du *De Abrahamo*, nᵒˢ 61-84', *REG* 84 (1972) 345-352.

Corrects Sandmel's study (**5519**) on a few points. We note in particular Cazeaux's interpretation, relative to the passages in question, of the superiority of seeing over hearing. These categories are traced back to the more general opposition between written law and oral law. Abstract in *StPh* 4 (1976-77) 89f. (= R780)

7209. J. CAZEAUX, 'Littérature ancienne et recherche des "structures"', *REAug* 18 (1972) 287-292.

This is an 'experiment' in the structural analysis of Philo's exegesis of Gen. 16:6-12 in *Fug.* 121-124, revealing a 'perfect coherence in its disparity and baroque nature' (292). (= R781)

7210. A. H. CHROUST, '"Mystical revelation" and "rational theology" in Aristotle's *On Philosophy*', *TF* 34 (1972) 500-512.

The road leading to the knowledge of God is twofold: by demonstration, starting from the cosmos, and by revelation, starting from God himself. The second road is preferred by Philo, but according to Chroust it finds an important antecedent in Aristotle's *De philosophia*. (= R782)

7211. P. COURCELLE, 'Verus homo', in *Studi classici in onore di Q. Cataudella*, vol. 2 (Catania 1972) 517-527, esp. 517-519.

Concisely illustrates the concept of 'true man' in Philo and many other pagan and Christian thinkers; the article is valuable for its extensive references to Philonic texts. (= R783)

7212. J. E. CROUCH, *The origin and intention of the Colossian Haustafel*, FRLANT 109 (Göttingen 1972) *passim*.

After collecting the principal Philonic texts concerned with the definition of social duties, the author points out that Philo allowed for the existence of two spheres in which the Law was transmitted: the synagogue and the family. In the latter case, the head of the family was the point of contact between both spheres, since he transmitted the Law to the women, children, and slaves who were not members of the synagogue. The Stoic influences on Philo's conception of social duties and the relations between Pseudo-Phocylides, Philo and Josephus on this theme are dealt with at some length in chapter 6 (84-101). (= R784)

7213. D. DELASSUS, *Le thème de la Pâque chez Philon d'Alexandrie* (diss. Lille 1972).

In Philo, according to the author, one cannot separate the theme of Passover from the overall interpretation of the Bible, an interpretation which is based on both allegory and an original ethical-religious doctrine. From this point of view Passover, which is connected to the more general theme of migration (cf. 24), corresponds to the first step of the soul's spiritual progress, which culminates in the moment of ecstasy. 'But to what extent is this Philonic conception related to the original conception of the feast?', the author asks (113). The Jewish Passover was essentially the record of a historical event corresponding to Jehovah's first intervention in the history of Israel (cf. 20). The Philonic interpretation in fact modifies the notion of Israel, which is no longer conceived as an ethnically and historically determined nation, but as a 'universal nation' (115). In this process of spiritualization Passover loses almost all its sacramental significance and assumes a psychological-moral meaning. (= R785)

7214. G. DELLING, 'Philons Enkomion auf Augustus: F. Paschke zum 60. Geburtstag in Verbundenheit zugeeignet', *Klio* 54 (1972) 171-192.

Philo's attitude to the Roman emperors is analyzed here with specific reference to the encomium to Augustus (*Legat.* 143-147). The author particularly emphasizes the feebleness of the epithets applied to the emperor, Philo being conditioned in the use of this terminology by the strict ties of his religion, which prevented him from assigning divine attributes to human beings. At the same time Philo was convinced that the sovereignty of the Roman emperor was not at all diminished by the fact that the Jews continued – as they had done under Augustus and Tiberius – to live in conformance with their own religious faith (cf. 191). Abstract in *StPh* 4 (1976-77) 91f. (= R786)

7215. J. P. DUMONT, *Le Scepticisme et le phénomène: essai sur la signification et les origines du pyrrhonisme*, Bibliothèque d'Histoire et de Philosophie (Paris 1972), esp. 147-154.

Ebr. 171-197 is traditionally held to be a source of prime importance for reconstructing the tropes of Aenesidemus. On the basis of a brief but rigorous analysis, the author claims that Philo's source was not in fact Aenesidemus, but an anonymous Sceptic, 'later than Timon, but earlier than Aenesidemus'. (= R787)

7216. M. J. FIEDLER, 'Δικαιοσύνη in der diaspora-jüdischen und intertestamentarischen Literatur', *JSJ* 1-3 (1970-72) 120-143.

The concept of δικαιοσύνη in Philo cannot be simply defined. The only constant element in the variety of meanings which it assumes is its close connection with the Greek philosophical world; but within this sphere its moves in all directions. Philonic *dikaiosune* 'has a Platonic side; especially a Stoic, but also a Pythagorean side. It is understood in a psychic-individual sense, but also in political-universal, mathematical, theological, legal and pedagogical senses' (128). (= R788)

7217. M. GIUSTA, 'ΑΝΕΥΠΡΟΦΑΣΙΣΤΟΣ: un probabile ΑΠΑΞ EIPHMENON in Filone *De aeternitate mundi* §75', *RFIC* 100 (1972) 131-136.

The passage in question is almost certainly corrupt. After examining the emendations proposed by earlier editors, the author offers and motivates his own reconstruction and interpretation of the text. Abstract in *StPh* 4 (1976-77) 92f. (= R790)

7218. C. GNILKA, *Aetas spiritalis: die Ueberwindung der natürlichen Altersstufen als Ideal frühchristlichen Lebens*, Theoph 24 (Bonn 1972), esp. 75-87.

The author collects and analyzes some Philonic texts on the allegory of the ages of man. Gnilka points out that it would be 'wholly false to understand the spiritualization of [the concept of] age as a mere exterior instrument of Philo's exegetical method. This spiritualization, like the transcendence of life's ages, should be seen against the background of Alexandrian religious philosophy' (82). In this specific context the particular cultural richness of Philo's thought – which the author interprets as a confluence of Platonism, the Peripatos, the Stoa, as well as of Jewish religiosity and Rabbinical erudition – is passed on, essentially unchanged, to Origen and, through him, to many other Christian thinkers (cf. 87-115). (= R791)

7219. P. GRELOT, 'La naissance d'Isaac et celle de Jésus: sur une interprétation "mythologique" de la conception virginale', *NRTh* 94 (1972) 462-487, 561-585, esp. 561-574.

The theme of virgin motherhood, as dealt with by Paul in Gal. 4:21-31 and in the Gospels, is not, as Dibelius would have it (*Botschaft und Geschichte*, vol. 1 (Tübingen 1953) 1-78), the restatement of a common and widespread *theologoumenon*, and even less a motif drawn from Philo's Alexandrian Judaism. An analysis of *Cher.* 45-47 (cf. 561-564) and of the allegorical meaning of Sarah (564-568) shows that this theme is used by Philo purely 'in support of a didactic exposition' related to the doctrine of the fertility of virtue (cf. 569). (= R792)

7220. R. G. HAMERTON-KELLY, 'Sources and traditions in Philo Judaeus: prolegomena to an analysis of his writings', *StPh* 1 (1972) 3-26.

This seminal contribution is mainly concerned with methodology, but in order to carry maximum conviction it also examines and assesses most of the major interpretations of Philo. In its entirety it is therefore an excellent reading guide to Philo. Among its many interesting observations, we cite the distinction drawn between 'formal tradition' or convention and 'material tradition', the former being defined as 'a custom governing the form or mode of a composition' and the latter as a 'congeries of words or ideas, whose substance is handed down in the community' (20). This specification would seem particularly relevant to the study of a philosopher like Philo, who is often reconstructed on the basis of poorly documented and largely hypothetical traditions, a process which paradoxically attempts to explain the known by the unknown. This paper was originally presented as a programmatic essay for the activities of the Philo Institute (see above **3301-6**). (= R793)

7221. M. HARL (with G. DORIVAL), *La chaîne Palestinienne sur le psaume 118 (Origène, Eusèbe, Didyme, Apollinaire, Athanase, Théodoret)*, vol. 1, *introduction, texte grec critique et traduction*, SC 189; vol. 2, *catalogue des fragments, notes et indices*, SC 190 (Paris 1972) *passim*.

Although Philo is not specifically dealt with in this work, we list it because he is often cited in the commentary to the text, and also because the exegetical chains often conceal important fragments from Philonic works, fragments which in part still need to be identified. Moreover the reader finds here much useful information on the relations between Philo and early Christian thought. (= R794)

7222. J. G. KAHN [ישר-כהן .י], הבעיות המיוחדות הכרוכות בתרגום כתבי פילון האלכסנדרוני לעברית ['Special problems in the Hebrew Translation of Philo's work'], *Proceedings of the Fifth World Congress of Jewish Studies* (Jerusalem 1972) 3.203-207 [Hebrew section]

The Hebrew translation of Philo's writings is a *desiderandum*, but the translator will have to pay attention to the following points: (a) Philo's quotations from the Bible follow the Septuagint and one must not render them in their traditional Hebrew version; (b) the etymologies can not be 'translated' but must be explained by notes; (c) the divine names have different connotations in Hebrew and in Philo's Greek; (d) philosophical and theological terms cannot always be rendered by those which medieval translators have coined; (e) the description of every-day-life given by Philo is foreign to the world of the Sages. Extensive English summary. (MM)

7223. J. LAPORTE, *La doctrine eucharistique chez Philon d'Alexandrie*, ThH 16 (Paris 1972); English translation *Eucharistia in Philo*, Studies in the Bible and Early Christianity 3 (New York-Toronto 1983).

The large scale of this work and especially the thoroughness of its introductory analyses – the term εὐχαριστεῖν and its derivatives are studied not only in Philo, but also in the biblical and Jewish (32-46) as well as non-Jewish contexts (23-32) – confer an undeniable authority to its conclusions. On this subject, therefore, the work reaches all but definitive results, even if some details remain subject to criticism. The study's guiding motif is an important one. The term *eucharistein* in Philo 'pervades the entire domain of theology and liturgy' (258) to the extent that its meaning threatens to be diluted and down-graded to the level of 'a notion of praise common to all branches of Hellenistic religiosity' (258). But that is only the exterior aspect of this theme. The richness which becomes obscured in a comprehensive survey reappears as soon as one manages to penetrate to its depths, using the Bible and the LXX as a starting-point. Then one discovers that Philonic thanksgiving is rooted in Mosaic law and in the sacrificial system of Leviticus. Its roots are not merely Jewish, therefore, but *wholly* Jewish, far removed even from the emancipated and Hellenizing Judaism of the synagogue (257). What Philo did was to emphasize and greatly extend the sphere of the Eucharist, ultimately transforming it into a universal 'eucharistic disposition'. Laporte has no difficulty in showing how this disposition has significant implications, not only for the theme of worship and religious feasts and for the celebrants of this worship, but also for cosmology and anthropology in general (the whole cosmos, through mankind and the high priest, gives thanks to God), for philosophy, since it 'affirms the existence of God at whom the Eucharist is directed' and finally, of course, for psychology, because 'the soul's interior life is the domain *par excellence* of divine activity' (263). REVIEWS: G. Delling, *ThLZ* 98 (1973) 593; J. Giblet, *RThL* 4 (1973) 119; M. Gilbert, *NRTh* 95 (1973) 789; R. G. Hamerton-Kelly, *JBL* 92 (1973) 630f.; C. Kannengiesser, *RecSR* 61 (1973) 374; E. J. Kilmartin, *ThS* 34 (1973) 498ff.; M. Messier, *MSR* 30 (1973) 195; C. M. Pifarré, *StudMon* 15 (1973) 498f.; H. Crouzel, *BLE* 75 (1974) 68; A. Paul, *RecSR* 62 (1974) 414; E. Starobinski-Safran, *RThPh* (1974) 223. Of the English edition: E. J. Kilmartin, *ThS* 46 (1985) 389. (= R796)

7224. J. C. H. LEBRAM, 'Eine stoische Auslegung von Ex. 3, 2 bei Philo', in *Das Institutum Judaicum der Universität Tübingen in den Jahren 1971-1972* (Tübingen 1972) 30-34.

Philo's commentary on Ex. 3:2 in *Mos.* 1.68-70, concerning the image of the burning bush which is not consumed, shows traces of Aristotelian and Stoic cosmology, particularly in the representation of fire as active element and the earth as passive element. Abstract in *StPh* 4 (1976-1977) 97ff. (= R797)

7225. B. L. MACK, 'Imitatio Mosis: patterns of cosmology and soteri-

CRITICAL STUDIES 1972   217

ology in the Hellenistic synagogue', *StPh* 1 (1972) 27-55.

Two metaphors are involved in *Mos.* 1.158-159: one dynamic (revolving around the concepts of guide and follower), the other graphic (relative to the concepts of paradigm and copy). The relationship between the two leads to the possibility of identifying Israel's journey, connected to the first metaphor, with the movement of the world, connected to the second, and, consequently, of interpreting the life of Moses from both historical-moral and cosmological points of view. Mack's aim is to show how the entire cosmological system is rooted in soteriological and theological concerns which reinterpret the Jewish credo and the nature and destiny of Israel in cosmic-universal terms (cf. 29). (= R798)

7226. J. W. MCKAY, 'The date of Passover and its significance', *ZAW* 84 (1972) 435-447.

Largely on the basis of Philonic evidence most scholars connect the original date of Passover with the phases of the moon, and specifically with the phase of full moon. In his discussion of these views the author points out that in the Philonic passages relevant to this subject a dominant role is played by the Greek philosophical notion of harmony, which is described as involving both the structure of the festive calendar and astronomical conceptions. (= R795)

7227. I. H. MARSHALL, 'The Jewish dispersion in New Testament times', *FaT* 100 (1972) 237-258.

Philo is regarded here as an orthodox Jew who was stubbornly faithful to the Law. He is cited at various times on account of the cultural and historical value of his work and his important role in the Jewish community of Alexandria. (= R799)

7228. G. MAYER, 'Aspekte des Abrahambildes in der hellenistisch-jüdischen Literatur', *EvTh* 32 (1972) 118-127.

Although it deals only briefly with Philo, this article is cited because in its examination of the subject of Abraham, it analyzes aspects of Hellenistic Judaism which are rarely explored, but are highly useful for an understanding of Philo's thought. Abstract in *StPh* 4 (1976-77) 98f. (= R800)

7229. A. MÉHAT, 'Clément d'Alexandrie et les sens de l'Écriture, Ier *Stromate*, 176, 1 et 179, 3', in J. FONTAINE and C. KANNENGIESSER (edd.), *Epektasis: mélanges patristiques offerts au Cardinal J. Daniélou* (Paris 1972) 355-365.

In *Strom.* 1.176.1 Clement discusses a four-part division of philosophy which is hard to understand without reference to Philo. The specifically Philonic aspect of the schema, however, is located in its structure rather than in its content. (= R801)

7230. S. MICHAELSON and A. Q. MORTON, 'The new stylometry: a one-word test of authorship for Greek writers', *CQ* 22 (1972) 89-102, esp. 95f.

Philo is one of the authors used as an example to test a new stylometric method based on the ratio of uses of the word αὐτός in the genitive compared with all uses of the word, a ratio which is claimed to be constant for any given author. (DTR)

7231. J. LE MOYNE, *Les Sadducéens* (diss. Paris 1972), esp. 60-62.

A brief but interesting note on Philo's position with respect to the dogmatic and cultural views of the Pharisees and Sadducees. (= R802)

7232. A. MYRE, 'La loi dans l'ordre moral selon Philon Alexandrie', *ScEs* 24 (1972) 93-113.

The author distinguishes three types of moral law in Philo: (a) a simple description of human action unrelated to any body of legislation; (b) 'a normative decree of right reason in contact with the divine Logos' (= natural law, 112); (c) the exemplary life of a perfectly virtuous man (= incarnate law). Especially the definitions under (b) and (c) imply an ontological foundation, a human means of access to 'the whole of being' from which the ethical principles of human behaviour must be deduced. Abstract in *StPh* 4 (1976-1977) 100f. (= R803)

7233. A. MYRE, 'La loi dans l'ordre cosmique et politique selon Philon d'Alexandrie', *ScEs* 24 (1972) 217-247.

One cannot distinguish in Philo between cosmic law and moral law. Strictly speaking, in fact, there is a single natural law deriving from God (who by nature stands above all laws) which, 'impressed in matter, governs the universe; written in man's heart ... rules his moral conduct; written in constitutions, governs political life' (245f.). At the centre of this system is man, who, inasmuch as he is corporeal, is subject to the law of nature; who, inasmuch as he is an ethical subject in accordance with the divine Logos, 'cannot but proclaim that which is in conformance with nature' (246); who, inasmuch as he is a political individual, is at once legislator and subject of the law. The latter case, however, involves a level of adherence to the law which is more external and superficial than the ethical level. Abstract in *StPh* 4 (1976-77) 100. (= R804)

7234. F. PARENTE, 'La "Lettera di Aristea" come fonte per la storia del giudaismo alessandrino durante la prima metà del I secolo a.C.', *ASNP* 2 (1972) 177-237, 517-567, esp. 524-567 *passim*.

In commenting on the *Letter of Aristeas* one can hardly avoid referring to Philo, who expresses a very similar cultural context. Parente, however, is not disposed to use Philo as a point of departure for reconstructing the influence of the Greek world on that of the Jews, as Goodenough did, since he holds that in the Hellenistic Judaic world Philo represents 'something absolutely individual' (545). (= R805)

7235. F. E. PETERS, *The harvest of Hellenism* (1972), esp. 300-306.

A supple and interesting account of Philo's role in Hellenistic and Jewish culture. Philo is regarded as a surprising example of Hellenized Judaism, i.e. quite the opposite of the clumsy anti-Hellenistic propaganda of the Maccabeans which was the rage in Jerusalem. Philonic Hellenism, based on the LXX and nourished by the various components of Greek thought, constitutes in the author's view an extremely interesting case of cultural openness. (= R806)

7236. *Reallexikon für Antike und Christentum*, edited by T. KLAUSER
et al., vol. 8 (Stuttgart 1972).

Cf. above **5016**. Contains: P. COURCELLE, art. 'Flügel (Flug) der Seele I', 29-65,
esp. 33-34 (wings or flight of the soul); E. DINKLER, art. 'Friede', 434-505, esp. 455-7
(peace, εἰρήνη); P. HADOT, art. 'Fürstenspiegel', 555-632, esp. 592-4 (ideal portrait of,
or advice given to, a ruler or king); J. HAUSSLEITER, art. 'Fruitio Dei', 538-55, esp. 543
('enjoyment of God', i.e. the relation of man to God in the religious or mystical sense);
B. KÖTTING, art. 'Fusswaschung', 743-777, esp. 758-9 (act or ritual of the washing of
the feet); O. MICHEL, art. 'Freude', 348-418, esp. 381-3 (joy); E. VON SEVERUS, art.
'Gebet I', 1134-1258, esp. 1168-9 (prayer).

7237. B. SCHALLER, Art. 'Philon von Alexandreia', *Der kleine Pauly*,
vol. 4 (Munich 1972) 772-776.

A brief but detailed account of Philo's life and thought, with bibliography, from the
viewpoint of classical scholarship. Abstract in *StPh* 4 (1976-77) 104. (= R807)

7238. A. N. SHERWIN-WHITE, 'Philo and Avillius Flaccus: a conun-
drum', *Lat* 31 (1972) 820-828.

Philo's work is used here only to reconstruct the political career of Flaccus, with
particular attention paid to questions of chronology. Abstract in *StPh* 4 (1976-77) 105.
(= R808)

7239. H. J. SPITZ, *Die Metaphorik des geistigen Schriftsinns: ein Beitrag zur allegorischen Bibelauslegung des ersten christlichen Jahrtausends*,
Münstersche Mittelalter-Schriften 12 (Munich 1972), esp. 14-19.

Philo is the great precursor of Christian allegorical interpretation. Origen in particular
is indebted to him. Both refer back to a Middle Platonic tradition, especially as regards
the interpretation of man's tripartite nature (man as body, soul, and spirit). This is in
turn strictly connected with the stratification of meaning in the biblical narrative (cf.
Contempl. 28, 78). (= R809)

7240. D. L. TIEDE, *The charismatic figure as miracle worker*, SBLDS
1 (Missoula 1972), esp. 101-137.

'The figure of Moses was one of the most important propaganda instruments that Jews
of the Hellenistic period appropriated for their competition with non-Jewish schools and
cults as well as inter-Jewish sectarian disputes' (101). At the same time this same figure
came to constitute the exact equivalent, in Jewish terms, of the Hellenistic sage, and thus
brought the two cultures closer to one another. On the basis of these assumptions it is
possible, in Tiede's view, to regard Philo's interpretation of Moses as a transposition of
the biblical text into a Hellenistic and, specifically, Stoic key (cf. 123), though one should
not ignore the important Middle Platonist influences on Philo's theories of ecstasy and
prophecy (cf. 112). The main point of this interpretation is that the 'divine' nature of
Moses does not lie in his power to perform miracles (in *Mos.* 1.85ff. this power is in fact
attributed to Aaron rather than to Moses), but in the fullness of virtue which he embodies.
On this basis it is possible to draw up a hierarchy – of degree and not of substance (cf.
120) – among the Patriarchs, who are essentially understood as models of ethical

perfection, from Enos, Enoch and Noah, to Abraham, Isaac, Jacob, and, finally, to Moses (109). (= R810)

7241. P. WENDLAND, *Die hellenistisch-römische Kultur, in ihren Beziehung zum Judentum und Christentum erweitert um eine Bibliographie von H. Dörrie*, Handbuch zum Neuen Testament 2 (Tübingen 1912, 1972⁴), esp. 201-211.

Dörrie's bibliography is a useful guide to historical and cultural aspects of Philo's *Umwelt.* (= R811)

7242. R. MCL. WILSON, 'Philo of Alexandria and Gnosticism', *Kairos* 14 (1972) 213-219.

In the author's view, 'the Bultmannian inclusion of Philo in the category of Gnosis is justified, *provided* that we remember that Gnosis is not yet Gnosticism' (219). Indeed, Gnosticism contains doctrinal elements which are not reflected to any significant extent in Philo's writings, and are moreover incompatible with the Old Testament revelation to which Philo remains faithful. It is true, however, that the philosophical substratum of the movement – i.e. Middle Platonism – is very close, though in a later stage of development, to Philonic thought, and this explains certain common features. But since Philo 'a new element has been introduced – the radical dualism which rejected this world and its creator, the divine tragedy, the tragic split in the Deity' (219). Abstract in *StPh* 5 (1978) 135f. (= R812)

1973

7301. Y. AMIR, 'Philo and the Bible', *StPh* 2 (1973) 1-8; German translation in *Die hellenistische Gestalt des Judentums bei Philon von Alexandrien*, Forschungen zum jüdisch-christlichen Dialog 5 (Neukirchen 1983) 67-76.

Under this rather general title the author offers some specific remarks on the meaning of Philo's allegorical interpretation. Clearly the latter is not be thought of as a mere play of images: the very fact that Moses is taken to be a philosopher drives Philo's entire exegetical system into the context of Greek philosophy. This does not occur without strain, however, since Mosaic philosophy is not purely speculative (like Greek philosophy), but religious in nature (cf. 7). (= R813)

7302. Y. AMIR, 'The Messianic idea in Hellenistic Judaism', *Immanuel* 2 (1973) 58-60; 'Die messianische Idee im hellenistischen Judentum', *FrRu* 25 (1973) 195-203 (= English summary and German version of Hebrew article, **7002**).

The passage at *Praem.* 163-172 is a vital source for our knowledge of the messianic idea in Hellenistic Judaism, for here Philo adopts popular traditions which he elsewhere generally refrains from using. Amir attempts a reading which detects popular motifs behind passages which Philo has transformed by means of more philosophical themes; e.g. the three advocates at §166 may have originally been the three Patriarchs. For Philo himself, however, such views represent no more than an exceptional sidetrack. (DTR)

7303. E. J. BARNES, 'Petronius, Philo and Stoic Rhetoric', *Lat* 32 (1973) 787-798.

Various passages of *Plant.* recall motifs from Petronius' *Satyricon.* In an overview of the two texts, the author isolates no less than six themes which they have in common. That does not imply a direct relationship between both writers, however, but simply that they follow a common critical tradition (cf. 793) which cannot be identified with an exact source. (= R814)

7304. H. D. BETZ, '2 Cor. 6:14-7:1: an anti-Pauline fragment?', *JBL* 92 (1973) 88-108.

The passage in 2 Cor. 6:16, where Lev. 26:12 is paraphrased, also has considerable resonances in Philo. Philonic texts variously related to this biblical text are briefly analyzed. Abstract in *StPh* 4 (1976-77) 88. (= R815)

7305. W. K. BIETZ, *Paradiesesvorstellungen bei Ambrosius und seinen Vorgängern* (inaug. diss. Giessen 1973), esp. 4-17.

Philo and Ambrose represent the beginning and the end of a single line of thought concerning the interpretation of Paradise. The whole structure of this dissertation conforms to this premiss. Bietz observes that, starting from God's act of creation, one sees in Philo's cosmology and anthropology a dualistic scheme of Platonic derivation which influences both his eschatological convictions and his conception not only of Paradise but also of man whose destination it is. The conception is spiritualized in Philo to such a degree that it is quite impossible to give it a precise location or definition. An examination of these themes in each of the authors discussed (Clement, Origen, Gregory of Nyssa, Tertullian, Ambrose) shows the repeated use of Philonic motifs. (= R816)

7306. J. E. BRUNS, 'The *Altercatio Jasonis et Papisci*: Philo, and Anastasius the Sinaite', *ThS* 34 (1973) 287-294.

Bruns cleverly reconstructs the history of an extremely difficult text quoted by Origen and others: the *Altercatio Jasonis et Papisci.* Philo enters into this discussion because, according to the evidence of Anastasius the Sinaite, the work in question had a different title which also included Philo's name. Philo, in fact, must have ousted the figure of Jason, at least from the title. In the author's view, this substitution can be explained by the high reputation which Philo enjoyed in the Christian world. (= R817)

7307. J. E. BRUNS, 'Philo Christianus: the debris of a legend', *HThR* 66 (1973) 141-145.

If we keep to the texts which have come down to us, the legend of Philo the Christian goes back to Eusebius. According to Bruns, however, it was probably created by Hegesippus, who was the author of a collection of legends about the Apostles and their contemporaries. Abstract in *StPh* 4 (1976-77) 89. (= R818)

7308. U. BURKHARD, *Die angebliche Heraklit-Nachfolge des skep-*

tikers Aenesidem, Habelts Dissertationsdrucke. Reihe klassische Philologie 17 (Bonn 1973), esp. 175-194.

In the opinion of H. VON ARNIM (*Quellenstudien zu Philo von Alexandria*, Berlin 1888), Philo's debt (*Ebr.* 167ff.) to Aenesidemus is made clear by the fact that both authors show the same Heraclitean influence. But Philo's Heraclitism has a quite specific character (182), is eclectic in form and profoundly original in content, so that it cannot be directly traced back to either Aenesidemus or the thought of the New Academy. On the other hand, Philo's systematic exposition of the tropes certainly goes back to the models of Aenesidemus (or one of his followers) (192ff.). One may therefore conclude that: (a) Philo regarded Aenesidemus as a genuine exponent of Sceptic philosophy; (b) Philo's Heraclitism can in no way be traced back to the supposed interpretation of Aenesidemus; (c) Philo's tropes testify against Aenesidemus' dependence on Heraclitus; (d) Philo himself did not think of Aenesidemus' philosophy as a synthesis of Heraclitism and Scepticism (194). (= R818/a)

7309. J. CAZEAUX, 'Aspects de l'exégèse philonienne', *RSR* 47 (1973) 262-269; reprinted in J. E. MÉNARD (ed.), *Exégèse biblique et Judaïsme* (Strasbourg 1973) 108-115.

Cazeaux gives here a sample of what one might call 'structuralist' analysis of Philonic texts. Philo, according to Cazeaux, proceeds by way of 'clusters (a text, an image, a biblical figure, a certain concept) which travel from one treatise to another and, like constellations seen from different planets, present themselves now from one angle, now from another' (268). Abstract in *StPh* 4 (1976-77) 89. (= R819)

7310. H. A. FISCHEL, *Rabbinic literature and Greco-Roman philosophy: a study of Epicurea and Rhetorica in early Midrashic writings*, SPB 21 (Leiden 1973), esp. 35-41.

A Targum passage denying the existence of compensatory justice is related by the author to *Det.* 1ff., where Philo allegorically interprets the quarrel between Cain and Abel. The author sees here traces of an anti-Epicurean polemic, for this philosophy, in Philo's view, opposes and denies all virtue. (= R822)

7311. G. FRIEDRICH (ed.), *Theologisches Wörterbuch zum Neuen Testament*, vol. 9 (Stuttgart 1973; English translation, Grand Rapids 1974).

Cf. above 3807. Contains: G. BERTRAM, art. φρόνησις κτλ (prudence), 224; art. ὠδίς κτλ (travail), 672; O. BETZ, art. φωνή κτλ (voice), 285-6; G. BRAUMANN, art. ψῆφος (verdict), 602; H. CONZELMANN, art. φῶς κτλ (light), 322-4; art. χαίρω (be glad), 355-7; art. χάρις κτλ (grace), 380-1; art. εὐχαριστέω κτλ (thank), 400; G. DELLING, art. χρόνος (time), 579-80; A. DIHLE, art. ψυχή κτλ (soul), 632-3; G. HARDER, art. φθείρω (perish), 101-2; H. KÖSTER, art. φύσις (nature), 261-3; U. LUCK, art. φιλανθωπία (love for man), 110; O. MICHEL, art. φιλοσοφία (philosophy), 178-9; G. STÄHLIN, art. φίλος κτλ (friend), 156; E. SCHWEIZER, art. χοϊκός (made of clay), 462-5; K. WEISS, art. χρηστός (useful, sound), 475; U. WILCKENS, art. χαρακτήρ (imprint), 409-10. (DTR)

7312. P. GEOLTRAIN, 'Quelques lectures juives et chrétiennes des premier versets de la Genèse de Qoumrân au Nouveau Testament', in *In*

Principio: interprétations des premiers versets de la Genèse, Études Augustiniennes (Paris 1973) 47-60.

Philo's interpretation of the first verses of Genesis is briefly analyzed, with particular reference to *Opif.* and *Aet.* (= R823)

7313. M. GRANT, *The Jews in the Roman world* (London 1973), esp. 120-146 *passim.*

Philo's evidence is used as a historical source of information on the famous embassy to Gaius and on the events connected with the reign of Agrippa. Philo is regarded as a representative of the wealthiest class of Jews in Alexandria. Within the community, this class was certainly the most favourably disposed towards the Romans. (= R824)

7314. R. G. HAMERTON-KELLY, *Pre-existence, wisdom, and the son of man: a study of the idea of pre-existence in the New Testament*, SNTSMS 21 (Cambridge 1973) *passim.*

Though no chapter is specifically devoted to Philo (contrast above **6614**), Philonic evidence is constantly used in order to illuminate and evaluate the role of pre-existence in the various books of the New Testament (cf. index of passages 302f.). (DTR)

7315. D. M. HAY, 'Philo's treatise on the Logos-Cutter', *StPh* 2 (1973) 9-22.

The very structure of *Her.*, with its long digression on the *logos tomeus* which appears to stray from the specific subject of the treatise, poses serious problems of interpretation. After an interesting literary and thematic analysis, the author concludes by interpreting the Philonic concept of the Logos-Cutter as a 'Jewish solution' (i.e. dependent on a Jewish tradition of the divine word as a sword to defend the faithful and punish the godless) to a Greek philosophical problem, namely the existence of infinite differences and conflicts in the universe. (= R827)

7316. H. HEGERMANN, 'Griechisch-jüdisches Schrifttum', in *Literatur und Religion des Frühjudentums: eine Einführung*, part 2, 'Sprache und Gestalt der früh-jüdischen Literatur', (Würzburg-Gütersloh 1973) 163-180, esp. 175-178.

Philo is regarded here as the most eminent figure of Alexandrian Judaism; both his cultural background and literary output are briefly outlined. The information about the latter, however, is very summary and general. (= R830)

7317. H. HEGERMANN, 'Das griechischsprechende Judentum' in *Literatur...* (**7316**), part 4, Religiöse Gruppierungen und Tendenzen in der Diaspora, 328-352.

Philo's work is used as a historical source for determining: (a) the nature and political position of the Jewish community in Alexandria; (b) the characteristics of Jewish-Alexandrian spirituality (here Philo is, as often, seen in conjunction with Aristobulus); (c) the acceptance or rejection of Jewish-Hellenistic thought on the part of the gentile world. (= R828)

7318. H. HEGERMANN, 'Philon von Alexandria' in *Literatur...* **(7316)** 353-369.

The first part of this synoptic study of Philo aims at establishing the chronology of the main events in his life, his social position, and his role in religion and culture. Next the general character of his works are analyzed. According to Hegermann these are based on a specific theological conception: man can know God only if God reveals himself, and therefore only by virtue of divine grace. The same concept of grace forms the basis of his ethical system. At the end of the study the author discusses Philo's relations with the gnosis and the political aspects of his personality and activities. Abstract in *StPh* 4 (1976-77) 93. (= R829)

7319. O. HOFIUS, 'Die Unabänderlichkeit des göttlichen Heilsratschlusses: Erwägungen zur Herkunft eines neutestamentlichen Theologumenon, D. O. Michel zum 70. Geburtstag am 28. August 1973', *ZNW* 64 (1973) 135-145, esp. 139ff.

Heb. 6:17f. shows clear parallels with some of Philo's statements on the immutability of divine judgements. The author points out, however, that these parallels are mainly formal, since it is clear that in Philo the immutability of God's will is made to depend on an adequate conception of the divine nature and, therefore, on a theological context which is absent in Hebrews. Abstract in *StPh* 4 (1976-77) 93-94. (= R831)

7320. G. E. HOWARD, 'The 'aberrant' text of Philo's quotations reconsidered', *HUCA* 44 (1973) 197-209.

The author discusses the difficult question of Philo's aberrant quotations, taking his starting-point, as is logical, from Katz's fundamental work **(5007)** on this subject. After a survey of Philo's biblical references and a review of the manuscript tradition of the LXX, Howard modifies Katz's conclusions on various points and confirms that Philo used a text which is in part different from the one we have today. Abstract in *StPh* 4 (1976-77) 95. (= R832)

7321. J. G. KAHN, "'Connais-toi toi-même' à la manière de Philon', *RHPhR* 53 (1973) 293-307.

Philo's interpretation of the Delphic maxim is wholly original. The author discusses here its essential outlines: from the initial training in paideia and through the recognition of his own insignificance man achieves a receptiveness towards God which climaxes in the acceptance of the universal harmony which is nothing other than the will of God. Abstract in *StPh* 4 (1976-77) 96. For subsequent Hebrew versions see **8339-40**. (= R833)

7322. K. KIESEWETTER, 'Philon d'Alexandrie', *RenOO* 10 (1973) 10-15.

A brief presentation of Philo which concentrates on his mysticism. (= R834)

7323. C. KRAUS REGGIANI, 'Aristobulo e l'esegesi allegorica dell'-Antico Testamento nell'ambito del giudaismo ellenistico', *RFIC* 101 (1973)

162-185 *passim*.

The article deals specifically with Aristobulus, but obviously the author's attention also turns to Philo, if only in order to lay a foundation for a genetic study of his allegorical interpretation. Aristobulus, certainly the greatest Jewish-Hellenistic exegete prior to Philo, represents – and here Kraus is in agreement with Walter – a more primitive stage of Alexandrian exegesis in which reference to Greek philosophy and in particular the theory of the Logos is still lacking, but in which two typically Philonic themes are already in evidence: the 'de-anthropomorphization' of God by means of allegorical interpretation, and the postulated dependence of Greek philosophy on Old Testament wisdom (cf. 185). (= R835)

7324. D. LÜHRMANN, 'Pistis im Judentum', *ZNW* 64 (1973) 19-38, esp. 29-32.

In the concept of πίστις, which also plays a central role in Philo, the author sees an 'audacious attempt to deposit the Jewish religious tradition into a context of alien, i.e. Greek, thought'. This was such a difficult operation that even Christianity moved along this road with great hesitation. Abstract in *StPh* 4 (1976-77) 98. (= R836)

7325. B. L. MACK, *Logos und Sophia: Untersuchungen zur Weis-heitstheologie im hellenistischen Judentum*, StUNT 10 (Göttingen 1973), esp. 108-195.

One of the characteristics of Jewish-Alexandrian thought, and also of Philo, is the substitution of logos for wisdom in some contexts. Wisdom, in fact, is located by Philo in an eschatological context, while the mediation between man and God is performed by the Logos. The latter, however, forms part of a series of identifications in which the typical function of mediation is transferred to other figures, such as Israel and the Patriarchs, according to a precise scheme: God – son of God (= Logos = Israel) – children of the son of God. Since man can only participate in the Logos and understand it if he assumes an attitude of listening, a second series emerges which, in a descending sequence, runs from God to the teacher to the pupil and, in a rising sequence, from the pupil of a teacher to the pupil of God to Moses in the presence of God. In this process Israel and its history, besides fulfilling a cosmological and religious function, play a psychological role in undergoing a process of interiorization which also involves the Patriarchs: the latter, in fact, lose their individual connotations and become paradigms of virtue. (= R837)

7326. F. E. MORARD, 'Monachos, moine: histoire du terme grec jusqu'au 4ᵉ siècle; influences bibliques et gnostiques', *FZPhTh* 20 (1973) 332-411, esp. 357-362.

Philo expresses the theme of solitude by means of various derivations of μόνος (notably μοναστήριον), but he never uses the term μοναχός. According to the author, that is due to the limited currency of the word in Philo's time. Nevertheless, although the corresponding term is absent, the concept of the monastic life, the search for God in solitude, does already occur in Philo. (= R838)

7327. R. MORTLEY, *Connaissance religieuse et herméneutique chez Clément d'Alexandrie* (Leiden 1973), esp. 5-11, 41-43, 62.

According to the author the concept of God's ineffability and unknowability did not originate with Philo, but was part of a wide-spread tendency in the Platonist schools (11, 62). At the same time it is true that Philo helped establish the concept by giving it theological consistency. At 41-43 Mortley also discusses Philo's method of allegorical interpretation, which he compares with that of Plutarch. (RR)

7328. E. MÜHLENBERG, 'Das Problem der Offenbarung in Philo von Alexandrien', *ZNTW* 64 (1973) 1-18.

Starting from Wolfson's statement that Philo substituted the concept of prophecy for the Platonic concept of recollection, the author traces Philo's thought on the relationship between prophecy and knowledge of God. Ultimately Philo leaves the problem of the basis of revelation, i.e. the essence of God, unsolved. In Philo, as is well-known, this essence is unknowable and, consequently, the road along which the soul raises itself to God is abruptly interrupted at this point. It is clear, in any case, that Philo's Platonic assumptions prevented him from drawing all the relevant consequences from the 'idea of the self-revelation of God' (18). Abstract in *StPh* 4 (1976-77) 99f. (= R839)

7329. P. G. MÜLLER, *ΧΡΙΣΤΟΣ ΑΡΧΗΓΟΣ: der religionsgeschichtliche und theologische Hintergrund einer neutestamentlichen Christusprädikation*, Europäische Hochschulschriften Reihe XXIII 28 (Bern-Frankfurt 1973), esp. 193-212.

In his writings Philo frequently refers to the theme of the guide characteristic of the book Exodus. But with the aid of Greek speculation and, in particular, the idea of the guide that is peculiar to Greek *paideia*, he considerably develops this motif, transposing it from the religious to the ethical level and, from there, to the level of theology and cosmology. For Philo the supreme guide is God the Creator, but below him it is possible to recognize two hierarchical lines which converge in God: one relating to the macrocosmos, formed by the intermediate Powers (Logos, Sophia, and *pneuma*), the other relating to the microcosmos, at the top of which stands Moses, but which includes all men who follow his example in aspiring to God. (= R840)

7330. A. MYRE, 'La loi et le Pentateuque selon Philon d'Alexandrie', *ScEs* 25 (1973) 209-225.

Though the term νόμος in Philo covers a wide semantic field, it has its central point of reference in the Pentateuch. The term serves to indicate: (a) the entire Pentateuch; (b) the lives of the Patriarchs; (c) the legislative part of the Pentateuch; (d) the Decalogue and all the laws of which it is composed and which derive from it; (e) any single legal prescription. Abstract in *StPh* 4 (1976-77) 101. (= R841)

7331. J. NEUSNER, *The idea of purity in ancient Judaism: the Haskell Lectures, 1972-1973*, with a critique and a commentary by M. DOUGLAS, SJLA 1 (Leiden 1973) *passim*.

With ample reference to the texts, the author describes the long series of purificatory laws which Philo derives from the Bible and interprets in various treatises. Philo was not the first to detach the concept of purity-impurity from the sphere of worship, but was anticipated in this respect by the author of the *Letter of Aristeas*. Nevertheless, his position, as Neusner observes, is a rather eccentric one in the context of the Jewish tradition, leading as it does to a radical allegorical transformation of the terms of purity and impurity. The same road is taken by the author of Hebrews, who 'like Philo ... treats the purity-rules as metaphorical or figurative of a higher reality' (63). (= R842)

7332. V. NIKIPROWETZKY, 'L'exégèse de Philon d'Alexandrie', *RHPhR* 53 (1973) 309-329.

The author anticipates here various fundamental themes which were later elaborated in detail and depth in his great monograph on Philo (**7731**); we refer to the latter for a comprehensive judgement. Here we confine ourselves to sketching some of the main points as summarized by Nikiprowetzky himself in the article's introduction. Philo's work is 'an exegetical exposition of the kind presented in the Alexandrian synagogue: a biblical text is the object of a commentary which step by step resolves all exegetical difficulties that it contains; next the commentator passes on to allegorical exegesis. The philosophical ideas are entirely put into the service of the interpretation of the text under study, which leads to the elaboration of original exegetical themes, such as that of spiritual migration' (309). Abstract in *StPh* 4 (1976-77) 101ff. (= R843)

7333. B. A. PEARSON, 'Friedländer revisited: Alexandrian Judaism and Gnostic origins', *StPh* 2 (1973) 23-39.

In his work *Der vorchristliche jüdische Gnosticismus* (Göttingen 1898), M. Friedländer maintained that Gnosticism was 'a pre-Christian phenomenon' (23) which arose in heterodox circles of the Jewish community in Alexandria. This view was not well received, and even came under radical attack. Today, however, as the result of a more profound analysis of the Philonic texts (esp. *Migr.* 86-93, where Philo polemicizes with the radical allegorists) and the recent discovery of the Nag Hammadi library, the situation has changed. Friedländer's basic contention has been vindicated, even if much of the detail of his argument is open to question. (= R844)

7334. B. A. PEARSON, *The pneumatikos-psychikos terminology in 1 Corinthians: a study in the theology of the Corinthian opponents of Paul and its relation to Gnosticism*, SBLDS 12 (Missoula 1973, 1976²), esp. 17-21.

Pearson makes some observations of particular interest at 17-21, where Philo's views on the immortality of the soul are reconstructed. For Philo, this immortality depends on God, but is made conditional on man's holiness: 'no Jew, not even Philo, could go so far as to affirm that the soul is immortal by its own nature and therefore incapable of mortality'. Philo is also adduced in relation to the entire question of the πνευματικός-ψυχικός terminology used by Paul in I Corinthians. (= R845)

7335. P. PETIT, 'Émerveillement, prière et esprit chez Saint Basile le Grand', *CCist* 35 (1973) 81-107, 218-238, esp. 220ff., 228.

Evidences various parallels between Philo and Basil, e.g. their philosophical and exegetical language, the themes of the admiration for the cosmos, the recollection of God, divine illumination and the image of God. (= R846)

7336. K. J. POPMA, 'Patristic evaluation of culture', *PhilRef* 38 (1973) 97-113.

Philo's importance in Patristic thought is such that two categories of philosophers can be distinguished within the latter, those who used Philo's work more or less extensively (Clement, Origen, Ambrose, Jerome) and those who made no use of it (Justin and Tertullian). This distinction largely corresponds to another, much vaster one, namely between the Christian thinkers who accepted pagan culture and those who rejected it. That serves to show that, for the Fathers of the Church, Philo's philosophical thought was identified *tout court* with Greek philosophy; and not without reason, if one bears in mind Philo's predominant philosophical eclecticism. (= R847)

7337. B. REICKE, *Die zehn Worte in Geschichte und Gegenwart. Zählung und Bedeutung der Gebote in den verschiedenen Konfessionen*, BGBE 13 (Tübingen 1973) 21-26.

Briefly highlights the arithmological motifs of the pentad and decad which influenced Philo's interpretation of the Decalogue. Also briefly discusses Philo's influence in this connection on the thought of the Christian Fathers. (RR)

7338. W. SCHWARZ, 'A study in pre-Christian symbolism: Philo, *De somniis* I, 216-218, and Plutarch, *De Iside et Osiride* 4 and 77', *BICS* 20 (1973) 104-117.

In Philonic allegory, linen is considered superior to wool. This symbolism also occurs in Plutarch, which suggests a common source, chronologically located between Aristotle and Philo. The same applies to the allegorical meaning of colours, here analyzed in a summary of the interpretations given by both thinkers. (= R848)

7339. E. STAROBINSKI-SAFRAN, 'Signification des noms divins – d'après Exode 3 – dans la tradition rabbinique et chez Philon d'Alexandrie', *RThPh* 6 (1973) 426-435.

The plurality of God's names corresponds in Philo to the different levels of knowledge which man can reach: the intuition of God as Being corresponds to the highest level. (= R849)

7340. M.-B. VON STRITZKY, *Zum Problem der Erkenntnis bei Gregor von Nyssa*, MBTh 37 (Münster 1973) *passim*, esp. 7f., 14f.

As a mediator between Greek and Jewish culture, Philo forms a true bridge between classical Greek and Christian thought (7-8). The author also discusses Philo in connection with his theories of the Logos, εἰκών (14 f.), πάθη (77), negative theology (82), and mysticism (84, 97), as related to the corresponding themes in Gregory of Nyssa. (RR)

7341. J. THURÉN, *Das Lobopfer der Hebräer: Studien zum Aufbau und Anliegen von Hebräerbrief 13*, AAAbo.H 47.1 (Abo 1973), esp. 110-115, 241-247.

Philo is often cited in this work in contexts too various to cover here. We draw attention to the detailed philological analysis of the term ἐξομολογεῖσθαι, on 110-112, and to the study of Philo's interpretation of the special laws, which is seen by Thurén as an attempt to codify and systematize synagogal teaching (243-246). (= R850)

7342. W. S. TOWNER, *The Rabbinic 'enumeration of scriptural examples': a study of a Rabbinic pattern of discourse with special reference to Mekhilta D'R. Ishmael,* SPB 22 (Leiden 1973), esp. 109-116.

In Philo's thought numbers not only have an arithmological value, but are also suitable instruments for giving a catalogic form to both philosophical doctrines and biblical data. The author sees parallels with the Rabbinic 'enumeration of scriptural examples' which cannot be regarded as coincidental, but are the result of Philo's Jewish education, the precise nature of which must remain speculative. (= R851)

7343. P. WALTERS (formerly KATZ), *The text of the Septuagint, its corruptions and their emendation,* edited by D. W. GOODING (Cambridge 1973) *passim.*

A purely philological work which continually uses Philonic texts to emend corruptions in the text of the LXX. The citations of Philo are listed on 416. (= R852)

7344. W. WARNACH, 'Selbstliebe und Gottesliebe im Denken Philons von Alexandrien', in H. FELD and J. NOLTE (edd.), *Wort Gottes in der Zeit: Festschrift K. H. Schelkle* (Düsseldorf 1973) 198-214.

Self-love (φιλαυτία) is condemned by Philo because it confirms man in the false conviction that he has exclusive control over his spirit and the faculties of his soul, whereas these in fact belong exclusively to God. This introduces the theocentrism of Philonic thought, in which not only the soul, but also the spirit and virtue itself derive from God. From this point of view, the philosopher no longer seeks knowledge autonomously, but looks to God for the content of his wisdom. Freedom is included in this interpretation too: it is understood as grace which, in view of the frailty of human nature, must be continually invoked from God. Warnach recognizes that Philo's emphatic devaluation of *philautia* goes beyond the norms of Greek thought, and for this reason he analyzes the views of Aristotle, Plato, Epictetus, and also, in passing, Scepticism. Abstract in *StPh* 4 (1976-77) 106f. (= R853)

7345. M. J. WEAVER, Πνεῦμα *in Philo of Alexandria* (diss. Notre Dame, Indiana 1973).

Before discussing the Philonic doctrine of πνεῦμα, Weaver analyzes the role of this concept in Stoic philosophy (7-25), Jewish thought (26-38), and the milieu of Alexandria (39-54). In this way we are given a precise idea of the semantic complexity of the term, which derives both from the materialist context of Stoic philosophy, where it is conceived as a vital substance as a vital substance 'which permeates and vivifies all reality' (25) and from Jewish and Jewish-Alexandrian culture. In the former *pneuma* loses all philosophical-religious connotations, in the latter, especially in Sap. Sal., it stands juxtaposed to a particularly enriched concept of soul (cf. 54). Philo makes extremely rich and basically unified use of the theme of *pneuma*, but one that is not systematically worked out. It furnishes, in fact, the foundation of his cosmology, anthropology, ethics, and doctrine of prophetic inspiration. In the process, however, it is profoundly spiritualized, clearly distinguished from ether, and placed at the centre of a Jewish religious ideology which 'provides the frame of reference for his confrontation of or adaptation to other doctrines'

(159). The unifying element of Philonic pneumatology which emerges from this analysis, it would seem, is the concept of *pneuma* as a free gift bestowed by God, which is the feature common to the various elaborations of Philo's system. (= R854)

7346. A. J. M. WEDDERBURN, 'Philo's 'heavenly man'', *NT* 15 (1973) 301-326.

The allegory of the heavenly man in Philo is important for two reasons: in the first place because it illuminates the background of 1 Cor. 15:44ff.; secondly because it has led many scholars to believe in the existence of a Gnostic myth of Anthropos in the pre-Christian period. As far as the first reason is concerned, the author underlines the difference between the points of view of Paul and Philo, drawing attention to the eschatological motives in Paul and their virtual absence in Philo. As regards the relationship with the Gnosis, Wedderburn observes that 'Philo's exegesis of the Old Testament, and indeed that of Judaism in general, does far more to explain Gnostic exegesis and mythology than vice versa' (324). Philo's motif of heavenly man does not reflect a 'heavenly man' figure or myth at all, and thus does no more than anticipate to some extent the Gnostic motif. Abstract in *StPh* 4 (1976-1977) 107. (= R855)

7347. J. WHITTAKER, 'Neopythagoreanism and the transcendent absolute', *SO* 48 (1973) 77-86.

The conception of God as 'transcendent absolute', which is the necessary presupposition of a negative theology, was a common heritage of the philosophical culture of Philo's time: it occurred both in the Neopythagorean and the Hermetic literature of his day. (= R856)

7348. D. S. WINSTON, 'Freedom and determinism in Greek philosophy and Jewish Hellenistic wisdom', *StPh* 2 (1973) 40-50.

Cf. **7555, 7647.** (= R857)

1974

7401. A. W. ARGYLE, 'Philo, the man and his work', *ET* 85 (1974) 115-117.

Philo is briefly presented from political, philosophical, and religious-theological points of view. (= R860)

7402. S. BELKIN, [בלקין .ש], פילון ומדרשי הגדול המדרש [= 'The Midrash Hagadol and the Midrashim of Philo'], in S. B. HOENING and L. D. STIT-SKIN (edd.), *J. Finkel Jubilee Volume* (New York 1974) 7-58.

Belkin reiterates his thesis (cf. **7204**) that 'the author of *Midrash Hagadol* may well have had access ... to the same early sources which Philo used – namely non-extant early Palestinian midrashic traditions which were (also) current in Egypt in ancient times' (7). Forty one additional examples of parallels are given. (NGC)

7403. O. BÖCHER, 'Die heilige Stadt im Völkerkrieg, Wandlungen eines apokalyptischen Schemas', in O. BETZ, K. HAACKER, M. HENGEL (edd.), *Josephus-Studien: Untersuchungen zu Josephus, dem antiken Judentum, und dem Neuen Testament. O. Michel zum 70. Geburtstag gewidmet* (Göttingen 1974) 55-76, esp. 63f.

The meaning of the holy city is examined in relation to the various historical phases of the Jewish-Christian religious tradition. Philo contributed more than anyone else to the spiritualization of this image. (= R861)

7404. P. BOYANCÉ, 'Le Dieu très haut chez Philon', in *Mélanges d'histoire des religions offerts à H. C. Puech* (Paris 1974) 139-149.

In Greek thought the epithet ὕψιστος is attributed both to Zeus and to θεός in general. In the latter form some scholars have seen a transfiguration of the Jewish God in terms of Olympic religiosity. The analysis of various Philonic passages, however, shows that this solution is improbable: Philo himself, though a Jew, adopted the epithet from a non-biblical, Aristotelian-Peripatetic context where it is linked to the theology of the Prime Mover. (= R862)

7405. R. CANTALAMESSA, 'Origene e Filone: a proposito di *C. Celsum* IV, 19', *Aev* 48 (1974) 132-133.

In *Contra Celsum* 4.19 the author sees a polemical allusion to the Philonic views expounded in *Somn.* 1.232-238. Abstract in *StPh* 4 (1976-77) 89. (= R863)

7406. H. C. C. CAVALLIN, *Life after death: Paul's argument for the resurrection of the dead in I Cor 15*, part 1, An enquiry into the Jewish background (Lund 1974), esp. 135-140.

Philo holds ambiguous views on the immortality of the soul: in some texts he seems to interpret death as the liberation of the soul from the prison of the body; in others it appears that he is in line with traditional Jewish eschatology, which foresees an end to history and a final glorification of Israel. In any case it is important to observe that 'the hope of personal immortality is not connected with the expressions of any national or universal collective eschatology' (139). (= R864)

7407. A. H. CHROUST, 'Some remarks about Philo of Alexandria, *De aeternitate mundi* V. 20-24: a fragment of Aristotle's *On Philosophy*', *ClF* 28 (1974) 83-88.

Aet. 20-24 'probably contains some Philonic additions, expansions or elaborations which did not occur in the original Aristotelian *De philosophia*' (88). Nevertheless, in the author's view, the essentials of what Aristotle had stated in the dialogue are faithfully reported by Philo. (= R865)

7408. A. H. CHROUST, 'A fragment of Aristotle's *On Philosophy* in Philo of Alexandria, *De opificio mundi* I, 7', *DT* 77 (1974) 224-235.

In the text under consideration – which Chroust considers to be a fragment of

Aristotle's *De philosophia* – Philo attacks those who hold that the world is neither generated nor destructible, since in this condition God and nature would be reduced to passive impotence. It is also noted that references to the same work may be present in *Prov.* 1. Abstract in *StPh* 5 (1978) 122f. (= R866)

7409. A. H. CHROUST, 'A fragment of Aristotle's *On Philosophy*: some remarks about Philo of Alexandria, *De Aeternitate Mundi* 8, 41', *WS* 87 (1974) 15-19.

In the author's view, the passage in question is 'a genuine and authentic fragment of the *De philosophia*. Of particular interest is the fact that Philodemus uses the same quote against women recorded by Philo. This shows how the Epicurean polemic against Aristotle on the subject of the indestructibility of the world exploited verbal ammunition supplied by the Stagirite himself. Abstract in *StPh* 4 (1976-77) 90. (= R867)

7410. P. COURCELLE, 'Tradition néo-platonicienne et tradition chrétienne des ailes de l'âme', in *Problemi attuali di scienza e di cultura. Atti del convegno internazionale sul tema: Plotino e il Neoplatonismo in Oriente e in Occidente, (Roma, 5-9 ottobre 1970)* (Rome 1974) 265-325, esp. 269-271.

Since Philo profoundly spiritualizes the image of the 'soul's flight' from earth to heaven, it is not necessary for him to postulate the literal image of the wings of the soul. Parallels with Philo's position are found in Plutarch (cf. 271) and Clement (283). (= R868)

7411. G. DELLING, 'Perspektiven der Erforschung des hellenistischen Judentums', *HUCA* 45 (1974) 133-176 *passim*.

The author warns that, in dealing with his subject, he has wished to avoid matters of detail and has virtually ignored three large areas of research on Hellenistic Judaism (Philo, Josephus, and the LXX), or rather, has only dealt with them insofar as they contribute directly and significantly to the understanding of the movement as a whole (cf. 134). Nevertheless, the references to Philo are very frequent and the article as a whole is of great interest, being one of the few to address this subject in an integral way. Abstract in *StPh* 5 (1978) 124ff. (= R869)

7412. H. DÖRRIE, 'Zur Methodik antiker Exegese', *ZNW* 65 (1974) 121-138, esp. 133ff.

A brief exposition of Philo's exegetical method, seen as a continuation and imitation of the Stoic exegesis of Homer. Abstract in *StPh* 5 (1978) 128. (= R870)

7413. I. ESCRIBANO-ALBERCA, *Glaube und Gotteserkenntnis in der Schrift und Patristik*, Handbuch der Dogmengeschichte, vol. 1, fasc. 2a (Freiburg-Basel-Vienna 1974), esp. 7-11.

Philo's work is a significant example of how biblical elements can be forced into a different context of thought, i.e. Greek thought. In the light of the ideal of *theoria* and the vision of God, many terms of Old Testament origin (the word of God, the concepts of faith, logos, and prophecy) take on new meanings. (= R871)

7414. V. R. L. FRY, *The warning inscriptions from the Herodian temple*, (diss. Southern Baptist Theological Seminary 1974).

A thorough investigation of the use of the word ἀλλογενής in Philo (and also in Josephus) reveals that the word is avoided when the authors concerned speak of death for the gentile desecrators of temple space, apparently because it had developed strong anti-gentile nuances. (DTR; based on *DA* 36-356A)

7415. L. GAZZONI, 'L''erede' nel *Quis rerum divinarum heres sit* di Filone Alessandrino', *RFIC* 102 (1974) 387-397.

The theme of the heir in *Her.* is much richer than the corresponding Old Testament theme: Philo extended its meaning to the extent of changing its connotations. Two aspects are important in this connection: (a) the concept of inheritance is spiritualized; (b) the inheritance is not obtained when God's gifts are obtained, but when they are 'restituted', i.e. in the act of the sacrificial offering. It is then that man acknowledges his own insignificance and obtains the wisdom of God, i.e. the true inheritance. (= R872)

7416. O. GIORDANO, 'Gesù e Barabbas', *Hel* 13-14 (1973-1974) 141-173 *passim*.

The episode of Carabas related by Philo in *Flacc.* shows extraordinary similarities with certain aspects of Christ's passion, in particular with the mockeries to which he is subjected. These probably refer to a popular custom, a kind of pantomime of the fool-king which is thought to inspire both episodes. (= R873)

7417. V. GUAZZONI FOÀ, 'Dalle origini alla chiusura della scuola d'Atene', in *Storia del pensiero occidentale*, vol. 1 (Milan 1974) 392-397.

Philo, defined as 'the most mature expression of Jewish-Alexandrian syncretism', is briefly presented here on the basis of his theological thought. Rapid attention is also paid to his allegorical method, epistemology, anthropology, and ethics. (= R874)

7418. D. HENNIG, 'Zu der alexandrinischen Märtyrerakte P. Oxy. 1089', *Chir* 4 (1974) 425-440.

A chiefly historical article in which Philonic evidence is used to identify a certain Flaccus mentioned in P. Oxy. 1089. (= R876)

7419. J. JERVELL, 'Imagines und Imago Dei: aus der Genesis-Exegese des Josephus', in *Josephus-Studien* (**7403**) 197-204, esp. 202f.

The Philonic theme of whether God can be represented in images is compared with the same theme in Flavius Josephus. (= R877)

7420. J.-G. KAHN [כהן-ישר .י], מקומו של פילון במחשבת ישראל [= 'Philo's place in Jewish thought'], *Sinai* 74 (1974) 275-284.

Taking as starting-point the Hebrew translation of Wolfson's *Philo* (**7038**), Kahn asks why Philo was forgotten in Jewish traditional literature. The Logos and the method of allegorical interpretation are compared to biblical and Rabbinic norms. (MM)

7421. H. KAISER, *Die Bedeutung des leiblichen Daseins in der paulinischen Eschatologie* (inaug. diss. Dresden 1974), esp. 73-258.

The author devotes two large sections to Philo: one – specifically dealing with Philo – discusses his anthropology and soteriology in comparison with 2 Cor. 5:1-10; the other – dealing with the relations between Paul and Philo – is concerned with the concept of *anthropos* in both thinkers, as seen from a soteriological and 'protological' point of view (cf. 258). In the first section Kaiser discusses four fundamental themes. (1) The theme of death (cf. 73-83): according to the author, death in Philo loses its character of caesura and constitutes for the pious man the final stage of purification. (2) The foundations of anthropology: particular emphasis is given here to the concepts of σῶμα, ψυχή, νοῦς (a large subsection is devoted to the latter, 98-118), and to the strongly dualistic structure of human nature. The author also underlines the ethical aspects of this dualism and devotes a brief excursus to the concepts of πάθη and ἡδονή and their relations with the body. (3) Man's aspiration towards the celestial and transcendent sphere (118-183): the various components of this theme are analyzed – Greek-Hellenistic (in which the mysteries are distinguished from philosophical-Platonic elements), Jewish, Iranian-Oriental, Egyptian, Hermetic. The crown of this aspiration, in Kaiser's view, is the spiritual vision of God and ecstasy. (4) The same process, previously illustrated from a philosophical point of view, is here reconsidered in terms of its allegorical translation (183-219), especially with regard to the figures of Abraham and Israel. (= R878)

7422. A. KASHER [כשר .א], הנסיבות לפרסום האדיקט של קלאודיוס קיסר ומכתבו אל האלכסנדרונים ['The circumstances of Claudius Caesar's edict and of his Letter to the Alexandrians'], *Zion* 39 (1974) 1-7.

Subsequently published in French; see **7624**.

7423. E. LANNE, 'La 'xeniteia' d'Abraham dans l'œuvre d'Irénée: aux origines du thème monastique de la 'Peregrinatio'', *Irén* 47 (1974) 163-187.

The quest for God, a motif represented by Abraham, is fundamental in Philo's thought and also occurs in Irenaeus. One therefore readily hypothesizes a direct debt to Philo, not in relation to details, 'but to the theme as a whole' (185). In fact, when one looks at particulars (for instance in the opposition between the city-dweller and the stranger), Philo's point of view seems much closer to the Gnosis than to Irenaeus (cf. 170). (= R879)

7424. G. LUONGO, 'Il ruolo del cristiano nel mondo. *Ad Diognetum* VI 10 e il motivo della diserzione', *AFLN* 16 (1973-1974) 69-79.

Briefly analyzes, with many references to the Philonic corpus, the metaphor of desertion and, more in general, images taken from military language and applied to wholly moral themes. (= R879/a)

7425. W. MAAS, *Unveränderlichkeit Gottes, zum Verhältnis von griechisch-philosophischer und christlicher Gotteslehre*, Paderborn Theologische Studien 1 (Munich-Paderborn-Vienna 1974), esp. 87-121.

The importance which the author attaches to Philo is explained by the fact that Philo was the first thinker to focus on the theme of God's immutability, to which in fact he devoted an entire treatise. Maas takes his starting-point from this work (i.e. *Deus*), which he considers in relation both to the whole Philonic corpus and to its specific subject-matter. The conclusions which he reaches are summed up as follows. (1) For Philo, God is ἀπαθές and ἄτρεπτον. (2) Statements to the contrary found in this work should be understood as 'improper' expressions, which, in their proper sense, mean something quite different. (3) These expressions are motivated by a pedagogical intention and form a concession to the weakness of the human mind. (4) Only those who keep to the proper sense of the divine attributes can grasp the true essence of God, and to these people God appears absolutely simple, indivisible, pure, and immutable. Next Maas collects a series of attributes from Philo's other works in order to complete and give depth to these basic conceptions. Thus he discusses the concepts of ἴδιον, absoluteness, impassibility, and other connected characteristics. After a section dedicated to the relations between Philonic thought and Greek philosophy, Maas discusses the subject of God's ontological nature and the biblical theme of divine faithfulness; the latter is regarded as an incidental theme, for the dominant perspective remains Greek-philosophical-theological. (= R880)

7426. G. MADEC, *Saint Ambroise et la philosophie*, Études Augustiniennes 47 (Paris 1974), esp. 52-60, 101-104.

An analysis is presented of certain passages in Ambrose which are clearly inspired by Philo. Particular attention is paid to the allegory of Abraham's sacrifice, the originally Platonic image of the heavens as a winged chariot, and the descriptions of the Chaldeans, the Egyptians, and the Gymnosophists. The author concludes that Philo was the intermediary from whom Ambrose drew many of his philosophical observations. (RR)

7427. P. G. MAXWELL-STUART, 'Pollux and the reputation of tax gatherers', *RSC* 22 (1974) 157-163, esp. 159ff.

The author confines himself to citing some passages from *Spec.* in which Philo 'denounces tax gatherers with that special hatred of the Jew for men who had placed themselves outside the Law or collaborated with the Roman enemy' (159f.). (= R881)

7428. A. J. MCNICOL, *The relationship of the image of the highest angel to the high priest concept in Hebrews* (diss. Vanderbilt University 1974), esp. 83-86.

For Philo the archetype of the earthly temple is not the heavenly temple, but the cosmos itself (83). For the rest the entire allegory of the temple is expressed in a spiritualized and philosophically refined language without precedent in Jewish literature. This language in fact takes an opposite direction compared with apocalyptic literature, which tends to 'materialize' its images. (= R882)

7429. A. NISSEN, *Gott und der Nächste im antiken Judentum: Untersuchungen zum Doppelgebot der Liebe*, WUNT 15 (Tübingen 1974), esp. 417-501.

The impression left by this book is that Philo's concept of the love of God (in the analysis divided into 'love for God' and 'love of God') is located in a cultural context of extreme complexity. It is true that Hellenism is the dominant element in this context (cf. 430), but it is also true that Nissen's attempt to define this element from a philosophical point of view results in a very elaborate formula: it is a form of Platonism mediated by Posidonius which shows traces of the religion of mysteries, tends towards mysticism, and is set in a context where biblical tradition shades off into Hellenism. In this vague framework of reference the author traces some fixed points: (a) ἔρως, as a liberation through the knowledge of God and the retreat from the world (cf. 440), constitutes 'the centre of Philo's discourse on the love of God' and, indirectly, of his anthropology and ethics (cf. 446). (b) The paired concepts of 'love and fear' expressing the love of God are of Jewish origin, but are incorporated into a theological hierarchy which is clearly Greek and which transforms their original characteristics (cf. 453). (c) Man cannot devote himself to God and to his neighbour at the same time, and he cannot ignore the fact that 'philanthropy and justice are only the first stage and 'worldly' form of the union with God' (502). This union forms the climax to the Philonic theme of *eros* and is philosophically justified by God's fatherhood and the transcendental nature of the human soul (429). (= R883)

7430. C. PERI, 'La *Vita di Mosè* di Gregorio di Nissa: un viaggio verso l'areté cristiana', *VetChr* 11 (1974) 313-332, esp. 315-321.

'In general, when dealing with the life of Moses by Gregory of Nyssa, one cannot avoid referring to the homonymous work by Philo' (315). That does not imply that the two texts are identical or even very similar; indeed, Peri observes that the didactic and exegetical trends of both works are quite different, like the audiences to which they are addressed: in Philo's case, the gentiles; in Gregory's case, a monk. (= R884)

7431. M. PETIT, 'Les songes dans l'œuvre de Philon d'Alexandrie', in *Mélanges...* (cf. **7404**) 151-159.

The ambivalence of dreams, understood on the one hand as a means of communicating with God, on the other hand as illusory visions, is found in the Old Testament as well as in Philo. Nevertheless in Philo the former aspect is a reason for giving dreams a dominant role, in virtue of the importance which he assigns to any form of communication with God. (= R885)

7432. S. PINES [פינס .ש], מפילון עד הרמב"ם :I תולדות הפילוסופיה היהודית [= *History of Jewish philosophy, I: From Philo to Maimonides*] (Jerusalem 1974) 1-22.

This work is essentially a diligent student's notebook record of the lectures of a noted historian of Jewish and Islamic philosophy. Pines presents an overview of Philonic thought, stressing its connections with the Hellenistic schools, and includes some explicit criticism (4-5) of Wolfson's interpretation. (DS)

7433. S. SAFRAI and M. STERN (edd.), *The Jewish people in the first century: historical geography, political history, social, cultural and religious life and institutions*, 2 vols., CRINT I 1-2 (Assen 1974-76) 1.420-463 and *passim*.

Compendia Rerum Iudaicarum ad Novum Testamentum has been planned as a large-scale reference work for Judaism at the time of the New Testament, which at the present time has not yet been brought to completion (see also **8411**). The first part described here consists of two volumes, but only the first is of concern for our bibliography. Although only a small amount of space is specifically devoted to Philo, there are many references to his work – used mostly as a historical source – in ch. 3 (by M. STERN on the Judaism of the Diaspora) and in chs. 8 and 9 (by S. APPLEBAUM on the legal and political situation of the Jewish community in Alexandria). (= R859)

7434. S. SANDMEL, 'Virtue and reward in Philo', in J. L. CRENSHAW, J. T. WILLIS (edd.), *Essays in Old Testament ethics: J. P. Hyatt, in memoriam* (New York 1974) 215-223.

In his analysis of the relations between virtue and reward, the author underlines the Philonic identification of virtue with wisdom. In this sense the reward of virtue must be virtue itself: reason and not the act is the essence of virtue, says the author, 'for deed is the consequence of reason, and deed appears to be a reflection of virtue, not a means of attaining it' (222). (= R887)

7435. L. H. SCHIFMAN, *The* Halakhah *at Qumran* (diss. Brandeis University 1974).

The author undertakes a detailed study and commentary on the Qumran Sabbath legislation in order to see how the law was developed and determine to what extent the legislation of Qumran may be compared with that of Philo, the Rabbis and other Jewish sects. (DTR; based on *DA* 36-2161A)

7436. J. W. THOMPSON, *'That which abides': some metaphysical assumptions in the Epistle to the Hebrews* (diss. Vanderbilt University 1974), esp. 47-62.

The author briefly inspects some basic terms in Philonic thought (such as logos, God, wisdom, progress). In his analysis he underlines the fundamental Platonically influenced dualism of Philo's thought, a dualism which originates in the concept of God's transcendence and the notion of the two universes (intelligible and sensible). The terms μένειν and αἰών, which are analyzed in greater detail, are said to be the main characteristics of God and the intelligible world, in contrast to the sensible world of becoming. (= R888)

7437. H. A. WOLFSON, 'Answers to criticisms of my discussions of the ineffability of God', *HThR* 67 (1974) 186-190; reprinted in I. TWERSKY (ed.), *Studies in the history of philosophy and religion*, vol.2 (Cambridge Mass. 1977) 525-37.

Contains a series of responses to various objections raised on the subject in question. We also draw attention to this article because it is Wolfson's last contribution to Philonic studies, 'written – as I. Twersky adds in a postscript – while he was convalescing from surgery, his body racked with disease, it symbolizes his relentless commitment to scholarship while it illustrates the triumph of the glorious mind over decaying matter' (190). (= R889)

7438. J. ZANDEE, *'Les enseignements de Silvanos* et Philon d'Alexandrie', in *Mélanges...* (cf. **7404**) 337-345.

The author points out some parallels between *The teachings of Silvanus* and Philo. Some of these parallels are theological, having a common point of reference to Platonism in the definition of God's transcendence; others are anthropological, sharing Stoic influence on their conception of man's intellectual faculties; yet others moral, having the conception – again Stoic in origin – of virtue as the struggle against passion. For these reasons, concludes Zandee, 'it is probable that the author who hides behind the name of Silvanus can be sought in the circle of Alexandrian theologians' (345). (= R890)

1975

7501. F. BOLGIANI, 'L'ascesi di Noè: a proposito di Theoph., *ad Autol.*, III 19', in *Forma futuri: studi in onore del cardinale Michele Pellegrino* (Turin 1975) 295-333, esp. 322-327.

Theophilus of Antioch makes reference to the themes of abstinence and continence and connects them with the figure of Noah. The origin of these ideas, according to the author, lies in Philo, and specifically in *QG* 2.49. Here, as elsewhere, Philo tends to spiritualize the content of the biblical account, so that 'the question of mere legal and ritual purity is bypassed in the interest of a more specifically ascetic-spiritual ideal' (326). Such a development makes it all the more suitable for appropriation by the nascent culture of early Christianity. (= R891)

7502. P. BOYANCÉ, 'Étymologie et théologie chez Varron', *REL* 53 (1975) 99-115.

For Varro, as for Philo, there are four levels of verbal interpretation, and of these the highest is attributed to the king, or rather 'to an initiation given by the king' (99). In Philo the wisest man is he who gave the things their names (Adam and Moses), and for this reason he is designated by royal attributes. These similarities between the two writers can only be explained by a common source, probably Antiochus of Ascalon. (= R892)

7503. J. M. VAN CANGH, *La multiplication des pains et l'Eucharistie*, LeDiv 86 (Paris 1975), esp. 50-53, 80f.

In the search for literary antecedents of the multiplication of the loaves, the evidence in Philo – although offering no direct parallel with the biblical episode – is considered important, in the first place because he sheds light on the figure of Moses, a figure which is later transferred and extended to Jesus in reference to this miracle; secondly because the conception of the divine man in the miracle of the manna and the quails as presented in Philo's interpretation constitutes a significant Old Testament parallel (50). A brief note is also devoted to the meaning of the terms εὐλογεῖν and εὐχαριστεῖν in Philo (cf. 80f.). (= R893)

7504. H. CAZELLES, 'Eucharistie, bénédiction et sacrifice dans l'Ancien Testament', *MD* 123 (1975) 7-28.

The notion of thanksgiving has an extended range of meaning in Philo, involving the liturgical sacrifices, the Paschal sacrifice, and the holocaust. The banquet of the Therapeutae, with its sacral character, has eucharistic connotations also. (= R894)

7505. A. H. CHROUST, 'Some comments on Philo of Alexandria, *De* *aeternitate mundi'*, *LThPh* 31 (1975) 135-145.

Returning to the subject of Philonic evidence for the lost works of Aristotle for the fourth time in short succession, the author argues the derivation of three arguments in *Aet.* 20-24, 28-34, 39-43 on the indestructibility of the cosmos from the *De philosophia*, as is proved by the internal coherence of the passages taken together and also by significant parallels at *Aet.* 78-84 and in Cicero and Simplicius. Abstract in *StPh* 4 (1976-77) 90f. (= R895)

7506. T. CONLEY, *'General education' in Philo of Alexandria*, CHSHMC 15 (Berkeley 1975).

The author's 'impression' is that a great proportion of what Philo says on the subject of general education conforms to what can be found in contemporary Greco-Roman authors, but that his concept of the *enkyklios paideia* and its place in man's life is peculiar to himself or to Alexandrian Judaic culture. An analysis is given of the most important material on the subject in Philo, with special attention paid to the Hagar story and the example of rhetoric. The final section is devoted to the Jewish-Alexandrian background which is characterized by the term 'scribism'. Responses by J. DILLON, A. MENDELSON, D. WINSTON, followed by a long discussion. (= R896/DTR)

7507. P. COURCELLE, *Connais-toi toi-même de Socrate à Saint Bernard*, Études Augustiniennes, 3 vols. (Paris 1974-75), esp. 1.39-47, 2.395-398, 3.567-569, 645-648.

In Philo, as in Plutarch, the Delphic precept is given a metaphysical meaning. It is interpreted as leading man to discover his special relationship with God and, consequently, to acknowledge his own insignificance. The author deals with this subject from two points of view: at 2.395ff., where the Philonic theme of the body as tomb of the soul is discussed, and at 3.567-569, where he refers to the image of the wings of the soul (restating views already advanced in **7410**) and the concept of 'true man' (645-648). The latter is generally understood by Philo – who thus goes much farther than Socrates – as the soul which despises the flesh and practises virtue, or as the nous which in all its purity is related to the Logos. It is evident that Philo's perspective is markedly religious. (= R897)

7508. P. COURCELLE, 'Le typhus, maladie de l'âme d'après Philon et d'après Saint Augustin', in *Corona gratiarum: miscellanea patristica, historica et liturgica E. Dekkers O.S.B. XII lustra complenti oblata*, (Bruges-The Hague 1975) 1.245-288, esp. 245-258.

Analyzes in detail the meaning of the term τῦφος in Philo. Essentially this term is used to indicate vanity and as such is frequently and diversely exemplified in Philo. Naturally, these examples are mostly taken from the Bible, where the figure of Jethro stands out on account of its allegorical significance. In the remaining instances Philo usually resorts to the expression to designate the pagan myths and idols. (= R898)

7509. R. A. CULPEPPER, *The Johannine school: an evaluation of the Johannine-school hypothesis based on an investigation of the nature of ancient schools*, SBLDS 26 (Missoula 1975), esp. 197-214.

As part of an investigation of whether the community responsible for the production of the Johannine writings can be regarded as a school, the author investigates the setting of Philo's teaching activities. Four aspects are analyzed: Philo's learning of Greek philosophy, the community of the Therapeutae, Bousset's hypothesis of a Jewish exegetical school in Alexandria, and Goodenough's thesis of a Jewish mystery cult. Culpepper's conclusion is that 'Philo was probably associated with a synagogue-school where he taught the higher vision of scripture to a select group of initiates whose ears were purified' (211). Nothing, however, is concretely known about the synagogue-school in which Philo worked. (DTR)

7510. H. DAVIDSON, 'Harry Austryn Wolfson: an appreciation', *StPh* 3 (1974-75) 1-9.

A penetrating and illuminating retrospective on Wolfson's method and achievement. (= R899)

7511. F. DEXINGER, 'Ein 'messianisches Szenarium' als Gemeingut des Judentums in nachherodianischer Zeit?', *Kairos* 17 (1975) 249-278, esp. 250-255.

There is no room for a Messiah in Philo's thought. That does not mean, however, that Philo was not confronted with the messianic tradition of his people: in the author's view Philo's writings show more than a trace of the latter. The main concept in this connection is Israel, but on the whole the messianic theme in Philo lacks a unified and linear development; its characteristic elements are dispersed and it is necessary to reorder them from the outside if one wishes to reconstruct 'the messianic scenario' peculiar to Philo (cf. 254f.). Abstract in *StPh* 5 (1978) 127. (= R900)

7512. L. K. K. DEY, *The intermediary world and patterns of perfection in Philo and Hebrews*, SBLDS 25 (Missoula 1975).

The basic thesis of this dissertation is that the series of comparisons in Hebrews, where Jesus, as 'son', is compared with the angels, heavenly man, Moses, Aaron, Levi, and Melchizedek, belongs to a single religious and speculative world which is rooted in the religious doctrine of Hellenistic Judaism and especially in Philo Judaeus (cf. 7). The series of identifications in Philo follows two converging roads which are united by the fact that both elaborate a process of mediation between God and man. The first, which can be defined as philosophical-cosmological, is characterized by the pre-eminence of the Logos and particularly involves the concepts of the Powers, *sophia*, the angels, *anthropos* and the son (cf. 7-30). The second, ethical-religious and strictly correlative to the first, demonstrates the different levels of 'religious status' and perfection of life (31). Each of the intermediaries, from this point of view, is presented as a stage in the ascent to God (cf. 42ff.). We should note in this connection, however, that Philo admits a double form of perfection: one typical of the progressing man, the other of those who are perfect by nature. Abraham, Jacob, Aaron (73ff.) represent in different ways the former, Isaac and Moses the latter. This double road to perfection is the essential characteristic of Philo's thought and also its main point of contact with Hebrews. As Dey observes (110): 'In the Old Testament, Testaments of the Twelve Patriarchs and in the literature of Qumran, there is no correlation between the concept of perfection and the immediacy to the divine in terms of going beyond the world of intermediaries. But it is precisely this correlation between perfection and immediacy which is central to the thought world of Philo and Hebrews.' REVIEWS: J. Coppens, *EThL* 52 (1976) 228; A. Paul, *RecSR* 64 (1976) 554;

G. Delling, *ThLZ* 102 (1977) 502f. (= R901)

7513. J. M. DILLON, *The transcendence of God in Philo: some possible sources*, CHSHMC 16 (Berkeley 1975).

The concept of transcendence in Philo is analyzed in this short paper only in relation to its possible sources; in Dillon's view, these are Speusippus and Neopythagorean tradition (which was probably indebted to Speusippus). The latter's conception of the one 'as reality superior to being and source from which being arises' (1) might form the remote origin of Philo's thought on this subject; just as a fragment from Pseudo-Archytas, which posits a principle superior to the monad and dyad, might be its immediate antecedent. Nevertheless Philo is the first to attribute 'unknowability' to God, and the author, who is not inclined to assign the paternity of this attribution to Philo (for otherwise it cannot be explained, observes Dillon, how Albinus, who almost certainly did not read Philo, could make such wide use of the principles of negative theology), is constrained in this connection to speculate on the contemporary currents of Alexandrian Platonism. At the end of the paper there are responses and discussions by G. E. CASPARY (9-18) and D. WINSTON (19-22), which elaborate and supplement Dillon's arguments, and a lively joint discussion on subjects relating to the theme in question (24-44). (= R902)

7514. C. ELSAS, *Neuplatonische und gnostische Weltablehnung in der Schule Plotins*, RVV 34 (Berlin-New York 1975).

Elsas frequently uses Philo as a source in reconstructing the philosophical background from which Plotinus drew both inspiration and thematic material. In particular he examines three lines of influence: (a) Philo–Middle Platonism–Plotinus (cf. 98, 121, 204); (b) Philo–Numenius–Plotinus (cf. 117, 121, 205); (c) Philo–Gnosis–Plotinus (118, 122). (RR)

7515. S. S. FOSTER, *The Alexandrian situation and Philo's use of dike* (diss. Evanston 1975).

After a chapter devoted to the legal position of the Jews and Greeks in Roman Egypt, and a primarily historical presentation of Philo and his work (49-106), the author discusses the figure of Dike. Foster observes that this figure has two slightly different meanings, according to whether it occurs in treatises relating to the Exposition of the Law, or in the Allegorical Commentary and historical works. In the first case Dike is the punisher of those who infringe the Jewish law, in the second of those who persecute the Jewish community. For the author, this justifies the hypothesis that the latter writings were written in a period of grave political tensions, and that, in a wider sense, the whole doctrine of dike, instead of being interpreted on the basis of a theological or philosophical model, should be read as the expression of a kind of quasi-political thought in which certain typical elements of Philo's speculation (God, Mosaic law, Israel) are to be understood as political categories (God = king; Mosaic law = state law; Israel = the political community of the Jews in Alexandria). (= R903)

7516. L. GINZBERG [ל. גינזברג], אגדות היהודים [*The Legends of the Jews*] 6 vols. (Ramat Gan 1966-1975) *passim*.

The classic work (**3804**) in a serviceable Hebrew translation with the copious additional notes appended to each volume. (DS)

7517. A. GRAESER, *Zeno von Kition: Positionen und Probleme* (Berlin 1975) 187-206.

Graeser analyzes the controversial final section of Philo's *De aeternitate mundi* (§117-149), in which Theophrastus is recorded as attacking four arguments put forward by the proponents of the genesis and destruction of the cosmos. He follows E. Zeller in interpreting it as the reflection 'of an attack by Zeno on Aristotle' (206), in particular on his theory of the eternity of the world. (RR)

7518. J. HELDERMAN, 'Anachorese zum Heil: das Bedeutungsfeld der Anachorese bei Philo und in einigen gnostischen Traktaten von Nag Hammadi', in M. KRAUSE (ed.), *Essays on the Nag Hammadi texts in honour of P. Labib*, NHS 6 (Leiden 1975) 40-55.

If we agree with Völker and take it for granted that Philo is the mediator between antiquity and Christianity, the question naturally arises of what kind of Christianity one is talking about. The Christianity of the Gnosis is closest to Philo, both from a chronological and geographical point of view. Although there are no actual Gnostic elements in Philo (his Jewish faith is too strong for that), the concept of ἀναχώρησις (retirement or withdrawal) as a means of salvation serves as the leading thread which connects Philo to the later Gnostic movement. Abstract in *StPh* 4 (1976-77) 93f. (= R904)

7519. M. HENGEL, *Der Sohn Gottes: die Entstehung der Christologie und die jüdisch-hellenistische Religionsgeschichte* (Tübingen 1975), esp. 82-89; English translation (London 1976), esp. 51-56.

Philo's *interpretatio graeca* of the Jewish tradition is reflected in many elements of his theology, especially in the synthesis between the typically Jewish doctrine of wisdom and the Platonic doctrine (expressed in the *Timaeus*) of the demiurge, as well as in the way he elaborates the figure of the 'son of God'. Hengel observes, however, that Philo is strangely reluctant to attribute this epithet to man, and that when he uses it in this sense he gives it an allegorical meaning far removed from its literal meaning. (= R905)

7520. B. S. JACKSON, *Essays in Jewish and comparative legal history*, SJLA 10 (Leiden 1975) *passim*.

Although on the whole Philo is not given a great deal of emphasis, the highly specific angle from which he is approached makes this study into an interesting contribution. Philo's work is used above all as a source for reconstructing, from a legal and moral point of view, the relationship between intention and responsibility in reference to the tenth commandment and to the originally Stoic opposition of reason and passion. Elsewhere (238-240) Philo provides a basis for reconstructing the legal difference between theft and robbery in Jewish law. (= R906)

7521. A. KASHER [כשר .א] ,עדות פילון על זכויותיהם של יהודי אלכסנדריה ['Philo on the rights of the Jews of Alexandria'], *Proceedings of the Sixth World Congress of Jewish Studies* (Jerusalem 1975) 2.35-45.

Subsequently expanded and published in English; see **8527**.

7522. R. A. KRAFT, 'The multiform Jewish heritage of Early Christianity', in J. NEUSNER (ed.), *Christianity, Judaism and other Greco-Roman cults: studies for Morton Smith at sixty*, part 3, *Judaism before 70*, SJLA 12 (Leiden 1975) 174-199, esp. 190-196.

Philo's allegorical method is briefly analyzed in relation to its intermediate position between the two opposite exegetical trends in Jewish culture: the literalists and the extreme allegorists. Other references to Philo are fleeting and concern the theme of Messianism and his evidence on the Essenes and the Therapeutae. (= R907)

7523. J. LAPORTE, 'Philo in the tradition of Biblical Wisdom literature', in R. L. WILKEN (ed.), *Aspects of Wisdom in Judaism and Early Christianity*, UNDCSJCA 1 (Notre Dame-London 1975) 103-141.

The author's aim in this article is not to offer an exhaustive study of the concept of wisdom in Philo, but to show the important role of Wisdom literature in his thought, a role which among Jewish writings is second only to the Pentateuch. The conclusions which he reaches can be summed up as follows. (1) Many motifs, images, and themes present in the biblical wisdom texts also occur in Philo. (2) The fact that he uses them widely and frequently shows that they form an essential component of his thought, to the extent that it would be incomprehensible without them. (3) These influences relate to both method and content, but at the same time Philo develops and expands them to a considerable extent. (4) Among the effects of this influence we should not underestimate the linguistic aspect; 'we find a philosophical language in biblical figures, highly developed, coherent, and creative' (135). Abstract in *StPh* 5 (1978) 130. (= R908)

7524. R. N. LONGENECKER, *Biblical exegesis in the Apostolic period* (Grand Rapids 1975), esp. 45-50.

A brief outline of Philo's allegorical interpretation in relation to the tradition of Old Testament exegesis. A few remarks are also devoted to the structure of Philonic thought, of which the Platonic foundation is emphasized. (= R909)

7525. B. L. MACK, 'Exegetical traditions in Alexandrian Judaism: a program for the analysis of the Philonic Corpus', *StPh* 3 (1974-75) 71-112.

The aim of this important contribution is explicitly programmatic, namely to find views shared by all scholars on which a collective analysis of the Philonic corpus can be constructed. The significance of Hellenistic Judaism has gradually increased in the eyes of scholars since it has become clear that it is precisely in this context that the origins of Gnosticism should be sought. What is urgently needed, therefore, is a rigorous definition of its exegetical tradition (cf. 75ff.), an analysis of the various kinds of interpretations it embraces (cf. 81ff.), and an in-depth analysis of the Philonic corpus and its individual treatises. The hypothesis underlying this programme is that Philo can be taken as a primary (if not exclusive) source of this tradition, and 'that a thorough analysis of the Philonic material with regard to the question of the exegetical method and traditions with which he worked may reveal the existence of various, perhaps contrasting or conflicting, theological traditions within the Hellenistic synagogue' (73). On 113-115 follows a summary of the discussion which took place, in which it was agreed that the programme deserved further exploration to be undertaken by the members of the Philo Institute. (= R911)

7526. A. MENDELSON, 'A reappraisal of Wolfson's method', *StPh* 3 (1974-75) 11-26.

The author analyzes the extent to which Philo was integrated in the cultural life of Alexandria, and on this basis indirectly discusses Wolfson's famous 'hypothetical-deductive' method. Mendelson notes that Wolfson oversimplified the cultural context of Alexandria on this point by distinguishing between believers (Pharisees) and apostates. In his opinion the Alexandrian situation must have been more complicated and segmented, so much so that somebody like Philo can not be reduced to one or the other category, but constitutes a *tertium quid*, a representative of intermediate positions and constraints (cf. 22). (= R912)

7527. J. MILGROM, 'On the origins of Philo's doctrine of conscience', *StPh* 3 (1974-75) 41-45.

Spec. 1.235-238 shows a concept of conscience which can be traced back to Jewish sources. In particular conscience is understood as being invested with the legal power to commute sentences. The main part of this article is also reproduced, as a response to Wallis, in **7553**. (= R913)

7528. A. MYRE, 'Les caractéristiques de la loi mosaïque selon Philon d'Alexandrie', *ScEs* 27 (1975) 35-69.

'Divine, revealed, inspired, immutable: Mosaic law is the best law' (69). On this certainty Philo constructed his entire cultural synthesis of Hellenism and Judaism. The author's interpretation of this synthesis is original and worth recounting. Philo, says Myre, 'was certainly not conscious of being Hellenized'. He did not at all try to save Judaism by Hellenizing it, but if anything tried to save paganism by Judaicizing it. Nor was he 'a poor, eclectic, second-hand philosopher'. On the contrary, 'he was *the philosopher* in full possession of divine wisdom, and therefore considered himself qualified to judge the various systems' (66). Abstract in *StPh* 5 (1978) 131. (= R914)

7529. J. NEUSNER, 'The idea of purity in ancient Judaism', *JAAR* 43 (1975) 15-26.

An important change in the interpretation of purity takes place in (a) Alexandrian Judaism and specifically Philo, and (b) Rabbinic Judaism. In both the concept is interpreted outside the context of worship, but in Philo 'the substance of the allegory [of purity] – the philosophical life – differs from that of the rabbis, which stresses practical and ethical behaviour' (24). (= R915)

7530. V. NIKIPROWETZKY, 'Note sur l'interprétation littérale de la loi et sur l'angélologie chez Philon d'Alexandrie', in *Mélanges André Neher* (Paris 1975) 181-190.

The author discusses the relations between the Sadducees and Philo with regard to the application of the Law and the doctrine of the angels. As far as the former is concerned, Nikiprowetzky concludes that Philo's intention in *Spec.* 'consists in justification pure and simple, certainly not always of the literal sense, but in any case of the letter of the Law' (183). With regard to the second subject, the author observes that from Philo's silence on Gabriel and Michael we cannot infer an attitude of 'repugnance' toward these figures.

See also further **8032**. (= R916)

7531. H. PAULSEN, 'Erwägungen zu *Acta Apollonii* 14-22', *ZNW* 66 (1975) 117-126, esp. 121-123.

The author notes 'surprising' parallels between the structure of Philonic cosmology and that of the *Acta Apollonii*, both being rooted in Stoic cosmology. (= R917)

7532. B. A. PEARSON, 'Hellenistic-Jewish Wisdom speculation and Paul', in *Aspects of Wisdom...* (cf. **7523**) 43-66, esp. 52-54.

The influence of Hellenistic-Jewish wisdom speculation on Paul becomes clear if his work is compared with that of Philo. The themes that emerge from this comparison are connected with the following concepts, which in Philo, according to the author, belong to a single line of development: τέλειος-νήπιος, πνεῦμα-ψυχή, πνευματικός-ψυχικός. Abstract in *StPh* 5 (1978) 132ff. (= R918)

7533. A. PELLETIER, 'La nomenclature du calendrier juif à l'époque hellénistique', *RB* 82 (1975) 218-233.

The names of the Jewish calendar passed unchanged into the Greek of the *koine*, where they were mostly transliterated. Philo in particular, in his allegorical interpretation, 'is only interested in the number of the months', and when considering a specific month, he indicates it by its ordinal numeral. (= R919)

7534. C. PERROT, 'Le repas du Seigneur', *MD* 123 (1975) 29-46.

In order to show the sacral meaning of meals in the Old and New Testament traditions, the author frequently turns to Philonic material. (= R920)

7535. E. DES PLACES, 'Numenius et la Bible', in L. ALVAREZ VERDES and E. J. ALONSO HERNANDEZ (edd.), *Homenaje a J. Prado: miscelanea de estudios biblicos y hebraicos* (Madrid 1975) 497-502.

Although Philo is only briefly mentioned, we cite this article by way of an exception because it is one of the few to discuss the relations between Philo and Numenius. Des Places hypothesizes that the intermediary between Numenius and the Bible might in fact be Philo, or the Jewish-Hellenistic tradition. (= R921)

7536. E. DES PLACES, 'Un terme biblique et platonicien: ΑΚΟΙΝΩ-ΝΗΤΟΣ', in *Forma futuri* (cf. **7501**) 154-158, esp. 156.

In this brief note the author suggests that the concept and term ἀκοινώνητος passed from Plato to Numenius through Philo. (= R922)

7537. G. QUISPEL, 'Jewish Gnosis and Mandaean Gnosticism', in J. E. MÉNARD (ed.), *Les textes de Nag Hammadi: colloque du Centre d'histoire des religions (Strasbourg, 23-25 octobre 1974)* (Leiden, 1975) 82-122, esp. 93f.

The author draws attention to some 'shocking and coarse erotic language' (94) used by Philo of Sophia in order to explain the description of Wisdom as a prostitute in the Gnostic treatise *Bronte*. (DTR)

7538. W. REISTER, 'Die Sophia im Denken Philons', in B. LANG, *Frau Weisheit. Deutung einer biblischen Gestalt* (inaug. diss. Düsseldorf 1975) 161-164.

Briefly illustrates some aspects of the concept of sophia in Philo: its character of ascetic virtue, the epithets attributed to it ('daughter of God', 'consort of God', 'mother of the world'), and the metaphors which Philo uses to represent it. (= R923)

7539. L. M. DE RIJK, 'Quaestio de Ideis: some notes on an important chapter of Platonism', in J. MANSFELD and L. M. DE RIJK (edd.), *Kephalaion: studies in Greek philosophy and its continuation offered to Professor C. J. De Vogel* (Assen 1975) 204-213, esp. 206f.

A survey of the *quaestio de ideis* from Plato to the modern age in which Philo also makes a brief appearance. The article is of interest because it enables us to place this Philonic theme in a very broad context. (= R924)

7540. H. SAVON, 'Saint Ambroise critique de Philon dans le *De Cain et Abel*', in E. A. LIVINGSTONE (ed.), *Papers presented to the Sixth International Conference on Patristic Studies held in Oxford 1971*, part 2, *Classica et hellenica, theologica, liturgica, ascetica*, StudPatr 13 (= TU 116; Berlin 1975) 273-279.

Far from being a slavish imitator of Philo, Ambrose departs substantially from Philo in the *De Cain et Abel*, even if this is sometimes difficult to detect. In this work, in fact, 'polemical preoccupations with regard to Philo are never absent, and ... Ambrose does not cease to defend himself against Philo when actually using him most' (278). (= R926)

7541. A. F. SEGAL, *Two powers in heaven: the significance of the Rabbinic reports about binitarianism, ditheism and dualism for the history of early Christianity and Judaism* (diss. Yale University 1975).

See **7741**.

7542. J. N. SEVENSTER, *The roots of pagan anti-semitism in the ancient world*, NT.S 41 (Leiden 1975).

A mainly historical work which deals with Philo only indirectly as a historical source. Nevertheless it is relevant to our study because it makes extensive analyses of Philo's works inasmuch as they for a long time constituted 'the prime sources for describing events and relationships in Alexandria' (15). This work points out, among other things, that anti-Semitism in antiquity was not racially oriented (cf. 36) and was only partly rooted in social-economic factors. Rather it was primarily a phenomenon related to cultural motives, in response to the strangeness of the Jews in ancient society (cf. 218). (= R927)

7543. F. SICILIANO, *Alla luce del 'logos': Filone d'Alessandria* (Cosenza 1975).

This work does not claim to be a scholarly inquiry, and is in fact far from up-to-date on the latest trends of interpretation. As an overall presentation of Philo, however, it has a certain lucidity and completeness, and as far as its views are concerned can be clearly set against those scholars who wish to make Philo into a 'mere mystic or even fanatic lacking appreciation of true philosophical issues' (2). There is no doubt that Siciliano moves along the lines of Wolfson's interpretation (though not without some substantial reservations, for instance on the nature of the Logos; cf. 45), an interpretation which places greater emphasis on Philo's philosophical dimension. Of specific interpretations we record the following. (1) God is also the creator of matter (35), while the Logos – it too created by God – has only an instrumental value in the act of creation (37). (2) The absolute priority of Being, and thus of God, gives a certain slant to Philo's thought, so that 'his philosophy is not pure theory, but existential enquiry' (53). (3) Given the essential incomprehensibility of God (61), however, philosophy as such needs the ecstatic moment in order to achieve its goal: hence Philo is both philosopher and mystic. It is the essentially problematic notion of Being which distinguishes Philo's position from that of Paul. REVIEW: A. de Vivo, *Vich* 5 (1976) 157ff. (= R928)

7544. C. SIRAT [סיראט .ק], הגות-פילוסופית בימי-הביניים [*Jewish philosophical thought in the Middle Ages*] (Jerusalem 1975) 11-16.

Subsequently published in English; see **8368**.

7545. A. R. SODANO, 'Ambrogio e Filone: leggendo il *De Paradiso*', *AFLM* 8 (1975) 65-82.

Ambrose's *De paradiso* shows clear Philonic influences, ranging from almost literal quotations to hidden and barely perceptible usage. The author concludes (82): 'Now if we take it to be certain that Ambrose knew Greek, these ambiguities [i.e. different ways of using Philo] ... might be attributed to the fact that Ambrose may not have had Philo's works directly at hand, but rather an exegetical draft already compiled on the basis of several interpreters of the Holy Scriptures'. (= R929)

7546. E. STAROBINSKI-SAFRAN, 'Sabbats, années sabbatiques et jubilés: réflexions sur l'exégèse juive et chrétienne de Lévitique 25', in *Mélanges Esther Bréguet* (Geneva 1975) 37-45, esp. 41-43.

The concepts of the Sabbath and the Sabbatical year cover a very wide range of meanings: religious, since they summon man to follow God; mystic and psychological, since they direct man toward the ideals of contemplation and introspection; ethical, because they promote spiritual progress; and, last but not least, social, because these occasions prescribe the remission of debts and the manumission of Jewish slaves. (= R930)

7547. G. STEMBERGER, 'Die Bedeutung des Tierkreises auf Mosaikfussböden spätantiker Synagogen', *Kairos* 17 (1975) 23-54, esp. 32ff.

Philo follows the apocalyptic writers in positing a correspondence of earthly liturgy to celestial liturgy. This is particularly clear in *Spec.* 1.88, where the twelve precious stones of the high priest's breastplate are associated both with the twelve tribes of Israel and the signs of the zodiac. (= R931)

7548. R. F. SURBURG, *Introduction to the Intertestamental period* (St. Louis 1975), esp. 153-161.

A general account of Philo without pretensions to originality, as part of a survey of inter-testamental literature. (DTR)

7549. C. H. TALBERT, 'The concept of immortals in Mediterranean antiquity', *JBL* 94 (1975) 419-436.

As part of the vast theme of this article (note its title), Philo is used as a source for making the distinction between the gods who are such by nature and those who have acquired divinity during their lives on account of special merits. The last category is linked to the Philonic theme of the *theios aner*. (= R932)

7550. J. W. THOMPSON, ''That which cannot be shaken': some metaphysical assumptions in Heb 12:27', *JBL* 94 (1975) 580-587.

The phrase in question is examined in relation to its historical-religious origins. Frequent references to Philo are inevitable here, since the theme of God's ontological stability and the instability of creation constantly reappears in Philonic thought. (= R933)

7551. E. E. URBACH, *The sages, their concepts and beliefs,* translated from the Hebrew by I. Abrahams, 2 vols. (Jerusalem 1975, 1979², Cambridge Mass. 1987³) *passim.*

It is impossible to give a full account of the many contexts in which Philo is cited in this work. Instead we draw particular attention to ch. 9 and 10 (184-254) on the creation of the cosmos and on God, where the references to Philo are more frequent and specific than elsewhere. The reader will find here copious – if somewhat scattered – examples of the points of contact between Philo and the main representatives of Jewish thought. Earlier version published in Hebrew; cf. **6925**. (= R935)

7552. C. DEL VALLE, 'Aproximaciones al método alegórico de Filón de Alejandría', *Helm* 26 (1975) 561-577.

According to the author Philo's allegorical method should not be interpreted as an isolated and individual phenomenon, but as a manifestation of the Jewish hermeneutical trend of the deraš, which underwent continuous development throughout the classical period until the later Middle Ages (cf. 577). (= R936)

7553. R. T. WALLIS, *The idea of conscience in Philo of Alexandria,* CHSHMC 13 (Berkeley 1975).

Wallis rejects *a priori* the Wolfsonian view that Philo's idea of conscience was absolutely original, and is thus left to specify the exact meaning of the term in Philo and the innovatory elements involved in it (cf. 1). If Philo's vocabulary on this theme is rather restricted (in effect he uses two terms to indicate conscience, ἔλεγχος and συνειδός), the contexts in which the concept occurs are many. They give rise to two opposite conceptions, one immanent and the other transcendent, which can be traced back in a number of ways: to the contrast between the Greek and Jewish components of Philo's thought; to a controversy about human faculties within Judaism; and, finally, to the general antithesis between nature and grace. Mediation between the two positions is in any case very difficult, and in Wallis's overall assessment (made with the help of a comparison of similar views in Neo-Stoicism, Plotinus, and Apuleius), Philo's position is limited to an incoherent metaphysical theory on the status of the conscience (cf. 8). At the same time, however, Philo is given merit for being the first to have emphasized the moral function of the conscience, to have specified its nature, and, in some degree, to have located it in a transcendent sphere. The publication in CHSHMC concludes with a series of further contributions by J. DILLON (9-13), W. S. ANDERSON (14-15), J. MILGROM (16-18, cf. 7527), S. SANDMEL (19), D. WINSTON (20-23), W. WUELLNER (24-28). These are followed by the usual debate on the subjects raised (30-47). Wallis's contribution alone was republished in *StPh* 3 (1974-75) 27-40 and in 8375. (= R938)

7554. J. C. M. VAN WINDEN, 'The early Christian exegesis of 'heaven and earth' in Genesis 1,1', in W. DEN BOER *et al.* (edd.), *Romanitas et Christianitas: studia J.H. Waszink ... oblata* (Amsterdam-London 1975) 371-382, esp. 373f.

Although he is not a Christian author, Philo's contribution to the development of the exegetical theme in question should not be overlooked because of his great influence on early Christian exegetes. Philo's interpretation is specifically referred to by Calcidius and echoed by Clement of Alexandria. (DTR)

7555. D. WINSTON, 'Freedom and determinism in Philo of Alexandria', *StPh* 3 (1974-75) 47-70 (cf. also above 7348).

The problem of free will emerges in every form of monotheism – and is therefore particularly prominent in Judaic religion – because it comes into violent conflict with the doctrine of God's infinite nature and goodness. The author analyzes this problem in the thought of Ben Sira (*StPh* 2 42-45), in the Sapientia Salomonis (*ibid.* 45f.), and finally in Philo. Winston's basic view is that the freedom discussed by Philo should not be considered absolute, but relative. Man does participate in the free will granted to him as a gift by God himself, but only to the extent in which he is capable of receiving it (cf. 61), an extent which, given man's essential *oudeneia*, cannot but be limited. In fact, the author observes, 'if God's gift [of freedom] is real (or absolute), then man's will is truly sovereign and independent... if however it is in some way unreal (or relative), then man does not indeed possess an absolute freedom of the will' (55). The whole tone of Philo's thought, therefore, is conditioned by determinism, following a general ethical conception which shows traces of Stoic influence (cf. 57). The article on Philo is reprinted in 7647, 8378. (= R939)

7556. D. WINSTON, 'Philo's theory of cosmogony', in B. A. PEARSON (ed.), *Religious syncretism in antiquity: essays in conversation with Geo Widengren*, American Academy of Religion and The Institute of Religious Studies University of California, Santa Barbara. Series on Formative Contemporary Thinkers 1 (Missoula 1975) 157-171.

After a brief presentation of Philo's cosmology, the author moves on to a critical analysis of Wolfson's views on this subject. Here Winston takes issue with Wolfson's interpretation of the Philonic theory of creation. In particular he denies that Philo had the concept of creation *ex nihilo*, and that God, in Philo's view, is the creator of matter. In addition to arguments based on textual analysis, Winston adduces the following philosophical proofs (167): 'First, if God created the copies of the four elements according to the pattern of the divine Forms, why should they be disordered? Second, how could God who, according to Philo, is never the source of evil, and is always introducing harmony and order, be the source of a pre-existent matter which is "contentious", "disordered", "dead", "chaotic", and "out of tune"?' (= R940)

7557. M. WINTER, *Pneumatiker und Psychiker in Korinth: zum religionsgeschichtlichen Hintergrund von 1. Kor. 2,6-3,4*, Marburger theologische Studien 12 (Marburg 1975), esp. 96-157.

One of the most important concepts in Philo is expressed by the term τέλειος, which is allegorically represented by the three Patriarchs: Abraham, who symbolizes the man who achieves perfection through learning-teaching; Isaac, who is perfect by nature; Jacob, who achieves perfection through training. Perfection is seen from a Stoic point of view as the last stage of a triadic process requiring both effort (cf. 116) – this motif is probably of Cynic origin – and abstinence, even if, in the final analysis, perfection remains a gift from God. Within this scheme Winter points out another hierarchy of concepts which plays on the following terms, though not always in the same order: ἀρχόμενοι, προκόπτοντες, τέλειοι. The defining characteristics of the perfect man are (a) perfect virtue and (b) the desire to know God (cf. 130ff.). The knowledge of God – which is for Philo in reality a revelation of God – can be achieved both through the practice of virtue and through the attainment of the moment of ecstasy. At this point (137ff.) the author raises the problem of Philo's debt to the mystery religions, and concludes that Philo neither drew on nor adhered to the mysteries directly, but depended on the Platonic tradition which, from Plato onwards, had absorbed many elements from this religion. Finally, attention is paid to the antitheses τέλειοι/πνευματικοί and ψυχικοί/σαρκικοί (143ff.) and to the corresponding antithesis σοφία-λόγος/σάρξ. The author points out that this antithesis is elaborated in a broader structure which no longer distinguishes two, but three classes of men: men of earth, men of heaven, and men of God (cf. *Gig.* 60). (= R941)

1976

7601. M. ALEXANDRE, 'L'exégèse de Gen. 1, 1-2a dans l'*In Hexa-emeron* de Grégoire de Nysse: deux approches du problème de la matière', in H. DÖRRIE, M. ALTENBURGER, U. SCHRAMM (edd.), *Gregor von Nyssa und die Philosophie: zweites Internationales Kolloquium über Gregor von Nyssa, Freckenhorst bei Münster 18.-23. September 1972* (Leiden 1976) 159-192, esp. 166f., 178, 181f.

The main difference between Gregory's and Philo's metaphysics is that the former completely lacks a hypostatic conception of God's thoughts and, consequently, also lacks the conception of a separate intelligible world (cf. 166f.). (= R942)

7602. Y. AMIR [עמיר .י], הסוואה ראציונאלית להגות אירראציונאלית אצל פילון האלכסנדרוני ['The rationalistic masking of irrational thought in Philo'], *Eshel Beer-Sheva* 1 (1976) 68-77.

Subsequently published in German; see **8309**.

7603. M. BALTES, *Die Weltentstehung des platonischen Timaios nach den antiken Interpreten*, vol. 1, PhilAnt 30 (Leiden 1976), esp. 32-38, 86-93.

The interpretation of the origin of the world as presented in Plato's *Timaeus* was the subject of a lively debate in Philo's time, traces of which are found in his work. Philo was forced in this connection to accommodate both (a) his Jewish faith and hence the biblical story of creation and (b) his Platonic background which drew on the contents of the *Timaeus*. The result was that although he regarded the act of creation as a real act (and not a mere metaphorical dependence of the world on God), he placed this act outside any chronological context. Baltes points out that Philo was acquainted with the figurative interpretations of the *Timaeus* (cf. 86), but kept to the literal interpretation of the treatise, thus showing a debt to Peripatetic thought (cf. 33). (= R943)

7604. J. R. BASKIN, *Reflections of attitudes towards gentiles in Jewish and Christian exegesis of Jethro, Balaam and Job*, (diss. Yale University 1976), esp. 52-66, 158-163, 273-4.

In the Rabbinic tradition the biblical figures Jethro, Balaam and Job represent the proselytizing gentile, the villainous gentile and the righteous gentile respectively. Baskin sets out to compare these exegetical treatments with the interpretations of the same figures found in Hellenistic Judaism (LXX, Philo, Josephus) and the Church Fathers. To this end a brief analysis is presented of all the passages in which Philo discusses the figures of Jethro and Balaam (Job is not mentioned in the Philonic corpus). Contrary to Rabbinic and Patristic exegetes, Philo and the other Greek-speaking writers do not emphasize the fact that these figures represent gentiles. Reasons suggested for this are: (a) the identification with gentiles is not an important theme in the passages devoted to these figures; (b) Philo's 'writings are highly individual attempts to communicate his unique Graeco-Jewish amalgam of commentary and philosophy' and do not reflect 'the practice and attitudes of an established religious community' (353). (DTR)

7605. P. BORGEN, 'Response concerning the Jewish sources', *NTS* 23 (1976) 67-75.

Borgen responds to B. LINDARS, 'The place of the Old Testament in the formation of New Testament theology', *NTS* 23 (1976) 59-66. Philo should be added as an important source for reconstructing the historical-religious milieu of the New Testament, firstly because of his evident relevance to John's Prologue and Hebrews, and secondly because his allegorical method, which probably drew on exegetical trends common to Judaism as a whole, also sheds light on the Jewish religious culture of Jesus' day. Abstract in *StPh* 5 (1978) 121f. (= R944)

7606. P. CARNY [פ. קרני], סיפור על מוצא לשון האדם [= 'The story of the origins of human language'], in הגות במקרא... לזכר י. רון [*Reflections on the Bible... in memory of Y. Ron*], vol. 2 (Tel-Aviv 1976) 223-232.

An interpretation of Gen 2:19-20. The modern interpreters are viewed against the background of the ancient versions, the midrashic literature and Philo (228-231). The Philonic sources discussed are: *Opif.* 136; *QG* 1.20-22; *Leg.* 3.14-18. Philo belongs to those interpreters of Gen 2:19f. who see here the story of the origin of man's language. Some parallels to midrashic literature are noted. English summary. (MM)

7607. A. CHASTAGNOL, 'Autour de la 'sobre ivresse' de Bonosus' in A. ALFÖLDI (ed.), *Bonner Historia Augusta-Colloquium 1972/1974*, Antiquitas IV. Reihe: Beiträge zur Historia-Augusta-Forschung 12 (Bonn 1976) 91-112.

There are certain similarities, especially of content, between the concept of *sobria ebrietas* in Philo and the character of Bonosus in the *Historia Augusta*. But these do not permit us to assume a direct relationship between the two texts. Rather they suggest an indirect influence possibly involving Origen, Cyprian, Eusebius, and in the final instance Ambrose. (= R945)

7608. G. L. COCKERILL, *The Melchizedek Christology in Heb. 7:1-28* (diss. Union Theological Seminary in Virginia 1976), esp. 388-412.

The author discusses Theissen's and Käsemann's interpretations of Hebrews and finds himself in disagreement with the latter, who sees in Philo a testimony, contemporary to the author of Hebrews, of a late Jewish tradition which supposedly identified the Gnostic *Urmensch* with the figure of the high priest (cf. 397). Cockerill's objections rest on three observations. (1) Philo's *logos archiereus* has nothing to do with the high-priest-who-sacrifices-himself of Hebrews. (2) The Philonic Logos cannot be identified with the *Urmensch*. (3) Philo did not identify the *logos archiereus* with Melchizedek, who is merely the symbol of man's logos (cf. 411). Moreover, Philo did not speculate independently on Melchizedek, whereas the latter does play an exceptional role in Hebrews, giving expression to the sacerdotal function of Christ (393). (= R946)

7609. I. ESCRIBANO-ALBERCA, 'Die spätantike Entdeckung des inneren Menschen und deren Integration durch Gregor', in *Gregor von Nyssa...* (cf. **7601**) 43-60.

The author talks at some length about the relations between the Gnostic and Philonic γνῶθι σαυτόν and reports the major scholarly views on this subject. In the discussion which follows the contribution the subject is also discussed by E. MÜHLENBERG, C. KANNENGIESSER and M. ALEXANDRE (59). (= R947)

7610. F. T. FALLON, 'The law in Philo and Ptolemy: a note on the Letter to Flora', *VChr* 30 (1976) 45-51.

Ptolemy's *Letter to Flora* presents a polyvalent interpretation of the Law involving multiple levels of understanding. The same is found in Philo, though details differ. Philo too supposedly ascribed different origins to different passages of the Law (cf. 45). Abstract in *StPh* 6 (1979-80) 207. (= R948)

7611. G. D. FARANDOS, *Kosmos und Logos nach Philon von Alexandria*, Elementa. Schriften zur Philosophie und ihrer Problemgeschichte 4 (Amsterdam 1976) 150-306.

For the first part of the book see **1110**. Philo's work is a demythologization or de-ideologization of the Old Testament by means of philosophy and allegorical interpretation. But at the same time it is the search for a system of principles on which a new social order can be constructed that is cosmopolitan and based on the Logos. Within this framework Philo's conception of philosophy is defined: it rests on the aspiration to contemplate being, which is achieved in a long process of μετανάστασις, i.e. transmigration from the sensible world to the *nous* (cf. the diagrams on 202) and to God. From here the author turns to the problem of God's nature and unknowability (203-230). The task of philosophy is the knowledge of Being, which in its essence coincides with God. Since God is unknowable for man, however, philosophical speculation will have to come to a stop at the Logos (image of God) and, secondly, at the world. The *metanastasis* of the spirit provides and makes possible, as an intermediate stage, knowledge of the world, the essence of which is becoming. The author makes the following points here. (1) The genesis of the world corresponds to a process from not-being to being; it is therefore a creation *ex nihilo* which does not, however, exclude a parallel and originally Platonic demiurgic conception of God. (2) The genesis of the cosmos corresponds to the genesis of time. (3) The creation of the cosmos presupposes an ideal plan which is the world of the ideas innate in the Logos (cf. the diagram on 296). (4) Creation, therefore, appears to be divided into a *kosmos noetos* and a *kosmos aisthetos*. On this point Farandos makes two further observations: (a) given the clear distinction between the two worlds, there is no room for a theory of recollection; (b) but this separation should not be considered absolute since the Logos is present in both worlds and there is moreover a paradigm-image relationship between the two. A diagram on 306 shows the various connections between the two kinds of cosmos. REVIEWS: C. Steel, *ThPh* 40 (1978) 354; P. Nautin, *RHR* 196 (1979) 208. (= R949)

7612. U. FISCHER, *Studien zur Eschatologie des hellenistischen Diasporajudentums* (inaug. diss. Lüneburg 1976), esp. 229-266.

Philo's statements on the afterlife show a strong Platonic influence: death is essentially conceived as the soul's ascent to heaven. Yet this ascent implies no eschatology, in the sense of hope for a new world which will come about at the end of time. In fact, neither eschatology nor the conception of death as a liberation from the body plays a central role in Philo. At the heart of his thought stands rather the conviction that man is already able in this world to rise to the contemplation of God, which is in a certain way an anticipation of the soul's fate after death. In order to prove this, the author adduces Philo's tendency to avoid categorical affirmations about man's afterlife and instead to take refuge in an allegorical interpretation which effectively transfers all affirmations onto the ethical level. Philo, in short, lacked an eschatology of the future but had an eschatology of the present. In the same way he lacked a 'national' eschatology, i.e. one limited to the chosen people. In Fischer's view, there are essentially three reasons for this: the ahistorical nature of Philo's thought, the central position of the figure of Moses in the context of a Jewish mystery, and, finally, his ethical-religious universalism. (= R950)

7613. V. GUAZZONI FOÀ, *Ricerche sull'etica delle scuole ellenistiche,* Pubblicazione dell'Istituto di Filologia Classica e Medievale 44 (Genoa 1976) 67-83.

Examining the concept of conscience in Philo, the author is led to define the wide semantic reach of the term ἔλεγχος in Philo (and to a lesser extent of the terms συνείδησις and σύνεσις). The analysis shows that the Philonic implications of this notion are much vaster than those of the Greek λόγος. In practice, for Philo, the fullness of being sought by man cannot be achieved by thought alone, but only if one adds to the latter the fruits of mystical experience, involving a leap from 'psychotherapy' to soteriology. (= R951)

7614. R. G. HAMERTON-KELLY, 'Some techniques of composition in Philo's *Allegorical Commentary* with special reference to *De agricultura*: a study in the Hellenistic Midrash', in R. HAMERTON-KELLY and R. SCROGGS (edd.), *Jews, Greeks and Christians: religious cultures in late antiquity: Essays in honor of W. D. Davies,* SJLA 21 (Leiden 1976) 45-56.

The allegorical technique according to which *Agr.* is structured can be reduced to two main principles: one related to a method of allegory and division which is of Greek-philosophical origin and consists in dividing an idea into two opposite sub-ideas; the other related to the originally Jewish technique of inference by analogy. The method used in *Agr.* is therefore a fine example of 'transcultural methodology' (54). Abstract in *StPh* 5 (1978) 129. (= R952)

7615. H. A. HARRIS, *Greek athletics and the Jews,* Trivium Special Publications 3 (Cardiff 1976), esp. 51-95.

According to the author, there is no 'other writer in Greece [like Philo] who so frequently and so effectively conjured up before the eyes of the reader a picture of what happened in a sports stadium at the beginning of the Christian era' (13). From this he concludes that Philo took part in the sporting activities directly, and not only as a spectator (cf. 72). The author collects and briefly explains the main Philonic passages discussing athletics and competitive sports in general. Of particular interest is Harris's demonstration of the ethical function of the sport metaphors, showing how Philo draws a clear distinction between the formative and pedagogical side of sport and its competitive and spectacular aspect (84). Philo judges the former favourably, the latter unfavourably. (RR)

7616. J. HOCHSTAFFL, *Negative Theologie: ein Versuch zur Vermittlung des patristischen Begriffs* (Munich 1976), esp. 33-35.

Philo places Greek metaphysics in the context of Jewish revelation and sees it in a mystical light. Hence Philo's negative theology, understood as the infinite effort of the spirit in search of its unreachable origins. (= R953)

7617. R. A. HORSLEY, 'Pneumatikos vs. psychikos: distinctions of spiritual status among the Corinthians', *HThR* 69 (1976) 269-288.

The terminological opposition *pneumatikos-psychikos* does not actually occur in Philo, who rather elaborates the contrast between the mortal body and the immortal soul. Nevertheless, Philo constitutes a significant antecedent of Cor. in that he anticipates the structure which underlies this religious text as a whole. The oppositions τέλειος/νήπιος, heavenly man and earthly man, πνευματικός/ψυχικός should be understood as parallel expressions 'for different levels of spiritual status or different religious types of men' (288). (= R954)

7618. F. L. HORTON, *The Melchizedek tradition: a critical examination of the sources to the fifth century and in the Epistle to the Hebrews*, SNTSMS 30 (Cambridge, 1976), esp. 54-60, 156-158.

The aspect of Philo's treatment of the figure of Melchizedek in the three passages analyzed which the author finds important is his emphasis on Melchizedek's lack of antecedents in the priest-kingship. This doctrine, which Philo uses as the basis of an equation of the priest with the Logos, is based on the observation that Melchizedek is the first priest to be mentioned in the Pentateuch. Philo is thus 'not allowing his imagination to run rampant' (158). (DTR)

7619. M. E. ISAACS, *The concept of spirit: a study of pneuma in Hellenistic Judaism and its bearing on the New Testament*, Heythrop Monographs 1 (London 1976) 1-64 *passim*.

There is a fundamental balance between the Platonic and Stoic elements in Philo's pneumatology. The Platonic influence (mainly recognizable in the interpretation of the biblical account of creation and in the entirely new interpretation of the ideas as the thoughts of God) reveals itself in a form of transcendentalism which nevertheless does not shirk the problem of the relationship between creator and created. The Stoic influence, on the other hand, reveals itself mainly in the terminology, which is typical of a materialistic context. Basically Philo used Stoic terms to express Platonic concepts, especially in the doctrine of the *pneuma*, but in this operation a synthesis of content was also involved. The *pneuma*, in fact, is the divine element in us – hence the theme of prophetic *pneuma* (cf. 47ff.); it is a reality 'in the world but not of it' (30). *Pneuma* is therefore a concept which serves to translate Philo's faith in a God who is beyond the world and at the same time a vital force which pervades the world from the inside. (= R955)

7620. I. JACOBS, 'The Midrashic background for James II. 21-3', *NTS* 22 (1976) 457-464.

In trying to show that the figure of Abraham in the passage under discussion corresponds to a model centuries older than James, the author also turns to Philonic evidence, where Abraham is characterized by 'his total submission to the Divine will' (461). (= R956)

7621. T. JAMES, 'Philo on circumcision', *South African Medical Journal* 50 (1976) 1409-1412.

A brief note on the practice of circumcision in various cultures and religions, with particular reference to Judaism and Philo's position. (RR)

7622. A. JAUBERT, *Approches de l'Évangile de Jean: parole de Dieu* (Paris 1976), esp. 157f., 168-174.

According to the author the parallels between John and Philo are twofold: (a) the metaphorical use of certain terms ('spiritual food', 'eyes of the spirit'); (b) certain applications of the term Logos. The second parallel is then further analyzed into the following: (1) the theme of man's kinship with the Logos; (2) the conception of the Logos as image of God; (3) the motif of the Logos as food for the soul and (4) its mediating function between God and humanity; (5) the metaphor of the Logos as light and (6) as medicine for the soul. At 157ff. the author discusses the Philonic meaning of the term θεῖος with reference to man. (RR)

7623. E. KAMLAH, 'Philos Beitrag zur Aufhellung der Geschichte der Haustafeln', in B. BENZING *et. al.* (edd.), *Wort und Wirklichkeit: Studien zur Afrikanistik, E. L. Rapp zum 70. Geburtstag* (Meisenheim am Glan 1976) 90-95.

Certain Philonic writings (especially *Decal.* 165-167 and *Spec.* 2.226-233) show clear traces of Stoic influence – relating to the doctrine of duty – on Jewish family ethics, especially with regard to the interpretation of the fifth commandment. (= R957)

7624. A. KASHER, 'Les circonstances de la promulgation de l'édit de l'empereur Claude et de sa lettre aux Alexandrins (41 ap. J.C.)', *Sem* 26 (1976) 99-108, esp. 102, 105, 108.

The author uses Philo's testimony (*Flacc.* 25-43) to throw light on the date and historical circumstances of the Claudian edict referred to by Flavius Josephus (*Ant. Jud.* 19.280f.) and of Claudius' letter to the Alexandrians (*P. Lond.* 1912). (RR)

7625. E. LUCCHESI, 'La division en six livres des *Quaestiones in Genesim* de Philon d'Alexandrie', *Muséon* 89 (1976) 383-395.

Discusses the difficult problem of the book division of *QG*. The most probable of three possible solutions is that, prior to the Armenian version, the work was divided into six books and two sections (the first containing books 1-4 and the second books 5 and 6). In any case we can rule out the division into four books which has come down to us. The division into two parts seems to be oldest, but there are insufficient grounds for making it go back to Philo. Abstract in *StPh* 5 (1978) 130f. (= R959)

7626. E. LUCCHESI, 'Réminiscence philonienne dans le discours de Paul devant l'Aréopage?', *REArm* 11 (1975-76) 179-181.

In Acts 17:28 reference is made to poets, probably of the Stoic school. It is likely that Paul is referring to something reported by Philo 'rather than to this or that text written by the poets in question' (180). Abstract in *StPh* 5 (1978) 131. (= R960)

7627. E. LUCCHESI, 'Un trait platonicien commun à Virgile et Philon d'Alexandrie', *REG* 89 (1976) 615-618.

The immortality manifested in the perpetuation of species is a Platonic theme which is also found, though in different contexts, in Philo (the posterity promised by God to Abraham) and in Virgil (*Georg.* 4.197-209). (= R961)

7628. J. C. MCLELLAND, *God the anonymous: a study in Alexandrian philosophical theology*, Patristic Monograph Series 4 (Cambridge Mass. 1976) 23-44.

The author's basic thesis is that the roots of Western thought, though buried in Greek soil, were nourished by Judaism and Christianity, from which they drew a new sense of history and time. The point at which these two movements converge is the Alexandrian philosophical theology represented by Philo, Clement, and Origen, a theology which, in philosophical terms, can be defined as 'classical theism' or 'Christian Hellenism'. McLelland states that Philonic thought – which he analyzes along general lines – shows three fundamental theological doctrines: (a) the namelessness of God; (b) his immutability and impassibility; (c) mystical union as a superior form of the knowledge of God. (= R958)

7630. W. A. MEEKS, 'The divine agent and his counterfeit in Philo and the fourth Gospel', in E. SCHÜSSLER FIORENZA (ed.), *Aspects of religious propaganda in Judaism and Early Christianity*, UNDCSJCA 2 (Notre Dame-London 1976) 43-67.

Although not wishing to postulate any direct relationship between Philo and John, the author holds that Philo is 'a fixed point of inestimable value in every study of first century Judaism and Christianity, not only because of the volume of his extant writings, but because he can be located precisely in place, time, and social class' (44). Meeks proceeds to concentrate on the comparison set up by Philo between the ideal divine agent, i.e. Moses the divine king, and the parody of the divine king, Caligula. Because 'what the Jews say about Jesus is rather like what Philo says about Gaius: that he, a man, makes himself God' (55), many of the theological and polemical aspects in John can be explained with reference to this Philonic context, though with a reversal of roles. Abstract in *StPh* 6 (1979-80) 210ff. (= R962)

7631. V. MESSANA, 'Caino ed Abele come εἴδη archetipali della città terrena secondo Agostino ed Ambrogio', *Sil* 4 (1976) 269-302, esp. 273-276.

Philo saw the rational and vital powers in man as two 'archetypal entities' expressed by the figures of Abel and Cain. The opposition between these two figures finds its limit in the creationistic context of Philo's thought, in which the earth too is a 'good creature' created by God. These themes were taken up and reworked by Ambrose, Augustine and the Fathers in general. (= R963)

7632. C. MÖLLER, *Die biblische Tradition als Weg zur Gottesschau: eine Hermeneutik des Judentums bei Philon von Alexandria* (diss. Tübingen 1976).

Philonic hermeneutics cannot be properly understood unless it is related to the way that Philo saw the function of the Jewish community and tradition in his time and world (cf. 2). For Philo 'presents himself as a Jew and his system as a form of Judaism' (2); he presents himself as an exponent of the theology of the Diaspora and as a passionate believer in the importance of the Jewish people for humanity as a whole. The latter idea, which Möller considers essential, is given a two-fold realization: (a) by demonstrating that the Bible has an answer for the problems of each individual person; (b) by explaining the inseparable connection between Scripture and the Jewish nation (cf. 116), one being the source and the other the guardian and mediator of the truth. Allegory and philosophy in Philo's work have a mediating function which is both missionary and apologetic in intent: missionary, because Philo wishes to be understood by a philosophically educated audience; apologetic, because by showing the similarities between Old Testament and Greek thought he implicitly demonstrates the truth and universality of the former (cf. 177). Möller's study is divided into three parts: (1) allegory and its functions: apologetic, polemic, cognitive; (2) the paradigmatic function of the history of the Patriarchs; (3) the role of the Jewish people in the ascent of the soul. These three parts clearly illustrate the essential elements of Philo's theory of knowledge with its typically religious objectives, and show how this theory involves the historical role of Israel. Philo, Möller observes, 'regards the Jewish tradition as a means of achieving the ideal of life which is common to all humanity and which corresponds to the highest form of knowledge' (79). (= R964)

7633. A. MYRE, 'La loi de la nature et la loi mosaïque selon Philon d'Alexandrie', *ScEs* 28 (1976) 163-181.

The concept of law in Philo comprises two fundamental categories: natural law and Mosaic law. These appear to be related in the following ways: (a) both are of divine origin; (b) their origin is in time; (c) they are immutable; (d) in their respective spheres, cosmological and human, both are universal; (e) they are concerned with ethical conduct; (f) they are susceptible to interiorization. As far as human behaviour is concerned, Philo gives the first place to natural law, 'but he assigns a position of relative pre-eminence to Mosaic law on account of man's moral and intellectual weakness' (181). (= R965)

7634. P. NAUTIN and L. DOUTRELEAU, 'Didyme L'aveugle sur la Genèse', *SC* 233, 244 (Paris 1976-78), esp. 1.27-28.

One of Didymus the Blind's sources for his commentary on Genesis was Philo, whom he cites by name on 6 occasions. Some of Philo's influence may have occurred via Origen, but the authors do not doubt that Didymus had a sound knowledge of Philo's writings. (DTR)

7635. V. NIKIPROWETZKY, 'Rébecca, vertu de constance et constance de vertu chez Philon d'Alexandrie', *Sem* 26 (1976) 109-136.

Philo's etymological and symbolical interpretation of Rebecca has caused disagreement among scholars. After an extensive linguistic and exegetical analysis (involving the secular tradition, the LXX, and the Philonic corpus), Nikiprowetzky reaches the following conclusions. (a) In Philo the terms ὑπομονή-ἐπιμονή used with reference to Rebecca do not carry the theological meaning which they had in the LXX. (b) The etymology ὑπομονή (constancy) proposed for Rebecca perhaps testifies to the existence of such an exegetical tradition in Alexandria, although Philo himself could have invented it on the basis of the episode of Rebecca's pregnancy. But all this need not imply that Philo knew 'the slightest trace of Hebrew' (136). Abstract in *StPh* 6 (1979-80) 216f. (= R966)

7636. M. PETIT, 'À propos d'une traversée exemplaire du désert du Sinaï selon Philon (*Hypothetica* VI, 2-3.8): texte biblique et apologétique concernant Moïse chez quelques écrivains juifs', *Sem* 26 (1976) 137-142.

The figure of Moses owes its exemplaristic role to the fact that it gradually came to be the apologetic centre of a long Jewish tradition, which was mainly a reaction to a series of accusations and attacks. Philo marks the culmination of this tendency, which explains his frequent deviations from the biblical account and the historical figure of Moses. Abstract in *StPh* 5 (1978) 133. (= R967)

7637. L. F. PIZZOLATO, 'La coppia umana in S. Ambrogio', in R. CANTALAMESSA (ed.), *Etica sessuale nel Cristianesimo delle origini*, Studia Patristica Mediolanensia 5 (Milan 1976) 180-211.

Ambrose, particularly in the *De paradiso*, alternates between Philo's strongly negative notion of women and the soteriological Christian notion which 'emancipates female nature' (182). When the former notion prevails, Ambrose appeals to a philosophical interpretation, according to which the feminine element, equated with *aisthesis*, is the cause of the guilt of the male element (the *nous*). Nevertheless Philo's pessimism with regard to female nature does not have the final word: man's original unity is restored when woman is prepared to subordinate herself to man, i.e. when the mind regains its rightful supremacy. (RR)

7638. *Reallexikon für Antike und Christentum*, edited by T. KLAUSER *et al.*, vol. 9 (Stuttgart 1976).

Cf. above **5016**. Contains: R. BOGAERT, art. 'Geld (Geldwirtschaft)', 797-907, esp. 814 (money, wealth and attitudes towards them); B. KÖTTING, art. 'Gelübde', 1055-1100, esp. 1065-6 (vows to God); G. D. G. MÜLLER, art. 'Geister (Dämonen)', 546-797, esp. 638 (demons; the section on Philo is clearly inadequate, but the rest of the long article reflects most usefully on Philo's views); W. SPEYER, art. 'Genealogie', 1145-1268, esp. 1212-3 (genealogies).

7639. J. M. RIST, *The use of Stoic terminology in Philo's Quod Deus immutabilis sit, 33-50*, CHSHMC 23 (Berkeley 1976); reprinted in *Platonism and its Christian heritage* (London 1985).

It is not by chance that Rist's study takes the form of a commentary, for in the author's opinion this form of exegesis is perhaps the only way of getting around the contradictory views put forward by interpreters of Philo. The work nevertheless has a unity of its own, as becomes apparent from the author's final summary. The section of *Deus* under discussion should be placed in the context of Stoic terminology, but shows lacunae, omissions, and often deviations which cannot be wholly imputed to Philo, but suggest an 'intermediate doxographical source' (12). This source is not to be located in the ancient Stoa, but in the Academy of Philo of Larissa and Antiochus of Ascalon. In examining the theme of free will, finally, Rist sees traces of a theory of innate ideas which has parallels in the Stoicism of Epictetus, but is probably much older; he is again inclined to think of Antiochus of Ascalon. The contributions which follow – by T. CONLEY (13-16), J. M. DILLON (17-20), V. NIKIPROWETZKY (21-26), and D. WINSTON (27-28) – supplement Rist's analyses in a useful way. The publication concludes with a discussion on the subjects raised. (= R968)

7640. K. G. SANDELIN, *Die Auseinandersetzung mit der Weisheit in 1. Korinther 15* (Abo 1976), esp. 26-44.

In examining Philo's exegesis of Gen. 2:7 and the cultural background which influenced it, Sandelin presents a very rigorous and schematic analysis which is divided into the following points: (a) the divinity of man's spirit or soul (man's soul becomes divine through God's act of creation); (b) the Logos as image and spirit of God, the soul as image of the Logos; (c) Sophia as the image and spirit of God, the soul of the perfect man as the image of Sophia. Two schematic representations of the points (b) and (c) show the correspondences between the series God-Logos-nous and the series God-Sophia-soul with relation to the figure of the wise man. (= R969)

7641. E. P. SANDERS, 'The covenant as a soteriological category and the nature of salvation in Palestinian and Hellenistic Judaism', in *Jews, Greeks and Christians* (cf. **7614**) 11-44, esp. 25-44.

In Philo's view the relationship between individual man and his salvation depends on whether or not he belongs to the covenant between God and Israel. In this sense he thinks that all Jews will be worthy of salvation, 'except those who sinned "incurably"' (40), i.e. apostates. Sanders calls this conception 'covenantal nomism', by which he means 'the view according to which salvation comes by *membership* in the covenant, while obedience to the commandments *preserves* one's place in the covenant' (41). (= R970)

7642. E. SCHWEIZER, 'Christianity of the circumcised and Judaism of the uncircumcised: the background of Matthew and Colossians', in *Jews, Greeks and Christians* (cf. **7614**) 245-260, esp. 249-260.

Certain Philonic passages are used to comment on Colossians and Matthew in relation to various subjects. We draw particular attention to the theme of 'girding oneself with virtue', related by the author to the Logos which 'girds itself' with the elements (252ff.) and the theme of abstinence understood as a fundamental component of the lifestyle of the Therapeutae (cf. 258). Abstract in *StPh* 5 (1978) 134. (= R971)

7643. E. SCHWEIZER, 'Gottesgerechtigkeit and Lasterkataloge bei Paulus (inkl. Kol und Eph)', in J. FRIEDRICH, W. PÖHLMANN, P. STUHLMACHER (edd.), *Rechtfertigung. Festschrift für E. Käsemann zum 70. Geburtstag* (Tübingen-Göttingen 1976) 461-477.

The author uses numerous Philonic passages to comment on Rom. 13:13 and Col. 3:5-8. In particular certain statements made by Paul are explained with reference to Philo's theory of the elements. Abstract in *StPh* 5 (1978) 135. (= R972)

7644. M. SIMON, 'Jupiter-Yahvé: sur un essai de théologie pagano-juive', *Numen* 23 (1976) 40-66.

Within Judaism there is a view which utterly rejects the pagan divinities. But in Alexandrian Judaism, and particularly in Philo, there is also an attitude which 'refuses to see nothing but error and perdition in paganism and is concerned to bring out the similarities rather than hurl anathemas' (66). (= R973)

7645. E. M. SMALLWOOD, *The Jews under Roman rule: from Pompey to Diocletian*, SJLA 20 (Leiden 1976), esp. 235-250.

The third chapter of this large work discusses the situation of the Jews in Egypt and naturally uses Philo's evidence as a prime historical source. This material is particularly important for reconstructing the riots of 38 A.D. and the subsequent embassy to Gaius, about which we are informed by the accounts in *Flacc.* and *Legat.* (= R974)

7646. E. STAROBINSKI-SAFRAN, 'La lettre et l'esprit chez Philon d'Alexandrie', *RenCJ* 44 (1976) 43-51.

The problem of mediating between letter and spirit is not only an exegetical question (here accurately placed in the context of Jewish biblical interpretation in antiquity and the Middle Ages); it is also a practical and theoretical question which involves 'the life of the body and the soul, the exigencies of the community, and the growth of the individual' (51): in short, a constant search for harmony. (= R975)

7647. D. WINSTON, *Freedom and determinism in Philo of Alexandria*, CHSHMC 20 (Berkeley 1976).

This contribution is also found published in *StPh* 2 & 3 (**7348, 7555**), to which we refer the reader. In addition to Winston's article, one finds here responses by J. M. DILLON and P. D. EISENBERG and a general discussion on the subject (24-35). (= R976)

7648. C. WOLFF, *Jeremia im Frühjudentum und Urchristentum*, TU 118 (Berlin 1976), esp. 152-155.

A brief section is devoted to the Philonic quotations of Jeremiah, which are in complete agreement with the Septuagint version. (= R977)

1977

7701. P. J. ALEXANDER, 'A neglected palimpsest of Philo Judaeus: preliminary remarks *editorum in usum*', in *Studia Codicologica*, TU 124 (Berlin 1977) 1-14.

The author draws attention to a valuable palimpsest in the library of Athens, but advises that he is not able to offer a complete description or exhaustive study. He confines himself to giving some notes of considerable interest, and at the end of the article draws up a synoptic table of contents in relation to the Philonic treatises as found in Colson's edition. These amount to mostly brief extracts from eleven works. Abstract in *StPh* 5 (1978) 121. (= R978)

7702. G. ALON, 'On Philo's Halakha', in *Jews, Judaism and the classical world: studies in Jewish history in the times of the second temple and Talmud*, translated by I. ABRAHAMS (Jerusalem 1977) 89-137.

The author analyzes Philo's interpretation of certain ritual laws and procedures and compares it with the Halachah on the following points: (a) the types and modes of offerings used by the priests, with particular reference to the rules set out in *Spec.* 1.132-150; (b) the legal structure and the organization of the priesthood in Jewish society, with particular reference to *Spec.* 3.52-63; (c) the description and allegorical interpretation of certain Jewish religious feasts (e.g. of the Passover, the Unleavened Bread, the Sheaves, and the Tabernacles) in *Spec.* 2.145-188, 204-209. Earlier version published in Hebrew; cf. **5702.** (= R979)

7703. B. J. BAMBERGER, 'Philo and the Aggadah', *HUCA* 48 (1977) 153-185.

This study 'is an effort to show that Philo had a modest knowledge of the Palestinian traditions later incorporated into Rabbinic literature' (154). The author draws this conclusion after first discussing methodological issues and then presenting a careful analysis of 41 examples in which there appears to be at least some evidence that Philo borrowed from the Palestinian tradition. Abstract in *StPh* 6 (1979-80) 202-203 (= R979/a)

7704. J. M. BAUMGARTEN, 'Studies in Qumran law', *SJLA* 24 (Leiden 1977), esp. 134-138.

The sacred nature of the number fifty in Philo shows affinity with Pythagorean doctrines as well as with certain Jewish religious and ritual ideas. These find a particular application in the way Philo presents the determination of the feast of Pentecost in the calendar of the Therapeutae (*Contempl.* 65). (= R980)

7705. J. BERNARD, 'La guérison de Bethesda: harmoniques judéo-hellénistiques d'un récit de miracle un jour de sabbat', *MSR* 33 (1976) 3-34 (esp. 15-27); 34 (1977) 13-44 (esp. 37-44).

The problem of the Sabbath rest is not given a definitive solution by Philo. The author shows that this ambiguity can be related to (a) the ambiguity of the biblical sources themselves and to (b) Philo's desire to compare the Old Testament account with the philosophical cosmologies in order to demonstrate the credibility and superiority of the Old Testament revelation. It seems evident in any case that 'for Philo God was not constrained by the limits of time' and that 'his creation continued on the day of Sabbath as well' (part I, 25). As far as John 5:1-30 is concerned, this seems to draw on a pre-Gnostic cultural context which is Philonic only in relation to the themes shared by Philo with the Jewish tradition of his time (cf. II 43). Abstract in *StPh* 6 (1979-80) 203f. (= R981)

7706. B. BOKSER, *Philo's description of Jewish practices*, CHSHMC 30 (Berkeley 1977).

The problem raised in this contribution is that of clarifying the relations between Philo and the Judaism of Jerusalem, its tradition, and the ideas of proto-Rabbinism. The author's starting-point is that even if Philo had taken Palestinian 'material', he would not have been able to reproduce it in its original form since the social-religious context to which he was referring was entirely different. Bokser then suggests that it is necessary to turn to a more proximate reference, to a Judaism which is also 'outside the temple' and which is as close as possible to the cultural context in which Philo operated. The choice falls on the Therapeutae and on the description of their banquet. The banquet of the

Therapeutae, however, – and here we come to the objection urged by V. NIKIPROWETZ-KY, Bokser's interlocutor in the discussion – can not be considered representative of Judaism in general, but is rather a specific rite which exists apart from Jewish practices and is, more specifically, a supplement *sui generis* to these practices. Besides Nikiprowetzky's response (14-18), there are responses by N. FORSYTH (12-13), L. H. SCHIFFMAN (19-27), and B. Z. WACHOLDER (28-29). The customary account of the discussion that followed Bokser's paper is found at 30-40. Abstract in *StPh* 6 (1979-80) 204. (= R982)

7707. P. BORGEN, 'Some Jewish exegetical traditions as background for son of man sayings in John's Gospel (Jn 3, 13-14 and context)', in *L'Évangile de Jean: sources, rédaction, théologie*, BEThL 44 (Louvain 1977) 243-258; reprinted as 'The son of man saying in John 3.13-14', in *idem, Logos was the true light and other essays on the Gospel of John* (Trondheim 1983) 133-148.

Borgen compares the passage from John's Gospel with various Philonic passages relating mainly to the theme of the 'descent from heaven'. Various similarities between the two authors are noted. (1) In both authors the ascent of Mount Sinai is interpreted as a birth. (2) This birth is a descent from heaven in which (3) God is postulated as a father and a mother is absent. (4) Thus this fact is regarded as a second birth. (5) Moreover there are undeniable correspondences between the opposition σάρξ-πνεῦμα in John and the opposition σῶμα-νοῦς in Philo. Finally Borgen speculates on the origin of the concept of 'rebirth' in Philo and on whether it is entirely of Hellenistic origin, or whether it carries traces of Hermetic doctrine. Abstract in *StPh* 5 (1978) 122. (= R983)

7708. P. BORGEN and R. SKARSTEN, '*Quaestiones et solutiones*: some observations on the form of Philo's exegesis', *StPh* 4 (1976-77) 1-15; reprinted in P. BORGEN, *Paul preaches circumcision and pleases men and other essays on Christian origins* (Trondheim 1983) 191-201.

The exegesis by question and answer typical of *QE* and *QG* also occurs, if less explicitly, in works like *Opif.* and *Decal.* It is clear, therefore, that at the basis of this exegesis stands a common method which constitutes a genuine 'exegetical formula'. (= R984)

7709. G. F. CHESNUT, *The first Christian histories: Eusebius, Socrates, Sozomen, Theodoret, and Evagrius*, ThH 46 (Paris 1977), esp. 147-155.

An idea that gained some popularity in the early imperial period identified the good emperor with 'incarnate reason'. This idea also influenced Philo's thought, if within the limits imposed by a strictly monotheistic faith. Chesnut repeatedly emphasizes important points of contact between Eusebius and Philo. (= R985)

7710. A. H. CHROUST, 'Some observations on Aristotle's doctrine of the uncreatedness and indestructibility of the universe', *RCSF* 32 (1977) 123-143.

Philo is used as a doxographical source in order to reconstruct the part of the *De philosophia* concerned with the theme under discussion. (= R986)

7711. C. DANIEL, "Le voyant', nom cryptique des Esséniens dans l'œuvre de Philon d'Alexandrie', *SAO* 9 (1977) 25-47.

The 'one who sees' is a term which Philo mostly uses to designate the wise man. Its original context is basically obscure, yet would be important for an understanding of Philo. By identifying the term with the Essenes, it is possible to shed light on many aspects of Philo's thought; this identification would in fact provide us with the key required to interpret a way of speaking which in the view of the author remains mysterious even today (25). (= R987)

7712. G. DELLING, 'Die Bezeichnung 'Söhne Gottes' in der jüdischen Literatur der hellenistisch-römischen Zeit', in J. JERVELL and W. A. MEEKS (edd.), *God's Christ and his people: studies in honour of N. A. Dahl* (Oslo 1977) 18-28.

In Philo the epithet 'son of God' usually refers to the Logos or the cosmos, and only rarely to the pious man. Philo tends to connect the expression with the ethical connotation of the ultimate goal of piety (cf. 23f.). (= R988)

7713. J. DILLON and A. TERIAN, 'Philo and the Stoic doctrine of εὐπάθειαι: a note on *Quaes. Gen.* 2.57', *StPh* 4 (1976-77) 17-24.

In an unmediated examination of the Armenian text of the passage in question, the authors are guided by the symmetry which the Stoics (and indirectly also Philo) aimed at in their search for rational equivalents of the passions. Dillon and Terian are thus led to suggest δηγμός as the fourth εὐπάθεια. When D. Winston drew attention to Cicero *TD* 3.83 as a parallel passage, however, Dillon felt inclined to withdraw his suggestion. (= R989)

7714. J. DILLON, *The Middle Platonists: 80 B.C. to A.D. 220* (London-Ithaca-New York 1977), esp. 139-183.

Philo's thought is analyzed here into its basic components, but in a form which 'is deliberately partial, attempting to isolate ... those elements which may derive from contemporary Platonism' (182). In this study, in fact, Dillon is easily able to condense almost the entire philosophical aspect of Philo's thought, chiefly because the deliberate exclusion of the Jewish element allows a great number of exegetical problems to recede, and also because Dillon holds that Philo's goal, apart from some concessions to Peripatetic philosophy, was essentially to adapt his own exegetical method to contemporary Alexandrian Platonism, which itself in turn was heavily influenced by Stoicism and Pythagoreanism. As regards the theory of the Powers and man's insignificance in the face of God – doctrines usually held to be original to Philo –, the author seems inclined to consider these the result of a mixture of influences. Dillon's study is significant, for it is one of the few recent noteworthy contributions on the relations between Philo and Middle Platonism, a field which is only gradually being explored in the way it deserves. (= R990)

7715. S. S. FOSTER, 'A note on the "Note" of J. Schwartz', *StPh* 4 (1976-77) 25-32.

Foster takes a close look at the article by Schwartz on Philo's family and shows that his justification of Philo's Roman citizenship is largely conjectural. That applies in particular to the hypothesis which traces this privilege back to the assistance given by Philo's grandfather to Mithridates. (= R991)

7716. A. GLIBERT-THIRRY, *Pseudo-Andronicus de Rhodes ΠΕΡΙ ΠΑΘΩΝ: édition critique du texte grec et de la traduction latine médiévale*, Corpus Latinum Commentariorum in Aristotelem Graecorum, Suppl. 2 (Leiden 1977), esp. 273-319.

In an appendix to this critical edition of the Περὶ πάθων, the author discusses at length the parallel tradition (273-319). Philo is extensively quoted, so that an accurate idea can be obtained of the relations beween him and Pseudo-Andronicus. (RR)

7717. C. R. HOLLADAY, *'Theios aner' in Hellenistic-Judaism: a critique of the use of this category in New Testament Christology*, SBLDS 40 (Missoula 1977), esp. 103-198.

The use of the expression θεῖος ἀνήρ in *Virt.* 177 is an exception in Philo's phraseology and thought. Various hypotheses have been advanced to justify it: it is a semitechnical expression, or an expression which designates the man who has had the vision of God, or, simply, an expression borrowed from the Stoic vocabulary related to the figure of the sage. For various reasons, however, none of these explanations is entirely convincing. The adjective θεῖος, though occurring frequently and variously in Philo, is in fact very rarely attributed to a man. The reason for this is to be found in the anthropological-metaphysical dualism which characterizes Philo's thought, the same dualism which justifies the opposition σῶμα-ψυχή in man. This conclusion is based on an in-depth analysis of diverse Philonic passages, especially those related to the presentation of Moses as θεός in Ex. 7:1. The author goes on to affirm: 'Deification, in Philo, takes place only insofar as detachment from the sensible world is possible' (196), whether it reveals itself in the (unrealizable) depiction of the Stoic sage, or is related to the subject of the meeting between divine and human (155-163) or human and divine (163-167), or, finally, is connected with the allegory of the high priest who enters into the Holy of Holies (170-173). The chapter concludes with the author explicitly agreeing with the statement of C. H. Dodd (cf. **5308**) that 'true to his Jewish upbringing, Philo keeps the distinction between God and man' (197). (= R992)

7718. R. A. HORSLEY, *'Wisdom of word and words of wisdom in Corinth'*, *CBQ* 39 (1977) 224-239.

Philo held eloquence and rhetoric in great esteem. The many critical attitudes which he adopts in this connection are not directed against eloquence and rhetoric as such, but against their degeneration. The concepts of language in general and rhetoric in particular cannot be separated from the broader subject of human perfection and the various levels which it involves. (= R993)

7719. D. JOBLING, *'"And have dominion...": the interpretation of Genesis 1, 28 in Philo Judaeus'*, *JSJ* 8 (1977) 50-82.

There are three basic aspects to Philo's interpretation of the passage in question: anthropological, ethical, and cultural. In each of these the influence of Greek thought is predominant: Stoicism and Middle Platonism in the anthropology and ethics; Sophistic thought and the Cynic school in the assessment of human culture. Jobling observes that Philo is strongly attracted here by the Cynic idea of the renunciation of culture. The Philonic interpretation of this passage is rather disorganized, but herein lies precisely its documentary value, since it draws together all the interpretations of Gen. 1:28 current in his time and considerably enriches them (cf. 81). Abstract in *StPh* 5 (1978) 129f. (= R994)

7720. J.-G. KAHN [ישר-כהן .י], על זמן ונצח במחשבתו של פילון האלכסנדרוני ['On time and eternity in Philo's thought'], *Proceedings of the Sixth World Congress of Jewish Studies* (Jerusalem 1977) 3.223-228 [Hebrew section]

Following his previous study (**6729**), Kahn wishes to check whether *Aet.* is in line with other statements of Philo regarding *creatio ex nihilo*. He accepts this work as Philonic, since the theory of creation is similar to the rest of Philo's work. Though the Alexandrian is not clear about this point and his terminology is not decisive, Philo certainly did believe in creation *ex nihilo*. English summary. (MM)

7721. A. F. J. KLIJN, *Seth in Jewish, Christian and Gnostic literature*, NT.S 46 (Leiden 1977) *passim*.

Klijn observes that Philo marks a turning-point in the Jewish tradition concerning Seth. He is in fact the first Jewish thinker to regard this figure as 'another seed', i.e. as the beginning of a new generation leading to Abraham and Moses. (= R995)

7722. E. LUCCHESI, *L'usage de Philon dans l'oeuvre exégétique de Saint Ambroise: une 'Quellenforschung' relative aux Commentaires d'Ambroise sur la Genèse*, ALGHJ 9 (Leiden 1977).

The object of this work is mainly philological, its aim being to reconstruct as accurately as possible the textual tradition of the Philonic corpus. The results which it reaches can be summed up as follows. (a) Ambrose certainly knew *Sacr.* and the first two books of the *Quaestiones* in the original Greek and used them in his *De Cain et Abel*, *De Noe*, and *De Abraham*. (b) His extensive use of these Philonic writings allows us to regard Ambrose 'as one of the authorized witnesses of the manuscript tradition of Philo' (118), and in this he is all the more interesting because he appears to have read and used a large section of the *Quaestiones* which has since been lost. (c) Ambrose was introduced to the writings of Philo by his teacher Simplicianus. (d) Apart from the three commentaries mentioned above, caution bids us posit an indirect relationship between Philo and Ambrosius, probably mediated through Origen. The work concludes with an interesting Appendix (122-126) in which a new classification of Philo's works is proposed, based largely on the catalogue in Eusebius' *Historia ecclesiastica*. Lucchesi suggests a three-part division of the corpus and limits the so-called Allegorical Commentary to *Opif.*, *Leg.*, *Cher.*, *Sacr.*, *Det.*, *Post.*, i.e. excluding all the other works usually considered to be part of this series. (= R996)

7723. E. LUCCHESI, 'Utrum Ambrosius Mediolanensis in quibusdam epistulis Philonis Alexandrini opusculum quod inscribitur *Quis rerum divinarum heres sit* usurpaverit an non quaeritur', *Muséon* 90 (1977) 347-354.

On the basis of a careful analysis the author concludes that Philo's influence (and specifically that of *Her.*) on Ambrosius' Ep. 1 and 2 was not direct, but almost certainly mediated through Origen. (= R997)

7724. E. LUCCHESI, 'Précédents non bibliques à l'expression néotestamentaire: "les temps et les moments"', *JThS* 28 (1977) 537-540.

Argues that the expression χρόνοι ἢ καιροί was not directly inspired by Dan. 2:21, but by a philosophical or Gnostic doctrine which was implicitly challenged by Philo as well as the Acts of the Apostles and Paul. (= R998)

7725. F. LUCIANI, 'Uso e significato del verbo εὐαρεστέω nei LXX e in Filone Alessandrino', *Verifiche* 2-3 (1977) 275-297, 557-588.

Philo is dealt with in the second part of the article. There the author analyzes all passages in which the verb εὐαρεστέω occurs and gives a very precise translation of each, thus bringing out the various semantic shades of the term. Next the same passages are subdivided into (a) texts in which biblical passages are quoted, (b) texts which simply refer to the Bible, (c) texts which do not refer to the Bible (cf. 584f.). In a further subdivision the material is considered according to the various meanings of the verb: (1) in its proper sense of 'to please' and 'to be agreeable'; (2) in the meaning 'to take pleasure in'; (3) in the moral and religious sense of 'to please, to be agreeable to God'. A philologically rigorous scholarly contribution. (= R999)

7726. G. LUONGO, 'Homo militans: la metafora della diserzione nella letteratura greca', *AFLN* 19 (1976-77) 109-142, esp. 125f.

Though quite brief, this contribution is interesting because it places the image of desertion – which in Philo interestingly shows the influence of Plato's *Apologia* rather than the *Phaedo* – in a wider referential framework, and thus throws new light on a particular theme of Philo's allegorical exegesis. (= R1000)

7727. M. MALINA, 'Sailing to Alexandria: Philo's imagery', *StPh* 4 (1976-77) 33-40.

An artistic and literary analysis of Philo's allegory, arguing that the absence of a narrative chain along Aristotelian lines is not a serious fault and that its 'textual density may be appreciated for the thematic amplification which it offers' (38). The latter involves 'the active participation of the reader's or viewer's imagination' (*ibid.*). (= R1001)

7728. J. P. MARTÍN 'Filón de Alejandría y el actual problema semiótico', *RFL* 3 (1977) 181-199.

As far as we know, this article constitutes a unique attempt to place Philonic exegetical discourse in the context of modern semiotics. The author appropriates Foucault's theory of the three ages of semiotics (resemblance, representation, and operation) and regards Philo's thought as 'the maximum theoretical expression of the semiotics of resemblance' (108). (= R1002)

7728a. J. P. MARTÍN, 'El texto y la interpretación: la exégesis según Filón de Alejandría', *RevBib* 39 (1977) 211-222.

Philo's interpretation of the biblical text can be characterized in the following manner. (1) 'The literal expression of Scripture is necessary, because it is the fruit of divine revelation, true philosophy, given to Israel as a universal meaning valid for all reasonable men' (222). (2) The meaning of Scripture has two aspects, a literal (superficial) one and an allegorical (profound) one. (3) The word of God has directive value, but the crown of spiritual progress is the vision of God. (4) Moses is prophet and legislator, God's instrument for communicating the truth to man. (5) God is the source of inspiration for both the author and the reader of the Bible, and ensures an authentic interpretation. (RR)

7729. M. DE MERODE, '"Une aide qui lui corresponde": l'exégèse de Gen. 2, 18-24 dans les écrits de l'Ancien Testament, du judaïsme et du Nouveau Testament', *RThL* 8 (1977) 329-352, esp. 341-343.

In the context of Judaism Philo was certainly the writer who most strongly emphasized the subordination of woman to man. Merode points out that in actual fact Philo merely legitimated, from a philosophical and exegetical point of view, the political marginalization of women which characterized the society of his day. (= R1003)

7730. R. H. NASH, 'The notion of mediator in Alexandrian Judaism and the Epistle to the Hebrews', *WThJ* 40 (1977) 89-115, esp. 105-109.

Intervening in the debate between Spicq and Williamson, the author points out that it is not possible to deny 'the common heritage of Hellenistic Judaism of Alexandria' (92) in Hebrews and Philo. This legacy can be reduced to five common themes: sophia, Logos, the intermediaries, the dominant role of the Logos, and the opposition between the earthly and the heavenly temple. At the same time Nash also indicates various essential differences, notably in relation to the theme of the Logos. (1) the Logos in Hebrews is not a metaphysical abstraction, but a person. (2) Philo's philosophical system is incompatible with the dogma of incarnation. (3) Christ's compassion for his brethren and his humanity cannot be reconciled with Philonic *apatheia*. (= R1005)

7731. V. NIKIPROWETZKY, *Le commentaire de l'Écriture chez Philon d'Alexandrie: son caractère et sa portée; observations philologiques*, ALGHJ 11 (Leiden 1977).

Though not claiming to be a state-of-the-art report on Philonic research (cf. 3), this indispensable study of Philo starts by discussing a multitude of interpretations which are shown to cancel one another out. But the reconstruction of these interpretations and the search for an objectivity which is not merely a compromise between extremes (some of Nikiprowetzky's views are close to Völker, cf. 241) do not stop at the bibliographical level. Nikiprowetzky in fact offers an original interpretation of Philo which can be summed up in two chief points. Firstly, the axis of Philo's thought is a particular 'exegetical intention' which reveals itself especially in the Allegorical Commentary (cf. 5). Secondly, the philosophical foundation of this exegesis consists in the common origin – in the reality of divine wisdom – of revelation and natural law. Just as *physiologia* interprets nature, therefore, so *philosophia* attempts to interpret the hidden and ultimately inscrutable meaning of Scripture and God. The instrument of this interpretation is allegory. These two principles have a number of fundamental consequences. (1) From a philosophical point of view, the centre of Philonic thought is the idea of migration (cf. 239), the structure of which is provided by the biblical account. (2) In this sense every *a priori* interpretation of Philo, e.g. the search for a rigorous and systematic unity of thought in his work, must be considered deceptive (162). (3) The use of Greek philosophy as an instrument for reading the Bible – a use which, among other things, accounts for Philo's apparent eclecticism and scepticism – does not rule out an apologetic intent. The latter, in fact, is responsible for the lack of rigour with which some terms are used. (4) Finally, the invocation of 'exegetical constraint' allows the author to explain the persistence of many contradictions on the philosophical level, but at the same time to show how this leads to a highly innovatory and powerful use of certain technical terms typical of Greek philosophy. Three other important subjects dealt with are Philo's knowledge of Hebrew (it is denied that he had any), the meaning of φιλοσοφία in Philo's writings, and the structure of Philo's commentaries on Scripture (it is argued that there are really only two series of commentaries, not three, as generally thought). Nikiprowetzky's work constitutes a fundamental point of reference in the study of Philo. The final chapter entitled 'Prolégomènes à une étude de Philon' points the way to important and fruitful areas of further study and interpretation. REVIEWS: A. Paul, *RecSR* 66 (1978) 360ff.; J. C. M. van Winden, *VChr* 32 (1978) 220f.; M. Bouttier, *ETR* 54 (1979) 701f.; R. P. C. Hanson, *JThS* 30 (1979) 310f.; A. V. Nazzaro, *Vich* 8 (1979) 387ff.; H. Savon, *REG* 92 (1979) 574ff.; D. A. Bertrand, *RHPhR* 60 (1980) 256; J. Murphy-O'Connor, *RB* 88 (1981) 147; A. Solignac, *ArPh* 54 (1981) 678ff.; W. Wiefel, *OLZ* 76 (1981) 552ff. Murphy-O'Connor's review provoked a reply on the part of the author, *RB* 89 (1982) 159f. See also **8443**. (= R1006)

7732. V. NIKIPROWETZKY, 'ΣΤΕΙΡΑ, ΣΤΕΡΡΑ, ΠΟΛΛΗ et l'exégèse de I Sam. 2, 5, chez Philon d'Alexandrie', *Sil* 3 (1977) 149-185.

Far from being a mere philological note, this article, starting from the expression in question (*Deus* 10-15) and from the translation usually given since Leisegang, gives a detailed account of the meaning of the two terms στεῖρα/στερρά in Greek antiquity and Philo's writings. Nikiprowetzky goes on to deal with the whole theme of sterility in Philo and the figures which express it (Sarah, Leah, Rachel), and also makes important observations on general methodology (cf. 184). Philo – the author concludes, thereby rejecting the current interpretations advanced by translators – 'could not give the double sense of 'sterile' and 'closed' to the word στεῖρα, for the simple reason that in Greek this word never involves the second meaning supposed here' (185). Instead the correct interpretation must be sought in the double meaning (positive and negative) which Philo assigns to sterility (cf. 176). (= R1007)

7733. B. A. PEARSON, *Philo and the Gnostics on man and salvation*, CHSHMC 29 (Berkeley 1977).

The aim of this work is to explain the relation between Philo's theology and religion on the one hand, and that between Gnosticism and Philo on the other (cf. 1). The author's view is that Philo is not a Gnostic in the technical sense of the word, nor was he influenced in any determinant way by Gnosticism. In order to demonstrate this, he singles out the theme of man and his salvation, common to Philo and Gnosticism, and sets up a comparison with the *Apocryphon of John*, which is taken as an example of Gnostic religiosity. The comparative analysis of the thought of both thinkers produces a series of similarities and differences. The similarities are the opposition πνεῦμα /ψυχή, the διάνοια/ἐπίνοια as an instrument of salvation, the interpretation of Gen. 1:26, the theme of the body formed from the four elements and seen as the tomb of the soul, the use of the allegorical method. The differences consist above all in Philo's greater fidelity to the biblical text and in the profound disagreement on the interpretation of God: one and transcendent in Philo, dualistically divided between negative and positive principles in Gnosticism. If we take these differences to be predominant, the similarities can only be explained by tracing them back to a common Jewish-Alexandrian exegetical tradition, and, as far as philosophical content is concerned, to Middle Platonism. Pearson's contribution is followed by the responses of T. CONLEY (18-22), J. DILLON (23-24), B. L. MACK (25-36), A. WIRE (37-38), E. N. LEE (39-41), and a brief account of the final discussion (43-58). Abstract in *StPh* 6 (1979-80) 217. (= R1008)

7734. J. RIAUD, *Les Thérapeutes d'Alexandrie dans la tradition et dans la recherche critique jusqu'aux découvertes de Qumran* (diss. Paris 1977).

This dissertation represents a vital contribution to research on the Essenes and Therapeutae in that it fills important gaps in our knowledge of Jewish religiosity and Philo. The subject under discussion has in fact given rise to a vast body of scholarly literature which, more even than the literature on Philo, contains many contradictory interpretations, to the extent that certain views 'on the Therapeutae, considered to be new, are in actual fact very old' (11). This goes to demonstrate the deadlock in which research on the subject finds itself, i.e. it is incapable of putting its own tradition in order and is exposed to the risk of unconsciously beating well-trodden paths. Riaud gives his work an anthological character, but at the same time imposes on it a rigorous structure provided by the material itself. He observes that, 'skimming through this literature, we found that the critics variously saw in the Therapeutae a utopia of asceticism, the first Christians of Alexandria, a branch of Essenism, and, finally, an original Jewish sect' (11). These points of view give the author the titles of the various sections in his work. A fifth chapter, by way of addition, deals with the question of the Therapeutae in our times. (= R1009)

7735. G. ROCCA-SERRA, *Le stoïcisme pre-imperial et l'esclavage*, Studi vari di storia greca ellenistica e romana: atti 7 (Milan 1976-77) 205-221, esp. 217ff.

Philo assigns both a psychological, and also a political meaning to the concept of slavery (*Prob.* 79, *Contempl.* 70), namely where he refers to a society without slaves which he sometimes identifies with the Essenes and other times with the Therapeutae. Citing the Dead Sea scrolls, the author notes that the second view of the concept does not derive from Judaism, which lacked 'a developed ideology against slavery' (200), but is rooted in Stoicism. (= R1010)

7736. J. R. ROYSE, 'The original structure of Philo's *Quaestiones*' *StPh* 4 (1976-77) 41-78.

Competently and clearly discusses the complex problem of the structure of the *Quaestiones*. A first solution to the problem was offerred by Wendland, who established that the fourth book of *QG* in the Armenian version must correspond to books 4, 5, 6 of the original Greek version. Later this view was criticized by Lucchesi and also to a certain extent by Marcus, who suggested that the division into books of *QG* need not depend on an internal criterion of symmetry and equilibrium of parts, but on a division relating to the customary cycle of weekly readings from the Pentateuch in the synagogues of Philo's time. Royse's further analysis confirms the basic validity of Marcus's suggestion, and so can shed further light 'on the difficult problem of the extent to which Philo is truly a product of contemporary Alexandrian Judaism' (62). Reconstruction of the extent of the commentaries on Genesis and on Exodus is aided by the many fragments and references found in the *catenae* of the Patristic tradition. Cf. also **8441**. (= R1010/a)

7737. E. P. SANDERS, *Paul and Palestinian Judaism: a comparison of patterns of religion* (Philadelphia, 1977), esp. 553ff.

At the end of Sanders's long book he briefly raises the question of Paul's relation to Hellenistic Judaism as represented by Philo. There is a similarity in that both thinkers are persuaded that man is in a state of bondage, but Paul's 'flesh' differs from Philo's body, and Paul's 'spirit' is not the same as Philo's soul. For Paul the conflict is between God's Spirit and the Flesh as the power that opposes God. (DTR)

7738. S. SANDMEL, 'The rationalist denial of Jewish tradition in Philo', in J. BEMPORAD (ed.), *A rational faith: essays in honor of Levi A. Olan* (New York 1977) 137-143.

A non-specialist contribution which attempts to present Philo as having achieved a balance between religious faith and philosophical knowledge. The author expresses himself with the usual incisiveness and clarity – qualities which never fail to make the contributions of this scholar interesting, even when these are of a non-scientific character. His conclusion is that Philo appears to affirm from a religious point of view what he in fact denies from a philosophical point of view (cf. 143). (= R1011)

7739. H. SAVON, *Saint Ambroise devant l'exégèse de Philon le Juif*, 2 vols., Études Augustiniennes (Paris 1977).

By means of an extremely detailed and extensive analysis of the *De Paradiso*, *De Cain*, *De Noe*, *De Abraham* 2, and *De fuga saeculi*, the author sets out to define the relationship between Ambrose and Philo, paying especial regard to its development. Philo's thought and above all his allegorical method was first discovered, later modified, and finally surpassed by Ambrose. This process did not, however, occur in a series of clear-cut breaks, but rather through the 'constant, minute, and careful vigilance' by which Ambrose, using a rigorous method, continually and sometimes imperceptibly corrected the Philonic model. One might say, Savon observes, that Ambrose's attitude to Philo was one of 'taking the words and leaving behind the content' (380). Having thus specified that Ambrose's thought must be sought beneath the apparent Philonism of some of his treatises (particularly the *De fuga*), and more in the differences than in the similarities, the author goes on to reach the following conclusions. (1) In the ethical realm Ambrose is harsher in his condemnation of pleasure than Philo; in contrast to Philo, he assigns to ethics an eschatological dimension; he denies astronomy any kind of propedeutic role with respect to religion, underlining the precariousness of creation; he makes no concession whatsoever to fate. (2) In the theological-philosophical realm he modifies the Philonic relationship between God and the Logos, and rejects the Platonic views – which were at the basis of Philo's thought – on the relation between ideas and reality ('what is real is the flesh of Jesus, and Plato's Ideas are nothing but vain shadows' (382)). (3) In the exegetical sphere Ambrose brought three changes to Philo's allegorical method. 'First he enriched it and made it more complex by multiplying the number of possible combinations. Next he firmly centred it around the person and mystery of Jesus. Finally, he constricted it by strictly associating it with orthodox doctrine and condemning the roads which the Alexandrian had left open' (384). REVIEWS: J. Doignon, *REL* 55 (1977) 586ff.; A. Solignac, *ArPh* 41 (1978) 499ff.; P. Courcelle, *Gn* 51 (1979) 292ff.; V. Nikiprowetzky, *REG* 94 (1981) 193-199 (= **8119**). (= R1012)

7740. G. SCARPAT, *Il pensiero religioso di Seneca e l'ambiente ebraico e cristiano*, Antichità classica e cristiana 14 (Brescia 1977), esp. 64-73.

Discusses certain themes common to Seneca and Philo which show 'that in his
religious thought Seneca may have drawn impulses from cultural accretions of Jewish-
Alexandrian provenance' (73). Interesting observations are also made on the relationship
between Philo and the treatise *On the Sublime* (cf. 64ff.). (= R1012/a)

7741. A. F. SEGAL, *Two powers in heaven: early Rabbinic reports
about Christianity and Gnosticism*, SJLA 25 (Leiden 1977), esp. 159-181.

The subject of this study is the mysterious group of Jewish heretics reported in our
Rabbinic sources who maintained the doctrine that there were 'two powers in heaven',
i.e. that the divine principal angel in heaven in some way was God. Philo's evidence is
of crucial importance, for it shows that such thinking existed already at the beginning of
our era. Diverse passages are analyzed in which Philo speaks of two Gods or of a first
and a second God, the latter referring to the divine Logos. Sometime Philo is aware of
the danger of his terminology for the doctrine of monotheism, sometimes not. In the
latter case he takes over ideas from the philosophical tradition involving the notion of
mediation. The choice of texts exploited by Philo clearly runs parallel to Rabbinic
tradition. Segal concludes that there must have been a basic tradition common to both
Philo and the Rabbis. (DTR)

7742. G. STEMBERGER, *Geschichte der jüdischen Literatur: eine Einführung* (Munich 1977), esp. 60-62.

An excessively brief outline of Philo's life and works in the context of a complete
survey of all Jewish literature from the Bible to the 20th century. (= R1013)

7743. J. W. THOMPSON, 'The conceptual background and purpose of
the Midrash in Hebrews VII', *NT* 19 (1977) 209-223.

A precise interpretation of the figure of Melchizedek, who is compared in Hebrews to
Christ, calls for a study of the sources in the light of the history of religion. Thompson
disagrees with Rusche (**5517**), who related Hebrews to apocalyptic literature rather than
to Philo, and assigns the thought expressed in this letter to the Philonic tradition, chiefly
on the basis of the 'dualistic reading of the Old Testament and its emphasis on the stability
of the deity' that the two writers share (222). The doctrine of creation provides an
adequate justification for the two motifs in both Hebrews and Philo. (= R1014)

7744. H. A. WOLFSON, 'What is new in Philo?', in *From Philo to
Spinoza: two studies in religious philosophy*, with an introduction by I.
TWERSKY (New York 1977) 17-38.

The purpose of the slender volume is to give an overview of Wolfson's contribution to
the history of philosophy. The chapter on Philo represents the final chapter of his
celebrated study (cf. **4714**). Twersky's introductory words provide a useful preview of
Wolfson's prodigious achievement. (DTR)

7745. J. ZANDEE, *'The teachings of Silvanus' and Clement of Alexandria: a new document of Alexandrian theology*, Mémoires de la Société
d'Études Orientales 'Ex Oriente Lux' 19 (Leiden 1977) *passim*.

The Teachings of Silvanus disclose themes typical of 2nd century Hellenized

Christianity. The author certainly did not attain to Clement's level of culture, but he was interested enough in philosophy to give us information about the philosophical-eclectic Alexandrian milieu of which Philo was an important exponent. Comparing the *Teachings* with passages from Clement, Zandee thus frequently needs to turn to Philo's works, and so gives a useful picture of the development of Alexandrian thought. (= R1015)

7746. H. ZIMMERMANN, *Das Bekenntnis der Hoffnung: Tradition und Redaktion im Hebräerbrief*, BBB 47 (Cologne 1977) esp. 91ff.

In Philo's writings Melchizedek is cited as king and high priest. Read allegorically, the two terms refer to the nous and the logos respectively. (= R1016)

1978

7801. Y. AMIR, 'Die Begegnung des biblischen und des philosophischen Monotheismus als Grundthema des jüdischen Hellenismus', *EvTh* 38 (1978) 2-19.

Although Philo is mentioned only briefly in this article, it makes an important contribution to the reflection on the Hellenization of Jewish thought and is thus of considerable interest to Philonic scholarship. The author argues that there is an essential difference between the conception of God's oneness in the Old Testament and in Greek philosophical theology. In the former God stands in relation to man and is to be worshipped and above all to be obeyed, whereas in the latter he is an object of knowledge. As diverse examples show, both sides tend to misunderstand each other in terms of their own assumptions. Philo is so influenced by the philosophical legacy of Hellenism that he softens the conception of God's oneness in the doctrine of the Logos and the Powers and becomes alienated from the conception developed in Jewish traditional belief (13-14). Nevertheless it would be simplistic to conclude that such Hellenization amounted to a total capitulation; Philo's Jewishness emerges in the selectivity of his approach to Greek philosophy. For the subsequent Hebrew version, cf. **8402**. (DTR)

7802. U. BIANCHI, 'Le Gnosticisme: concept, terminologie, origines, délimitation', in B. ALAND *et al.* (edd.), *Gnosis: Festschrift für H. Jonas* (Göttingen 1978) 33-64, esp. 53-55.

Philo is not a Gnostic, because he firmly maintains the unicity and transcendence of God. Nevertheless he contains Gnostic elements to the extent that he accepts the dualistic foundation of anthropology and the consequent ontological necessity of evil which are implicit in the Orphic-Pythagorean and Platonic traditions. (= R1017)

7803. U. BIANCHI, 'La 'doppia creazione' dell'uomo come oggetto di ricerca storico-religiosa', in U. BIANCHI (ed.), *La 'doppia creazione' dell'uomo negli Alessandrini, nei Cappadoci e nella Gnosi* (Rome 1978) 3-23.

The author interprets the theme of the 'double creation' – which is a Philonic doctrine, but also recurs frequently in Patristic thought – as a philosophical category, the meaning and limits of which he carefully defines. By means of these reflections the continuation of Philo's thought in early Christian philosophy is also illuminated. (= R1018)

7804. U. BIANCHI, 'Presupposti platonici e dualistici nell'antropogonia di Gregorio di Nissa', in *La 'doppia creazione'* ... (cf. **7803**) 83-115.

The direct line which connects Philo with the Alexandrian theologians and Gregory of Nyssa on the theme of the 'double creation' should not be understood as a mere 'transmission' of contents, but rather as a series of 'variations on a theme', in which an original allegorical-conceptual motif is elaborated according to the religious and philosophical contexts in which it occurs. The theme of the moulded man and man 'according to the image', for instance, loses most of its Platonic connotations in the passage from Philo to Gregory. (= R1019)

7805. U. BIANCHI, 'Le "Gnosticisme syrien", carrefour des fois', in *Paganisme, Judaïsme, Christianisme: influences et affrontements dans le monde antique; mélanges offerts à M. Simon* (Paris 1978) 75-90.

With regard to the supposed relations between Philo and Gnosticism, the author states that 'one cannot, in Philo's doctrine relating to the demiurgic assistants of God, identify true tendencies toward Gnosticism: all they have in common is perhaps an original form of dualism' (77). (RR)

7806. P. BILDE, 'The Roman emperor Gaius (Caligula)'s attempt to erect his statue in the temple of Jerusalem', *StTh* 32 (1978) 67-93.

The author addresses his subject clearly and fully, paying special attention to the following problems: (1) the motives which led Gaius to change his policies towards the Jews; (2) the behaviour of Petronius; (3) the Jewish opposition; (4) Agrippa's intervention; (5) the ultimate failure of Gaius' plans; (6) the question of chronology. The article discusses Philo mainly because he is a source of basic and indispensable information on the relevant historical facts. But the author also engages in a comprehensive examination of tendencies and literary forms characteristic of Philo. (= R1020)

7807. A. BROADIE and J. MACDONALD, 'The concept of cosmic order in ancient Egypt in dynastic and Roman times', *AC* 47 (1978) 106-128, esp. 107-121.

This article is mostly devoted to explaining the concept of logos in Philo. The analysis dwells on two main points. One emphasizes, besides the many similarities, certain basic differences between the Philonic and the Stoic logos, differences which can basically be traced back to the ontological subordination and immateriality of the Philonic logos. The other, underlining the double meaning – i.e. both transcendent and immanent – of this concept and the 'passive' role of the ideas, concludes that mediation between human and divine freedom and the immanent necessity of the logos is impossible or in any case very difficult. But the most original contribution of this study is the discovery of important antecedents of the Philonic logos, which reflect identical philosophical tensions, in the religious thought of ancient Egypt. The concept of *Maat*, for instance, which in Egyptian thought represents cosmic order (cf. 120f.), is said to reveal the same function, the same degree of ambivalence, and the same aporetic results as the logos in Philo. (= R1021)

7808. G. J. BROOKE, *4 Q Florilegium in the context of early Jewish exegetical method*, (diss. Claremont Graduate School 1978).

See below **8508**.

7809. C. CARLSTON, 'The vocabulary of perfection in Philo and Hebrews', in R.A. GUELICH (ed.), *Unity and diversity in New Testament theology: essays in honor of George E. Ladd* (Grand Rapids 1978) 133-160.

An exhaustive study is presented of the occurrence of words with the τελ-stem in Philo and the Epistle to the Hebrews. We note especially the following words: τέλος, τελετή, τέλειος, τελειόω. On the basis of his analysis Carlston concludes that the Platonic heritage is basic to both authors but much more fundamental to Philo, whose main emphasis falls on the soul's ascent and whose religious pedagogy is intrinisically ethical. In the Epistle the 'Platonic' contrast between the heavenly and the earthly realm has been modified by the Christian *kerygma*, so that crucial Philonic emphases, such as the stress on the ethical, are missing. Thus even if the two writers lived in the same general thought world, according to the author the analysis of perfection makes clear that 'they were citizens of quite different countries' (148). (DTR)

7810. P. CARNY [פ. קרני], התיאוריה האלגוריסטית של פילון [*Philo Alexandrinus' theory of allegory*] (diss. Tel-Aviv University 1978).

This thesis, prepared under the supervision of Y. Amir, attempts to define Philo's allegories anew, since the few discussions to date have dealt more with the allegorical technique of Philo and not with his theory of allegory and its place in his thought. Philo not only stresses the allegorical meaning of the Bible, but keeps its literal sense as well, as is demonstrated by a discussion of his uses of the concept of shadow. If Philo abandons the literal meaning, this is due to difficulties in the text. Short analyses of Philo's theory of ideas and his use of the concept of τύπος are also offered. (MM)

7811. G. F. CHESNUT, 'The ruler and the Logos in Neopythagorean, Middle Platonic, and late Stoic political philosophy', *ANRW* II 16.2 (Berlin 1978) 1310-1332, esp. 1326-1329.

This survey article briefly stops at Philo and observes that in his writings the quasi-divine character of the earthly monarch is described in traditional Hellenistic philosophical language, even though he is acutely aware of the danger of idolatry. The notion of the ruler as embodied Law or Logos of God 'was simply a part of the general atmosphere' (1329). (DTR)

7812. N. A. DAHL and A. F. SEGAL, 'Philo and the rabbis on the names of God', *JSJ* 9 (1978) 1-28.

The authors reopen the debate, first introduced by Z. Fraenkel and later challenged by A. MAMORSTEIN in a well-known article (*JQR* 22 (1931) 295-306) on the names of God θεός and κύριος in Philo and their relation to the names given to God in the Rabbinic tradition. These appear to indicate opposite connotations, but the authors draw attention to evidence that suggests there may have been an earlier Rabbinic tradition parallel to what is found in Philo. The article ends with a discussion on the debate concerning God's unity, which appears to have reached its most intense point in the second century A.D.

The root problem here is whether the names are to be regarded as attributes of God or as independent divine realities (25). Philo finds himself involved in this debate on account of his double role of philosopher and Jewish believer. 'The God of the Torah did not tolerate any one beside him, while the God of philosophy was raised above all passions and intervened in worldly affairs by means of a plurality of divine powers' (26). Of the two approaches, i.e. theological and the religious, the former, which 'saves' the figure of God but jeopardizes his unity, prevails in Philo; the other, moving in the opposite direction, gains the upper hand in Rabbinism. Abstract in *StPh* 6 (1979-80) 205f. (= R1022)

7813. R. J. DALY, *Christian sacrifice: the Judaeo-Christian background before Origen*, The Catholic University of America Studies in Christian Antiquity 18 (Washington 1978), esp. 389-422.

In richness and depth, the author claims, Philo's theology of sacrifice was surpassed in early antiquity only by that of Origen. Moreover in terms of influence on early Christian ideas Philo comes second only to Scripture itself. After selecting and commenting on a number of important texts, Daly concludes with a summary (421f.): 'Philo's spiritualizing, allegorical interpretation of sacrifice pays little attention to the idea of sacrifice as such, but rather concentrates on showing how the offering of spiritual sacrifice plays a major role in the soul's progress towards God. Our treatment examined the expression of this "progress of the soul" under the headings of the Passover, the idea of sacrifice as an offering of the whole self, the theology of priesthood and universalism, and the spiritual interpretation of temple and altar. Our major finding ... is that the ethical moment is clearly subordinate to the "gnostic". In sharp contrast to the strongly incarnational NT idea of the sacrifice of the Christian which emphasized the sacrificial aspects of the practical, down-to-earth Christian life of virtue, Philo's thrust was almost exclusively vertical. For him, true sacrifice consisted in the soul being freed from things material and elevated to the contemplation of things divine.' (DTR)

7814. J. DILLON, 'Philo Judaeus and the *Cratylus*', *LCM* 3 (1978) 37-42.

Some of Philo's apparently extravagant etymologies are more comprehensible if seen against the theory of language set out in the *Cratylus*. Certainly Philo must have had in mind the existence of a natural and correct form of language which, as Moses tells us, was taught by God to Adam. By referring to this form it is possible to establish an 'order of purity' which incorporates the various languages. (= R1023)

7815. J. DILLON, 'Some thoughts on the commentary', in E. C. HOBBS, *The commentary hermeneutically considered*, CHSHMC 31 (1978) 14-16.

Expounds what Dillon thinks should be the methodology of a Philonic commentary, as carried out in practice in the commentary on *Gig.-Deus* then in preparation (cf. **3101**). (DTR)

7816. R. B. EDWARDS, 'The pagan dogma of the absolute unchangeableness of God', *RelSt* 14 (1978) 305-313.

The few remarks about *Deus* in this article have the merit of putting its themes in a broadly philosophical context with a Kierkegaardian slant. (= R1024)

7817. H. E. FABER VAN DER MEULEN, *Das Salomo-Bild im helle-nistisch-jüdischen Schrifttum* (diss. Kampen 1978).

The figure of Solomon does not play a significant role in Philo's work. In Jewish-Alexandrian literature generally, however, he is often presented as a symbol of wisdom (cf. 79-107), and Philo is thus frequently cited by the author as a term of comparison and reference. (RR)

7818. U. FISCHER, *Eschatologie und Jenseitserwartung im hellenisti-schen Diasporajudentum* (Berlin-New York 1978), esp. 184-213.

The nationalistic eschatology present in the Bible is given a psychological interpretation by Philo, i.e. as the symbol of a shared spiritual process. 'Philo thus shows not only a clear lack of interest in national-eschatological expectations, but also a certain implicit distance with respect to this type of expectation' (199). This attitude can be attributed to the fact that the very concept of Israel, its vicissitudes and its protagonists have lost all their historical connotations in Philo and have come to express 'the salvation of the pious man'. In attempting a synthesis of Judaism and Hellenism, Philo was pushed beyond Jewish particularism and espoused an ethical-religious universalism which transcends any historical category. (= R1025)

7819. R. D. HECHT, 'Preliminary issues in the analysis of Philo's *De Specialibus Legibus*', *StPh* 5 (1978) 1-55.

This extensive analysis of *Spec.* addresses a programme containing three points. (1) In his interpretation of the legal regulations contained in the Pentateuch Philo uses the Decalogue as a fundamental structure, so that 'each commandment ... is understood to be a general category' (1) around which all other commandments and prohibitions are organized. (2) The true nature of Philo's discussion in *Spec.* immediately raises the problem of the extent to which it resembles or differs from the Palestinian Halachah (cf. 2). Here the work of Belkin is crucial and needs to be further re-examined. (3) To support these views, Hecht undertakes to arrange certain elements taken from *Spec.* and related to the interpretation of Num. 19 in a 'comparative exegetical context', showing what a unit of interpretation in this treatise may amount to and also suggesting the most suitable methods of analysis (cf. 3). (= R1026)

7820. R. A. HORSLEY, 'The background of the confessional formula in 1 Kor 8, 6', *ZNW* 69 (1978) 130-135.

The Pauline formula in 1 Cor. 8:6 which has played such an important role in Christian doctrine is of Philonic origin. The author finds traces of it in many Philonic texts, which mostly deal with the Logos and Sophia. (= R1027)

7821. R. A. HORSLEY, 'The law of nature in Philo and Cicero', *HThR* 71 (1978) 35-59.

Reacting against the position of H. Koester (**6816**), the author affirms Philo certainly played an important role in developing and explaining the concept of natural law, but his views are neither original (those of Cicero are very similar) nor isolated, being part of a development which departs from a Stoic tradition and comes to full growth in an eclectical Platonic sphere. The Platonism referred to is probably that of Antiochus of Ascalon, who assimilated many features of Stoic ethics. The main characteristic of this philosophical direction is said to be the attempt to justify natural law on the basis of a concept of God-as-Legislator. (= R1028)

7822. R. A. HORSLEY, '"How can some of you say that there is no resurrection of the dead?": spiritual elitism in Corinth', *NT* 20 (1978) 203-231.

Although he does not intend to solve the problem of the sources from which the underlying religious conception of Corinthians is derived, the author is constrained to observe that 'all of the Corinthians' language and principles, except perhaps the *pneumatikos-psychikos* contrast, are extensively paralleled in the writings of Philo of Alexandria and much of it occurs significantly in Sap. Sal.' (207). The subject under discussion and Paul's thought in general can only be understood adequately if put in the context of Alexandrian Judaism, of which Philo and Sap. Sal. are the major surviving representatives. The notion common to both Corinthians and Philo is that of the various levels of religious perfection, a notion which occurs in different forms but is essentially identical. The philosophical foundation of this theory is formed by the concepts of Sophia and the two *anthropoi* (cf. 216ff.). In Horsley's view, the latter in particular represents a part of the symbolism and theology of the various levels of spiritual status, and certainly not the postulated proto-Gnostic figure of the *Urmensch* (cf. 221). (= R1029)

7823. B. JAY, *Le monde du Nouveau Testament* (Yaounde 1978), esp. 153-161.

A brief synoptic presentation of Philo, in which there is an almost exclusive concentration on the theological aspect of Philo's philosophical thought. In Jay's view the key to Philo's thought is his universalism, which ousts the historical-eschatological-Messianic tradition typical of Judaism. (= R1030)

7824. A. KASHER [כשר .א], יהודי מצרים ההלניסטית והרומית במאבקם על זכויותיהם [*The Jews in Hellenistic and Roman Egypt*] (Tel-Aviv 1978), esp. 212-237.

Subsequently published in English; see **8527**.

7825. R. A. KRAFT, 'Philo (Josephus, Sirach and *Wisdom of Solomon*) on Enoch', *SBLSPS* 13 (1978) 1.253-257.

For Philo Enoch represents virtue in solitude and ecstatic knowledge. Nevertheless, he takes second place to Abraham or Moses, perhaps because of the social-political significance which Philo associates with the figures of these two patriarchs. (= R1031)

7826. J. LARCADE, 'Les images des jeux et de l'entraînement des athlètes chez Philon d'Alexandrie', in *Centre Jean Palerne: Mémoires* 1 (Saint Étienne 1978) 67-81.

The metaphors of the game and the training of athletes are culturally significant because they document the continuation, in the Hellenistic period and particularly in Alexandria, of the Greek-classical literary tradition from which they originate. (= R1031/a)

7827. J. P. LEWIS, *A study of the interpretation of Noah and the flood in Jewish and Christian literature* (Leiden 1978), esp. 42-74.

'Philo has found an arbitrary existential meaning in the flood episode. Under the form of a narrative of the past, it depicts occurrences that may happen in the present day experience of any person. This value is not a unified thing. The flood may either be an overwhelming of evils or it may be a cleansing of the soul; but either way, the narrative displays contemporary religious values which Philo wishes to sell his readers' (74). (= R1032)

7828. L. LIES, *Wort und Eucharistie bei Origenes: zur Spirituali-sierungstendenz des Eucharistieverständnisses*, Innsbrucker Theologische Studien 1 (Munich 1978), esp. 59-62.

Origen's concept of the Eucharist finds its historical roots in Philo, from whom he borrows the following meanings of the term: the Eucharist as εὐλογία (= benediction); as ἐξομολόγησις (= confession, assent, promise); as remembrance and εὐχή (= vow, consecration); and as an offering. (RR)

7829. B. L. MACK, 'Weisheit und Allegorie bei Philo von Alexandrien: Untersuchungen zum Traktat *De congressu eruditionis*', StPh 5 (1978) 57-105.

The greatest merit of this article is the rigorous structure of its analysis, which allows the content of *Congr.* to be condensed in a systematic schematization (83-93), and thus illustrates the methods of analysis suggested by the author above in **7525**. In the figures of Abraham, Hagar, and Sarah and the events in which they are involved the author discovers as many as five levels of allegorical meaning, each of which relates to different themes, though all using the same elements. The result is a semantic structure which is stratified into the following levels: (a) the motif of the encomium of Sarah and Abraham; (b) the allegory of wisdom; (c) the allegory of the *encyclia*; (d) the first allegory of the soul; (e) the second allegory of the soul. On each of these levels each character assumes a specific meaning, so that ultimately it is possible to delineate 'the diverse levels of explanation' of the story of Sarah and Hagar (cf. 82). (= R1033)

7830. G. W. MACRAE, 'Heavenly temple and eschatology in the Letter to the Hebrews', *Semeia* 12 (1978) 179-199, esp. 184-188.

While apocalyptic literature metaphorically locates the temple in heaven, Hellenistic Judaism compares it with the structure of the universe. Philo, in particular, regards the space outside the temple as a symbol of the sensible world and the sanctuary as a symbol of the intelligible world. (= R1041)

7831. G. MAY, *Schöpfung aus dem Nichts: die Entstehung der Lehre von der creatio ex nihilo*, AKG 48 (Berlin-New York 1978), esp. 9-21.

The author does not propose to discuss *ex novo* the complex issue of creation in Philo, but merely to run through the most important Philonic texts on the subject in search of 'general indications'. Yet the conclusions which he reaches are deserving of close attention. Philo, says May, 'did not represent creation *ex nihilo* in the same way as the doctrine of later Christianity and does not seem to have found contradictions between the philosophical model of the formed world and the biblical model of the created world' (9). But that does not imply a dualistic theory which opposes pre-existent matter to God (creation as 'formation' of matter is for Philo merely a conventional concept; cf. 15), for the material principle's passivity and lack of form do not make it a positive principle, but essentially a 'nullity'. (= R1034)

7832. A. M. MAZZANTI, 'L'aggettivo ΜΕΘΟΡΙΟΣ e la doppia creazione dell'uomo in Filone di Alessandria', in *La 'doppia creazione'*... (cf. **7803**) 25-42.

The term μεθόριος in Philo is rich in meaning. It does not reflect a superficial idea about the human condition, but forms, so to speak, the peak of a vast 'ontological-anthropological' (38) discourse, the ethical implications of which are secondary. The basic assumptions of this discourse are certainly dualistic and Platonic, and the liminal condition which characterizes human behaviour cannot be understood without reference to man's essential structure and his 'ontological mediate condition which, though it includes two different entities, nevertheless reaffirms their discontinuity and hence their mutual exclusion' (33). (= R1035)

7833. D. L. MEALAND, 'Philo of Alexandria's attitude to riches', *ZNW* 69 (1978) 258-264.

The author points out the discrepancy between Philo's social and economic ideas and his professed contempt of wealth. But in his view there is no trace of hypocrisy in Philo's attitude, since Philo is motivated by a constant process of identification with the politically marginalized and vulnerable Jewish people. See further **8365, 8532**. (= R1036)

7834. H. R. MOEHRING, 'Arithmology as an exegetical tool in the writings of Philo of Alexandria', *SBLSPS* 13 (1978) 1.191-229.

The aim of this article, which represents a much wider context of research (cf. 191), is to show that the number seven – and, in a broader sense, Philo's arithmology as a whole – should be understood as an integral part of the exegetical arsenal used by Philo (cf. 191). The author also discusses at some length the bibliography of recent contributions on this question, concluding that the subject has been largely neglected. Abstract in *StPh* 6 (1979-80) 212. (= R1037)

7835. S. C. MOTT, 'Greek ethics and Christian conversion: the Philonic background of Titus II, 10-14 and III, 3-7', *NT* 20 (1978) 22-48.

The Pastoral Epistles combine an elaborate and typically Hellenistic doctrine of virtue with a conception of God-as-benefactor which is definitely non-Greek in character (22). This necessitates a study of sources, and here Philo's writings are an indispensable point of reference. The author does not examine all the parallels between Philo's work and the letters, because these parallels include Hellenistic elements already present in Philo. Instead, he confines himself to those aspects which are present in both the Letters and

Philo, but do not occur in Hellenism. This method brings out the difference between the Stoic attitude, which describes God 'in terms of cosmic functions', and that of the Letters and Philo, who use 'the virtues of God as powers' (47). 'The total effect of the parallels between Philo and the Pastoral Epistles, therefore, argues for dependency rather than parallelism' (47). (= R1038)

7836. B. MACNEIL, 'The narration of Zosimus', *JSJ* 9 (1978) 68-82, esp. 77ff.

The *Narration of Zosimus* mentions a sect of Rechabites, which the author identifies with the Therapeutae. He reaches this conclusion after making extensive use of the Philonic evidence, in particular that of *Contempl.* (= R1039)

7837. A. PELLETIER, 'La philanthropia de tous les jours chez les écrivains juifs hellénisés', in *Paganisme, Judaïsme, Christianisme* (cf. above **7805**) 35-44.

The contemporary sense of the term φιλανθρωπία (i.e. generosity, gentleness) is found in Philo, particularly in *Legat.* One must turn to this meaning in order to understand the exact sense of the term in Sap. Sal. (RR)

7838. L. F. PIZZOLATO, *La dottrina esegetica di sant'Ambrogio*, Studia Patristica Mediolanensia 9 (Milan 1978) *passim.*

Frequently refers to Philonic texts which play a fundamental role in Ambrose's thought. Two particularly important doctrines common to both thinkers emerge in this connection: the tripartition of philosophy (cf. 163) and allegorical exegesis. In the latter, however, Ambrose seems to move away from Philo and what the author calls 'Jewish ethical exclusivism' (246). (= R1040)

7839. G. REALE, 'Filone di Alessandria e la "filosofia mosaica"', in *Storia della filosofia antica*, vol. 4, *Le scuole dell'età imperiale* (Milan 1978, 1987⁵), esp. 247-306.

To our knowledge this is the longest contribution devoted to Philo by a history of ancient philosophy. In Reale's opinion Philo is at once a turning-point in the philosophy of the imperial age (cf. 248) and, from the viewpoint of the scholar, a fundamental point of convergence in which the main lines of classical thought meet and separate. Thus as a Middle Platonist, Philo released Hellenistic philosophy from the limits of materialism; as a Jew, he introduced a monotheistic (271ff.) and creationistic (279ff.) conception of God unknown to the Greeks. As a man of faith, finally, he raised for the first time the problem of the relationship between revelation and reason (261ff.), thus anticipating themes and solutions essential to early Christian speculation. The author emphasizes that Philonic thought was also original from an ethical point of view, since it contained (299ff.) the first – and in Greek culture perhaps the only – successful victory over moral intellectualism. (= R1042)

7840. *Reallexikon für Antike und Christentum*, edited by T. KLAUSER *et al.*, vol. 10 (Stuttgart 1978).

Cf. above **5016**. Contains: H. CHADWICK, art. 'Gewissen', 1025-1107, esp. 1062-

3 (conscience). (DTR)

7841. N. ROTH, 'The "theft of philosophy" by the Greeks from the Jews', *ClF* 32 (1978) 53-67.

The polemics conducted by early Christian thinkers against Greek philosophy was based on the conviction that the latter was merely an offshoot of Jewish wisdom. Philo in particular helped to fuel this conviction by identifying Moses as the source of all philosophical knowledge. His aim in doing so certainly was not to emphasize the originality of Greek philosophy, but in the final analysis, by giving it his validation, 'it is not Greek philosophy that must conform to the Torah, but rather Torah that must be made to conform to Greek philosophy' (67). (= R1044)

7842. S. SANDMEL, 'Philo's knowledge of Hebrew: the present state of the problem', *StPh* 5 (1978) 107-112.

The author briefly examines the difficult problem of Philo's knowledge of Hebrew and summarizes the major scholarly points of view. He acutely observes that this question is 'only a single facet of the more complex problem, namely, where does Philo fit into Judaism?' (107). The conclusion is that 'whether he knew Hebrew or not does not affect either the form or, more importantly, the substance of what he wrote and thought' (111). (= R1045)

7843. S. SANDMEL, *Judaism and Christian beginnings* (New York 1978), esp. 279-301.

An overall presentation of Philo's work which takes its starting-point in a clear and straightforward way from the ethical-anthropological themes summed up in the figure of Abraham, and then touches on the main points of Philo's thought. The structure of this study might suggest that Philo's philosophy is systematic and coherent, but that, says Sandmel, is a result of expository necessity, and does not depend on the nature of Philonic discourse. With regard to the latter, indeed, 'any presentation of Philo's thought in a topical, systematic way is fraught with insuperable difficulties' (296). The reference to Wolfson here is unmistakable. (= R1046)

7844. A. SCATTOLON, 'L'ΑΓΑΠΗΤΟΣ sinottico nella luce della tradizione giudaica', *RivBib* 26 (1978) 3-32, esp. 20ff.

The biblical term ἀγαπητός carries a very wide range of meanings which Philo, for the benefit of a non-Jewish audience, is forced to render by a series of almost synonymous adjectives. (= R1047)

7845. L. W. SCHWARZ, *Wolfson of Harvard: portrait of a scholar* (Philadelphia 1978), esp. 141-156.

A sympathetic and well-informed account of the life and scholarly achievement of H. A. Wolfson. Chapter five, entitled 'The Alexandrian mystery', recounts how Wolfson's discovery of the crucial importance of Philo in 1941-2 solved, to his own satisfaction, the mysterious problem at the heart of his theory of the development of the history of philosophy. Note also the bibliography of Wolfson's writings at 259-269 which is complete up to 1963. (DTR)

7846. E. STAROBINSKI-SAFRAN, 'Exode 3, 14 dans l'oeuvre de Philon d'Alexandrie', in *Dieu et l'être.:exégèses d'Exode 3, 14 et de Coran 20, 11-24*, Centre d'études des religions du Livre 152, Études Augustiniennes (Paris 1978) 47-55.

Philo's interpretation of Ex. 3:14 bears the stamp of Platonism in its implicit ontological dualism between that which changes and that which is immobile. In this interpretation, however, Philo incorporates a number of elements which go far beyond the Platonic horizon: the possibility of different degrees of knowledge of God, the mystic intuition of Being, the unknowability of the divine entity, and negative theology. These last two aspects, in particular, do not contradict God's infinite goodness: God 'is good, and precisely in his goodness does not allow man to perceive the mystery of his being' (55). (= R1048)

7847. E. STAROBINSKI-SAFRAN, 'La prophétie de Moïse et sa portée d'après Philon', in R. MARTIN-ACHARD *et al.* (edd.), *La figure de Moïse: Écriture et relectures*, Publications de la Faculté de Théologie de l'Université de Genève 1 (Geneva 1978) 67-79.

Moses is without doubt the central figure in Philo's work and as such sums up the defining characteristics of Philo's ethical-religious ideal, namely those of the king, legislator, high priest, and prophet. Besides this series of attributes derived directly from the biblical account, Philo posits another relating to the theme of virtue: Moses is the prototype of the virtuous man, the ascetic, the sage; the man blessed with the kind of wisdom that does not stop at the intelligible world, but transcends it in prophecy and in the ecstatic vision of God (76). (= R1049)

7848. A. TERIAN, 'The implications of Philo's dialogues on his exegetical works', *SBLSPS* 13 (1978) 1.181-190.

Agreeing with M. ADLER (*Studien zu Philo von Alexandria* (Breslau 1929) 66f.) that Philo's writings develop from a strictly exegetical to a primarily philosophical phase, the author assigns *Anim.* to the final period of Philo's literary production. Abstract in *StPh* 6 (1979-80) 220. (= R1050)

7849. L. TROIANI, 'Osservazioni sopra l'Apologia di Filone: gli *Hypothetica*', *Ath* 56 (1978) 304-314.

The historical works and the fragments of *Hypoth.* reveal Philo's political views on the role of the Jews in the Empire. In particular it is evident that Jewish theocracy, inasmuch as it places religion above politics, is for Philo wholly compatible and even faithful to the programme of pacification and civil progress undertaken by the Julian-Claudian house. (= R1051)

7850. R. McL. WILSON, 'Jewish literary propaganda', in *Paganisme, Judaïsme, Christianisme* (cf. **7805**) 61-71.

The apologetic aim of Philo's work is directed at Greeks as well as Jews: at the former, since Philo assimilates a large part of Greek philosophy, and at the latter inasmuch as he tends to confirm them in their traditional faith (cf. 68 f.). (RR)

7851. J. C. M. VAN WINDEN, 'Quotations from Philo in Clement of Alexandria's *Protrepticus*', *VChr* 32 (1978) 208-213.

In order to prove the close connections between Clement and Philo, the author compares passages of the *Protrepticus* with *Plant*. 3-9, *Somn*. 2.193, 258, and *Cher*. 94. It can be shown that the Church Father 'had Philo's works on his desk, so to speak' (208). (= R1052)

7852. D. WINSTON, 'Was Philo a mystic?', *SBLSPS* 13 (1978) 1.161-180.

The mystical dimension of Philo's personality and work is not, as certain scholars would have it, the 'combination of a poetic flowering and an apologetic intelligence', but is the expression of an authentic experience. Therefore we must hold that 'Philo was at least a "mystical theorist" (if not a "practicing mystic") in the very core of his being and that his philosophical writings cannot be adequately understood if this signal fact is in any way obscured' (175). Abstract in *StPh* 6 (1979-80) 221f. (= R1053)

7853. H. A. WOLFSON [וולפסון .א.צ], המחשבה היהודית בימי הביניים [*The Jewish philosophy in the Middle Ages*] (Jerusalem 1978) *passim*.

An anthology of important studies, including **5021** (38-56), **6021** (20-37), **6121** (75-103), **6758** (11-19). (DS)

1979

7901. H. W. ATTRIDGE, '"Heard because of his reverence" (Heb. 5:7)', *JBL* 98 (1979) 90-93.

Christ's prayer in Hebrews 5:7 recalls, in its immediacy, Abraham's boldness of speech as described in *Her*. (= R1054)

7902. R. VAN DEN BROEK, 'The Authentikos logos: a new document of Christian Platonism', *VChr* 33 (1979) 260-286, esp. 280ff.

In analyzing the third treatise of Codex 6 in the Nag Hammadi library, the author attempts to demonstrate that this text is not Gnostic but Platonic, and that its prospective readers were Christians acquainted with the New Testament. In the course of the article the author adds further specific characteristics, e.g. that the treatise was composed in Alexandria, as is demonstrated by its significant parallels with the analogous doctrines in Philo. (= R1055)

7903. M. BUSCEMI, ''Εξαιρέομαι, verbo di liberazione', *SBFLA* 29 (1979) 293-314, esp. 304f., 314.

The metaphorical sense of the verb ἐξαιρέομαι, viz. 'liberate', is widespread in the world of the Old Testament. The author demonstrates that this sense occurs in Philo too. (RR)

7904. B. BYRNE, 'Sons of God' - 'seed of Abraham': a study of the idea of the sonship of God of all Christians in Paul against the Jewish background, AnBib 83 (Rome 1979), esp. 57-59.

Brief remarks on God's fatherhood and the sonship of creation and the truly wise man. Philo's employment of the sonship idea has more in common with Stoic-Platonic models than with the Jewish usage seen in other intertestamental literature. (DTR)

7905. H. C. C. CAVALLIN, 'Leben nach dem Tode im spätjudentum und im frühen Christentum', *ANRW* II 19.1 (Berlin-New York 1979) 240-345, esp. 288-293.

In Philo the subject of immortality is strictly connected to anthropological presuppositions. Philo defines man's nature on the basis of the (philosophical) exegesis of Gen. 2:7 and 1:26 ff., which concludes that the nous possesses a form of immortality (in being of divine origin), but not an immortality that is possessed 'automatically' by all men. In short, immortality is only given to the wise man as a divine reward for his virtue. In the course of the article Cavallin examines many Philonic passages related to this subject, and concludes that Philo allows for 'a personal life after death, if in a totally transformed, spiritual form' (293). (RR)

7906. C. J. CLASSEN, 'Der platonisch-stoische Kanon der Kardinaltugenden bei Philon, Clemens Alexandrinus und Origenes', in A. M. RITTER (ed.), *Kerygma und Logos: Beiträge zu den geistesgeschichtlichen Beziehungen zwischen Antike und Christentum; Festschrift für C. Andresen zum 70. Geburtstag* (Göttingen 1979) 68-88.

In Philo's aretalogy the cardinal virtues play a central role because they are the means by which man can fully realize his potential. Although they show signs of Platonic and Stoic influence, Philo's abiding aim was to connect these virtues with the Jewish tradition by tracing them back, through allegorical exegesis, to biblical thought. (= R1056)

7907. C. COLPE, 'Von der Logoslehre des Philon zu der des Clemens von Alexandrien', in *Kerygma und Logos* (cf. **7906**) 89-107.

Philo's theory of the Logos separates into a plethora of concepts and figures which are held together by the common mediating function between God and the world, a function which is fundamentally expressed by the concept of εἰκών. But apart from its intrinsic value, the theory of the Logos is, from a historical point of view, also related to three other concepts: the concept of reason typical of late-classical Greek philosophy, the Jewish concept of God's creative word, and the concept of the liberating potency characteristic of Gnosticism. One would be overly ambitious, in Colpe's view, in wanting to explain the exact relations existing between the innovatory Philonic concepts of *logos, eikon, anthropos, nous, logismos, sophia, pneuma, phronesis, kosmos noetos* (cf. 97), given the extent to which their meanings fluctuate. (= R1057)

7908. D. DAUBE, 'The Rabbis and Philo on human rights', in D. SIDORSKY (ed.), *Essays on human rights: contemporary issues and Jewish perspective* (Philadelphia 1979) 234-246.

A vivid but not very profound discussion of Rabbinic and Philonic attitudes to what we now call 'human rights'. Specific subjects discussed are discrimination (e.g. the indictments of Cain and Er), the right to a fair hearing (Eve and the serpent), the rights of a runaway slave. In a note Daube affirms that if the Rabbis and Philo coincide on an idea, priority belongs to the Rabbis. (DTR)

7909. J. C. ENGELSMAN, *The feminine dimension of the divine* (Philadelphia 1979), esp. 95-109.

Philo's loyalty to Judaic traditions means he has to retain the figure of Sophia. But his antipathy for the feminine leads him to reduce her importance in comparison with the masculine Logos. Philo's elevation of Sophia helps to explain later Mariology, but also shows why Mary could never become a true goddess figure like Isis or Demeter. Regrettably Philo's repressive attitude towards the feminine came to predominate in Christian theology. (DTR)

7910. R. FERNHOUT, *Woord en naam in de religies: een vergelijkend onderzoek* (diss. Amsterdam, Kampen 1979).

Philonic ideas on God's word and name and the way they reach man are frequently, if not profoundly, dealt with in this phenomenologically orientated study, but the reader is going to work hard to find them all on account of the systematic structure of the work. Cf. esp. 163f. (Logos), 183f. (Sophia), 223f. (prophecy), 285f. (transcendence). The most interesting aspect of the study is the frequent comparison with themes, in other religious cultures (including those of ancient Egypt and India). (DTR)

7911. T. W. FRANXMAN, *Genesis and the 'Jewish antiquitites' of Flavius Josephus*, BibOr 35 (Rome 1979).

Philo is one of the 'literary parameters' against which Josephus' reshaping of the Genesis narrative can be determined. Throughout the analysis, but especially in relation to the earlier chapters, Philonic parallels are constantly adduced. But the study is not easy to exploit, for it lacks a proper index, and moreover at no stage summarizes the results that it reaches in relation to Josephus' use of source material. The impression gained, however, is that the material collected supports the view that Josephus did in fact make use of Philo's works (cf. Feldman **1115**, 937). (DTR)

7912. A. B. GARCÍA, 'La concepción filoniana de eiréne y pólemos: ideas sobre el pensamiento antropológico del filósofo de Alejandría', *CD* 193 (1979) 193-238.

After a general presentation of Philo and a rapid outline of his anthropology, the author proceeds to discuss the subject of Philo's politics, a theme which is regarded as leading directly to the heart of his thought, namely his conception of God as the prototype of all wisdom and, consequently, of all royal dignity. From here it also possible to specify the close connection between God and peace, since if God 'is the archetype on which every law is modelled' (208), he himself also symbolizes true peace (cf. 217). This theological structure is ambivalent, however, in the sense that it is significant both on a political level and on an interior and ethical level. On the latter level peace is ultimately identical with virtue, while war corresponds to the assault and dominion of the passions. There is a correspondence between the two types – i.e. exterior and interior – of peace (and also war), but within this relation the interior level predominates, because external peace is a reflection and copy of internal peace (230). (= R1058)

7913. A. GRILLI, 'Sul numero sette' in *Studi su Varrone, sulla retorica, storiografia e poesia latina: scritti in onore di B. Riposati*, vol. 1 (Rieti 1979) 203-219.

With Philo, observes the author (204), 'we stand before the oldest text [i.e. on the hebdomad] which we have, and chronologically we stand rather close to Varro'. In all probability this complex arithmological theme found 'a great catchment basin' in the 2nd century B.C. Philo's evidence is said to show that, in the arithmological tradition – especially with reference to the relationship Varro-Favonius – the role of Antiochus of Ascalon should not be underestimated. (= R1058/a)

7914. R. GRYSON, 'Le vêtement d'Aaron interprété par saint Ambroise', *Muséon* 92 (1979) 273-280.

Analyzes the Philonic passages in which the high-priestly robe is interpreted allegorically and demonstrates the many parallels between Philo and Ambrose. (RR)

7915. E. HALL, 'Philo of Alexandria', *Hermes* (Santa Barbara) 5 (1979) 232-239.

A brief yet balanced and lucid presentation of Philo's thought written from a theosophical perspective. (DTR)

7916. D. M. HAY, 'What is proof? rhetorical verification in Philo, Josephus and Quintilian', *SBLSPS* 17 (1979) 2.87-100.

Mission is an essential component of Judaism and in it the apologetic element predominates (87). A comparative analysis of the rhetorical aspects of *Flacc.* and Josephus' *Contra Apionem* shows a common legacy typical of Jewish-Hellenistic apologetics (97). (= R1058/b)

7917. M. C. HOROWITZ, 'The image of God in man – is woman included?', *HThR* 72 (1979), esp. 190-192.

The author, writing from a feminist viewpoint, wishes to show that the argument that woman, as well as man, was created in God's image has deep historical roots within both Jewish and Christian religious traditions. In Philo's reading the categories 'male' and 'female' do not exist in the part of man that is in the image of God. 'While Philo allowed the possibility that both woman and man would through ascetic life approximate the Logos, or image, of God, the association of actual women with derogatory notions of woman as sense-perception made it less likely that they would be in the image of God' (192). (DTR)

7918. R. A. HORSLEY, 'Spiritual marriage with Sophia', *VChr* 33 (1979) 30-54, esp. 32-40.

The image of spiritual marriage in Philo involves the relationship between God, divine Sophia, and the individual soul. There are three reasons that this symbolism is not 'merely a complex of standard traditional metaphors' (35). (1) Sophia is both object and means of salvation. (2) Philo's dualism causes him to view the body and sense-perception as a problem soteriologically. (3) The higher, spiritual kind of intercourse with Sophia or God involves a change in one's marital status and sexual behaviour. Such beliefs on spiritual marriage with Sophia tend to push Philo's thought in the direction of an asceticism in relation to worldly affairs and also sexuality (compare these themes in Philo's description of the Therapeutae). The article concludes with a discussion of the same themes in earliest Corinthian Christianity. (= R1059)

7919. K. JANÁČEK, 'Das Wort σκεπτικός in Philons Schriften', *LF* 102 (1979) 65-68.

The author thoroughly examines the term under discussion in Philo's works and concludes that it is impossible to reconstruct the specific terminology of Aenesidemus on the basis of Philo. It is clear, however, that Philo was not acquainted with the official name of the Sceptic school, οἱ σκεπτικοί. (= R1060)

7920. A. KASHER [כשר .א], ירושלים כ"מטרופולים" בתודעתו הלאומית של פילון ['Jerusalem as "metropolis" in Philo's national consciousness'], *Cathedra* 11 (1979) 45-56.

Developing a point made briefly in his book (**7824**, cf. **8527**), Kasher analyzes the political terminology which Philo uses to describe the Diaspora Jew's respective loyalities to Jerusalem, his μητρόπολις, and to the city in which he resides, his πατρίς. He notes especially *Flacc.* 46, *Legat.* 281-283, and the more philosophical usage of the same terminology in *Conf.* 77-78. In this connection, other aspects of the links between Diaspora Jewry and Jerusalem, and between the Jewish nation and religion, as perceived by Philo, are also studied. English Summary. (DRS)

7921. C. KRAUS REGGIANI, *La lettera di Aristea a Filocrate, introduzione, esame analitico, traduzione* (Rome 1979), esp. 20f., 42, 46-48.

The translation of the *Letter of Aristeas* is preceded by an extensive analysis (7-63) which frequently refers to Philo, particularly in connection with: (a) the legend of the translation of the LXX (20f.); (b) Philo's criticism of Egyptian polytheism (42); (c) the subject of unclean animals and the metaphor of 'rumination' (46-48). (RR)

7922. M. KÜCHLER, *Frühjüdische Weisheitstraditionen: zum Fortgang weisheitlichen Denkens im Bereich des frühjüdischen Jahweglaubens*, Orbis Biblicus et Orientalis 26 (diss. Freiburg-Göttingen 1979), esp. 222-235.

The summary of Mosaic law found in *Hypoth.* 7.1-9 deserves our attention because it reveals the cultural matrix of Philo's thought. In particular this text shows the gradual opening up toward Greek tradition, which leads to its integration in early Judaism (235). This development becomes even clearer when related to parallel passages in Josephus (where the Greek element is much less in evidence; cf. 225) and in the light of an examination of the Greek νόμοι ἄγραφοι as a whole. (= R1060/a)

7923. E. LUCCHESI, 'Nouvelle parallèle entre Saint Paul (Gal. III, 16) et Philon d'Alexandrie (*Quaestiones in Genesim*)?', *NT* 21 (1979) 150-155.

Ambrose, *De Abrahamo* 2.7.39-41 can be regarded as an ample paraphrase of a now lost passage from Philo's *Quaestiones*, which by this means can to some degree be reconstructed. The resultant text shows surprising parallels with Gal. 3:16, which are to be explained on the basis of a common Rabbinical source. (= R1061)

7924. J. MANSFELD, 'Providence and the destruction of the universe in early Stoic thought', in M. J. VERMASEREN (ed.), *Studies in Hellenistic religions*, EPRO 78 (Leiden 1979) 129-188, esp. 141ff., 159ff., 186-188.

The evidence of Philo's treatise *Aet.* is quite indispensable to the argument of this long article. The author argues that Chrysippus' revival of the old Stoic arguments of Zeno against the position of Plato and Aristotle on the indestructibility of the cosmos occasioned the revival of traditional arguments which could be used against him, and this led to Philo's preservation of the arguments from Aristotle's *De philosophia* (fr. 18-19), which otherwise would have been lost to us. (DTR)

7925. B. L. MACK, 'Weisheit und Allegorie bei Philo von Alexandrien: Untersuchungen zum Traktat *De congressu eruditionis*', *Theok* 3 (1973-75); = *Festgabe für H. Koch zum 70. Geburtstag* (Leiden 1979) 23-59.

Cf. **7829.** (= R910)

7926. D. MENDELS, 'Hellenistic utopia and the Essenes', *HThR* 72 (1979) 207-222.

Starting from the assumption that the Essenes described by Philo and Josephus are none other than the members of the Qumran community, the author analyzes the parallels between their convictions and ideals and the classical utopias (particularly that of Iambulus as summarized by Diodorus Siculus). The following conclusions are reached. (a) The Qumran rule of life was influenced by the Hellenistic utopias. (b) Philo and Josephus idealized these communities in their descriptions in order to impress their pagan audiences. (c) As far as we know, the Essenian way of life cannot be included in the genre of the classical and Hellenistic utopias. (= R1062)

7927. M. MINNITI COLONNA, 'Sul *De aeternitate mundi* di Filone Alessandrino', *Nicolaus* 7 (1979) 61-89.

This article represents an important contribution. The author's aim is to improve and supplement the OPA edition of *Aet.* (**2224**), which she observes to be deficient and inaccurate in various places. She goes on to discuss the authorship of the work, its manuscript tradition, and its philosophical sources, i.e. the various problems which Philo's treatise has always raised. *Aet.*, it is concluded (88), 'is nothing but a preparatory excursus written with a view to the real refutation to follow, in which Philo proposed to explain his own theories with regard to the diverse and contrasting views on the subject of the world's indestructibility'. (= R1062/a)

7928. H. R. MOEHRING, 'Moses and Pythagoras: arithmology as an exegetical tool in Philo', in E. A. LIVINGSTONE (ed.) *Studia Biblica I: Sixth International congress on Biblical studies,* JSOT.S 11 (1979) 205-208.

Philo knows three realms of the sacred: the cosmos, the people of Israel, the sanctuary. Each is arranged according to the same coherent pattern, which is not esoteric or mysterious, but is accessible to the use of arithmology and is therefore of universal validity. Pythagoras rediscovered what Moses had recognized as the key to the understanding of the harmony of the cosmos. Philo rediscovered Pythagoras and so located the key to the universal understanding of the Torah. (DTR)

7929. L. A. MONTES PERAL, *Akataleptos theos: eine Untersuchung über die Transzendenz und Immanenz im Gottesbegriff bei Philo von Alexandrien* (diss. München 1979); republished as *Akataleptos Theos: der unfassbare Gott,* ALGHJ 16 (Leiden 1987).

Philo's theology is based on two opposite principles, the transcendence and the immanence of God. It therefore develops in two different directions: one vertical, emphasizing the distance between God and the world, and one horizontal, concerned with the mediation between God and creation (164). The first part of this book (1-163) is devoted to the former, and analyzes the 'modes' of God's transcendence, viewed mainly in ontological terms and distinguished by the following characteristics: 'only God is *true* Being', 'only Being is fundamental', 'only Being is the true and one God', 'only Being is eternal, immutable, and perfect'. The following conclusions are reached. God is transcendent not only with regard to creation, but also with regard to man, the superior spiritual realities (e.g. the angels), and his own Powers. In this sense he is the 'wholly other' (cf. 3). At this point Montes-Peral raises a fundamental problem: how can Philo proclaim the absolute alterity of God, and yet continually use God as a term of comparison in relation to human nature? The origin of this contradiction is said to lie in Holy Scripture, which presents God as 'a God for man'. But, the author observes, 'Philo is a philosopher and a thinker; on the one hand he therefore views God in his absoluteness, and on the other he views God as "a God for man"' (39 ff.). In this way the pure theological unity of the Bible is ruptured, and this also explains the ambivalence of Philo's theological conception. The second part of the work addresses the same problem in different terms: how can the transcendent aspect and the immanent aspect of God be reconciled? The author's answer is that a distinction must be made between God's nature and God's activity (and to the latter must be related the concepts of Logos, Powers, cosmos, and man, which Montes-Peral proceeds to analyze). Only the first is wholly transcendent; the second, on the other hand, is immanent, as is demonstrated first and foremost by the biblical story of creation (204 ff.). The above summary is based on the new edition of 1987 (= **8727***). (RR)

7930. M. MORANI, 'Due frammenti di Eschilo e la traduzione armena del *De providentia* di Filone Giudeo', *RIL* 113 (1979) 489-495.

The Armenian translation of the *De Providentia* reproduces some fragments of Aeschylus not known from other sources. Given the strict correspondence between the translated version and Greek text, it is possible to obtain a more accurate idea of the original text than is allowed for by Aucher's Latin version, which is the only one reproduced in the edition of Aeschylean fragments. (RR)

7931. V. NIKIPROWETZKY, 'Le *De vita contemplativa* revisité', in

Sagesse et Religion: colloque de Strasbourg (Octobre 1976), Travaux du Centre d'Études Supérieures Spécialisé d'Histoire des Religions de Strasbourg (Paris 1979) 105-125.

A perceptive and thorough article on the Therapeutae. Starting from a brief report of research on the subject, the author discusses in detail the study by M. ELIZAROVA, *Obchtchina Terapeutou* (Moscow 1972). This discussion is of great interest because it brings to public attention one of the more important works of recent Russian scholarship. Nikiprowetzky's views on the difficult question of the Therapeutae are as follows. The greatest possible prudence is called for in using *Contempl.* as a source of information on the Therapeutae on account of the 'purely symbolic character' (115) of Philo's descriptions, especially those of the rites and the banquet, which in this treatise are described in 'exclusively Sabbatical terms' (122). Abstract in *StPh* 6 (1979-80) 214ff. (= R1063)

7932. F. PASTOR, 'Libertad helénica y libertad paulina, II', *MCom* 37 (1979) 219-237.

For Philo freedom is primarily identical with virtue, understood mainly in the Stoic sense of ἀπάθεια and ἀταραξία. On a second level, it is identical with adherence to the law and to reason, and ultimately with friendship with God. In this sense freedom and submission to God in the end amount to the same thing (231), the more so since, for Philo, God himself is the active cause of freedom, which is thus to be regarded as a form of 'liberation'. (RR)

7933. M. PATILLON, 'Les sources du Livre III', in J. BOUFFARTIGUE and M. PATILLON (edd.), *Porphyre, De l'abstinence,* tome II, livres II et III, Collections des Universités de France (Paris 1979) 138-143.

Chapters 2.1–18.2 of the third book of Porphyry's treatise *De abstinentia* offer an argument in favour of the existence of reason in animals which is very similar to that presented in *Anim.* 11-70. An analogous argument is found in Sextus Empiricus, *PH* 1.62-77, on which basis the author suggests a common source for both philosophers, possibly Carneades or one of his followers. (RR)

7934. G. M. POZZO, s.v. 'Filone di Alessandria', in *Enciclopedia filosofica* (Rome 1979²) 608-611.

Philo is seen here essentially as an eclectic exegete who resolved the relationship between faith and reason in favour of faith. Historically, Philo represents a decisive moment in the spiritualistic trend which leads to Neoplatonism, in spite of the many gaps and obscurities of his philosophical thought. (= R1064)

7935. J. R. REA, 'Paper hats', in J. BINGEN, and G. NACHTERGAEL (edd.), *Actes du XVe Congrès international de papyrologie* (Brussels 1979) 3.34-38.

Discussion of the meaning of βύβλος in *Flacc.* 37. (DTR)

7936. G. REALE, 'Filone di Alessandria e la prima elaborazione filosofica della dottrina della creazione', in R. CANTALAMESSA and L. F. PIZZOLATO (edd.), *Paradoxos politeia: studi patristici in onore di G. Lazzati* (Milan 1979) 247-287.

Reale carefully analyzes the diverse Philonic texts on creation (with particular attention paid to *Prov.* 1.6-9), also referring to Plato's *Timaeus*, since it is an essential source of Philo's thought on this subject. He draws the following conclusions. (1) A correct interpretation of the problem of creation in Philo must take into account the biblical data – though it lacks unity on this issue – and Platonic thought, and, consequently, the author's effort to mediate between these two sources. (2) The theory of a double creation, which is a solution to this very problem, requires in its first phase a further subdivision into two 'events': the creation of the Logos followed by the creation of matter. Reale is thus in essential agreement with Wolfson that Philo developed a doctrine of *creatio ex nihilo*. (3) The limits of this theory lie in the inadequate philosophical development of the concept of God, especially with regard to the ontological aspect. (4) Given the central position of theology in Philo, the innovative purport of this theory has repercussions on all aspects of his thought. (= R1065)

7937. J. R. ROYSE, 'The text of Philo's *Quis rerum divinarum heres* 167-173 in Vaticanus 379', in *Festgabe...* (cf. **7925**) 217-223.

After carefully examining the manuscript tradition of the passage in question, Royse reconsiders and copiously annotates the critical solutions adopted by Wendland. (= R925)

7938. S. SANDMEL, 'Apocalypse and Philo', in A. I. KATSH and L. NEMOY (edd.), *Essays on the occasion of the seventieth anniversary of the Dropsie University (1909-1979)* (Philadelphia 1979) 383-387.

The role of the prophet is important in Philo's thought, yet the theme of prophecy is marginal to it. This is no doubt due to Philo's intellectualistic background. In fact there is even an attitude of 'false piety' for everything connected with this subject in the Bible. This clearly brings out the difference between Philo and Apocalyptic literature, which concentrates almost exclusively on the prediction of future events. (= R1065/a)

7939. S. SANDMEL, *Philo of Alexandria: an introduction* (New York-Oxford 1979).

A balanced and lucid introduction to Philo which describes at length the contents of his works (this takes up about the first third of the book) and then proceeds to touch on all the main points of his thought. The final four chapters place Philo in relation to his *Umwelt* (Palestinian Judaism, Gnosticism, Christianity), and also include a chapter on the interpretations of Sandmel's teacher E. R. Goodenough. We draw attention here to what seem to be the author's two fundamental assumptions. (a) Philo is regarded as the voice of a culture in which Hellenism and Judaism interpenetrate completely. 'There are two sides to Philo's accomplishment. One is his Hellenization of Judaism in that he presents Scriptural matters in Grecian categories. But the other side is possibly even more important: Philo also Judaizes Grecian ideas. That Philo accomplishes this double process is the most significant testimony to the profundity of the Hellenization found in the thought of this loyal Jew. It is a Hellenization not just in form but also in substance' (122). (b) Both the religious and the ethical-anthropological elements in Philo share a single objective: the communion and vision of God (cf. 88 and 101). This objective fulfils what Sandmel calls the 'mystical-philosophical' (124) side of Philo's personality. REVIEWS: A. Mendelson, *SR* 8 (1979) 334f.; L. H. Feldman, *JAOS* 100 (1980) 197f.; H. R. Moehring, *JBL* 100 (1981) 138f.; D. Winston, *JAAR* 48 (1981) 138f. (= R1066)

7940. S. SANDMEL, 'Palestinian and Hellenistic Judaism and Christianity: the question of the comfortable theory', *HUCA* 50 (1979) 137-148.

'A comfortable theory is one which satisfies the needs of the interpreter, whether theological or only personal, when the evidence can seem to point in one of two opposite directions' (139). Examples of such theories, the author contends, are the refusal to acknowledge significant Hellenization in Philo or in the New Testament and Early Christianity. (DTR)

7941. J. DE SAVIGNAC, 'Religion et sagesse dans le prologue johannique', in *Sagesse et Religion* (cf. **7931**) 135-146.

The author is convinced that the thought of the writer of John 1:1-18 is, with regard to its adaptation of Greek philosophical ideas, parallel to that of Philo, and that the evangelist may have read him or even been his disciple. (DTR)

7941a. E. SCHÜRER, *The history of the Jewish people in the age of Jesus Christ (175 B. C. - A. D. 135)*, a new English version revised and edited by G. VERMES, F. MILLAR, M. BLACK, vol. 2 (Edinburgh 1979), esp. 557-595.

A thorough handbook account of the Essenes and Therapeutae, making extensive use of the Philonic evidence, the various aspects of which are judiciously weighed. The Appendix at 591-597 deals explicitly with the account of the Therapeutae given by Philo in *Contempl.* and the relation which his account has to what we know about the Essenes. The conclusion is worth citing (597): 'In the light of the ancient data, therefore, and the fresh support they have received from the Dead Sea discoveries, the hypothesis that the Therapeutae were members of an Egyptian branch of the Palestinian movement deserves serious consideration'. (DTR)

7942. E. TAGLIAFERRO, 'Nota linguistica filoniana (Cher.1-10)', *Hel* 18-19 (1978-79) 415-424.

A detailed analysis of *Cher.* 1-10, particularly with reference to the two verbs ἐκβάλλω and ἐξαποστέλλω, which are opposed to one another in this context, but are elsewhere considered equivalent. (RR)

7943. A. C. THISELTON, 'The "interpretation" of tongues: a new suggestion in the light of Greek usage in Philo and Josephus', *JThS* 30 (1979) 15-36, esp. 18-24.

The term ἑρμηνεύω should be understood in terms of 'articulation' or 'simply putting something into words' and not as the equivalent of 'expression' (cf. 24). The author reaches these conclusions after a brief analysis of Philo's theory of language which also takes into account the important contributions made by Otte (**6827**). (= R1068)

7944. J. W. THOMPSON, 'Hebrews 9 and Hellenistic concepts of sacrifice', *JBL* 98 (1979) 567-578, esp. 576ff.

The author argues that Hebr. 9:11-14 on the nature of adequate sacrifice shares metaphysical assumptions with writers in the Platonic tradition and with Philo. Although Philo is a loyal apologist for the Jerusalem cultus, he is clearly under the influence of the 'Hellenistic enlightenment' (576). Philo and Hebrews share an uneasiness with the earthly or material cult of sacrifice. What really matters for Philo is the spiritual cult offered by the soul to God. Thompson agrees with Nikiprowetzky (**6741**) that the author of the Epistle in fact proceeds beyond Philo in the direction of those who would allow no earthly cult at all. (DTR)

7945. R. WILLIAMSON, 'Philo and New Testament Christology', *ET* 90 (1979) 361-365; also published in a slightly different version in E. A. LIVINGSTONE (ed.), *Studia Biblica 1978 III: sixth international congress on Biblical studies Oxford 3-7 April 1978*, JSNT.S 3 (Sheffield 1980) 439-445.

New Testament scholars should look to Philo not only for what he says about the Logos, but also his treatment of Moses, for it is likely that Philo was struggling with the same fundamental problem of expression in relation to Moses that the NT writers wrestled with in the case of Jesus. The author gives a summary of Philo's depiction of Moses; four topics are of special importance: his 'second birth', his association with the Logos, his 'translation', and the remarkable prayer addressed to him at *Somn.* 1.164ff. Philo remains fully aware that Moses was a real, human being. The fact that he feels the need to add a 'mythological story' to the human account may help us to understand the language of the NT writers concerning Jesus. (DTR)

7946. J. C. M. VAN WINDEN, 'The first fragment of Philo's *Quaestiones in Genesim*', *VChr* 33 (1979) 313-318.

Contains relevant remarks on and corrections of Marcus's (and Aucher's) translation of *QG* 1.1 on the basis of a comparison with the corresponding Greek fragment published by F. Petit in her collection of fragments (**1814**). (= R1069)

7947. D. WINSTON, *The Wisdom of Solomon*, The Anchor Bible 43 (New York 1979), 59-63 and *passim*.

The chief thesis of this major commentary on the Sapientia Salomonis is that it should not be dissociated from the Philonic corpus and the tradition of Hellenistic philosophy, as has generally been done by scholars hitherto. The book thus abounds with discussions of passages that disclose ideas held in common with Philo. A summary of such themes is given at 59-63. On the chronological relation Winston concludes (59): 'I have attempted to demonstrate that Wisd[om] was written sometime between 30 BCE and 50 CE, and have further conjectured that it was likely to have been composed ca. 37-41 CE. If this dating should turn out to be correct, then we must conclude that (barring dependence on common sources) it was the author of Wisd[om] who was deeply influenced by Philo rather than the other way around.' (DTR)

7948. E. ZELLER, R. MONDOLFO, *La filosofia dei Greci nel suo sviluppo storico*, part 3, *La filosofia post-aristotelica*, vol. 4, *I precursori del neoplatonismo*, ed. by R. DEL RE, Il pensiero storico 73 (Florence

1979), esp. 468-577.

As G. REALE emphasizes and demonstrates in his review article, 'In margine all' aggiornamento italiano di *La Filosofia dei Greci nel suo sviluppo storico* dello Zeller dedicato ai precursori del neoplatonismo', *Elenchos* 1 (1980) 333-361, esp. 357-360, this work lacks an adequate up-to-date bibliography, and thus catches only faint echoes of the extensive and lively debate in which Philonic scholars have been involved in more recent times (even while the work was being prepared for publication). From this point of view, the final section on Philo (572-577) is sensibly written, but has nothing significantly new to offer. It presents with certainty views which recent students of Philo have called into question. (= R1069/a)

1980

8001. Y. AMIR [עמיר .י], העלייה-לרגל נוסח פילון ['Philo's version of the pilgrimage to Jerusalem'], in A. OPPENHEIMER, U. RAPPAPORT, M. STERN (edd.), פרקים בתולדות ירושלים בימי בית שני. ספר זיכרון לא. שליט [*Jerusalem in the Second Temple period... A. Schalit memorial volume*] (Jerusalem 1980) 154-165.

Subsequently published in German; see **8303**.

8002. Y. AMIR [עמיר .י], משה כמחבר התורה אצל פילון ['Moses as author of the Law in Philo'], *Proceedings of the Israel Academy of Sciences and Humanities* 6.5 (Jerusalem 1980, 1984) 83-103.

Subsequently published in German; see **8304**.

8003. M. L. ARDUINI, 'Il tema "vir" e "mulier" nell' esegesi patristica e medievale di Eccli., XLII, 14; a proposito di una interpretazione di Ruperto di Deutz', *Aev* 54 (1980) 315-330, esp. 324-330.

Deals with two aspects of the exegetical categories of 'male' and 'female' in Patristic literature: the connections between Philo and Ambrose, and the theme's origins. These may lie in Gnostic thought, which radically contrasts man, symbol of absolute truth, with woman, symbol of absolute falsehood. After successive elaborations, this resulted in the Philonic-Patristic and medieval theme (typical, for instance, of Rupert of Deutz) of Adam-*nous* and Eve-*aisthesis*. (RR)

8004. Y. F. BAER [בער .י], קצירת העומר ['Harvesting of the Omer'], in H. BEINART, S. ETTINGER, M. STERN (edd.), ספר זכרון ליצחק בער [= *Yitzhak F. Baer memorial volume*] (Jerusalem 1980) xxi-xxxiii [Hebrew pp. כא-לג].

In this, his final article, Baer continues his discussion (see **5201, 5304, 5502**) of the social and religious ideals of Judaism in the period of the Second Temple. He explains Philo's description of the harvesting of the omer sheaves (*Spec* 2.162ff.) as being conceived in direct opposition to certain Platonic views (28-30). English summary. (DS)

8005. U. BIANCHI, 'Presupposti Platonici e dualistici di Origene, *De Principiis*', in H. CROUZEL and A. QUACQUARELLI, (edd.), *Origeniana Secunda: second colloque international des études origéniennes (Bari 20-23 septembre 1977)*, QVetCh 15 (Rome 1980) 33-56, esp. 42-45.

The ontology put forward in Origen's treatise *De principiis* is dualistic in conception. This view is supported by passages in Philo, in particular *Opif.* 151 and *Fug.* 62. In Philo the notion of 'original sin' is based on anthropological, cosmological, and also ontological considerations, as is shown by connections with many passages in Plato's dialogues. (RR)

8006. R. BIGATTI, 'Sui significati del termine "logos" nel trattato *Le allegorie delle leggi* di Filone di Alessandria', *RFN* 72 (1980) 431-451.

The author analyzes with great accuracy the instances of the term logos and its synonyms in *Leg.* 1-3. The semantic field of the term is reconstructed by regrouping the material according to the different meanings which it assumes: (a) metaphysical-ontological; (b) cosmological; (c) anthropological-ethical; d) epistemological; (e) biblical. Having underlined the novelty of Philo's use of the term compared to its meaning in Greek philosophy, and having indicated its central role in Philo's thought, Bigatti makes the following observation: 'one could say that the whole philosophical scaffolding of Philo's system is nothing but the formal structure through which Philo did justice to a faith: such a representation clarifies the function of a logos which is at the same time a philosophical concept and a term of faith' (449). (= R1071)

8007. P. BORGEN, 'Observations on the theme "Paul and Philo": Paul's preaching of circumcision in Galatia (Gal. 5:11) and debates on circumcision in Philo', in S. PEDERSEN (ed.), *Die paulinische Literatur und Theologie: anlässlich der 50. jährigen Gründungs-Feier der Universität von Aarhus*, Skandinavische Beiträge (Aarhus-Göttingen 1980) 85-102; reprinted as 'Debates on circumcision in Philo and Paul', in *Paul preaches circumcision and pleases men and other essays on Christian origins* (Trondheim 1983) 15-32.

There is a close link between Paul and Philo on the theme of circumcision: the thought of both (in Gal. 5:11-6:10 and *Migr.* 86-93, *QE* 2.2) is characterized by a tension between circumcision in its physical and ethical senses (86). After a careful analysis of Paul in particular (the author is mainly interested in Paul and uses Philo only to clarify Paul's views; cf. 85), Borgen reaches conclusions of general interest: although Paul and Philo reflect parallel conflicts between the rite of circumcision in its physical sense, it would be wrong to see behind these a broader opposition between Hellenistic and Palestinian Judaism. In actual fact, as the author demonstrates, identical tensions are recognizable in the Judaism of Palestine (cf. 102). (= R1072)

8008. J. CAZEAUX, 'Système implicite dans l'exégèse de Philon: un exemple: le *De praemiis*', *StPh* 6 (1979-1980) 3-36.

Analyzing *Praem.*, the author applies in a highly elaborate and subtle way his particular method of interpreting Philo, a method which makes use of a kind of meta-structure that serves to explain the actual structure of each treatise. In this case Cazeaux uses two principles: (a) the *code of identification*, which is the meaning that each figure carries in

Philo's allegorical interpretation as a result of the overall context of his works; (b) the *idiom*, which is the specific function that the same figure fulfils in the individual treatises as a result of a variation of the code. Such an exegesis, it would seem, presupposes on the one hand the recognition of the essential semantic unity and completeness of each text, and on the other a clear subordination of philosophical to exegetical intent. (= R1073)

8009. R. R. CHAMBERS, *Greek athletics and the Jews: 165 B.C. - A.D. 70* (diss. Miami University, Oxford Ohio 1980), esp. 136-144.

The central question of the study is how Paul in 50 A.D. could apparently accept Greek athletics when there had been such antagonism on the part of Jews towards the gymnasium in 165 B.C. and towards Herod's athletic festivals c. 25-13 B.C. The traditional view that Palestinian Judaism abhorred athletics is criticizable, though H. A. Harris (cf. **7615**) goes too far in affirming a 'general enthusiasm' for it (he is also reprimanded for regarding Philo as an orthodox Jew *tout court*). In fact the evidence suggests significant accommodation on the part of the Jews in both Palestine and the Diaspora to the practice and especially the cultural ideal of athletic competition. Philo's evidence needs to be considered. He is important because he takes accommodation to the extreme: 'he is an example of a Jew who crossed over the line into Hellenism but who still thought of himself as a Jew!' (143). This conclusion is based almost wholly on the secondary literature. There is virtually no analysis of individual Philonic texts. (DTR)

8010. B. P. COPERHAVER, 'Jewish theologies of space in the scientific revolution: Henry More, Joseph Raphson, Isaac Newton and their predecessors', *Annals of Science* 37 (1980) 489-548, esp. 495f.

According to the author Philo seems to have tried to reconcile the Rabbinic custom of calling God māqôm with his essentially Peripatetic understanding of τόπος, the equivalent Greek term. The likeness of Philo's language, especially at *Somn.* 1.63-64, to that of the Rabbis is beyond dispute. (DTR)

8011. J. DILLON, 'Ganymede as the logos: traces of a forgotten allegorization in Philo', *StPh* 6 (1979-80) 37-40.

Three passages in Philo – *Deus* 155-158, *Somn.* 2.183, 249 – suggest that Ganymede symbolizes the Stoic logos through his activity as Zeus' wine-steward. The image indicates the Logos as a divine outpouring from God, bringing order to all creation. See also **8104.** (= R1074)

8012. C. ELSAS, 'Das Judentum als philosophische Religion bei Philo von Alexandrien', in K. W. TRÖGER (ed.), *Altes Testament - Frühjudentum - Gnosis: neue Studien zu 'Gnosis und Bibel'* (Gutersloh 1980) 195-220.

In an article containing copious bibliographical references the author proposes to define Philo's conception of Judaism and how it relates to the history of the Gnosis and late classical spirituality. Elsas's theme is certainly vast, but he reduces it to its essence in the following way. (1) From the Philonic themes he chooses the allegory of the wine in *Ebr.* (2) He considers three different contexts relating to Philo's position: the Christian Gnosis, religious philosophy, and the philosophy of the mysteries. (3) He sums up in three opposite pairs the themes which emerge from *Ebr.*: drunkenness-spirituality, foolishness-wisdom, moral disorder-practice of virtue. It is true, the author observes, that 'Philo chooses his point of departure in the sacred text of his religion, just like the Gnostics do; but the content of his allegory of foolishness and disorder opposed to practical and theoretical virtue is much more philosophical than the positions of the Gnosis and the philosophy of the mysteries' (198). (= R1074/a)

8013. H. E. FABER VAN DER MEULEN, 'Zum jüdischen und hellenistischen Hintergrund von Lukas 1,31', in W. HAUBECK and M. BACHMANN (edd.), *Wort in der Zeit: neutestamentliche Studien: Festgabe für K. H. Rengstorf zum 75. Geburtstag* (Leiden 1980) 108-122, esp. 114-116.

The author relates Luke 1:31 to various texts in Philo on the giving of names and, more penetratingly, on predestination as the fruit of divine prescience. (RR)

8014. D. FLUSSER [פלוסר .ד] (ed.), ספר יוסיפון [*The Josippon (Josephus Gorionides)*], 2 vols. (Jerusalem 1978-1980) 1.272-274, 434-435.

Flusser's edition of the medieval 'Hebrew Josephus' includes two passages of direct interest to students of Philo: an account of the embassy to Gaius and a version of the entry on Philo from Jerome's *De viris illustribus*. There is also a brief discussion of these passages at 2.7-8. (DS)

8015. F. R. GAHBAUER, 'Die Erzieherrolle des Logos Christus in der Ethik des Klemens von Alexandrien auf dem Hintergrund der (mittel) platonischen und stoischen Anthropologie', *MThZ* 31 (1980) 296-305.

The link laid by Clement between Christ the Logos and the human mind (διάνοια, λογισμός, νοῦς) finds precedents in Philo, especially in the contrasts between irrational (ἄλογον) and rational (λογικόν), sense-perception (αἴσθησις) and intellection (νόησις), flux and stability, impurity and purity, opinion (δόξα) and knowledge (ἐπιστήμη), desire (ἐπιθυμία) and insight (φρόνημα). (DTR)

8016. R. M. GRANT, 'War – just, holy, unjust – in Hellenistic and early Christian thought', *Aug* 20 (1980) 173-189, esp. 182-184.

Philo's political convictions are characterized by a fundamental pacifism which leads him to humanize the decrees of Deuteronomium and, essentially, to refute the idea of the holy war. (= R1075)

8017. R. GRYSON, 'Les Lévites, figure du sacerdoce véritable, selon Saint Ambroise', *EThL* 56 (1980) 89-112.

'While for Philo and, ultimately, for Origen too, the Levites symbolize the wise and the perfect, Ambrose sees in them a prefiguration of Christ, founder of a new priesthood, and of his ministers' (111). Such are the conclusions reached by the author; but it should be pointed out that these differences occur in contexts which coincide to a large degree and which are undoubtedly evidence of Ambrose's debt to Philo. (= R1076)

8018. R. GRYSON, 'La médiation d'Aaron d'après saint Ambroise', *RThAM* 47 (1980) 5-15.

Philo's allegorical interpretation of the figure of Aaron (the Logos, the priest, the man of progress) is paralleled in Ambrose and also Origen. For Philo, however, the priestly mediation of the Logos (symbolized by Aaron) is a result of its ontological status, whereas for Ambrose it is related to Christ's redemptive incarnation (15). (RR)

8019. W. Z. HARVEY [הרוי .ז.], העבריות והפילוסופיה המערבית בתורת ההסטוריה של צבי וולפסון ['Hebraism and western Philosophy in H. A. Wolfson's theory of history'], *Daat* 4 (1980) 103-109.

Subsequently published in an English version; see **8220**.

8020. D. M. HAY, 'Philo's references to other allegorists', *StPh* 6 (1979-80) 41-75.

The problem of the relations between Philo and the other allegorists is important because its solution can provide valuable information about the Alexandrian context and, in particular, about Philo's position within the exegetical tradition. The author collects all Philo's references to other allegorists and concludes that 'the casualness with which Philo mentions other exegetes, his evident carelessness in defining where their ideas stop and his own begin, tends to support the hypothesis of a long-standing school tradition behind his writings' (60). (= R1077)

8021. R. D. HECHT, 'Patterns of exegesis in Philo's interpretation of Leviticus', *StPh* 6 (1979-80) 77-155.

The author proceeds from Nikiprowetzky's views (cf. **6741**) on the Philonic interpretation of the sacrifice – which he regards as representing the 'state of the art' in Philonic studies – and isolates within Philo's thought the specific theme of ritual sacrifice as described in Leviticus. His aims are the following: (1) to examine, in a large section of Leviticus, what he calls 'groups of interpretation', from which it is possible to extract specific exegetical models; (2) to isolate, from the rest of the book, chapter ten, which contains the story of Nadab and Abihu and their death, since the Philonic exegesis on this point is without antecedents; (3) to pay particular attention to the interpretation of the holocaust (as it emerges from Lev.), because the analysis of this subject, taking him beyond the limits of the Philonic corpus, might help to place Philo more adequately in the history of biblical exegesis (cf. 86). (= R1078)

8022. F. D. HOFFNUNG, *The family of Jesus: a sociological analysis* (diss. University of California at Irvine 1980).

It is argued that, contrary to the Christian tradition, Jesus was a Shammaite Pharisee from the priestly family of Abijah-Phabi. Evidence from Philo is used to demonstrate that Jesus was called the 'Logos' and 'son of God' because he was the chief priest of his division. (DTR; based on *DA* 41-1168A).

8023. H. KÖSTER, *Einführung in das Neue Testament im Rahmen der Religionsgeschichte und Kulturgeschichte der hellenistischen und römischen Zeit* (Berlin-New York 1980), esp. 284-293.

Brief outlines of Philo's life and work, the latter following the order and contents of his writings, but without coming to an adequate synthetic analysis of his thought. (RR)

8024. E. LANNE, '"La règle de la vérité": aux sources d'une expression de saint Irénée', in J. BÉKÉS and G. FARNEDI (edd.), *Lex orandi, lex credendi: miscellanea in onore di P. C. Vagaggini*, StAns 79, Sacramentum 6 (Rome 1980) 57-70.

Irenaeus is the first Christian writer to use the expression 'rule of truth'. The closest (and perhaps only) antecedent of Irenaeus is Philo, who uses this formula four times: in *Det.* 125, *Conf.* 2, *Ios.* 145, and *Leg.* 3.233. The author examines these texts and finds that they express slightly different meanings of the term κάνων (meanings largely neglected by students of this important concept). Taken together, however, they do show that Irenaeus is to some degree indebted to Philo in relation to this specific theme. (= R1078/a)

8025. R. LORENZ, *Arius judaizans? Untersuchungen zur dogmen-geschichtlichen Einordnung des Arius*, FKDG 31 (Göttingen 1980), esp. 103-106, 145-146.

Wolfson's interpretation of the Philonic Logos (in particular its tripartition into God, itself, and the world) seems to equate Philo's position with that of Arius. It is unlikely, however, that Arius based himself on Philo's views, since these are anything but clear and unambiguous, and since there remain considerable differences in the theological thought of both philosophers, especially the structural distinction which Arius posits between God and the Logos-Son. (RR)

8026. J. T. MATTHEWS, 'Reflections of Philo Judaeus in the Septuagint illustrations of the Joseph story', *ByS* 7 (1980) 35-56.

Although late ancient, Byzantine and medieval illustrations of the Joseph story rely mainly on the Septuagint account, elements from outside are also sometimes incorporated. The author argues that Philo's account of the life of Joseph in *Ios.* has influenced both the sequence of illustrations in the story and certain detailed motifs. Such influence is found in some *Octateuchs*, on the ivory plaques from the throne of Maximinanus in Ravenna (6th century), in the *Paris Gregory*, on Coptic textiles, the marble plaques in Santa Restituta in Naples, and on the cupola of San Marco in Venice (illustrations 46-56). Philo's influence was literary rather than visual (it is not likely that Philo's works were illustrated), and probably occurred largely via the *catenae*. (DTR)

8027. A. MÉASSON, 'Un aspect de la critique du polytheisme chez Philon d'Alexandrie: les acceptions du mot μῦθος dans son œuvre', *Centre Jean Palerne Mémoires* 2 (Saint-Étienne 1980) 75-107.

The article is divided into two parts: (a) a main section (77-99) which considers the various meanings of the term μῦθος (word, story, legend, invention of the spirit, appearance) on the basis of an extensive analysis of the relevant Philonic texts; (b) a second section (100-107) which considers the relation between μῦθος and ἀλήθεια. Here two aspects in particular are emphasized: namely that myths are not invariably negative (100f., 105), but that nevertheless they are opposed to truth and reality (105). It must be concluded that myths, too, may be of some value, to the extent that they contain the seed of truth (106f.). (RR)

8028. R. MELNICK, 'On the Philonic conception of the whole man', *JSJ*

11 (1980) 1-32.

The subject dealt with in this article – a subject only roughly indicated by the title – is in our opinion too vast for the limited space devoted to it. The author's first concern is to specify the terms of the synthesis between Judaism and Hellenism in Philonic anthropology; his second is to examine Philo's views on the nature of man and on immortality in particular. Melnick specifies further that central to his discussion will be the role which Philo gives to sexual imagery. From this point on (5ff.) the article constitutes a careful and thorough reading of Baer's fundamental study on this subject (7005). The themes of immortality and sexual allegory converge in the motifs of 'becoming virgin' (the ultimate stage of the soul's progress), of 'becoming man', and, in a broad sense, of 'becoming one'. These together form conscious efforts of the soul to achieve an immortal state (cf. 27). But note that man's initiative is neither absolute nor decisive: immortality remains a divine gift (cf. 28). (= R1079)

8029. A. MOMIGLIANO, 'Interpretazioni minime', *ASNP* 10 (1980) 1221-1231, esp. 1225-1226; reprinted in *Settimo contributo alla storia degli studi classici e del mondo antico* (Rome 1984) 105-114, esp. 190-110.

A brief analysis of *Flacc.* 93 which sheds light on various aspects of Roman politics in Egypt with regard to the maintenance of public order. (= R1079/a)

8030. H. MOXNES, *Theology in conflict: studies in Paul's understanding of God in Romans*, NT.S 53 (Leiden 1980), esp. 130-164.

The section of the book relevant to our purpose is wholly devoted to the way Philo interprets God's promise of an innumerable posterity to Abraham (Gen. 17:4-5; 15:6 etc.). The author carefully reconstructs the meaning of this exegesis by comparing Philo's thought to the Jewish tradition, and reaches the following conclusions (163f.). The story of Abraham was aimed at the various groups for which Philo was preaching: Jews, proselytes, and God-fearers. He reminded the Jews in particular of their duty to stand firm in their faith and not to follow the deviations of popular beliefs. For Philo, as for all Jews, Abraham was a symbol; but beyond his historical, religious, and nationalistic significance, Abraham was also the example of pure faith. Philo's exegesis proves that in Judaism Abraham's faith was not understood as a 'work' only, but more importantly as a gift from God. (= R1080)

8031. H. G. VON MUTIUS, 'Die Trennung von Licht und Finsternis in Philo von Alexandriens *De opificio mundi*', *BibNot* 11 (1980) 32-34.

Opif. 33-34, and the division between light and darkness represented there, does not involve a simple distinction between elementary substances, but rather the opposition of two powers, according to a notion which, in the author's opinion, is typically Jewish. (= R1080/a)

8032. V. NIKIPROWETZKY, 'Sur une lecture démonologique de Philon d'Alexandrie, *De gigantibus*, 6-18', in G. NAHON and C. TOUATI (edd.), *Hommage à G. Vajda: études d'histoire et de pensée juives* (Louvain 1980) 43-71.

In the author's view the Wolfsonian interpretation of *Gig.* 6-18 is inaccurate. Wolfson interprets this passage in terms of the myth of the fall of the angels, and thus attributes an originality to Philo which in this case he does not deserve. In Philo's writings there is in fact no room for evil spirits and demonology. The angels of God alluded to in this passage are 'erring spirits that preferred terrestrial passions, symbolized by women, above their divine origin, as demonstrated by the very name Scripture gives them' (70). It is possible that Philo, in accordance with Stoic views, rejected the very idea of demons as contradicting the goodness of Providence that governs the world. (= R1081)

8033. P. L. PARROTT, *Paul's political thought: Rom. 13:1-7 in the light of Hellenistic political thought* (diss. Claremont Graduate School 1980).

Philo furnishes one of the Greco-Roman political philosophies which represent the primary analogues for Paul's political thought. (DTR; based on *DA* 41-3625A)

8034. G. QUISPEL, 'Ezekiel 1:26 in Jewish mysticism and gnosis', *VChr* 34 (1980) 1-13.

After a few remarks on Philo's interpretation of the heavenly man as being neither male nor female, the author draws attention to: (a) the spiritualization of this theme, no doubt as a result of the effort to mediate between the Greek (and particularly Platonic) idea of man and the biblical figure of Adam; (b) the existence of a lively debate on this subject in the Jewish world as well. Thus Jewish heterodox circles are the source for the Gnostic *Anthropos*. (= R1082)

8035. J. R. ROYSE, 'Philo and the immortality of the race', *JSJ* 11 (1980) 33-37.

Briefly draws attention to the theme of the immortality of the race, in which both Aristotelian and Platonic influences can be traced. (= R1084)

8036. S. SANDMEL, 'Some comments on providence in Philo', in J. L. CRENSHAW and S. SANDMEL (edd.), *The divine Helmsman: studies on God's control of human events presented to Lou H. Silberman* (New York 1980) 79-85.

The theme of Providence intervening in human affairs is prominent in both *Flacc.* and *Legat.* Presumably the missing 'palinode' of the second work would have shown how the wicked Gaius was punished by God, just as happened in the case of Flaccus. The theme of Providence leads directly to the problem of theodicy, which is dealt with in the surviving fragments of *Prov.* The general superficiality of the treatment is somewhat striking, however, for that is a quality usually not found in Philo. No concern is shown for the unfortunate individual innocently caught up in events beyond his control. Such concern is found in Rabbinic literature. (DTR)

8037. A. F. SEGAL, 'Heavenly ascent in Hellenistic Judaism, Early Christianity and their environment', *ANRW* II 23.2 (Berlin 1980) 1333-1394, esp. 1352-1358.

Though Philo works in a scriptural framework, specific exegeses are secondary to an overarching system of ascent to God expressed in terms of a heavenly journey. By this means Philo can fully actualize the philosophical possibilities of the ascension structure such as were developed in the Hellenistic period. Segal's treatment of Philo is brief, but it is placed in the framework of a penetrating critique of the History of Religions school. Note also the excellent bibliography. (DTR)

8038. R. M. SELTZER, *Jewish people, Jewish thought: the Jewish experience in history* (New York-London 1980), esp. 205-213.

An elementary, but useful summary of Philo's place in Judaism. Philo is preoccupied with the same questions that were later to engage medieval Jewish thinkers, although he had no direct influence on them. (DTR)

8039. P. SIGAL, *The emergence of contemporary Judaism*, vol. 1 The foundations of Judaism from Biblical origins to the sixth century A.D., Part one From the Origins to the separation of Christianity, PThMS 29 (Pittsburgh 1980), esp. 311-326.

A general account of Philo's thought from the Jewish perspective, with emphasis on his theology and his knowledge of contemporary Halachah. The author concludes (325): 'Scholars who deny his affinities with agadic and halakhic traditions that eventually appear as "rabbinic Judaism" miss the mark'. (DTR)

8040. T. H. TOBIN, *The creation of man: Philo and the history of interpretation* (diss. Harvard University 1980).

See **8373**.

8041. L. TROIANI, 'Gli Ebrei e lo stato pagano in Filone e in Giuseppe', *Ricerche di Storia Antica II*, Biblioteca di Studi antichi 24 (Pisa 1980) 193-218.

Judaism as it existed during the lives of Philo and Josephus seems to be characterized by two different aspects, i.e. it seems to undergo the transition from loyalty to the pagan state to a separation based on 'respectful and reciprocal tolerance' (195). The aim of this work is to recover from Philo's historical writings the traces of this evolution. Troiani concludes (218) that Philo 'seems to be witness to an age in which the political and cultural relations between Judaism and paganism seem at times to be deteriorating, but not entirely jeopardized'. (RR)

8042. L. URBAN and P. HENRY, '"Before Abraham was I am": does Philo explain John 8: 56-58?', *StPh* 6 (1979-80) 157-195.

John 8:56-58, a highly problematical passage, gains in clarity if it is compared with Philo's thought and exegetical method, and, in particular, with his concept of logos. Such a comparison immediately shows what the Johannine identification of Christ with the Logos means and how the expression attributed to Jesus of 'my day' is to be understood (in Philo's terminology) as one of the attributes of the Logos, particularly connected with the theme of light. Yet the authors are reluctant to postulate a direct relation between Philo and John. They are more inclined to allow that both are representatives of a common theological tradition. (= R1086)

8043. F. VILLENEUVE, 'Philon d'Alexandrie et le judaïsme antique', *L'Histoire* 23 (1980) 45-54.

This general introduction to Philo is not an in-depth scientific study, but a fresh and lively presentation of Philo's thought and work against the background of Jewish-Hellenistic culture in Alexandria. Philo, according to Villeneuve, wished to explain Judaism as a mystery (in the religious sense of the term, cf. 50), in which the theme of migration predominates. (= R1087)

8044. D. S. WINSTON, 'Philo's theory of eternal creation: *De Prov.* 1, 6-9', *PAAJR* 46-47 (1980) 593-606.

The Philonic doctrine of creation clearly takes its cue from Platonism, and more specifically from the *Timaeus*. But within these limits it is characterized by a great degree of originality. Philo, in fact, was not able to accept a theory of creation in time, since this would entail inactivity (prior to creation) and thus subsequent mutability on the part of God. Nor on the other hand could he simply share the view of a creative activity *ab aeterno*, since that would presuppose another originating principle besides God. (We note that in Winston's view Philo interprets the creative act as a precise and accurate division of formless matter by the *logos tomeus*, and, therefore, as a demiurgic activity and not as a creation *ex nihilo*.) The solution formulated by Philo is rather as follows. The creative act is identical with divine thought. Thus God directly created the intelligible world and only indirectly the sensible world, as shadow and copy of the former. In this way – notwithstanding some undeniable obscurities and ambiguities – Philo saved both the principle of God's activity and immutability and that of his unicity. (= R1088)

1981

8101. D. A. CARSON, 'Divine sovereignty and human responsibility in Philo: analysis and method', *NT* 23 (1981) 148-164.

The question of free will is taken here as a significant example of a larger philosophical problem, namely the antagonism between divine sovereignty and human responsibility. Carson underlines the following aspects of Philo's thought on the subject. (1) Philo imposes a measure of control on the concept of providence, so that man's freedom is not structurally denied. (2) Freedom is in Philo essentially freedom from passion. (3) Only God is truly active, while man is passive. Yet this passivity is not impotence, but the possibility of collaboration with God. Free will consists in man's power to put himself 'outside God' through sin. (4) Election and divine grace are not the results of a discriminatory activity on God's part, but are destined for all men. (= R1089)

8102. A. V. CERNUDA, 'La introducción del Primogénito según Hebr. 1,6', *EstB* 39 (1981) 107-153.

A careful analysis of the terms expressing the incarnation of God in Heb. 1:6. Given the relation between the author of Hebrews and Philo, Philo's texts are particularly relevant, and a number of these are analyzed with great precision. (RR)

8103. R. LE DEAUT, 'Le thème de la circoncision du coeur (Dt. XXX

6; Jér. IV 4) dans les versions anciennes (LXX et Targum) et à Qumrân', in *Congress Volume: Vienna 1980*, VT.S 32 (Leiden 1981) 178-205, esp. 187-189.

The circumcision of the heart, a popular theme in Jewish literature, is spiritualized to an extreme degree in Philo. It is significant, however, that even more extreme tendencies existed in Philo's time, such as the radical allegorists, who unlike Philo denied any value to the actual rite of circumcision. (RR)

8104. J. DILLON, Ganymede as the Logos: traces of a forgotten allegorization in Philo?', *CQ* 31 (1981) 183-185.

Cf. **8011.**

8105. H. DÖRRIE, 'Die andere Theologie: wie stellten die frühchristlichen Theologen des 2.-4. Jahrhunderts ihren Lesern die "Griechische Weisheit" (= den Platonismus) dar?', *ThPh* 56 (1981) 1-46, esp. 6-15.

In order to demonstrate Philo's role in mediating between 'Greek wisdom' and the Platonism of the Christian Fathers (14), Dörrie touches on many allegorical and philosophical themes in Philo's work. Philo's openness to Hellenism, he observes, does not involve the relinquishing of his Jewish orthodoxy: the avenue which he opens up between both worlds leads from Hellenism to Judaism, and not vice versa (12f.). (RR)

8106. L. GREENSPOON, 'The pronouncement story in Philo and Josephus', *Semeia* 20 [= R. C. TANNEHILL (ed.), *Pronouncement stories*] (1981) 73-80.

A pronouncement story – a literary genre containing a brief narrative in which the climactic element is a pronouncement which is presented as a particular person's response to something said or observed on a particular occasion in the past – is comparatively rare in Philo, only 17 instances having been located by the author. In fact 11 are found in the last third of *Prob.* This distribution links up with the fact that almost all such stories deal with characters from Greek history or mythology (favourites Diogenes, Socrates), and not with Jewish figures from biblical or later periods (only exception at *Abr.* 260f.). (DTR)

8107. H. GUEVARA, *La resistencia judía contra Roma en la epoca de Jesus,* Tesis presentada al Pontificio Instituto Biblico (diss. Metingen 1981), esp. 183-196.

Philonic evidence, in particular derived from *Legat.*, is used to reconstruct the historical-political situation of Alexandria and the events in which Philo played a leading role. The author emphasizes that at the time of the rebellion the Jewish community showed unity and respect for its internal hierarchies, and that Roman sovereignty was never questioned (195). (= R1090)

8108. R. D. HECHT, 'Scripture and commentary in Philo', *SBLSP* 20 (1981) 129-64.

The question addressed in this well-researched paper is: where does Scripture end and commentary begin for Philo? In the introductory section a survey is given of scholarly studies devoted to the biblical text in Philo. The remainder of the paper falls into three parts. In the first Hecht observes that Philo describes Scripture by using terms – such as χρησμός and θεσπισθὲν λόγιον – that evoke its authority and veracity and also by emphasizing the role of Moses as transmitter of the authoritative material. The second part illustrates Philo's method of dealing with Scripture by examining his interpretation of Lev. 19. Noteworthy is that most references are not literal quotes but involve paraphrase and interpolation of the biblical text. Certain 'exegetical phenomena' emerge which Hecht regards as typical of Philo's use of the biblical text: (a) the interpretation is not a line-by-line commentary; (b) it is structured by the demands of allegorical interpretation; (c) central ideas inform the reading of the text; (d) the use of the biblical text is governed by the logic of association. In the third and final part Hecht reaches conclusions on Philo's method of scriptural interpretation. The notion of 'hermeneutical prophecy' is crucial: 'Philo and any other person interested in real wisdom all have equal access as Moses himself to the divine truths. Moses ... or Philo could by-pass the written text altogether... The written text only 'jogs' the rational soul' (150). Thus Scripture does not exist apart and independently from commentary. In an appendix Philo's citations and allusions to Lev. 19 are compared with the LXX text. (DTR)

8109. M. HENGEL and H. LICHTENBERGER, 'Die Hellenisierung des antiken Judentums als *Praeparatio Evangelica*', in *Humanistische Bildung*, Württembergischer Verein der Freunde des humanistischen Gymnasiums 4 (1981) 1-30, esp. 18-21.

Philo contributed more than anyone else to the transition from Judaism to early Christian philosophy. This is above all due to the synthesis which he was able to achieve between biblical revelation and Greek thought. In this sense he may be considered the first theologian. (RR)

8110. R. A. HORSELY, 'Gnosis in Corinth: I Corinthians 8.1-16', *NTS* 27 (1981) 32-51.

The author argues that it is possible to determine with some degree of precision the nature and background of the 'proto-Gnosticism' in Corinth, namely a distinctive Hellenistic Jewish religiosity focussed on *sophia* and *gnosis* (cf. 32). The chief evidence for this thesis is drawn from Philo's writings (and the Sapientia Salomonis), which, it is argued, provide an analogy for nearly every aspect of the Corinthians' religious language and viewpoint. The conflict in the letter is thus rooted in two differing Jewish religious viewpoints: some of the Corinthians are caught up in spiritual exaltation through possession of *sophia*, whereas Paul maintains an apocalyptic perspective connected primarily with Palestinian Judaism. (DTR)

8111. R. KRAFT, 'Philo on Seth: was Philo aware of traditions which exalted Seth and his progeny?', in B. LAYTON (ed.), *The rediscovery of Gnosticism*, 2 vols., SHR 41 (Leiden 1980-81) 2.457-458.

The author, in what is more a summary than an article, notes that Seth and his descendants are symbols rather than historical figures, and outlines the chief interpretations with which Seth is associated in Philo's works, but does not explicitly answer the question in his title. (DTR)

8112. J. P. LÉMONON, *Pilate et le gouvernement de la Judée: textes et monuments*, Études Bibliques (Paris 1981), esp. 205-230.

The author examines *Legat*. 299-305, which he sees as an important document for reconstructing Pilate's career. Basically three problems present themselves: (a) is it possible to establish exactly the date of the Jewish-Alexandrian embassy to Gaius? (b) can the date of the publication of *Legat*. be determined? (c) what is the nature of this section of *Legat*.? is it an 'echo' of a letter or free composition written by Philo himself? Lémonon deals carefully with each of these questions by analyzing the Philonic texts and comparing them with the information in Flavius Josephus. (RR)

8113. A. LOUTH, *The origins of the Christian mystical tradition* (Oxford 1981), esp.18-35.

The fact that a chapter on Philo is flanked by chapters on Plato and Plotinus is an indication of the importance that the author accords to his influence on the Platonizing mystical tradition among the Church Fathers. In Philo the doctrine of God is central; despite many similarities to Middle Platonist ideas, it breathes a different spirit, since God is not only a philosophical spirit, but One who reveals himself to his people. In his account of the doctrine of God, the Powers and the Logos, Louth stresses the role of grace and the connection Philo makes between the Logos and God's self-disclosure in Scripture, both themes that the Fathers would take up. The chapter ends with a description of the soul's quest for knowledge and experience of God. Philo develops 'a mysticism of love and yearning for God in Himself, in his unknowability' (32). In spite of much ecstatic language (esp. 'sober drunkenness'), however, he does not envisage mystical union with God. (DTR)

8114. J. MANSFELD, 'Bad world and demiurge: a "Gnostic" motif from Parmenides and Empedocles to Lucretius and Philo', in R. VAN DEN BROEK and M. J. VERMASEREN (edd.), *Studies in Gnosticism and Hellenistic religions presented to Gilles Quispel on the occasion of his 65th birthday*, EPRO 91 (Leiden 1981) 261-314, esp. 301-309.

Discussion of Philo's account of the arguments between Plato and Aristotle and the further reaction of the Stoa as recorded in *Aet*. 'Philo does not just report, in doxographical fashion, the views of others, but emphatically takes part in the discussion himself; he continuously interpolates and adds arguments of his own, and argues at length against the Stoics at 85ff.' (308). (DTR)

8115. J. P. MARTÍN, 'El Cosmos - hijo de Dios: el desarrollo judeohelenista de un tema platónico', *OrOcc* 2 (1981) 75-81.

The metaphor of the cosmos as the perfect son of God has Platonic origins and is specifically linked to the figure of the Demiurge. Philo, however, elaborates this theme considerably, incorporating in it the theme of worship (cosmic liturgy) and the theme of the progress of creation, in particular of man. The foundation of the concept, observes Martín at 79ff., lies in the theory of the identity between *eidos* and *telos* inherited from classical Greece. (RR) (RR)

8116. A. M. MAZZANTI, 'ΘΕΟΣ e ΚΥΡΙΟΣ: i "nomi" di Dio in Filone d'Alessandria: questioni storico comparative', *SSR* 5 (1981) 15-30.

Gives a broad analysis of Philo's conception of God, often in comparison with parallel themes in Gnostic (22, 26f.), Neoplatonic (22f.), Middle Platonist (23f.) and early Christian (25f.) literature. Mazzanti thinks it is possible to speak 'of a duality of the divine owing to the existence of *dynameis* which, though genetically dependent and having a collaborating role, are nevertheless not ontologically assimilable to Being in all aspects, but represent the divine at a lower level' (29). This conception clearly exercises a strong influence on Philo's anthropology and ethics as well. (RR)

8117. R. MORTLEY, *Womanhood: the feminine in ancient Hellenism, Gnosticism, Christianity and Islam* (Sydney 1981), esp. 6-19.

Philo's views on womanhood (and the relation to manhood) take their cue from the Adam and Eve story, but it is the way the biblical account in interpreted – with reference to philosophical ideas, and to a lesser extent current Alexandrian social conditions – that is determinative. The difference between man and woman, according to Philo, is based on nature (φύσις) and not convention (νόμος), and is epitomized in the relation between reason and sensuality. The image of womanhood for Philo is not entirely negative, the author stresses, since woman contributes to reality and has a necessary function. It is illuminating, however, that only through virginity, i.e. the repression of her sensual nature, can woman aspire to the higher status of the man. (DTR)

8118. J. MURPHY-O'CONNOR, '"Baptized for the dead" (I Cor., XV, 29): a Corinthian slogan', *RB* 88 (1981) 532-543, esp. 536ff.

The author follows Horsely (cf. **7617**) in attributing a spiritual elitism to the Corinthians involving contempt of the body. This attitude was best articulated in Philonic thought, but what the Corinthians knew was probably mediated by Apollos. (DTR)

8119. V. NIKIPROWETZKY, 'Saint Ambroise et Philon', *REG* 94 (1981) 193-199.

Though this article is essentially a review of Savon's study on Philo and Ambrose (**7739**), the author also incorporates, by way of introduction, an illuminating *status quaestionis* on the relations between the two thinkers. (= R1091)

8120. J. NOLLAND, 'Uncircumcised proselytes', *JSJ* 12 (1981) 173-194, esp. 173-179.

A detailed reading of *QE* 2.2 shows, contrary to the view of N. J. MCELENEY (*NTS* 20 (1974) 327) and other scholars, that Philo does not allow uncircumcised proselytes. (DTR)

8121. E. F. OSBORN, 'Negative theology and apologetic', in D. W. DOCKRILL and R. MORTLEY, *The via negativa*, Prudentia supplementary number 1981 (Auckland 1981) 49-63, esp. 54-56.

In Philo divine transcendence and incomprehensibility do not entail separation from man, but rather determine the way that man can be joined to God. (DTR)

8122. M. PUCCI, 'Il significato del termine apoikia nell'opera di Filone', *Ath* 59 (1981) 498-499.

The term ἀποικία in Philo does not involve any precise and specific legal meaning and is therefore of no value for a reconstruction of the historical and legal position of the Jewish community in Alexandria. (= R1091/a)

8123. *Reallexikon für Antike und Christentum*, edited by T. KLAUSER et al., vol.11 (Stuttgart 1981).

Cf. above **5016.** Contains: C. COLPE, art. 'Gnosis II (Gnostizismus)', 537-659, esp. 566-570 (Gnosticism, of which Philo (together with Plato) is regarded as a precursor); H. DITTMANN, art. 'Gnade', 313-446, esp. 345-6 (grace, χάρις); J.-C. FREDOUILLE, art. 'Götzendienst', 828-95, esp. 863-4 (worship of idols); D. LÜHRMANN, art. 'Glaube', 48-122, esp. 63 (faith, πίστις); R. MORTLEY, art. 'Gnosis I (Erkenntnislehre)', 446-537, esp. 476-81 (knowledge, epistemology); K. THRAEDE, art. 'Gleichheit', 122-164, esp. 140-2 (equality).

8124. S. H. RINGE, *The Jubilee proclamation in the ministry and teaching of Jesus: a tradition-critical study in the synoptic gospels and Acts* (diss. Union Theological Seminary New York 1981).

As background to Jesus' pronouncement of 'good news for the poor', 'release', or 'forgiveness', Jubilee references are traced through the literature of the late Second Temple Judaism, including Philo. (DTR; based on *DA* 42-1214A)

8125. J. R. ROYSE, 'A Philonic use of πανδοχεῖον (Luke X 34)', *NT* 23 (1981) 193-194.

The New Testament word πανδοχεῖον, which according to Bauer is not found in Philo, in fact occurs in a Greek fragment recording a brief portion of *QG* 4.33. The negative attitude towards the wayside inn concurs with later Jewish usage. (DTR)

8126. D. T. RUNIA, 'Philo's *De aeternitate mundi*: the problem of its interpretation', *VChr* 35 (1981) 105-151.

As Sandmel already pointed out, the difficulty of understanding *Aet.* is caused by the fact that the eternity of the world which it posits is hard to reconcile with Philo's doctrine of creation. In the past interpreters have solved this contradiction in two ways: by questioning the treatise's authenticity, or by minimizing its importance. In order to go beyond these two positions, the author reconstructs – with greater precision than Sandmel – the major scholarly views on this subject from the end of the 19th century until the present day (107-112). After a careful analysis of the style and content of *Aet.*, the following conclusions are drawn. The contents of the treatise, if correctly interpreted, are wholly in line with Philo's thought as it is found in the remainder of his writings. The arguments at *Aet.* 20-149 do not represent his true thought, but rather contrary views belonging to a dialectical debate of which the part expressing his own thought has unfortunately been lost (cf. 139). The treatise is authentic and makes its own contribution to an understanding of Philo. Runia also rejects the suggestion that it is an immature work belonging to the period of Philo's philosophical studies. 'This would be to beg the entire question of the relation between exegesis and philosophy in Philo's achievement' (140). (= R1093)

8127. M. SIMONETTI, *Profilo storico dell'esegesi patristica*, Sussidi patristici 1 (Rome 1981) *passim*.

Philo's allegorical exegesis is related to Greek and in particular Stoic allegorical exegesis, but differs from these in its typically religious aims. Philo in fact regards Scripture as a divine and revealed work much superior to the myths which the Greek allegorists interpreted (13f.). For this reason the literal meaning of the biblical text also retains a certain value for Philo. The author also briefly sketches the impact of Philo's exegesis on Christian thinkers, particularly Clement and Origen. (RR)

8128. G. C. STEAD, 'In search of Valentinus', in *The rediscovery of Gnosticism* (cf. **8111**) 75-103.

Even though this article does not deal with Philo explicitly, we have included it because it is one of the scholarly writings which relates Philo to an individual Gnostic thinker. Philonic evidence is adduced at numerous points in order to support the thesis that on the basis of the preserved fragments of Valentinus' writings he should be regarded as a biblical Platonist. (DTR)

8129. S. K. STOWERS, *The diatribe and Paul's letter to the Romans*, SBLDS 57 (Chico California 1981), esp. 12-17, 68-69, 75-78.

Discussion of P. Wendland's famous monograph (1895) and Philo's evidence on the 'diatribe' in the context of an examination of R. Bultmann's application of the theory to the interpretation of Paul's Letter to the Romans. The evidence of Greco-Roman authors shows that the diatribe type of discourse has its source in the philosophical school situation and generally contains dialogical elements. In the case of both these aspects the Philonic evidence is somewhat anomalous. (DTR)

8130. G. STROUSMA, 'Le couple de l'ange et de l'esprit: traditions juives et chrétiennes', *RB* 88 (1981) 42-61, esp. 46, 53-55.

The function of the two Cherubim in the divine hierarchy must be considered that of a hypostatic rather than symbolic representation of God. The exegesis of the two Cherubim (in *Cher.* 21ff. and *QE* 2.68) shows Platonic and Jewish influences. (RR)

8131. B. WARDY, *Philo and the Haggada as treated in modern scholarship* (diss. McGill University Montreal 1981).

The study consists of two parts. In the first Wardy presents brief biographical sketches of eight Philonic scholars – C. Siegfried, L. Treitel, E. Stein, J. Pépin, Y. Amir (= H. Neumark), E. R. Goodenough, H. Wolfson, S. Sandmel –, followed by an analysis of their views on the subject of the relationship between Philo and the Palestinian Haggadah. Critical comments are made, but no clear-cut conclusions reached. The second part consists of a summary (and not very original) account of the author's own views on Philo, concentrating on the relation of Greek and Hebrew elements in his thought. 'Philo, in my opinion, is best viewed as representing a relatively self-contained Jewish-Hellenism, not totally severed from Palestinian Judaism, yet clearly distinct from it' (195). (DTR)

8132. M. A. WILLIAMS, 'Stability as a soteriological theme in Gnosticism', in *The rediscovery of Gnosticism* (cf. **8111**) 819-829, esp. 824ff.

Philo's attribution of a God-like stability to the Patriarchs Abraham and Moses is invoked as a significant parallel for the stability attained by Allogenes in the Gnostic treatise of the same name. The author finds evidence of a cross-fertilization of Jewish wisdom tradition with a Platonic theme, and sees no reason to regard the theme as original with Philo. (DTR)

8133. *Philo of Alexandria: The contemplative life, The giants and selections*, translation and introduction by D. WINSTON, preface by J. DILLON, The Classics of Western Spirituality (New York-Toronto 1981).

This work opens with a brief preface by Dillon (xi-xiv), followed by a short but compact and valuable introduction in which Winston sets out the main lines of his interpretation of Philo (1-37). Philo, in Winston's view, is a convinced and enthusiastic follower of Plato (interpreted, of course, according to the canons of contemporary Platonism, i.e. Middle Platonism) who lacks a systematic philosophical mind, but who must at least be credited with an extensive and profound knowledge of the Greek philosophical tradition, which he synthesized, elaborated, and amplified with remarkable depth and breadth of vision. More precisely, it is the mystical aspect of Platonism which is in tune with Philo's sensibility (the author calls him a 'mystical theorist' (35)) and allows him to assimilate the legacy of Judaism to Platonic philosophy. This synthesis even extends to formal aspects, it seems, for Winston is able to relate the particular structure of Philo's writings to Plato's dialogical method (cf. 2). Winston concentrates on two subjects in his analysis: Philo's doctrine of creation (cf. above **8044**) and his mysticism (cf. above **7852**). Cf. also **1117**. The remainder of the book is a splendid anthology of Philonic texts presented in a copiously annotated English translation (cf. above **3013**). Besides a complete translation of *Gig.* and *Contempl.* (cf. **2154**), it further contains selected texts from other Philonic writings grouped under the following headings: (1) autobiographical texts; (2) exegesis: (3) the Logos; (4) cosmogony; (5) soul, angels and demons; (6) divine transcendence; (7) knowledge and prophecy; (8) worship, (9) mysticism; (10) Providence, theodicy, miracles; (11) ethics; (12) Moses and the Law; (13) universalism and particularism. REVIEW: W. C. Heiser, *ThD* 30 (1982) 187. (= R1094/a)

8134. S. ZAÑARTU, 'El origen del universo y del hombre según Filón de Alejandría en su libro *De Opificio Mundi*', *TyV* 22 (1981) 31-50.

A detailed analysis and exposition of the theology and anthropology of *Opif.* The author does not address the fundamental problems of Philo's theology, but limits himself to explaining some of the themes which emerge from this treatise. Philo is seen as an exponent of the philosophical-eclectic thought which permeated the rhetorical culture of his day but which which he successfully subordinated to his own religious and exegetical purposes. (= R1095)

1982

8201. Y. AMIR, 'Wie verarbeitete das Judentum fremde Einflüsse in hellenistischer Zeit?', *Jud* 38 (1982) 150-163, esp. 155-159.

In Philo's work the contact between Hellenistic and Jewish culture results, among other things, in a new interpretation of Mosaic law as the culmination of Greek ethics. Philo relates the political organization of the Jews to the Platonic theory of the state, opting for a theocratic form of government which resolves the problem of the state's unity left unanswered by Plato. For if the head of the state (God) is one, the temple and also the priestly caste which administrates the state will be one. (RR)

8202. J. M. BASSLER, *Divine impartiality: Paul and a theological axiom*, SBLDS 59 (Chico, California 1982), esp. 77-119.

Chapter 3, entitled 'The Philonic interpretation of divine impartiality', discusses the following problem: 'does Philo present an adequate statement of Greek universalism, or is it subordinated to Jewish nationalistic interests?' (109). The solution proposed by Bassler is quite complex and allows no unambiguous or categorical answers. Philo's work certainly contains universalistic motifs deriving mainly from Stoicism, but these motifs determine the presuppositions of his ethics rather than his political views. As in the case of the Stoa, the equality of men is for Philo based on the 'common possession of divine Reason' and on the affinity of all men (119). But it is precisely the theme of virtue that Philo uses to distinguish the good from the evil and thus to justify, from a clearly nationalistic point of view, the excellence of the Jewish people. (= R1095/b)

8203. B. BELLETTI, 'La dottrina dell'assimilazione a Dio in Filone di Alessandria', *RFN* 74 (1982) 419-440.

In an exhaustive study of specific passages, the author analyzes the concepts of συγγένεια and ὁμοίωσις and the problem of the assimilation with God. The concept underlying this relationship is that of the image. The original Platonic meaning of this concept, however, has been substantially modified by being incorporated into a creationistic frame of reference. (RR)

8204. G. BISSOLI, 'Es 15, 17-18 nell'interpretazione di Filone Alessandrino', *SBFLA* 32 (1982) 147-154.

A collection and discussion of all the basic Philonic texts commenting on Ex. 15:17-18, the final words of the song of Moses, including their relation to the Jewish exegetical tradition. Philo's interpretation of the 'mountain of inheritance' is dominated by an ethical perspective and specifically by the theme of the passage from passion to virtue. (RR)

8205. R. A. BITTER, *Vreemdelingschap bij Philo van Alexandrië: een onderzoek naar de betekenis van πάροικος* (diss. Utrecht 1982).

This dissertation takes the form of a lexical inquiry. Through the examination of texts the occurrence of the word πάροικος and words of the same root in the Septuagint and Philo is determined and the Philonic usage is analyzed. This conception is based on the original meaning of 'sojourner', interpreted in almost all cases in a metaphorical sense.

The following themes are dealt with in sequence: πάροικος as indicating the relation of man to God; πάροικος as indicating the temporary involvement with the encyclical studies in preparation for attaining to knowledge of God; πάροικος as indicating the relation of the wise man (who has learnt to know God) to earthly existence. In each case Bitter relates the themes involved to Philonic texts and the biblical figures interpreted in them (with particular emphasis on Abraham, the archtypal 'sojourner'). The final chapter discusses original aspects of Philo's conception in comparison with that of his contemporaries (especially the Stoic and Middle Platonist philosophers). 'To summarize, πάροικος is used by Philo to express man's situation in this world, where he is neither a complete stranger nor a native citizen, but an alien resident, who originally comes from on high and is therefore always eager to return to his native country and in his physical existence labours to become what he is, God's image, through an ever-deepening intellectual and existential knowledge of God' (190-1, conclusion of the English summary). An appendix discusses the possibility suggested by G. Quispel and other scholars that behind some of Philo's remarks on alienship more radical Gnosticizing views can be discerned. It is not impossible, according to the author, that some of Philo's remarks may tacitly correct such views. REVIEWS: J. C. M. van Winden, *NTT* 36 (1982) 337f.; A. Hilhorst, *JSJ* 14 (1983) 186f. (RAB/DTR)

8206. G. BOCCACCINI, 'L'interpretazione di Gen. 1,26 in Filone Alessandrino', *QVM* 31 (1982) 33-41.

Philo's exegesis of Gen. 1:26 in *Opif.* is analyzed as a significant example of his allegorical interpretation and theology. Two important themes emerge: the Logos and God's assistants in the creation of man. These themes, together with many others of Platonic origin, show the profundity of the synthesis which Philo achieved by merging Greek thought and Jewish religiosity. (RR)

8207. P. BORGEN, 'Paul preaches circumcision and pleases men', in M. D. HOOKER and S. G. WILSON, *Paul and Paulinism: essays in honour of C.K. Barrett* (London 1982) 37-46; reprinted in *Paul preaches circumcision and pleases men and other essays on Christian origins* (Trondheim 1983) 33-46.

Evidence on the ethical interpretation of circumcision in Philo is invoked to explain an exegetical crux at Gal. 5:11. When Paul exhorted the heathen Galatians to depart from the desire of the flesh, he effectively preaches ethical circumcision, but this does not mean that bodily circumcision is to follow. (DTR)

8208. P. CARNY [פ. קרני], מצרים המקראית בתפיסתו הפרשנית של פילון ['Biblical Egypt as a symbol in Philo's allegory'], *Shnaton* 5-6 (1982) 197-204.

Part of a larger study on Philo's allegories based on the author's theory of a principal difference between Philo and the Greek allegorists, and illustrated here by the various allegorical meanings of Egypt. An attempt is also made to delineate Philo's major hermeneutical criteria. English summary. (MM)

8209. A. DIHLE, *The theory of will in classical antiquity*, Sather Classical Lectures 48 (Berkeley 1982), esp. 90-98.

A discussion of Philo's views on divine will, human will and human conscience in the wider context of the development of the concept of will in ancient thought. Dihle argues that both in Philo and Paul this concept as we know it today is not yet present, although it is badly needed. In an appendix (145-149) it is noted that Philo, unlike the LXX, prefers βούλομαι to θέλω, presumably because in more literary Greek the former denotes decision based on rational deliberation, the latter arbitrary volition. (DTR)

8210. J. J. DILLON, *Lapsus: a study of the word and its synonyms from the classical age to St. Cyprian* (diss. The Catholic University of America 1982).

As part of a primarily lexical study of the *lapsus* (apostasy) used by Cyprian for people who did not stand firm in their convictions during the period of persecution, the third chapter discusses the Greek equivalents ὀλισθάνω, πταίω, πίπτω, as used in the Septuagint, New Testament, Philo and the Greek Church Fathers up to the middle of the third century A.D. (DTR; based on *DA* 43-1136A)

8211. P. DONINI, *Le scuole, l'anima, l'impero: la filosofia antica da Antioco a Plotino*, Sintesi 1 (Turin 1982), esp. 100-102, 252-258.

Philo is concisely presented in the context of the evolution of Platonism and, more precisely, in the context of Middle Platonism and its 'Pythagoreanizing embellishments'. A few pages are also devoted to Philo's influence on Clement. (RR)

8212. F. G. DOWNING, 'The resurrection of the dead: Jesus and Philo', *JSNT* 15 (1982) 42-50.

Jesus' puzzling appeal to Ex. 3:15f. in Mark 12:24-27 is illuminated by a Philonic text, *Abr.* 50-55. 'At least one Jewish near-contemporary of Jesus found himself bound by an interpretation of Exodus 3.6 and 15f. which took the words to mean that God had related himself so closely to mortal men as to raise awkward and inescapable questions about mortality as such' (47). (DTR)

8213. J. D. DUBOIS, 'Le Préambule de l'Apocalypse de Pierre (Nag Hammadi VII, 70, 14-20)', in J. RIES *et al.* (edd.), *Gnosticisme et monde hellénistique: actes du colloque de Louvain-la-Neuve (11-14 mars 1980)*, Publications de l'Institut Orientaliste de Louvain 27 (Louvain 1982) 384-393, esp. 390f.

The meaning of certain numerical references in the Preamble of the *Apocalypse of Peter* is clarified on the basis of various arithmological parallels in Philo. (RR)

8214. K. EYSELEIN, 'Kosmogonische Mythen im Unterricht der Oberstufe', *Der altsprachliche Unterricht* 25 (1982) 39-51, esp. 49-51.

The author briefly explains Philo's cosmology in the *De opificio mundi* in relation to the cosmology in the fragments of Aristobulus, placing special emphasis on its Platonic elements. (RR)

8215. S. C. FELDMAN, 'The continuity of the Jewish tradition in philosophy', *JRJ* 29 (1982) 65-76.

The author endeavours to illustrate the continuity of the Jewish tradition in philosophy by briefly discussing the philosophies of Philo, Spinoza and Feibleman (cf. above **5906**), with also a passing reference to Wolfson. Philo's genius was to find a means of retaining the Platonic theory of ideas, but at the same time subordinate it to Jewish religious revelation. (DTR)

8216. J. E. FOSSUM, *The name of God and the angel of the Lord: the origins of the idea of intermediation in Gnosticism* (diss. Utrecht 1982).

See below **8524**.

8217. G. FUKS, 'Again on the episode of the gilded Roman shields at Jerusalem', *HThR* 75 (1982) 503-507.

The puzzles concerning Pontius Pilate's introduction of the gilded shields in Jerusalem can be solved by taking into account Philo's description at *Legat.* 299. The official name of the Emperor was inscribed on the shields, part of which contained reference to his deified father. Hence the name of an alien deity was engraved within the precincts of the holy city, and it was this that enraged the Jews. (DTR)

8218. E. E. HALLEWY [הלוי .א.א], ערכי האגדה וההלכה לאור מקורות יווניים ולאטיניים [= *Facets of the Aggadah and the Halakhah in light of Greek and Latin sources*], 4 vols. (Tel Aviv 1979-1982) *passim*.

These volumes attempt a comprehensive survey of Rabbinic thought, legal reasoning, and biblical exegesis within the context of the literature of the Greco-Roman world. Philo, like many other authors, is cited widely, though only with the briefest accompanying discussion. Furthermore, the absence of any form of indices in these volumes detracts from their usefulness. Mention should be made of a series of earlier studies (all in Hebrew), very much in the same spirit, from which Hallewy draws freely: *The gates of the Aggadah* (1963), *The world of the Aggadah* (1972), *Passages in the Aggadah* (1973), *The historical-biographical Aggadah* (1975), *Aggadot of the Amoraim* (1977). In all cases no indices and no English summaries. (DS)

8219. S. A. HANDELMAN, *The slayers of Moses: the emergence of Rabbinic interpretation in modern literary theory*, SUNY series on modern Jewish literature and culture (Albany NY 1982), esp. 93-96.

The two sources of the modern science of interpretation are biblical hermeneutics and Greek philosophy. The author argues that modern literary theorists such as Freud, Lacan, Derrida and Bloom have reacted against the finality of Christian interpretation of the text and reverted to the principles of multiple interpretability of the Scripture found in the Jewish tradition. This revisionist conception of Jewish thought, pursued in a heretical and profane spirit, has the effect of subverting the Greco-Christian conception of meaning. On her path through the tradition the author makes a brief stop at Philo. In that he regards the scriptural text as divine revelation, Philo differs from the Greek philosophers. At the same he gives the native Jewish midrashic method a philosophical turn. This means that he adopts an entirely different way of thinking about meaning and truth, which has an implicit antilinguistic and anti-scriptural attitude at its centre (cf. 96). (DTR)

8220. W. Z. HARVEY, 'Hebraism and Western philosophy in H. A. Wolfson's theory of history', *Immanuel* 14 (1982) 77-85.

In a youthful essay for G. Santayana Wolfson sharply distinguished between Hebrew and Greek thought, criticizing Maimonides for succumbing to the latter. In his later scholarly corpus he developed a novel view of the history of philosophy in which he gives up the earlier position and argues that Jewish thought through Philo caused a Jewish revolution in philosophy, i.e. Greek philosophy is remade in accordance with a Hebrew view of life. We cite the author's concise conclusion (85). 'The old historian did not betray the young Hebrew. Wolfson's work in the history of philosophy is justly known for the breadth of its impressive erudition, and is distinguished by its precise philological analyses in Hebrew, Greek, Latin, and Arabic. Yet, for all that Wolfson's theory of the history of philosophy is preeminently scientific, it is in its soul *Hebrew*. If you will, it is a Hebraic revolution in the study of the history of Western philosophy.' Earlier version published in Hebrew; cf. **8019**. (DTR)

8221. K. JANÁČEK, 'Philon von Alexandreia und skeptische Tropen', *Eirene* 19 (1982) 83-97.

Philo's reliability as a doxographical source of Aenesidemus (*Ebr.* 169-205) has recently been questioned in fundamental works by Burkhard (**7308**) and Dumont (**7215**). The author discusses the views of these scholars, and criticizes not so much their conclusions (which he nevertheless seems to qualify) as their method of inquiry. A selection of particularly significant Philonic expressions and a comparison with the corresponding Sceptic terms and Philo's philosophical vocabulary as a whole show the significant changes which Philo applies to originally Sceptic themes. These are caused by the far from negligible influence of Philo's political, religious, and cultural ideas (96f.). (= R1095c)

8222. J. P. KENNEY, *Plotinus and the via antiqua: a study in philosophical theology* (diss. Brown University 1982), esp. chap. 2.

The thesis examines the importance of Platonic realist ontology for western philosophical theology. The second chapter traces the doctrine of the divine ideas in pre-Plotinian Platonism. Philo must be placed in the realist tradition of Platonist theology on account of his description of the first principle as τὸ ὄντως ὄν. But he represents a new type of realism in that he does not follow the general Middle Platonist trend to resolve the problems of divine demiurgic activity by means of a degree of divinity theology. Instead he retains the stress on divine uniqueness (from his Jewish background), and is led to a two-stage theory of the ideas and of divine production. Moreover the very structure of his cataphatic theology causes him to develop a strong emphasis on negative theology, which reflects an awareness that the nature of the Deity cannot be adequately expressed. 'It is no wonder that Philo considered God to be fundamentally incomprehensible, given the assumptions of his system' (59). (DTR)

8223. H.-J. KLAUCK, 'Gütergemeinschaft in der klassischen Antike, in Qumran und im Neuen Testament', *RQ* 11 (1982) 47-79, esp. 52-55.

Basing himself mainly on *Prob.*, the author briefly illustrates the principal features of Essenian morality and rules of life, with particular reference to the custom of holding goods in common possession. It is to be noted, however, that Essenian ethics have a tendency to alternate between the ideals of absolute poverty and a collective use of goods. (RR)

8224. H.-J. KLAUCK, *Herrenmahl und hellenistischer Kult: eine religionsgeschichtliche Untersuchung zum ersten Korintherbrief*, NTA 15 (Münster 1982), esp. 168-172.

Philo's use of the image of the meal is briefly analyzed under four headings: (a) the topos of spiritual food; (b) allegorization of manna; (c) spiritual drink; (d) mystically interpreted sharing of food. Philo is acquainted with the terminology of the mysteries, also in relation to food and drink. Others could easily give them a sacramental role, which he himself never intended. (DTR)

8225. C. KRAUS REGGIANI, 'I frammenti di Aristobulo, esegeta biblico', *Bollettino dei Classici* 3 (1982) 87-134.

In an extensive commentary on the fragments of Aristobulus, the author continually uses Philo's work as a point of reference. Her article is thus an indispensable contribution to research on the relations between Aristobulus and Philo. (RR)

8226. E. M. LAPERROUSAZ, *Les Esséniens selon leur témoignage direct*, Religions et cultures (Paris 1982), esp. 7-20.

The first chapter of this book, 'Knowledge about the Essenes prior to the Qumran discoveries', describes the evidence in Flavius Josephus, Pliny, and Philo, the latter mainly in *Hypoth.* and *Prob.* (RR)

8227. B. J. LILLIE, *A history of the scholarship on the Wisdom of Solomon* (diss. Hebrew Union College, Ohio 1982).

No clear scholarly consensus has emerged with regard to the dating of this work, suggestions ranging from the 3rd century B.C. to the first A.D. The Philonic concept of logos appears, though it is not nearly so well developed as in Philo himself. (DTR; based on *DA* 43-2377A)

8228. B. L. MACK, 'Under the shadow of Moses: authorship and authority in Hellenstic Judaism', *SBLSPS* 21 (1982) 299-318, esp. 316ff.

Philo is one of three authors used to illustrate theses which the author, inspired by the views of the critic H. Bloom, develops on the subject of authorship and authority. Under the influence of Greek literary practice increased emphasis is placed on the authorship of Moses during the period in question. Philo recognizes, indeed glories in the authority of Moses, but at the same time, by undertaking to write an interpretation of Moses, takes his own place in the roster of authoritative authors as well. (DTR)

8229. G. MANTOVANI, 'Acqua magica e acqua di luce in due testi gnostici', in *Gnosticisme et monde hellénistique* (cf. **8213**) 429-439, esp.

436-438.

The 'water of light' metaphor used to express the divine essence relates the *Apocryphon of John* to Philo on account of a common relation to a 'Sapiential context'. (RR)

8230. J. MARCUS, 'The evil inclination in the Epistle of James', *CBQ* 44 (1982) 606-621, esp. 613-615.

It is argued that the phrase ἡ ἰδία ἐπιθυμία at James 1:14 corresponds to the OT and Jewish concept of yeṣer. Various aspects of Philo's use of ἐπιθυμία are adduced as parallels to James, including his great emphasis on the voluntariness of desire (in which he departs from the Stoics). (DTR)

8231. J. L. MARSHALL, 'Melchizedek in Hebrews, Philo and Justin Martyr', in E. A. LIVINGSTONE (ed.), *Studia Evangelica VII: Papers presented to the Fifth International Congress on Biblical Studies held at Oxford, 1973*, TU 126 (Berlin 1982) 339-342.

Philo bases his interpretation of the figure of Melchizedek on Gen. 14:18 and not Ps. 110, and there is no evidence to suggest that he had any influence on either Hebrews or Justin. (DTR)

8232. J. P. MARTÍN, 'Fragmentos de Aristóbulo, el primer filósofo del Judaismo: introducción, traducción y comentarios', *OrOcc* 3 (1982) 65-95 *passim*.

In commenting on the fragments of Aristobulus, the author frequently cites Philo for purposes of comparison. The relations between Aristobulus and Philo are assessed on 90 ff. (RR)

8233. J. P. MARTÍN, 'L'interpretazione allegorica nella Lettera di Barnaba e nel guidaismo alessandrino', *SSR* 6 (1982) 173-185.

Certain aspects of the *Letter of Barnabas* regarding the creation of man can be traced back to Jewish-Alexandrian exegesis and specifically to Philo. This particularly applies to the allegorical themes of 'earth-body' and of the creation of man 'in the image of God' (Gen. 1:26) after all other beings. But these parallels, though remarkable, are not enough to prove a direct relation between Barnabas and Philo and to establish the *Letter of Barnabas* as an Alexandrian document. (RR)

8234. J. P. MARTÍN, 'Sobre la conceptión ontológica de physis-natura en Philón y en Spinoza', *Actas del Tercer Congreso Nacional de Filosofia, Buenos Aires, 13 al 18 de octubre de 1980*, Sesiones de Comisión y Homenajes (Buenos Aires 1982) 2.136-144.

If one takes Spinoza's philosophy to be a 'philosophical radicalization of biblical monotheism' (136), then Philo is no doubt one of the most ancient antecedents of this view. The closest connections between the two thinkers concern the theme of nature. Characteristics to some degree shared are: (a) the idea that the first principle is Being itself; (b) the conception of the first cause as efficient cause; (c) 'the comprehensive concept of *physis* as the universal creative force identified with the infinite God' (138). (RR)

8235. A. MENDELSON, *Secular education in Philo of Alexandria*, Monographs of the Hebrew Union College 7 (Cincinnati 1982).

The author returns to the subject of his dissertation (see above **7115**), having further developed his views and now presenting them with greater clarity and succinctness. The study consists of four chapters. In the first the diverse disciplines of the ἐγκύκλιος παιδεία are briefly outlined, with most attention being paid to the science of astronomy. Philo did not contribute in an original way to these himself; his task is to give them a place in a wider religious and philosophical framework. In the second chapter Mendelson places his subject in both a social (i.e. Alexandrian) and philosophical context. A positive appreciation of the encyclical sciences entails a positive attitude to the world, even if there is always the danger of excessive involvement. The place of these sciences becomes clearer in the third chapter, in which the author presents Philo's 'typology of mankind', basically a tripartite scheme consisting of a hierarchy of men of earth (Nimrod), men of heaven (Abraham, Bezalel), men of God (Isaac, Moses). Through the study of Scripture it is possible to move up in the hierarchy, if God's grace and man's talents and efforts allow. In the final chapter the place of the sciences is made clear. The man of progress Abraham dwells but briefly at the stage of the encyclical studies and then moves upwards. It is the 'class of ordinary men' (77) such as Bezalel who remain at the level of ἐγκύκλιος παιδεία and draw benefit from it. Philo thus accords a positive value to the encyclical studies in their own right, and herein lies his contribution to their history. Philo thus departs from the elitism of Plato and shows concern for the religious progress of ordinary men. The *encyclia* are offered as common ground between the Greek and Jewish worlds. The study ends with some comments on the social and intellectual dangers of total assimilation for the Jews in the context of Alexandrian life. REVIEWS: J. L. Houlden, *ET* 94 (1982-83) 248; L. H. Feldman, *SR* 12 (1983) 229f.; W. Adler, *JAAR* 52 (1984) 172f.; D. Bourget, *ETR* 59 (1984) 103f.; J. Morris, *JJS* 35 (1984) 87ff.; D. T. Runia *Mnem* 39 (1986) 493ff.; S. Schreiner, *Jud* 40 (1984) 195f.; J. G. Kahn, *Tarbiz* 54 (1985) 306ff. (cf. **8526**); F. Siegert *JThS* 37 (1986) 208f. (DTR)

8236. V. NIKIPROWETZKY, 'Quelques observations sur la répudiation de l'esclavage par les Thérapeutes et les Esséniens d'après les notices de Philon et de Flavius Josèphe', in *Mélanges à la mémoire de Marcel-Henri Prévost* (Paris 1982) 229-271.

The author takes his starting-point in the views of the Russian scholar M. Elizarova. Apart from certain valid intuitions and analytical principles, these views are all but demolished by Nikiprowetzky's penetrating criticisms. He reaches the following conclusions (270): 'Certainly, participation in the suffering of the poor and awareness of the injustice of the rich were very much alive, but what was being awaited [i.e. by the Essenes] was not the advent of a socialist revolution, but the inauguration of God's kingdom, of which the freedom of Israel, happiness, and social justice were to be the main characteristics.' The religious nature and theological foundation of their rejection of slavery marks off the views of the Essenes from similar attitudes in classical antiquity. (RR)

8237. E. E. PASETTI, 'I temi di Abramo "peregrinus" e "advena"

(Gen. XII. 1-3; 9-10): alla ricerca di una tradizione esegetica antica', *Studi e ricerche sull'oriente cristiano* 5 (1982) 13-46, 103-124, 141-155, esp. 13-46.

Abraham's migration is a 'classic *topos* of monastic hagiography' (13). Searching for its sources involves therefore specifying the nature of a tradition which unites Philo, Origen, and Ambrose; but it also means showing the variations in meaning which the theme gradually underwent. In particular the author points out the following. (a) Philo's Abraham is not 'a model of ascetic choice' (17) but the expression of an anthropological typology. (b) Therefore his migration should be understood as 'a paradigm of the journey which every man must pursue ... in order to reach God' (37). (c) This interpretation is based 'on an undoubtedly favourable view of man's cognitive capacity' (33), a view which is lost in the Christian tradition. (d) Abraham's migration in Philo furthermore involves epistemological considerations and is the result of an allegorical technique (etymology) which by Origen's time has fallen into disfavour. In his analysis Pasetti emphasizes Philo's attitude towards Chaldean astrology, which he accepts, though with due reservations, whereas Origen and Ambrose reject it decisively. (= R1095/d)

8238. P. PERKINS, '"An ailment of childhood": spiritual pediatrics for adults', in F. A. EIGO (ed.), *Dimensions of contemporary spirituality* (Villanova Pa. 1982) 79-115, esp. 99-108.

The whole of I Corinthians attacks a Hellenistic Jewish version of the spiritual tendency to identify wholly with the heavenly and divine to the neglect of a participation in this world. Various passages from Philo are adduced to illustrate such a spirituality. Paul insists that the spiritual condition so prized by the Corinthians comes only in the future through assimilation to the risen Christ. Thus the alliance between the spiritual and conditions in this world as symbolized in the death of Christ is preserved. (DTR)

8239. D. PESCE, *La Tavola di Cebete: testo, traduzione, introduzione e commento*, Antichità classica e cristiana 21 (Brescia 1982), esp. 33-37.

A three-way comparison between Seneca, Philo (*Congr.*), and the author of the *Tabula Cebetis* illustrates the views of these three thinkers on the *encyclia*: favourable, in the sense of an introduction to wisdom, in Philo; favourable, but secondary to ethics, in Seneca (36); unfavourable and subject to an outright rejection in the anonymous author, since wisdom, for him, is devoid of content that is properly theoretical (cf. 37). (= R1095/e)

8240. M. PHILONENKO, 'Essénisme et misogynie', *Academie des Inscriptions & Belles Lettres* (1982) 339-353, esp. 339 ff.

'The misogyny of the Essenes presented to us by Philo (cf. *Hypoth.* 11.14-17), Josephus, and Pliny presupposes a fundamental doctrinal reflection on men's place in society. This reflection has a double concern: to exculpate man from sin and put the blame on womankind' (341). (RR)

8241. E. DES PLACES, *Eusèbe de Césarée commentateur: Platonisme et Écriture sainte*, ThH 63 (Paris 1982), esp. 73-75.

A list, virtually without commentary, of passages taken from Philo in the *Praeparatio*

Evangelica of Eusebius. Of particular importance are the texts relating to the Logos. (DTR)

8242. D. ROKEAH, *Jews, Pagans and Christians in conflict*, SPB 33 (Jerusalem-Leiden 1982), esp. 95-97, 173-176.

Discusses Philo's apologetic works in the wider context of the interrelations between Judaism, Paganism and Christianity. Philo's contribution to Christian polemic against paganism was more positive, Josephus' more negative. (DTR)

8243. J. R. ROYSE, 'Two problems in Philo's *Quaestiones*', *REArm* 16 1982) 81-85.

Two short but obscure passages in the Armenian translation of *QG* 1.41 and 4.35 are illuminated through comparison with surviving Greek fragments. (DTR)

8244. G. RUIZ, 'Profetas y profecía en la obra de Filón Alejandrino', *MCom* 77 (1982) 113-146.

This extensive and well-documented article deals with the following points, which are held to constitute the theme of prophecy in Philo: (a) the nature of the prophet; (b) the nature of inspiration and the concept of ecstasy in relation to the theme of prophecy (122f.); (c) the function of prophecy, understood as the cognitive and hermeneutical function of the divine will. Ruiz concludes that Philo profoundly reinterpreted the prophetic world of the Old Testament by reducing the phenomenon of prophecy almost exclusively to the figure of Moses (117) and by stressing its cognitive nature, which reaches its culminating moment in the state of ecstasy. (RR)

8245. D. R. SCHWARTZ [שוורץ .ד], כרונולוגיה: פילאטוס פונטיוס השעיית ומקורות. ['Pontius Pilate's suspension from office: chronology and sources'], *Tarbiz* 51 (1982) 383-398.

An attempt to solve the problems arising from the assumption that Vitellius, the Roman govenor of Syria, visited Jerusalem *twice* in 36-37 CE (Josephus, *Antiquities* 18. 90-95, 122-126) by reviving a suggestion originally offered by W. OTTO (*RE* I 18 (1916) 2515), according to which Josephus used two accounts of the same visit. In addition to these two sources, Josephus also had access to a third, reflected in *Ant.* 15.403-409 and 20.6-14, stemming from a lost section of Philo's *Legatio* (where Vitellius' visit is mentioned, in the extant text, in § 231). (DRS)

8246. D. R. SCHWARTZ [שוורץ .ד], בתרגום מהאלהה ההימנעות לשאלת ויקרא לספר השבעים ['Avoidance of deification in the Septuagint version of Leviticus?'], *Shnaton* 5-6 (1982) 205-218, esp. 216.

It is suggested that the version of Leviticus in the Septuagint goes out of its way to avoid appearing to ascribe divinity to the priests, to Moses, and to the Temple. This reflects Hellenistic-Jewish debates on these issues, as is demonstrated by Philo's various and conflicting statements on the status of Moses. English summary. (DRS)

8247. D. R. SCHWARTZ [שוורץ .ד], על האלכסנדרוני ופילון מתתיהו בן יוסף
פילטוס פונטיוס ['Josephus and Philo on Pontius Pilate'], in U. RAPPAPORT
(ed.), יוסף בן מתתיהו – היסטוריון של ארץ-ישראל בתקופה ההלניסטית והרומית
[*Josephus Flavius: historian of Eretz-Israel in the Hellenistic-Roman period.*] (Jerusalem 1982) 217-236.

Subsequently published English; see **8366**.

8248. G. SELLIN, 'Das "Geheimnis" der Weisheit und das Rätsel der "Christuspartei" (zu 1 Kor 1-4)', *ZNW* 73 (1982) 69-96, esp. 90-92.

The adjectives σοφός, τέλειος and πνευματικός in 1 Cor. 2:6-3:4 clearly go back to Alexandrian and in particular to Philonic terminology. In Philo, however, one does not find the distinction between ψυχικός and πνευματικός; nevertheless a similar form of dualism – which is in fact alien to Greek thought – may be found expressed in the concepts of ψυχή and πνεῦμα. The latter term is especially important in Philo, both from an anthropological and a religious point of view, since πνεῦμα transforms man into 'man of God'. (RR)

8249. M. D. VAN VELDHUIZEN, *'Philanthropia' in Philo of Alexandria: a scriptural perspective* (diss. University of Notre Dame 1982).

The analysis of Philo's notion of φιλανθρωπία commences with an exploration of sources and parallels found in his milieu, thereby setting Philo's thought in the context of considerable intellectual diversity. Two chapters are then devoted to divine *philanthropia* in relation to Philo's anthropology and the theory of divine Powers. Not only is God *philanthropos* but his *philanthropia* is adjusted to the moral condition of the individual person. As in Stoicism, the sage becomes a representative of the divine *philanthropia*. Those who share the more common condition of man are trained in *philanthropia* and other virtues by the Law of Moses. The allegorical or moral interpretation confers on the detail of the legislation a deeper meaning which gives it relevance for the life of virtue. The analysis is also related to the views of modern ethicists and biblical scholars, with a focus on the way Scripture can be used in the development of ethics. (DTR; based on *DA* 43-3349A).

8250. J. R. WEGNER, 'The image of woman in Philo', *SBLSPS* 21 (1982) 551-563.

Philo's depiction of women is compared with some Greek sources that were certainly available to him and also to some Jewish talmudic and midrashic texts. Four main topics are touched upon: (1) gender attributes in allegory; (2) gratuitous depreciation of women; (3) the anomaly of the virtuous woman; (4) the social status of women under law. Of Philo's sources some are Greek (and especially Platonic), some Jewish (maybe via oral traditions native to Alexandria), while others were common to the entire Near East of his day. (DTR)

8251. D. WINSTON, 'Was Philo a mystic?', in J. DAN and F. TALMAGE (edd.), *Studies in Jewish mysticism: Proceedings of regional conferences held in 1978* (Cambridge Mass. 1982) 15-41.

Cf. above **7852**.

8252. W. WUELLNER, 'Tradition and interpretaton of the "wise-powerful-noble" triad in I Cor. 1, 26', in *Studia Evangelica VII* (cf. **8231**) 567-572.

Philonic evidence drawn exclusively from *Opif.* is invoked in order to show that the Pauline triad 'wise-powerful-noble descent' is based on established tradition. (DTR)

1983

8301. Y. AMIR, *Die hellenistische Gestalt des Judentums bei Philon von Alexandrien*, Forschungen zum jüdisch-christlichen Dialog 5 (Neukirchen 1983).

Over the years the author (whose dissertation is listed above at **3713** under his former name H. NEUMARK) published various articles on Philo, mainly in the Hebrew language. These have been translated into German and collected together in this volume. Three of the articles have not been published elsewhere. There are some unifying themes joining up the various contributions, but on account of their diverse origin we will present them as separate items. REVIEWS: M. Mach, *FreibRund* 35 (1983) 139f.; H. W. Attridge *RelStR* 10 (1984) 405; R. Trevijano *Salm* 31 (1984) 361ff.; A. Paul, *RecSR* 74 (1986) 156. (DTR)

8302. Y. AMIR, 'Philon und die jüdische Wirklichkeit seiner Zeit', in *Die hellenistische Gestalt...* (cf. **8301**) 3-51.

The author takes his starting-point in the observation that Philo's influence within the Jewish tradition was weak, not to say inexistent (3). The following problem therefore poses itself: how is it possible that the same writings 'which carried no weight in the Jewish literary tradition and also failed to arouse any interest in the Hellenistic and Roman world, did assume a role of prime importance in Christian literature', to the point of being translated both into Latin and Armenian (5)? Amir answers this question in an overall presentation of Philo (5-10), his work (10-17), and his thought (17-21). The final section of the article deals with the relations between Philo and the Jewish world (21-37) and between Philo and the Mosaic Law (37-51). Concurrently published in Hebrew; cf. **8310**. (RR)

8303. Y. AMIR, 'Die Wallfahrt nach Jerusalem in Philons Sicht', in *Die hellenistische Gestalt...* (cf. **8301**) 52-64.

The pilgrimage to Jerusalem is obviously a religious theme (63). But in order to understand its exact meaning, this theme must also be considered from a historical-political point of view, since that is the context from which its terminology is derived (e.g. μητρόπολις, ἱερόπολις). Amir notes that this terminology is mostly based on Greek history, and in particular on its period of colonization, rather than on the period of Roman imperialism, although the latter was more topical in Philo's time (53). Earlier version published in Hebrew; cf. **8001**. (RR)

8304. Y. AMIR, 'Mose als Verfasser der Tora bei Philon', in *Die hellenistische Gestalt...* (cf. **8301**) 77-105.

This extensive and penetrating article sets out to examine certain views held by Wolfson on the subject expressed in the title. The author deals with the following points. (1) The problem of the author of the Torah: according to a view also shared by the Rabbis, Philo saw the Torah as both the work of Moses and as the work of God (81f.). (2) The nature of the Torah: in this connection Amir observes that Philo refers to the Torah by the Greek term νόμος, which means 'book' as well as 'collection of laws' or 'legal codex' (86f.). (3) The status of Moses as compiler of the Torah: here Amir notes that just as there is no legislation without a fundamental divine dimension, so there is no legislation without a human dimension, and this also applies to Mosaic Law (93f.). Finally (4) the role of Moses in drawing up the Law and in general the problem of prophecy in Philo (101ff.): Moses, in Philo's view, is not merely an unconscious and impersonal instrument in the hands of God, but a man loved by God who himself contributes to the drawing up of the Law (cf. 106, 87). Earlier version published in Hebrew; cf. **8002**. (RR)

8305. Y. AMIR, 'Rabbinischer Midrasch und philonische Allegorie', in *Die hellenistische Gestalt...* (cf. **8301**) 107-118.

For the Rabbis the Torah is divine because the divine word is spoken in it. For Philo, in contrast, the Torah is the human word of the perfect man inspired by God (111). Furthermore, Midrash and allegory have a different relation to the biblical text. The former tends to make the text topical 'by transferring it to a different time', whereas allegory goes beyond the temporal dimension and formalizes the contents of Scripture in an abstract and philosophical sense. Hence the different functions of exegesis, which in Philo is addressed to an intellectual elite, while in the case of the Rabbis the audience envisaged is the believers in the synagogue (118). Subsequently published in Hebrew; cf. **8605**. (RR)

8306. Y. AMIR, 'Die Übertragung griechischer Allegorien auf biblische Motive bei Philon', in *Die hellenistische Gestalt...* (cf. **8301**) 119-128; English translation also published as 'The transference of Greek allegories to Biblical motifs in Philo' in F. E. GREENSPAHN *et al.* (edd.), *Nourished with peace: studies in Hellenistic Judaism in memory of Samuel Sandmel* (Chico California 1984) 15-25.

According to the author, the relation between Greek and Philonic allegorical interpretation should be one of the foremost subjects of Philonic research. Amir demonstrates Philo's tendency to superimpose elements from Greek mythology on scriptural themes. The following instances are noted: (a) Penelope in relation to the episode of Hagar and Sarah; (b) the Graces in relation to the Patriarchs (c) the Dioscuri (hemispheres) in relation to the Cherubim; (d) the hydra in relation to the serpent. Subsequently published in Hebrew; cf. **8604**. (RR)

8307. Y. AMIR, 'Die Zehn Gebote bei Philon von Alexandrien', in *Die hellenistische Gestalt...* (cf. **8301**) 131-163.

Amir repeatedly stresses the essential role of the ten commandments in Philo's work. This role basically depends on the fact that Philo puts the Decalogue at the head of the

Mosaic legislation, since it is a direct revelation from God (163). In fact, the very structure of the Law seems to have a preordained unity, so that the commandments merge 'into a single commandment, that is to say, into a single Law' (137). All this also finds expression in Philo's approach to Greek philosophy, where he reduces multiple norms to a single matrix, that of the Logos. In analyzing this subject, the author emphasizes that the special position accorded to the Decalogue does not disqualify the rest of the Law, which retains its sacral character and authority (cf. 163). For the subsequent Hebrew translation, cf. **8604**. (RR)

8308. Y. AMIR, 'Philons Erörterung über Gottesfurcht und Gottesliebe in ihrem Verhältnis zum palästinischen Midrasch', in *Die hellenistische Gestalt...* (cf. **8301**) 164-185.

The relation between fear and love of God, which is an important theme in Philo's thought, has significant antecedents in the Greek world, especially in Seneca and Posidonius (165). Philo adopts various important characteristics from the Greek context (166) and transfers them to a conception based on the following elements. (1) Love is superior to fear. (2) Both depend on man's conception of God. (3) In particular, fear results from a wrong opinion about God and (4) is overcome when replaced by an authentic religious knowledge. (5) Fear of God only has a pragmatic value in that it helps to uphold the Law. The final part of the article deals with the relations between Philo's thought on this subject and the Palestinian Midrash, which Amir considers important and influential (185). Earlier version published in Hebrew; cf. **6503**. (RR)

8309. Y. AMIR, 'Irrationales Denken in rationalem Gewande bei Philon von Alexandrien', in *Die hellenistische Gestalt...* (cf. **8301**) 189-199.

The dialectical relationship between rational and irrational in Philo is examined by the author on various levels: (1) in Philo's theology, which continually oscillates between divine transcendence and immanence (192f.); (2) in his ethics (195-198); (3) in his allegorical method. In all these contexts a substantial Stoic influence is present, but also a tendency on Philo's part to go beyond the limits of pure rationality and ascend to the level of a 'supra-rationality', i.e. to pour 'new wine in the old wineskins of classical rationalism' (199). Earlier version published in Hebrew; cf. **7602**. (RR)

8310. Y. AMIR, 'Die religiöse Umdeutung eines philosophischen Begriffs bei Philon', in *Die hellenistische Gestalt...* (cf. **8301**) 200-206; English translation also published as 'Philo's religious interpretaton of a philosophical concept', *Immanuel* 17 (1983-84) 22-29.

Philo's thought must also be considered in the context of the reaction to Greek culture shown by oriental religious thought, i.e. in the specific historical phase which led to the end of classical antiquity and to the birth of the Middle Ages. Amir substantiates this view by examining the Philonic concept of εὐστάθεια, which takes on a typically religious meaning with respect to its Greek antecedents (in particular Democritus and the Stoa, cf. 201f.). At the same time this is not merely an isolated example, but forms part of Philo's general tendency to reduce each virtue (in particular faith and joy) to a form of divine grace (206). Earlier version published in Hebrew; cf. **7001**. (RR)

8311. Y. AMIR, 'Die Umformung des εὐδαίμων in den θεοφιλής bei

Philon', in *Die hellenistische Gestalt...* (cf. **8301**) 207-219.

Classical Greek literature regarded εὐδαίμων (blessed) as a synonym of θεοφιλής (God-beloved), and one tends to find the same situation in philosophy, especially in the Stoa and in Plato. Philo, however, in virtue of his special conception of the relationship between God and man (210), goes beyond the Stoa, and also beyond Plato. For the latter man can be considered θεοφιλής in so far as he is εὐδαίμων; for Philo man is εὐδαίμων in only so far as he is θεοφιλής (212), and this is justified only by Philo's characteristic view of grace. (RR)

8312. Y. AMIR [עמיר .י], פילון מאלכסנדריה] ['Philo of Alexandria'], in M. STERN (ed.), הפזורה היהודית בעולם ההלניסטי-רומי [*The Diaspora in the Hellenistic-Roman World*], World History of the Jewish People 10 (Jerusalem 1983) 238-264.

Concurrently published in German; see above **8302**.

8313. D. AUNE, *Prophecy in early Christianity and the ancient Mediterranean world* (Grand Rapids 1983), esp. 147-153.

As part of a comprehensive survey of prophecy in the Greco-Roman, biblical and early Christian world the author reaches the following conclusion on Philo (153): 'Philo was a prophet only in the sense that he consciously regarded the prophetic revelatory experience as the highest source of knowledge, and he himself had experienced the heightened vision into supranormal reality. Because of Philo's close association of vision with prophetic inspiration, he appears to have transformed some of the speeches of Moses into visionary announcements of salvation or judgment.' (DTR)

8314. B. BELLETTI, 'La concezione dell'estasi in Filone di Alessandria', *Aev* 57 (1983) 72-89.

After a careful and exhaustive examination of all the passages in which Philo alludes to or elaborates the doctrine of ecstasy and a full comparison of the technical Platonic and Philonic terms, the author attempts to determine the scriptural and Platonic elements in Philo's discourse. The conclusion is that there are indubitably points of contact, mostly lexical, between the themes of ecstasy and enthusiasm and the Platonic θεῖα μανία, but that these themes are also perfectly consistent with the Bible, in particular with Philo's interpretation of the Old Testament theophanies. (RR)

8315. P. BORGEN, 'The Early church and the Hellenistic synagogue', *StTh* 37 (1983) 55-78; reprinted in *Paul preaches circumcision and pleases men and other essays on Christian origins* (Trondheim 1983) 75-97.

Evidence from Philo on the themes of conversion, prosyletism and circumcision of the heart is invoked as support for the thesis that the Early church emerged within the context of Hellenistic synagogal communities. Traditions and practices of Jewish prosyletism were Christianized and so the Early church gradually grew into a new form of community comprising both Jews and Gentiles. (DTR)

8316. P. BORGEN, 'Philo, Luke and geography' in *'Paul preaches*

circumcision and pleases men' and other essays on Christian origins
(Trondheim 1983) 59-71.

A survey of Philo's geographical outlook on the inhabited world. The world centres for Philo are religiously and culturally Jerusalem and Athens, politically Rome. At the centre of Philo's own world is Alexandria, the significance of which for Jewry is made manifest above all in the Septuagint translation of the Hebrew Bible. For Luke the same world three centres hold, but the geographical perspective is based on Ephesus at the centre rather than Alexandria. (DTR)

8317. R. E. BRACEWELL, *Shepherd imagery in the synoptic gospels* (diss. Southern Baptist Theological Seminary 1983).

As a preliminary to studying the use of shepherd imagery in the Synoptic gospels (and especially in relation to the figure of Christ), an examination is made of the shepherd imagery in ancient literature preceding the New Testament, including the writings of Philo. (DTR; based on *DA* 45-2489A)

8318. P. CARNY [פ. קרני], דמויים מרכזיים בתאוריה האלגוריסטית של פילון
['Rhetorical figures in Philo's allegory'], *Te'uda* 3 (Tel Aviv 1983) 251-259.

An attempt to define the specific character of Philo's biblical interpretation against its Greek background. Philo's allegories differ from the common Greek ones, since Philo never gives up the literal meaning of the text, but wishes to keep it alongside the allegorical one. Philo's interpretations of 'the body and the shadow' and 'the body and the soul' serve as examples. English summary. (MM)

8319. J. CAZEAUX, *Philon d'Alexandrie: de la grammaire à la mystique*, Supplément au Cahier Évangile 44 (Paris 1983); Spanish translation by A. ORTIZ GARCÍA (Estella 1984).

Though written in a popular manner, this work is worthy of notice, especially for those who wish to grasp Cazeaux's original (and extraordinarily difficult) hermeneutical scheme. The author presents Philo from a historical point of view (1-17), and goes on to offer an outline of his work, first in general terms (18-20), and then with specific reference to his characteristic method of allegorical exegesis. Here Cazeaux presents a number of *topoi* in a very effective way, using an accurate and felicitous choice of Philonic texts. The conclusion (77ff.) synthesizes the author's hermeneutical theories with particular clarity. REVIEWS (of the Spanish translation): V. Muñiz, *NatGrac* 31 (1984) 201; M. Sáenz Galache, *Biblia y Fe* 10 (1984) 335; R. de Sivatte *ActBibl* 21 (1984) 311. (RR)

8320. J. CAZEAUX, *La trame et la chaîne: structures littéraires et exégèse dans cinq traités de Philon d'Alexandrie*, ALGHJ 15 (Leiden 1983).

The aim of this massive study is indicated by its subtitle. It undertakes to examine the nature and methods of Philo's exegesis as revealed in the literary structure of his allegorical writings. In the first part of the study, amounting to three-quarters of its length, elaborate analyses are given of *Migr.*, *Her.*, *Congr.* 81-121, *Fug.*, *Mut.* 1-38. The second part adopts a 'manière synthétique' and presents a relatively concise summary of the procedures of Philonic exegesis which came to the fore in the earlier analyses. This study thus constitutes the most extensive presentation of the author's radical views on the nature of Philo's writings. Influenced by the structuralist views on 'discourse' developed by critics and philosophers such as R. Barthes and M. Foucault, Cazeaux attempts to discover whether such insights can be profitably applied to Philo's exegesis of Scripture. Careful analysis shows that Philo's treatises are not, as most scholars have thought, an accumulation of loosely associated ideas. Cazeaux unconditionally posits the total coherence of the literary composition and structure of Philo's treatises. In his exegesis Philo imitates the slowly unfolding unity and 'spatiality' of the biblical narrative. The resultant structure is best described as a tapestry (cf. *Sacr.* 83, from which the warp and the woof of the title are derived). Two main principles and a number of exegetical techniques allow this structure to be constructed. The first principle is that of substitution ('suppléance'), i.e. in order to explain one text another is substituted in an artfully devised chain. The second principle is that of redundance ('redondance'). Philo's exegesis is fundamentally teleological; the second text is partly redundant, repeating aspects of the first but also adding new elements. The various techniques that Cazeaux discovers are largely based on the notions of symmetry and movement. Philo organizes the texts and exegetical figures which he selects into tightly and usually symmetrically organized units, amounting to chapters, which the reader moves through as he reads. These basic structures, often in the form of 'cradles' or 'curves', occur time and time again during the analyses that Cazeaux gives of the five allegorical treatises. The book contains about 140 diagrams in which they are schematically made plain to the reader. Philo thus does not submit to the 'iron collar' of deductive logic or psychology (208) in the mode of Hellenic thought. His exegesis follows the logic of Scripture, exploring and articulating, but not filling in the spaces of the biblical narrative. Unlike the later Patristic exegetes Philo does not try to prove preconceived ideas. He presupposes only the unity and self-sufficiency of Scripture, allowing its contents gradually to unfold. REVIEWS: J. Pouilloux, *CRAI* (1983) 467f.; J. Lust, *EThL* 60 (1984) 396; M. J. Pierre, *RB* 91 (1984) 294f.; D. T. Runia, *VChr* 38 (1984) 211ff. (= **8447**); R. A. Bitter, *NTT* 39 (1985) 244ff.; E. des Places, *RPh* 59 (1985) 129f.; M. Petit, *REJ* 145 (1986) 141ff. (DTR)

8321. J. CAZEAUX, *L'épée du Logos et le soleil de midi*, Collection de la Maison de l'Orient Méditerranéen 13, Série Littéraire et Philosophique 2 (Lyon 1983).

The main part of this work is devoted to a structural analysis of the *De Cherubim* and the *De Abrahamo*, but the author's aim is much more ambitious: by means of the logical scheme implied in both writings, Cazeaux wishes to define the essence of Philo's allegorical method. The work's initial and final pages are essential in this regard, since they deal with the problem of allegorical interpretation from a general and formal viewpoint. Proceeding from the axiom that in Philo the whole prevails over the part (172ff.), Cazeaux points out four basic rules: (a) the pre-eminence of the biblical text; (b) 'the biblical text is endowed with a particular life: it partly repeats itself' (that is, every following lemma continues and clarifies the preceding lemma); (c) each specific allegorical development can be read psychologically and ethically; (d) these moral itineraries often take the form of a curved line, along which the arguments are symmetrically arranged (5 ff.). The entire analysis of the two treatises (11-171) aims to verify these assertions. REVIEWS: R. Joly, *AC* 53 (1984) 367f.; E. des Places, *RPh* 59 (1985) 130f.; M. J. Pierre, *RB* 93 (1986) 465ff. (RR)

8322. S. J. D. COHEN, 'From the Bible to the Talmud: the prohibition of intermarriage', *HebAR* 7 [= R. AHRONI (ed.), *Biblical and other studies* *in honor of Robert Gordis*] (1983) 23-39, esp. 26-27, 33.

The prohibition of intermarriage is not biblical, but emerges in the post-exilic period. Philo in an implicit reference to Deut. 7:3-4 at *Spec.* 3.29 is the first extant continuator of Ezra's exegesis of that text in terms of prohibition. His strict exegesis of Deut. 23:9 in terms of the discouragement of proselytism agrees with Rabbinic commentators, but not with the Jews of Qumran. (DTR)

8323. J. J. COLLINS, *Between Athens and Jerusalem: Jewish identity in the Hellenistic Diaspora* (New York 1983), esp. 111-117.

In spite of what the title suggests, this book deliberately excludes the Philonic contribution to Hellenistic Judaism, except a brief passage on Philo's politics, which the author needs in order to explain the political/ethnic understanding of Judaism in the Hellenistic Diaspora. The main question is how far Philo's sacramental and symbolic view of Judaism requires its exclusive exaltation and actual triumph over the gentiles. The eschatology of *Praem.* 79-172 is primarily spiritual, but its political dimension cannot be entirely dismissed. The chief difference with apocalyptic thought is the lack of urgency. Jerusalem and the homeland remain largely in the background of Philo's thought. (DTR)

8324. T. CONLEY, 'Philo's use of topoi', in D. WINSTON and J. DILLON (edd.), *Two treatises of Philo of Alexandria: a commentary on De gigantibus and Quod Deus sit immutabilis* (cf. also above **3101**), BJudSt 25 (Chico California 1983) 171-178.

In the texts of *Gig.* and *Deus* Conley traces three kinds of *topoi*, which he classifies as follows: 'commonplaces', 'philosophical *topoi*', and 'dialectical *topoi*'. These categories (especially the last one) can be divided further into subordinate genres, and of each of these the author finds various examples in the two treatises. (RR)

8325. J. DILLON, 'Philo's doctrine of angels', in *Two treatises...* (cf. **8324**) 197-205.

As stated by the author (197), this article addresses the following questions: (a) is the origin of Philo's angelology mainly Greek or Jewish? (b) what is the role of the stars in Philo's theological scheme? (c) what is the ethical nature of angels, or, do evil angels exist in Philo's view? In order to solve these problems, Dillon turns in particular to the evidence in *Gig.* 6ff. (RR)

8326. J. DILLON, 'The formal structure of Philo's allegorical exegesis', in *Two treatises...* (cf. **8324**) 77-87.

According to the author, 'the tradition of commentary with which Philo on the one hand, and the Neoplatonists [in particular Proclus, *in Tim.*] on the other, are working is essentially the same' (86). This similarity is ultimately a question of common origin, namely in the tradition of commentary developed by Stoic scholars of the last two centuries B.C., in particular Crates of Mallos, Herodicus of Babylon, and Heraclitus. (RR)

8327. J. DILLON, 'The nature of God in the *Quod Deus*', in *Two trea-*

tises... (cf. **8324**) 217-227.

The main subject of this article is the relation between the supposed unknowability of God and the large number of attributes and connotations which Philo assigns to him. As is well-known, the solution to this problem lies in the distinction which Philo draws between God's essence and his activity. Dillon makes some interesting observations on the attribution of εὐπάθειαι (in particular joy) to God (222ff.), an attribution which certainly goes beyond the horizon of Stoic thought. (RR)

8328. J. DILLON, 'Plotinus, Philo and Origen on the grades of virtue', in H.-D. BLUME and F. MANN (edd.), *Platonismus und Christentum: Festschrift für Heinrich Dörrie*, JbAC.E 10 (Münster 1983) 92-105, esp. 102f.

In order to offer a comparison with Plotinus' distinction between lower civic virtues and higher kathartic virtues, the author adduces some Philonic texts – notably *Leg.* 1.59-65, 3.125ff. – in which similar ideas on grades of virtue are implied, but not coherently worked out. (DTR)

8329. F. FABBRINI, *Storiografia della speranza: Filone ed Enos* (Lanciano 1983).

Despite repeated efforts we have been unable to obtain this study, reported in *APh* 54 (1984) 346 (no. 5534). (RR)

8330. R. FREUND, 'The ethics of abortion in Hellenistic Judaism', *Helios* 10 (1983) 125-137, esp. 131-132.

Philo's position on abortion, namely that foeticide must be linked to homicide is discussed as part of a wider discussion, which stresses the importance of the LXX translation in Ex. 21:22-23. (DTR)

8331. J. GAGER, *The origins of anti-semitism: attitudes toward Judaism in Pagan and Christian antiquity* (New York-Oxford 1983), esp. 47-52.

Philo's evidence on the anti-Jewish violence in Alexandria in 38-41 A.D. is discussed in the larger context of anti-Semitism in the ancient world. (DTR)

8332. W. GODZICH, 'De l'œil à l'oreille: les voies de l'allégorie de Philon d'Alexandrie' in L. BRIND'AMOUR and E. VANCE (edd.), *Archéologie du Signe*, Recueils d'Études Médiévales 3 (Toronto 1983) 45-61.

Using the texts of *Conf.* and *Migr.*, the author interprets the allegorical procedure followed in these writings from a very general point of view, but also specifically to the extent that it can clarify certain aspects of the nature and function of language. His interpretation is based on an analysis of the relations between literal and allegorical sense and on a semiological exegesis of the symbolism contained in the two treatises. (RR)

8333. W. L. GOMBOCZ, 'Gott als hyperano theos bei Philo Judaeus', in I. SEYBOLD (ed.), *MEQOR HAJJIM: Festschrift für Georg Molin zu seinem*

75. Geburtstag (Graz 1983) 107-114.

Analyzes the basic elements of Philo's doctrine of divine transcendence, the epithets which define it, the concept of God the creator, negative theology, and the doctrine of the two Powers. With regard to the latter Gombocz observes that, no matter how one interprets the two Powers envisaged by Philo, 'these constitute a special Philonic contribution to theology: a theology which is rigorously aligned to the monism of the highest God, but which nonetheless leaves room for the dogma of the Trinity in the typically Christian transformation of the doctrine of God' (114). (RR)

8334. A. C. J. HABETS, *Geschiedenis van de indeling van de filosofie in de oudheid* (diss. Utrecht 1983), esp. 102-108.

Philo is dealt with as part of a methodical analysis of the diverse schemata of division of the subjects of philosophy devised in antiquity. He is seen to reflect a number of these. In his philosophical and theological thought he chiefly exploits the tripartition logic, physics, ethics for purposes of allegorical explanation, but does not adhere to it in a rigid and dogmatic way. Preferences are determined by factors of exegetical convenience. (RAB/DTR)

8335. M. E. HOPPER, *The Pauline concept of imitation (mimesis)* (diss. Southern Baptist Theological Seminary 1983), esp. chap. 4.

As background to a study of imitation in the Pauline tradition the concept of mimesis is analyzed in Greek and Jewish thought. Its use in Philo, the Apocrypha and Pseudepigrapha is similar to what is found in the Greek world, whereas Qumran, Tannaitic Judaism and the Old Testament reveal an entirely different understanding of imitation. (DTR; based on *DA* 45-206A)

8336. W. HORBURY, 'The Aaronic priesthood in the Epistle to the Hebrews', *JSNT* 19 [= *Essays in honour of Ernst Bammel*] (1983) 43-71.

The views of the author of the Epistle to the Hebrews on the subject of the priesthood (esp. with respect to Levi and tithing) are closer to Josephus than Philo, which might constitute a marginal consideration in favour of Palestinian rather than Alexandrian authorship. (DTR)

8337. P. W. VAN DER HORST, 'Moses' throne vision in Ezechiel the dramatist', *JJS* 34 (1983) 21-29.

Adduces Philonic evidence in support of the thesis that the dream vision ascribed to Moses in Ezechiel's play implies a deification of the Jewish lawgiver. (DTR)

8338. H. J. DE JONGE, 'Traditie en exegese: de hogepriester-christologie en Melchizedek in Hebreeën', *NTT* 37 (1983) 1-19, esp. 4-7.

Argues that it is not possible to explain the high-priestly christology in Hebrews by means of the decisive intervention of a speculative Logos-doctrine such as that of Philo, even if the letter does bear some traces of a similar Judaeo-Hellenistic tradition. The motif developed through the reciprocal influence of tradition and exegesis in the early church. (DTR)

8339. J. G. KAHN [ישר-כהן .י], עמדתו – ביהדות הכללית ההשכלה מעמד פילון של ['Philo's view of the status of general knowledge in Judaism'], *Proceedings of the Eighth World Congress of Jewish Studies* (Jerusalem 1983) Division C, 69-72; reprinted in M. STERN (ed.), *Nation and history* (Jerusalem 1983) 51-54.

A compressed version of an article originally published in French; cf. **7321**.

8340. J.-G. KAHN [ישר-כהן .י], פילון של כוונתו סוד – "עצמך את הכר" האלכסנדרוני ['"Know thyself" – the secret of Philo's meaning'], in A. A. GREENBAUM and A. L. IVRY (edd.), ראבידוביץ לש. זכרון ספר .ומעשה הגות [*Thought and action: essays in memory of S. Ravidowicz*] (Tel Aviv 1983) 17-21.

A compressed version of an article originally published in French; cf. **7321**.

8341. R. KIRSCHNER, 'The Rabbinic and Philonic exegesis of the Nadab and Abihu incident (Lev. 10:1-6)', *JQR* 73 (1983) 375-393.

The author undertakes to compare the exegesis of the incident in which Nadab and Abihu are consumed by divine fire given by Philo and the Rabbinic Midrash (primarily Sifra, Pesikhta de-Rab Kahana, Leviticus Rabbah) in order to elucidate similarities and differences between them. Both take the canonical text as starting-point. Philo offers a wholly positive interpretation, which is consistent with his philosophical views on the relation between soul and body and the nature of priestly sacrifice. There are two strands of Rabbinic interpretation: the majority view tries to determine what improper conduct or cultic transgression on the part of the priests brought about the punishment; a minority view attempts to exonerate them, but this view is less closely tied to the text. The analysis corroborates E. Stein's observation that 'Philonic exegesis is more systematic while Palestinian exegesis is more concerned with confirming judgments already rendered in the text of Scripture' (391). (DTR)

8342. C. LANDMAN, 'The etymological and allegorical functioning of Cain, Abel and Seth in the exegetical methods of Philo and Augustine', *Ekklesiastikos Pharos* (Alexandria) 65 (1983) 17-26.

Comparison is made between certain passages in *Post.* and Augustine's *De civitate Dei.* (DTR; based on *APh* 54 (1983) no. 3723)

8343. J. LEOPOLD, 'Philo's knowledge of rhetorical theory', in *Two treatises...* (cf. **8324**) 129-136.

Philo's acquaintance with rhetorical theory can be inferred from his use of technical terminology in *Gig.* and *Deus.* This terminology is briefly analyzed on 133-135. (RR)

8344. J. LEOPOLD, 'Philo's vocabulary and word choice', in *Two treatises...* (cf. **8324**) 137-140.

A brief analysis of Philo's vocabulary in *Deus* and *Gig.* leads to the following conclusion: 'Philo seems to preserve for us something of the quality of educated and literary prose before the strong influence of the Atticist movement of the first century B.C.' (139). (RR)

8345. J. LEOPOLD, 'Characteristics of Philo's style in the *De Gigantibus* and *Quod Deus*', in *Two treatises...* (cf. **8324**) 141-154.

The variety of subjects with which he deals suggests to Philo a variety of styles, presumably based on different models (Plato, the late Academy, the Stoic-Cynic diatribe). But Philo also manages to infuse a poetic vein into his style, especially in his use of metaphors. (RR)

8346. J. LEOPOLD, 'Rhetoric and allegory', in *Two treatises...* (cf. **8324**) 155-170.

Discusses the allegorical tradition running parallel with Philo, and in particular the methods of exegesis found in Plutarch. Philo differs from Plutarch in that he regards the Bible not as a myth that must be rationalized, but as a truth which must be made manifest. In the appendix at 163-170 Leopold provides a full list of allegorical terms in the Greek tradition and Philo. (RR)

8347. H. LEWI, 'Actualité de Philon d'Alexandrie', *NouvC* 18 (1983) 47-48.

Addresses the problem of Philo's cultural and religious identity. Following Nikiprowetzky, Lewi holds that Philo, though not knowing Hebrew and profoundly Hellenized, never ceased to be an orthodox Jew. (RR)

8348. F. LUCIANI, 'Le vicende di Enoc nell'interpretazione di Filone Alessandrino', *RivBib* 31 (1983) 43-68.

In Hebrew literature there are two traditions about Enoch: an Enochian (i.e. one presenting Enoch in positive terms) and an anti-Enochian. Philo was certainly acquainted with the first (cf. *Mut.* 34ff.), but also, it seems, with the second (cf. *Abr.* 17 ff., *QG* 1.82-86, where Enoch is seen as the symbol of repentance). According to Luciani, this second interpretation originated with Philo, and was subsequently adopted and developed by the exegetical tradition. Underlying it is the theme of 'the individual's progress from sin to sanctity through repentance and conversion' (67 f.). This theme is to be regarded as a specific contribution by Philo, anticipating the morality propagated in the Gospels. (RR)

8349. F. MANNS, *Le symbole eau-Esprit dans le judaisme ancien*, SBFA 19 (Jerusalem 1983), esp. 152-168.

A straightforward discussion, based on direct analysis of texts, of Philo's use of the symbolism of water: the spring points to the Logos, Sophia, creator and prophecy; the well to knowledge; rivers to the virtues; rain, dew, and washing to the purification and mystical journey of the soul. Because Philo does not comment on prophetic texts, the symbolism of water representing the Spirit is limited in his writings, surfacing only briefly in the exegesis of Gen. 1:2. More often water points in the direction of the Logos and Sophia, a conception more congenial to philosophers and Alexandrian Jews. (DTR)

8350. J. MANSFELD, 'Two Heraclitea in Philo Judaeus', in L. ROSSETTI (ed.), *Atti del Symposium Heracliteum 1981* (Rome 1983) 1.63-64.

Two passages in Philo are reminiscent of preserved fragments of Heraclitus: *Conf.* 80 of fr. 63 Diels, *Somn.* 2.253 of fr. 67 Diels. (DTR)

8351. T. MARIANI, 'Sangue e antropologia biblica in Filone di Alessandria', in F. VATTIONI (ed.), *Atti della Settimana Sangue e Antropologia nella Letteratura Cristiana (Roma, 29 novembre – 4 dicembre 1982)*, Centro Studi Sanguis Christi 3.1 (Rome 1983) 545-563.

After some statistics on Philo's use of the term αἷμα (blood), the author carries out a semantic analysis of the term, the meaning of which appears to have at least four areas of application: social, medical-biological, liturgical, and philosophical. On the basis of this analysis Mariani concludes (563) that Philo was no doubt highly educated, but incapable of philosophical synthesis. (RR)

8352. J. P. MARTÍN, 'La primera exégesis ontológica de "Yo soy el que es" (Exodo 3,14 – LXX)', *Stromata* (Argentina) 39 (1983) 93-115.

After systematically analyzing Philo's exegesis of Ex. 3:14, which he holds to be the first ontological exegesis of this text (102ff.), Martín provides an outline of Philo's philosophical thought in relation to his Greek antecedents. Philo, it is stated at 111f., has affinities with Parmenides (the conception of being), Plato (ontological dualism), Aristotle (the concept of *nous*), the Stoa (the theory of two principles), and the Neoplatonists (the concept of hypostasis). Yet his thought can be identified with none of these philosophies, because it contains elements which distinguish it from each. For this reason it is necessary to reconsider carefully Philo's position in the history of metaphysics. (RR)

8353. S. MAVROFIDIS, 'Gal 2,6b: l'imperfetto e le sue conseguenze storiche', *Bib* 64 (1983) 118-121.

A passage in *Legat.* 245 serves to explain Gal. 2:6b with reference to the use of the continuous imperfect in New Testament texts. (RR)

8354. P. MIRRI, 'La vita di Mosè di Filone Alessandrino e di Gregorio Nisseno: note sull'uso dell'allegoria', *AFLPer* 20 (1982-1983) 31-53.

Analyzes and compares the various allegorical themes in Philo's *De vita Moysis* and the work of the same name by Gregory of Nyssa. After conceding that *Mos.* 'constitutes a real exception in the general panorama of Philo's other works' (32), since it contains little in the way of allegory, Mirri highlights some fundamental differences between the two works. Above all there is a difference in thematic focus, in that Gregory discusses the perfect virtue of which Moses is a symbol, whereas Philo's subject is the person of Moses as legislator, king, prophet, and priest. In the second place the two treatises are aimed at different groups of readers: Gregory addresses his work to his religious brothers, Philo to the non-Jews. Finally, according to the author, 'Philo's interpretative method in the *Life of Moses* differs from the genuine allegory employed by Gregory in his homonymous work' (53). The latter is in fact much more similar to the treatises of the Allegorical Commentary. (RR)

8355. J. L. MORENO MARTINEZ, 'El atardecer y el amanecer de Gen. 1,5, según Filón de Alejandría', *Salm* 30 (1983) 231-239.

The theme of 'evening and morning' (*Opif.* 33-35) can be related to the parallel theme of the separation of good from evil. This relation is justified by the principle of the analogy between microcosmos and macrocosmos, and God's function as separator of day and night, good and evil, sin and holiness. (RR)

8356. J. L. MORENO MARTINEZ, 'El logos y la creación: la referencia al Logos en el "principio" de Gen. 1, 1 según Filón de Alejandría', *ScrTh* 15 (1983) 381-419.

If reference is made to the texts of *Opif.* and *Leg.*, the phrase 'in the beginning' of Gen. 1:1 can be related, from a philosophical point of view, to the Logos. Moreno gives three reasons for this interpretation. (1) The instrumental function of the divine Logos in creation; this function reveals itself above all in the fact that the Logos is 'the place of the ideas', or the plan of the world. In this aspect one recognizes an implicit reference to Prov. 8:22. (2) The epithet ἀρχή given to the Logos in *Leg.* (3) The term ἀρχέτυπος, which is used more than once to define the Logos. In the latter case precedents are readily found in Judaism and especially in Sap. Sal. (RR)

8357. V. NIKIPROWETZKY, 'L'exégèse de Philon d'Alexandrie dans le *De Gigantibus* et le *Quod Deus sit Immutabilis*', in *Two treatises...* (cf. **8324**) 5-75.

Nikiprowetzky's well-known theory on the essence of Philonic thought – i.e. the priority of exegetical intention – is both applied and verified here, since on the one hand it provides the key for interpreting the relation between the two treatises, and on the other hand helps to explain their structure. As the author observes (8): 'In effect, the obscurity of the analysis and the atomization of the text are due to the fact that the guiding principle, the true woof, the essential form ... 'the mother cell' of Philo's exegetical developments has been forgotten; that is, the *quaestio* followed by the *solutio*...'. The two treatises are thus interpreted as a chain of *quaestiones* and *solutiones* (14 in all) which extends itself without interruption from *Gig.* to *Deus* as based on the text of Gen. 6:1-12. This is then proven by means of a section-by-section analysis of the thematic content of the single work. (RR)

8358. V. NIKIPROWETZKY and D. GOODING, 'Philo's Bible in the *De Gigantibus* and the *Quod Deus sit Immutabilis*', in *Two treatises...* (cf. **8324**) 89-125.

Nikiprowetzky deals with the explicit and implicit quotations from the Bible in *Gig.* and *Deus* (which are listed together with the Philonic text and also systematically annotated; cf. 98-118). Gooding discusses the problem of the relations between Philo and the original Hebrew of the biblical text (119-125). (RR)

8359. B. A. PEARSON, 'Philo, Gnosis and the New Testament', in A. H. B. LOGAN and A. J. M. WEDDERBURN (edd.), *The New Testament and Gnosis: essays in honour of Robert McL. Wilson* (Edinburgh, 1983) 73-89.

An important synthesizing article, in which the author attempts to find a connecting thread between the three areas in his title. The link between the Christianized Hellenistic Jewish wisdom found in the early Corinthian church may well be the teaching activity of Apollos, who comes from Alexandria. But to what extent can Philo be called a 'Gnostic'? Pearson gives a positive critique of Wilson's study (cf. **7242**), contrasting Philo's modified Platonism with the radical dualism of the Gnostics. This basic difference is further illustrated by two second century Alexandrian documents, the *Teachings of Silvanus* (in the Philonic tradition, though Christian) and the *Testimony of Truth* (Gnostic). (DTR)

8360. R. RADICE, 'Nota al *De posteritate Caini* 64-65 di Filone di Alessandria', *RFN* 75 (1983) 119-123.

The author, adducing a large number of parallel texts, puts forward an unusual interpretation of the passage in question (and of other passages which cite or comment on Gen. 2:4), viewing it in the broader perspective of the metaphysics of the Logos. (RR)

8361. *Reallexikon für Antike und Christentum*, edited by T. KLAUSER et al., vol. 12 (Stuttgart 1983).

Cf. above **5016**. Contains: C. COLPE, art. 'Gottessohn', 19-58, esp. 35-6 (sonship of God); P. COURCELLE, art. 'Grab der Seele', 455-467, esp. 456-8 (grave or tomb of the soul); P. KRAFFT, art. 'Gratus animus (Dankbarkeit)', 732-752, esp. 742-3 (thankfulness to God); W. SCHOTTROFF, art. 'Gottmensch I (Alter Orient und Judentum)', 155-234, esp. 229-231 (the divine man in the Near East and Judaism).

8362. D. ROKEAH, 'The temple scroll, Philo, Josephus, and the Talmud', *JThS* 34 (1983) 515-526

The author criticizes some of Y. Yadin's conclusions on the temple scroll found at Qumran which might appear to weaken the hypothesis of an identification of the Dead Sea sect with the Essenes described by Philo and Josephus. (DTR)

8363. D. T. RUNIA, *Philo of Alexandria and the* Timaeus *of Plato*, 2 vols., (diss. Free University Amsterdam 1983).

This study was first published in a provisional edition, and three years later in a slightly revised second edition. We summarize the latter below at **8656**. REVIEWS (of first edition): C. Lefèvre *MSR* 40 (1983) 207; J. den Boeft *PhilRef* 49 (1984) 92ff.; R. Radice *RFN* 76 (1984) 32ff. (cf. **8443**); P. van der Horst *NTT* 39 (1985) 247; A. Solignac *ArPh* 48 (1985) 475ff.; E. des Places *BAGB* 44 (1985) 408; A. Pattin, *TF* 48 (1986) 122.

8364. B. SCHALLER, 'Philon von Alexandreia und das "Heilige Land"', in G. STRECKER, *Das Land Israel in biblischer Zeit: Jerusalem-Symposium 1981 der Hebräischen Universität und der Georg-August Universität*, Göttinger Theologische Arbeiten 25 (Göttingen 1983) 172-187.

There can be no doubt that Philo tends to psychologize or at any rate to interpret in an individualistic sense the notion of the 'Holy Land'. But this tendency is not exclusive, since there are instances in which the ethical significance of the Holy Land is combined with an eschatological and universal meaning more consonant with the religious tradition and culture of the Jews. (RR)

8365. T. E. SCHMIDT, 'Hostility to wealth in Philo of Alexandria', *JSNT* 19 [= *Essays in honour of Ernst Bammel*] (1983) 89-97.

Argues against Mealand's assumption (cf. **7833**) that there is a causative relation between socio-economic circumstances and a critical evaluation of wealth. On the basis of a detailed analysis of Philonic passages dealing with wealth the following conclusions are reached. (1) Philo writes from an aristocratic point of view. (2) Philo consistently expresses hostility to wealth. (3) This hostility is not determined by sympathy for oppressed Jews. (4) Philo's affinities to Greek thought (esp. of the Cynics) are limited in scope to those that he perceives to be consistent with Jewish tradition. (DTR)

8366. D. R. SCHWARTZ, 'Josephus and Philo on Pontius Pilate', *The Jerusalem Cathedra* 3 (1983) 26-45.

A detailed comparison of the accounts in Philo (*Legat.* 299-305) and Josephus of Pilate's dispute with the Jews when he brought to Jerusalem symbolic items of a military and religious nature in honour of Tiberius Caesar, i.e. the so-called incident of the gilded shields. Schwarz argues that the discrepancies in the two accounts should not lead to the conclusion that there were two separate incidents. The basic accounts are very similar, and the discrepancies can be explained by Philo's apologetic bias which leads him to distort the story to such a degree that it would have been unintelligible, had we not had Josephus' simpler and more convincing version. Two appendices give an extensive bibliography, the first of modern interpretations arguing for two separate incidents, the second of interpretations published before 1802. Earlier version published in Hebrew; cf. **8247**. (DTR)

8367. P. SIGAL, 'Further reflections on the "begotten" Moses', *HebAR* 7 [cf. **8322**] (1983) 221-233, esp. 226f.

Are there Jewish antecedents for the notions of the pre-existence and the divine conception of the Messiah, as espoused by Christians in the case of Jesus? Sigal discusses the evidence of a theory of divine conception hinted at by Philo at *Cher.* 43-45, which he, contrary to P. Grelot and R. Brown, is inclined to regard as a serious precedent. (DTR)

8368. C. SIRAT, *La philosophie juive au Moyen Âge selon les textes manuscrits et imprimés*, Institut de Recherche et d'Histoire des Textes (Paris 1983), esp. 18-21.

Philo is briefly presented as the precursor of Jewish medieval philosophy, i.e. as the first to attempt a synthesis between Judaism and philosophy, especially in the context of theology. Nevertheless there seems to be no specific relation between Philo and non-Hellenistic Judaism, since the latter essentially ignored Philo's thought, regarding it as excessively Hellenized. Earlier version published in Hebrew; cf. **7544**. (RR)

8369. W. H. SMITH, *The function of 2 Corinthians 3:7-4:6 in its epistolary context* (diss. Southern Baptist Theological Seminary 1983).

There are clear parallels among 2 Corinthians 3:7-4:6, Philo, and the Palestinian

Midrashim in such details as exegetical method, patterns of contrast, and terminology. (DTR; based on *DA* 44-1481A)

8370. R. SORABJI, *Time, creation and the continuum: theories in antiquity and the early Middle Ages* (London 1983), esp. 203-209.

The author frequently cites passages in Philo's work which deal with the problem of time. At 203-209 he discusses in particular the creation of time, with specific reference to *Prov.* 1-2 and *Opif.* His conclusion is 'that Philo has not given careful thought to any idea of a duration before measured time. He presupposes sometimes its existence and sometimes its non-existence' (209). (RR)

8371. H. TARRANT, 'The date of Anon. *In Theaetetum*', *CQ* 33 (1983) 161-187, esp. 173-178.

Philo's thought and especially its sceptical element are examined and adduced in support of the thesis that the anonymous author of the *Commentary on the Theaetetus* is to be dated to the early 1st century A.D. and may even be earlier (perhaps Eudorus). The commentator's 'kind of Platonism is also Philo's kind of Platonism' (177). See further **8657**. (DTR)

8372. H. TARRANT, 'Middle Platonism and the *Seventh Epistle*', *Phronesis* 28 (1983) 75-103, esp. 77, 80.

Philo's evidence is used to support the thesis that the philosophical digression in Plato's *Seventh letter* is a later Middle Platonist or Neopythagorean addition, perhaps by Thrasyllus; see further **8657**. (DTR)

8373. T. H. TOBIN, *The creation of man: Philo and the history of interpretation*, CBQ.MS 14 (Washington 1983).

The aim of this important study 'is to understand Philo's interpretation of the story of the creation of man in Genesis 1-3 against the background of the exegetical traditions which were available to him' (viii). In Tobin's view the contradictions inherent in the Philonic *kosmopoiia* cannot be resolved in terms of philosophical interpretation, but owe their existence to the composite nature of Philo's work. Each element of each contradiction corresponds to a 'level' of interpretation, mostly pre-Philonic, which was incorporated without substantial changes into the nucleus of Philo's treatment. In particular two caesuras can be traced in Philo's cosmology: one between day 'one' and days two to six, and the other between days 'one' to six and the seventh day (124). This double caesura reflects two different levels of interpretation: the first goes back to an older, mainly cosmological tradition of exegesis, the second interprets the two biblical passages Gen. 1:27 and Gen. 2:7 as if they were two different acts of creation relating to 'heavenly man' and 'earthly man' respectively (108). In the transition from one model to the other (both pre-Philonic) the anthropological aspect comes to prevail over the cosmological aspect. Philo's own contribution is seen above all in the application of the allegory of the soul. The reason Philo feels constrained to preserve the various interpretations is the respect he feels for the traditions established by his exegetical predecessors. The study is also important on account of the correlations made between Philonic material and contemporary Greek philosophical developments (especially Middle Platonism). Cf. also **8443, 8651, 8656**. REVIEWS: G. Bissoli, *SBFLA* 33 (1983) 475f.; J. Lust, *EThL* 40 (1984) 395; M. Whittaker, *JThS* 35 (1984) 500f.; G. Delling,

ThLZ 110 (1985) 183ff.; D. Winston, *JBL* 104 (1985) 558ff. (RR)

8374. C. J. DE VOGEL, 'Der sog. Mittelplatonismus, überwiegend eine Philosophie der Diesseitigkeit?', in *Platonismus und Christentum* (cf. **8328**) 277-302, esp. 280-282.

The author briefly analyzes Philo's metaphysics in relation to the problems discussed in the *Timaeus*. She lists the differences and similarities in respect to Platonic thought, in particular emphasizing the transcendence of God in Philo, which she holds to be the dominant theme of his theology. (RR)

8375. R. T. WALLIS, 'The idea of conscience in Philo of Alexandria', in *Two treatises...* (cf. **8324**) 207-216.

A reprint, with some slight changes, of the article first published in 1975; cf. **7553**.

8376. J. C. M. VAN WINDEN, 'The world of ideas in Philo of Alexandria: an interpretation of De opificio mundi 24-25', *VChr* 37 (1983) 209-217.

A detailed analysis of *Opif.* 24-25, paying particular attention to the state of the Greek text and Philo's mode of argumentation. Van Winden rejects the alterations made to the text in C-W and follows the readings of Eusebius and the ms. V. He furthermore argues that Philo's argumentation, based on the double image relation between God, Logos and cosmos-man, is coherent, but that this is not immediately apparent because he jumps to his conclusion without formulating all the steps of his argument. (DTR)

8377. J. WHITTAKER, 'ΑΡΡΗΤΟΣ ΚΑΙ ΑΚΑΤΟΝΟΜΑΣΤΟΣ', in *Platonismus und Christentum* (cf. **8328**) 303-306.

The negative attributes used of God in *Somn.* 1.67 are important evidence for tracing the development of negative theology in Middle Platonism. (DTR)

8378. D. WINSTON, 'Philo's doctrine of free will', in *Two treatises...* (cf. **8324**) 181-195.

Cf. **7555** and **7647**.

8379. D. WINSTON [ד. וינסטון], החכם בתורתו של פילון ['The Philonic sage'], *Daat* 11 (1983) 9-18.

Philo's portrayal of the sage is in virtually every respect identical with that developed in Stoic philosophy: a citizen of the universe whose inner tranquility marks him as an embodiment of virtue. Of no little significance, therefore, is Philo's attempt at 'oneupmanship' (17), the claim that Moses, in his perfection, exceeded even the extreme ideal of the Stoic sage. English summary. (DS)

1984

8401. Y. AMIR, 'The transference of Greek allegories to biblical motifs in Philo', in *Nourished with peace* (cf. **8423**) 15-25.

Cf. above **8306**.

8402. Y. AMIR [עמיר .י], הפגישה בין אמונת היחוד הישראלית לבין המונותאיזם הפילוסופי כנושא־היסוד של היהדות ההלניסטית ['The monotheistic problem of Hellenistic Jewry'], *Daat* 13 (1984) 13-27.

Originally published in German; see above **7801**.

8403. R. ARNALDEZ, 'La Bible de Philon d'Alexandrie', in C. MON-DÉSERT (ed.), *Le monde grec et la Bible*, Bible de tous les temps (Paris 1984) 37-54.

In a rapid analysis of Philo's method of interpreting the Bible, Arnaldez is able to show why Philo was virtually ignored by Jewish culture, but very favourably received by the Christian Fathers. There are essentially three reasons for this: (a) the fact that Philo refers to the Greek version of the LXX; (b) Philo's markedly Hellenistic spirituality, essentially alien to Palestinian Judaism; (c) Philo's extensive use of allegorical exegesis, which distorts the historical sense of the Bible. (RR)

8404. R. ARNALDEZ, 'L'influence de la traduction des Septante sur le Commentaire de Philon', in R. KUNTZMANN and J. SCHLOSSER (edd.), *Études sur le Judaïsme hellénistique. Congrès de Strasbourg (1983)*, LeDiv 119 (Paris 1984) 251-266.

An analysis of the etymologies in *Leg.*, *Conf.*, *Sacr.*, *Her.*, *Congr.*, and *Fug.* shows how Philo often takes great liberties with the LXX text, to the point of suggesting that his thought does not derive from the exegesis of Scripture, but is imposed on it, even at the cost of violating the text (266). In Philo, in short, the *text* of the Bible is often a *pretext* for legitimizing his thought. (RR)

8405. R. BARRACLOUGH, 'Philo's politics: Roman rule and Hellenistic Judaism', in *ANRW* II 21.1 (cf. **8424**) 417-553.

Although Philo's political ideas do not amount to a genuine political theory, they are unified and supported by the pre-eminent position which Philo gives to the contemplative life. This ideal also accounts for Philo's attitude to the Roman empire and the authorities which embodied it: Augustus and Tiberius on the one hand, and Gaius, Flaccus, Pilate, and Sejanus on the other. The former he valued for their ability to maintain law and order, the latter he condemned for their lack of this ability. Philo's love of the law and his abhorrence of mob rule can be explained in the same way. All in all Philo's politics were essentially based on a static ideal and defence of the *status quo* which has little to do with the experiences of the major figures in Jewish history (in particular Moses and Joseph; cf. 487-506). In short, Barraclough concludes, 'his static view of history undergirds his static political ideals' (551). (RR)

8406. P. BENOIT, 'Le Prétoire de Pilate à l'époque byzantine', *RB* 91 (1984) 173-177.

Analyzes some passages in *Legat.* which help to locate the Praetorium where Jesus was judged by Pilate. (RR)

8407. R. M. BERCHMAN, *"The periarchon (De principiis)"*, *Origen of Alexandria's "Apodeixis euaggelike": a study in logical and rhetorical types of argument and the demonstration of a Christian ontology* (diss. Brown University 1984).

See the following entry.

8408. R. M. BERCHMAN, *From Philo to Origen: Middle Platonism in transition*, BJudSt 69 (Chico California1984) esp. 23-53.

In the early phase of Middle Platonism, according to the author, we must distinguish between two different trajectories, one represented by Antiochus of Ascalon, and the other, Pythagorean in character, represented by Eudorus of Alexandria (2). 'With Antiochus the Platonic distinction between Being and Becoming is reduced to the Stoic distinction between that which is active and that which is passive', so that with him 'there is no distinction between sensible and intelligible, corporeal and incorporeal' (27). Eudorus, on the other hand, 'adopts the Academic categories of Absolute and Relative'. Philo, according to Berchman, achieves a synthesis of the two trajectories and 'whereas the Pythagorean trajectory emerges in his theology, the Antiochean emerges in his physics' (27). REVIEWS: C. Kannengiesser, *RecSR* 74 (1986) 605ff.; A. Meredith, *JThS* 37 (1986) 557ff. (RR)

8409. U. BIANCHI, 'Dieu unique et création double: pour une phénomenologie du dualisme', in *Orientalia J. Duchesne-Guillemin emerito oblata*, Acta Iranica 23, 2nd series Hommages et opera minora 9 (Leiden 1984) 49-60, esp. 52-55.

'Dualism' is understood by the author in a fundamental ontological sense. A 'dualistic' doctrine (a) accepts a duality of principles on which (b) is founded the existence of that which is in the world, while (c) these principles may or not be coeternal. On this basis the duality of creators in Philo must be related to the analogous duality proposed by Plato in the *Timaeus* (demiurge and the 'young gods'), both themes of which in fact have an anthropological orientation. (RR)

8410. G. BOCCACCINI, 'Il concetto di memoria in Filone Alessandrino', *Annali dell'Istituto di Filosofia dell'Università di Firenze* 6 (1984) 1-19.

Philo's synthesis of Jewish faith and Greek philosophy recognizably also influenced his concept of memory. The μνήμη of which Philo speaks can be related to the traditional classical sources (esp. Plato and Aristotle, cf. 6ff.); at the same time it shows traces of the Jewish meaning of the term. In this sense memory is equivalent to 'preserving the sacred Law in one's spirit', and therefore corresponds to the virtues of faithfulness and perseverance (15-17) and, ultimately, to the 'remembrance of God', which implies 'self-forgetfulness' (19). (RR)

8411. P. BORGEN, 'Philo of Alexandria', in M. E. STONE (ed.), *Jewish writings of the Second Temple period: apocrypha, pseudepigrapha, Qumran sectarian writings, Philo, Josephus,* CRINT II 2 (Assen 1984) 233-282

A masterly survey of Philo's writings, thought and *Sitz im Leben,* parallel to Borgen's other survey (**1114**), but with less direct discussion of scholarly views. The first part of the article recounts the organization of Philo's writings, the second part summarizes his thought, the third concentrates on the relation to his predecessor Aristobulus. Although the author emphasizes Philo's debt to Greek culture, his chief emphasis is on his direct participation in Jewish culture (233): 'Philo's aim was definitely practical – to bring his readers to follow the revealed Law of the Pentateuch. Here, as elsewhere, no sharp distinction should be drawn between Hellenistic and Palestinian Judaism.' Philo is primarily an exegete; the exegetical debates that Philo is engaged in are not just those of Alexandria, but are part of the wider Jewish situation. Specific subjects treated in some detail are Philo's views on God as architect, heavenly nourishment, Moses' ascent, the cosmic significance of Jewish existence ('it is specifically the Jewish people which intermediates between God and man' (269)), and the Logos. (DTR)

8412. G. L. BRUNS, 'The problem of figuration in antiquity', in G. SHAPIRO and A. SICA (edd.), *Hermeneutics: questions and prospects* (Amherst 1984) 147-164, esp. 148-153.

Thought-provoking observations on aspects of Philo's use of allegory in the context of a discussion that distinguishes radically between the ancient hermeneutical way of reading texts and our post-Enlightenment analytical approach. For Philo allegory is not a method of interpretation but rather a form of mental or spiritual life. To know what a text means is to know what the text would say if it were able to speak. For us moderns it is hard to imagine that figuration may not be a textual or a linguistic phenomenon – i.e. a certain kind of correspondence between two terms –, but rather a form of prophecy or mystery. (DTR)

8413. F. W. BURNETT, 'Philo on immortality: a thematic study of Philo's concept of παλιγγενεσία', *CBQ* 46 (1984) 447-470.

An examination of Philo's use of the concept of παλιγγενεσία based chiefly on an in-depth analysis of *Cher.* 113-115 (the instances in *Aet.* are left out and the question of Philo's sources is but briefly touched on). The conclusions are summarized as follows (470): 'Παλιγγενεσία is the rebirth of the soul into incorporeal existence. Although the migrating soul can envision the intelligible world and experience an ethical rebirth while still in mixture with the body, it is after the mixture is dissolved, i.e., after physical death, that παλιγγενεσία occurs... Philo does not present a clear, systematic statement about what incorporeal existence for the soul means, but he seems to imply that the soul continues to exist as a distinct entity in the presence of God. Incorporeal existence in the presence of God, however, is only for virtuous souls. Souls which did not allow God to free them from the world of sense-perception are doomed to perish with it.' No evidence is found for a Stoic understanding of the concept, nor does it imply a doctrine of reincarnation. Philo draws from several traditions, but never clearly aligns himself with any single one. (DTR)

8414. P. CAMBRONNE, 'Loi et législateur chez Philon d'Alexandrie:

remarques sur la formation d'un concept judéo-hellénistique', *CCGR* 4 (1984) 45-63.

An unusual article, the contents of which differ from what the title might lead one to expect. Starting-point is the opening passage of *Opif.*, of which §1-6 are cited. The task of 'the interpreter of God is to decipher the Law by means of the order of the cosmos and its characters' (46). This order is then analyzed at some length, with separate sections devoted to order as beauty of number (including some remarks on Philo's exemplarism), order as finality (as seen in the sequence of creation and the divine will), and order as hierarchy (here man has his place and through his inclination to the irrational evil enters and causes rupture). The article concludes with some more general remarks. Philo is profoundly imbued with all the ideas which flourished in his milieu. He should not, however, be called a syncretist, for he uses this material to illuminate the Bible which in fact belongs to another culture. He can thus be called the first 'apologist of continuity', opening the way to Patristic writers. It is worth noting that Cambronne perceives a strong debt incurred by Minucius Felix to Philo's *De Providentia*. (DTR)

8415. J. CAZEAUX, 'Philon d'Alexandrie, exégète', in *ANRW* II 21.1 (cf. **8424**) 156-226.

This study summarizes the distinctive view of Philo's allegorical exegesis expounded by the author at greater length elsewhere (cf. **8319, 8320**). We shall limit ourselves, therefore, to explaining its structure, particularly with reference to the first part, which discusses Philo's allegory from a general and formal point of view and determines the scheme of the whole article. Cazeaux distinguishes four levels through which the exegesis of Philo's work must pass: (1) a more exterior and obvious level, guided 'by the procedures of allegorical grammar and rhetoric'; (2) a level of 'complete interpretation', showing the connection between the parts and the whole; (3) a more profound level, based on the procedures of dialectic and philosophy; (4) a general level enabling us to arrive at various allegorical categories (e.g. 'symmetry', 'substitution', 'redundance'; cf. 211ff.) which show the original structure of Philonic allegory. (RR)

8416. J. CAZEAUX, 'Philo, l'allégorie et l'obsession de la totalité', in *Études sur le Judaïsme hellénistique* (cf. **8404**) 267-320.

Cazeaux's article consists of a brief theoretical introduction followed by a long analysis which sets out to verify, on the basis of suitable examples, the general rules formulated in the introduction. The introduction (267-278) makes the following points. (1) Philonic allegory is a search for unity which is conducted on increasingly higher levels until a kind of all-embracing allegory is reached (269f.). (2) In this Philo is 'an independent creator' (268), even if his work forms part of a tradition which is in the process of consolidation. (3) The level of all-embracing allegory is achieved through a series of codes (anthropological, moral, cosmic, exegetical; cf. 277), which must be seen as instruments that unify the meaning of numerous biblical texts. (4) Philo's allegorical interpretation is finalized in the anthropological and psychological meanings it conveys. (RR)

8417. G. H. COHEN STUART, *The struggle in man between good and evil: an inquiry into the origin of the Rabbinic concept of yeṣer hara'* (diss. Amsterdam, Kampen 1984), esp. 101-114.

A large number of Philonic texts dealing with the struggle in man between good and evil are cited and briefly analyzed. It is highly questionable, however, whether Philo uses expressions that are in any way parallel to those of the 'good inclination' and 'evil inclination' (yeṣer) in Rabbinic thought. (DTR)

8418. T. M. CONLEY, 'Philo's rhetoric: argumentation and style', in *ANRW* II 21.1 (cf. **8424**) 343-371.

The author's aim in this article is to examine 'some of the stylistic phenomena in Philo as rhetorical phenomena, not as mere ornament; and as deliberate and intentional aspects of his argumentation, not simply as matters of habitual or idiosyncratic usage' (345). To this end Conley first (345-350) deals with the grammatical aspects of Philo's rhetoric, and next (351-358) with its 'figures of thought'. Finally in the third part (359-369) the theoretical results of the first two sections are applied to an analysis of *Cher*. (RR)

8419. M. DEAN-OTTING, *Heavenly journeys: a study of the motif in Hellenistic-Jewish literature*, Judentum und Umwelt 8 (Frankfurt 1984), esp. 31-33.

'Perhaps a kind of heavenly journey is described by Philo but it can only be called one in the broadest definition of the motif' (33). For this reason Philo's evidence is only used indirectly in this study of heavenly journeys in Jewish apocalyptic literature. (DTR)

8420. G. DELLING, 'The "one who sees God" in Philo', in *Nourished with peace* (cf. **8423**) 27-41.

After an extensive and thorough analysis of the etymological and allegorical meaning of 'Israel' in Philo, Delling reaches the following conclusions. 'In accordance with a firmly fixed tradition which was inherited by Philo, the name Israel designates the ancestor of the people of God. According to a younger tradition, which also was in Philo's possession, the name indicates the relationship of the bearer to God. The declaration contained in the name was carried over from the forefather to the Jewish people. Whoever says "Israel" says "seeing God"' (41). (RR)

8421. C. GIANOTTO, *Melchisedek e la sua tipologia; tradizioni giudaiche, cristiane e gnostiche (sec. II a.C. - sec. III d.C.)* RivBib.S 12 (Brescia 1984), esp. 87-99.

Philo devotes many passages to Melchizedek (*Congr.* 99, *Abr.* 235, *Leg.* 3.79-82, as well as a fragment of *QG* relating to Gen. 14:18-20). The most important and also most problematical of these is *Leg.* 3.79-82, where Melchizedek is identified with the Logos-priest. Gianotto examines the possible motives of this interpretation, and makes the following points. (1) Both the Logos and Melchizedek play the role of mediator between man and God, a role which is typical of the priest. (2) Melchizedek is regarded as the man who naturally possesses the blessing of priesthood, and this relates him to the nature of the Logos, the oldest of God's creatures. We add that the latter view has been contested by N. CASALINI in his review article 'Ancora su Melchisedek', *SBFLA* 35 (1985) 107-130, esp. 115f. (cf. **8511**). (RR)

8422. S. GORANSON, '"Essenes": etymology from עשׂה', *RQ* 11 (1984) 483-498.

Yet another discussion of the etymology of the name of the Essenes, with copious reference to previous scholarly discussion. Philo's evidence is a better starting-point than might be thought, for he, in addition to taking over the received name Ἐσσαῖοι, also retains the sound approximated by ὅσιοι. Goranson uses this as support for his suggestion of an etymology from the Hebrew root 'SH, meaning 'to do, make, prepare, bring forth, bear (fruit)'. (DTR)

8423. F. E. GREENSPAHN, E. HILGERT, B. L. MACK (edd.), *Nourished with peace: studies in Hellenistic Judaism in memory of Samuel Sandmel*, Scholars Press Homage Series 9 (Chico, California 1984).

A memorial volume in honour of the distinguished Philonic scholar Samuel Sandmel, who died in 1979. In addition to the scholarly articles it contains, which will be listed under the names of the individual authors, the book also contains tributes to Sandmel, correspondence between him and V. Nikiprowetzky, and a complete bibliography of his writings compiled by F. E. Greenspahn. Noteworthy is the short introductory piece by M. J. COOK, 'Samuel Sandmel on Christian origins: common sense, uncommon grace' (1-4), which clarifies the underlying pattern in Sandmel's interpretation of Philo. The essential problem for Sandmel was that of defining the relations between Greek and Jewish culture in the overall context of Judaism. With regard to Philo his view was that the degree of integration between philosophy and religion 'was so extensive as to have produced in Hellenistic Judaism a religious flavor markedly distinct from all varieties of Palestinian Judaism' (2). REVIEWS: D. Winston, *JR* 66 (1986) 212f.; F. de Meyer, *Bijdr* 48 (1987) 81f. (RR)

8424. W. HAASE (ed.), *Hellenistisches Judentum in römischer zeit: Philon und Josephus,* Aufstieg und Niedergang der römischen Welt, II Principat vol. 21 (Berlin-New York 1984).

Volume 21 of the second part of this encyclopedic series actually consists of two hefty tomes, one devoted to Philo, the other to Josephus. The various contributions to the Philo volume, each of which is listed under the respective author's name (see also **1019**, **1114**), give a good indication of the state of Philonic research *circa* 1977 (when most were written), though no attempt is made to integrate the volume into a coherent whole. REVIEW: J. C. M. van Winden, *VChr* 39 (1985) 90f. (DTR)

8425. I. HADOT, *Arts libéraux et philosophie dans la pensée antique*, Études Augustiniennes 79 (Paris 1984), esp. 282-287.

Philo's contribution to the subject lies in his extensive use of the terms ἐγκύκλιος παιδεία, ἐγκύκλια προπαιδεύματα, μέση παιδεία etc. It represents an intermediate stage, halfway between elementary instruction and perfection represented by philosophy. The perspective is wholly Platonic, for the aim is gradually to liberate the soul from the constraints of the body and sense-perception. (DTR)

8426. R. D. HECHT, 'The exegetical contexts of Philo's interpretation of circumcision', in *Nourished with peace* (cf. **8423**) 51-79.

Spec. 1.1-11 is an essential passage with regard to Philo's views on circumcision, while *QG* 3.46-52 adds significant points. Hecht mainly discusses the first text, in which connection he pays a good deal of attention to bibliographical matters (cf. esp. §1 (53-61) entitled '*De specialibus legibus* in the history of Philonic studies'). In his opinion the text is basically apologetic (79) and aims at showing the 'reasonableness of the Law'. As for circumcision this practice is justified by Philo on four grounds: (1) its hygienic usefulness; (2) its purificatory value; (3) its procreative value; (4) its symbolical meaning (68). (RR)

8427. J. HELDERMAN, *Die Anapausis im Evangelium veritatis*, NHS 18 (Leiden 1984) *passim*.

Although no specific discussion of Philo's use of the term ἀνάπαυσις is furnished in this study, in the commentary on passages using the term in the Gnostic treatise such extensive use is made of Philonic material that the index of reference occupies more than 5 columns (399-401). Note the discussion on the spiritualization of Sabbath rest and the theme of divine stability (108ff.), divine and human πνεῦμα, the interpretation of paradise (148ff.). (DTR)

8428. L. D. HURST, 'Eschatology and "Platonism" in the Epistle to the Hebrews', *SBLSPS* 23 (1984) 41-74.

A detailed discussion, with frequent reference to the scholarly literature, of the 'heavenly sanctuary' in Hebr. 8:5 leads to the conclusion that 'there is little reason to turn aside from Jewish Old Testament literature to literature directly influenced by Platonic-type metaphysical concerns [i.e. Philo] in seeking to find the key to the writer's eschatology', which differs little from the 'mainstream apocalyptic tradition, for which there is a future heavenly Jerusalem to be manifested on earth' (74). (DTR)

8429. C. KRAUS REGGIANI, 'I rapporti tra l'impero romano e il mondo ebraico al tempo di Caligola secondo la "Legatio ad Gaium" di Filone Alessandrino', in *ANRW* II 21.1 (cf. **8424**) 554-586.

This study amounts to a detailed analysis of the *Legatio ad Gaium*. The fourth section (571-582) deals with the problems of composition and structure inherent in this treatise, while in the final part Kraus Reggiani sets out some general interpretative views with regard to the principles of Philo's political and religious philosophy (rather than to his ideology or political practice). Noteworthy is the recognition in Philo's work of the concept of 'spiritual *civitas* which transcends all earthly concerns', namely a '*civitas* precious to God in which Moses includes every man of virtue, without distinguishing between those who belong or do not belong to Judaism' (586). (RR)

8430. S. LÉGASSE, 'Morale hellénistique et morale chrétienne primitive: les rapports interhumains illustrés par deux exemples', in *Études sur le Judaïsme hellénistique* (cf. **8404**) 321-338, esp. 327f., 329ff.

Greek friendship and Christian friendship operate on different planes: one is horizontal (between man and man), the other vertical (between man and God). In Christianity, moreover, Greek φιλία broadens out into a form of φιλανθρωπία. Philo's point of view can be located between the two extremes, but comes closer to the Christian attitude. (RR)

8431. B. L. MACK, 'Decoding the scripture: Philo and the rules of rhetoric', in *Nourished with peace* (cf. **8423**) 81-115.

The viewpoint presented by the author in this work is that Philo 'was not only trained in the Hellenistic school through its secondary curriculum', but that 'he was trained in the art of rhetorical composition as well'. Hence it follows that 'Philo regarded all of Moses' writings to be crafted according to canons of rhetorical composition' (84). Mack verifies this theory by turning to the rhetorical canons of Theon of Alexandria and Hermogenes, and showing how these canons can be fruitfully applied to the first ten paragraphs of *Sacr*. (RR)

8432. B. L. MACK, 'Philo Judaeus and exegetical traditions in Alexandria', in *ANRW* II 21.1 (cf. **8424**) 227-271.

The author's thesis is that in the cultural milieu in which Philo was formed 'the intellectual activity was essentially hermeneutical debate which was carried on by means of exegetical traditions which had roots in theological systems'. Hence it follows that 'Philo's work can be seen to be both a repository for such traditional exegetical accomplishments, and a result of systematic efforts of his own' (227). Given these premisses, it appears that Philo's thought cannot be reconstructed 'by using only the models of the Hellenic and Hellenistic schools' (229); in the first place we must reconstruct the hermeneutical principles which governed the biblical exegesis of the Alexandrian Jews. Therefore Mack proposes in this study 'to review the scholarship on Philo in such a way as to clarify the question with regard to his relationship to exegetical traditions in Alexandria' (229). (RR)

8433. J. P. MARTÍN, 'El encuentro de exégesis y filosofia en Filón Alejandrino', *RevBib* 46 (1984) 199-211.

In *Conf.* 97 Martín distinguishes three types of biblical propositions about God, each of which can be related to a corresponding type of exegesis: pedagogical exegesis (200-202), relational exegesis (202-206), and absolute exegesis. Only the latter properly represents the nature of God, which it expresses in ontological terms. (RR)

8434. W. J. MCCARTHY, *Sol salutis, arbor mundi, lucerna Christi: cosmic cross and cosmic Christ in a second century A.D. Paschal homily (a literary interpretation)* (diss. Catholic University of America, Washington 1984), esp. chap. 2.

As background to the interpretation of the 2nd century Easter homily *In sanctum pascha* the author examines macrocosmic and microcosmic applications of the concept of the tree in Plato and the curious ramifications of these ideas among Stoics, Philo and certain Christians. (DTR; based on *DA* 44-3376A)

8435. J. MONTSERRAT I TORRENTS, 'Filó d'Alexandria, de la saviesa a la contemplació', *Enrahonar* 7-8 [*Homenatge a J. M. Calsamiglia*] (1984) 103-107.

Philo was not a mystic in the true sense of the word. Nevertheless, he hypothetically puts forward in his work 'a mystical-intellectual way' to contemplation which is in essential terms not dissimilar to the Platonic way. Philo goes beyond Plato, however, in holding that intuitive contemplation of divinity is impossible. (RR)

8436. P. MORAUX, *Der Aristotelismus bei den Griechen von Andro-nikos bis Alexander von Aphrodisias*, vol. 2, *Der Aristotelismus im I. und II. Jh. n.Chr.*, Peripatoi: philologisch-historische Studien zum Aristotelismus 6 (Berlin-New York 1984), esp. 42-44.

Philo belongs to the circle of thinkers (including the author of the *De mundo*, Pseudo-Aristeas, Aristobulus) committed to surmounting the theological immanentism of the Stoics. Both the theory of the Powers and the distinction between God's *ousia* and his *dynamis* must be seen in this perspective. In the preface (xxviii) Moraux speaks of his 'umfangreichen Lesenotizen' on Philo, which he declined to convert into a chapter on Philo and Aristotle. This material remained unpublished, to our knowledge, at the time of his death in 1985. (RR)

8437. R. H. NASH, *Christianity and the Hellenistic world* (Grand Rapids 1984), esp. 81-112.

The author's aim is to examine whether the Christianity found in the New Testament is in any way dependent for its essential beliefs and practices on the pagan philosophical and religious systems of belief current in the first century A.D., a thesis which he vigorously denies. In two areas it might be asked whether Philo, whose thought is regarded as heavily influenced, if not wholly determined, by Hellenistic philosophy, is a source of New Testament ideas. In the case of the Logos doctrine of John's Gospel two alternative sources are given, namely Jewish wisdom speculation and personification of God's word in the Old Testament. In the case of the Epistle to the Hebrews a weak dependence on the thought world of Alexandrian Judaism is not to be denied. It is likely that the author knew the writings of Philo. But he has no intention of importing alien ideas into the Christianity to which he had been converted; rather he exploits his knowledge of Alexandrian terminology and ideas for apologetic purposes. The conception of Christ's incarnation, his compassion and suffering is quite incompatible with the philosophical presuppositions of Philo's Logos theology. (DTR)

8438. V. NIKIPROWETZKY, '"*Moyses palpans vel liniens*": on some explanations of the name of Moses in Philo of Alexandria', in *Nourished with peace* (cf. **8423**) 117-142.

Nikiprowetzky is concerned here with Philo's etymologies, a subject of great importance, since it is the starting-point of every attempt to demonstrate Philo's knowledge – or ignorance – of the Hebrew language. Besides a perceptive analysis of the various etymologies of Moses' name (two of which are indicated in the title), the author's conclusions seem particularly significant. (1) 'No one has yet been successful in showing that any of the etymologies used by Philo were imagined by him.' (2) 'The most fantastic or the most "barbarous" of them do not prove that their real authors were ignorant of Hebrew, but only that they were concerned with other matters than an exercise in philology and that they were not under the same constraints as we are today.' (3) With regard to Philo and his knowledge of Hebrew, 'consideration of the etymologies ... proves nothing at all...' (4) 'Whether plausible or grammatically absurd, Philo's etymologies are vehicles for theological concepts' (141-142). (RR)

8439. V. NIKIPROWETZKY and A. SOLIGNAC, 'Philon d'Alexandrie', in *Dictionnaire de Spiritualité*, vol. 12 (Paris 1984) 1352-79.

The section devoted to Philo and his work (1351-1366), presented by Nikiprowetzky, first discusses Philo's works and then the cultural influences, both Jewish and Alexandrian, which shaped him. A second part then discusses Philo's spiritual personality, paying particular attention to his place in the philosophical tradition and his conception of philosophy. The contribution is also valuable from a bibliographical point of view, since Nikiprowetzky constantly refers to the various scholarly positions. The subject of Philo's influence on the Fathers, presented by Solignac (1366-79), is discussed under three headings: (a) the circulation of Philo's works; (b) the relations with Clement, Origen, and Gregory of Nyssa; (c) the relations with the Latin Fathers, Ambrose, and Augustine. (RR)

8440. B. A. PEARSON, 'Philo and Gnosticism', in *ANRW* II 21.1 (cf. **8424**) 295-342.

The relation between Philo and the Gnosis, the author observes, can hardly be called into question. The problem is rather in what way it must be understood, since critics have regarded it either 'as representing a stage in the development of Gnosticism, or even as a formative factor in certain mythico-philosophical systems of second-century Gnosticism' (295). Pearson observes that 'in general, more recent scholarship has tended toward the latter alternative', a conclusion which he reaches after considering a large part of the literature on the subject, and in particular the works of Jonas (cf. **5408**) and Friedländer (cf. **7333**). (RR)

8441. C. PERROT, 'La lecture de la Bible dans le Diaspora hellénisti- que', in *Études sur le Judaïsme hellénistique* (cf. **8404**) 109-132, esp. 125- 132.

The problem of the form and manner in which Philo's Bible was read can only be solved after correctly analyzing the structure of the *Quaestiones*. In this connection Perrot criticizes the theories of Royse (cf. **7736**) and, without reaching definite conclusions, restates the problem clearly by putting it in the context of sabbatical reading practices during the Hellenistic Diaspora (125-128). (RR)

8442. J. PIGEAUD, 'Le problème de la conscience chez Philon d'Alex- andrie', in E. A. LIVINGSTONE (ed.), *Papers presented to the Seventh International Conference on Patristic Studies held in Oxford 1975*, part 1, StudPatr 15 (= TU 128) (Berlin 1984) 486-488.

The Philonic notion of conscience goes beyond the limits of Greek thought, for it makes reference to the notion of sin, which certainly has a Jewish origin. (RR)

8443. R. RADICE, 'Filone di Alessandria nella interpretazione di V. Nikiprowetzky e della sua scuola', *RFN* 74 (1984) 15-41.

Compares Nikiprowetzky's hermeneutical views with the most recent and important developments in Philonic research. Besides Nikiprowetzky, the author considers the views put forward by scholars of the Philo Claremont Project, by Tobin (cf. **8373**), and particularly by Runia (cf. **8363, 8656**), of whose study a detailed and amply docu- mented synthesis is presented. (RR)

8444. H. E. REMUS, 'Authority consent law: *nomos, physis*, and the striving for a 'given'', *SR* 13 (1984) 5-18, esp. 13-16.

Philo's views on the law(s) of nature are discussed in the context of Hellenic thought on νόμος and φύσις. The author, mainly following Koester (cf. **6816**), concludes (16): 'The bringing together of nomos and physis in a significant way in Philo is part of an extremely nuanced mode of thought that enables him to employ nomos physeos as a way of expressing the divinely given even while treating departures from it as reinforcements of that given.' (DTR)

8445. D. T. RUNIA, 'In den beginne...: een Joodse uitleg van Genesis 1-2 uit Alexandrië', *Beweging* 48 (1984) 52-55.

The article contains a summary, intended for the general reader, of Philo's exegesis of Gen. 1-2 in *Opif.*, preceded by an introductory section outlining the historical importance of Hellenistic Judaism. The conclusion gives a brief evaluation of Philo's contribution to the history of exegesis. Although one can admire Philo's attempt to exploit cosmological ideas from Greek philosophy in his exegesis, from the philosophical and theological point of view Philo does not allow the Bible to speak in its own language. His exposition of the creation of the cosmos and of man one-sidedly emphasizes the spiritual above the sense-perceptible realm. (RAB/DTR)

8446. D. T. RUNIA, 'History in the grand manner: the achievement of H. A. Wolfson', *PhilRef* 49 (1984) 112-133.

The article consists of two parts. In the first the career and scholarly achievement of H. A. Wolfson is outlined, with particular emphasis on the development of the planned series of studies *Structure and growth of philosophic systems from Plato to Spinoza*. In the second part an evaluation is attempted of Wolfson's main thesis, with particular attention paid to his methodology and the role of Philo. The author concludes: 'The grand thesis of H. A. Wolfson ... consists of two half-truths. It is true that Philo initiates a new era because in his work two traditions of thought flow together for the first time, but it cannot be said that an articulated Philonic system dominates seventeen centuries of philosophy. It is true that medieval philosophy presents an essential unity in the guise of three languages, but it cannot be said that this philosophy is a Philonic philosophy and is adequately circumscribed in terms of a (Philonically inspired) subordination of reason to faith... The Achilles' heel of Wolfson's thesis lies in his conception of Judaism and the role he assigns to Judaism in the history of philosophy' (130). (DTR)

8447. D. T. RUNIA, 'The structure of Philo's allegorical treatises: a review of two recent studies and some additional comments', *VChr* 38 (1984) 209-256.

The starting-point of this lengthy article is a critique of the monograph of Cazeaux, *La trame et la chaîne* (**8320**), and the commentary of Winston and Dillon (**3101**) on *Gig.-Deus* (including especially the structural analysis presented by Nikiprowetzky, cf. **8357**). These studies bring forward in an acute form the problem of the structure of Philo's allegorical treatises – a problem that has received insufficient attention in Philonic studies –, and the remainder of the article is addressed to this subject. First four principles that need to be recognized when reading Philo's exegesis are outlined (primacy of biblical text, opacity of biblical text, finality of Philonic text, modesty of Philonic text). Then Runia points out the crucial role played by the enchainment of primary and secondary biblical lemmata in the way that Philo's exegesis proceeds. An analysis of *Deus* confirms this observation and reveals that the transitions between the lemmata are frequently motivated by verbal as well as thematic parallels. A question that remains unresolved is the extent to which Philo aims at a thematic unity in a single treatise. (DTR)

8448. S. SANDMEL, 'Philo Judaeus: an introduction to the man, his writings, and his significance', in *ANRW* II 21.1 (cf. **8424**) 3-46.

Sandmel's introduction to Philo follows the classic pattern: a reconstruction of his life (3-6) and works (6-13), followed by an explanation of his method (i.e. of allegorical interpretation, 13-22) and thought (22-30). The latter is summed up in nine essential subjects which touch on the main themes of Philo's theology, anthropology, and ethics. Next, a brief section entitled 'Jew or Greek' deals in a synthetic way with the essential problem of Philo's cultural position. This problem is resolved by Sandmel in the following terms (36): '... Philo, Fourth Maccabes, the Fragments from Aristobulus, and the Wisdom of Solomon can be described as a blend of Judaism and Hellenism, and this blend is neither identical with any Palestinian Judaism, nor with pagan Hellenism. It is a unique blend, a cultural anomaly.' In conclusion, Sandmel devotes some pages (36-46) to the relations between Philo and early Christian thought. (RR)

8449. H. SAVON, 'Saint Ambroise et saint Jérôme, lecteurs de Philon', in *ANRW* II 21.1 (cf. **8424**) 731-759.

Reassesses Philo's influence on the Latin Fathers and in particular on Ambrose and Jerome. Savon's view is that 'Philo's influence on the Latin West at the end of the 4th century was largely exercised in an indirect manner', namely 'through Christian allegorism and, specifically, through the mediation of Origen' (759). This hypothesis is supported by an analysis of the relations between Philo and Ambrose (743ff.), which shows substantial differences between the two thinkers, particularly in the appraisal – basically negative in Ambrose – of Platonist metaphysics. (RR)

8450. D. R. SCHWARTZ, 'Philo's priestly descent', in *Nourished with peace* (cf. **8423**) 155-171.

Jerome's testimony, according to which Philo descended *de genere sacerdotum*, has hitherto been regarded with scepticism. The author, by adducing further indirect evidence (cf. 170), makes a case for accepting it and thus accepting that Philo 'was of a priestly family', possibly belonging to the Sadducees. This conclusion 'should encourage us to compare his writings specifically with other remnants of the literature of the priestly tradition' (171). (RR)

8451. A. F. SEGAL, 'Torah and *nomos* in recent scholarly discussion', *SR* 13 (1984) 19-27.

The author takes issue with the view of scholars such as Dodd and Sandmel that the (mis)translation of Torah by νόμος contributed to the separation of Judaism and Christianity. Hellenistic Jews, including Philo, were perfectly aware that *nomos* in the Greek tradition could refer to both human law and divine or transcendent Law. Philo's position is only exceptional because of the influence of Platonism on his thought, i.e. he felt the need to defend the Law as the 'closest embodiment to platonic forms' (27). (DTR)

8452. J. R. SHARP, 'Philo's method of allegorical interpretation', *EAJTh* 2 (1984) 94-102.

A competent survey of Philo's allegorical method, with copious references to scholarly literature. Philo had various predecessors – Alexandrian, philosophical, and possibly Palestinian –, but his apologetic interest motivated him to develop the method further in his application to the Scriptures. His influence on early Christian scriptural interpretation was strong and is seen at its most pervasive in Origen. (DTR)

8453. J. R. SHARP, 'Philonism and the eschatology of Hebrews: another look', *EAJTh* 2 (1984) 289-298.

Spatial dualism (between the transient earthly world and the eternal heavenly realms) is less important in Hebrews than eschatological dualism, which is central to the work as a whole. The background for the 'idealism' that is undeniably present is the spatial dualism found in Apocalyptic idealism and primitive Christian thought rather than in Platonic or Philonic idealism. Similarities between Philo and Hebrews are primarily of a verbal kind. (DTR)

8454. P. SIGAL, 'Manifestation of Hellenistic historiography in select Judaic literature', *SBLSPS* 23 (1984) 161-185, esp. 170-174.

Although the accounts of Moses in Philo and Josephus contain elements in common with the aretalogies of Hellenistic historiography, it should not be concluded, as done by M. Smith (cf. **6528**), that these accounts were themselves written as actual aretalogies. (DTR)

8455. D. R. SILLS, *Re-inventing the past: Philo and the historiography of Jewish identity* (diss. University of California, Santa Barbara 1984).

The question addressed by this study is why it took until the 19th century before Philo became an object of study in Jewish historical research. The two Jewish scholars taken as indicative of a more pervasive trend are H. Graetz and H. A. Wolfson. For Graetz, the outspoken critic of Reform, Philo became the champion of orthodoxy, i.e. in spite of his affection for Greek philosophy, his primary concern was with the coherence of religious observance. For Wolfson, whose critique of modern Jewry rested on a Zionist programme, Philo both as social historian and biblical exegete prefigured the Zionist call. Both scholars regard the urban pluralism of 1st century Alexandria as a prefiguration of the post-Emancipation experience of modern Jewry. Philo is a 1st century ally who, like themselves, opposes the process of acculturation to the prevailing non-Jewish environment. (DTR; based on *DA* 46-1314A)

8456. H. SIMON and M. SIMON, *Geschichte der jüdischen Philosophie* (Munich 1984), esp. 26-36.

'Philo's philosophy is a blending (*Mischung*) of Greek and Jewish elements. But this blending is not to be understood in terms of a mechanical mixing in which the components remain separate; rather we have to do with a chemical reaction resulting in a new and autonomous quality' (26). The authors argue this view in a brief analysis of Philo and his thought. They conclude that Philo's work can be seen as the apex of Jewish thought in antiquity, but also as its conclusion (34), since virtually no continuation was provided by the other traditions of Jewish thought (34). (RR)

8457. G. STROUMSA, *Another seed: studies in Gnostic mythology*, NHS 24 (Leiden 1984), esp. 27-29.

Gnostic thought was obsessed with the problem of evil. The author attempts to show that the basis of the Gnostic consciousness of evil was formed through a radical transformation of the myth of the fallen angels in Gen. 6:1-4. Whereas in Apocalyptic literature the myth is 'remythologized', Philo is the first witness of a demythologizing exegesis, which after him is continued in the Patristic tradition. (DTR)

8458. A. TERIAN, 'A critical introduction to Philo's Dialogues', in *ANRW* II 21.1 (cf. **8424**) 272-294.

Presents an analytical examination of *Prov*. 1-2 and *Anim*. The author also tackles the problem of the dating of these two treatises. It is convincingly argued that they belong to Philo's maturity or old age and that their relation with the treatises of the Allegorical Commentary is much closer than has been thought until now (276). (RR)

8459. F. TRISOGLIO, 'Filone alessandrino e l'esegesi cristiana: contributo alla conoscenza dell'influsso esercitato da Filone sul IV secolo, specificatamente in Gregorio di Nazianzo', in *ANRW* II 21.1 (cf. **8424**) 588-730.

The aim of this work is 'to do for Gregory of Nazianzus what has already been done for the majority of the great Christian Greek authors' (599), namely a systematic comparison with the work of Philo. Trisoglio examines *Or*. 14 on the love of the poor, comparing it with Philo on conceptual (600-679) and lexical (679-687) levels, and also referring to a series of external considerations (mostly related to Gregory's biography and personality, cf. 687ff.). All in all the thesis that Gregory depends on Philo is confirmed. The final part of the work (696ff.), which contains many references to the scholarly literature, gives a general evaluation of Philo's influence on Christian thought in the 2nd to 4th centuries. (RR)

8460. L. TROIANI, 'Filone Alessandrino e la XIV regio augustea', *Ath* 62 (1984) 268-275.

Legat. 155 refers to the Augustan division of Rome into 14 quarters and to the concession made to the Jews, allowing them residence in the 14th quarter and complete freedom of worship. (RR)

8461. G. VERMES and M. GOODMAN, 'La littérature juive intertestamentaire à la lumière d'un siècle de recherches et de découvertes', in *Études sur le Judaïsme hellénistique* (cf. **8404**) 19-39 *passim*.

This article devotes few words to Philo, but does offer some general analyses of Alexandrian Judaism which help to throw light on him. The authors point out that there are two different critical attitudes to Jewish-Hellenistic literature, one optimistic and one sceptical (30). The first tends to stress the importance of this literary movement, relating to it a large number of minor authors. The second, on the other hand, tends to reduce its substance to Philo's oeuvre and the Septuagint (36). The authors appear to show a preference for the latter view. (RR)

8462. D. WINSTON, 'Philo's ethical theory', in *ANRW* II 21.1 (cf. **8424**) 372-416.

Philo's ethics are rooted in his conception of God as being at once transcendent and immanent in reality. This duality is also present in his conception of the human soul, sometimes seen as 'a divine fragment', other times as a reality opposed to God and sunk in obscurity. Ultimately, on the ethical level, this opposition devolves into an alternative between the presumption of the intellect which believes in its own autonomy and the intellect's surrender to God, acknowledging itself as an instrument of his power. In this perspective Winston analyzes various prominent themes in Philo's ethics, such as freedom and determinism (377-381), natural law (381-388), the conscience (389-391), the concepts of φιλανθρωπία, ἀπάθεια and εὐπάθεια (391-405) and, finally, asceticism (405-414). (RR)

1985

8501. Manuel ALEXANDRE, 'Argumentaçâo retórica no Comentário de Filón de Alexandria ao Pentateuco', *Euph* 13 (1985) 9-26.

For Philo rhetoric is not merely a matter of aesthetics (i.e. as embellishment of the discourse) and even less a purely sophistic artifice designed to convince the reader, regardless of the truth of the premisses (20). It is a 'holy rhetoric' (25), i.e. an apologetic-pedagogic and at the same time hermeneutic instrument. In this sense rhetoric cannot be distinguished from allegorical interpretation and from the philosophical content communicated by allegory. At the same time, however, rhetoric also has a technical aspect, and this can be traced in the structure of many treatises and constitutes their code of interpretation. (RR)

8502. J. M. BASSLER, 'Philo on Joseph: the basic coherence of *De Iosepho* and *De somniis* II', *JSJ* 16 (1985) 240-255.

The portraits of Joseph in *Ios.* and *Somn.* II are given from different perspectives (whole versus single episode) and the mode of presentation is different (literal with political allegory versus allegory of the soul). Yet the two presentations are argued to be 'completely congruent' (255) and the congruence is bestowed by Philo's exegetical consistency in dealing with Joseph's dreams on both the literal and allegorical levels (this emerges especially in the treatment of the scene with Potiphar's wife). There is no need to invoke complex historical or psychological explanations in order to resolve the apparent discrepancies between the accounts in the two treatises. (DTR)

8503. P.-M. BEAUDE, 'Autour du Nouveau Testament: la crise du sacerdoce aaronide et sa ruine', *Supplément au Dictionnaire de la Bible* vol. 10 (Paris 1985) 1254-1306, esp. 1295-1300.

Priesthood is a vast theme in Philo. Indeed, one can say that 'Philonic spirituality as a whole is sacerdotal' (1296), in the sense that Philo succeeded in interiorizing the theme of priesthood and thus greatly extending its range (though this does not mean that Philo held the priestly rites and precepts to be without value). The themes of worship and priesthood are allegorized by Philo through important symbolical figures such as Moses, Aaron, the Logos, and of course Israel, which stands for a kind of universal priesthood.

Beaude also discusses the relations between Philo and the Letter to the Hebrews, with reference to priesthood and the figure of Melchizedek. (RR)

8504. R. BECKWITH, *The Old Testament canon of the New Testament church and its background in early Judaism* (London 1985) *passim.*

Philo contributes copious evidence for the task this study sets itself, namely to bring together all the truly ancient evidence for a collection of Jewish scriptures that existed during the New Testament period, consisting of books that were believed to be divinely inspired and possessed divine authority. More specific discussions at 115ff. (the reading matter of the Therapeutae), 383f. (prophetic inspiration). Philo's overwhelming concentration on the Pentateuch, however, is not discussed. (DTR)

8505. B. BELLETTI, 'Analisi e valutazione di una recente bibliografia generale su Filone di Alessandria', *Sap* 38 (1985) 89-97.

A laudatory appraisal of Radice's bibliography (**1113**), the predecessor of this work. (DTR)

8506. U. BIANCHI, 'La tradition de l'enkrateia: motivations ontologiques et protologiques', in U. BIANCHI (ed.), *La tradizione dell' enkrateia: motivazioni ontologiche e protologiche; atti del Colloquio Internazionale, Milano, 20-23 aprile 1982* (Rome 1985) 293-315, esp. 293-297.

Many themes of the *enkrateia* tradition in early Christianity are also found in Philo (e.g. in *Opif.* 151ff.). A crucial role is played, according to the author, by metaphysical anthropology, which is 'an essential foundation of all the groups who in the tradition of *enkrateia* appeal to protological motives' (296). In Philo, however, the soteriological dimension is entirely lacking and instead a pessimistic view of history prevails. (RR)

8506a. R. A. BITTER, 'De betekenis van *hyponoia* en *allègoria* bij Philo van Alexandrië', *Bijdr* 46 (1985) 363-380.

The article demonstrates that Philo uses both ὑπόνοια and ἀλληγορία in the special sense of 'underlying or hidden meaning', but that he has a preference for the former, usually in the expression δι' ὑπονοιῶν. ὑπόνοια is an old term with philosophical connotations, much used long before Philo. It is able to convey the process whereby the hidden meaning of a text is discovered. ἀλληγορία on the other hand is a grammatical term indicating the practice of saying something but meaning something quite different. From the 1st century B.C. onwards it pushes aside the older term ὑπόνοια. Philo's preference for the latter can be explained by the fact that in his exegesis he wishes to exploit philosophical concepts that enable him to penetrate to the deeper meaning of the text. (RAB/DTR)

8507. G. BOCCACINI, 'Il valore della verginità in Filone Alessandrino', *QLB* [*Parola Spirito e Vita*] 12 (1985) 217-227.

Philo shares the negative view of sexuality typical of late Judaism, where its function is confined to procreation within marriage. Virginity, in the sense of abstention from the sexual act, thus becomes equivalent to virtue. Besides this negative meaning of virginity, however, Philo also introduces a positive one, that of virginity accepted for the sake of

God. Far from being equivalent to sterility, this is a necessary condition for receiving the gifts and blessings of God and allowing them to grow in oneself. (RR)

8508. G. J. BROOKE, *Exegesis at Qumran: 4Q Florilegium in its Jewish context*, JSOT.S 29 (Sheffield 1985), esp. 17-25.

Philo is part of the background of Jewish exegesis against which the Qumran document must be read; it is no longer legitimate to dismiss him as an irrelevant allegorist. Stress is laid on the centrality of scriptural exposition in Philo and his use of Jewish exegetical techniques, e.g. the use of etymology. But in the actual analysis of the document Philonic material is used but sparingly. (DTR)

8509. J. D. BUTIN and J. SCHWARZ, 'Post Philonis legationem', *RHPhR* 65 (1985) 127-129.

An unpublished papyrus from the Library of Strasburg gives information about the situation in Egypt in 40 A.D. and throws light on some episodes – in particular Claudius' letter to the Alexandrians and the trial of Isidorus and Lampone – discussed by Philo in *Flacc.* (RR)

8510. P. CARNY [קרני .פ], היסודות ההגותיים של דרשנות פילון האלכסנדרוני ['Philo's theory of allegory'], *Daat* 14 (1985) 5-19.

Another attempt by the author to come to terms with Philo's allegorical method. The basic difference between Philo and the Homeric allegorists is the fact that for Philo the biblical text remains constant, whereas man's interpretation is relative. Philo identifies 'ideas' with Plato's *typoi*. The different uses of τύπος are by no means equal to the later Christian use of the term. In Philo's thought such ideas are 'created' by God and function as archetypes. Philo presents three stages of creation or spheres of being: God, the world of *typoi*, and the sense-perceptible world. For Philo biblical stories are a new historical manifestation of the same structure and signal hints to the other realm: the *typos* to the sense-perceptible, then back to the *typos* and to God. The author sees parallelisms in Philo's interpretation, i.e. there are historical, earthly, and legal dimensions of eternal ideas. These may exist simultaneously as allegories and should not necessarily be regarded as alternatives. (MM)

8511. N. CASALINI, 'Ancora su Melchisedek', *SBFLA* 35 (1985) 107-130, esp. 115f.

A review article on **8421**, which see. (RR)

8512. J. CAZEAUX, 'Peuple ou personne dans la mystique juive', *REJ* 144 (1985) 382-394, esp. 388-393.

The relation between 'people' and 'person' is already a fundamental problem in the Bible and 'can be formulated in political terms' (394). In Philo this problem assumes a wholly individual form, since after allegorical transposition the person – above all symbolized by the three Patriarchs, Abraham, Isaac, and Jacob – becomes an ethical and psychological type, and thus an immanent category in the soul of every man. (RR)

8513. N. G. COHEN [ן.כ.נ], בדיקה מחודשת – פילון "נומוס בכתבי "אגראפוס נומוס
['"Agraphos nomos" in Philo's writings – a reconsideration'], *Daat* 15 (1985) 5-20.

A new evaluation of the thesis, formulated primarily by I. Heinemann, that the Greek term ἄγραφος νόμος in Philo never means the oral Law but only the Greek νόμος φύσεως as based on Aristotle's *Rhetoric*. The text of Aristotle does not allow for the interpretation given by Heinemann; Plato and Aristotle use the term *agraphos nomos* as unwritten, but binding law. The major text under discussion is *Spec.* 4.149. See the further contributions **8514, 8708***. English summary. (MM)

8514. N. G. COHEN, ''Al taseg gevul 'olim' (Peah 5:6, 7:3)', *HUCA* 56 (1985) 145-166, esp. 164f.

The saying cited in the title may be a non-biblical aphorism from Ben Sira or from his vintage. Philo's allusion to Prov. 22:28 in his exegesis of Deut. 19:14 in *Spec.* 4.149 is called in as evidence, but the question is said to deserve a separate study. (DTR)

8515. J. J. COLLINS, 'A symbol of otherness: circumcision and salvation in the first century', in J. NEUSNER and E. S. FRERICHS (edd.), *"To see ourselves as others see us": Christians, Jews, "Others" in late antiquity'*, Scholars Press Studies in the Humanities (Chico, California 1985) 163-186, esp. 170-176.

In this survey of the spectrum of opinions held on the subject of circumcision by Jews in the Greco-Roman Diaspora Philo's evidence is discussed especially in relation to the question of proselytism and conversion. Philo defends literal observance of circumcision. Presumably he regards it not as a prerequisite for entry to the Jewish community, but as duty consequent upon admission. But practical monotheism is a more important dividing line between Jew and Gentile than the ritual act of circumcision. (DTR)

8516. M. G. CREPALDI, 'Giudaismo ed Ellenismo: il kairos della salvezza in Filone di Alessandria', *ArFil* 53 (1985) 209-219.

Unlike the Jewish tradition, which emphasizes the historical dimension of salvation, Philo tends to devalue this aspect by spiritualizing history in an individual and moral sense. Fundamental consequences are: (a) a cosmopolitan ideal which transcends geographical limits (214); (b) a universalistic interpretation of the Law; (c) an overall devaluation of human history and in general a transcendence of the temporal dimension; (d) a transformation of historical providence into individual providence. All these transformations, according to Crepaldi, are due to the influence of Stoic and Platonic philosophy. (RR)

8517. M. G. CREPALDI, *La concezione del tempo fra pensiero biblico e filosofia greca: saggio su Filone di Alessandria* (Padua 1985).

The author conducts an extended analysis of the Philonic concept of time, distinguishing three dimensions of the term in Philo's work: cosmo-physical (27-38), historical (39-50), and ethical (51-82). Crepaldi's research can be summed up in the following points (set out on 85ff.). For Philo temporality culminates in the absolute transcendence of God's eternity, while its lower limit is formed by the time of the world of becoming (= χρόνος). Between these two extremes lies an intermediate sphere (the αἰών of the intelligible world and the 'duration' of the ethical world) which accounts for the relation between man and God. Two important consequences follow from this tripartition: firstly the devaluation of χρόνος; secondly the priority of the ethical aspect of temporality. And precisely the prevalence of the latter aspect is responsible for the fact that Philo almost completely neglects the historical and worldly dimension of time, though this dimension is typical of the Bible, in favour of its moral and individual dimension, in which the personal relation between God and man prevails, as is implicit in the doctrine of grace (86 f.). See also **8611**. REVIEW: M. Jori, *StudPat* 32 (1985) 629f. (RR)

8518. F. G. DOWNING, 'Philo on wealth and the rights of the poor', *JSNT* 24 (1985) 116-118.

Diverse texts are cited in order to show that Philo displays a more sensitive and caring awareness of the situation of the poor than allowed for by T. E. Schmidt (cf. **8365**). (DTR)

8519. P. E. EASTERLING and B. M. W. KNOX (edd.), *The Cambridge history of Classical literature*, vol. 1 Greek literature (Cambridge 1985), esp. 639, 854-855.

We include this item in order to indicate the treatment of Philo in a high-quality handbook on Greek literature. The results are meagre. A. A. LONG devotes a (not uncomplimentary) paragraph to Philo in his chapter on post-Aristotelian philosophy, while in an appendix M. DRURY sets out a short bibliography. (DTR)

8520. R. S. ECCLES, *Erwin Ramsdell Goodenough: a personal pilgrimage*, Society of Biblical literature: Biblical scholarship in America (Chico California 1985), esp. 11-65.

A somewhat stiff but informative intellectual biography of one of America's leading Philonic scholars. In chapters 2-4 competent (though wholly uncritical) summaries are presented of all Goodenough's scholarly works that deal with Philo's thought. (DTR)

8521. D. FLUSSER and S. SAFRAI [ספראי ש. – פלוסר .ד], נדב ואביהוא במדרש ובדברי פילון ['Nadab and Abihu in the Midrash and in Philo's writings'], *Milet* 2 (Tel Aviv 1985) 79-84.

The authors examine Philo's treatment of the death of the sons of Aaron (Lev 10:1-3), particularly at *Somn.* 2.67. The positive portrayal of the 'sacrifice' of Nadab and Abihu is shown to bear a significant relationship to a number of (unduly ignored) traditions in Rabbinic literature. English summary. See also **8654**. (DS)

8522. S. FOCARDI, 'Anthropos ed eros nell'ideologia religiosa tardo-antica', *SMSR* 51 (1985) 43-71, esp. 61-66.

The double creation of man set out in *Opif.* is used by the author to interpret the theme of sexuality in Philo. It would seem that Philo took a moderately negative view of the sexual act – the result of a balance between two elements, one biblical, the other Platonic –, the necessity of procreation and the fall from reason involved in carnal union. Focardi draws these conclusions after a concise analysis of the allegory in *Opif.* and in particular of the figures of Adam and Eve. (RR)

8523. J. FOSSUM, 'Gen.1, 26 and 2, 7 in Judaism, Samaritanism, and Gnosticism', *JSJ* 16 (1985) 202-239, esp. 203-208.

In order to recover the original form of the Haggadah on Gen. 1:26, it is necessary to compare the Rabbinic evidence with traditions preserved in Philo, Gnostic and Samaritan texts. Philo's discussions of the creation of man indicate a widespread scriptural tradition of intermediate figures. If these texts are stripped of their Platonizing associations and transferred to a less sophisticated setting, it is clear that the tradition behind them maintained that angels were the creators of the material body. (DTR)

8524. J. FOSSUM, *The name of God and the angel of the Lord: Samaritan and Jewish concepts of intermediation and the origin of Gnosticism,* WUNT 36 (Tübingen 1985), esp. 197-204.

A similar discussion to the preceding entry. Further evidence from Philo on the heavenly man as Adam (286f.) and the doctrine of the Powers (335f.) is invoked to support the thesis that the origins of Gnosticism are to be sought in Samaritan and Jewish religion. (DTR)

8525. E. HILGERT, 'The dual image of Joseph in Hebrew and early Jewish literature', *BR* 30 (1985) 5-21, esp. 7-13.

In order to understand Philo's double, ambiguous and often contradictory presentation of Joseph it is not enough to look at the Old Testament background and Philo's contemporary position in Egypt (Goodenough). It is also necessary to take into account the development of traditions in Alexandrian allegorical exegesis. But Philo does not stand alone in his picture of Joseph, for a similar duality is found in a wide range of Hebrew and Jewish writings from the 8th century B.C. to the 2nd century A.D. (DTR)

8526. J. G. KAHN [ישר-כהן .י], הלימודים הכלליים במשנתו של פילון האלכסנדרוני ['Philo on secular education'], *Tarbiz* 54 (1985) 306-314.

A review of A. Mendelson, *Secular education in Philo of Alexandria* (**8235**), stressing Philo's attitude towards secular education as a first step towards wisdom. The example of Moses is adduced. English summary. (MM)

8527. A. KASHER, *The Jews in Hellenistic and Roman Egypt: the struggle for equal rights,* TSAJ 7 (Tübingen 1985), 233-261 and *passim.*

This important study is a translation of a monograph originally published in Hebrew (cf. above **7824**, and previously **7521**), which in turn was based on a Tel Aviv doctoral dissertation (1972). The author takes a stand on the problem of the civic status of Alexandrian Jews in strong opposition to the views of Tcherikover (cf. esp. **5723**), whom he regards as having projected the emancipatory struggle of 18th and 19th century Jews back to a completely different situation. In chapter VII the Philonic evidence is discussed, based mainly on *Flacc.* and *Leg.,* but with corroboratory material drawn from *Spec.* and even some allegorical treatises. From Philo's writings it can be inferred that the Jews were called Ἀλεξανδρεῖς without any implications of citizenship in the polis.

In fact when they are described as πολῖται, this must be taken to mean that they have their own independent πολιτεία, i.e. they constituted a πολίτευμα, with the right to practice their own customs and to participate in the general civic rights of all those classified as πολῖται. This situation was radically altered by Flaccus' edict which abolished the Jewish πολιτεία. Other subjects dealt with are Jewish neighbourhoods, leadership and decision-making in the Jewish community, Jewish educational institutions (Kasher thinks that these may have been organized separately from Greek institutions), and the aims and demands of the embassy to Rome headed by Philo ('it is inconceivable, even ridiculous, to think that Philo and his delegation aspired to attain citizenship in the Greek polis...' (261)). In an appendix at 358-361 Philo's use of the term πολιτεία is analysed. (DTR)

8528. J. R. LEVISON, *'Adam' in major authors of Early Judaism* (diss. Duke University 1985), esp. chap. 4.

Philo is one of the seven early Jewish sources examined in relation to the treatment of the figure of Adam (others Sirach, Wisdom of Solomon, Jubilees, Josephus, 4 Ezra, 2 Baruch). A comparative analysis focusses on the exegeses of Gen. 1:26-28 and 2:7, Adam's original nature, the nature and the effects of his transgression. The author concludes that the common thread between the documents is the common texts, for there are virtually no correspondences in interpretation between the various traditions. (DTR; based on *DA* 47-558A)

8529. L. A. LEWIS, *'As a beloved brother': the function of family language in the letters of Paul* (diss. Yale University 1985).

As background to an examination of Paul's family language, made with reference to the study of kinship in anthropological theory, the writings of Philo, Josephus and Qumran are analyzed in order to show how 'pseudo-family language' was understood by more or less restrictive groups within Judaism. (DTR; based on *DA* 46-3379A)

8530. J. MANSFELD, 'Heraclitus, Empedocles, and others in a Middle Platonist cento in Philo of Alexandria', *VChr* 39 (1985) 131-156.

The starting-point is a detailed analysis of *QG* 1.69-76 (exegesis Gen. 4:8-15), in which the author permits himself to follow Philo's chains of interrelated scriptural passages wherever they lead. In §70-71 he identifies a cento of motifs from Plato, Heraclitus and Empedocles, focussing on the death of the soul and its entombment in the body as experienced by Cain. This cento derives from Middle Platonist contemporaries, and is also found in Plutarch, Clement, Plotinus and Hierocles. Similar exegetical themes are also adduced when the same biblical texts are used in treatises of the Allegorical Commentary. Especially the passage *Fug.* 53-64 is 'beautifully constructed' (144). The comparison between Cain and the first sinner, Adam, is also strengthened by allegorical references to earthly Hades and motifs from Empedocles' *Katharmoi*. The article concludes with a brief discussion of the Philonic theme of the punishment of the wicked by means of the elements, in which two doctrines of different origin – the one Stoic-Platonic-cosmological, the other Middle Platonist-Empedoclean-psychological – conjoin. Philo the eclectic exegete is happy to conclude that his various philosophical sources agree with one another. (DTR)

8531. A. M. MAZZANTI, 'Motivazioni protologiche nell' antropologia di Filone di Alessandria, con riferimento al tema della distinzione dei sessi', in *La tradizione dell'enkrateia* (cf. **8506**) 541-559.

In Philo the concepts of 'male' and 'female' function as hermeneutical categories and thus carry a complex of valid meanings on various levels. Mazzanti deals with the ethical and psychological levels, concentrating particularly on the anthropological aspect and the problem of Philo's attitude toward sexuality. This problem ultimately leads to the theme of spiritual asceticism and the related concepts of 'sterility', 'fertility', 'virginity', 'unity'. In general it would seem that the basis of Philo's anthropology is ontological, but that, in addition to an ontological interpretation of anthropology, he also achieved an anthropological interpretation of ontology. (RR)

8532. D. MEALAND, 'The paradox of Philo's views on wealth', *JSNT* 24 (1985) 111-115.

A response to an attack on the author's article (cf. **7833**) by T. E. Schmidt (**8365**). Two points of difference are stressed. (1) The discrepancy between Philo's wealth and Philo's views on wealth is not an apparent puzzle but a real paradox. (2) Philo cannot be simply seen as an aristocrat writing from an aristocrat's point of view; he identifies with the Jewish people of Alexandria when under attack. (DTR)

8533. V. NIKIPROWETZKY, 'Brève note sur le Commentaire Allegorique et l'Exposition de la Loi chez Philon d'Alexandrie', in A. CAQUOT, S. LÉGASSE, M. TARDIEU (edd.), *Mélanges bibliques et orientaux en l'honneur de M. Mathias Delcor*, Alter Orient und Altes Testament (Neukirchen-Vluyn 1985) 321-329.

According to the author in this post-humously published article, there are no valid grounds for distinguishing between and contrasting the works of the Allegorical Commentary and those of the Exposition of the Law within the Philonic corpus. Nikiprowetzky examines some of the differences assumed by certain scholars (e.g. the superiority of the Commentary over the Exposition) and shows that they are unfounded. In assessing Philo's works, he observes, attention should focus on the fundamental distinction between the 'concrete' and the 'abstract', i.e. between ἄνθρωπος and τρόπος ψυχῆς as drawn by Philo in *Ebr.* 144. (RR)

8534. V. NIKIPROWETZKY, 'Texte et discours dans l'interprétation de Philon d'Alexandrie', *Sil* 11 [*Studi in onore di A. Barigazzi*] (1985) 2.105-128.

Certain passages from above all *Migr.*, *Leg.* and *Her.* are problematical from a philosophical point of view since they are in contradiction with other texts. These passages are used by the author to introduce a methodological exposition of great importance. Nikiprowetzky draws a distinction between 'texte' and 'discours': discourse is *what Philo aspires to*, while the text is purely instrumental. Hence it is impossible to reconstruct Philo's thought on a given question on the basis of the text alone: one must keep in mind 'the discourse', or the real subject. In this connection, Nikiprowetzky considers the function of secondary (i.e. scholarly) literature, which is indispensable on the one hand, since it continually opens new avenues to the heart of Philo's thought, but is extremely dangerous on the other, because through its considerable extension and variety it risks 'confusing ideas'. The approach necessary in Philo's case, therefore, is erudite as well as critical, direct as well as indirect. (RR)

8535. *Reallexikon für Antike und Christentum*, edited by E. DASS-MANN *et al.*, Supplement-Lieferung 1-3 (Stuttgart 1985).

From now onwards the *Reallexikon* intends to publish Supplementary articles on a regular basis. These will supplement, but not replace existing articles. Relevant to Philo in the first 3 issues are: K. HOHEISEL, art. 'Aegypten II (literaturgeschichtlich)', 12-88, esp. 62-63 (Egypt in literary perspective); H. GÖRGEMANNS, art. 'Anfang', 401-447, esp. 413-4 (beginning). (DTR)

8536. D. T. RUNIA, 'Philo van Alexandrië en het begin van de christelijke exegese', in C. DATEMA *et al.* (edd.), *Kerkvaders: teksten met toelichting uit de vroege kerk* (Bruges-The Hague 1985) 201-227.

As background to the study of the beginnings of Christian exegesis an introductory account is presented of Philo's life, writings and thought, with special emphasis on his use of the allegorical method of scriptural interpretation. There follows a Dutch translation of *Abr.* 60-88, *Migr.* 1-4 and *QG* 3.1, preceded by some remarks on the philosophical themes used by Philo to expound the biblical account of Abraham's double migration. (DTR)

8537. G. SFAMENI GASPARRO, 'Le motivazioni protologiche dell' enkrateia nel Cristianesimo dei primi secoli e nello gnosticismo', in *La tradizione dell'enkrateia* (cf. **8506**) 149-237, esp. 231-237.

The tradition of *enkrateia* typical of early Christianity has antecedents in Philo. In particular one finds in Philo an allegorical structure which links the theme of *enkrateia* to that of 'Adamite protology'. Thus it is necessary to interpret correctly the figure of 'man created in the image' presented in *Opif.* 134, i.e. not as an androgynous figure, but as a figure transcending the categories of 'male' and 'female'. (RR)

8538. M. SIMON, 'L'ascétisme dans les sectes juives', in *La tradizione dell'enkrateia* (cf. **8506**) 393-426.

If it is true that asceticism is not an essential element of Jewish religiosity, which holds a basically optimistic view on the value of life in the body and in the world, it is also true that Essenian thought expresses an entirely different attitude and thus reveals a strong element of tension. In order to illustrate this view, Simon frequently refers to Philonic texts (esp. *Contempl.*), as he considers Philo not only a true representative of Judaism but also a prime source for our knowledge of Essenian thought and practice. (RR)

8539. M. SIMONETTI, *Lettera e/o allegoria: un contributo alla storia dell'esegesi patristica*, StEAug 23 (Rome 1985), esp. 16-19, 24f.

Discusses the general characteristics of Philonic allegory, in particular the relation between the literal and the allegorical sense of the biblical text. Although Philo habitually acknowledges a significance on both levels, he in fact tends to devalue the first in favour of the second (18). (RR)

8540. H. TARRANT, *Scepticism or Platonism?: the philosophy of the Fourth Academy*, Cambridge Classical Studies (Cambridge 1985).

As part of a provocative analysis of epistemological developments in the first centuries B.C. and A.D. Tarrant examines Philo's use of the terms σκέψις and σκεπτικός (23ff.) and discusses the doctrine of the ideas as thoughts of God (116ff.). (DTR)

8541. A. TERIAN, 'Some stock arguments for the magnanimity of the Law in Hellenstic Jewish apologetics, in B. S. JACKSON (ed.), *Jewish Law Association Studies* I (Chico, California 1985) 141-149.

In attempting to demonstrate the excellence of the Law Jewish apologists paid particular attention to the dietary laws, which *inter alia* illustrated the Law's magnanimity. The author discusses in this connection a curious Halachah in *Hypoth.* 7.9, which is related to Deut. 22:6 and Lev. 11:15 (a similar passage is found in Josephus). The dietary laws thus gain an ethical and even an anthropocentric dimension. (DTR)

8542. M. D. VAN VELDHUIZEN, 'Moses: a model of Hellenistic philanthropia', *RefR* 1985 (38) 215-224.

Although the word φιλανθρωπία is not common in the Septuagint, Philo bases his interpretation of the concept, which was familiar to philosophers and often connected to the ideology of Hellenistic kingship, on his interpretation of Scripture. It thus becomes a virtue (though not found in traditional lists of virtues found in Greek philosophy), and serves as an expression of God's grace through Moses and the Law. The article explores how Moses, as living law, suppliant, righteous sage and prophetic legislator, functions as an archetype of *philanthropia* in Philo's thought. (DTR)

8543. C. J. DE VOGEL, 'Platonism and Christianity: a mere antagonism or a profound common ground?', *VChr* 39 (1985) 1-61, esp. 7-18.

A final look by this distinguished Dutch historian of ancient philosophy at the relation between the heritage of Platonism and Christianity leads to a brief examination of Philo's doctrines of God, the Logos and creation. Special emphasis is placed on the role of the images of εἰκών and τύπος. This imagery is later taken over by Athanasius, but is understood quite differently. Although such language is not far removed from Plato's intentions in the *Timaeus* and other dialogues, Philo was probably influenced in his use of τύπος imagery by the notion of καταληπτικὴ φαντασία developed by the founder of the Stoa, Zeno. (DTR)

8544. A. DE VOGÜÉ, 'Échos de Philon dans la Vie de Saint Sulpice de Bourges et dans la Règle d'Abélard pour le Paraclet', *AB* 103 (1985) 359-365.

The *Life of St Sulpice of Bourges* offers a vivid image of the faithful gathering around the saint and listening to his teaching. This description is not taken from life, but has a literary origin, being based on a passage from Eusebius' *Ecclesiastical history*, which in turn goes back to Philo's *De vita contemplativa*. The monks of St Sulpice thus share features with Philo's Therapeutae. Similar points of contact are found in Abélard's eighth letter to Héloïse. All this demonstrates the wide occurrence of Philonic themes in the Middle Ages. (RR)

8545. R. A. WILD, '"Be imitators of God": discipleship in the Letter to the Ephesians', in F. F. SEGOVIA (ed.), *Discipleship in the New Testament* (Philadelphia 1985), 127-143, esp. 128-132.

Comparison with Philo's use of the themes of ὁμοιώσις θεῷ and μίμησις θεοῦ shows that 'in its formulation of the goal or end of Christian discipleship [especially the injunction at 5:1] the Letter of Ephesians stands in a clear Platonic tradition mediated through Hellenistic Judaism' (138). (DTR)

8546. M. A. WILLIAMS, *The immovable race*, NHS 29 (Leiden 1985), esp. 14-27, 43f. and *passim.*

What Philo has to say on the subject of two types of persons, the stable and the unstable, 'is probably one of the most illuminating pieces of evidence we now have for reconstructing the possible roots of the gnostic immovable race designation' (14). Discussing the terms 'unshakeable' (ἀσάλευτος) and 'standing' (ἑστάναι), the author exploits Philo's use of the theme of stability with reference both to God and, more importantly, to the sage Moses who receives the Law as an image of the heavenly immutable and paradigmatic ideas. Philo also supplies evidence on the race of Seth as a spiritual type, but this material is insufficient on its own to demonstrate a Sethian Gnostic origin for the theme of the 'immovable race' (204f.). (DTR)

8547. J. C. M. VAN WINDEN, '"Idee' en 'materie' in de vroeg-christelijke uitleg van de beginwoorden van Genesis: een hoofdstuk uit de ontmoeting tussen Griekse filosofie en christelijk denken', *Mededelingen der koninklijke Nederlandse akademie van wetenschappen,* afdeling Letterkunde 48 (1985) 1-27, esp. 7-10.

A brief summary of how Philo reads an ideal world into Gen. 1:1-5, concluding with some remarks on how we should interpret the relation between God and his Logos. (DTR)

8548. D. WINSTON, *Logos and mystical theology in Philo of Alexandria* (Cincinatti 1985).

This volume contains the Efroymson Memorial lectures delivered at Hebrew Union College, Cincinatti, in 1984, the three chapters each corresponding to a single lecture. In the first Winston gives a general portrait. Philo is passionately loyal to Judaism, but the deepest roots of his soul draw their nourishment from philosophy, and especially Platonism. This emerges more concretely in an analysis of the doctrine of the Logos. In the second lecture man's place in the cosmos and in the hierarchy of living beings is discussed, with reference to such problems as the reason for the soul's descent and the fate of souls who do not attain perfection and soar up to God. In the third lecture the themes of 'logology' and anthropology converge in an account of Philo's mystical theology. An account of the doctrine of creation emphasizes that Philo's thought, constrained by biblical monotheism, must be read in terms of a mystical monism that anticipates Plotinus. On this foundation Philo builds a mystical view of the nature of reality, which may correspond to a genuine inner experience. The study concludes with some remarks on Philo's relations to the nationalistic and messianic aspects of Judaism. Here tensions in his thought emerge: 'we may thus conclude that when Philo is justly described as "a man between two worlds", that metaphor needs to be understood in a double sense, for not only does he join Athens with Jerusalem, but also the supernal, celestial Jerusalem with its lower, terrestrial image' (58). REVIEWS: A. H. Armstrong, *JThS* 38 (1987) 293; D. T. Runia, *VChr* 41 (1987) 93f. (DTR)

1986

8601. Manuel ALEXANDRE, 'A elaboraçâo de uma Chreia no código hermenêutico de Fílon de Alexandria', *Euph* 15 (1986) 77-87.

The logical structure of *Mut.* 252-263 is rhetorical and related to a didactic genre, the elaboration of a *chreia*. The author shows how this passage specifically applies the rhetorical canons of the rhetorician Theon of Alexandria. (RR)

8602. Manuel ALEXANDRE, 'Rhetorical argumentation as an exegetical technique in Philo of Alexandria', in *Hellenica et Judaica* (cf. **8608**) 13-27.

The author has no difficulty in showing the importance of rhetoric in Philo's work, a conviction which he bases on the authority of numerous scholars. He goes on to stress three specific characteristics of Philo's rhetoric: its exegetical function (21f.), its strict relation to ethics and truth (23f.), and its profound connection with philosophy (25f.). (RR)

8603. Monique ALEXANDRE, 'L'épée de flamme (Gen. 3,24): textes chrétiens et traditions juives', in *Hellenica et Judaica* (cf. **8608**) 403-441, esp. 410-422.

Philo, particularly in the treatise *De Cherubim*, stands at the origin of a vast exegetical tradition which evolved in the Christian world (the author refers in particular to Didymus, Augustine, Origen, Gregory of Nyssa, Tertullian, and Thomas Aquinas) on the basis of the biblical report of the Cherubim and the flaming sword. (RR)

8604. Y. AMIR [עמיר .י], .עשרת הדברות פל פי פילון מאלכסנדריה ['The Ten Commandments according to Philo from Alexandria.'], in B. Z. SEGAL (ed.), עשרת הדברות בראי הדורות [*The Ten Commandments*] (Jerusalem 1986) 95-125.

Originally published in German; see **8307**.

8605. Y. AMIR [עמיר .י], דרשנות חז"ל ואלגוריה פילונית ['Rabbinical Midrash and Philonic allegory.'] *Daat* 18 (1986) 5-14.

Originally published in German; see **8305**.

8606. R. VAN DEN BROEK, 'Jewish and Platonic speculations in early Alexandrian theology: Eugnostus, Philo, Valentinus, and Origen', in B. A. PEARSON and J. E. GOEHRING (edd.), *The roots of Egyptian Christianity*,

Studies in Antiquity and Christianity (Philadelphia 1986) 190-203.

The Nag Hammadi library can tell us much about Hellenistic Judaism in Alexandria before the advent of Christianity. The Gnostic writing *Eugnostus the Blessed* 'demonstrates the existence of a Jewish tradition according to which the heavenly Adam reveals God in his creative and royal powers as God and Lord. And this shows that Philo, in attributing this function to the Logos, was not original, but simply Hellenizing a Jewish myth, which, though in itself not gnostic at all, could easily be interpreted in a gnostic sense' (195). (DTR)

8607. M. CANEVET, 'Remarques sur l'utilisation du genre littéraire historique par Philon d'Alexandrie dans la *Vita Moysis*, ou Moïse général en chef-prophète', *RSR* 60 (1986) 189-206.

The *De vita Moysis* is idiosyncratic in not being an exegetical work, but 'an apologetic and moral biography' (189). The representation of Moses in this treatise is therefore particularly significant, differing from the others, which are mainly allegorical. Although Philo might seem to present Moses as a leader and general of the Greek and pagan type, essentially he is conceived as a prophet. And by prophet is not meant a 'sham wizard' (206), but the political as well as religious leader of a people. The greatness of Moses consists in his having assisted the divine will which fulfils itself in history. (RR)

8608. A. CAQUOT, M. HADAS-LEBEL, J. RIAUD (edd.), *Hellenica et Judaica: hommage à Valentin Nikiprowetzky* ל"ז (Leuven-Paris 1986).

A memorial volume in honour of the distinguished scholar of Hellenistic Judaism and Philonic thought, who died in 1983. The first part consists entirely of contributions dealing with Philo, while some articles in other sections are also relevant. These will be listed under their authors' names. The book also contains two memorial notices by A. CAQUOT and M. HADAS-LEBEL, and a complete bibliography of Nikiprowetzky's scholarly oeuvre compiled by J. RIAUD. (DTR)

8609. J. H. CHARLESWORTH, 'Greek, Persian, Roman, Syrian and Egyptian influences in early Jewish theology: a study of the history of the Rechabites', in *Hellenica et Judaica* (cf. **8608**) 219-243, esp. 238 f.

Underlines a few points of contact between *The history of the blessed sons of the Rechabites* and the passages in *Contempl.* dealing with the Therapeutae. An indirect relation between the two works is hypothesized. (RR)

8610. N. G. COHEN, 'Philo's Tefillin', in *Proceedings of the Ninth world congress of Jewish studies*, Division A (Jerusalem 1986) 199-206.

A discussion of problems arising from Philo's mention of the Tefillin in the paraphrase of Deut. 6:6-8 at *Spec.* 4.137. It would appear that Philo knew of these from experience, and not just on the basis of literary knowledge, and that he did not regard them as 'charms' or 'amulets' (cf. Matt. 23:5). His conception of the function of the Tefillin differs from that of the Rabbinic Halachah, but 'in spirit he is one with traditional Judaism as we know it' (204). (DTR)

8611. M. G. CREPALDI, 'Tempo ed esperienza religiosa in Filone di

Alessandria', in *Tempo ed esperienza religiosa*, StudFilGal 9 (Padua 1986) 91-103.

An article summarizing the contents of Crepaldi's previously published study (**8517**), *La concezione del tempo fra pensiero biblico e filosofia greca* (Padua 1985). (RR)

8612. P. S. DAVIES, 'The meaning of Philo's text about the gilded shields', *JThS* 37 (1986) 109-114.

Some lexical notes on the precise meaning of *Legat*. 299 lead the author to an interpretation closer to that of Lémonon (**8112**) than that of Fuks (**8217**). The cause of offence was the actual dedication of the shields, not the inscription on them. (DTR)

8613. J. DILLON, 'Female principles in Platonism', *Itaca: Quaderns Catalans de Cultura Clàssica* 1 (1986) 107-123, esp. 117f.

Although Philo's monotheism should leave no place for an independent female principle in the universe, both the influence of Platonism and the already established Wisdom tradition in Hellenistic Judaism combine to carve out a place in his system for such a principle, i.e. Sophia. (DTR)

8614. E. S. FRERICHS and J. NEUSNER (edd.), *Goodenough on the history of religion and on Judaism*, BJudSt 121 (Atlanta 1986).

The brief introduction discusses Goodenough's career and in particular the scholarly evaluation of his great work *Jewish symbols in the Greco-Roman period* (cf. **5309**). The remainder of the work reprints nine articles, three of which specifically deal with Philo (our **3705**, **4808**, and the article entitled 'Philo's Exposition of the Law and his *De vita Mosis*', *HThR* 27 (1933) 109-125). (DTR)

8615. D. GEORGI, *The opponents of Paul in Second Corinthians* (Philadelphia-Edinburgh 1986), 358ff, 390, 422ff.

See above **6407**.

8616. R. GOETSCHEL, 'Philon et le Judaïsme hellénistique au miroir de Nachman Krochmal', in *Hellenica et Judaica* (cf. **8608**) 371-383.

Presents the interpretation of Philo's work given by Nachman Krochmal, a 19th century Jewish scholar. This interpretation is considered important because it gives us an example of Philo's reception in the Jewish world. The author stresses the fact that Krochmal strictly associated Philo's thought with Judaism (383). (RR)

8617. R. M. GRANT, *Gods and the one God: Christian theology in the Graeco-Roman world* (London 1986), esp. 84-92.

The Christian doctrines of God's creatorship and immutability have their roots in Philo and in early Middle Platonist authors whom Philo may have read. (DTR)

8618. R. M. GRANT, 'Theological education at Alexandria', in *The* *roots of Egyptian Christianity* (cf. **8606**) 178-189.

Less is actually known about the procedures in higher education at Alexandria than many modern scholars suggest. The best precedent for the Christian schools appears to lie not in Philo but among the Therapeutae which he describes in *Contempl.* (DTR)

8619. I. GRUENWALD [גרינולד .א], התורה ליוונית תרגום בעניין הפולמוס ['Polemical attitudes toward the Septuagint'], *Te'uda* 4 (Tel Aviv 1986) 65-78.

Discussion of Aristeas, Philo, and Josephus as background for the polemical attitudes of the Sages towards the Septuagint. All three are themselves seen as reacting to polemic against the Septuagint. The section on Philo (67-69) rests mainly on *Mos.* 2.12-52. English summary. (MM)

8620. M. HARL, *La Bible d'Alexandrie. La Genèse: traduction du texte grec de la Septante, introduction et notes* (Paris 1986) *passim.*

This is the first volume of an ambitious series which aims to present an annotated translation of the entire Septuagint. It is of particular value for Philonic studies because in its annotations on the lemmata of Genesis it makes copious reference to the interpretations found in Philo's writings, which then can be compared with developments in the Patristic period. But also the long introduction (29-82) makes valuable observations on the Greek Genesis as a literary, historical and theological work. (DTR)

8621. E. HILGERT, 'A survey of previous scholarship on Philo's *De Josepho*', *SBLSPS* 25 (1986) 262-270.

After some preliminary remarks on editions, translations and studies of the *De Josepho*, the author concentrates on the main issue facing scholars in the interpretation of this work, namely the tensions that exist between the portrait of Joseph here and that presented in the Allegorical Commentary. The trend of recent scholarship is to regard these tensions as less irreconcilable than hitherto thought. (DTR)

8622. L. HOGAN, *Healing in the Second Temple period* (diss. Hebrew University, Jerusalem 1986) 170-215.

Philo's use of the language and imagery of 'healing' is examined from a number of different viewpoints. Topics discussed by Hogan include the relationship between physical and spiritual health (174ff.), God as the source of health (177ff.), and the Therapeutae (185ff.). A lengthy excursus (192-208) investigates 'Philo's medical background.' The author elaborates Bréhier's conviction that Philo must have had a personal acquaintance with the Hippocratic corpus, yet demonstrates that there are also idiosyncratic elements which closely resemble specific aspects of Rabbinic medical knowledge. Nevertheless he concludes that for Philo 'the subject of healing is primarily concerned with spiritual healing, or healing of the soul' (209). (DS)

8623. W. HORBURY, 'Ezechiel tragicus 106: δωρήματα', *VT* 36 (1986) 37-51, esp. 42-45.

In order to explain the mention of God's gifts to the Patriarchs in line 106 of Ezechiel's tragedy the author invokes Philo's equation of gifts with covenant, which leads to a discussion of what διαθήκη means in Philo and Hellenistic Judaism. (DTR)

8624. K. W. HUGGHINS, *An investigation of the Jewish theology of sexuality influencing the references to homosexuality in Romans 1:18-32* (diss. South Western Baptist Theological Seminary 1986).

In order to explicate the background to Paul's reference to homosexuality in Rom. 1:18-32 the writings of Philo are interrogated on the following points: (a) what was prohibited sexually? (b) what was permitted sexually? (c) what were the roles of the sexes? (DTR; based on *DA* 47-4114A)

8624a. J.-G. KAHN [ישר-כהן .י], במשנתו של פילון (טבע) "פיסיס" המושג על האלכסנדרוני ['The concept of "Physis" in the philosophy of Philo'], in *Proceedings of the Ninth World Congress of Jewish Studies* (Jerusalem 1986) Division A, 139-143 [Hebrew section].

One may define φύσις either as the world and the phenomena within it or as the inner meaning of the individual phenomena. The Sages normally employed the first of these definitions whereas Philo uses both. Philo did not have a negative attitude towards *physis*, but seems to have returned to a Presocratic level of the concept. English summary. (MM)

8625. J. KAMPEN, 'A reconsideration of the name "Essene" in Greco-Jewish literature in light of recent perceptions of the Qumran sect', *HUCA* 57 (1986) 61-81.

The dominant view in recent literature that the name 'Essene' used by Philo is derived from a Semitic root is rejected. Instead the author advocates a look at the use of the term in Greek literature and inscriptions. It is chiefly used to designate certain important functionaries in the cult of Artemis at Ephesus. The description of these officials in Pausanias shows not only great differences, but also certain similarities with the descriptions of the Essenes in Philo and Josephus. The hypothesis can be developed that both writers may have been dependent on a prominent Greek observer of Jewish life in Palestine, Nicolaus of Damascus, who could have applied to the Jewish sectaries a term that he knew from the famous Ephesian cult. (DTR)

8626. A. KASHER [כשר .א], לנזירת ישראל בארץ ההלניסטיות הערים של זיקתן קאליגולה נאיוס של הצלם ['The connection between Hellenistic cities in Eretz-Israel and Gaius Caligula's receipt to install an idol in the Temple'], *Zion* 51 (1986) 135-151.

This study of Gaius' attempt to introduce an image in the Temple focusses on the roles of the Gentile population of Jabneh (Philo, *Legat.* 200-202) and of Gaius' advisor Apelles of Ashkelon (*ibid.* 203-205). Evidence from Josephus on Gentile-Jewish hostilities in first-century Judaea supports the idea that these played an important role in manipulating the emperor into his decree. (DRS)

8627. H.-J. KLAUCK, 'Die heilige Stadt: Jerusalem bei Philo und Lukas',

Kairos 28 (1986) 129-151.

Philo's writings (esp. *Prov.* 2, *Spec.* 1, *Legat.*) contain useful elements for gaining a historically founded insight into the worship of the temple and its relation to the Jewish Diaspora. The author discusses somes of these elements in detail (visits, pilgrimages, administration of the temple, and the dramatic events connected with the pogrom of 38 A.D.), stressing above all the temple's uniqueness, which clearly has a theological foundation (i.e. 'one God, one temple'). This uniqueness entails, as Klauck observes, that the spiritualization of the temple, in which this entire theme is usually summed up, cannot constitute Philo's sole or final word on the subject. Some discussion (136ff.) is also devoted to the relations with Apocalyptic literature and with eschatology in general. Philo's tendency to conceive an ideal Jerusalem makes the relationship between history and eschatology problematic and marks him off from Apocalyptic thinkers. The final part of the article (esp. 147) compares the same themes in the Gospel of Luke. (RR)

8628. B. KOOLE, *Man en vrouw zijn één: de androgynie in het Christendom in het bijzonder bij Jacob Boehme* (diss. Utrecht 1986), esp. ch. 5 'De androgynie bij Philo en haar kontekst' (139-170).

On the basis of an analysis of the texts on the creation of man (Gen. 1:26, 2:7) in *Opif.* and *Leg.* 2.13 the author concludes that Philo's source material contained the concept of androgyny. Philo applies the concept only to his interpretation of Gen. 2:7; because he rejects any connection between God and sexuality, the other biblical text is interpreted in an asexual manner. Philo does in fact frequently use sexual metaphors for the relation to God, but this is due to the fact that such language was prevalent in his intellectual milieu and, moreover, Philo only uses it in an allegorical sense. Philo opposes, without explicitly saying so, the positive evaluation of sexuality found at this time in the Gnosticizing concept of the androgyne *Anthropos*. (RAB/DTR)

8629. R. LAMBERTON, *Homer the theologian: Neoplatonist allegorical reading and the growth of the epic tradition*, The transformation of the classical heritage 9 (Berkeley, 1986), esp. 44-54.

Philo's importance for this study lies in the fact that he has absorbed currents of Middle Platonist allegorical interpretation of Homer and thus furnishes otherwise unattested material. His allegorical method is primarily indebted to Stoic exegesis, yet in his writings an increased concern is shown for locating texts that can be interpreted in terms of the fate of the soul, a concern central to later Neoplatonist exegesis. An analysis is given of all the Philonic passages which give evidence of allegorical interpretation of the Homeric poems; the most important of these is *Prov.* 2.40-41. (DTR)

8630. J. LAPORTE, 'The ages of life in Philo of Alexandria', *SBLSPS* 25 (1986) 278-290.

A dozen passages in Philo dwell on the theme of the ages of life. An analysis is given of the Greek philosophical sources on which Philo drew and the way he adapts the theme to his own purposes. The ages of man are not reduced to a single typology, for Philo posits a number of different types of men. Philo's views on the first stages of the development of man – similar to that found in Origen – differ from the doctrine of original sin as later formulated by Augustine. (DTR)

8631. J. LAPORTE, 'Philonic models of eucharistia in the eucharist of Origen', *LThPh* 42 (1986) 71-91.

The article undertakes to examine Origen's doctrine of the Eucharist in relation to the Philonic notion of εὐχαριστία, using as tools of investigation the chief biblical themes (laws, ritual, events, characters) through which Philo develops his thought on the subject. The fact that these themes and images reappear in Origen points to the conceptual identity existing between the two theologians. But the differences between them clearly show how Origen, because he refers to the incarnated Christ, deeply transforms the Philonic themes in the light of the Last Supper, of the Gospel of John, of Paul, and of the Epistle to the Hebrews. The biblical themes successively dealt with are: (a) the first-fruits and sacrifices as images of thanksgiving; (b) the word of God as bread of life; (c) the Pascha; (d) the high priest as mediator of prayer and (e) of propitiation. Laporte concludes by noting that both Philo and Origen, because of their emphasis on the contemplation and the elevation of the mind, have difficulty in accommodating the role of the 'simple' among the believers. (DTR)

8632. J. LAPORTE, 'Forgiveness of sins in Origen', *Worship* 60 (1986) 520-527.

Origen's teaching on forgiveness is interpreted in the light of Philo. The Philonic models which Origen develops in his theology of forgiveness are: (a) the sacrifice for sin, particularly in the ritual of Yom Kippur; (b) the confession of sin; (c) the word of God as a source of divine energy; (d) asceticism, or the struggle against the passions; (e) divine punishment; (f) intercession, and the care of the community for sinners; (g) public penance. (DTR)

8633. C. LÉVY, 'Le "scepticisme" de Philon d'Alexandrie: une influence de la Nouvelle Académie?', in *Hellenica et Judaica* (cf. **8608**) 29-41.

Having recognized the importance of the sceptical element in Philo's work (24), the author considers whether the language in which it is expressed goes back to the New Academy (30). After a careful analysis of the technical terms used by Philo (ἐποχή, εὔλογον, πιθανόν), Lévy concludes that he is not directly indebted to Academic scepticism, but takes over from it a 'conceptual material' which remains recognizable in spite of the modifications imposed by a 'religious reading of philosophy' (41). (RR)

8634. S. P. LOGAN, *The background of παιδεία in Hebrews* (diss. Southern Baptist Theological Seminary 1986), esp. ch.3.

The concept of παιδεία in the Jewish literature, including Philo, is examined as part of the attempt to discover the religious and cultural background against which παιδεία in Hebrews is best understood. (DTR; based on *DA* 47-3084A)

8635. M. MACH [מ. מאך], היהודית (אנגלולוגיה) המלאכים בתורת מחקרים רומית.-ההלניסטית בתקופה [*Studies in Jewish angelology in the Hellenistic-Roman Period*] (diss. Tel Aviv University 1986) 198-283.

Within the framework of the Judaism of the Second Temple period Philo's angelology is remarkable, for though it shares the common trend of linking Jewish angels with Greek traditions about demons, it does not share the development towards the new angel-figure common in Jewish theology. Philo's angels are identified with the Stoic logoi, although a certain Middle Platonist influence is felt as well. Attention is paid to the differentiation between angels and 'divine powers': Philo does not introduce angels into his exegesis unless they are mentioned in the biblical text, though he does introduce divine powers where none are mentioned at all. Likewise, he uses angels mainly for the purpose of divine messages, whereas divine powers are also used for punishing and 'theodicy'. It is also to be noted that Philo makes no distinction between the two when it comes to the question of visibility. English summary. (MM)

8636. J. P. MARTÍN, *Filón de Alejandría y la génesis de la cultura occidental* (Buenos Aires 1986).

The declared aim of this work is to search for the unity of Philo's thought and to compare it with the development of Western thought with a view to determining its value from a historical-philosophical point of view. This ambitious objective makes it necessary for the author to give broad – though for the most part accurate – summaries of Philo's thought, focussing mainly on anthropological themes. Self-knowledge in particular constitutes Philo's fundamental theme: through it man knows himself and at the same time recognizes above himself and as cause of himself the transcendent God. But although absolutely pre-eminent in Philo, this motif is expressed by a series of apparent contradictions (cf. ch.1) which are resolved only in the fundamental relationship between man and God (ch.3). Nevertheless, Martín observes, a purely theoretical and historical-philosophical assessment of Philo's thought fails to bring out all its richness and peculiarity, which above all consists in the allegorical method as synthesis of reason and revelation (145). This method establishes a hermeneutical circle between philosophy and exegesis (134) which transforms both and gives way to a *tertium quid*, a true innovation in the history of ideas (136). It is also worth noting that, in the author's view, Philo is by no means an isolated thinker in the field of cultural philosophy. In fact his thought was fully absorbed not only by Christianity, as is obvious, but also by Judaism and Neoplatonism (141). (RR)

8637. J. P. MARTÍN, 'La presencia de Filón en el Exámeron de Teófilo de Antioquía', *Salm* 33 (1986) 147-177.

In the introduction the author advances the theory that Theophilus of Antioch's *Ad Autolycum* is directly indebted to Philo. In the rest of the article he tries to find confirmation of this theory in the texts of Philo and Theophilus. He emphasizes the following points of contact: (a) the role of light in creation (153-155); (b) the term and concept of a *hexameron* (155); (c) the characteristics of the seventh day (156); (d) the genesis of the four elements (156-159); (e) the double creation of the heavens (159-160); (f) the separation of the waters from the earth (160 f.); (g) the didactic function of certain moments in creation (161-162); (h) the function of the triad in the order of creation (163 f.); (i) the symbolism of the creation of the animals (164 f.); (j) some motifs related to the creation of man (165-171); (k) the synthesis of the *hexameron* (171f.). On the basis of these parallels, Martín regards his initial hypothesis as verified *ad abundantiam*. (RR)

8638. A. MÉASSON, *Du char ailé de Zeus à l'Arche d'Alliance: images et mythes platoniciens chez Philon d'Alexandrie* (Paris 1986).

The aim of this long and complex book is to examine Philo's debt to Plato by studying a 'privileged example', namely his use and application of the imagery derived from the myth of the *Phaedrus*. The method and procedure followed involves three main areas of inquiry: (a) to analyze the particular vocabulary, images and ideas that Philo draws from Plato; (b) to determine the ways in which Philo deviates from Plato's original ideas in relation to the tradition of later Platonist interpretation; (c) to examine Philo's own adaptation and development of these ideas and motifs, particularly with regard to his own task of giving biblical exegesis. It emerges that Philo does not use the images of the *Phaedrus* myth in isolation, but rather entwines them with much other material from the Platonic corpus. The study accordingly also deals *in extenso* with themes from other Platonic works (especially the *Timaeus* and *Phaedo*, also *Theaetetus*, *Politicus*, *Republic*, *Ion*, *Alcibiades* I). The results of the investigation are divided into two parts. In the first the images of God as reinsman and God as pilot are analyzed, as well as the revelation of these two images to the Patriarchs Abraham and Jacob. The second part concentrates on the history of the soul from a double perspective: firstly the allegories of the incarnated soul (image of the horses, submersion of the soul, ascent of the soul); secondly the myth of the soul's descent and return to God its origin. The book contains many fine analyses of passages from Philo's allegorical works, among which we might mention *Opif.* 69-71, *Cher.* 21-30, *Gig.* 6-18, *Plant.* 11-14, *Conf.* 168-182, *Her.* 237-243, 277-293, *Somn.* 1.134-137, and also the autobiographical passage *Spec.* 3.1-6. Philo is an important witness to developments in the interpretation of the Platonic legacy by later interpreters. But his own contribution lies especially in the application of Platonic ideas to biblical exegesis and Jewish faith. (DTR)

8639. J. MILLER, *Measures of wisdom: the cosmic dance in classical and Christian antiquity* (Toronto, 1986), esp. 56-80.

This ambitious work presents a lengthy exploration of the interrelation between the notions of choral dance, cosmos and culture (παιδεία) in Greek thought from Plato to Pseudo-Dionysius. A chapter entitled 'The leap of the corybant' is devoted to Philo, 'for no Platonist of the Greco-Roman era observed the chorus of the stars with greater delight' than he (57). Miller's starting-point is *Opif.* 69-71, the themes of which he explicates at some length, making frequent references to other Philonic texts which refer to the dance of the stars and their contemplation by the aspiring soul. Central to Philo's thought was the relation between model and image which he derived from the *Timaeus* (in fact he was so dazzled by the correspondences between Genesis and Plato's craftsman myth that he failed to notice their significant differences). Miller emphasizes Philo's awareness of the limitations of imagery and metaphor. Positive imagery affirms the relation between man and the cosmos, negative imagery (i.e. imagery that falls significantly short) is used to express man's relation to God and the intelligible world. It is the image of the corybant that conveys how the soul proceeds beyond the measured order of the heavenly dancing stars and in pious revelry attains the philosophical vision of the ideal world and the mystical experience of divine union. Such corybants or bacchoi are the Therapeutae, who in their nocturnal dance join together the Platonic cosmos and the Mosaic exodus as they celebrate the liberation of the soul from the bondage of the body and its ascent to the divine realm. (DTR)

8640. R. MORTLEY, *From word to silence*: vol. 1 The rise and fall of logos, vol. 2 The way of negation, Christian and Greek, Theoph 30 (Bonn 1986), esp. 1.39-46, 86-89, 103-107, 2.149-150.

The main thesis of the study is that in the 1200 years from Parmenides to Damascius the concept of discourse (logos) is put forward as the key to human intellectual activity, examined at great length and ultimately found to be wanting. Philo too has a role to play.

He exploits to the full the dual meaning of λόγος as both speech and reason, but also adds a third, logos as hypostasis. The word of God has as specific function the guidance and composition of the cosmos, a task based largely on the world-soul of Plato's *Timaeus*. Philo also shows a keen interest in the subject of names and language in general. Indeed his commitment to language is stronger than we find among later Christian philosophers. A connection here is made between Philo and the unorthodox thinker Eunomius attacked by Gregory of Nyssa. (DTR)

8641. J. A. MUNITIZ, 'Fragments of Philo on Genesis', *HeyJ* 27 (1986) 63-65.

An enthusiastic account of the discovery of new fragments of *QG* published by J. Paramelle (cf. **1820**). (DTR)

8642. O. MUNNICH, 'Note sur la Bible de Philon: κλοποφορεῖν/- *κλοποφρονεῖν en *Gen*. 31, 26 et en *Leg. All*. III, 20', in *Hellenica et Judaica* (cf. **8608**) 43-51.

The passage *Leg*. 3.20f. authorizes us to believe that Philo's Bible used at Gen. 31:26 the verb κλοποφρονεῖν instead of κλοποφορεῖν, the traditional reading. Munnich reaches this conclusion after a careful philological analysis and thorough examination of the Philonic text. (RR)

8643. A. NEHER, 'Les références à Philon d'Alexandrie dans l'œuvre du Rav Hanazir, disciple du Rav Kook (*Qol Hanevoua*, 1970)', in *Hellenica et Judaica* (cf. **8608**) 385-390.

Rav Hanazir is one of the writers in the Jewish world who gives a position of central importance to Philo; remarkably, he does so in the name of Philo's orthodoxy and faithfulness to the Jewish tradition. Neher, formulating the basic theory of Rav Hanazir's exegesis, concludes his article as follows (389): 'The disappearance of Philo deviated medieval Jewish philosophy toward a Hellenization which Philo would have been able to resist. Only the Cabbalah remained faithful to Philo...' (RR)

8644. J. NEUSNER, 'Philo and the Mishnah: the matter of the soul after death', in *Hellenica et Judaica* (cf. **8608**) 53-59.

A comparative analysis of the Mishnah tract *Ohalot* with *Spec*. 3.206 f. allows the author to show that 'at the foundations, the Mishnah's original philosophers and Philo in quite distinct ways turn out to have been saying pretty much the same thing about the character of the soul after death' (54). (RR)

8645. J. VAN OORT, *Jerusalem en Babylon: een onderzoek van Augustinus' De stad van God en de bronnen van zijn leer der twee steden (rijken)* (diss. Utrecht, The Hague 1986), esp. ch. IVB 'Platonisme, Stoa en Philo' (198-212).

Philo is acquainted with the Stoic distinction between the megalopolis (the universe) and individual cities, and also with the Platonic division between κόσμος νοητός and κόσμος αἰσθητός, but not the radical opposition between a heavenly and an earthly city

375

such as we find in Augustine. (RAB/DTR)

8646. A. PAUL, 'Le récit de la création dans les *Antiquités Juives* de Flavius Josèphe: traduction et commentaire', in *Hellenica et Judaica* (cf. **8608**) 129-137.

In commenting on Josephus' account of creation (*Ant.* 1.27-36), the author frequently turns to the corresponding exegesis in Philo's *Opif.* (RR)

8647. B. A. PEARSON, 'Earliest Christianity in Egypt: some observations', in *The roots of Egyptian Christianity* (cf. **8606**) 132-159, esp. 145-151.

Philo's writings provide valuable evidence on the variegated Jewish milieu in which the origins of the Christian community in Alexandria are to be located. (DTR)

8648. B. A. PEARSON, 'Christians and Jews in first-century Alexandria', *HThR* 79 (1986) 206-216.

In discussing the subject of the relations between Jews and Christians in first century Alexandria, Philo's evidence must play a substantial role. Pearson concludes (216): 'Philo's role, and that of like-minded Jews of his day, was incalculably important in the development of Christianity. It is the Philo-like Christianity of *Silvanus*, rather than the primitive apocalypticism of *Barnabas*, or the acosmic radicalism of the Gnostics, that ultimately carried the day in the development of Christian theology in the Patristic age.' (DTR)

8649. M. PHILONENKO, 'Philon d'Alexandrie et l'"instruction sur les deux esprits"', in *Hellenica et Judaica* (cf. **8608**) 61-68.

In the author's view, the text of *QE* 1.23, which refers to the presence of the powers (of good and evil) in the soul of every man, shows the influence of Iranian dualism and 'reminds us that Philo belongs not only to the history of philosophy, but also to the history of religion' (67). (RR)

8650. L. RADCHIK, 'Una aproximación a Filón de Alejandría', *Logos* (Mexico) 14 (1986) 59-71.

A brief synoptic presentation dealing with the main aspects of Philo's work (theology, anthropology, doctrine of creation, cosmology). The essential contribution of Philo's thought, in the view of the author, is the theory of grace as the encounter of the immanent (historical) dimension and the transcendent (theological) dimension. (RR)

8651. R. RADICE, 'Ipotesi per una interpretazione della struttura della *kosmopoiia* nel *De opificio mundi* di Filone di Alessandria', in *Hellenica et Judaica* (cf. **8608**) 69-78.

Analyzing the structure of the *De opificio mundi*, and especially its presentation of the 'cosmological week', the author stresses the divide which exists between cosmogony and anthropogony and which rules out the possibility of unifying the entire Philonic interpretation of creation in a single philosophical and exegetical category. (RR)

8652. *Reallexikon für Antike und Christentum*, edited by E. DASS-MANN *et al.*, vol. 13 (Stuttgart 1986).

Cf. above **5016**. Contains: J. PÉPIN, art. 'Harmonie der Sphären', 593-618, esp. 610-1 (harmony of the spheres); K. THRAEDE, art. 'Hauch', 714-734, esp. 720-1 (breath, divine and human); M. WACHT, art. 'Güterlehre', 59-150, esp. 102-6 (doctrine of goods). (DTR)

8653. A. REINHARTZ, 'The meaning of *nomos* in Philo's *Exposition of the Law*', *SR* 15 (1986) 337-345.

Analyzes Philo's use of the concept of *nomos* in the Exposition of the Law, and especially in relation to the programmatic doctrinal summary in *Opif.* 170-172. The law of Moses is superior to other legislations because (a) it has a divine origin, (b) it exhorts rather than commands, (c) it is equivalent to the law of nature, (d) it offers philosophical instruction, and (e) it shows the way to a life of virtue. It cannot be said, therefore, that the use of the concept *nomos* to translate Torah in Philo's case leads to a narrow emphasis on the purely legalistic aspects of the Pentateuch. (DTR)

8654. D. ROKEAH [רוקח .ד], פילון האלכסנדרוני, המדרש וההלכה הקדומה [('Philo of Alexandria, the Midrash, and the primitive Halacha'], *Tarbiz* 55 (1986) 433-439.

A reaction to the article by D. Flusser and S.Safrai (**8521**), discussing Philo's interpretation of the death of Nadab and Abihu. It is concluded that Philo knew neither Hebrew nor midrashic material. English summary. (MM)

8655. H. ROUILLARD, 'Et si Caïn voulait que l'œil le regardât? étude des transformations de *Gen.* 4,14 à travers la LXX et Philon d'Alexandrie', in *Hellenica et Judaica* (cf. **8608**) 79-83.

A curious error made by Victor Hugo in the quotation and interpretation of Gen. 4:14 may have a precedent in Philo, *Det.* 150f. (RR)

8656. D. T. RUNIA, *Philo of Alexandria and the* Timaeus *of Plato*, PhilAnt 44 (Leiden 1986).

This lengthy and detailed study has as its main point of focus the philosophical aspects of Philo's thought, but it also makes allowance for the fact that this thought is primarily conveyed by means of exegesis of Scripture. Its subject is Philo's Platonism, as it emerges in his knowledge and use of Plato's celebrated cosmological dialogue, the *Timaeus*. The work falls into four parts. In the first brief sketches are given of recent Philonic research (with emphasis on questions of methodology, cf. **1117**), Philo's historical and cultural setting, and the history of interpretation of the *Timaeus* from Plato up till the Middle Platonic period. The second part, entitled Analysis, consists of an extensive 'commentary' on all the passages of the *Timaeus* referred to by Philo, presented in the order of the dialogue. At the end of this section an Appendix lists all the Pentateuchal texts in relation to which Philo invokes the *Timaeus*. The third part, entitled Synthesis, collects and discusses in a synoptic way all the evidence collected in the previous section. Its first chapter evaluates the way Philo uses the *Timaeus*. It emerges that Philo is intimately acquainted with much of the dialogue, but utilizes especially its theological, metaphysical, cosmological and anthropological aspects, ignoring for the most part its mathematical and physiological/medical doctrines. The dialogue is used as 'a kind of blueprint that offers partial guidance to the exegete in the construction of his edifice of scriptural commentary' (409). The next chapter discusses the influence of the *Timaeus* on Philo's thought, with emphasis on the doctrines of creation, God the creator, the Logos, matter, man the microcosm, and the correct evaluation of the created order. The final chapter of the section looks at Philo's interpretation of Plato's work in the light of interpretative tradition. Influence of the early Academy, Aristotle, and the Stoa is not as strong as that of the incipient Middle Platonist school. But Philo should not be regarded as a Middle Platonist. In the fourth and final section some conclusions on the relation between philosophy and exegesis in Philo's work are reached, and some brief comparisons are made with contemporary thinkers. Philo is presented as a pioneer, whose 'attempt to bring together Scripture and philosophy marks a pivotal point in the history of thought' (552). The book is a lightly revised edition of the dissertation listed at **8363**. A short Appendix has been added on research carried out by scholars on relevant topics since the completion of the dissertation (especially the study of Tobin, cf. **8373**). REVIEWS: R. Radice, *Elenchos* 8 (1986) 481ff.; E. des Places, *BAGB* 46 (1987) 408; A. Sheppard, *CR* 37 (1987) 222ff. (DTR)

8657. D. T. RUNIA, 'Redrawing the map of early Middle Platonism: some comments on the Philonic evidence', in *Hellenica et Judaica* (cf. **8608**) 85-104.

Philo's writings give valuable evidence for the beginnings of the Middle Platonist movements, the precise developments of which remain obscure on account of the poverty of our sources. This contribution examines two suggestions made by the Australian scholar H. Tarrant (cf. above **8371-72**) in the light of the Philonic evidence. The argument that the famous philosophical digression in Plato's Seventh letter was a product of early Middle Platonism (perhaps by Thrasyllus) is not contraverted, for Philo does not allude to it. The second thesis is that the *Anonymous commentary on the Theaetetus* is much earlier than hitherto supposed, probably ante-dates Philo, and may have been written by Eudorus of Alexandria. This is examined from the following angles: (1) Philo's use of the *Theaetetus*; (2) the papyrus' suggested neglect of the *Timaeus*; (3) its perspective on the history of philosophy; (4) the direction of philosophical interests; (5) epistemology and mild scepticism; (6) parallels in methods of commentary and exegesis. Runia concludes that the earlier dating of the papyrus is probable; but on the basis of the Philonic evidence he is less convinced by philosophical conclusions which Tarrant draws from it, especially in the area of epistemology. (DTR)

8658. D. T. RUNIA, 'How to read Philo', *NTT* 40 (1986) 185-198.

A guide to the reader who is about to tackle Philo's voluminous writings or wishes to do research on them. Problem areas in Philonic research are highlighted and the various instruments of research available are briefly outlined. From a sound methodological viewpoint the following four procedures are recommended: (1) when a particular subject is dealt with, all the relevant passages must be taken into account; (2) special attention should be paid to the exegetical context; (3) the exegetical problem underlying the discussion must be determined; (4) the philosophical ideas called on by Philo should be identified, and then related to the exegetical *locus* under discussion. The article ends with two examples, one on the idea-numbers in *Opif.* 102, the other on Philo's use of the divine epithet ὕψιστος. (DTR)

8659. D. T. RUNIA, 'Mosaic and Platonist exegesis: Philo on 'finding' and 'refinding'', *VChr* 40 (1986) 209-217.

A explanation (and defence in the light of recent criticism) of Philo's distinction between εὕρεσις and ἀνεύρεσις at *Deus* 86. Factors that have to be taken into account are a similar distinction between finding and recollection (ἀνάμνησις) in Platonist exegesis, and also ancient theories of homonymy and synonymy. (DTR)

8660. K.-G. SANDELIN, *Wisdom as nourisher: a study of an Old Testament theme, its development within early Judaism and its impact on early Christianity*, AAAbo.H 64.3 (Abo 1986), esp. chap. 5 'Wisdom as a hostess and nourisher in Philo of Alexandria' (82-150).

A comprehensive and penetrating analysis of the theme, originating in Prov. 9:1-6, of Sophia as nourisher in Philo. The chapter divides roughly into two halves. In the first numerous passages are analyzed in which Wisdom is presented as hostess of a banquet, as nourisher (by means of diverse metaphors, such as heaven, tree of life, vine, mother), and with reference to the activity of the divine Logos. Also in the case of the texts associating light and vision with Wisdom the nourisher Sandelin opts primarily for a metaphorical interpretation. In the second half the question is asked as to what this theme means in a more practical sense. The theoretical framework here is the conception of the royal road that has as its goal the land of Wisdom in which Israel comes to see God. Wisdom as nourisher must thus be seen as a reality in the life of the individual Jew, and can be said to be spiritually present in the life of the Jewish community on the Sabbath. The Passover meal is viewed by Philo as a symbolical (i.e. earthly) representation of the heavenly meal furnished by Wisdom (though the food is not sacramental, as Goodenough maintained). Finally Sandelin argues that the theme is concretely present in Philo's depiction of the life of the community of the Therapeutae (and especially their banquet), giving expression to Philo's religious ideal. (DTR)

8661. A. F. SEGAL, *Rebecca's children: Judaism and Christianity in the Roman world* (Cambridge Mass. 1986), esp. 54-58, 154ff.

Philo holds many views that are similar to those of the Sadducees in Judea, but in other ways he is like the Pharisees. But what sets him apart, as a Diaspora Jew, is the attempt to show that Scripture and Greek philosophy are in harmony. At 154ff. Segal repeats his thesis (cf. **7741**) that Philo's talk of a 'second god' runs counter to the warnings of the Rabbis and anticipates developments in the direction of Christianity. (DTR)

8662. R. STARK, 'Jewish conversion and the rise of Christianity: rethinking the received wisdom', *SBLSPS* 25 (1986) 314-329, esp. 321ff.

It is argued from the theoretical sociological point of view that Hellenized Jews, because they were highly secularized, were most responsive to the message of early Christianity. Philo and his writings are a prime example of the secularization process, especially because there is evidence to suggest that he gave expression to fashionable views. (DTR)

8663. R. W. THURSTON, 'Philo and the Epistle to the Hebrews', *EvQ*

58 (1986) 133-143.

The author attempts somewhat speculatively to answer the question of how C. Spicq and R. Williamson could reach diametrically opposed views on the relation between Philo and Hebrews. The reason both dwell on the same subjects is that Hebr. 1-4 is reacting against a Christology that draws on Philonic ideas and thus identified Christ with the Logos, an angel, Moses, Adam and the 'great high priest'. The founder of such a movement must have been a Jewish Christian and may well be Cerinthus, who is said to have studied philosophy in Egypt. (DTR)

8664. T. H. TOBIN, 'Tradition and interpretation in Philo's portrait of the patriarch Joseph', *SBLSPS* 25 (1986) 271-277.

At the literal level Philo's portrait of Joseph is an encomium, probably based on material drawn from Hellenistic Judaism. In the non-literal sections Philo wanted to convey to his reader some sense of the ambiguous role of the statesman, but the material from the allegory of the soul was unsuitable on account of its extremely negative emphasis. He thus uses material from Greek philosophical traditions on the superiority of the sage over the instable world of sense-perception. (DTR)

8665. W. WIEFEL, 'Das dritte Buch über "Moses": Anmerkungen zum Quaestionenwerk des Philo von Alexandrien', *ThLZ* 111 (1986) 865-882.

An unusual but stimulating article, partly giving a review of Philonic scholarship (very much from the German-French perspective, references to English-American and Italian contributions almost completely lacking), partly discussing the nature and value of the *Quaestiones*. These have been badly neglected in Philonic studies. They are in method closer to Hellenistic scholarship than Jewish Midrash, and from the formal point of view would have been the most perfect of Philo's writings, had they but survived in a complete and original state. In them Philo speaks, not as preacher or apologist, but first and foremost as teacher, situated perhaps in a Jewish predecessor of the later Christian catechetical school. The author gives a systematic sketch of Philo's thought as presented in the *Quaestiones*, to our knowledge the first of its kind ever attempted. (DTR)

8666. R. McL. WILSON, art. 'Philo Judaeus', in G.W. BROMILEY (ed.), *The International Standard Bible Encyclopedia* (Grand Rapids 1986) 3.847-850.

A brief but judicious synoptic portrait of Philo, introducing his life and work and some of the leading themes in his thought. Philo helps towards a balanced judgment of contemporary Judaism, and provides valuable insights into a range of aspects of ancient thought which would otherwise be closed to us. (DTR)

8667. D. WINSTON, 'Philo on the contemplative life', in A. GREEN (ed.), *Jewish spirituality: from the Bible through the Middle Ages*, World spirituality: an encyclopedic history of the religious quest, vol. 13 (New York 1986) 198-231.

A beautifully written and documented introduction to the subject of Philo's spirituality, drawing together themes treated at length in other contributions by the same author (cf. **7852, 8133, 8462**). The main topics dealt with are: (1) God and Logos; (2) worship through sacrifice, thanksgiving, prayer; (3) action versus contemplation; (4) Philo's mysticism. (DTR)

8668. D. WINSTON, 'Theodicy and the creation of man in Philo of Alexandria', in *Hellenica et Judaica* (cf. **8608**) 105-111.

Gathers some particularly important passages in which Philo alludes to the 'participated creation' of the soul. The problem emerging from these texts concerns the definition of which part of the soul (irrational or rational) God created directly. More profoundly, it concerns the function of the two parts of the soul in relation to moral choice. (RR)

1987

For the years after 1986 we give references to studies on Philo that have come to our attention, but these are not summarized or indexed. The asterisk indicates that the numbering is provisional. See further the Introduction, section 2 (i).

8701*. J. A. BAZELEY, *The correlation of salvation and creation according to Philo of Alexandria* (thesis University of Melbourne 1987).

8702*. B. BELLETTI, 'Idea e creazionismo in Filone di Alessandria', *Sap* 40 (1987) 277-304.

8703*. B. BELLETTI, 'La creazione delle idee e dell'uomo nel trattato *De opificio mundi* di Filone Alessandrino', *Hum* 42 (1987) 273-279.

8704*. R. BERCHMANN, 'Arcana mundi: magic and divination in the De *Somniis* of Philo of Alexandria', *SBLSPS* 26 (1987) 403-428.

8705*. F. F. BRUCE, "To the Hebrews: a document of Roman Christianity?', *ANRW* II 25.4 (Berlin-New York 1987) 3496-3521, esp. 3506ff.

8706*. J. CAZEAUX, 'Le voyage inutile, ou la création chez Philon', in L. DEROUSSEAUX and F. BLANQUART (edd.), *La création dans l'Orient ancien: congrès de l'ACFEB*, LeDiv 127 (Paris 1987) 345-408.

8707*. J. CAZEAUX, 'Mystique et sagesse: le repas des trois anges et d'Abraham à Mambré, vu par Philon d'Alexandrie, in *Prière, mystique et Judaïsme: actes du Colloque de Strasbourg, 12-14 Septembre 1984* (Paris 1987) 21-41.

8708*. N. G. COHEN, 'The Jewish dimension of Philo's Judaism: an elucidation of *de Spec. Leg.* IV 132-150', *JJS* 38 (1987) 165-186.

8709*. M. G. CREPALDI, 'Ai confini del linguaggio: il discorso teologico in Filone di Alessandria', in *I linguaggi della comunicazione*, StudFilGal 15 (Padua 1987) 157-167.

8710*. G. DELLING, 'Die Begegnung zwischen Hellenismus und Judentum', *ANRW* II 20.2 (Berlin 1987) 3-39.

8711*. G. DELLING, *Die Bewältigung der Diasporasituation durch das hellenistische Judentum* (Berlin-New York 1987) *passim*.

8712*. J. H. ELLENS, 'Philo Judaeus and the ancient library of Alexandria', *SBLSPS* 26 (1987) 439-442.

8713*. H. FELD, 'Der Hebräerbrief: literarische Form, religionsgeschichtlicher Hintergrund, theologische Fragen', *ANRW* II 25.4 (Berlin-New York 1987) 3522-3601, esp. 3548ff.

8714*. L. H. FELDMAN, 'Philo's views on music', *JJML* 100 (1986-87) 36-52.

8715*. H. FROHNHOFEN, *Apatheia tou theou: über die Affektlosigkeit Gottes in der griechischen Antike und bei den griechischsprachigen Kirchenvätern bis zu Gregorios Thaumaturgos*, Europäische Hochschulschriften Reihe XXIII Theologie 318 (Frankfurt 1987), esp. 108-115.

8716*. J. G. GRIFFITHS, 'Egypt and the rise of the synagogue', *JThS* 38 (1987) 1-15.

8717*. R. GOULET, *La philosophie de Moïse: essai de reconstitution d'un commentaire philosophique préphilonien du Pentateuque*, Histoire des doctrines de l'Antiquité classique 11 (Paris 1987).

8718*. A. G. HAMMAN, *L'homme image de Dieu, essai d'une anthropologie chrétienne dans l'église des cinq premiers siècles*, Relais-études 2 (Paris 1987), esp. 106-113.

8719*. D. M. HAY, 'The psychology of faith in Hellenistic Judaism', *ANRW* II 20.2 (Berlin-New York 1987) 881-925.

8720*. D. M. HAY, 'Politics and exegesis in Philo's treatise on dreams', *SBLSPS* 26 (1987) 429-438.

8721*. E. HILGERT, 'A survey of previous scholarship on Philo's *De Somniis* 1-2', *SBLSPS* 26 (1987) 394-402.

8722*. A. VAN DEN HOEK, 'Mistress and servant: an allegorical theme in Philo, Clement and Origen', in L. Lies (ed.), *Origeniana Quarta*, IThS 19 (Innsbruck-Vienna 1987) 344-349.

8723*. V. HUROVITZ, 'Salted incense Exodus 30,35; Maqlû VI 111-112, IX 118-120', *Bib* 68 (1987) 178-194.

8724*. A. A. LONG and D. N. SEDLEY, *The Hellenistic philosophers*, 2 vols. (Cambridge 1987), cf. esp. 1.497, 506.

8725*. J. MÉNARD, 'Philon d'Alexandrie', *Gnostica* 5 (1987).

8726*. J. MÉNARD, *La gnose de Philon d'Alexandrie* (Paris 1987).

8727*. L. A. MONTES-PERAL, *Akataleptos theos: der unfassbare Gott*, ALGHJ 16 (Leiden 1987).

See above **7929**.

8728*. E. F. OSBORN, 'Philo and Clement', *Prudentia* 19 (1987) 35-49.

8729*. M. PETIT, 'Exploitations non bibliques des thèmes de Tamar et de Genèse 38: Philon d'Alexandrie; textes et traditions juives jusqu'aux Talmudim', in *ΑΛΕΞΑΝΔΡΙΝΑ: hellénisme, judaïsme et christianisme à Alexandrie; mélanges offerts à Claude Mondésert S.J.* (Paris 1987) 77-115.

8730*. G. REALE and R. RADICE, 'La genesi e la natura della "filosofia mosaica": struttura, metodo e fondamenti del pensiero filosofico e teologico di Filone di Alessandria; monografia introduttiva ai diciannove trattati del Commentario allegorico alla Bibbia', in *La filosofia mosaica* (cf. **2405***) (Milan 1987) v-cxli.

8731*. *Reallexikon für Antike und Christentum*, edited by E. DASS-MANN *et al.*, Lieferungen 105-107 (Stuttgart 1987).

W. BEIERWALTES, art. 'Hen (ἕν)´, 445-472, esp. 460-1 (the One, unity); A. DIHLE, art. 'Heilig', 1-63, esp. 33-35 (holy); R. KLEIN, art. 'Hellenen', 375-445, esp. 417-8 (Greeks). (DTR)

8732*. J. RIAUD, 'Les Thérapeutes d'Alexandrie dans la tradition et dans la recherche critique jusqu'aux découvertes de Qumran', *ANRW* II 20.2 (Berlin-New York 1987) 1189-1295.

8733*. C. RIEDWEG, *Mysterienterminologie bei Platon, Philon und Klemens von Alexandrien*, UALG 26 (Berlin-New York 1987), esp. 70-115.

8734*. C. J. ROETZEL, *The world that shaped the New Testament* (London 1987), esp. 80-83.

8735*. M.-J. RONDEAU, *'Pragmatologeîn*: pour éclairer Philon *Fug.* 54, *Somn.* I, 228-231', in *ΑΛΕΞΑΝΔΡΙΝΑ* (cf. **8729***) 117-150

8736*. D. T. RUNIA, 'Further observations on the structure of Philo's Allegorical treatises', *VChr* 41 (1987) 105-138.

8737*. R. SCHMITT, 'Ist Philo, Vita Moysis (Mos) II 251 ein Peristasencatalog?', *NT* 29 (1987) 177-182.

8738*. E. SCHÜRER and J. MORRIS, 'Philo the Jewish philosopher', in E. SCHÜRER, *The history of the Jewish people in the age of Jesus Christ (175 B.C. – A.D. 135)*, a new English version revised and edited by G. VERMES *et al.* (Edinburgh 1973-87) 809-889.

8739*. M. SIMON, Philons Philosophie als Modelfall für das mittelalterliche Problem des Verhältnisses von Glauben und Wissen', in *Beiträge zu Wissenschaftsgeschichte: Wissenschaft in Mittelalter und Renaissance* (Berlin 1987) 79-93.

8740*. E. M. SMALLWOOD, 'Philo and Josephus as historians of the same events', in L. H. FELDMAN and G. HATA, *Josephus, Judaism and Christianity* (Detroit 1987) 114-129.

8741*. C. SPICQ, 'L'Épître aux Hébreux et Philo: un cas d'insertion de la littérature sacrée dans la culture profane du Ier siècle (Hébr. V,11 – VI,20 et le 'De sacrificiis Abelis et Caïni' de Philon', *ANRW* II 25.4 (Berlin-New York 1987) 3602-18.

8742*. E. STAROBINSKI-SAFRAN, 'La communauté juive d' Alexandrie à l'époque de Philon', in *ΑΛΕΞΑΝΔΡΙΝΑ* (cf. **8729***) 45-75.

8743*. H. DE VRIES, 'Philosophia ancilla theologiae bij Philo', *Stoicheia* (Amsterdam) 2.3 (1987) 27-52.

8744*. R. D. WILLIAMS, *Arius: heresy and tradition* (London 1987), esp. 117-124.

8745*. D. WINSTON, art. 'Philo', *The Encyclopedia of Religion*, vol. 11 (New York-London 1987) 287-291.

1988

8801*. H. BURKHARDT, *Die Inspiration heiliger Schriften bei Philo von Alexandrien* (Giessen 1988).

8802*. J. CAZEAUX, 'Etre juif et parler grec: l'allégorie de Philon', in B. DUPUY *et al.*, *Juifs et chrétiens: un vis-à-vis permanent*, Publications des Facultés Universitaires Saint-Louis 42 (Brussels 1988), 67-109.

8803*. A. VAN DEN HOEK, *Clement of Alexandria and his use of Philo in the Stromateis: an early Christian reshaping of a Jewish model*, VChr.S 3 (Leiden 1988).

8804*. J. MANSFELD, 'Philosophy in the service of scripture: Philo's exegetical strategies', in J. M. DILLON and A. A. LONG (edd.), *The question of "eclecticism": studies in later Greek philosophy* (Berkeley 1988) 70-102.

8805*. M. J. J. MENKEN, 'The provenance and meaning of the Old Testament quotation in John 6:31', *NT* 30 (1988) 39-57, esp. 49ff.

8806*. D. T. RUNIA, 'God and man in Philo of Alexandria', *JThS* 39 (1988) 48-75.

INDICES

The method used in the compilation of the six indices has been described in section 2 (h) of the Introduction, which the reader is advised to consult before making extensive use of them. Throughout the indices bold type is used to refer to particularly important studies by the author or on the subject concerned.

1. INDEX OF AUTHORS

Numbers followed by a bullet sign indicate that the author was the editor or co-editor of the work concerned. Where authors have given different forms of their name (especially in the case of initials), we place all references under the most common form.

Badt B. 2001
Baër D. 7004
Baer R. A. 6505, **7005**
Baer Y. 5201, 5303, 5502, 8004
Balch D. L. 7201
Baltes M. 7202, 7603
Balz H. 6906
Bamberger B. J. 4901, 7703
Barbel J. 4102
Barnard L. W. 6302, 6707
Barnes E. J. 7303
Baron S. W. 3004, 5202
Barraclough R. **8405**
Barrett C. K. 3007
Bartelink G. J. M. 5801, 6001
Barth E. M. 7203
Barth P. 4103
Barthélemy D. 6708
Baskin J. R. 6603, 7604
Bassler J. M. 8202, 8502
Batey R. 6709
Bauer J. B. 6002
Bauerfeind O. 4202, 5405, 6406
Baumgarten H. 7006
Baumgarten J. M. 5304, 7704
Beauchamp P. 6710
Beaude P.-M. 8503
Beckaert A. 2203, **4301**, 4302
Beckwith R. 8504
Behm J. 3807, 4202, 5405
Beierwaltes W. 5703
Beinart H. 8004*
Békés J. 8024*
Belkin S. 3701, **4002**, 4601, 5103,
  5601, 5602, 5802, 5803, 5804, 6003,
  6401, 6402, 6506, 6711, 7007, 7204,
  7404
Belletti B. 8203, 8314, 8505
Bemporad J. 7738*
Bengio A. 3202, 7102
Benoît A. 3209
Benoit P. 8406
Benzing E. 7623*
Berchmann R. M. 8407, 8408
Bergh van Eysinga G. A. van den 1105,
  5302, 5603
Bernstein S. 5802*
Berkowitz L. 3210
Bernard J. 7705
Berthold H. 1007
Bertram G. 3807, 3901, 4003, 4202,
  5405, 5805, 6406, 6906, 7311
Bertrand D. A. 3209

Betz H. D. 6604, 7008, 7205, 7304
Betz O. 6004, 6303, 7311, 7403
Beus C. de 5116*
Bianchi U. 7802, 7803, 7804, 7805,
  8005, 8409, 8506
Bieder W. 4104, 5907
Bienert W. A. 7206
Bietenhard H. 5104, 5405
Bietz W. K. 7304
Bigatti R. 2401, 8006
Bilde P. 7806
Bingen J. 7935*
Bissoli G. 8204
Bitter R. A. **8205**, 8506a
Black M. 5105, 6102, 7941a*
Blau J. L. 3004
Blin G. 3001
Bloomfield M. W. 4303
Blume H.-D. 8328*
Boas G. 4801
Boccaccini G. 8206, 8410, 8507
Böcher O. 7011*, 7403
Boer W. den 4005, 7554*
Bogaert R. 7638
Bogner H. 3702
Bokser B. 7706
Bolgiani F. 7501
Bolkestein H. 3902
Bolognesi G. 6901, 7009, 7010
Bonafede G. 4902
Bonner C. 4105
Borgen P. **1114**, 3206, 6304, **6507**,
  6804, 7207, 7605, 7707, 7708, 8007,
  8207, 8315, 8316, 8411
Borig R. 6712
Bormann K. 2007, **5503**
Botte B. 5401, 6313
Box H. 2151, 3100
Boyancé P. 4602, 5902, 6005, **6305**,
  6306, 6307, 6713, 6714, 7404, 7502
Bracewell R. E. 8317
Brandenburger E. 6202, 6805
Braumann G. 7311
Braun F. M. 5903, 6403
Braun H. 5704, 5907, 7011, 7103
Brayer M. M. 6902
Bréhier E. 2205, 4714, 5505, 5506
Broadie A. 7807
Brock S. P. 1010
Broek R. van den 7902, 8114*, 8606
Bromiley G. 3807
Brongers H. A. 6203
Brooke G. J. 7808, 8508

Daniel S. 2231, 2601, 3100, 6717
Daniélou J. 4401, 4702, 4804, 4805,
    5001, 5002, 5305, 5706, 5809, **5810**,
    6105, 6718, 6719, 7014
Dassmann E. 6510, 8535*, 8652*
Daube D. 5606*, 7908
Daumas F. 2210, 3100, 6720
Davidson H. 7510
Davies P. S. 8612
Davies W. D. 5606*
Dean-Otting M. 8419
Deaut R. le 8103
Del Medico H. E. 5708, 5811
Del Re R. 7948
Delassus D. 7213
Delatte L. 4201
Delcor M. 6610, 6809
Delcuve G. 4503
Delling G. 1007, 1012, 5003, 5405,
    5707, 5907, 6406, 6511, 6906, 7105,
    7214, 7311, 7411, 7712, 8420
Delobre P. 2207
Devivaise C. 5313
Devreesse R. 1800, 1809
Dexinger F. 7511
Dey J. 3703
Dey L. K. K. **7512**
Di Napoli G. 5306
Dihle A. 6627, 7311, 8209
Dillon J. 3013, 3101, 7506, 7513,
    7553, 7647, 7639, 7713, **7714**, 7733,
    7814, 7815, 8011, 8104, 8133, 8324,
    8325, 8326, 8327, 8328, 8613,
Dillon J. J. 8210
Dinkler E. 7236
Dittman W. 5307
Dittmann H. 8123
Dockrill D. W. 8121*
Dodd C. H. 3704, 5308
Donini P. 8211
Dorival G. 7221
Dörrie H. 5510, 6905, 7241, 7412,
    7601*, 8105
Doutreleau L. 7634
Downing F. G. 8212, 8518
Dreyer O. 7015
Drury M. 8519
Dubois J. D. 8213
Duchrow U. 7016
Dumont J. P. 7215
Dungan D. 3011
Dupont J. 4806, 4904
Dürr L. 3801

Earp J. W. 2110, 3203
Easterling P. E. 8519*
Eccles R. S. 6810, 8520
Edwards R. B. 7816
Effe B. 7017
Ehrhardt A. 6811
Eigo F. A. 8238*
Eisenberg P. D. 7647
Eisenstein J. D. 5107, 5107
Elsas C. 7514, 8012
Eltester F. W. 5812, 6404
Engelsman J. C. 7909
Ernst J. 7018
Ervin H. M. 6206
Escribano-Alberca I. 7413, 7609
Ettinger S. 8004*
Eydoux E. 5403
Eyselein K. 8214

Fabbrini F. 8329
Faber van der Meulen H. 7817, 8013
Facher E. 5918
Faggin G. 6611
Fallon F. T. 7610
Farandos G. D. 1110, **7611**
Farnedi G. 8024*
Fascher E. 6405
Feibleman J. K. 5906
Feldman L. H. 1108, 1115, 6008
Feldman S. C. 8215
Fernhout R. 7910
Ferrabino A. 6731
Festugière A. J. **4905**, 5404
Feuer I. 2216
Feuillet A. 6601
Fiedler M. J. 7216
Finkel J. 6207, 6512
Fischel H. A. 7310
Fischer U. 7612, 7818
Fitzer G. 6406
Flasch K. 6531*
Flusser D. 8014, 8521
Foakes Jackson F. J. 3903
Focardi S. 8522
Foerster W. 3807, 6406
Fontaine J. 7229*
Forsyth N. 7706
Fossum J. E. 8216, 8523, 8524
Foster S. S. 7515, 7715
Fraccaro P. 4006
Fränkel H. 3802
Franxmann T. W. 7911
Fredouille J.-C. 8123

Harrison P. N. 4010
Harvey W. Z. 8019, 8220
Haubeck W. 8013*
Hauck F. 5907
Hausherr I. 5205
Hausleiter J. 1002, 5716, 6627, 7236
Hay D. M. 7315, 7916, 8020
Hecht R. D. 7819, 8021, 8108, 8426
Hegermann H. 6107, 6514, 7316, 7317, 7318
Heinemann.I. 2001-7, 2002, 2003, 2004, 2006, 3708, 4008, 4809, 4810, 4907, 4908, 5005, 5006, 5206, 6210
Heitmann A. 4009
Helderman J. 7518, 8427
Hemmerdinger B. 6312
Henao Zapata L. 7107
Hendrix P. 7108
Hengel M. 6907, 7109, 7403, 7519, 8109
Hennig D. 7418
Henrichs A. 6815
Henry P. 8042
Hering J. 5606
Hermaniuk M. 4704
Herrmann L. 6615
Heyke W. 1004
Hilgert E. 1009, 1011, 1013, 1015, 1016, 1017, **1019**, 1111, 1822*, 3301-6, 8423*, 8525, 8621
Hitchcock F. R. M. 4010
Hobbs E. C. 7815
Hochstaffl J. 7616
Hoening S. B. 7402*
Hoffnung F. D. 8022
Hofius O. 7021, 7319
Hogan L. 8622
Hoheisel K. 8535
Holladay C. R. **7717**
Holtz T. 5707*, 6511*
Hombert M. 1806
Hommes N. J. 3709
Hopper M. E. 8335
Horbury W. 8336, 8623
Horn H. J. 7022
Horowitz M. C. 7917
Horsley R. A. 7617, 7718, 7820, 7821, 7822, 7918, 8110
Horst J. 4202, 5405
Horst P. W. van der 8337
Horton F. L. 7618
Howard G. E. 7320
Hoyle R. B. 3806

Hruby K. 6313
Hugedé N. 6616
Hugghins K. W. 8624
Huonder Q. 5407
Hurst L. D. 8428

Isaacs M. E. 7619
Ivánka E. von 5918
Ivry A. L. 8340*

Jackson B. S. 7520
Jacobs I. 7620
Jaeger W. 5916, 6108
James T. 7621
Janáček K. 7919, 8221
Jaubert A. 6314, 6727, 7622
Javierre A. M. 6315
Jay B. 7823
Jellicoe S. 1010, 6109
Jeremias G. 7109*
Jeremias J. 5907
Jervell J. 6009, 7419, 7712*
Jobling D. 7719
Johannson N. 4011
Jonas H. 4909, **5409**, 5814, 6409
Jonge H. J. de 8338
Jossa G. 6728
Jost W. 3908
Junés E. 6617
Junod E. 1818, 3209

Kahle P. 5917
Kahn J. G. 2209, 2652, 3100, 6515, 6729, 7110, 7222, 7321, 7420, 7720, 8339, 8340, 8526, 8624a
Kaiser H. 7421
Kamlah E. 6410, 7623
Kampen J. 8625
Kannengiesser C. 6730, 7229*, 7609
Kasch W. 5907
Käsemann E. 3909
Kasher A. 7422, 7521, 7624, 7824, 7920, **8527**, 8626
Katsh A. I. 7939*
Katz P. 4605, 4910, **5007**, 5207, 5607, 5608
Kaufmann P. 5711
Kaufmann-Bühler D. 6627
Kelber W. 5815
Kenney J. P. 8222
Kiesewetter K. 7322
Kirschner R. 8341
Kittel G. 3807*, 4202*

Lührmann D. 7324, 8123
Luneau A. 6217
Luongo G. 7424, 7726
Lyonnet S. 6012

Maar O. 6413
Maas W. 7425
McCarthy W. J. 8434
McCasland S. V. 5013
McClain M. 6819
McDiarmid J. B. 4013
MacDonald J. 7807
McEleney N. J. 8120
Mach M. 8635
McKay J. W. 7226
Mack B. L. 1116, 1822*, 3301-6, 7225,
    7325, 7525, 7733, 7829, 7925,
    8228, 8423, 8431, 8432
McLelland J. C. 7628
MacNeil 7836
McNicol A. J. 7428
MacRae G. W. 7830
Maddalena A. 6820, 7025
Madec G. 7426
Maguire J. P. 3912
Mahmud Ahmad M. 3913
Maier P. L. 6911
Maimon I. L. haCohen 6309*
Malina M. 7727
Malingrey A. M. 6111
Mann F. 8328*
Manns F. 8349
Mansfeld J. 7113, 7539*, 7924, 8114,
    8350, 8530
Mantel H. D. 6316
Mantovani G. 8229
Maraval P. 3209
Marcus J. 8230
Marcus R. 1003, 1807, 2111-2, 3003,
    3207, 3811, 4403, 4811, 4812, 4911,
    4912, 5014, 5210, 5612
Mare W. H. 6912
Mariani T. 8351
Marlowe J. 7114
Marshall I. H. 7227
Marshall J. L. 8231
Martín J. P. 7728a, 7728, 8115, 8232,
    8233, 8234, 8352, 8352, 8433, 8636,
    8637
Martin-Achard R. 6913, 7847
Maser M. 1012
Matthews J. T. 8026
Maurer C. 6406

Mavrofidis S. 8353
Maxwell-Stuart P. G. 7427
May G. 7831
Mayer G. 3207, 6627, 7228
Mayer R. 6821
Mazzanti A. M. 7832, 8116, 8531
Mazzantini C. 2403, 4913
Mealand D. L. 7833, 8532
Méasson A. 2220, 3100, 6621, 8027,
    8638
Meeks W. A. 6734, 6822, 7630, 7712*
Méhat A. 6622, 7229
Melnick R. 8028
Ménard J. E. 6601, 6823
Mendels D. 7926
Mendelson A. 7115, 7506, 7526, 8235
Mercado L. F. 6735
Mercier C. 2233, 2234, 6914
Merell J. 1803
Merki H. 5211
Merode M. de 7729
Messana V. 7631
Meyer G. 3914
Meyer R. 3712, 5907
Michaelis W. 3807, 4202, 5405, 5907,
    6406
Michaelson S. 7230
Michel A. 6736, 6915
Michel O. 4202, 5405, 7236, 7311
Michl J. 6222
Middleton R. D. 3915
Milgrom J. 7527, 7553
Millar F. 7941a*
Miller J. 8639
Minniti Colonna M. 7927
Miquel P. 2210
Mirri P. 8354
Moehring H. R. 7834, 7928
Möller C. 7632
Momigliano A. 5613, 8029
Mondésert C. 2201-34*, 2205, 2223,
    4404, 6601, 8403*
Mondin B. 6737, 6738, 6824, 6916,
    7116
Mondolfo R. 5015, 5614, 5817, 6317,
    7948
Montes Peral L. A. 7929
Montserrat I Torrents J. 2353, 8435
Mor M. 1014, 1018
Morani M. 7930
Morard F. E. 7326
Moraux P. 4813, 6318, 8436
Moreno Martinez J. L. 8355, 8356

2. REVIEWERS INDEX

Bevan E. 4002
Bienert W. A. 6903
Bikerman E. 2005
Bissoli G. 8373
Bitter R. A. 8320
Boeft J. den 8363
Bogaert M. 1601, 1814, 2204, 2208,
    2210, 2212, 2214, 2216, 2217, 2219,
    2220, 2225, 2226, 2227, 2228, 2229,
    2230, 2231, 2233, 2234
Boismard M. E. 6507
Bolkestein H. 1108
Boman T. 6827
Bonnard P. 2202, 2204, 2205, 2210,
    2211, 2225, 2227
Botte B. 1601, 3817, 4714, 5007
Boularand E. 2214, 5810
Boulluec A. le 2234
Bourget D. 8235
Bouttier.M. 2231, 6903, 7731
Bouwen F. 2202, 2204, 2205, 2206,
    2207, 2211, 6747
Bovon F. 7005
Bovon R. 7037
Boyancé P. 1108, 6212
Brock S. P. 1704
Bruce F. F. 6827, 6903
Brunner A. 4714
Burkile T. 4714
Butler C. 5810

Cadbury H. J. 4714
Calderini A. 3805
Camelot P. T. 2204, 2205, 2207, 2208,
    2210, 2211, 2214, 2219, 5810, 2201,
    2202, 2203
Caplan H. 4002
Carmignac J. 1108
Carrea G. de 2225
Cartechini S. 6916
Cataudella Q. 2202, 2205, 2209, 2211,
    3805
Cattaneo E. 1814, 2233
Cazeaux J. 7025
Celada B. 4714
Chadwick H. 1814, 1820, 2221, 2233,
    4714
Chirat H. 1551
Churgin G. A. 4714
Cilleruelo L. 2210, 6529
Collart P. 3805
Collette 1113
Colson F. H. 4007

Coppens J. 7512
Coulon G. L. 2220, 2219
Courcelle P. 1551, 1814, 2201, 2203,
    2204, 2205, 2206, 2207, 2209, 2210,
    2211, 2212, 2214, 2216, 2217, 2219,
    2220, 2221, 2222, 2223, 2224, 2225,
    2226, 2226, 2227, 2228, 2230, 2231,
    7025, 7739
Cox C. 1704
Crepaldi M. G. 1113
Croatto J. S. 6827
Crouzel H. 1814, 2201, 2202, 2203,
    2204, 2205, 2206, 2207, 2211, 2218,
    2218, 2219, 2219, 2220, 2220, 2222,
    2223, 2227, 2231, 2233, 6747, 7223

Daniélou J. 2201, 2202, 2219, 2221,
    2224, 2253, 4714, 6747, 6812, 7005,
    7025, 7037
Daoust G. 5810
Daris S. 2202, 2204, 2205, 2206, 2207,
    2211
Daube D. 4002
Davids A. 2229
Debrunner A. 5007
Delcor M. 2210, 6747
Delehaye H. 3817
Delling G. 1113, 1814, 2111, 2201-
    34n., 2233, 5519, 6212, 6507, 6827,
    7223, 7512, 8373
Devriendt M. 2233
Diaz D. 1551
Doignon J. 7739
Doornik P. van 2206, 2210, 2214
Dörrie H. 5519
Drexler H. 2005
Dudley D. R. 3805
Dumont C. 2210
Dupont J. 4714

El Molar N. de 2202, 2205, 2206, 2207,
    2209, 2210, 2214, 2216, 2217, 2218,
    2219, 2220, 2221, 2222, 2223
Elliger W. 2209

Feldman L. H. 2152, 3207, 5519, 7939,
    8235
Ferrua A. 2451
Fidio P. de 2224, 6212, 6827
Filoramo G. 2230
Filson F. V. 4714
Fohrer G. 1108, 6507
Fraine J. de 2202, 2204, 2205, 2206,

3. INDEX OF BIBLICAL PASSAGES

See also general references to Bible books under separate headings in the Subject index.

4. INDEX OF PHILONIC PASSAGES

See also general references to Philo's treatises under the heading Corpus Philonicum in the Subject index.

1.77-88	4501		3.1	8536
2.40-41	8629		3.46-52	8426
			3.56	6705
QG			4.2	7010
1.1	7946		4.33	8125
1.18-20	7606		4.154-245	1601
1.35	8243		4.195-196	2234
1.41	8243		4.238	5014
1.69-76	8530			
1.82-86	8348		*QE*	
1.89-99	2403		1.23	8649
2.1-7	1820		2.2	8007, 8120
2.5	3802		2.46	3703
2.31	4403		2.62-68	1820
2.49	7201, 7501		2.68	8130
2.57	7713			

5. INDEX OF SUBJECTS

It is imperative that the reader, before making extensive use of this index, consult the explanatory and methodological comments made in the Introduction, section 2 (h). The references 1501-08n., 2001-07n., 2101-12n., 2201-34n. refer to the preliminary comments preceding the detailed descriptions of the edition and translation series in question.

Aaron
  as intermediary 7512
  interpretation of 8018
  and priesthood 8503
  as progressing 7512
  symbolism of 5309
  see also high priest; priesthood
Abel, *see* Cain and Abel
Abelard, and Therapeutae 8544
abortion 8330
Abraham
  and Ambrose 7426
  and audience, Philo's 8030
  boldness of speech of 7901
  and Christ in Hebrews 7901
  descent from 6407
  as embodied law 5718
  interpretation of **5519**, 6913, 7228,
    7829, 7843
  in Irenaeus 7423
  and James, Epistle of 7620
  and Joseph and Aseneth 6828
  knowledge of God 5113, 7421
  migration of 8237, 8536
  name

    interpretation of 6405
    change of, and Rabbinic tradition
      6711
  posterity, promise of 8030
  as progressing 7512
  and remnant, theme of 6727
  and sojourning, theme of 6735
  stability, God-like 8132
  and typology of man 8235
  see also Patriarchs; sage
abstinence
  marital, and Rabbinic tradition 6711
  and Noah 7501
  and Therapeutae 7642
abstracts of articles 3301-6
accommodation, cultural in Philo 8009
acknowledgement, and praise-verbs 6818
Acta Apollonii, parallels with 7531
Acta Isidori et Lamponis 4506
action
  in Vico, and Philo 6317
  versus contemplation 8667
  see also contemplation
Acts of Apostles, and 'times of seasons'
  7724

Adam
  allegory of in *Opif.* 8522
  and Christ 8663
  double creation of 7129
  and enkrateia 8537
  as heavenly man 3814, 8034, 8606
  interpretation of 6210, **7129**, 8528
  and language, origin of 7502, 7814
  as lord of world 6009
  as nous 8003
  original nature of 8528
  and Pauline thought 6202, 6634
  transgression of 8528
  two Adam-anthropoi 6202
  typology of 5002
  see also Anthropos; heavenly man; man, creation of
Adler M. 7848
Aenesidemus
  as sceptic 7308
  terminology of 7919
  tropes 7215, 7308, 8221
  see also scepticism
aeons, theology of 6107
Aeschylus, fragments in *Prov.* 7930
affinity, *see* God, and relation to man; συγγένεια in Greek index
agape, concept of 5522
ages of life 7218, 8630
ages of the world 6217
agon motif, and Paul 6746
Agrippa 6535, 7806
Albinus
  influence on 5216
  and negative theology 5216, 5727, 7513
Alexander the Alabarch 5108
Alexandria
  and anti-Semitism 7542
  catechetical school at 7509
  Claudius' letter to Alexandrians 7624
  early Christian community 8647
  and geography, Philo's 8316
  and Hebrews 3911
  higher education at 8618
  Jewish neighbourhoods 8527
  Jews and Christians in 8648
  and Platonism, contemporary 7714
  religious cosmopolitanism 7114
  riots 38 A.D. at 7645
  see also Egypt
Alexandrian culture
  Philo's place in 7526

  and Seneca 6524
Alexandrian Jews
  and acculturation, problem of 8235, 8455
  audience
    for apologetic literature 5617
    as Philo's 6108
  and Christian origins 8647
  citizenship of 4407, **8527**
  and Claudius, Emperor 4506
  decision-making by 8527
  and education 7115, 8235
  and educational institutions of 8527
  evidence on in Philo 6302, 7317
  identification with 7833, 8532
  integration in society 5601
  internal strife among 5617
  legal status of 2451, 6752, 7433, 7515
  orthodoxy of 6008
  place of Philo in 5723
  place of Philo's family in 5521
  political situation of 1107, 2222, 6323, 6752, 7433, 8107
  and post-emancipation Jewry 8455
  situation in 40 A.D. 8509
  social status 1107, 2226
Alexandrian Judaism
  and enkyklios paideia, concept of 7506
  evidence on, Philo's 3710, 7316
  and exegetical traditions 5710, **7525**, 7635, **8432**
    and Gnosticism 7733
    and Letter of Barnabas 8233
    and references to other allegorists 8020
  and Hebrews 5114, 6413, 7730
  and midrashic tradition 5804, 6506
  and Medieval Judaism 6516
  and Nag Hammadi Library 8606
  and paganism, attitude to 7644
  Philo's place in 5617, 6015, 6216, 6751, 7227, 8461
  Philo's relation to 1107, 4816
  place in Diaspora, its 6754
  and pneuma, concept of 7345
  and pre-Christian Gnosticism 7333
  and *Quaestiones*, evidence of 7736
  and 'Religionsphilosophie' 6020
  and 'scribism' 7506
  and Seneca 6525
  in H. A. Wolfson's interpretation 7526
  and women, views on 8250
  see also Diaspora; Hellenistic Judaism

Apocalyptic literature
  and heavenly journeys 8419
  and Jerusalem 8627
  and prophecy 7938
Apocalyptic thought
  and angels, myth of fallen 8457
  and Hebrews 8428, 8453
  and intermediaries 6722
  and language, 'materialization' of 7428
  and Paul 8110
  Philo's relation to 6728, 8323
Apocryphon of John
  comparison with 7733
  and 'water of light' image 8229
Apollos
  and Alexandria 8359
  and Corinthians 8118
apologetic literature
  analysis of **5617**
  and Jewish-Pagan-Christian relations
    8242
  and Sapientia Salomonis 6830
apologetics
  and Alexandrian Jews 5723
  and allegorical method 5206
  centrality of in Philo 3702, 6107
  and cosmological theory 6637
  early Christian 7123
  Jewish 6407
  and Law's magnanimity 8541
  and Moses, presentation of 7636
  and philosophy 7632, 7731
  and rhetoric 7916
  and writings, Philo's 7850
apostasy
  and Alexandrian Judaism 7526
  and covenant, exclusion from 7641
  and judgment 7124
  terminology of 8210
Apuleius, and conscience, concept of
    7553
Aquila
  fragment in Philo 4605
  and Philo's Bible quotations 5917,
    6708
archangel, and logos 4102
Archive of Nicanor 5108
archons, planetary
  in Gnosticism 6714
Ares, symbolism of 5309
aretalogical literature 6528
aretology
  in Allegorical Commentary 2403

  and cardinal virtues 7906
argumentation, method of
  and Hebrews 5019
Argyle A. W. 5315
Arianism, influence on 5823
Aristeas, *see Letter of Aristeas*
Aristo, and philosophy as handmaiden of
  theology 6815
Aristobulus
  and Alexandrian-Jewish spirituality
    7317
  and allegorical method 5915
  commentary on 8225, 8233
  and cosmology in *Opif.* 8214
  and creation account 6115
  Philo's relation to 5402, **6426**, 7323,
    8411
aristocrat, Philo as
  and attitude to poor 8532
  and views on wealth 8365
Aristotelianism
  and allegorical method 6903
  cosmology, and interpretation of
    burning bush 7224
  and Philo's thought 5810, 8436
  and theory of creation 6637
Aristotle
  arguments in *Aet.* 8114
  attack by Zeno on 7517
  and cosmos' indestructibility 7924
  demonology, source for 5111
  De philosophia 4110, 4813, 5301,
    6324, 6416, 7017, 7210, 7408,
    7409, 7505, 7710, 7924
  De philosophia, and *Aet.* 20-24 7407
  and God as ὕψιστος 7404
  and immortality of the race 8035
  influence of in metaphysics 5313
  influence on theory of ideas 5409
  and law of nature 8513
  lost works 4813
  and memory, concept of 8410
  and negative theology in Albinus and
    Plotinus 5727
  and nous, concept of 8352
  Protrepticus 5701
  Rhetoric 8513
  and self-love, theme of 7344
  and *Timaeus*, interpretation of 8656
arithmetic, Philo's knowledge of 6701
arithmology
  general account **7834**
  and allegorical interpretation of Homer

Augustus
  and Alexandrian Jews 6752
  attitude towards, Philo's 8405
  encomium of 7214
  and Jews in Rome 8460
  see also Roman rule
Authentikos logos, and Alexandrian
    provenance 7902
authorship
  and authority 8228
  stylometric test 7230
autobiographical texts, anthology of 8133
Azariah dei Rossi, interpretation of Philo
    4811

Baer R. A. 8028
Balaam, interpretation of 7604
banquet
  of Essenes and Therapeutae 6809
  and Passover meal 6321
  of Therapeutae 7706, 7931
  of Wisdom, and Therapeutae 8660
Barnabas, Letter of
  and origins of Christian theology 8648
Barnard L. W. 6302
Barthes R. 8320
Basil
  and exegetical method 6326
  parallels with 7335
basilikos hodos, *see* royal highway
Bauer B. 5302
beginning, concept of
  in creation account 6811
  in exegesis 8535
  in philosophy 8535
  see also cosmos; creation
Being
  doctrine of 7543
  mystic intuition of 7846
  and Pauline thought 7543
Belkin S. 6207, 6309, 7120, 7819
  critique of 5921
Bellier P. 5403
Belloni G. 2451
Ben Sira
  aphorism of 8514
  and free will, problem of 7555
benediction, Eucharist as 7828
Bernays J. 4204
Bertoli G. 2451
Betz H. D. 6604
Bezalel, and typology of man 8235
Bible

Alexandrian canon 6422
  and children, education of 3811
  importance of love for 4905
  interpretation of, general account
    7728a, 8318, 8403
  and Jewish people, role of 7632
  Philo's 1114, 6601
  quotations from, aberrant 7320
  quotations from in *Gig.-Deus* 8358
  as sacred text 6903
  text used by Philo **5007**
  texts cited by Philo, index of **3203**
  see also Scripture
biblical exegesis
  and allegorical interpretation 7301
  centrality of 2201-34n.
  and commentary 8108
  hermeneutical principles of 8432
  and motifs from Plato's Phaedrus 8638
  see also allegorical exegesis; exegesis
biblical narrative, and exegesis, Philonic
    8320
biblical quotations, and Septuagint text
    5917
biblical references, index of **3209**
biblical text
  and Hebrew original 8358
  in Philo, scholarship on 8108
  Septuagint and Hebrew 6739
  used by Philo **5007**
  see also Septuagint
bibliographies
  annotated 1101-17
  on historical subjects 1008, 1014,
    1018
  of Philo's *Umwelt* 7241
  unannotated 1001-20, 6601
biographical genre, and *De vita Moysis*
    4815, 5401, 6528, 8607
biographical information
  on Philo 5521
  see also family, Philo's
blessedness, *see* eudaimonia
blood, concept of, semantic analysis 8351
Bloom H. 8219, 8228
body
  contempt of, and Corinthians 8118
  and four elements, and Gnosticism
    7733
  as prison 6509, 7406
  and relation man-society 3808
  relative value 4807
  renunciation of, and theme of

divisions of 7722, 8533
fragments
  on computer 3210
  identification, problems of 1822
  of lost Philonic texts 1800-1901
historical-apologetic treatises 5617
how to read 8658
introduction to 7939
lost writings 3810
  and *Aet.*, sequel of 3711
  De numeris 1901
  Περὶ εὐσεβείας 1816
  Περὶ μεθῆς I 1816
numeration, changed for *Spec.*, *Virt.*,
  Praem. 2107-8
order of treatises 1103
philosophical treatises 4304, 5504,
  8126
structure of 7731
textual tradition of **7722**
translations
  Castilian 2352
  Dutch 2500
  English 2101-52, 8133
  French 2201-53
  German 2001-51
  Hebrew 2601-55
  Italian 2401-52
  Spanish 2301-53
  see also under individual treatises
Corpus Philonicum, individual treatises
De Abrahamo
  Greek text 1504
  translations
    English 2106
    French 2218
    German 2001
    Hebrew 2655
    Italian 2452
    Spanish 2303, 2353
  commentary
  structural analysis 8321
De aeternitate mundi
  Greek text 1506
  translations
    English 2109
    French 2224
    German 2007
    Spanish 2305
  commentary 3100
  analysis 3711, 7927
  and Aristotle's *De philosophia* 7017
  authenticity of 2224, 7927, 8126

cosmos' destructibility 7924
and creation *ex nihilo* 7720
historical context 5504
interpretation of 6636, 7927, 8126
manuscript tradition 7927
observations on 4304
philosophical evidence 8114
philosophical sources of 7927
scholarship on 8126
De agricultura
  Greek text 1502
  translations
    English 2103
    French 2201
    German 2004
    Spanish 2302
  analysis compositional technique
    7614
De animalibus
  Greek fragments 1817
  translations
    Armenian 1701, 1703-4
    English 2153
    Latin 1701
  commentary 3100
  analysis of 8458
  biblical references 3209
  dating 1704, 7848, 8458
  historical context 5504
  and Porphyry 7933
De Cherubim
  Greek text 1501
  translations
    English 2102
    French 2208
    German 2003
    Italian 2403
    Spanish 2301
  interpretative tradition 8603
  rhetorical analysis 8418
  structural analysis 8321
De confusione
  Greek text 1502
  translations
    English 2104
    French 2209
    German 2005
    Spanish 2302
  commentary 3100
  allegorical procedure in 8332
De congressu eruditionis gratia
  Greek text 1503
  translations

Roman rule 8029
situation in 40 A.D. 8509
Upper, Philo's family connected with
    5108
see also Alexandria
Egyptian religion, comparisons 7910
election, not discriminatory 8101
elements
    and cosmology, in Revelation of John
        6604
    and Pauline thought 7032, 7643
elitism
    and allegorical exegesis 8305
    spiritual 7822
Elizarova M. 7931, 8236
eloquence, held in esteem 7718
emanation, and concept of light 6212
embassy to Gaius
    aims and demands of 8527
    and author of *De sublimitate* 4504,
        5513, 6524
    and chronology 2152, 2226, 6319,
        6421, 8112
    and historical context 7313
    in Josippon 8014
    number of members 6421
    and Philo's politics 3805
    and Philonic influence on Roman
        culture 6524
    reconstruction of events 7645
embodied law
    and kingship 7811
    Patriarchs as 5718
Empedocles, in Middle Platonist cento
    8530
emperor, as incarnate reason 7709
Emperors, Roman
    attitude towards 7214
    see also Augustus; Gaius; gilded
        shields, incident of; Tiberius
encomium
    as exegetical technique 7829
    and Joseph, portrait of 8664
encyclia, *see* enkyklios paideia
enkrateia
    and Early Christianity 8506
    tradition of 8537
enkyklios paideia
    in allegorical interpretation 7829
    choric terminology 6523
    concept of 2221, 6523, 7506, 8425
    place in Philonic thought 2221, 7115,
        8235

relation to philosophy 7115, 8235
    social context of 8235
    and sojourning, theme of 8205
    subjects of 6701, 8235
Enoch, interpretation of 7825, 8348
Enos, and hope 8329
Ephesians, Letter to
    and discipleship 8545
Ephesus
    and geography, Luke's 8316
Epictetus
    anthropology 5013
    ideas, doctrine of innate 7639
    and lamentation model 7125
    and self-love, theme of 7344
Epicureanism
    ethics and Hercules myth 5516
    influence of on theology 4205
    polemic against, Philo's 7310
    polemics of against Aristotle 7409
epinoia, and Gnosticism 7733
epiphany, concept of 5514
epistemology
    and language 6828
    and self-knowledge 7027
    developments in 8540
    knowledge of 3813
    RAC article 8123
    see also knowledge
Epstein A. 5103
equal rights, and Alexandrian Jews 8527
equality, concept of 8123
Er, discrimination of 7908
error, concept of in Philo 5012
eschatology
    decline of interest in 6728
    in Diaspora Judaism 7612
    doctrine of **7612**, 7818
    and immortality of soul 4604, 7406
    and Jerusalem 8627
    and Pauline thought 3709, 3816
    Platonist assumptions 5606
    spiritual and political 8323
    and temple 8627
    see also Apocalyptic thought
esotericism, of exegesis 4503
Essenes
    and asceticism 6110, 7126, 8538
    banquet as cultic act 6809
    and Christian monasticism 6626
    economic rules 7012
    emendation of text on 5920
    evidence on, Philo's 5704, 5708,

Gaius
  attitude towards 8405
  eulogy of 3810
  and Macro 6425
  palace of 6423
  and Providence, theme of 8036
  reign of, and Philo 5110
  and temple, desecration of 5722, 7806,
    8626
  see also embassy to Gaius; gilded
    shields, incident of
Ganymede, allegorical interpretation of
  8011, 8104
Gelenius, Latin translation of Philo 4811
genarch, office of 7033
genealogy 7638
generation, concept in Heraclitus 3802
Genesis
  interpretation of in Septuagint 8620
  Josephus' reshaping of 7911
  see also creation account; Septuagint
Gentiles
  and hostilities towards Jews 8626
  and Jews, dividing line between 8515
  little emphasis in interpretation biblical
    figures 7604
geography, Philo's outlook 8316
Geoltrain P. 6320
geometry, knowledge of 6701
Gfrörer A. 1105
gift
  concept of 5711
  of God to man 3713, 7345
  to Patriarchs, and Ezechiel tragicus
    8623
  terminology of 5711
gilded shields, incident of 6911, 8217,
  8366, 8612
  comparison Josephus and Philo 8366
  lexical notes 8612
  scholarship on 8366
  see also Gaius
Gnosis
  and Abraham, interpretation of 7423
  anticipates, Philo 5923
  and Clementine thought 5215
  and John, influence on 6507
  origin of 6617, 6748
  Philo's relation to 7242, 7318, 7518,
    8012, 8359, 8440
  and Plotinus 7514
  and proto-Gnosticism at Corinth 8110
  and rest, theme of 7021

Gnosticism
  Alexandrian 5603
  anthropos myth 7346
  and Christian theology 8648
  and cosmology 6812
  and Delphic maxim 7027, 7609
  and Dionysius Zagreus, myth of 6823
  and exegesis of tree of life 6620
  and fate, concept of 3914
  and God, conception of 8116
  and immovable race designation 8546
  and intermediaries 6722
  and interpretation Gen. 1:26 8523
  and Logos doctrine 7907
  and male-female contrast 8003
  mythological-sexual speculation 7005
  origins of 4706, 7333, 8524
  Philo's relation to 4916, 5822, 6807,
    7242, 7733, 7802, 7805, 7939,
    8440
    scholarship on 8440
  planetary archons 6714
  and Platonism 6219
  precursor of, Philo as 5912, 6753,
    7102, 8123
  and prepositional metaphysics, system
    of 6905
  and retirement, concept of 7518
  and sexuality, positive evaluation 8628
  and sojourning, theme of 8205
  and Sophia 6760
    as prostitute 7537
  and stability, theme of 8132
  and 'times or seasons' 7724
  Valentinian 4709
  and virtue, concept of 5814
  see also Gnosis; Pre-Gnosticism;
    Valentinus; Valentinians
God
  general account, see theology
  'abides', that which 7436
  Abraham's quest for 7423
  activity 7021
  activity versus nature 7929
  anthropomorphic language 7323
  architect 8411
  assimilation to, see assimilation to God
  assistants of, in creation of man 8206
  attributes 5216, 6602, 6737, 7015,
    7103, 7425
    and encomium to Augustus 7214
    ethical 4009
  be pleasing to 7725

God (*continued*)
  Being 7103, 7543, 7929
  as benefactor, in Pastoral Epistles 7835
  contemplation of 4205, 5923
  and cosmology 6824
  cosmos, relation to 6501, 6614, 7018
    and Gnosis 6748
  creation
    and doctrine of 7936
    and thought 8044
  creationistic conception of 7839
  as creator
    and Christian doctrine 8617
    and *Timaeus*, influence of 8656
  as demiurge **6637**
  doctrine of **4714**, **5503**, 6824, 8116
    critical evaluation of **7103**
    and Gnosticism 7733
    and Rabbinic thought 7551
  dominion of over creation 6730
  dreams, communication via 7431
  and dualism, radical 7242
  enjoyment of 7236
  epiphany of 5514
  epithets of 4606
  essence of, and revelation 7328
  and eupatheiai 8327
  and exegesis, inspiration of 7728a
  existence of 6737
  faithfulness of 7425
  as father 7707
  and the feminine 7909
  fear of, and Rabbinic thought 8308
  filling cosmos 5907, 7018
  first and second 7741
  fitting or proper to 7015
  friendship with man **3713**, 8430
    and freedom 7932
  glory, *see* Shekhina
  as the Good 7102
  goodness of 7015, 7846
    and free will, problem of 7555
  guide, supreme 7329
  and health, source of 8622
  highest 8658
  hypostases, and Cherubim 8130
  hypsistos 7404
  ideas, theory of 6121
  ideas, thoughts as 5409
  image, doctrine of God's 5013
    and Basil 7335
    see also man as image
  images, representation of 7419

imitation of 4009, 6226
immanence of 7929
immutability of **7425**, 7628, 7816, 7846, 8617
impassibility of 7111, 7425, 7628
incomprehensibility 7543, 8222
ineffability of 5713, 7004, 7327, 7437
infinity of 6021
  denied 6623
intelligible world 7601
interpretation of Ex. 3:14 7846
Israel, in relation to 5707
joy of 6603, 8327
knowledge of (as object) **4301**, 5408, 5511, 5923, 6813
  and Aristotle *De philosophia* 7210
  degrees of 7339, 7846
  and Delphic maxim 7027
  and Heidegger 6409
  and John 5308
  mystical-intuitive 4711
  and perfection 7557
  and revelation 7328
  and scepticism 6120
  see also negative theology 5727
as Legislator 7821
and Logos
  and Ambrose 7739
  and logos endiathetos-prophorikos 6218
  relation to 6730, 7025
  see also Logos
lordship of 3805
love and fear of 8308
love of 5106, **7429**
  and Rabbinic thought 8308
  and self-love 7344
and male and female 6415
man, becoming 7019
man as image 6225
man, relation to **3713**, 5018, 5514, 5523, 5614, 7929
  and creation account 7129
  dialectic of **7102**
  distinguished from 7717
  and sojourning, theme of 8205
mercy symbolized by menorah 5109
miracles 5707
and monotheism 7839
mystic vision of 4301, 7020
  see also God, vision of; mysticism
name(s) of 7339, 7910
  hypostasization 7812

7512
and God's unknowability 7004
and interpretation Gen. 1:26 8523
Logos and others 7325
Platonist influence 5822
see also Logos; Logos doctrine;
   Powers; Sophia
intermediation
   and Hebrews 7730
   and man's relation to God 5525
   and Melchizedek as priest 8421
   and Valentinian gnosis 4709
interpolations
   in Philo, on Essenes 5811
   in Philo's Bible text 5007, 5917, 6708
   see also Septuagint, text of
inventor, topos of 6222
involuntary sin 7035
Iranian thought
   influence of 6410
   and two powers in soul of man 8649
Irenaeus
   Abraham, interpretation of 7423
   Cherubim and Seraphim, theme of
      5512
   direct knowledge of Philo 5821
   and expression 'rule of truth' 8024
irrational, place in Philo's thought 8309
Isaac
   allegorical interpretation of 4702, 5002
   as embodied law 5718
   laughter of soul, theme of 4814
   marriage of 5002
   offer of, interpretation of 5011
   and perfection 7512
   and typology of man 8235
   see also Patriarchs
Isaiah, vision of 6726
Isidore of Pelusium, lexical and thematic
   parallels 3803
Isidorus, trial of 8509
Isis 7909
Islam, and mysticism 6703
Israel
   and arithmology 7928
   dehistoricization of 7818
   election of 6314
   and eschatology, national 7818
   etymology of 6409, 7110, 8420
   history, role in 7632
   interiorization, process of 7325
   interpretation of 4107, 7119
   and messianic traditions 7511

and Moses as saviour 7225
and Passover, interpretation of 7213
and Prayer of Joseph 6835
redemptive function 6727
and Sophia 8660
and universal priesthood 8503
and vision of God 5923, 6219, 7421
   in John 6804
and universalism 7213
see also Judaism
Israel, land of
   Philo's views on 4907

Jabneh, Gentile-Jewish hostilities 8626
Jacob
   as embodied law 5718
   as progressing 7512
   see also God, vision of; Israel;
      Patriarchs
James, Letter of
   parallels to 7620
   and evil inclination, concept of 8230
Jeremiah, quotations from 7648
Jerome
   evidence on priestly descent 8450
   influence on 4803, 7336, 8449
   on Philo in *De vir. ill.* 8014, 8450
Jerusalem
   conception of 5017, 8323, **8627**
   and geography, Philo's 8316
   Diaspora Jew's loyalty to 7920
   and gilded shields, incident of 6911,
      8217
   Judaism of, relation to 7706
   pilgrimage to 8303
   psychologization of 5017
   residence of Roman governors 6223
   sacrificial cult 3816, 6741
   spiritualization of 5017
   and temple 5706, 8627
   terminology for 5017, 8303
   see also Temple
Jerusalem cultus, and Hebrews 7944
Jesus
   and Carabas in *Flacc.* 7416
   God, making himself 7630
   and multiplication of loaves 7503
   as Shammaite Pharisee 8022
Jethro
   etymology of 6201, 6316
   interpretation of 7604
   and vanity, concept of 7508
Jew-pagan antithesis, and Pauline thought

and Gregory of Nyssa 7804
in Pauline thought 6009
and woman 7203
imitation of God 6226
insignificance, *see* oudeneia
interior 7016
as intermediate figure 7014
kinship to God, *see* affinity to God
knowledge of God 6020
and logos doctrine 6607
as microcosm 8656
and Christ's body 6404
moulded 7129, 7804
nature of 8028
oudeneia 5523, 5814, 7321, 7555
and Middle Platonism 7714
and Pauline thought 7205
and Paradise, interpretation of 7304
passive nature of role 5711
and self-love 7344
structure, dualistic 7421
tripartite nature, and biblical exegesis
7239
true, concept of 7211, 7507
typology of 7024, 7617, 8235
will 8209
and woman 7203, 8117
see also divine man; heavenly man;
male and female
Mangey T., edition of 1501-08n.
manna
interpretation of 6507, 6710, 8224
in John 6507, 6920
and Logos 6926
and Moses' intercession 6926
and multiplication of loaves 7503
and Rabbinic tradition 6711
Targum Neofiti 6926
see also food
manuscripts
of fragments and sources 1810
lost, of Latin translation 1819
neglected palimpsest 7701
Vaticanus 379 7937
Vatopedinus 659 1820
Marcion, diminished Philonic influence
5603
Marcus Julius Alexander 5108
Marcus R. 2233, 7736
fragment collection 1814, 1822
translation from Armenian 7010, 7946
marriage
levirate and agnate 7007

spiritual 7918
Mary, and feminine dimension of divine
7909
mathematics, of *Timaeus* ignored 8656
mathesis, concept of 3817
matter
concept of in New Testament 5720
God creator of 7543
and Plato's *Timaeus*, influence of 8656
pre-existent 6614, 6637, 6638, 7556,
7642, 7831
as principle 7831
see also creation, *ex nihilo*
Matthew parallels to 7642
maxims 7026
see also Delphic maxim
Maximus the Confessor, influence on
anthropology 6532
Maximus Tyrius 6531
Mayer G. 3201
māqôm 8010
Mealand D. L. 8365
meals, sacral meaning of 7534
meaning, and truth 8219
mediation, *see* intermediation
medical doctrines
and Hippocratic *Peri hebdomadon*
7113
knowledge of 8622
in *Timaeus* ignored 8656
medieval Jewish philosophers
influence on **4714**, 6207
and Karaites 6516, 7122
Philo's relation to 6401
precursor of 8368
medieval philosophy
influence on 4714
and Philo, Wolfson's thesis 5005,
8446
Philo in 6228
Melchizedek
antecedents, lack of 7618
and Hebrews 7608, 7618, 7743, 7746,
8231
and high priest 6836
interpretation of 4015, 5517, **8421**
and Justin Martyr 8231
and Logos-priest 8421
and mediator 7512, 8421
and priesthood, concept of 8503
see also Hebrews, Letter to
memory
conception of 8410

and remembrance of God 8410
menorah, symbolism of 5109
Messiah, divine conception of 8367
Messianism
    in Alexandrian Judaism 5807
    and angelology 4102
    and Christianity, acquaintance with
        7019
    decline of 6728
    in Hellenistic Judaism 7302
    lacking in Philo 5915, 6322, 7511
    nature of Philo's 6014, 7302, 8548
    traditions of present in Philo 7511
metaphors
    bibliography of 1004
    and John 7622
    and theological language 7116
metaphysics
    history of, place in 8352
    prepositional, two series of 6905
Metatron, name's origin 5105
methodology
    dangers of secondary literature 8534
    how to read Philo 8658
    importance of 1117, 3904, **7220**,
        7732
    in Philonic scholarship 6220, 8656
    and Palestinian Judaism, relation to
        7703
    and Wolfson H. A. 4714, 8446
metriopatheia
    and Clement 7111
    and Middle Platonism 6215
Michael, silence on 7530
Middle Ages, Philo in 6228, 8544
Middle Platonism
    and allegorical method 6713, 7239
    and angelology 8635
    and *Anonymous Commentary on the
        Theaetetus* 8371, 8657
    and assimilation to God 5211
    beginnings of 6305, 6531, 8657
    in Alexandria 5902
    cento on death of soul **8530**
    and Chaldean oracles 5611
    and cosmology **6812**
    and creation account 8373
    double trajectory of 8408
    ethical themes **6215**
    and Gnosis 7242
    and Gnosticism 7733
    and God, conception of 8116
    and Homer, allegorical exegesis of

    8629
    and ideas, theory of 5409
    and Moses, figure of 7240
    negative theology 8377
    Philo's relation to **6305**, 6619, **7714**,
        7839, 8113, 8133, 8211, **8408**,
        8656
    and Plato's *Phaedrus*, interpretation of
        8638
    and Plato, Seventh letter 8372
    and Plato's *Timaeus*, interpretation of
        8656
    and Pythagorean influence 8408
    and sojourning, theme of 8205
    and Timaeus Locrus 7202
    and transcendence 8374
    see also Neoplatonism; Pre-neoplato-
        nism; Neopythagoreanism; Plato;
        Platonism
Middle Stoicism, and theology 5822
Midrash
    and ancient oral tradition 5103, 5804,
        7204, 7402
    and etymological exegesis 5602
    exegesis, relation to 8219
    in Hebrews 7 7743
    Hellenistic, theory of M. (or E.) Stein
        7034
    and John 6304
    and manna, theme of 6920
    medieval commentators 7204
    and Nadab and Abihu, interpretation of
        8341, 8521, 8654
    Palestinian, relation to **5804**, 6401,
        6506, 6507, 7402, 8305
    symbolic 6506
    see also Haggadah
Midrash Exodus Rabbah, parallels in Philo
    5914
Midrash ha-Ne'elam
    parallels with Philo **5803**
    Philonic influence on denied 5921
    and Sapientia Salomonis 6207
Midrash Hagadol 7204, 7402
Midrash Numbers Rabbah 15
    and symbolism of menorah 5109
Midrash Tadshe 5103
migration
    centre of Philo's thought, theme as
        7731
    and exegesis 7332
    and Passover, theme of 7213
    see also transmigration

and rhetoric 6736
sophia, preparatory to 6111
sources, nature of Philo's **6305**
theft of by Greeks from Moses 7323,
7841
and women, attitude to 7729
see also Philo, introduction to
philosophical thought; Platonism;
Stoicism; etc.
phronesis, meaning fluctuates 7907
physiology, in Plato's *Timaeus* ignored
8656
physis, *see* nature
piety
centrality of 4405
concept of 6627
embodied in Moses 5919
and son of God 7712
and two trees in Paradise 6210
and virtues, placed in catalogue of
6910
Pilate
attitude towards 6911, 8405
career of 8112
and gilded shields incident 8217, 8366
and Jesus' trial 8406
pilgrimage, to Jerusalem 8303
pious man, God's relationship to 3713
place, concept of 8010
Plato
Alcibiades I, themes from 8638
and allegorical method 6529, 6903
Apology, image of desertion 7726
and Aristotle in *Aet.* 8114
and assimilation to God 8203
body as tomb or prison 6509, 6608
cave, image of 6504
and cosmos, indestructibility of 7924
Cratylus 7814
and creation, doctrine of 6636, 6637
debt to, Philo's 8638
demiurge, concept of 6637, 7015
demonology, source for 5111
dialogue method 8133
and dialectic of God and man **7102**
and dialectic of sensibility 6703
and ecstasy, concept of 8314
elitism rejected 8235
eudaimonia 8311
and faith and reason, problem of 6738
and genuine coin, image of 6817
ideal numbers, and creation account
6520

Ion, themes from 8638
knowledge of, Philo's 6305, 8656
light image 4713
and matter, pre-existent 6638
and memory, conception of 8410
in Middle Platonist cento 8530
and mystical tradition 8113, 8435
and Numenius 7536
and ontological dualism 8352
Phaedo 4905, 6306, 8638
Phaedrus 1704, 6307, 6520, 6531
Phaedrus myth 6305, **8638**
political thought 5017, 8201
Politicus, themes from 8638
Republic 4905, 8638
and self-love, theme of 7344
Seventh letter 8372, 8657
style, model for 8345
Symposium 4905
Theaetetus 6120, 8638, 8657
and theological language 3202, 7116
Timaeus
28c 6219
37c-38c, exegesis of 7131
and *Anonymous Commentary on the
Theaetetus* 8657
and creation, doctrine of 6520,
7936, 8044
duality of creators 8409
and ideas, theory of 6121
interpretation of 1117, 4905, 5822,
6305, **7127**
knowledge and use of 6305, 8638,
8656
and metaphysics 8374
and planetary archons 6714
and τύπος imagery 8543
see also creation account
vocabulary, influence of 3203, 7102
see also Middle Platonism; Neoplatonism; Platonism
Platonism
Alexandrian 7513, 7714, 7902
and cardinal virtues 7906
and Christianity 5813, 8543
commentaries 6531, 7127
and cosmos as son of God 8115
and creation doctrine 8044
dualism, anthropological 7832
and Paradise, interpretation of 7304
and enkyklios paideia 8425
and eschatology 7612
exegesis 8659

and female principle 8613
and Gnosticism 7802, 8359
and God, infinitude of 6623
and God, ineffability of 7327
and God, knowledge of 5511
and God, love of 7429
and Good, the 7022
and E. R. Goodenough, interpretation
   of 5309
and heavenly man 6802
and Hellenistic Judaism 8201
ideas, theory of 7539
and image, concept of 6221
and immortality, doctrine of 4604,
   8035
influence on Philo 1117, 4714, 6715,
   8548
and interpretion of Ex. 3:14 7846
and justice, concept of 7216
and law 8451
and Logos doctrine 6411
and man, double creation of 7804
and natural law 7821
of Patres 8105
and Paul, Ephesians 8545
and perfection, theme of 7557
and pneumatology 7619
and prepositional metaphysics 6905
and Providence 5913
religious 5906, 6632
and sacrifice, concept of 7944
and salvation, concept of 8516
and sanctuary in Hebrews 8428
and scepticism 6120, 8540
and sonship, concept of 7904
and Sophia, figure of 6760, 8613
Stoicizing 4204
and theology 5822
and transcendence 6020
and Virgil 7627
and women, views on 8250
see also dualism; Middle Platonism,
Pre-neoplatonism; Neoplatonism
play, concept of 4814
pleasing God, terminology of 7725
pleasure, condemnation of
   and Ambrose 7739
pleroma, and God's relation to the cosmos
   7018
Pliny the Elder, on Essenes 5708, 5811
Plotinus
   and conscience, concept of 7553
   and ecstasy, concept of 5614, 6419

and God's ineffability 5713
influence on, Philo's 5216, 7514
and light imagery 5725
and Logos doctrine 6749
and Middle Platonist cento 8530
and mysticism 6922, 8113
and negative theology 5216, 5727
Philo's relation to 4001, 6749
virtue, grades of 8328
see also Neoplatonism
Plutarch
   and allegorical method 7327, 8346
   and Delphic maxim 7507
   and linen, symbolism of 7338
   Middle Platonist cento 8530
   and prepositional metaphysics 6905
   and soul, wings of 7410
pneuma
   concept of 3806, **4504**, **4508**, 5112,
      7025, **7345**, **7619**
   in Ambrose 5820
   divine and human 4302, 8652
      and rest 8427
   and faith in God 7619
   Hellenistic background 4504
   as intermediary 6745
   and man as image 5812
   and man of God 8248
   meaning fluctuates 7907
   and Pauline thought 6805, 7737
   and royal highway 5923
   and soul 6820, 7733
   and water symbolism 8349
   see also inspirtation; prophecy;
poem, didactic,
   on Philo 5403
poetic allusions, index of 3204
Poimandres, and Delphic maxim 7008
political thought **3805**, 4104, **8405**
   and Diaspora Judaism 8323
   and Dike, interpretation of 7515
   and Pauline thought 8033
   principles of 8429
   and ruler, concept of 7811
   see also Roman rule
Polybius 6512
polytheism, Egyptian
   and *Letter of Aristeas* 7921
poor, the
   care for 3902
   compassion for 8236
   love for, and Gregory of Nazianzus
      8459

Proseuché of Joseph, see Prayer of Joseph
Proto-Rabbinism
  relation to, Philo's 7706
protreptic
  elements, importance of 6534
  genre, and *Contempl.* 5701
Providence
  general account **3914,** 5913, 8036
  anthology of texts on 8133
  defence of in lost part of *Aet.* 3711
  in *Flacc.* 2451
  historical and individual 8516
  in *Legat.* 3810
  and man's freedom 8101
  and miracles 5913
  and natural law 5913
  and pre-existence, concept of 6614
Prudentius, influence on 4303
Pseudo-Andronicus
  Περί Πάθων, relation to 7716
Pseudo-Archytas, and transcendence 7513
Pseudo-Aristotle, *see De mundo*
Pseudo-Longinus, *see* De sublimitate, Ps.
  Longinus
Pseudo-Philo, *Liber Antiquitatum*
  Biblicarum
  and Moses' burial 7105
Pseudo-Phocylides
  and social duties, conception of 7212
psychological interpretation of Philo,
  dangers of 6826
psychology
  general account **4302,** 4711
  and Pauline thought 4904
  see also soul
punishment, divine
  by elements 8530
  and forgiveness of sin 8632
purity, concept of 7331, 7529
Pythagoras
  arithmology 7928
  and Logos doctrine 5815
  and Moses 7928
  and parable of Panegyrion 6518
Pythagoreanism
  and celestial harmony 7128
  and fifty, number 7704
  and Gnosticism 7802
  harmony of spheres 4602
  influence on ethics 5817
  and justice, concept of 7216
  and Middle Platonism 7714, 8211
  myth of muses 4602

see also Neopythagoreanism

Qirqisani, Jacob 6516, 7122
quaestio et solutio, and exegetical
  structures 7708
Quaestiones
  audience of 6003
  book division of 7625
  form of exegesis 7708, 8357
  method of 6003, 8665
  and Rabbinic Midrash 6003, 6402
  structure, problem of 7736
    and Sabbath readings 8441
  see also Corpus Philonicum
Quispel G. 8205
Qumran
  and creation *ex nihilo* 6729
  evidence on Essenes 5719, 6004, 8362
  exegesis at 8508
  and Hebrews 6205, 7512
  and Hellenism 7926
  and intermarriage, prohibition of 8322
  legislation on Sabbath 7435
  and sin, conception of 6805
  writings
    4Q *Florilegium* 8508
    Manual of discipline 6517
  see also Essenes; Therapeutae
quotation, methods of 7026

Rabbinic exegesis
  Balaam, interpretation of 7604
  catalogues, and numbers in Philo 7342
  and commentaries on Homer 6209
  Jethro, interpretation of 7604
  and Nadab and Abihu, account of
    8521, 8654
  and 'one flesh', interpretation of 6709
  Philo's knowledge of 5519, 6527
  techniques of 5915, 7614
  see also Haggadah; Halachah; Midrash
Rabbinic Judaism
  concepts and beliefs of sages 7551
  and human rights 7908
  and inheritances 7007
  and intermarriage, prohibition of 8322
  and legal exegesis 4601
  and levirate and agnate marriages 7007
  and mystical Judaism 6755
  and Paul's allegorical method 5618
  Philo's relation to **4002,** 4901, 6015,
    6308, 6601, 6725, **7741,** 8302,
    8305, 8661

6. INDEX OF GREEK TERMS